THE LAW OF COMPULSORY PURCHASE AND COMPENSATION

This book is a statement of the current law of compulsory purchase of land and compensation for that purchase. It covers all major aspects of the procedure for the compulsory acquisition of land and deals in full detail with all aspects of the law of compensation for such an acquisition. The many and diverse statutory provisions are organised into a series of chapters containing all principles and rules and there is a full analysis and explanation of the leading authorities on the subject and the principles derived from those authorities without which the subject cannot be understood.

The aim of the book is not only to explain the statutory provisions and to organise the various possible claims for compensation into different heads, but also to explain and analyse the substantial body of case law which has built up, particularly in recent years, and the relationship between that body of law and the underlying statutory provisions. The book also attempts to explain the purpose of the statutory provisions and the reason for the rules that are derived from the authorities. Chapters of the book are devoted to the procedure for formulating and pursuing a claim for compensation and to the valuation principles which must be applied in advancing claims. An Appendix is provided by Mr Nicholas Eden FRICS, a leading valuer in the field, which contains examples of different types of compensation valuation with annotations as to how the valuations are prepared and built up. A further aim of the book is to provide, where possible, practical advice to public authorities and landowners involved in the process of compulsory purchase and compensation as well as to explain the legal principles.

The Law of Compulsory Purchase and Compensation

Michael Barnes

·HART·
PUBLISHING

OXFORD AND PORTLAND, OREGON
2014

Published in the United Kingdom by Hart Publishing Ltd
16C Worcester Place, Oxford, OX1 2JW
Telephone: +44 (0)1865 517530
Fax: +44 (0)1865 510710
E-mail: mail@hartpub.co.uk
Website: http://www.hartpub.co.uk

Published in North America (US and Canada) by
Hart Publishing
c/o International Specialized Book Services
920 NE 58th Avenue, Suite 300
Portland, OR 97213-3786
USA
Tel: +1 503 287 3093 or toll-free: (1) 800 944 6190
Fax: +1 503 280 8832
E-mail: orders@isbs.com
Website: http://www.isbs.com

Hart Publishing is an imprint of Bloomsbury Publishing plc.

British Library Cataloguing in Publication Data
Data Available

ISBN: 978-1-84946-448-2

Typeset by Hope Services, Abingdon
Printed and bound in Great Britain by
CPI Group (UK) Ltd, Croydon CR0 4YY

This book is for Rachel, who is so very far away.

Foreword

It is a great pleasure to be introducing a book which deals with an important topic, and which plainly meets a need and does so very well.

Compulsory purchase of land is an important topic for a number of reasons. First, in an island which is very heavily populated, and has a growing population, land is an increasingly scarce and valuable resource. Secondly, for the same sorts of reason, the ability of public authorities to acquire land for beneficial purposes is ever more challenging. Thirdly, this challenge is reinforced as developments in technology, transport and industry become increasingly sophisticated and occur increasingly rapidly. Fourthly, compulsory purchase gives rise in a particularly acute form to the constitutionally important tension between public interest and private interests. Fifthly, particularly in the modern world of human rights, the need to protect those people from whom land is sought to be compulsorily acquired requires close attention.

Coupled with these factors, the law, as developed by parliament through statutes, by the executive through statutory instruments, and by the courts through decided cases, is becoming more and more complex in most areas, and compulsory purchase law is by no means an exception. Further, it is not just lawyers who are routinely involved in compulsory purchase issues: it is at least as much a field for surveyors, and valuation techniques and other aspects of surveying expertise are also becoming more sophisticated and complex. So a modern book dealing with the topic in detail is of considerable value on that score as well.

The need which this book satisfies, therefore, at least expressed in broad terms, is for a comprehensive and in-depth treatment of the modern law and practice of compulsory purchase and valuation. There are books which cover the topic, but they are either many decades out of date or relatively brief. In a fast-changing and socially-important area such as compulsory purchase, it is particularly important not only to professional lawyers and surveyors, but also in the wider public interest, that there is a wide-ranging, reliable, penetrating and up-to-date book on the topic.

In more specific terms, what is required is a book which not only goes into the modern law and practice comprehensively, but does so in a clear and structured way. Ideally, such a book should not simply identify those aspects of the law and practice which are clear and settled, but it should also identify those which are unclear or controversial. Further, while many otherwise excellent books on legal topics fail to do this, the best books go on to set out the competing arguments on the unresolved issues, and give the author's view as to which is correct and why. In addition, a good law book will be well structured and signposted, so that readers can find what they want relatively easily, and clear, so that readers can understand what is being said once they find the passage dealing with the topic on which they are seeking guidance.

It should come as no surprise to anyone who has come across him professionally (as I have done, over the past thirty five years, first at the Bar and more recently as a judge) that Michael Barnes QC has managed to produce a book on compulsory purchase, a topic on which he is an acknowledged leading expert and practitioner, which passes all these requirements with flying colours.

What particularly appeals to me about this book is that it manages to be both practical and reflective. Thus, not merely is there an appendix which contains a number of helpful worked examples prepared by a highly experienced chartered surveyor, Nicholas Eden FRICS, but throughout the text, there is a clear awareness of the need for practicality as well as intellectual rigour. On the other hand, not only does the book go into unresolved and problem questions, but, particularly in the first and last chapters, the author characteristically describes both the past and the future in characteristically instructive, thorough and thoughtful terms.

Finally, I must confess that the part of the book which is of most interest to me is chapter 4, which is on valuation. This is because it is the aspect of compulsory purchase with which I have had easily the most experience, both at the bar and since becoming a judge. I read it with particular enjoyment and can say with particular confidence that it amply justifies what I have said in the preceding paragraphs.

David Neuberger
Ides of March 2014

Preface

In any modern and democratic society there will be occasions on which land is needed for use for the public good but where the landowner refuses to sell it or to sell it on reasonable terms. It is recognised that, subject to important safeguards, there should be a power to compel the owner to sell his land. The safeguards are important. One is that the landowner should have the right to some form of independent consideration of whether the acquisition of his land against his will is justified in any particular case. Another is that the landowner should receive fair compensation for the land taken from him, that compensation being equivalent to the whole of the loss which he suffers as a result of that acquisition. The purpose of this book is to explain the law on how this system with its safeguards works in England and Wales.

Landowners whose land is acquired and public bodies exercising a power of compulsory acquisition are entitled to a rational and coherent body of law which regulates these matters. The law on the subject is wholly statutory. That law originates in early Victorian legislation, often repeated with little modification in modern statutes, and in a series of later enactments the effect of which is sometimes a sporadic bolting on of new rules to old principles. A substantial body of decisions of the courts on the meaning of these provisions means that the law can only be understood by reference to a body of case law. The system in fact operates more fairly than might be supposed from this description of its origins and development. Nonetheless it is generally recognised that a wholesale restatement of the law on the subject is needed.

The task which is attempted in this book is to provide an account of the law of compulsory purchase and compensation, and particularly of the latter, which imposes a pattern on the subject and explains not only the content of the various rules and principles and decisions of the courts but also their purpose and justification and how they fit into the total corpus of the law on the subject. Those who practice in this area of public law are mainly lawyers and valuers. All but the simplest of cases will need the input of both disciplines. My aim has been to make this book useful to both categories of practitioners. Chapters are included towards the end of the book which explain the basic principles of valuation and explain the procedure for making and resolving claims for compensation. A final chapter provides some suggestions for reform. An appendix contains a number of worked examples of valuations for the assessment of compensation with explanations of what is done.

I take this opportunity to thank those who have given me help. My old friend, Mr Nick Eden, FRICS, senior partner of Kenney Green, has provided the appendix and, much more than that, has read large parts of the remainder of the text and made many valuable suggestions.

Others of my colleagues have given me help with suggestions and discussion whenever I have asked. I refer particularly to Mr Eian Caws, Barrister, and Mr Michael Rich QC.

I also wish to thank Hart Publishing whose friendly and efficient work has made the task of writing this work easier and more pleasant.

Finally I express my gratitude to Janet Steel who has typed the whole of this material with speed and accuracy. Without her assistance the production of this book would not have been possible.

Michael Barnes QC
Wilberforce Chambers
April 2014

The Appendix material has been provided by Mr Nicholas Eden FRICS,
Senior Partner in Kinney Green.

Table of Contents

Abbreviations

The following abbreviations of Acts of Parliament and other instruments are used from time to time.

The Land Clauses Consolidation Act 1845	The 1845 Act
The Acquisition of Land (Assessment of Compensation) Act 1919	The 1919 Act
The Land Compensation Act 1961	The 1961 Act LCA 1961
The Compulsory Purchase Act 1965	The 1965 Act
The Land Compensation Act 1973	The 1973 Act LCA 1973
The Town and Country Planning Act 1990	The 1990 Act
The Tribunal Procedure (Upper Tribunal) (Lands Chamber) Rules 2010	The Rules
Practice Directions of the Lands Chamber of the Upper Tribunal of 29 November 2010	The Practice Directions

Table of Cases

Table of Legislation

1

Introduction

The carrying out of many projects of development, certainly the carrying out of major projects, is likely to require the acquisition of land by the developers. In the case of ordinary commercial developments the implementation of the project may, therefore, depend on the willingness of landowners to sell their land and on an agreement being reached as to the price to be paid for that land. It is for this reason that housing and other developers may build up a 'land bank' of land suitable for development as economic circumstances become right. The value of land for development is often much greater than its value for the continuation of an existing use and in such circumstances landowners may need little encouragement to sell the land. Even so in the end if the necessary land or rights over land cannot be acquired by agreement the development project may founder. It has long been considered that where there is a public interest in carrying out development to provide significant public facilities, for example roads, railways or schools, and where agreement cannot be reached for the acquisition of the necessary land by the body promoting the development, there should be a residual power to compel landowners to sell their land at a proper price so as to enable the public benefits which are expected to accrue from the project to be realised.   1.1

It is this last situation which has given rise to the law of compulsory purchase and compensation for compulsory purchase. The expressions compulsory purchase and compulsory acquisition are used interchangeably and have the same meaning. The subject has two areas, the first being the process of the compulsory purchase of land and the second being the assessment of the compensation to be paid to the person whose land has been compulsorily taken from him. It is obvious that a person's land should only be taken from him against his will if there is a real and genuine public interest in the scheme or project for which the land is needed and that there should be reasonable procedural safeguards before this is done. It is equally obvious that the compensation should be assessed on principles that result in a fair recompense for the dispossessed landowner. It is the purpose of this book to explain and illustrate the principles and the provisions which govern these two areas of the law.   1.2

It is sometimes said that the use of powers of compulsory purchase is only justified if there is a compelling public need for land. Whereas in general that proposition is no doubt correct legislation has provided what are in substance powers of compulsory acquisition of interests in land or rights for the benefit of private persons. Two examples are the Leasehold Reform Act 1967 under which landlords can be compelled to sell their interests to certain tenants and section 84 of the Law of Property Act 1925 under which the owner of the benefit of a restrictive covenant can in certain circumstances be deprived of the benefit of his covenant. In both cases compensation may be payable for the loss of the benefit. The compulsory acquisition of interests in land and of rights for the benefit of private persons under legislation of this nature is outside the scope of this book. Even when one refers to the   1.3

compulsory purchase of land for a particular project or use the distinction between public bodies and private interests may be blurred. Many organisations providing public utilities such as water or electricity or telecommunications have power to acquire land for the purposes of their undertaking. When these undertakings were public or nationalised bodies the connection between the acquisition of land and the public interest was more clear than it is when, as today, the providers of public utilities are mainly commercial enterprises. Any dividing line between public and private purposes is further compromised by acquisitions which take place by public authorities in order to assemble land for wholly or largely private development under powers in town and country planning and similar legislation.[1] Private developers often participate closely in this process and a large developer may agree to fund the process of compulsory purchase including the payment of compensation. On occasions the close connection between an acquiring authority and a commercial body can lead to a successful challenge to the validity of a compulsory purchase.[2] The body which exercises a power of compulsory purchase is usually called the acquiring authority although when it is the amount of compensation for the purchase which is in issue the description of the body liable to pay the compensation is sometimes that of the compensating authority. Compensation is sometimes available for damage (usually called injurious affection) to land even when the land is not acquired so that there is no acquiring authority as such.

1.4   The first area of law just mentioned, the provisions on the procedure for a compulsory purchase, is not difficult to understand although in some ways the law seems unduly complicated. Apart from the detailed statutory provisions applicable to compulsory purchase the procedural safeguards which the law has built up are largely common to most aspects of administrative law, for example the rules of natural justice such as the right to a fair hearing. The provisions governing the assessment of compensation are more arcane. The underlying principle is said to be the principle of equivalence which is described as the touchstone by reference to which all claims for compensation succeed or fail,[3] although this principle is never stated as such in the statutes. The principle of equivalence is that a person who is compulsorily deprived of his land in the public interest is entitled to compensation equivalent to his true and actual loss, no more and no less.[4] A principle of such wide generality is easy to state and commands general approbation but its application to the many varieties of circumstances which in practice arise is not straightforward.

1.5   The whole of the law of compulsory purchase and the whole of the law on the assessment of compensation are statutory.[5] A person cannot be required to sell his land against his will

---

[1] See s 226 of the Town and Country Planning Act 1990 and s 142 of the Local Government Planning and Land Act 1980.

[2] See ch 2, para 2.10 et seq. In *R (Sainsbury's Supermarkets Ltd) v Wolverhampton City Council* [2010] UKSC 20, [2011] 1 AC 437, a proposal by a local authority to acquire land from one large supermarket operator in order to assist development by another large supermarket operator with a view to obtaining public benefits from the second operator was held to be unlawful.

[3] *Director of Buildings and Lands v Shun Fung Ironworks Ltd* [1995] 2 AC 111, [1995] 2 WLR 904, per Lord Nicholls at p 125.

[4] *Horn v Sunderland Corporation* [1941] 2 KB 26, per Scott LJ at p 49. The principle of equivalence was said in this decision to be 'at the root of statutory compensation'.

[5] It was pointed out by Lord Scott in *Waters v Welsh Development Agency* [2004] UKHL 19, [2004] 1 WLR 1304, at para 84 that compulsory appropriation of land is a creature of statute and that there is no common law right or extant Royal Prerogative that allows such a thing. The same was said by Lord Collins in *R (Sainsbury's Supermarkets Ltd) v Wolverhampton City Council* [2010] UKSC 20, [2011] 1 AC 437, at para 9, citing Lord Pearson in *Rugby Joint Water Board v Shaw-Fox* [1973] AC 202, [1972] 2 WLR 757, at p 214. See however the remainder of this paragraph and its footnotes.

unless the person acquiring the land can point to a statutory provision, including a provision in delegated or subordinate legislation, which authorises the acquisition. There was in previous times a doctrine of eminent domain (the *dominium eminens* of the sovereign) under which the Crown could compel a citizen to give up his land at times and for purposes of national need subject to making reasonable compensation but in practice today statutory authority is nearly always essential.[6] There is a sole remaining component of the right of eminent domain in that property may still be requisitioned by the Crown where it is essential to do so at times of war or of grave national emergency pursuant to the Royal Prerogative. The Royal Prerogative means the residual powers of the Crown which have not perished from disuse or been removed or taken away by statute. An example of the modern day use of this residual Crown Prerogative power is the destruction of property in wartime ahead of an enemy advance so as to deny the use of the property to the enemy.[7] If this power is exercised compensation is still payable to the owner of the land.[8] In modern times the extensive emergency powers given by statute to the Government in wartime normally provide all necessary authority to requisition land.

The earliest statutory intervention was to permit the construction of canals, railways and highways at the end of the eighteenth and the beginning of the nineteenth century. Some of the major railway routes now in use originated under private Acts of Parliament which authorised a company as the promoters of the scheme to acquire land by agreement or by compulsion and to construct the new railway. This process has continued and major projects such as the Channel Tunnel rail link and the Crossrail project in London have been or are authorised by a specific Act.[9] In these cases the Act itself identifies certain areas within

1.6

---

[6] It has been recognised at least since Tudor times that a person cannot save in grave national emergency be deprived of his property by the Crown except by the authority of Parliament. The Crown once had powers such as the power to raise taxes (*Bate's* case (1606) 2 ST Tr 371) and to imprison people (*Darnel's* case (1627) 3 St Tr 1) but these elements of the Royal Prerogative have disappeared by reason of statutory restriction or disuse. In addition it is established that where a particular power is granted or regulated by statute the statutory power wholly supersedes any former prerogative powers vested in the Crown: *A-G v De Keyser's Royal Hotel* [1920] AC 508.The power of eminent domain was recognised by natural law jurists such as Grotius and Pudendorf. The power is recognised by the 5th and 14th amendments to the American Constitution subject to due process of law. The 5th amendment states that private property shall not be taken for public use without just compensation. Other jurisdictions have similar basic principles. For example, art 105 of the Basic Law in force in Hong Kong since the transfer of sovereignty from the British Crown to the People's Republic of China states:

> The Hong Kong Special Administrative Region shall, in accordance with law, protect the rights of individuals to the acquisition, use, disposal and inheritance of property and their right to compensation for lawful deprivation of their property. Such compensation shall correspond to the real value of the property concerned at the time and shall be freely convertible and paid without delay. The ownership of enterprises and the investments from outside the Region shall be protected by law.

There are limits to the protection of property afforded by constitutional provisions of this nature. A deprivation of property normally means a deprivation of specific private rights in property and not the limitation of rights generally available to the public such as the right to use a public highway free of charge: see *Grape Bay Ltd v A-G of Bermuda* [2000] 1 WLR 579. It is possible that some protection is available to landowners in England and Wales from the European Convention for the Protection of Human Rights and Fundamental Freedoms and the Human Rights Act 1998 although this appears to fall short of that protected by other systems of constitutional safeguards. See para 1.13.

[7] *Burmah Oil Co Ltd v Lord Advocate* [1965] AC 75, [1964] 2 WLR 1231. The opinion of Lord Reid contains a full analysis of the principle of eminent domain relating to property rights.

[8] *Burmah Oil Co Ltd v Lord Advocate*, ibid.

[9] See the Channel Tunnel Rail Link Act 1996 and the Crossrail Act 2008. The Wandsworth to Croydon Railway Act 1801 is said to be the first Act which gave power to acquire land compulsorily for a railway. It is sometimes observed that in modern times private rights in land are often removed or overridden in the interests of the community but the Victorians had no hesitation in using a similar process to facilitate the construction of railways and

which land can be compulsorily purchased. During Victorian times, and increasingly since then, the state through central and local government has intervened in ever wider areas of life by the provision of public facilities such as schools, housing and drainage, and the pattern has been that public and general Acts covering these subjects have contained a general power of compulsory purchase of land. In these cases the Act does not usually itself specify the area within which land may be acquired but confers a general power of compulsory purchase for the purposes of the legislation with responsible public bodies such as a Minister or a local authority being allowed to select the specific areas of land as to which the power is exercised.[10] A terminology has arisen under which the Act which authorises the compulsory purchase, whether it falls into either of the categories described, is called the special Act.[11]

1.7　　The law of compensation has also developed considerably since its inception. The earliest Acts of Parliament which authorised the compulsory purchase of land for a specific scheme each contained their own provisions for putting a purchase into effect and for assessing compensation payable to persons deprived of their land.[12] This was inconvenient with the number of such Acts increasing and in 1845 and 1847 Parliament enacted legislation which contained a series of standard provisions which could be incorporated into or applied by each new special Act. The legislation was the Lands Clauses Consolidation Act 1845, the Railways Clauses Consolidation Act 1845, the Waterworks Clauses Act 1847 and the Cemeteries Clauses Act 1847. This legislation was called compendiously 'the Lands Clauses Acts'.[13] The complicated procedural provisions in this legislation for the assessment of compensation by arbitrators, juries and justices have passed away and today all questions of disputed compensation are decided by the Lands Tribunal. That body was set up under the Lands Tribunal Act 1949 and is today technically the Lands Chamber of the Upper Tribunal established under the Courts, Tribunals and Enforcement Act 2007 although it is still colloquially described as the Lands Tribunal. It will generally continue to be described as the Lands Tribunal in this book. However, many of the substantive provisions in the 1845 legislation remain the basis of the current law on the principles for the assessment of compensation, having been re-enacted in subsequent legislation. For example, section 63 of the Lands Clauses Consolidation Act 1845 stated that compensation was to be assessed for: (a) the value of the land acquired and (b) damage to other land of the owner retained by him but injuriously affected by the acquisition of the land acquired. This basic provision was repeated in section 7 of the Compulsory Purchase Act 1965 with only minor modernisation of the language and remains the ultimate basis of much of the law of compensation today.

---

other projects (eg the embankment of the Thames and the provision of a sewerage system in London) which underpinned the economic expansion and prosperity of Britain in the mid 19th century.

[10] There are instances of old local Acts giving a power of compulsory purchase without defining the exact geographical area within which the power could be exercised. An example is the Metropolitan Paving Act 1817 under which land could be acquired in order to widen and improve London streets.

[11] Section 1(2) of the Compulsory Purchase Act 1965 provides that in Pt I of the Act the enactment under which the purchase is authorised and the compulsory purchase order shall be deemed to be the special Act. See also ss 1 and 2 of the Lands Clauses Consolidation Act 1845.

[12] See, eg the Defence Act 1842.

[13] By virtue of sch 1 to the Interpretation Act 1978 the expression 'Lands Clauses Acts' today means the Lands Clauses Consolidation Act 1845 and the Land Clauses Consolidation Acts Amendment Act 1860 and any Act for the time being in force amending those Acts.

Sometimes modern legislation has continued or repeated the terse language of the 1845   1.8
Act. On other occasions complex language has been used. It has recently been said that in
some instances the 'stark simplicity' of the 1845 Act has been replaced in modern legislation
by 'provisions displaying the least attractive features of statutory draftsmanship in the second half of the twentieth century'.[14] It is a curiosity of the legislation that while section 63
of the Lands Clauses Consolidation Act 1845, and now section 7 of the Compulsory
Purchase Act 1965, state what is the basis of the assessment of compensation there is no
provision which in express terms states that a person whose land is compulsorily acquired
is entitled to compensation. It may be that this omission is of little significance having
regard to the principle that when a body is empowered to acquire land compulsorily there
is a presumption that compensation is to be payable to the owner assessed in accordance
with the general statutory provisions which govern the assessment of compensation even
though no express right of compensation is stated in the empowering legislation.[15] The
entitlement is simply assumed to exist. A right to compensation, reasonably related to the
value of the land acquired, is now guaranteed under the Human Rights Act 1998.[16]

Whereas the law of compulsory purchase and compensation is, and always has been, wholly   1.9
statutory it has been the subject of a substantial body of case law which in some instances
has paid scant regard to the language of the legislation or has superimposed new rules and
principles on that language. The modern law cannot be understood without close examination of the detailed authorities and what they decide. The most obvious example of this
process is section 68 of the Lands Clauses Consolidation Act 1845 which can be mentioned
in outline now and is considered in full later.[17] That section provided for the payment of
compensation to persons whose land had not been taken but whose land had been injuriously affected by works carried out by the acquiring authority. No guidance was given in the
sparse language of the section as to the exact circumstances in which the compensation
could be claimed or as to how the compensation was to be assessed. In a series of cases following the Act the courts established a group of rules stating conditions which had to be
satisfied before a claim under section 68 could succeed. It has been commented that this
judicial legislation bore little relation to the language of section 68.[18] Section 68 remained
the law for 120 years until it was replaced and re-enacted with little change in the language

---

[14] *Transport for London Ltd v Spirerose Ltd* [2009] UKHL 44, [2009] 1 WLR 1797, per Lord Walker at para 22.
This particular criticism was directed at the notoriously complex provisions of s 6 and sch 1 in the Land
Compensation Ac 1961. These provisions are examined in section (d) of ch 5.

[15] There is a general canon of statutory construction that an intention to take away the property of a subject
without giving to him a legal right to compensation for the loss of it is not to be imputed to the legislature unless
that intention is expressed in unequivocal terms: *A-G v Horner* (1884) 14 QBD 245; *Commissioner of Public Works
(Cape Colony) v Logan* [1903] AC 355; *Western Counties Rly Co v Windsor and Anapolis Rly Co* (1882) 7 App Cas
178. In *Central Control Board (Liquor Traffic) v Cannon Brewery Co* [1919] AC 744 a public house was acquired
from its owner under wartime legislation in force during World War 1. It was held that, although there was no
specific provision providing for compensation, compensation should be assessed under the ordinary and general
principles as contained in the Lands Clauses Consolidation Act 1845. See also *Burmah Oil Co Ltd v Lord Advocate*
[1965] AC 75, [1964] 2 WLR 1231 in which it was held that compensation was payable for property taken in pursuance of the Royal Prerogative in emergency at time of war: see para 1.5.

[16] See para 1.13.

[17] See ch 10.

[18] In *Argyle Motors (Birkenhead) Ltd v Birkenhead Corporation* [1975] AC 99, [1973] 2 WLR 487, at p 129 Lord
Wilberforce said 'The relevant section of the Act of 1845 (section 68) has, over one hundred years, received through
a number of decisions, some in this House, and by no means easy to reconcile, an interpretation which fixed upon
it a meaning having little perceptible relation to the words used'. See also *Wildtree Hotels Ltd v Harrow London
Borough Council* [2001] 2 AC 1, [2000] 3 WLR 165, per Lord Hoffmann at p 6.

by section 10(1) of the Compulsory Purchase Act 1965 which remains in force today. The Compulsory Purchase Act 1965 was an Act to consolidate the Lands Clauses Acts and other legislation but in this case no opportunity was taken to state in statutory form the state of the law as it had become as a result of judicial intervention. Instead section 10(2) of the Compulsory Purchase Act 1965 states that section 10

> shall be construed as affording in all cases a right to compensation for injurious affection to land which is the same as the right which section 68 of the Lands Clauses Consolidation Act 1845 has been construed as affording in cases where the amount claimed exceeds fifty pounds.

1.10   The totality of the statutory law on compulsory purchase and compensation falls into three categories. First, there are the statutes which confer a power of compulsory purchase, either in relation to defined areas of land required for a specific project or in general terms such as the power to acquire land needed for the construction or improvement of highways. The legislation often not only permits the acquisition of interests in land which give a right to possession of the land, such as freehold or leasehold interests, but also permits the creation and acquisition of new interests or rights over land such as easements. It is not appropriate in a book of this nature to attempt to itemise the many different powers of compulsory purchase which now exist and these powers and their limits are often described in specialist books dealing with the general area of law involved.[19] The major importance of the statute conferring powers, the empowering Act, is that a compulsory purchase of land may only be carried out if the land is in truth being acquired for the purpose for which the power of compulsory purchase was granted. An Act conferring powers of compulsory purchase will usually apply the general provisions of other legislation which contains the detailed procedures for exercising the power and the rules for the assessment of compensation. Normally the legislation which gives power to purchase land for particular purposes authorises a purchase by agreement for that purpose so that compulsion is to be regarded as a last resort.[20] The second category of the statutory law is the provisions which set out the procedure for the exercise of the power of compulsory purchase. A central part of these procedures is that in most cases when a general power of acquisition is conferred, without specifying particular land which may be acquired and a particular project for which it may be acquired, a person against whom the power is sought to be exercised has a right to object and to have his objection considered at a public local inquiry or hearing. The third category of legislation is the statutory provisions for assessing the amount of the compensation. The greater part of this book is taken up with an explanation of this last category of statutory rules and provisions.

1.11   The statutory law of compulsory purchase and compensation, having originated in the Lands Clauses Acts in the nineteenth century, is now contained almost wholly in five modern statutes.[21] The process of statutory intervention since 1845 has been spasmodic. The first, and perhaps the most major, intervention was the Acquisition of Land (Assessment of

---

[19] The 11th edn of *Cripps on the Compulsory Acquisition of Land* (1962), the last published edition of that work, contains in Pt 1 a long list of powers of compulsory acquisition as then existing. The list would be longer today.
[20] Section 120(2) of the Local Government Act 1972 states that a principal Council may acquire by agreement any land for any purpose for which they are authorised by this or any other enactment to acquire land, notwithstanding that the land is not immediately required for that purpose. By s 120(5) an acquisition by agreement means acquisition for money or money's worth as purchaser or lessee.
[21] See para 1.13.

Compensation) Act 1919. This Act followed the report in 1918 of the Scott Committee[22] and introduced six rules for the assessment of compensation which aimed to put into effect, with some alterations, various principles which had been bolted on to the provisions of the Lands Clauses Acts by decisions of the courts. The 1919 Act also abolished the rule of practice whereby the compensation based on the value of the land acquired was increased by 10 per cent as a type of solatium for a person losing his land against his will.[23] These six rules have been re-enacted in section 5 of the Land Compensation Act 1961 and remain a foundation of the assessment of compensation under today's legislation. A procedure for the exercise of powers of compulsory purchase was introduced by the Acquisition of Land (Authorisation Procedure) Act 1946. Further important rules were introduced by the Town and Country Planning Act 1959 including a statutory formulation of the important principle worked out by the courts that in assessing the value of the land acquired the effect on value of the scheme of the acquiring authority was to be left out of account.[24] The provisions on assessing compensation in force today are sometimes referred to as the compensation code although the aggregation of different provisions in different pieces of legislation bears little resemblance to a code as that expression is normally used.

The essential principle for the assessment of compensation became that the compensation should be equal to the value of the land acquired in the sense of the amount which that land would fetch if sold in the open market with all its advantages and disadvantages including its potential for development. In many cases the potential of developing the land adds considerably to, or even forms the predominant part of, the value of the land. In 1947 there began a period in which the development potential of land was to be ignored in assessing compensation. The political and economic view of the labour government of the time was that the development value of land should belong to the community as a whole and not to the private owner of the land. The consequence was that the Town and Country Planning Act of 1947 provided that the compensation payable following the compulsory purchase of land should not include any element attributable to the development value of the land. The measure of compensation became the value of the land in its existing use. There were obvious difficulties in such a system but it was not until the Town and Country Planning Act 1959 that the former basis of compensation as a sum which included all the potentialities enjoyed by the land acquired including its potential to be developed was fully restored. These matters are fortunately now of largely historical interest.[25]

1.12

---

[22] *Second Report to the Ministry of Reconstruction of the Committee dealing with the Law and Practice Relating to the Acquisition and Valuation of Land for Public Purposes* (L Scott QC, Chairman), Cd 9229.

[23] See r (1) of s 2 of the 1919 Act, now repeated in r (1) of s 5 of the Land Compensation Act 1961. Curiously the principle of an additional fixed payment or payments, that is payments additional to the value of the land, was reintroduced by ss 33A–33E of the Land Compensation Act 1973, inserted by the Planning and Compulsory Purchase Act 2004. These additional payments are considered in ch 11. In Hong Kong a wholly non-statutory process has grown up whereby what is described as ex gratia compensation is paid as an alternative to compensation on the statutory basis where land is taken for development, the ex gratia compensation being based on the unit area taken multiplied by a published rate in Hong Kong dollars with different rates applied to land in different locations.

[24] This principle is an important aspect of the 'value to the owner' or 'value to the seller' rule worked out by the courts following the Lands Clauses Consolidation Act 1845, and is sometimes known as the Pointe Gourde principle after the decision of the Privy Council in *Pointe Gourde Quarrying and Transport Co Ltd v Sub-Intendent of Crown Lands* [1947] AC 565. The principle is of cardinal importance to the assessment of compensation and is examined in ch 5.

[25] Even so the reasoning in recent cases in the House of Lords on the value to the owner or disregard of the scheme principle has been assisted by historical reference to the changing basis of compensation over the last half century: see ch 5 and see *Waters v Welsh Development Agency* [2004] UKHL 19, [2004] 1 WLR 1304 and *Transport*

1.13   As with most areas of public law the Human Rights Act 1998 with its application of the European Convention for the Protection of Human Rights and Fundamental Freedoms has a potential effect on the interpretation of the legislation just described, although as yet the impact has not been as great as in other areas such as deportation and immigration. Article 1 of the First Protocol to the Convention states:

> Every natural and legal person is entitled to the peaceful enjoyment of his possessions. No-one shall be deprived of his possessions except in the public interest and subject to the conditions provided for by law and the general principles of public international law.

It is said that in general this provision means that a person deprived of an interest or rights in land is entitled to compensation and that the compensation shall be reasonably related to the value of that taken, but that this does not mean that in all circumstances the compensation must be equal to the full market value of the interest or rights taken or affected.[26] The principle of equivalence does not appear to have found its way fully into human rights law. Article 6 of the Convention states that in the determination of his civil rights and obligations everyone is entitled to a fair and public hearing within a reasonable time by an independent and impartial tribunal. The Court of Appeal has been willing to use its power under section 3 of the Human Rights Act 1998 to interpret section 19(3) of the Land Compensation Act 1973 (compensation for the depreciation in the value of land caused by the use of a new highway) in a fashion not apparent from the statutory language in order to bring the provision into compliance with article 1 of the Convention.[27] A failure to determine proceedings resulting in a compulsory purchase within a reasonable time may be a violation of the convention rights of a landowner.[28] The generally established procedure in this country under which a Minister decides certain planning applications and appeals and decides whether to confirm a compulsory purchase order or to make an order prepared by him in draft has been held by the House of Lords to be in accord with article 6(1) of the Convention since, although a Minister was not himself a fair and impartial tribunal, the requirement of the article was satisfied provided the decision of the Minister was itself subject to review by a fair and impartial tribunal such as the High Court with full jurisdiction to deal with the case.[29]

1.14   The five statutes which together contain nearly all of the current statutory law on the subject of compulsory purchase and compensation are:

(a) the Land Compensation Act 1961;
(b) the Compulsory Purchase Act 1965;
(c) the Land Compensation Act 1973;
(d) the Acquisition of Land Act 1981; and
(e) the Compulsory Purchase (Vesting Declarations) Act 1981.

for London Ltd v Spirerose Ltd [2009] UKHL 44, [2009] 1 WLR 1797. The system whereby the development value of land was recouped by the state by way of a development charge was abolished in 1953 but the full open market value of land compulsorily acquired including its development value was not restored as the basis of compensation until 1959.

[26]   *James v United Kingdom* (1986) 8 EHRR 123 (relating to the Leasehold Reform Act 1967); *S v United Kingdom* [1984] 41 DR 226 (decision of the Commission).

[27]   *Thomas v Bridgend County Borough Council* [2011] EWCA Civ 862, [2012] QB 512. See section (b) of ch 13.

[28]   *Guillemin v France* (1997) 25 EHRR 435.

[29]   *R (Alconbury Developments) v Secretary of State* [2003] 2 AC 295, [2001] 2 WLR 1389. The making of a compulsory purchase order is not in breach of art 8 of the Convention simply because it is not the least obtrusive measure available: *Smith v Secretary of State* [2008] 1 WLR 394.

Further amendments to the Land Compensation Act 1961 of some significance have recently been made by the Localism Act 2011. In the main the provisions governing the assessment of compensation are in the Land Compensation Acts of 1961 and 1973 whereas the procedure for exercising the power of compulsory purchase of land is spread among the provisions of the other Acts. The statutory provisions emanate from different sources and cannot be said to have a tidy arrangement. An instance of the piecemeal arrangement of the legislation is that the provisions for the service of a notice to treat, an essential step in many compulsory acquisitions, are in the Compulsory Purchase Act 1965 whereas the provisions for the withdrawal of notices to treat are in the Land Compensation Act 1961. The reason for this division of provisions on the same subject is that the provisions on the service of a notice to treat go back to the Land Clauses Consolidation Act 1845 while the right to withdraw a notice to treat originated in the Acquisition of Land (Assessment of Compensation) Act 1919.

While the law of compulsory purchase and compensation is wholly statutory, disputes involving aspects of the application of that law can involve the consideration and application of legal principles which have effect throughout the whole of English civil law. For example, questions of the entitlement of a person to compensation or to certain components of compensation can involve such matters as the existence of constructive or resulting trusts, the doctrine of proprietary estoppel, and the principles which govern the lifting of the corporate veil so as to look behind the structure of companies.[30] The procedural requirements which are a part of the process of a compulsory acquisition may be the subject of arguments on the application of the general law of estoppel. It is not practical in a book of this nature to do more than draw attention to decisions and situations in which these general principles have become relevant and to explain how the principles have assisted in the determination of specific issues relating to compulsory purchase or compensation.

1.15

In 2003 and 2004 the Law Commission published two reports, one on compensation for compulsory purchase and one on the procedure for compulsory purchase, the aim being to produce a new statutory code.[31] Unfortunately no draft bill was included as sometimes appears in Law Commission publications although the text contains a number of rules which could form the basis of comprehensive new statutory provisions. The Government subsequently announced that it did not propose to introduce new legislation to give effect to the proposals in the reports. Thus an opportunity to produce a new and comprehensive code was lost. It seems inevitable that eventually such a new code will be enacted and although not all of the proposals of the Law Commission are to be welcomed[32] these reports will form a valuable input to any comprehensive reform.

1.16

---

[30] See section (b) of ch 12. There is a valuable analysis of the background to some of the current legislation in the decision of the then President of the Lands Tribunal, Mr George Bartlett QC, in *Pentrehobyn Trustees v National Assembly for Wales* [2003] RVR 140, although parts of it may be affected by later decisions.

[31] Law Com No 286 (2003) and No 281 (2004). Previous suggestions for reform had been contained in a review carried out by the Compulsory Purchase Policy Review Advisory Group, *Fundamental Review of the Laws and Procedures relating to Compulsory Purchase and Compensation*, published by the Department of the Environment, Transport and the Regions in 2000.

[32] For example, the proposals for the making of assumptions on the grant of planning permission for development of the land acquired seem inordinately complex when they appeared in legislative form, as they in part have in the Localism Act 2011 as explained in ch 7. Following the reports of the Law Commission some minor amendments to or clarification of the law were made by the Planning and Compulsory Purchase Act 2004 and these are noted as necessary in this book. They fall far short of the comprehensive reform suggested by the Law Commission and which is certainly needed.

1.17   This book describes the law of compulsory purchase and compensation as today applicable in England and Wales. There are some references in the book to the law in England or to English law. These are to be taken to refer to England and Wales. The underlying principles of the law have been extended to many areas of the British Commonwealth where legislation has been enacted for many years which in its essentials is similar to that in force in England and Wales. Many of these jurisdictions have or had final appeals to the Privy Council and the result has been a corpus of case law from that Court which, although not directly applicable in this country and although sometimes based on statutory provisions which are not entirely the same as those in force in England and Wales, has profoundly affected the law in this country. Similar legislation to that in England and Wales has been enacted by Parliament from the nineteenth century onwards so as to apply to Scotland and decisions of the higher Scottish courts have established principles of law which can be applied in England and Wales. As an example of the cross-fertilisation of legal authority reference may be made to the probable rule that in determining the value of a leasehold interest in land for the purposes of assessing compensation for the acquisition of that interest any expectation that the lease will be renewed by the agreement of the parties is to be left out of account. This somewhat controversial rule, originating or at least expounded in a Scottish decision, has been applied in recent years in Hong Kong.[33]

1.18   Other important principles have been established by, or have been clarified by, decisions of the Privy Council on appeals from countries in the Commonwealth. For example, the principle that all potentialities for changes of use and other development of the land acquired as at the date of acquisition are to be taken into account in assessing the value of that land is established or endorsed by decisions on appeals from New Zealand[34] and India.[35] The so-called Pointe Gourde principle, which has had great influence in the development of the law in the present field, takes its name from a decision of the Privy Council in 1947 on an appeal from Trinidad and Tobago.[36] A further leading case on the same topic arose from an appeal from Queensland in Australia to the Privy Council.[37] These decisions and their effect on the law of England and Wales are, of course, explained fully later in this book. Today the law of compensation in Hong Kong, a Special Administrative Region of the People's Republic of China, depends largely on a statute, the Lands Resumption Ordinance, which is closely based on English statute law and is applied in Hong Kong with the assistance of English and Commonwealth decisions. A leading authority on the ambit and limits of 'disturbance'

---

[33] See *Corporation of Glasgow v Lynch* (1903) 11 SLT 263 and *Director of Lands v Yin Shuen Enterprises Ltd* [2003] 6 HCFAR 1 (Hong Kong, Court of Final Appeal): see ch 4, para 4.99. For a further important Scottish decision upholding the principle that the expectation of making a future profit from land is a part of the value of that land, see *McEwing & Sons Ltd v Renfrew County Council* 1960 SC 53, (1959) 11 P & CR 306 discussed in ch 4, para 4.53, itself a decision which relied on an earlier decision of the Privy Council on appeal from New South Wales in *Pastoral Finance Association Ltd v The Minister* [1914] AC 1083. Recent decisions in courts in present or former British Colonies can assist in the understanding of the law of compensation in England and Wales. Examples discussed later in this book are *Penny's Bay Investment Co v Director of Lands* (2010) 13 HKCFAR 287 (Hong Kong, Court of Final Appeal) and *National Roads Authority v Bodden* (2013: CICA10 of 2012) (Court of Appeal of the Cayman Islands).
[34] *Maori Trustee v Ministry of Works* [1959] AC 1, [1958] 3 WLR 536.
[35] *Gajapatiraju v Regional Divisional Officer, Vizagapatam* [1939] AC 302. The principle as applied in England can be traced back at least to *R v Brown* (1867) LR 2 QB 630, per Cockburn CJ at p 631.
[36] *Pointe Gourde Quarrying and Transport Co Ltd v Sub-Intendent of Crown Lands* [1947] AC 465.
[37] *Melwood Units Pty Ltd v Commissioner of Main Roads* [1979] AC 426, [1978] 3 WLR 520. This decision established the principle that the rule which requires the disregard of the effect of the scheme of the acquiring authority on the value of the land acquired applies to decreases as well as increases in value brought about by the scheme. See ch 5.

compensation is the decision of the Privy Council on an appeal from Hong Kong just before it ceased to be a British Crown colony and general guidance on this subject was given in that decision.[38] The law of compensation as today applied in England and Wales therefore has a wide geographical reach as well as having been fructified by decisions from a wide area of present and former British possessions. On the other hand there can be important differences between parts of the legislation in force in former British possessions and the statutory provisions today in force in England and Wales such that decisions from other jurisdictions cannot necessarily be regarded as applicable in all respects to compensation claims in England and Wales.[39]

It is obvious to anyone concerned with the present area of the law that the legislation on compensation is in need of substantial amendment. The statutory provisions derive from a series of sources going back to 1845. They are found spread amongst a number of separate statutes between 1961 and 1973 which have themselves been amended from time to time so that new provisions are bolted on to what was there before. In important respects the legislation is what it was in 1845 with no more than a limited modernisation of the language. In some instances what is written in the legislation is difficult to comprehend save with the assistance of a number of decisions of the courts which give to the language of the statutes a meaning which is radically different from that which appears from an initial and untutored reading of that language. Distinctions are drawn in the application of the provisions as a whole which it is impossible to justify except for historical reasons which have no force today. For instance, different statutory provisions apply to the assessment of compensation when the dispossessed owner has a short leasehold interest such as an annual tenancy of the land as compared to the provisions which apply when the dispossessed owner has a more substantial interest such as a freehold or even a lease for two years. This distinction goes back to the Lands Clauses Consolidation Act 1845 and while there may have been reasons for it then there are none today. Other procedures are antiquated and are little if ever used such as the procedure for obtaining a right to possession of land being compulsorily acquired by the payment into court of the compensation claimed and the giving of a bond, a procedure which may have been significant under the Lands Clauses Consolidation Act 1845 and in the days of Victorian railway promoters but is not needed today.[40] The law of compulsory purchase and compensation is an important aspect of the relations between the citizen and the state, and both those to whom the power of compulsory purchase is entrusted and persons required in the public interest to give up their land are entitled to a rational, comprehensive and fair system of rules for the determination of the compensation which has to be paid. The sentiments just expressed are likely to be shared by most practitioners in this area of the law whether lawyers or valuers and have been echoed by the courts charged with the interpretation and application of the current disorganised legislation.[41]

1.19

---

[38] *Director of Buildings and Lands v Shun Fung Ironworks Ltd* [1995] 2 AC 111, [1995] 2 WLR 904.

[39] See *Director of Buildings and Lands v Shun Fung Ironworks Ltd*, ibid, where aspects of the decision depended on parts of the Lands Resumption Ordinance in force in Hong Kong which have no equivalent in English statutes. See ch 4, para 4.84.

[40] See section (k) of ch 2. This procedure which originated in the Lands Clauses Consolidation Act 1845 was repeated in the Compulsory Purchase Act 1965 even though that latter Act contained a new and simple procedure for obtaining possession by the giving of a notice of entry, and it is that procedure which is today normally used to gain entry to land prior to the determination and payment of compensation. Yet a further procedure for gaining entry was introduced in 1981 by the Compulsory Purchase (Vesting Declarations) Act of that year (see section (q) of ch 2) but the old procedure remains in the statute book.

[41] See *Waters v Welsh Development Authority* [2004] UKHL 19, [2004] 1 WLR 1304.

1.20   Following this introduction this book contains the following structure. The book is divided into four parts.

(i)   The first part, chapter 2, deals with the process and machinery of compulsory purchase which are described. This is largely a matter of organising the statutory provisions into a helpful sequence and the description contains little that is contentious. The main elements of the process are described, from a consideration of the power to effect a compulsory purchase to the limited opportunity given to challenge in the High Court the validity of a compulsory purchase order and the taking possession of the land by the acquiring authority.

(ii)   The second part is a series of chapters, chapters 3–13, which describe the main rules on the assessment of compensation. This is the core of the book. It starts in chapter 3 with a description of the general principles and concepts which underlie the law of compensation and an itemisation of the seven main heads of compensation. The three main components of compensation due when land is acquired are explained in subsequent chapters, these components being the value of the land acquired, compensation for injurious affection to land retained when only a part of a person's land is acquired, and disturbance compensation. This is followed by a description of the remaining four heads of compensation which are: (a) compensation for injurious affection under section 10 of the Compulsory Purchase Act 1965, (b) disturbance payments, (c) additional statutory payments, and (d) compensation for the use of public works under Part I of the Land Compensation Act 1973. It may be noted that two of the heads of compensation described, those under section 10 of the Compulsory Purchase Act 1965 and Part I of the Land Compensation Act 1973, are generally regarded as a part of the overall compensation code even though they do not involve the acquisition of any land from the claimant.

(iii)   The third part is an examination of the important subjects of procedure and valuation. This includes the procedure for establishing disputed claims and the main principles of the valuation of land which are likely to be of practical help especially to non-valuers who are concerned with compensation claims. These subjects are relevant to all the main heads of compensation. The Appendix contains worked examples of different methods of valuation with explanatory material.

(iv)   Lastly in the fourth part certain suggestions for reform of the law are made.

1.21   This book is likely to be of greatest assistance to lawyers and surveyors advising landowners and public authorities on claims for compensation. The central component of such claims is the valuation of land and the calculation of other forms of compensation. One of the difficulties in producing an overall description of the law of compulsory purchase and compensation is that the legislative basis of the subject is spread in what sometimes appears an haphazard fashion between a series of statutes some of which have been heavily amended by later statutes. It is hoped that the 16 chapters of this book form a reasonably logical sequence of the description. A completely logical arrangement is probably impossible in the light of the statutory material. For instance, no statutory provision contains a complete list of the persons entitled to compensation. One result of these difficulties is that matters which are in part substantive, such as the right to advance payments of compensation, are explained in chapter 15 under the general heading of procedure. There are a number of rules applicable to assessing compensation which do not fit easily into any major division of the subject and these are covered in chapter 6 under the heading of 'Other Valuation Rules'.

The concept of the liability to pay compensation for the acquisition or removal of interests and rights in land is widely found in law. Instances in private law relating to the relation of landlord and tenant and to restrictive covenants have been mentioned earlier in this chapter.[42] Other examples in public law are the payment of compensation for orders revoking a planning permission or requiring the discontinuance of a use of land. The specific compensation provisions vary from case to case. It is not practical in a book of this nature to cover all such instances of compensation even though in some cases the fundamental principles of the assessment of compensation and the valuation techniques used are the same as, or similar to, those which apply to the compulsory purchase of land.[43] It has been a general constitutional practice to compensate landowners when rights in land are removed or modified in the public interest. Even so major areas of the deprivation of property rights have occurred without compensation. The most notable is the general town and country planning system in force since 1 July 1948 which severely constrains the rights of landowners to deal with their land as they think fit. Another example is the statutory controls which reduce the ordinary contractual rights of landlords where land is let for business, agriculture or residential purposes. Provisions which restrict rights available generally to the public without compensation being payable, such as the right to own restaurants or the right to use particular highways free of charge or tolls, are not normally a breach of constitutional safeguards against the deprivation of property without compensation.[44] This book is therefore confined to the general law of the compulsory purchase of land by public bodies and of the assessment of compensation payable for such purchases.[45]   1.22

Of its nature a compulsory purchase of land is normally a process which enables a public authority to acquire land from an owner in the public interest even though the owner is unwilling to sell the land. There are certain procedures under which an owner of land can compel a public authority to acquire his land such as by a purchase notice where the land has become incapable of reasonably beneficial use in its existing state or by a blight notice when the disposal of land is affected by certain public proposals, both procedures arising under the Town and Country Planning Act 1990. This book does not deal with the details of the procedures in question which will be found in specialised books on town planning. However, the acquisitions in these cases operate to some extent as if they were a compulsory purchase of land and the compensation is generally assessed on the same principles as would apply if there had been an ordinary compulsory purchase. The treatment of those principles in this book will therefore be relevant to the compensation aspects of these procedures in the town planning legislation. There are also numerous statutory powers under which organisations providing public and utility services can obtain rights, called wayleaves, to run pipes and cables over private land or to install equipment such as   1.23

---

[42] See para 1.3.

[43] See, eg s 237 of the Town and Country Planning Act 1990 which provides for the payment of compensation when certain rights over land, such as easements or restrictive covenants, are overridden in order that a development for which planning permission has been granted may be carried out. The legislation specifically applies s 7 and s 10 of the Compulsory Purchase Act 1965 to the assessment of compensation.

[44] *Grape Bay Ltd v A-G of Bermuda* [2000] 1 WLR 574; *Ampbell-Rodriquez v Jamaica* [2007] UKPC 65, [2008] RVR 144.

[45] As mentioned in para 1.20(ii) there are certain areas of the overall compensation code which apply even though no land is acquired from the claimant for compensation.

telecommunications equipment on private land. The relevant statutes often contain their own provisions for compensation which may or may not repeat or apply general provisions applicable to compensation for the compulsory acquisition of land. These individual compensation processes are not described in this book save where decisions on them throw light on the general law of compensation.[46]

---

[46] An example of this situation is *Welford v EDF Energy (LPN) Ltd* [2007] 2 EGLR 1 where it was agreed by the parties that general principles of compensation applied to provisions in sch 4 to the Electricity Act 1989 when a wayleave to run underground electricity cables under land was granted and the Court of Appeal examined general principles applicable to compensation claims (see paras 4.74 et seq of ch 4). A further example is *Bocardo SA v Star Energy UK Onshore Ltd* [2010] UKSC 35, [2011] 1 AC 380, referred to in para 5.78 of ch 5.

2

The Law of Compulsory Purchase

(A) INTRODUCTION

In order to gain an understanding of the law of compensation it is necessary to have at least   2.1
an outline appreciation of the procedure or machinery of compulsory purchase. The assessment of compensation sometimes depends on aspects of the operation of that machinery. For example, a cardinal rule in the assessment of compensation is that the value of the land acquired is usually to be determined as its value at the date of entry onto the land by the acquiring authority and the right to make a physical entry onto the land is an aspect of the machinery of compulsory purchase. The giving to the landowner of a notice known as a notice to treat is a part of many compulsory purchases and some rules relating to compensation are linked to these notices. This chapter provides an account of the procedures which have to be followed if a compulsory purchase is to be effected with the aim of providing a background to the law of compensation. All main matters and all matters of central importance are explained but the chapter does not cover every detail of those procedures. The exercise of powers of compulsory purchase is an aspect of administrative law and is subject to the general law on that subject which is examined in specialist textbooks on the subject. For example, the process of public local inquiries is used widely in public aspects of property law such as town and country planning and a specialist jurisprudence, as an aspect of administrative law, has grown up in relation to that procedure which is described in specialist books on administrative law and on town planning. This jurisprudence applies in general to public local inquiries held in connection with objections to compulsory purchase orders which is explained in outline later in this chapter.

The statutory provisions governing the procedures to be applied in effecting a compulsory   2.2
purchase of land are contained mainly in three statutes, the Compulsory Purchase Act 1965, the Acquisition of Land Act 1981, and the Compulsory Purchase (Vesting Declarations) Act 1981. In general terms the acquisition of a piece of land by compulsory means involves a series of stages.

- The acquiring authority must satisfy itself that there is statutory power to acquire compulsorily the land in question for the purpose for which it proposes to acquire the land.
- The acquiring authority must make a decision, usually by way of a resolution of the council or a decision by a committee or officer pursuant to delegated powers where the acquiring authority is a local authority, to acquire the land.
- Where the acquisition is of land under a power of acquisition which does not itself identify the land which may be acquired the acquiring authority makes and gives

notice of a compulsory purchase order which identifies the land to be acquired. Where the statute conferring the power of acquisition itself identifies the exact area within which land may be acquired for a particular project the making of a compulsory purchase order is not normally necessary.

- There is then a process of confirmation of the compulsory purchase order when the making of an order is necessary. The process of confirmation varies depending on whether the order is made by a local authority or other public body or by a Minister and on whether the publication and notification of the making of the order have resulted in objections which are not withdrawn. In technical terms when the acquisition is by a Minister the order is first prepared in draft by the Minister and then after consideration of objections may finally be made by the Minister. It is at this stage that the important right to object to the order arises.

- Once the order has been confirmed, or made by the Minister, the acquiring authority has the choice of serving a notice to treat or implementing the general vesting declaration procedure. The process is further complicated by the fact that a vesting declaration operates for many purposes as a constructive or deemed notice to treat. Of course if no compulsory purchase order is needed, because land within specific and prescribed geographical limits is authorised to be acquired by the empowering Act, the acquiring authority may proceed directly to the giving of notice to treat or the making of a general vesting declaration.

- At this stage the authority generally has the right to enter the land being acquired.

- If the vesting declaration procedure has been used title to the land will vest in the acquiring authority on a date specified as the vesting date in the vesting declaration. Otherwise the authority will need to have a conveyance or transfer executed in its favour as occurs in the ordinary way when there is a purchase of land.

- The amount of compensation payable to the dispossessed landowner may be agreed between him and the acquiring authority but if it is not agreed following the service of an actual or constructive notice to treat the matter may be referred by either party to the Lands Tribunal for determination.

2.3   The procedure just described may seem to many to be of considerable complexity. The situation does not improve when the details of some of the stages are explained. One reason for the complexity is that the procedure owes its origin to different statutes. A part of what is required, for instance the central feature of the giving of a notice to treat, goes back to provisions in the Lands Clauses Consolidation Act 1845 whereas much of the detailed procedure started in the Acquisition of Land (Authorisation Procedure) Act 1946 before being repeated in the current Acquisition of Land Act 1981. A new and substantially different procedure was then provided, as an alternative method of gaining entry onto and title to the land, by the Compulsory Purchase (Vesting Declarations) Act 1981. The remainder of this chapter explains the machinery and procedure of compulsory purchase in more detail following the general sequence and pattern of the steps just mentioned.

(B) POWER OF COMPULSORY PURCHASE

1. General Extent of the Power

Compulsory purchase means that a person's property is taken from him against his will   2.4
because it is considered to be in the public interest to do so. Whether a particular compulsory purchase is within the boundaries of the power in the empowering Act is in many
instances a question of the correct interpretation of that Act in the light of the facts. The
approach of the courts to this question is to scrutinise carefully the meaning of the relevant
legislation and, in the words of a recent opinion delivered in the Supreme Court, 'The
courts have been astute to impose a strict construction on statutes expropriating private
property'.[1] The same approach to this area of the law has often been commended as a matter
of principle.[2]

Since all powers of compulsory purchase are statutory it follows that a purported compul-   2.5
sory purchase will be void if the acquisition does not fall within the terms of the statutory
power.[3] This statement is no more than a repetition of the classic underlying principle of
ultra vires in administrative law, namely the rule that a public authority may not act outside
its powers. If it is alleged that an authority has acted outside its powers in purporting to
acquire land compulsorily the correctness of that allegation will be tested by considering
the facts and construing the statute which confers the power of purchase. It is rare that an
authority attempts to acquire land which is blatantly outside the power in the statute.
Sometimes a geographical boundary within which land may be acquired is specified such as
where a local authority has power to acquire land within its administrative area. A local
authority would be unlikely in such a case to try to acquire land outside its administrative
area. An occasion on which an authority did seek to acquire rights which it could not
acquire under the empowering Act was an attempt by a housing authority to acquire flats in
a building and to acquire newly created easements and ancillary rights over other parts of
the building not acquired but needed for the use of the flats. The compulsory purchase
order was quashed since there was no power to acquire rights not in existence at the time of
the compulsory purchase.[4] Sometimes where the legislation is directed to a specific project

---

[1] R (Sainsbury's Supermarkets Ltd) v Wolverhampton City Council [2010] UKSC 20, [2011] 1 AC 437, per Lord
Collins at paras 9–11.
[2] See, eg Prest v Secretary of State for Wales [1982] 81 LGR 193, per Lord Denning MR at p 198 and, more
recently, French CJ in the High Court of Australia in R & R Fazzolari Pty Ltd v Parramatta City Council [2009]
HCA 12 at paras 40, 42 and 43, citing Blackstone's Commentaries.
[3] See ch 1, para 1.5. The only exception today appears to be the power of the Crown under the Royal Prerogative
to requisition property at times of war or grave national emergency.
[4] Sovmots Investments Ltd v Secretary of State for the Environment [1979] AC 144, [1977] 2 WLR 951. See section
(c) of this chapter for the present law on the acquisition of ancillary rights. A further example is that a compulsory
purchase order was quashed in White and Collins v Minister of Health [1939] 2 KB 838, when the acquiring authority purported to acquire for housing purposes 23 acres out of 35 acres of land which surrounded a large house
when the empowering legislation excluded the acquisition of land forming part of a park or garden. A recent
example of an attempt to exercise a power of compulsory purchase which was held to be outside the ambit of the
empowering Act was R (Barnsley Metropolitan Borough Council) v Secretary of State [2012] EWHC 1366 (Admin),
[2012] 2 EGLR 1, in which a Council made a compulsory purchase order over land registered as a village green and
owned and occupied by Irish travellers for what was in substance the benefit, improvement or development of the
area relying upon powers of compulsory purchase conferred by the Local Government Act 1972 and the Local
Government Act 2000 when the exercise of the power of compulsory purchase for that specific purpose was

there is a time limit on the power of acquisition and a purported exercise of the power out-side the period prescribed would be ultra vires and void.[5] On occasions an empowering Act permits an authority to take temporary possession of land, for example for use as a tempo-rary storage area while permanent works are being carried out. In such cases the normal process of the compulsory purchase of land is not necessary. In these cases there is provi-sion for compensation to be paid to a person who is temporarily deprived of his land equal to the loss which he suffers.[6] It is a principle of constitutional law that a body entrusted with powers and discretions in the public interest cannot fetter its power by entering into con-tracts not to exercise those powers and this principle is applicable to the exercise of powers for the compulsory acquisition of land.[7] However, the principle is applied in a flexible rather than rigid fashion.[8]

2.6   The delineation of the purpose for which a power of compulsory acquisition may be exer-cised is framed in different ways in different legislation. Acts of Parliament not concerned with a specific project often give a general power of acquisition for a particular purpose, such as the improvement of a highway, to local authorities who are highway authorities to exercise generally on such land as they think fit.[9] Where an Act is concerned with a specific project the power may be framed differently. A modern example of this latter type of case is the Crossrail Act 2008 which is concerned with the construction of a new railway running from the west to the east of London and passing in a tunnel through central London. This Act is used generally in this chapter and elsewhere as an illustration of this latter type of case. Under the Crossrail Act certain plans known as the deposited plans were deposited in Parliament which showed limits of deviation and limits of land to be acquired and used. These limits were drawn by reference to the works proposed, called the scheduled works, which were specified in schedule 1 to the Act. It was then provided that the Secretary of State is authorised to acquire compulsorily land within the two limits just mentioned which is required for or in connection with the works or the Crossrail project.[10] The effect is that the Secretary of State may proceed directly to acquire the land by the service of notice to treat or under the general vesting declaration procedure. In most cases a compulsory pur-chase of a specific area of land, pursuant to a general statutory power to acquire such land, as the acquiring authority decides that it needs for a particular purpose, needs to be autho-rised by a compulsory purchase order made by the acquiring authority to which landown-

expressly excluded by s 121(2)(b) of the 1972 Act. The Minister refused to confirm the order and his decision was upheld in the High Court.

[5] See, eg s 6(6) of the Crossrail Act 2008 which prescribes a five year period from the date of the passing of the Act for the service of a notice to treat or the initiation of the vesting declaration procedure. An older example is *Tiverton and North Devon Rly Co v Loosemore* (1883) 9 App Cas 480, where the empowering Act required that the powers of compulsory purchase had to be exercised within three years of the passing of the Act and that the works of construction of the railway had to be completed within five years of the passing of the Act.

[6] An example of a provision permitting the temporary taking of possession of land is sch 5 to the Channel Tunnel Rail Link Act 1996 which required that the possession taken temporarily should be given up within one year from the completion of the works and stated that the owners and occupiers of the land were entitled to com-pensation for any loss which they might suffer by reason of possession having been taken. The compensation was to be determined under and in accordance with Pt I of the Land Compensation Act 1961, that is by the Lands Tribunal.

[7] *Ayr Harbour Trustees v Oswald* (1883) 8 App Cas 623.

[8] *Stourcliffe Estate Co v Bournemouth Corporation* [1910] 2 Ch 12. A discussion of this aspect of general consti-tutional law will be found in works on administrative law such as *De Smith on Judicial Review*, 7th edn (London, Sweet and Maxwell, 2003) paras 9-022, 9-023.

[9] Highways Act 1980, s 239(3).

[10] Crossrail Act 2008, s 6(1).

ers may object and this process is considered later. No compulsory purchase order authorising the acquisition need be made under the above provisions in the Crossrail Act or under
similar Acts because authorisation for the acquisition is already given by the Act and consequently there is no opportunity for a landowner to object to the acquisition of his land.[11]

However, in the Crossrail Act 2008 the Secretary of State is given a further power to acquire   2.7
land outside the limits of deviation, and outside the limits of the land to be acquired and
used, with that power to be exercised for the same purposes of the works and the Crossrail
project, but in this case the acquisition is not authorised by the Act itself and must become
authorised by a compulsory purchase order made by the Minister.[12] The theory behind
these provisions is that owners of land within the two limits in the deposited plans had an
opportunity to object to the acquisition of their land during the progress of the Bill through
Parliamentary procedures whereas those with land outside the limits have an opportunity
to object to a compulsory purchase order relating to their land when it is made. Objections
at the Bill stage are presented by way of petitions to Parliament which are heard by a select
committee but the time available and the need to observe a timetable mean that not all
objections may be heard or heard as fully as petitioners might wish. The process of defining
the works to be carried out and establishing limits of deviation and limits of land to be
acquired and used is a familiar procedure with the construction of a project such as a railway and where the acquisition of land for the work is authorised by an Act of Parliament
and this procedure has been in use since the nineteenth century.

2. Purpose of Acquisition

A public authority needs to take care not only that the land it proposes to acquire is within   2.8
the prescribed geographical and time limits of the power of acquisition and within any
other limitation on that power but also that the acquisition is for the prescribed purpose. A
purported acquisition of land for some purpose other than that stated in the empowering
statute, sometimes called a collateral purpose, is ultra vires and void. Thus if an authority is
empowered to acquire land for the purpose of providing housing an acquisition which is in
truth for the purpose of constructing a road will be quashed.[13] The acquisition of land by a

---

[11] Certain parts of the procedure for putting into effect a compulsory purchase refer to a compulsory purchase
order and a frequent method of dealing with this in provisions of the present nature is that such other provisions
are specifically applied to the acquisition. For example, para 2 of sch 6 to the Crossrail Act applies Pt I of the
Compulsory Purchase Act 1965 to acquisitions as it applies to a compulsory purchase order albeit with certain
modifications. Paragraph 4 of the same schedule applies the Compulsory Purchase (Vesting Declarations) Act
1981 to acquisitions under the Crossrail Act 2008 as if that Act were a compulsory purchase order.

[12] Crossrail Act 2008, s 7(1). Section 7(6) applies the Acquisition of Land Act 1981 to acquisitions outside the
specified limits so that an acquisition of such land is only authorised if a compulsory purchase order is made
covering the land in question: see para 2.23.

[13] *Merravale Builders v Secretary of State* (1978) 36 P & CR 87. Other examples can be found of this obvious
principle. In *Lynch v Commissioners of Sewers of the City of London* (1886) 32 Ch D 72, it was held that an authority could not acquire land under a power of acquisition to widen a road if the true intention of the authority was
to alter the level of a road. The court will where necessary investigate on the evidence what is the true intention of
an acquiring authority: ibid. In *Webb v Minister of Housing and Local Government* [1965] 1 WLR 755, [1965] 2 All
ER 193, an order was quashed when its purpose was in part to construct a promenade whereas the empowering
Act permitted compulsory acquisition only for the purposes of coast protection works. A change of intention
by an acquiring authority after the service of a notice to treat may mean an implied abandonment of the right
to proceed with the notice if the new intention is to put into effect a purpose for which the land could not be

railway company was held to be unlawful when the land was acquired not for the purposes of the railway undertaking but in order that it could be given free of charge to a third party from whom the company had bought stock and pursuant to a contractual obligation to that person.[14] In an appeal from Australia the Municipal Council of Sydney was empowered to acquire land for 'carrying out improvements in or remodelling any portion of the City'. A resolution to acquire land was held to be unlawful on the basis that the true motive for the acquisition was to secure an anticipated increase in the value of the land.[15]

2.9   There is a tendency in modern statutes to frame powers of acquisition in very wide terms. Under the Town and Country Planning Act 1990 land may be acquired by a local planning authority for 'a purpose which it is necessary to achieve in the interests of the proper planning of the area in which the land is situated'.[16] It would not be easy to contend that any acquisition was not within this wide formulation. In addition public purposes merge into each other. Land acquired to be made available for housing in a particular area might equally well be said to be acquired for the purposes of planning in that good planning of an area no doubt requires that there is a sufficiency of land available for housing development in that area.[17] A statutory power, including a power of compulsory purchase, may be exercised for more than one purpose and a court will generally only uphold the validity of the exercise of the power if it is satisfied that the true and dominant purpose of the exercise was that authorised by the statute.[18]

3. Relevant Considerations

2.10   The decision by a public body to exercise its power of compulsory acquisition is a discretionary decision. It is a fundamental tenet of administrative law that any public body exercising a discretion must act lawfully and one of the criteria of lawfulness is that the body in question takes into account all relevant considerations and leaves out of account all irrelevant considerations.[19] This rule therefore applies to an authority making a compulsory

---

compulsorily acquired: *Simpson's Motor Sales (London) Ltd v Hendon Corporation* [1964] AC 1088, [1963] 2 WLR 1187. The classic expression of the underlying principle is that of Lord Cranworth LC in *Galloway v Mayor and Commonalty of London* (1886) LR 1 HL 34, at p 43 where he said: 'The principle is this, that when persons embarking in great undertakings, for the accomplishment of which those engaged in them have received authority from the legislature to take compulsorily the land of others, making to the latter proper compensation, the persons so authorised cannot be allowed to exercise the powers conferred on them for any collateral object; that is for any purposes except those for which the legislature has invested them with extraordinary powers'.

[14] *Lord Carrington v Wycombe Rly Co* (1868) 3 Ch App 377.
[15] *Municipal Council of Sydney v Campbell* [1925] AC 338.
[16] Town and Country Planning Act 1990, s 226(1)(b).
[17] See *Hanks v Minister of Housing and Local Government* [1963] 1 QB 999, [1963] 1 All ER 47.
[18] *Westminster Corporation v London and North Western Rly* [1905] AC 426. For example, in *R v Inner London Education Authority, ex parte Westminster City Council* [1986] 1 WLR 28, [1986] 1 All ER 19, the Inner London Education Authority had power to publish information on matters relating to local government but its actions were held to be unlawful when it carried out a major publicity campaign against expenditure cuts by central government.
[19] *Associated Provincial Picture Houses Ltd v Wednesbury Corporation* [1948] 1 KB 223, [1947] 2 All ER 680, per Lord Greene MR at p 234. The statement of Lord Greene has been described by Lord Scarman in the House of Lords as the classical review of the circumstances in which the courts will intervene to quash as being illegal the exercise of administrative discretion: see *R v Secretary of State for the Environment, ex parte Nottinghamshire County Council* [1986] AC 240, [1986] 2 WLR 1, at p 249.

purchase order with the result that if there is a failure to take into account relevant considerations, or if irrelevant considerations are taken into account, the actions of the authority are liable to be quashed.[20] Quashing is not of course automatic and the court will exercise its discretion so that if the error is minor, or could not conceivably have affected the decision of the authority, it is unlikely that a court would quash the action of the authority.[21] In most cases where a public authority makes a compulsory purchase order the benefits which it believes will flow from the compulsory acquisition of a piece of land in question are related in some way to the development of that particular piece of land and to the public benefit which will accrue from the development or other use of that land. The acquisition of land for the provision on it of a part of a highway, or for housing, or for some other form of regeneration of the land, or for some public project such as an airport, clearly falls within this category. However, it is permissible for an acquiring authority to take account as a relevant consideration in its decision to acquire compulsorily a particular piece of land benefits which may accrue to other land through the acquisition of the land in question. That having been said, the circumstances in which the securing of benefits for other land, off-site benefits, is a relevant consideration and are carefully restricted as a matter of principle.

The law has developed in this area by drawing from principles in the law of town and country planning. In that area of law the courts have often considered whether benefits which may accrue to the public from the development or use of a different site are a relevant consideration when permission is granted for a particular development on a particular site. For example, a local planning authority may decide to grant permission for the development of site A in circumstances in which that development might not otherwise be acceptable because the development of site A will in some way bring about some development or have some other effect on site B which is perceived to be in the public interest. The general principle which the courts have worked out in relation to planning cases of this sort is that the prospect of a benefit to site B is only relevant if the development and benefit on site B are reasonably related to the development of site A which is being permitted. The same general principle has been applied to decisions to make a compulsory purchase order. If a compulsory purchase order is made to acquire site A in order that as a result benefits may accrue to site B which are seen as being in the public interest then those benefits to site B, the off-site benefits, must be related to or connected with the development to secure which the compulsory acquisition of site A is taking place. Furthermore, the connection has to be a real rather than a fanciful or remote connection.[22] The fact that in cases of this type the compulsory acquisition by a public authority of site A will mean that, through the development of that site by a developer, a commitment and funds will be available for the development in the public interest of site B – what is called a cross-subsidy situation – will not by itself and in the absence of some other connection between the two sites amount to a sufficient connection between the site being compulsorily acquired and the site to which the benefits will accrue. In such a case a compulsory purchase order made to acquire site A, or a decision in

2.11

---

[20] See section (i) of this chapter for the procedure available to secure the quashing of a compulsory purchase order and the strict time limit for starting proceedings for this purpose. There is a discussion by Glidewell J of the principles applicable in this area of the law in *Bolton MBC v Secretary of State for the Environment* (1991) 61 P & CR 343.
[21] See para 2.78.
[22] *R (Sainsbury's Supermarkets Ltd) v Wolverhampton City Council* [2010] UKSC 20, [2011] 1 AC 437.

principle to make such an order, is likely to be quashed.[23] This is a stark example of the process of compulsory acquisition being vitiated by the acquiring authority taking into account an irrelevant consideration but, of course, there could be many other instances where that was done so that the validity of the order was in jeopardy.

2.12   Acquiring authorities sometimes carry out compulsory acquisitions as part of an overall arrangement with a developer whereby the acquiring authority uses its statutory powers to acquire land and then transfers the land to the developer on terms that the developer indemnifies the authority against the costs of the acquisition. It appears that such arrangements are generally lawful provided that the authority complies with the restriction on disposals of land contained in section 123(1) of the Local Government Act 1972, namely that the disposal is not for a consideration which is less than the best that can reasonably be obtained, and with the similar requirement in section 233 of the Town and Country Planning Act 1990 as regards land which has been acquired or appropriated by a local authority for planning purposes. The type of indemnity arrangements just described are colloquially called a 'back to back' arrangement and provided that the authority takes care that it is obtaining the best commercial arrangement that it can with a developer such arrangements are lawful.[24] One matter to which attention should be paid in such arrangements is that land may be acquired from a landowner at a price which disregards the overall scheme of development whereas the land which is disposed of by the acquiring authority, after its acquisition from the owner, to the developer may have a value which reflects the value of the scheme. Matters of this sort must be taken into account in considering whether the best commercial arrangement reasonably possible has been made and whether the land acquired is being disposed of for the best consideration reasonably obtainable.[25] What seems objectionable in principle is that land should be acquired from an owner at a price which does not reflect the value given to the land by a scheme of development and that the land is then acquired by a developer at the same reduced value so that he can profit from the scheme of the development.

4. Works Orders

2.13   Most powers of compulsory purchase derive from an Act which confers general powers without specifying the exact land which may be acquired, so that the exact land has to be

---

[23] In the *Wolverhampton* case, above, a site in Wolverhampton suitable for supermarket development was owned as to 86% by Sainsbury and as to the balance by Tesco. Both supermarket companies wished to develop the site. Tesco owned a further site in Wolverhampton about 850m away which contained a number of listed buildings and required regeneration. Tesco offered to carry out the regeneration of the nearby site if the local authority would make a compulsory purchase order to acquire the part of the site to be developed as a supermarket owned by Sainsbury so that Tesco could, with ownership of the whole site passed to them, carry out that supermarket development. The local authority made the compulsory purchase order for this overall purpose. It was quashed by the Supreme Court on the basis of the principles which have been explained. As a matter of legal analysis two fundamental aspects of the law of ultra vires actions by public bodies, (a) the principle that a power cannot be exercised wholly or mainly for an unauthorised purpose (see para 2.8), and (b) the principle that the decision to exercise a power must not be taken having regard to immaterial considerations (such as achieving some unauthorised or collateral purpose), merge into each other.

[24] *Standard Commercial Property Services Ltd v City of Glasgow* [2006] UKHL 50, 2005 SLT 144.

[25] The general disregard of the scheme of the acquiring authority in valuing the land acquired for the purposes of assessing compensation is explained in ch 5.

the subject of a compulsory purchase order made under the Act, or from an Act which authorises a specific major project such as the Crossrail Act 2008 or the Channel Tunnel Rail Link Act 1998, in which case the Act itself generally defines a limited area within which land which may be acquired. There is a further procedure under which powers to acquire specific land may be obtained which is that under the Transport and Works Act 1992. The Act is intended to apply to substantial transport projects, the construction and operations of railways, tramways, trolley vehicle systems, other systems of guided transport, the construction and operation of inland waterways and certain other works.

The person intending to carry out the project may apply to the Secretary of State for Transport for a works order which may be made by the Minister by statutory instrument. The Transport and Works (Applications and Objections Procedure) Rules 2006 state the procedure governing applications for an order, the making of objections to the order and the holding of an inquiry or hearing into objections. If the order is made it may, among other matters, authorise the compulsory purchase of land and rights in land for the purposes of the project. The owner or occupier of any land to be acquired has a right to object to the order and to have his objection heard at an inquiry or hearing.[26] As with compulsory purchase orders there is a right to challenge the validity of an order in the High Court within six weeks of the publication of notice of the making of the order on the same grounds as apply to challenging the validity of compulsory purchase orders, that is that the works order is not within the powers of the Act or that there has been a failure to comply with a procedural requirement.[27]   2.14

The Transport and Works Act 1992 gives an opportunity for a substantial transport project to be considered as a whole and to be authorised without the need for primary parliamentary legislation and subject to reasonable procedural safeguards. An order made under the Act is therefore a further possible source of powers of compulsory purchase of land.   2.15

5. Nationally Significant Infrastructure Projects

There has long been concern over the very lengthy legal and administrative processes involved with authorising projects such as new transport facilities or nuclear power stations which may be the subject of considerable political and social objection.[28] The delay is caused in part by the need to hear many objections to the grant of planning permission or other necessary consent for the project. The Planning Act 2008 sought to meet these difficulties by establishing the Planning Infrastructure Commission which would consider major projects of the above nature but without the huge delays and formalities created by long public inquiries. The procedure was amended by the Localism Act 2011 in that the Commission was abolished and the functions under the Planning Act 2008 relating to nationally significant infrastructure projects are now carried out by the Planning Inspectorate before a final decision is made by the relevant Secretary of State. The Planning Inspectorate is a body of   2.16

---

[26] Transport and Works (Applications and Objectors Procedure) (England and Wales) Rules 2006, (SI 2006/1466), s 11.

[27] Ibid, s 22. For the process of statutory challenge to the validity of a compulsory purchase order see section (i) of this chapter.

[28] Examples are the Sizewell Nuclear Power Station in the 1980s and more recently the Fifth Terminal at Heathrow Airport. Both in the end were permitted but only after massive and unacceptable delays.

permanent inspectors who hold inquiries and hearings into matters such as appeals to the Secretary of State against the refusal of planning permission under the Town and Country Planning Act 1990. At one time inspectors held the inquiry and then reported to the Secretary of State with their recommendation with the Secretary of State making the decision. Today in the great majority of cases the decision is made by the inspector.

2.17   The process involves the examination of major proposals relating to energy, transport, water, waste and waste water. The result of the examination may be that a development consent is issued by the Secretary of State. The consent will have the effect of a planning permission and other necessary statutory consents for the project and it may include provision for authorising the compulsory acquisition of land. Such an authorisation operates as a confirmed compulsory purchase order. The exact procedure involved is described in an Advice Note issued by the Planning Inspectorate.[29] There is the usual right to challenge the validity in law of a development consent within six weeks of the decision of the Secretary of State, in this case by a claim for judicial review.[30] A considerable number of major projects have been accepted for examination under the procedure such as the Thames Tideway Tunnel and the M1 Junction 10a Grade Separation at Luton. The issue of a development consent is therefore a further possible source of a power of compulsory purchase of land.

6. Limited Power to Sell

2.18   There are a number of reasons why land or an interest in land may not be alienable or freely alienable by its owner. Such restrictions on alienation do not prevent the compulsory purchase of the land.

2.19   Sometimes land is made inalienable by statute. An example is land belonging to the National Trust which is made inalienable by the National Trust Acts of 1907 and 1939. A power to acquire land under a compulsory purchase order is exercisable notwithstanding any enactment providing that the land shall be inalienable. This provision can only be overridden by an express statement in the enactment which makes the land inalienable that the land shall not be subject to compulsory acquisition.[31]

2.20   Other forms of restriction on alienation may exist such as covenants against alienation in a lease or restrictions on corporations disposing of land or restrictions on sale by the trustees of a charitable trust. Persons with an interest in land subject to such restrictions are entitled to sell or convey or release their interest to the acquiring authority.[32] There are provisions whereby in some cases in which the above entitlement has to be relied upon to sell the land the compensation is to be determined by a surveyor appointed by one of the parties or by the Lands Tribunal and paid into court to be applied for such purposes as the High Court shall order. On the money being paid into court the owner of the interest in question must convey it to the acquiring authority or, if he fails to do so, the authority may execute a deed

---

[29] See Advice Note 8 issued by the Planning Inspectorate.
[30] See Planning Act 2008, s 118.
[31] Acquisition of Land Act 1981, s 9.
[32] Compulsory Purchase Act 1965, sch 1, para 2; *Slipper v Tottenham and Hampstead Junction Rly Co* (1867) LR 4 Eq 112.

poll vesting the interest in the authority.[33] These provisions in schedule 1 to the Compulsory Purchase Act 1965 are made subject to section 42(7) of the Law of Property Act 1925.[34] Section 42(7) provides that where a purchaser has power to acquire land compulsorily and enters into a contract to do so or has served a notice to treat (which will include a deemed notice to treat under section 7 of the Compulsory Purchase (Vesting Declarations) Act 1981) the seller can make title without the compensation money being paid into court unless the acquiring authority requires that the money shall be paid into court. The overall position is that in most cases where the landowner is under some restriction or disability as regards the sale of the land the compulsory purchase can proceed in the ordinary way as though that restriction or disability did not exist.

7. The Crichel Down Rules

Although they do not relate to the acquisition of land as such it is useful to draw attention briefly at this point to the Crichel Down Rules. The rules relate to the disposal of land acquired under compulsion by a public authority when that land subsequently becomes surplus to the requirements of the authority and so is to be sold. The rules arose out of events in 1954 when land acquired before the war was not offered back to the original land-owner. It led to the resignation of the Minister of Agriculture at the time.   2.21

The substance of the rules is now stated in Part 2 of Circular 06/2004 issued by the Office of the Deputy Prime Minister.[35] The nature of the rules is that when land has been acquired compulsorily (including a voluntary sale where a power of compulsory purchase existed) and the land has become surplus to the requirements of the acquiring authority it should be offered back to the former owner or someone to whom the property would have passed by will or intestacy if it had not been acquired from that owner. Of course if the former owner does not wish to take advantage of the offer to him the land may be offered for general sale. The offer must be for a sale back at the current market value of the land at the time of that sale. This is an aspect of the statutory provision in section 123 of the Local Government Act 1972 that save with the consent of the Secretary of State a local authority must dispose of land for the best consideration reasonably obtainable. The offer should be made to the former freeholder but if he does not wish to purchase back the land an offer may be made at the discretion of the authority to a leaseholder who held a term the unexpired residue of which was more than 21 years at the time of the acquisition. The rules are not rules of law but are said to be a recommendation to local authorities and bodies other than central government. They will of course be observed by central government.[36]   2.22

---

[33]   Ibid, paras 4, 6 and 10.
[34]   Ibid, para 1.
[35]   The Circular in Pt 1 offers extensive general guidance on compulsory purchase procedures. Previous guidance on the Crichel Down Rules had been issued in 1992.
[36]   Circular 06/2004, Pt 2, paras 1, 4, 7, 12, 13, and 26. It is presumably open in law to an authority to reject the recommendation in a particular case although a decision to do so could be impugned as a failure to have regard to all material considerations unless there were solid reasons in that particular case for refusing to follow the guidance in the Circular.

2.23   There are substantial exceptions to the duty to make the offer back:

    (a) Where the land is other than agricultural land the duty to offer it back does not apply to a disposal more than 25 years after the date of the acquisition.[37]

    (b) The duty does not apply if the character of the land has materially changed since the date of the acquisition, for example by substantial development having taken place on it.[38]

    (c) The duty does not apply if the land is so small that its sale would not be commercially worthwhile.[39]

These are a few of the main exceptions but there are other significant exceptions beyond those mentioned. An authority which has acquired land which has become surplus to requirements and which it proposes to sell should consider carefully the advice in Part 2 of Circular 06/2004 before deciding whether and how to dispose of the land.

(C) ACQUISITION OF LIMITED INTERESTS AND OF RIGHTS

1. General and Preliminary Matters

2.24   In most cases a public authority will wish to acquire the whole of a particular piece of land in the sense of acquiring all interests in that land and all strata of the land comprising the surface, the underlying strata, and the airspace above the surface. However in some cases the authority may wish to acquire only a limited part of the totality of the land such as only a leasehold interest or only the surface of the land without the underlying strata and minerals. An authority may sometimes wish to acquire only rights over a particular piece of land such as a right of way. It is necessary to consider the power of an authority to put into effect compulsorily such a limited purpose.

2.25   A single piece of land by reason of its permanent nature is capable of being the subject of limited interests held by different persons, the most obvious example being freehold and leasehold interests. As far as such limited interests in land are concerned five categories of case can arise which are

    (a) the acquisition of single or limited interests or rights in the land involved;

    (b) the acquisition of existing rights over other land which are appurtenant to the land acquired;

    (c) the acquisition of existing rights over land when no land is acquired;

    (d) the acquisition of new (as opposed to already existing) rights over land other than the land acquired; and

    (e) the acquisition of strata of land.

2.26   Before coming to these five categories a preliminary matter to mention is the distinction relevant to the present subject which is sometimes drawn in land law before corporeal and

---

[37] Ibid, para 14(3).
[38] Ibid, para 10.
[39] Ibid, para 15(3).

incorporeal interests, sometimes called corporeal and incorporeal hereditaments, in land. A corporeal interest means an interest in land which gives a right to possession of the land either currently or in the future. Thus the freehold and leasehold owners of land both have corporeal interests in land, the leaseholder because he currently has the right to possession of the land and the freeholder because he will become entitled to possession of the land at the expiry of the lease. An incorporeal interest is a proprietary right over land which does not give the right, currently or in the future, to possession of the land. In this context the word 'incorporeal' means not admitting of physical possession.[40] An obvious example of an incorporeal interest is a right of way or other easement over land.

A further preliminary matter to mention as regards limited interests is the distinction drawn in land law between proprietary interests and non-proprietary rights. A proprietary interest in land is an interest which is capable in principle of binding not only the owner of the land in which the interest exists at the time of its creation but successors in title of that owner. Whether the interest will in fact bind a successor in title in any particular case may depend upon other matters such as the terms of the interest and its proper protection by registration under the Land Registration Act 2002. Leases, easements and the right to enforce restrictive covenants are proprietary interests in this sense. A non-proprietary right over land is a right which has land as its subject matter but which is in principle incapable of binding a successor in title to the land over which it is created. The best example is a contractual licence. If A grants a licence to B to enter A's land, and then A sells the land to X, B is in principle not entitled to enforce the licence against X and it does not matter whether at the time of his acquisition of the land X knew of the existence of the licence.[41] As a result an acquiring authority does not acquire the rights of licensees in the land acquired. The licence does not bind the authority after it has acquired the proprietary interests in the land just as it would not bind an ordinary purchaser of those interests. This distinction is mentioned now as it is relevant to the process of acquisition but it is also of considerable importance when aspects of the law of compensation are explained. A licensee in possession of land who is dispossessed as a consequence of the compulsory acquisition of the land is not entitled to compensation under the general provisions providing for compensation but may be entitled to a disturbance payment under provisions introduced in the Land Compensation Act 1973.[42]

2.27

---

[40] See *Great Western Rly Co v Swindon and Cheltenham Rly Co* (1884) 9 App Cas 787, per Lord Bramwell at pp 807–08. In this case the right of one railway company to construct a bridge over the line of another railway company was classified as the acquisition of a perpetual easement and not the acquisition of land. There is a further important consideration of incorporeal interests in section (f) of ch 10 under the subject of claims for compensation pursuant to s 10 of the Compulsory Purchase Act 1965.

[41] *Ashburn Anstalt v Arnold* [1989] Ch 1. This decision resolved a number of previously conflicting decisions. It is possible that in some circumstances a purchaser of land subject to a licence could become bound by the licence by reason of a constructive trust. More is required than mere notice of the licence by a purchaser for there to be a constructive trust: see per Fox LJ at p 26. It is also possible in exceptional circumstances that that which starts as a licence can become a proprietary interest in land, and so something which creates an entitlement to compensation on the part of the holder of that interest, under the doctrine of proprietary estoppel: see *Plimmer v Mayor of Wellington* (1883–84) LR 9 App Cas 699 and see ch 12, para 12.5, n 9. It was held in *Pennine Raceway Ltd v Kirklees Metropolitan Borough Council* [1983] QB 382, [1982] 3 WLR 987, that a licensee was 'a person interested in the land' for the purposes of the right to compensation for the revocation of a planning permission under s 164 of the Town and Country Planning Act 1971. It was accepted that in the legislation dealing with compensation for compulsory purchase the meaning of an interest in land was narrower and more technical.

[42] See ch 12. The matter of the interest in or entitlement to land which may create a right to the various forms of compensation is explained in section (c) of ch 3.

2. Limited Interests in the Land Acquired

2.28   As regards the first category of case mentioned in paragraph 2.25, in most cases an acquiring authority which has power to acquire an area of land also has power to acquire only a single or limited proprietary interest in that land as opposed to all subsisting interests in the land. The reason this is so is that in nearly all cases the word land when used in the empowering statute will include an interest in land. In many empowering statutes there is an express definition of land to this effect. Even if there is no such express definition unless a contrary intention appears in the empowering statute the Interpretation Act 1978 operates so that in that statute the word 'land' includes buildings and other structures, land covered by water, and any estate, interest, easement, servitude, or right in or over land.[43] Thus it is normally open to an acquiring authority to acquire the freehold interest in land without acquiring the leasehold interest and to acquire a leasehold interest without acquiring the freehold interest.[44] Such a course could sometimes be of advantage to an acquiring authority. It is possible that the authority needs the land only for a limited time and can achieve its purposes by acquiring a subsisting lease with an appropriate period to run. Another situation in which only one interest might be acquired is that when the freehold is acquired it is subject to a lease with only a short period to run before its expiry. In such a case it would be open to the authority to acquire only the freehold and, provided this accords with the timing of the purpose behind the acquisition, the authority might be content to wait for the lease to expire without any intervention of its own or, if that is possible, to determine the tenancy in accordance with its nature or terms by a notice to quit given by it.[45] There may, of course, be cases in which the acquiring authority already owns an interest in land and needs to acquire an existing interest held by someone else such as a lease.

2.29   It is explained later in this chapter that when a compulsory purchase order has been confirmed the acquiring authority may take one or other of two procedural courses to implement its rights under the order. It may serve a notice to treat or use the general vesting declaration procedure.[46] Assuming that the power of acquisition in the empowering Act permits the acquisition of an interest in land as opposed to the whole of the land or all interests in the land it is necessary to see how that power can be put into effect. It has been said in the Lands Tribunal that once an area of land is included in a confirmed compulsory purchase order the acquiring authority must either serve notices to treat on all persons having an interest in the land or not serve any notice to treat in respect of that area of land.[47]

---

[43] Interpretation Act 1978, sch 1.

[44] An example of the acquisition of a leasehold property only is *Slipper v Tottenham and Hampstead Rly Co* (1867) LR 4 Eq 112.

[45] *London Borough of Newham v Benjamin* [1968] 1 WLR 694, [1968] 1 All ER 1195, per Lord Denning MR at p 700. See para 4.97 of ch 4 and n 144 to that paragraph.

[46] See sections (j) and (q) of this chapter.

[47] *Union Rlys Ltd v Kent County Council* [2008] 2 EGLR 183 (Lands Tribunal). In its decision the Tribunal considered a number of older authorities decided when the relevant provision, the predecessor of s 5(1) of the Compulsory Purchase Act 1965, was s 18 of the Lands Clauses Consolidation Act 1845. None of these decisions provided any decisive guidance on the question. See *Stockton and Darlington Rly Co v Brown* (1860) 9 HLC 246; *Stone v Commercial Rly Co* (1839) 4 May & Cr 122 (decided before the 1845 Act); *Ecclesiastical Commissioners v Commissioners for Sewers for City of London* (1880) 14 Ch D 305; *Abrahams v Mayor of London* (1868) LR 6 Eq 625; the Scottish cases of *Davidson's Trustees v Caledonian Rly Co* (1894) 21 R 1060 (Ct of Session) and *Caledonian Rly Co v Davidson* [1903] AC 22 (HL); *Martin v London, Chatham and Dover Rly Co* (1866) LR 1 Ch App 501.

This conclusion was founded on the language of section 5(1) of the Compulsory Purchase Act 1965 which states that when the acquiring authority requires to purchase any of the land subject to compulsory purchase (ie land within the confirmed compulsory purchase order[48]) it

> shall give notice (hereafter in this Act referred to as a 'notice to treat') to all the persons interested in, or having power to sell and convey or release, the land, so far as known to the acquiring authority after making diligent enquiry.

This provision was said to dictate the 'all or nothing' rule. If this rule is correct then in practice it prevents the acquisition of a limited interest such as a leasehold interest in the land by itself when the notice to treat procedure is used since no notice to treat can be served on the leaseholder alone. Such a situation could plainly be of some inconvenience. The Tribunal in its reasoning did not consider the fact that in section 5(1) the word 'land' includes anything within the definition of that word in the empowering Act.[49] Since the empowering Act will generally define land as including an interest in land the same meaning will apply to section 5(1) so that it appears that in general a notice to treat may be served on a person with only a limited interest in an area of land specified in a confirmed compulsory purchase order. The decision of the Lands Tribunal went to the Court of Appeal but that Court found it unnecessary to comment on this aspect of the decision of the Tribunal.[50] In the light of the reasoning in this paragraph, and until the matter is reconsidered by the Tribunal or decided by some higher court, acquiring authorities may feel justified in serving a notice to treat on a person with only a limited interest in an area of land, without serving a notice to treat on other persons with an interest in the same land, when they wish to acquire only one interest in the land and when the empowering statute permits this and it is convenient to do so.

The same reasoning applies when the general vesting declaration procedure is used. Under the Compulsory Purchase (Vesting Declarations) Act 1981 an acquiring authority may execute a general vesting declaration in respect of any land which they are authorised to acquire by the compulsory purchase order.[51] The word 'land' has the same meaning as in the empowering Act.[52] It follows that if the empowering Act permits the acquisition of a limited interest in land a general vesting declaration may be executed in relation to that interest alone. If this reasoning is correct it would make it all the more curious if a limited interest cannot be acquired under the notice to treat procedure. This is especially so since a general vesting declaration operates for many purposes as a deemed notice to treat.[53]

2.30

---

[48] Compulsory Purchase Act 1965, s 1(3).

[49] Ibid.

[50] *Union Rlys Ltd v Kent County Council* [2009] EWCA Civ 363, [2009] 30 EGLR 68. The decision of the Lands Tribunal appears to make impossible the procedure of an acquiring authority acquiring just the freehold of a property and waiting for a lease with a little over a year to run to expire, the procedure described by Lord Denning in *London Borough of Newham v Benjamin* above n 45. If the law is indeed as stated by the Lands Tribunal one possible course would be for the acquiring authority to attempt to frame the compulsory purchase order (when such an order is needed) so that it applies only to the interest in land which the authority wishes to acquire. In the case of some shorter leasehold interests, such as an annual or monthly periodic tenancy, no notice to treat need be served on the tenant: see para 2.87.

[51] Compulsory Purchase (Vesting Declarations) Act 1981, s 4(1). The general vesting declaration procedure is explained in section (q) of this chapter.

[52] Ibid, s 2(1).

[53] Compulsory Purchase (Vesting Declarations) Act 1981, s 7.

3. Rights Appurtenant to the Land Acquired

2.31   The second category of case mentioned in paragraph 2.25 creates no difficulty. Where plot A is purchased and it has appurtenant to it an easement such as a right of way over plot B the benefit of that easement will automatically pass to the purchaser unless it is expressly excluded. The same rule applies where the purchase of plot A is by way of a compulsory acquisition.[54]

4. Acquisition of Existing Rights

2.32   Turning to the third category of case mentioned in paragraph 2.25, the most usual instances of the acquisition of a limited interest in land will be the acquisition of corporeal interests as mentioned under the first category. Nonetheless there is no reason in principle why an authority should not acquire an existing incorporeal interest such as a right of way over land. Easements such as rights of way over a piece of land (the servient land) are necessarily appurtenant to another piece of adjoining or nearby land for which they provide a benefit (the dominant land). If the dominant land is acquired by the authority the right to exercise the easement will become available to the authority in any event (and an acquisition in these circumstances is the second category of case just considered). If the dominant land is not acquired by the authority the easement cannot become exercisable by the authority since it remains appurtenant to the dominant land and it will be exercisable only by those with an interest in that land. The situation examined in this paragraph is, therefore, not likely to arise in practice.

2.33   It is convenient at this point to consider problems which can arise where an acquiring authority acquires only a part of an owner's land. A question which may occur is what rights the acquiring authority will have over the part of the land not acquired, that is the remaining land of the owner. Prior to the acquisition the owner may have used the remaining land as an access from the land acquired to a public highway or for some other purpose connected with the land acquired. As a matter of general law, and in the absence of any specific provision in the transfer which deals with the matter, a purchaser of a part of the land of a seller may acquire implied rights for the benefit of the land purchased against the retained land of the seller

    (a) as an easement of necessity (for example a right of way where the land purchased would otherwise be landlocked),

    (b) as an implied easement under the rule in *Wheeldon v Burrows*[55] (this arises where there is a prior use of the retained land for the purposes of the land purchased which was 'continuous and apparent' such as the access of light or the use of an access route), and

---

[54]   *Godwin v Schweppes Ltd* [1902] 1 Ch 926. The benefit of an easement will also pass to the acquiring authority under s 62 of the Law of Property Act 1925. In *Sovmots Investments Ltd v Secretary of State for the Environment* [1979] AC 194, [1977] 2 WLR 951, Lord Edmund Davies said at p 178: 'A right of way appurtenant to Blackacre will undoubtedly pass to the acquiring authority when a compulsory purchase of Blackacre is confirmed'.
[55]   (1879) 12 Ch D 31.

(c) by the operation of section 62 of the Law of Property Act 1925 (the automatic transfer of rights without express mention when land is conveyed).

Where the purchase is by way of a compulsory acquisition the rule in *Wheeldon v Burrows*
has no application since it is founded on the implied intention of a voluntary grantor and
so cannot be applied against a person whose land is taken from him against his will.[56] It is
doubtful whether section 62 will be of any assistance since that section passes rights available to the land transferred and existing prior to the transfer but where land is under one
ownership and occupation it is not possible to speak intelligibly of rights existing in favour
of one part of the land against another part of the land.[57] It is possible that the doctrine of
an implied easement of necessity could apply to a compulsory acquisition.[58] The result of
these considerations is that when an acquiring authority acquires a part of a person's land
it should take care that any necessary rights over the remaining land are expressly acquired
by the creation of new rights under the terms of the compulsory purchase order.[59]

5. Acquisition of New Rights

The fourth category of case mentioned in paragraph 2.25, the acquisition of newly created   2.34
rights over land, that is rights not previously existing but created by the compulsory purchase order and acquired under it, has in the past created difficulty. The House of Lords has
held that a right given to acquire land, even when the definition of land includes rights in
or over land as it normally will by reason of the definition of land in the empowering Act or
by reason of the Interpretation Act 1978, permits the acquisition of existing rights but does
not extend to the creation and acquisition of new rights over land not acquired.[60] This
difficulty led to the enactment in the Local Government (Miscellaneous Provisions) Act
1976 of a provision which permits a local authority to acquire compulsorily new rights over
land for a particular purpose where it has a right to acquire compulsorily the land for that

---

[56] *Sovmots Ltd v Secretary of State for the Environment* [1979] AC 144, [1977] 2 WLR 951, per Lord Wilberforce
at p 169.
[57] Ibid. It therefore remains arguable that where a part of the land of an owner is acquired, and despite the common ownership different persons were prior to the acquisition in occupation of the part acquired and the part
retained, the acquiring authority may acquire rights in favour of the part acquired, for instance a right of way, over
the land retained under s 62 of the Law of Property Act 1925. In addition it appears that even when there was unity
of ownership and of occupation prior to the transfer an easement in favour of the property sold over the property
retained may come into being under s 62 where the 'right' in question was 'continuous and apparent' such as the
enjoyment of the access of natural light: see *Long v Gowlett* [1923] 2 Ch 177; *P&S Platt Ltd v Crouch* [2003] EWCA
Civ 1110, [2004] 1 P & CR 18.
[58] However the creation of an implied easement of necessity also depends on the implied intention of a voluntary grantor so that the coming into existence of an easement by this doctrine may be excluded for the same reason
as in respect of the rule in *Wheeldon v Burrows*. It must also be remembered that an easement of necessity only
arises where the easement is necessary for the use of the land conveyed not where it is merely convenient for that
use.
[59] See para 2.34 of this chapter.
[60] *Sovmots Investments Ltd v Secretary of State for the Environment* [1979] AC 144, [1977] 2 WLR 951. Of course
the empowering legislation may confer an express right to acquire an easement over particular land: see n 64. The
right to acquire a portion of land for the construction of a tunnel without acquiring the whole of the land is perhaps best categorised as a right to acquire a stratum of land but is sometimes described as a right to acquire an
easement: *Hill v Midland Rly Co* (1882) 21 Ch D 143. However in *Metropolitan Rly Co v Fowler* [1893] AC 418 the
right to construct a railway tunnel under a road was said to be a right to acquire a hereditament or tenement (and
so something subject to land tax) rather than a right to acquire an easement. The acquisition of a stratum of land,
such as may be needed for the construction of a tunnel, is discussed in paras 2.35 and 2.36.

purpose.[61] New rights means rights not in existence when the compulsory purchase order is made.[62] If the acquiring authority acquires plot A and there is an existing proprietary right such as a right of way or of support over plot B then as already mentioned that right will pass to the authority by reason of the general law. The effect of the provision just mentioned is that the local authority can include in the compulsory purchase order, and thus acquire, a new right such as a right of way over plot B. It should be noted that the general power to acquire new rights is conferred only on local authorities[63] and that the land over which the new right is created must be land which can be acquired compulsorily by the authority for the purpose for which the new right is created. To take the above example, if the authority acquired plot A for housing purposes and wished to create a new easement of way over plot B to accommodate plot A it could only do so compulsorily if it had power to acquire compulsorily plot B for housing purposes. Some empowering legislation contains a specific power to create and acquire new rights over land.[64] The legislation relating to the assessment of compensation is applied to the compulsory purchase of newly created rights with the modifications necessary for this type of purchase. There are also modifications to the procedure for effecting a compulsory purchase when new rights are created and acquired.[65] Acts which confer a power of compulsory purchase sometimes expressly confer a power to acquire newly created rights. Legislation conferring powers on public utility companies generally contain such rights since the acquisition and operation of rights over land as opposed to the land itself is often necessary for the provision of public utility services.[66]

6. Acquisition of Strata of Land

2.35   The fifth category of case mentioned in paragraph 2.25 is the acquisition of strata of land. Just as land can be divided by vertical division into different plots, and just as each plot can

---

[61] Local Government (Miscellaneous Provisions) Act 1976, s 13(1).

[62] Ibid.

[63] Local Government (Miscellaneous Provisions) Act 1976, s 44(1) defines local authorities to mean county councils, county borough councils, district councils, London borough councils, the Common Council of the City of London, the Council of the Isles of Scilly and certain other defined bodies such as in London the Mayor's Office for Policing and Crime.

[64] See, eg the Crossrail Act 2008, s 7(5). Legislation enacted in recent years often contains a provision to this effect. The usual statutory language is that a specific power to acquire land compulsorily 'shall include power to acquire an easement or other right over land by the grant of a new right'. An early example of a statute expressly conferring a right to acquire an easement of way is *Great Western Rly Co v Swindon and Cheltenham Rly Co* (1884) 9 App Cas 787 in which one railway company was given a right to acquire a right of way across the line of another railway company. The right was to be exercised by the construction of a bridge.

[65] Local Government (Miscellaneous Provisions) Act 1976, s 13(2), (3). Certain specific additions to the Compulsory Purchase Act 1965, to apply to a compulsory purchase of new rights, are made by sch 1 to the 1976 Act. For example, where a new right over the land of a landlord is sought to be acquired the landlord can, in certain circumstances, compel the acquiring authority to acquire the whole of his land. This is brought about by the substitution of a new form of s 8 of the Compulsory Purchase Act 1965. Section 8 of the 1965 Act is considered in ch 9. Where the new right is acquired under a specific provision in an Act that Act usually applies sch 3 to the Acquisition of Land Act 1981 to the compulsory acquisition: see, eg s 7(6) of the Crossrail Act 2008. Paragraph 2 of sch 3 to the Acquisition of Land Act 1981 provides that that Act shall have effect with the modifications necessary to make it apply to the compulsory acquisition of a right as it applies to the compulsory acquisition of land. Part II of sch 3 contains a series of substituted provisions applicable to certain special kinds of land such as land of statutory undertakers whose rights are being compulsorily acquired. See section (h) of this chapter.

[66] Operators who provide telecommunication services enjoy the benefit of a special code in sch 2 to the Telecommunications Act 1984 which enables them to install and maintain equipment on the land of others.

have separate interests belonging to different persons in it, so land can be divided by horizontal division into different strata. A stratum may be a level of ground beneath the surface,
for example seams of coal, or may be different floors or storeys within buildings. English
land law permits the ownership of the freehold (or lesser interests) in a particular stratum
of land as just described.[67] Of course leasehold interests in a part or stratum of a building
are frequent, the best examples being lettings of flats in a block of flats or particular floors
in an office building. Given that this is so there seems no reason in principle why a compulsory purchase should not be of the freehold of a separate stratum. The acquisition of such
strata may be needed for the construction of tunnels or underground railways. In the case
of such projects the empowering Act may specifically permit the acquisition of strata.
Where the Act confers a power to acquire rights over or under the land of a person it
may sometimes be that as a matter of construction what is intended is the acquisition of
incorporeal interests such as easements rather than the acquisition of a corporeal interest
constituted by a particular stratum of the land.[68]

Nonetheless it is sometimes suggested that a stratum of land cannot as a matter of law be   2.36
acquired by compulsion unless there is clear authority in the empowering Act that this can
be done.[69] A decision sometimes prayed in aid in support of this proposition is a decision
of the Court of Appeal in which it was said to have been agreed by Counsel that a stratum
of land could be acquired only by agreement.[70] Earlier authority of the Court of Appeal is
to the contrary effect since it was pointed out that the word 'land' in the Lands Clauses
Consolidation Act 1845 included mines or strata.[71] There seems every reason for the same

---

[67] Co Litt 48b: 'A man may have an inheritance in an upper chamber though the lower buildings and soil be in
another'. Where the stratum is of a floor or floors in the building a freehold interest may be described as a flying
freehold. Flying freeholds exist in Lincoln's Inn in London. The owner of an underground room has been called
the owner of a 'subterranean flying freehold': see *Corbett v Hill* (1870) LR 9 Eq 671; *Grigsby v Melville* [1974] 1
WLR 80, per Russell LJ at p 83. Although there may be obvious practical difficulties such as a right of support there
seems no reason in principle why a person should not own (and why an acquiring authority should not acquire)
a volume of air space such as an area within which a bridge is constructed or within which a part of a building
overhangs other land.

[68] *Great Western Rly Co v Swindon and Cheltenham Rly Co* (1884) 9 App Cas 787. In *Hill v Midland Rly Co*
(1882) 21 Ch D 143 the right to construct a tunnel through land was described as an easement: see per Fry J at
p 148. Cf *Metropolitan Rly Co v Fowler* [1893] AC 418, and see n 60. A difficulty in describing something such as
the use of a tunnel under the land of a landowner as an easement is that generally an easement is a right which does
not give exclusive possession of the land the subject of the easement (cf *Moncrieff v Jamieson* [2007] UKHL 42,
[2007] 1 WLR 2620, in relation to a right to park vehicles). It is difficult to conceive of a railway company running
trains through a tunnel without having exclusive possession of it. The best assessment is that the acquisition of
land to construct and use a tunnel should be considered as an acquisition of a stratum of land of which the vertical
and horizontal dimensions are defined. The sensible and logical way forward on this somewhat confused subject
is that: (a) the power to acquire land or rights for the exclusive possession by the acquiring authority of tunnels or
bridges should be regarded as the acquisition of a stratum of land, and (b) that the empowering legislation should
be interpreted as permitting the compulsory acquisition of such a stratum unless of course such an acquisition is
expressly excluded.

[69] See, eg para 534 of *Halsbury's Laws of England*, 5th edn (LexisNexis, 2009). The authorities cited in that paragraph do not support this proposition and the first authority is to the contrary effect.

[70] *English Property Corporation v Royal Borough of Kingston Upon Thames* (1999) 77 P & CR 1, at p 5. Propositions
of this nature put to and accepted by a court without argument or consideration do not gain legal authority and
are not a part of any binding decision. A further old decision also sometimes cited in favour of the same proposition is that of Pollock CB in the Court of Exchequer in *Ramsden v Manchester, South Junction and Altrincham Rly
Co* (1848) 1 Ex 723. It was held that the company was not entitled to construct a tunnel under a public road and
through the soil under the road which belonged to the plaintiff. However, the basis of the decision was that the
company could not act without purchasing the soil from the plaintiff and paying him compensation before entry.
It was not held that a stratum of the soil as necessary for the tunnel could not have been purchased.

[71] *Errington v Metropolitan District Rly Co* (1882) 19 Ch D 559.

rule and reasoning to apply to current legislation. The better view is therefore that as a matter of law and principle an acquiring authority which is empowered to acquire land can
acquire a particular stratum of the land needed for a particular purpose such as the construction of a tunnel even when there is no express or specified power to acquire a stratum
in the empowering Act. Of course the owner of the remainder of the land may be entitled
to compensation for injurious affection caused to his retained land by reason of the acquisition of the particular stratum.[72] As mentioned an empowering Act may confer an express
power to acquire what amounts to a particular stratum or portion of land, for example for
the purpose of constructing a tunnel.[73] There are general provisions relating to the special
case of mines and minerals. Section 3 and schedule 2 to the Acquisition of Land Act 1981
provides that unless they are expressly purchased the acquiring authority is not entitled to
any mines (coal, ironstone, slate and other materials) under land within a compulsory purchase order. The owner who retains the mines and minerals must thereafter give to the
acquiring authority 30 days notice of his intention to work them. The authority is then able
to prevent the working subject to the payment of compensation.

(D) DECISION TO EXERCISE POWERS

1. Making and Recording the Decision

2.37   A public authority which is entitled to make a compulsory purchase order must make a
decision to do so in relation to specified land. A decision by a Minister may be constituted
by no more than the formal making of a draft of the order. In the case of local authorities
and some other bodies a resolution or other manifestation of the decision of the body is
needed. In the case of local authorities the resolution or other form of decision may be by
the full council or by a committee or sub-committee or by a member or an officer to whom
the power to make the order has been delegated. The normal procedure adopted by local
authorities is that resolutions and decisions of the present nature are preceded by a written
report from an officer or officers of the authority. One importance of a properly compiled
and reasoned report setting out the purpose and justification for making a compulsory
purchase order is that if there is an objection to the order or a legal challenge to its validity
the report may play a central part in any defence of the order. A challenge to the validity of
a compulsory purchase order can be made to the High Court under a statutory procedure
described later and must be made within six weeks of the publication of notice of confirmation of the order. No other form of legal challenge to the validity of the order is possible
whether before or after the order has been made or confirmed.[74] The reasons for making the
order, possibly as revealed by a report from an officer of the council or other body, may be

---

[72] See ch 9 for compensation available under s 7 of the Compulsory Purchase Act 1965 where only a part of a
person's land is compulsorily acquired.

[73] *Hill v Midland Rly Co* (1882) 21 Ch D 143; *Metropolitan Rly Co v Fowler* [1893] AC 418 (see n 60). See, eg para
11 of sch 6 to the Crossrail Act 2008 which provides that in certain defined areas the right of compulsory acquisition shall only be exercised in relation to so much of the subsoil or under-surface of the land as lies more than 9m
beneath the level of the surface of the land. Thus an upper limit of the stratum but not the lower limit is prescribed.
See n 68 and the cases just cited for the possible construction of such provisions as permitting the acquisition of
an easement rather than giving the right to acquire a stratum of land.

[74] See section (i) of this chapter.

of importance if the notice is in due course questioned in legal proceedings. A report may also be important as a means of demonstrating that all relevant considerations have been taken into account in the decision to make the order.[75] Such a report may form the basis of the statement of reasons which the acquiring authority is recommended to serve with its notification to persons affected of the making of the compulsory purchase order.[76] In a leading modern case on the validity of the exercise of a power to effect a compulsory purchase which was challenged in the courts the challenge was to a decision of a local authority to proceed with a compulsory purchase and in such a case the background to the decision will usually be of cardinal importance.[77]

2. Obtaining Information

The procedure for the making of a compulsory purchase order involves the service of notices at different stages on the owners and occupiers of the land being acquired. To do this may be difficult for an acquiring authority if it does not have full information on the ownership of interests in the land. Therefore an acquiring authority, having decided to make a compulsory purchase order, may consider whether to put in train a procedure which enables it to gather information on land ownership within the area of the order. It may do this before or after making the order. An authority which is entitled to acquire a piece of land compulsorily may serve a written notice on the freeholder or lessee or mortgagee of the land, on anyone who directly or indirectly receives rent for the land, on the occupier of the land, and on any person authorised to manage the land or to let it, requiring the recipient of the notice to state the name and address of any person he believes to be an owner, lessee, tenant or occupier of the land and of any person he believes to have an interest in the land. The notice must specify the land, the power of compulsory purchase, and the enactment which confers that power. A period of at least 14 days must be specified for the giving of the information.[78] It is a criminal offence to fail without reasonable excuse to comply with the notice or knowingly to give information which is materially false.[79] A general power is available to local authorities to survey land which they propose to acquire compulsorily and there is a further general power available to local authorities to require that owners and occupiers provide to them the name and addresses of persons with an interest in land where that information is needed with a view to the authority performing its statutory functions.[80] At certain points in the compulsory purchase process an acquiring authority is required to make diligent enquiry such as in ascertaining the persons to be served with a notice to treat and the exercise of the right given by statute as here described may be a part of fulfilling that duty. A matter of particular importance is that a notice to treat must be served within three years of a compulsory purchase order becoming operative

2.38

[75] See paras 2.10–2.12. In an appropriate case the reasons may be derived from other sources such as internal memoranda or policy documents of the authority making the order or even from a record of what was said in discussions at committee meetings.

[76] See para 2.44.

[77] *R (Sainsbury's Supermarkets Ltd) v Wolverhampton City Council* [2010] UKSC 20, [2011] 1 AC 437. See para 2.11.

[78] Acquisition of Land Act 1981, s 5A. See s 6 of the Act for provisions on the service of notices. Service by post should be by registered letter or by the recorded delivery service: see s 6(1). See n 96.

[79] Ibid, s 5B.

[80] Local Government (Miscellaneous Provisions) Act 1976, ss 14 and 15.

on all persons interested in, or having power to sell or convey or release, the land so far as known to the acquiring authority after making diligent enquiry so that if the enquiry has not been sufficiently thorough the authority may be left after three years with a person who has not been served with notice to treat and whose interest they cannot acquire.[81] The use of the power to gather information may also be important in operating the general vesting declaration procedure.[82]

(E) THE MAKING AND NOTIFICATION OF A COMPULSORY PURCHASE ORDER

1. Authorisation of the Compulsory Purchase

2.39   The making of compulsory purchase orders is in most cases governed by the Acquisition of Land Act 1981. The usual statutory process is that an Act which confers a power of compulsory purchase applies the 1981 Act to a compulsory purchase order made under that power. The 1981 Act replaced similar procedural provisions in the Acquisition of Land (Authorisation Procedure) Act 1946. References to the 1946 Act in Acts conferring powers of compulsory purchase enacted prior to the 1981 Act were amended by the 1981 Act so as to substitute references to that Act.[83] The 1981 Act is also applied to a number of Acts mainly passed between 1886 and 1946.[84] The end result is that the provisions in the 1981 Act apply to compulsory purchases made under a small number of specified Acts conferring powers of compulsory purchase passed mainly before 1946 and to most compulsory purchases made under Acts passed since that date which confer powers of compulsory purchase and which, in their original or amended form, apply the 1981 Act. Some modern Acts do not apply the Acquisition of Land Act 1981 but contain their own procedures for the making and confirmation of a compulsory purchase order.[85]

2.40   When the 1981 Act applies the basic provision is that a particular compulsory purchase of land pursuant to a power in an Act must be authorised and that that authorisation is conferred by a compulsory purchase order made by the authority exercising the power of compulsory purchase.[86] The whole process of making a compulsory purchase order, the making of objections to the order, and the securing of the confirmation of the order, derives from this basic rule. Following on from the basic rule there are two different procedural paths one of which has to be followed before the order becomes operative. The first procedure applies to orders made by an authority other than a Minister and the second applies to orders made by a Minister. Despite these differences the two procedures have the common feature that they permit objections to be made to the order and permit an objector to support his objection at a public local inquiry or hearing or by making written representations.

---

[81] See section (p) of this chapter for the procedure where an acquiring authority has taken possession of land but through a mistake has failed to acquire a particular interest in the land.

[82] See para 2.85 for service of a notice to treat, and see section (q) of this chapter for the general vesting declaration procedure.

[83] Acquisition of Land Act 1981, sch 4.

[84] Ibid, s 2(2).

[85] An illustration is s 10 and Pt I of sch 4 in the New Towns Act 1981.

[86] Acquisition of Land Act 1981, s 2(1).

Therefore in procedural terms the exercise of powers of compulsory purchase falls into one of three types of case. First there are acquisitions where the authority to acquire specified land is conferred by the empowering Act itself. Powers to acquire land for a specific project within precisely defined geographical limits specified in the Act are usually of this sort and the Crossrail Act 2008 has been described earlier as an instance of this type of case. In this type of case no compulsory purchase order is necessary and the Acquisition of Land Act 1981 is not applied to such acquisitions.[87] The second type of case is where a compulsory purchase of a particular area or areas of land has to be authorised by a compulsory purchase order made by a local authority or some other person or body other than a Minister in whom the power of acquisition is vested. The third type of case is where a compulsory purchase of a particular area or areas of land has to be authorised by a compulsory purchase order made by a Minister in whom the power of acquisition is vested. The compulsory purchase order procedure applicable in the second and third types of case is now described. The procedure applicable to purchases by authorities other than Ministers is described first in the remainder of this section.[88]

2.41

2. Making the Compulsory Purchase Order

The forms prescribed for a compulsory purchase order made by an acquiring authority are forms 1–6 in the schedule to the Compulsory Purchase of Land (Prescribed Forms) (Ministers) Regulations 2004.[89] The prescribed forms have a schedule in which there must be described the land authorised to be purchased and any new rights to be created and purchased. The schedule requires that the land is identified by way of a reference number on a map and by a statement of its extent, description and situation, and requires that there be stated the names of the persons who are qualifying persons (that is owners, lessees, tenants and reputed tenants, and occupiers) as defined in section 12(2)(a) of the Acquisition of Land Act 1981. In addition the form must state certain particulars of the persons to whom the acquiring authority would be required to give notice to treat if they proceeded under the notice to treat procedure.[90] Many compulsory purchase orders cover an area or areas of land in various different ownerships and reference numbers are attributed to different lots with details given of the persons with interests in each lot.

2.42

---

[87] Certain other legislation may be specifically applied by legislation in this category: see n 11 to para 2.6 which refers to such provisions in the Crossrail Act 2008 as an example. In addition the empowering Act sometimes states that the process of acquisition of land shall operate as if there had been a compulsory purchase order over it. Certain provisions relevant to the assessment of compensation depend on there being an order. For instance, para 2 of Pt 2 of sch 6 to the Crossrail Act 2008 provides that Pt I of the Compulsory Purchase Act 1965 applies to a compulsory purchase under s 6(1) of the Crossrail Act as if the Act were a compulsory purchase order under the 1965 Act.

[88] The procedure for the making of orders by Ministers is described in section (g) of this chapter.

[89] Acquisition of Land Act 1981, s 10(2). The title of the Regulations (SI 2004/2595) is somewhat misleading since they apply to orders made by local authorities and other bodies.

[90] See section (j) of this chapter for the notice to treat procedure.

3. Notification of the Making of the Order

2.43   Having made the compulsory purchase order in the prescribed form the next step for the acquiring authority is to give notice in the prescribed form of the making of the order. Notices must be published in a newspaper, affixed to a conspicuous object, and given directly to persons affected. The authority must publish a notice in the prescribed form in two successive weeks in one or more local newspapers circulating in the locality of the land comprised in the order. The notice must state that the order has been made and is about to be submitted for confirmation, must describe the land and state the purpose of the acquisition, must name a place within the locality where a copy of the order and the map may be inspected (this will generally be the offices of the acquiring authority), and must state the time and manner in which objections to the order can be made. The time specified for objections must be at least 21 days from the first publication of the notice. The manner specified for making the objection will normally be that it shall be made in writing to the acquiring authority.[91] In addition the acquiring authority must affix a notice in the prescribed form to a conspicuous object or objects on or near the land comprised in the compulsory purchase order.[92] The form of notice prescribed is the same for publication in a newspaper and affixation to a conspicuous object.[93]

2.44   The duty to serve notice on persons affected by the compulsory purchase order is to serve notice on what are called qualifying persons. A person is a qualifying person if

    (a) he is the owner, lessee, tenant for any period, or occupier of the land, or

    (b) he is a person to whom the acquiring authority would be required to give a notice to treat if it follows the notice to treat procedure, or

    (c) he is a person who may be entitled to make a claim for compensation under section 10 of the Compulsory Purchase Act 1965 as described in the next paragraph.[94]

Again the notice has to be in the prescribed form.[95] Persons in category (b) include persons such as mortgagees or persons with equitable interests in the land who are entitled to be served with a notice to treat.[96] Circular 06/2004 issued by the Government and giving

---

[91] Acquisition of Land Act 1981, s 11(1), (2).

[92] Ibid, s 11(3). Obviously if the order covers a large area of land it would be sensible to affix a number of notices in separate locations.

[93] See form 7 in the schedule to the Compulsory Purchase of Land (Prescribed Forms) (Ministers) Regulations 2004 (SI 2004/2595).

[94] Acquisition of Law Act 1981, s 12(1), (2), (2A) and (2B). Where the land is ecclesiastical property the notice must be served on the Church Commissioners. Where two or more persons are co-owners of property as joint tenants or tenants in common notice of the making of the order should be served on all co-owners. An inadvertent failure to do so will not lead to the quashing of the order if there has been no substantial prejudice to the persons not served: *George v Secretary of State* (1979) 38 P & CR 609.

[95] The forms prescribed are forms 8 and 9 in the schedule to the Compulsory Purchase of Land (Prescribed Forms) (Ministers) Regulations 2004 (SI 2005/2595).

[96] See section (j) of this chapter. Section 6 of the Acquisition of Land Act 1981 contains provisions for the service of documents under the Act. Service on a person may be effected by delivering the document to him or by leaving it at his proper address (his last known address or an address he has provided for service) or by post. Service by post must be by registered letter or by the recorded delivery service. Service on an incorporated company or body may be effected by service on the secretary or clerk of the company or body. If the name and address of a person cannot be ascertained after reasonable enquiry service may be effected by addressing the document to the 'owner', 'tenant', etc, and delivering it to some person on the land or by leaving it or a copy of it on or near the land. The statutory provisions are a complete code for the service of notices so that service on an agent is not good service: *Fagan v Knowsley Metropolitan Borough Council* (1985) 50 P & CR 363.

general guidance on the procedure for a compulsory purchase recommends that when notices are served on qualifying persons the notices should be accompanied by a statement of reasons for the making of the order.[97]

The acquiring authority must serve notice on any person whom it thinks likely to be enti-   2.45
tled to make a claim under section 10 of the Compulsory Purchase Act 1965 if the order is confirmed and the compulsory purchase takes place, so far as that person is known to the acquiring authority after making diligent enquiry. Section 10 of the Compulsory Purchase Act 1965 entitles a person to make a claim for compensation for injurious affection to his land caused by the execution of works carried out by a public body in certain circumstances even though no land has been acquired from him.[98]

(F) CONFIRMATION OF THE ORDER AND OBJECTIONS TO THE ORDER

1. Introduction

What is described under this section is the procedure for the confirmation of a compulsory   2.46
purchase order which applies where an order is made by a local authority or other body except a Minister. The procedure applicable to orders made by Ministers is described under the next section. On the expiry of the period for objections specified in the notices of the making of the order the acquiring authority may submit the order to the confirming authority for confirmation. The confirming authority is the Minister who under the empowering Act has power to authorise the compulsory purchase.[99] The next procedural steps depend on whether an objection to the order has been made within the period speci-fied in the published notices. There are three procedures which may lead to the confirma-tion of the order, the first being confirmation by the Minister without a public local inquiry or hearing or the consideration of written representations into or on the objections, the second being confirmation by the Minister after consideration by him of objections follow-ing a public local inquiry or hearing or written representations into or on the objections, and the third being confirmation by the acquiring authority itself. In the first two cases the Minister may confirm the order with or without modifications or, of course, may simply refuse to confirm it at all. A modification will usually mean that some land is removed from the order. The power of modification cannot be used to alter or limit the purpose for which the order was made.[100] In all cases, unless all interested persons consent, the order cannot be modified by adding land which was not within the order as made. If the acquiring authority wishes to add further land and cannot obtain the consent of those persons interested (which must include any owners or tenants of the additional land but may also include others) the

---

[97] See para 35 of Pt I of the Circular.
[98] Acquisition of Land Act 1981, s 12(2A)(b), (2B). See ch 10 for claims under s 10 of the Compulsory Purchase Act 1965. Modern authority suggests that a claim for compensation may be made by a person whose land is injuri-ously affected by works executed by the authority provided a power of compulsory purchase exists for the pur-poses of those works even though no land is actually acquired by compulsion: see *Moto Hospitality Ltd v Secretary of State for Transport* [2007] EWCA Civ 764, [2008] 1 WLR 2822, and see section (c) of ch 10.
[99] Acquisition of Land Act 1981, s 7(1).
[100] *Proctor & Gamble Ltd v Secretary of State* (1991) EGCS 123. See para 51 of Circular 06/2004 where it is said that the power of modification will be used sparingly.

only recourse open to it is to make and publish a further compulsory purchase order relating to the additional land. The explanation of the confirmation procedure involves the concepts of relevant objections, objections which may be disregarded, and remaining objections. These categories of objection are explained in the following paragraphs.

2. Confirmation: No Relevant Objections

2.47   The first procedure, the confirmation of the order by the Minister without the consideration of objections by one of the methods just stated, applies when either there is no relevant objection to the order or every relevant objection is withdrawn or is disregarded.[101] A relevant objection is an objection made by one of the persons on whom a notice of the making of the order has to be served.[102] If the Minister is satisfied that an objection relates exclusively to matters which can be dealt with by the Lands Tribunal in assessing compensation he may disregard the objection even though it is a relevant objection.[103] The existence of such a disregarded objection does not prevent the confirmation of the order with modifications under this first procedure. Nor does it prevent the Minister refusing to confirm the order although this is an unlikely result in the absence of relevant objections. The type of objection which may be disregarded under this rule is an objection that a particular person is likely to receive insufficient compensation for the acquisition of his interest. However, a more general objection to the merits of a compulsory purchase order on the ground that the cost of the project is excessive may validly be put forward and one of the grounds for saying that the cost of the project is excessive may be that the total compensation which will become payable to persons who are dispossessed as one of the components of that cost is high.[104] Therefore to this limited extent objections which go to the general amount of compensation likely to be payable for land acquisitions may still be put forward and may not be capable of being disregarded in the way just mentioned. If an objector puts forward an alternative site as that which ought to be acquired for the purposes of the scheme of the acquiring authority the cost of acquiring that site may be a relevant consideration when it comes to the confirmation of a compulsory purchase order, and a failure by the confirming authority to take into account that cost may lead to the quashing of the order.[105] Before confirming an order under this procedure the Minister must be satisfied that the requirements as to publication of notice of the making of the order have been complied with.

---

[101]   Acquisition of Land Act 1981, s 13(1), (2).

[102]   Ie a 'qualifying person': see para 2.44. If a person is only a qualifying person because he has been identified as someone who is likely to be entitled to make a claim under s 10 of the Compulsory Purchase Act 1965 (see para 2.45) his objection will not rank as a relevant objection if the confirming Minister concludes that that person is not likely to be entitled to make a claim under s 10: Acquisition of Land Act 1981, s 13(6). Presumably further information, perhaps the form of the objection itself, may lead the Minister to a conclusion on this matter different to that previously formed by the acquiring authority.

[103]   Acquisition of Land Act 1981, s 13(2)(b), (7).

[104]   *Sovmots Investments Ltd v Secretary of State for the Environment* [1977] QB 411, at p 424 (per Forbes J at first instance); *Green v Secretary of State for the Environment* [1984] 2 EGLR 27.

[105]   *Prest v Secretary of State for Wales* [1983] RVR 11, and see section (i) of this chapter.

3. Confirmation: Consideration of Objections

The second procedure is the confirmation of the order by the Minister where there is what   2.48
is called a remaining objection. The procedure applies where there is any remaining relevant objection which is not withdrawn or which cannot be disregarded as explained in the
last paragraph. The Minister should first consider whether the written representations procedure can be or should be applied. The written representations procedure for dealing with
objections can be applied (save in certain special instances such as where the order is subject
to special parliamentary procedure) provided any person who has a remaining relevant
objection consents to the procedure.[106] In the absence of such consents there must be a
public local inquiry or a hearing into objections.[107] The purpose of the written representations procedure is to enable objectors, the acquiring authority, and any other person permitted by the Minister, to make written representations to the Minister as to whether the
order should be confirmed. The details of the procedure to be adopted are laid down in
Regulations.[108] The Regulations provide for a timetable for the exchange of representations,
the possible appointment of an inspector to consider the representations and to report to
the confirming Minister, site visits by an inspector, the notification of the Minister's decision and other matters. The advantage of the written representations procedure is that it is
usually quicker and less costly than an inquiry or hearing. Providing that the conditions for
its application are satisfied the Minister has a discretion on whether to follow the written
representations procedure and so may, if he wishes, still proceed instead by way of a public
local authority or hearing. The usual practice of a confirming Minister is to offer the written representations procedure to objectors except where it is clear from the outset that the
scale or complexity of the order makes it unlikely that the procedure would be acceptable
or appropriate.[109] Where the Minister follows the written representations procedure there
are ancillary provisions which entitle him to make orders as to the costs of the parties to the
procedure and which enable him to recover from the acquiring authority the costs which he
has incurred in connection with that procedure.[110]

If the Minister is not able to follow the written representations procedure, or decides not to   2.49
do so, he must cause a public local inquiry to be held into objections or give every person
who has made a remaining relevant objection an opportunity of appearing before and
being heard by a person appointed by him at a hearing. A hearing is intended to be less
formal than an inquiry and there are procedural differences such as that persons cannot be
compelled to attend or produce documents at a hearing. Hearings are not frequent and are
suitable for cases where there is only a small amount of objection. The conduct of public
local inquiries is governed by procedure rules.[111] It will be conducted by an inspector

---

[106] Acquisition of Land Act 1981, s 13A(1), (2). As stated the written representations procedure cannot be used
where the order is subject to special parliamentary procedure: ibid, s 13A(2)(a). For the special parliamentary
procedure see section (h) of this chapter.

[107] Ibid, s 13A(3).

[108] The Compulsory Purchase of Land (Written Representations Procedure) (Ministers) Regulations 2004 (SI
2004/2594).

[109] See para 40 of Circular 06/2004.

[110] Acquisition of Land Act 1981, s 13B(2)–(5).

[111] The Compulsory Purchase (Inquiries Procedure) Rules 2007 (SI 2007/3617). In the following footnotes
these are generally referred to as the Rules.

appointed by the Minister who may be someone drawn from a panel of permanent inspectors or may be a person appointed *ad hoc* to hold the particular inquiry.

2.50   The main elements of the procedure to be followed before the start of the inquiry are described by the Inquiries Procedure Rules and are as follows:

> (i)   The Minister (called the authorising authority in the Rules) must inform the acquiring authority and objectors that he intends to hold an inquiry.[112] The date of the notification is the relevant date and is a date which is important for subsequent time limits in the Rules.
>
> (ii) In longer inquiries a pre-inquiry meeting may be held presided over by the inspector at which matters of procedure and timetabling will be discussed.[113]
>
> (iii) The acquiring authority must provide its statement of case within eight weeks of the relevant date and the Minister may require any objector to provide a statement of case within the same eight weeks.[114]
>
> (iv) Statements of evidence and summaries of these statements may be required to be sent to the inspector and other parties not less than three weeks before the start of the inquiry.[115]

2.51   Many elements of the procedure at the inquiry are in the discretion of the inspector or other person appointed[116] but a typical procedure would be for the acquiring authority to open its case through its advocate and to call its evidence in support of the order and in resisting the objections. It is for the authority to justify its use of powers of compulsory purchase and so it must lay before the confirming authority information which will enable the authority to conclude that the purchase is necessary, and this may include some consideration by the acquiring authority of alternative schemes such as a possible alternative route for a road.[117] Objectors will be allowed to cross-examine the witnesses of the acquiring authority and to present their own case calling evidence if they wish with their witnesses also being subject to cross-examination. Final submissions may be made first by, or on behalf of, the objectors and then by the acquiring authority. In practice the procedure varies substantially depending on the size of the compulsory purchase and the number of objectors. An inquiry or hearing with only one or a few objectors may be over in a morning whereas a large compulsory purchase order which attracts many objectors with legal representation may result in an inquiry or hearing which takes weeks. In the latter case the inspector will often arrange a programme at the beginning of the proceedings so that particular objectors need only attend when their objection is being presented. A particular objector will at that time have the opportunity to call evidence or make representations in support of his objection and to ask questions of the witnesses called by the acquiring authority. The inspector will make arrangements to view the land sought to be acquired and other relevant areas.

---

[112] Ibid, r 3.
[113] Ibid, rr 5, 6.
[114] Ibid, r 5.
[115] Ibid, r 15.
[116] Unless otherwise stated by the Rules the inspector shall determine the procedure at the inquiry: r 16(1).
[117] *R v Secretary of State, ex parte Melton Borough Council* (1986) 52 P & CR 318; *Prest v Secretary of State for Wales* [1983] RVR 11; cf *London Welsh Association v Secretary of State* (1980) 255 *Estates Gazette* 1095.

The content of an objection may be anything relevant to the order. It could, for example, be   2.52
that the acquiring authority has not demonstrated a real need for the land for the purpose
stated or that a particular piece of land is not needed to fulfil that purpose or that a particular objector will suffer particular hardship if he has to give up his land. It might be
contended by objectors that the proposals of the acquiring authority were not sufficiently
advanced or sufficiently clear or detailed to justify the taking of land. An acquiring authority will often try to arrange or suggest alternative premises to which objectors can move. An
objection can be made at this stage to the legal validity of an order. Such an objection might
persuade the Secretary of State that the order is not valid and so cannot be confirmed. If the
Secretary of State concludes that the power of compulsory purchase is being used for a
purpose not authorised by the empowering Act he should of course refuse to confirm the
order.[118] If the Secretary of State does confirm the order its legal validity can still be challenged in the courts by way of the statutory procedure described later. An objection to the
underlying scheme of the acquiring authority which justifies a compulsory purchase order
may be difficult in some cases since the merits of the scheme may have been dealt with by
some earlier administrative procedure such as an order establishing the line of a new road
by a scheme under section 16 of the Highways Act 1980 or by the grant of planning permission for the proposals of the acquiring authority after the consideration of objections. An
extreme example of the difficulties which confront objectors who wish to object to the
principle of a scheme is where a highway has been in part constructed and a compulsory
purchase order is made for a further length of the highway or for a connecting road.
Obviously an objector cannot reasonably assert that the highway or part of the highway
already built should be removed. As mentioned an objection which relates exclusively to
the amount of compensation which a particular objector is likely to receive may be
disregarded.[119]

The Government has published a lengthy circular referred to earlier setting out its general   2.53
policy in relation to the confirmation by a Minister of compulsory purchase orders including special provisions which apply to certain types of order such as those made for the
regeneration of areas of land.[120] Any objector to a compulsory purchase order or his professional representatives should read carefully any relevant parts of this circular before presenting the objection. An inspector holding an inquiry or hearing is likely to follow closely
the guidance given in the circular. A circular is not a statement of law but an expression of
policy and in exceptional cases a Minister is free to depart from the generally stated policy.
An inspector will not consider material such as evidence or representations produced after
the close of the inquiry, but there is nothing to prevent persons sending such material to the
Secretary of State who may consider it and in an appropriate case may order the re-opening
of the inquiry for certain purposes. A compulsory purchase order may be quashed if the
inspector hears evidence after the close of the inquiry and at a site visit if there is a risk of
prejudice to objectors.[121] An inspector is bound to hear and consider all relevant evidence

---

[118] *London and Westcliff Properties v MHLG* [1961] 1 WLR 519, (1961) 12 P & CR 154; *R (Barnsley Metropolitan Borough Council) v Secretary of State* [2012] EWHC 1366 (Admin), [2012] 1 EGLR 1 (see n 4 to para 2.5). See Circular 06/2004, para 50.
[119] See para 2.47.
[120] Circular 06/2004, *Compulsory Purchase and the Crichel Down Rules*, issued by the then Office of the Deputy Prime Minister.
[121] *Hibernian Property Co Ltd v Secretary of State* (1974) 27 P & CR 197. See section (i) of this chapter.

put to him at an inquiry into objections and in an exceptional case a procedural error in the course of an inquiry may be the subject of immediate proceedings for judicial review.[122]

2.54   After the close of the inquiry or hearing the inspector prepares a report of the proceedings which is submitted to the Minister.[123] The inspector in the report summarises the case for the acquiring authority in support of the order and the cases put forward by objectors who oppose the order and then reaches a series of conclusions and makes a recommendation to the Minister on how the Minister should deal with the question of confirmation. The Minister is not bound to accept the conclusions or the recommendation of the inspector. There is, however, one procedural limitation on the discretion of the Minister. If he disagrees with a finding of fact by an inspector or takes into account any new evidence or new matter of fact not raised at the inquiry, and for that reason does not accept a recommendation of the inspector, the minister must notify the acquiring authority and persons who appeared at the inquiry and give them an opportunity to make written objections. Where in these circumstances the minister has taken into account any new evidence or new issue of fact the same parties are entitled to seek a re-opening of the inquiry. These steps must of course be taken by the Minister before he reaches his decision.[124] The Minister then decides whether or not to confirm the order and, if he does confirm it, whether to do so with modifications. As stated earlier modifications will generally be the omission from the order of certain areas of land. In some instances a particular piece of land may be removed from the order without the removal having a great effect on the project underlying the order as a whole, such as where a small piece of land at the edge of a large regeneration scheme is removed, whereas in other cases, such as a road project, to remove from the order a piece of land in the line of the road could obviously prevent the whole scheme from being implemented. If the latter type of case occurred the Minister, if sufficiently impressed by the objection, might think it preferable to refuse to confirm the order as a whole. A successful objector who was entitled to object will be awarded the costs of his objection against the acquiring authority unless there are exceptional reasons why he should not have his costs.[125]

2.55   A Minister carrying out his function as the confirming authority may conclude that the order should be confirmed as to a part of the land within it without reaching a decision on whether the order should be confirmed as to the remaining part. This process is known as confirmation in stages.[126] The Minister may act in this way if there are no remaining objections to the order, or if he has considered all outstanding objections by way of the written representations procedure, or following an inquiry or hearing, or if any remaining objections relate solely to the part of the land as regards which the order is not at that time being confirmed.[127] If an order is confirmed in stages then the Minister must give a direction postponing consideration of the confirmation of the remaining part until a time which he

---

[122] *R v Secretary of State, ex parte Royal Borough of Kensington and Chelsea* (1987) 19 HLR 161.
[123] The Compulsory Purchase (Inquiries Procedure) Rules 2007 (SI 2007/3617), r 18(1).
[124] r 18(4).
[125] See Circular 8/93, *Awards of Costs Incurred in Planning and Compulsory Purchase Order Proceedings*. The power to award costs derives from s 5(3) and 5(4) of the Acquisition of Land Act 1981 which apply s 250 of the Local Government Act 1973. Section 5(4) of the 1981 Act was added by s 3 of the Growth and Infrastructure Act 2013, and permits orders for costs to be made where arrangements are made for an inquiry but the inquiry does not take place and for orders to be made relating to the costs of a party who does not attend the inquiry. A Minister may direct that the costs incurred by him in relation to holding an inquiry shall be paid by a local authority.
[126] Acquisition of Land Act 1981, s 13C.
[127] Ibid, s 13C(2), (3), (4).

specifies and the order is to be treated as a separate order in so far as it relates to each part of the land.[128] One possible result of this last provision is that an application to the High Court to quash the order as it relates to one part of the land will not jeopardise the validity of the purchase of the other part which is taken to be the subject of a separate order. The deemed existence of separate orders also means that the six week time limit within which an application to the High Court to question the validity of the order must be made runs, as regards a particular part of the order confirmed, from the date of the confirmation of that part of the order and thus from the coming into operation of the order as to that part.[129] The power to confirm an order in stages may be useful in circumstances where it is clear that much of the order may be confirmed so as to allow a scheme to commence but it remains uncertain whether a particular piece of land is needed for or should be a part of the scheme. An order may be confirmed in two or more successive stages where the conditions for staged confirmation are satisfied.

The position of a Minister deciding whether to confirm a compulsory purchase order, or   2.56
even more the position of a Minister who has to decide whether to make an order which he has himself prepared in draft, is not the same as that of a judge who has to decide between the cases of two opposing litigants. The judge has no input of his own to the result and so must decide the case on the evidence put before him as the exercise of a purely judicial function. A confirming authority is entitled to consider its own policies and the interests of the public as a whole and so is carrying out to an extent an administrative and political function. The position of a confirming authority can sometimes be described as quasi-judicial, an expression which gives recognition to the duty of that authority to have regard to public policies and to the wider interests of the public. The proper reconciliation of these dual capacities of a confirming authority has been the subject of a number of decided cases and a discussion of the details will be found in general works on administrative law.[130] What can be said as a matter of generality is that the confirming authority: (a) must allow a fair opportunity for objections to a compulsory purchase order to be put forward, and (b) in its ultimate decision on whether to confirm the order is entitled to have regard to ministerial and government policy as well as the views of the acquiring authority and of objectors to the order.

4. Confirmation by the Acquiring Authority

The third procedure is that the acquiring authority may confirm its own order.[131] For this to   2.57
occur the Minister must notify the authority that it may act in this way.[132] This process of confirmation can only operate if there are no objections to the order or all objections have

---

[128] Ibid, s 13C(5).

[129] See section (i) of this chapter for the right of challenge to an order in the High Court.

[130] *Johnson & Co (Builders) Ltd v Minister of Health* [1947] 2 All ER 345; *Bushell v Secretary of State* [1981] AC 75, [1980] 3 WLR 221. As it was put in *De Rothschild v Secretary of State for Transport* [1989] 1 All ER 933, [1989] 1 EGLR 19, the decision of a Minister on whether to confirm a compulsory purchase order is not akin to a *lis inter parties*, that is a dispute between persons over rights in private law. For a general account of these principles and of their historical development, see *De Smith on Judicial Review*, 7th edn (London, Sweet and Maxwell, 2003) paras 5.010 and 6.038–6.040.

[131] Acquisition of Land Act 1981, s 14A.

[132] Ibid, s 14A(1).

been withdrawn and the order is capable of being confirmed without modification.[133] For this purpose an objection means an objection made by anyone and not just objections made by persons entitled to be served with notice of the making of the order. The concepts of irrelevant objections and of objections which may be disregarded are not applied for the purposes of the self-confirmation of orders. There is no power under this type of confirmation to confirm an order with modifications and no power of staged confirmation or confirmation of an order in part only. The power of self-confirmation by the acquiring authority may be useful where the order is small and non-contentious. Even so a direction by the Minister allowing such a process of confirmation is needed and in the absence of outstanding objections it is not apparent what is gained from the Minister directing the authority that it may confirm the order as opposed to the Minister confirming the order himself.

5. Notice of Confirmation

2.58   Once the order has been confirmed following any of the above procedures the acquiring authority must serve and affix and publish a confirmation notice.[134] This is a notice in the prescribed form which describes the land, states that the order has been confirmed, states that a person aggrieved by the order may apply to the High Court for an order quashing the order, and in the case of a notice affixed as about to be described states a place where a copy of the order and the map may be inspected.[135] Where there has been a confirmation in stages the notice must also state that a direction has been given by the Minister postponing consideration of the rest of the order. If the acquiring authority intends to implement the order by using the general vesting declaration procedure under the Compulsory Purchase (Vesting Declarations) Act 1981 it must include in the confirmation notice a statement in a form prescribed of the effect of Parts I and III of that Act and an invitation to persons who would be entitled to claim compensation if a general vesting declaration were made in respect of all the land in the order to give information to the acquiring authority in the prescribed form with respect to their name and address and the land in question. The general vesting declaration procedure is described later.[136] The confirmation notice must be served on owners, lessees and tenants and occupiers who were entitled to be served with notice of the making of the order and a notice must be affixed to a conspicuous object or objects on or near the land and so far as practicable kept in place for six weeks after the order becomes operative.[137] This period is chosen since it is the period during which any challenge to the validity of the order in the High Court may be made.[138] In addition a confirmation notice must be published in one or more local newspapers circulating in the locality of the land. A compulsory purchase order becomes operative on the date on which confirmation of the order is first published in accordance with these provisions. The date on which the order

---

[133] Ibid, s 14A(3). This procedure for confirmation by the acquiring authority is not available where the land is that of statutory undertakers or forms part of a common, open space or fuel or field garden allotment: ibid, s 14A(2).

[134] Ibid, s 15.

[135] See form 10 in the schedule to the Compulsory Purchase of Land (Prescribed Forms) (Ministers) Regulations 2004 (SI 2004/2595). For the requirement of a map as a part of a compulsory purchase order, see para 2.42.

[136] The prescribed form is form 2 in the Compulsory Purchase of Land (Vesting Declarations) Regulations 1990 (SI 1990/497). For vesting declarations see section (q) of this chapter.

[137] Acquisition of Land Act 1981, s 15(1), (2).

[138] See section (i) of this chapter.

becomes operative is important for a number of purposes such as the rule that the power of compulsory purchase has to be exercised within three years of this date.[139] Acquiring authorities are asked in paragraph 57 of Circular 06/2004 to notify the confirming authority of the date on which notice of the confirmation of the order is first published.

(G) ORDERS MADE BY MINISTERS

Where the compulsory purchase is carried out by a Minister there is a separate procedure   2.59 which mirrors the essential elements of the procedure applicable to a compulsory purchase by a local authority or other body.[140] The important difference is that instead of making the compulsory purchase order the Minister prepares it in draft. Instead of confirming the order the Minister, after considering objections, may make the order so that the order when made by a Minister authorises the compulsory purchase of the land in question. In effect, therefore, the Minister decides on the strength of objections to the order which he has himself prepared in draft before deciding whether, despite the objections, to make the order. In a real sense the Minister is judge in his own cause. An element of impartial scrutiny remains in that the Minister may be obliged to cause a public local inquiry or a hearing to be held into objections and to consider the report of the person who has held the inquiry or hearing. Again the Minister is not bound to accept the conclusions or recommendation of the person who has held the inquiry or hearing. Where the acquisition is in the exercise of highway land acquisition powers the persons who decide whether to make the order prepared in draft are the Minister who prepared the draft order and the Planning Minister (the Planning Minister is the Secretary of State who for the time being has general responsibility in planning matters) acting jointly. The Minister having general responsibility in planning matters has varied over the years but is currently the Secretary of State for Communities and Local Government.

Leaving aside these differences in the process the overall procedure for the preparation in   2.60 draft and making of orders by a Minister is in nearly all respects the same as that which applies to the making and confirmation of orders where the acquiring authority is a local authority or other body. It is not necessary to set out again the details of the procedure but the following points may be noted:

(a) There is in this case no prescribed form of compulsory purchase order and the form of the order may be such as the Minister may determine save only that it must describe by reference to a map the land to which it applies.[141] In practice orders prepared in draft by a Minister follow closely the form prescribed for orders made by other authorities.

(b) The Minister must publicise the preparation of the draft order by notices in the prescribed form in local newspapers, by affixation to a conspicuous object and by

---

[139] Thus a notice to treat is only valid if served within the three year time limit: see s 4 of the Compulsory Purchase Act 1965 and see para 2.88. The same time limit applies to the making of a general vesting declaration: see para 2.131.

[140] Acquisition of Land Act 1981, sch 1.

[141] Ibid, sch 1, para 1.

notice given to the owners, lessees, tenants and occupiers of the land in the same way as such notices have to be given or published by other authorities.[142]

(c)   There is the same opportunity for the Minister to make the order if either there is no relevant objection or any relevant objection is withdrawn or may be disregarded since it relates solely to the amount of compensation.[143]

(d)   There is also the same opportunity for the Minister to consider objections by way of the written representation procedure if every objector consents and then to make the order with or without modifications after considering the representations.[144]

(e)   In all other cases of subsisting objections the Minister must cause a public local inquiry or hearing to be held and consider the report of the person who held the inquiry or hearing before deciding whether to make the order with or without modifications.[145]

(f)   There are provisions for the making of the order by stages equivalent to those which have been described for the confirmation by stages of orders promoted by other authorities.[146]

(g)   As with orders promoted by other authorities the order may not be modified when it is made by including land not within the draft order unless all persons interested consent.[147]

(h)   After the order has been made the Minister must give notice of the making of the order in the prescribed form as with orders made by other authorities which have been confirmed. An order made by a Minister comes into operation on the date on which notice of the making of the order is first published.[148]

(i)   The prescribed forms to be used for many purposes in the case of orders made by Ministers are the same as for orders made by other authorities and the Regulations governing the written representations procedure are the same.[149]

(H) SPECIAL PARLIAMENTARY PROCEDURE AND SPECIAL CASES

1. Special Parliamentary Procedure

2.61   There are three categories of land now to be described where the compulsory purchase of the land may be subject to special parliamentary procedure. The special procedure is designed to provide an additional protection for the owners of the categories of land to which it applies. The procedure is that described in the Statutory Orders (Special Procedure) Act 1945 as amended by the Statutory Orders (Special Procedure) Act 1965. A compulsory purchase order to which the procedure applies has no effect until it is laid before Parliament

---

[142] Ibid, sch 1, paras 2, 3.
[143] Ibid, sch 1, para 4.
[144] Ibid, sch 1, para 4A.
[145] Ibid, sch 1, para 4A(3).
[146] Ibid, sch 1, para 4B.
[147] Ibid, sch 1, para 5.
[148] Ibid, sch 1, para 6.
[149] See the Compulsory Purchase of Land (Prescribed Forms) (Ministers) Regulations 2004 (SI 2004/2595) and the Compulsory Purchase of Land (Written Representations Procedure) (Ministers) Regulations 2004 (SI 2004/2594).

and brought into operation in accordance with the provisions of the 1945 Act. The procedure applies to many other types of administrative order as well as certain compulsory purchase orders of land as specified in the Acquisition of Land Act 1981. Special parliamentary procedure applies in addition to, and not in place of, the procedures under the 1981 Act and no order may be laid before Parliament until these procedures, such as the publication of orders and the consideration of objections, have been carried out.

Special parliamentary procedure is linked to a compulsory purchase order coming into effect. It therefore has no application to compulsory acquisitions which are authorised without the need to make a compulsory purchase order. Consequently it applies to the second and third of the types of procedure for putting a power of compulsory purchase into effect as described in paragraph 2.41. Special parliamentary procedure is not applicable to the first type of procedure where the empowering Act itself delineates the area of land within which land may be compulsorily acquired. There is no compulsory purchase order in such a case. Those persons who would otherwise have been entitled to the protection of the special parliamentary procedure are considered to have had their opportunity to petition Parliament in opposition to the passing of the empowering Act.   2.62

A petition against the order may be made within 21 days of the order being laid before Parliament. A petition may be a general objection to the order or may seek modification of the order. The chairmen of the appropriate parliamentary committees consider petitions and may certify that the petition is proper to be received.[150] It is then open to either House within 21 days to resolve that the order be annulled and if this is done the order becomes void.[151] If the order is not so annulled any petitions certified by the chairmen as proper to be received are referred to a joint committee of both Houses of Parliament.[152] The joint committee then 'reports' the order. The report may state that effect ought to be given to the order with or without modifications or that the order be not approved. The report is laid before both Houses. If it is stated in the report that effect ought to be given to the order then the order comes into operation on the date on which the report of the committee is laid before Parliament with any modifications so reported. If the report of the joint committee is that the order be not approved the order shall not take effect unless it is confirmed by Act of Parliament.[153] Standing orders of the two Houses regulate the proceedings of any committee upon the consideration of an order.[154] A joint committee may award costs.[155]   2.63

A compulsory purchase order may include land which is subject to special parliamentary procedure and other land which is not so subject and there seems to have been some doubt over whether Parliament could consider petitions relating to land within the order but which was not subject to the special procedure. Any inconsistency between the Statutory Orders (Special Procedure) Act 1945 and the Acquisition of Land Act 1981 has now been removed by provisions inserted into the former Act by the Growth and Infrastructure Act 2013. This was done by defining the provisions in the 1981 Act which apply the special parliamentary procedure as 'special acquisition provisions' and by stating that where those provisions apply 'the special authorisation' means the compulsory purchase order only so   2.64

---

[150] Statutory Orders (Special Procedure) Act 1945, s 3.
[151] Ibid, s 4(1).
[152] Ibid, s 4(2).
[153] Ibid, ss 5, 6.
[154] Ibid, s 9.
[155] Ibid, s 7.

far as it authorises the compulsory acquisition of land to which the special acquisition provisions apply. The 1945 Act is thus in general applied as though its references to petitions
presented to Parliament referred only to petitions presented against the special authorisation provisions of the order.[156]

2.65   The first category of land to which this procedure applies is where land forms part of a common, open space or fuel or field garden allotment. The application of the special parliamentary procedure does not operate if the Secretary of State is satisfied that, and gives a certificate that, one of a certain set of circumstances exists. The circumstances are (a) that land
has been or will be given in exchange for the land acquired which is at least as large and
equally advantageous as the land acquired,[157] or (b) that the land is being acquired in order
to secure its preservation or improve its management, or (c) that the land does not exceed
250 square yards or is required wholly or partly for the widening or drainage of an existing
highway and that the giving of exchange land is unnecessary in the interests of the persons
entitled to rights of common or other rights or in the interests of the public. The Secretary
of State must direct the acquiring authority to give public notice of his intention to give a
certificate as just described and must give persons interested an opportunity to make representations and objections. He must consider any representations or objections made before
giving a certificate and he may cause a public local inquiry to be held on the matter. A decision of the Secretary of State not to hold an inquiry before deciding whether to give a certificate is, like all discretionary administrative decisions, subject in principle to control by
judicial review but the person seeking to challenge a decision not to hold an inquiry would
need to establish one of the normal grounds of challenge to the exercise of a discretion such
as a failure by the Secretary of State to take into account all relevant considerations.[158] A
compulsory purchase order of land in the present category may provide for the vesting of
the exchange land and for the discharge of the land acquired from all rights, trusts and
incidents to which it was previously subject. It needs to be remembered that the application
of the special parliamentary procedure or the giving of a certificate by the Secretary of State
applies to this category of land automatically and without the need for an objection to the
compulsory purchase order by persons interested in the common or other land affected.[159]

2.66   The second category of land is land held inalienably by the National Trust. A compulsory
purchase order of such land is subject to special parliamentary procedure if there is an
objection to the order by the National Trust which is not withdrawn.[160]

2.67   The third category arises when the land being acquired is the property of a local authority
or has previously been acquired by statutory undertakers who are not a local authority for
the purpose of their undertaking. Local authorities in England are the councils of counties,
districts, London Boroughs and the City of London together with certain other specified
bodies such as police authorities. In Wales local authorities are county or county borough

---

[156] See s 1A of the Statutory Orders (Special Procedure) Act 1945 inserted by s 25(4) of the Growth and
Infrastructure Act 2013 as from 25 June 2013.
[157] It is for the Secretary of State to make a general evaluation of whether the exchange land is equally advantageous as the land to be acquired when deciding whether to issue a certificate: *Yates v Secretary of State* [1993] Env
LR 344.
[158] *Waltham Forest District Council v Secretary of State* [1993] EGCS 34. A common includes a town or village
green. Open space means any land laid out as a public garden, or used for the purposes of public recreation, or land
which is a disused burial ground: Acquisition of Land Act 1981, s 19(4).
[159] Acquisition of Land Act 1981, s 19.
[160] Ibid, s 18.

authorities and police authorities.[161] Statutory undertakers are defined as persons authorised by an enactment to construct, work or carry out various transport, dock or postal
services, the civil aviation authority and certain other bodies which the Secretary of State
may specify.[162] The rule is that a compulsory purchase order made of land of any of these
persons is subject to special parliamentary procedure if that person has made an objection
and it is not withdrawn.[163] The rule is subject to a wide exception in that it does not apply
where the acquiring authority is a local authority, a statutory undertaker or one of certain
other specified bodies, or a Minister.[164] Most compulsory purchase orders are made by one
of these last mentioned persons so that the width of the exception deprives the rule of much
of its effect.

2. Special Cases

In addition to the possible application of the special parliamentary procedure to an acquisi-   2.68
tion of their land statutory undertakers are protected from the compulsory purchase of
their land in a further way. When land has been acquired by a statutory undertaker for the
purpose of its undertaking and a compulsory purchase order has been made or made in
draft in respect of the land the undertaker may make a representation to the appropriate
Minister during the period specified for the making of objections. The Minister can then
state that he is satisfied that the land or any interest in the land is used for the purposes
of the carrying on of the undertaking. The result of the Minister so stating his satisfaction
is that unless the representation is withdrawn the compulsory purchase order cannot be
confirmed, or made if prepared in draft, unless the Minister is also satisfied that either the
land can be purchased without replacement and without serious detriment to the carrying
on of the undertaking or that if the land is purchased it can be replaced by other land
belonging to, or available for acquisition by, the undertaking without such serious detriment.[165]

It has been explained that while a power to acquire land does not include a power to create   2.69
and acquire new rights over land a general power is conferred on local authorities to do this
and some statutes confer a specific power to acquire and create new rights. Some modification of the procedural provisions in the Acquisition of Land Act 1981 is required so as to
apply the procedure in the Act to cases of acquisitions of new rights over land. This is
brought about by a general provision that the Act shall have effect with the modifications
necessary to make it apply to the compulsory acquisition of a right as it applies to the compulsory acquisition of land. The modifications are applied to compulsory acquisitions of
new rights under the general power given to local authorities and under certain other specified statutes. In addition the provisions which restrict the compulsory acquisition of land
of statutory undertakers and which apply the special parliamentary procedure to the compulsory acquisition of land of local authorities and statutory undertakers, national trust

---

[161] Ibid, s 17(4).
[162] Ibid, ss 8(1), (12A), (1A), 17(4).
[163] Ibid, s 17(2).
[164] Ibid, s 17(3).
[165] Ibid, s 16. Under s 16(3) a number of further public bodies are included within the meaning of statutory
undertakers for this purpose.

land, and commons and open spaces, etc, do not apply to statutory acquisitions of rights but are replaced by other specific and generally equivalent provisions.[166]

2.70   Certain special provisions apply to compulsory rights orders under the Opencast Coal Act 1958 (which applies the Acquisition of Land Act 1981) and to the compulsory purchase of a right to store gas in an underground gas store under the Gas Act 1965.[167]

(I)   CHALLENGES TO THE VALIDITY OF ORDERS

2.71   The ordinary power to challenge the validity of the actions of a public authority by seeking a remedy by way of judicial review, such as an order quashing the action or a declaration as to its validity, is removed in the case of compulsory purchase orders and is replaced by a specific statutory right to challenge orders in the High Court which is in many ways akin to the general process of judicial review.[168] The two grounds of challenge under this procedure are examined here.[169] It is provided that save by the use of the specific statutory procedure a compulsory purchase order shall not, either before or after it has been confirmed or made, be questioned in any legal proceedings whatsoever.[170] There is a six week time limit running from the date on which the order becomes operative for the use of the statutory procedure for challenge which, since it is a statutory time limit, cannot be extended by the court. The draconian nature of the exclusion of ordinary remedies is demonstrated by the fact that an order cannot be questioned after the end of the six week period even if the person wishing to challenge it had no opportunity within that period to ascertain the facts which would found any challenge and even if the order was tainted by bad faith.[171] A similar special procedure for challenge in the High Court is provided in other areas of public law such as decisions on planning appeals where there is also an exclusion of ordinary remedies.[172]

2.72   It is questionable what is gained by this type of restricted right of challenge. It is obvious that an acquiring authority needs to know with certainty at an early stage where it stands and to be protected from late legal challenges after the compulsory purchase order has been acted on by the authority. This is true of many actions of public bodies and the flexible time limits and discretionary nature of judicial review, with the need to apply promptly for permission to apply for judicial review, already provides a general protection to public bodies. In addition the specific grounds of the statutory right of challenge are not greatly different from the grounds which are available when any action of a public body is questioned in judicial review proceedings. The broad effect of the above provisions is, therefore, to impose a short, rigid and inflexible, time limit for challenges to the validity of compulsory purchase orders.[173] The prohibition on a legal challenge is one which applies to the validity of a com-

---

[166]   See Acquisition of Land Act 1981, s 28 and sch 3. See also n 65 to para 2.34.
[167]   Ibid, ss 29, 30.
[168]   Acquisition of Land Act 1981, s 23.
[169]   See para 2.74 et seq.
[170]   Acquisition of Land Act 1981, s 25.
[171]   *Smith v East Elloe District Council* [1956] AC 736, [1956] 2 WLR 888; *R v Secretary of State for the Environment, ex parte Ostler* [1977] QB 122, [1976] 3 WLR 288. Cf *Anisminic v Foreign Compensation Commission* [1969] 2 AC 147, [1969] 2 WLR 163.
[172]   Town and Country Planning Act 1990, ss 284–88.
[173]   In *Smith v East Elloe District Council*, above n 171, Lord Radcliffe described the six week period as pitifully inadequate. The law discussed under this section of this chapter raises matters of general importance in adminis-

pulsory purchase order. There appears to be no restriction on a challenge to the validity in law of some preliminary administrative action such as the resolution by a local authority to make a compulsory purchase order, and ordinary proceedings by way of judicial review are in principle available to enable such preliminary steps to be challenged.[174] Other administrative actions of an acquiring authority carried out in the course of the process of compulsory purchase may also be challenged by way of judicial review provided the challenge is not one as to the validity of the compulsory purchase order. For example, an entry onto the land by the acquiring authority without the service of a notice of entry or the use of some other appropriate procedure could be challenged by way of judicial review.[175] In an exceptional case some unfairness or procedural error at an inquiry into objections to a compulsory purchase order might be challenged by way of judicial review.[176] A decision by a confirming authority not to confirm a compulsory purchase order can be challenged by judicial review sought by the authority which made the order since in such a case there is ex hypothesi no order the validity of which is being questioned.[177] Steps taken by an authority following the confirmation of an order such as the service of a notice to treat may in principle be challenged in legal proceedings as long as the validity of the order itself is not being questioned. A possible ground of challenge might be that the acquiring authority was proceeding to acquire the land for a purpose other than that for which the compulsory purchase order was made.[178]

A challenge to an order may be brought by 'a person aggrieved' by the order. Plainly persons with an interest in any land being acquired under the order fall within this description. It is likely that anyone who has a genuine concern regarding the order and who can be said to be someone aggrieved by it in the ordinary sense of that word will be found to have sufficient standing to proceed in the High Court. The question of who is a person aggrieved in the context of this and other provisions creating a right of statutory challenge to an action of a public body is akin to the general question of what persons have sufficient standing, often called *locus standi*, to apply for judicial review to challenge decisions of public bodies. The modern tendency has been to extend the ambit of persons who have a sufficient interest to seek the intervention of a court.[179] For instance, when a planning decision is in issue it has been held that a local amenity society is a person aggrieved within the meaning of a similar   2.73

trative law and a full discussion of the nature and effect of exclusive statutory remedies will be found in *Wade & Forsyth on Administrative Law*, 10th edn (Oxford, Oxford University Press, 2009) pp 621–31.

[174] See, eg the leading recent decision on the use of the power of compulsory acquisition for improper purposes or with immaterial considerations taken into account where a resolution to make a compulsory purchase order was challenged in judicial review proceedings: *R (Sainsbury's Supermarkets) Ltd v Wolverhampton City Council* [2010] UKSC 20, [2011] 1 AC 437. See also *R v Camden LBC, ex parte Comyn Ching & Co Ltd* [1984] JPL 661. It is not wholly clear what is meant by the restriction on challenging the validity of a compulsory purchase order before it is made.

[175] See section (k) of this chapter for the provisions on gaining entry to the land being acquired. A wide range of remedies is available in proceedings for judicial review including injunctions, declarations and interim relief: see Civil Procedure Rules, Pt 54.

[176] *R v Secretary of State, ex parte Royal Borough of Kensington and Chelsea* (1987) 19 HLR 161.

[177] *Islington LBC v Secretary of State* (1982) 43 P & CR 300; *R (Barnsley Metropolitan Borough Council) v Secretary of State* [2012] EWHC 1366, [2012] 2 EGLR 1.

[178] See paras 2.75 and 2.8.

[179] *R v Inland Revenue Commissioners, ex parte National Federation of Self-Employed and Small Businesses Ltd* [1982] AC 617, [1981] 2 WLR 722. The Federation was held to have a sufficient status to challenge by way of judicial review the actions of the Revenue in making an agreement to deal with the various and curious practices which at one time were employed as regards their tax affairs by printers and others.

provision creating a statutory challenge to the validity of certain planning decisions.[180] A neighbour may have a sufficient interest to challenge a decision to grant planning permission by the ordinary process of judicial review.[181] It is important to distinguish in this area of law two questions, the first being whether a person has sufficient status to challenge the compulsory purchase order by virtue of being a person aggrieved and the second being whether, assuming a person has such a status, his interest is such that the court in its discretion should grant him the remedy of quashing the order.[182]

2.74   There are two grounds of challenge.[183] The first is that the authorisation of a compulsory purchase is not empowered to be granted under the Acquisition of Land Act 1981. This ground allows a challenge on the basis that the empowering Act did not permit the making or preparing in draft of the compulsory purchase order or that it was made or prepared in draft for a purpose other than that for which the power to make it was conferred.[184] A failure by the confirming Minister to take account of a material consideration in reaching his decision to confirm the compulsory purchase order could also amount to a breach of the first ground.[185] The second ground is that there has not been compliance with the requirements of the 1981 Act or of any regulation made under that Act or with any requirement of the Tribunals and Inquiries Act 1992.[186] This ground refers generally to a failure to observe a procedural requirement such as the duty to publish the making of a compulsory purchase order or such as that an objector has not been given proper opportunity to make representations under the written representations procedure. It may sometimes be difficult to distinguish between a breach of the law within the first and the second grounds. It appears that a breach of the rules of natural justice, for example a failure to allow an objector a fair opportunity to present his objection, would be a breach within both of the grounds.[187] Such

---

[180] *Turner v Secretary of State for the Environment* (1973) 28 P & CR 123.

[181] *R v Hendon RDC, ex parte Chorley* [1933] 2 KB 696.

[182] See the discussion in *Wade & Forsyth on Administrative Law*, 10th edn (Oxford, Oxford University Press, 2009) at p 630.

[183] There are many decided authorities on challenges in the courts to compulsory purchase orders. The purpose of this chapter is to explain the main principles which apply and where appropriate to illustrate those principles by reference to the more important decided cases. A list of many of the decisions will be found in the annotations to s 23 of the Acquisition of Land Act 1981 in vol 1 of the *Encyclopaedia of Compulsory Purchase and Compensation* (London, Sweet & Maxwell). One general matter that should be kept firmly in mind by anyone seeking to question the validity of a compulsory purchase order under these provisions is that the court will be concerned with seeing that the law has been observed and that there has been procedural fairness. The court will not involve itself in the detailed merits of the compulsory purchase or of objections to it since these matters lie within the province of the acquiring authority: see the observations of Beatson J in *Boland v Welsh Ministers* [2011] EWHC 629 (Admin).

[184] See paras 2.4–2.9 of this chapter.

[185] *Eckersley v Secretary of State for the Environment* (1977) 34 P & CR 124. See *Bolton MBC v Secretary of State for the Environment* (1991) 61 P & CR 343 for the discussion by Glidewell J of a series of principles to be applied in cases where matters had been left out of account in the process of confirming a compulsory purchase order. In *Crest v Secretary of State for Wales* [1983] RVR 11, an order was quashed because the confirming authority failed to take into account the acquisition costs of alternative sites. It was held in *Smith v Secretary of State* [2008] 1 WLR 394, that the making of a compulsory purchase order could not be impugned as a failure to comply with art 8 of the European Convention on Human rights simply because it was not the least obtrusive measure available.

[186] Under s 10 of the Tribunals and Inquiries Act 1992 the Minister is required to state the reasons for his decision if requested, on or before the notification of his decision, to do so. Rule 19(1) of the Compulsory Purchase (Inquiries Procedure) Rules 2007 (SI 2007/3617) requires the authorising authority to give reasons in writing of its decision. The reasons given must be proper, intelligible and adequate: *Westminster City Council v Great Portland Estates* [1985] AC 661, [1984] 3 WLR 1035.

[187] *Fairmount Investments Ltd v Secretary of State for the Environment* [1976] 1 WLR 1255, [1976] 2 All ER 865. An example of a breach of the rules of natural justice is where an inspector hearing objections into a housing compulsory purchase order asked questions of residents during a site visit without objectors being present: *Hibernian Property Co Ltd v Secretary of State* (1974) 27 P & CR 197.

a breach is usually considered to render the actions of the public body involved void in law. There are many procedural faults and breaches of the requirements of the legislation or of delegated legislation such as inquiry procedure rules which could occur. It was at one time thought useful to divide such procedural requirements into those called mandatory (in the sense that a breach of the requirement always renders an administrative action or decision void) and those called directory (in the sense that a breach did not render the administrative action or decision void). However, the modern tendency has been to deprecate such a dichotomy and to adopt a more flexible approach to the consequences in law of a breach of a procedural requirement.[188]

It may be possible to challenge not the validity of the compulsory purchase order itself but the validity in law of subsequent actions by the acquiring authority in implementing the compulsory purchase authorised by the order. Such a challenge will be by way of judicial review rather than under the statutory procedure in the Acquisition of Land Act 1981. A possible ground of challenge might be that the acquiring authority had failed to observe an undertaking given when objections to the order were being considered.[189] A practice which is sometimes followed is that objectors may withdraw their objection on some particular undertaking being given to them such as that they will not be removed from the land until the acquiring authority has made available to them certain specified alternative premises to which they can move. The challenge to subsequent actions of the acquiring authority may be to the service of a notice to treat or to the making of a general vesting declaration or to physical entry under the order. Other grounds of such a challenge might in principle and in an appropriate case include: (a) that the compulsory purchase order was being implemented for a purpose different to that for which it was made or confirmed, (b) that the acquiring authority was guilty of inordinate delay in proceeding with the compulsory purchase, and (c) that the conduct of the acquiring authority was such as to lead to the inference that the compulsory purchase was being abandoned.[190]

2.75

The period of six weeks for the making of the application runs from the date on which the order became operative, that is the day on which notice of the confirmation or making of the order was first published as already explained. Consequently an application made after the confirmation of the order but before publication of notice of the confirmation could not be heard.[191] Where the order is subject to special parliamentary procedure the six weeks runs from the date on which the order became operative under the Statutory Orders (Special Procedure) Act 1945. The application must be made in accordance with the procedure under Part 8 of the Civil Procedure Rules and is heard by a single judge of the

2.76

---

[188] *London & Clydeside Estates Ltd v Aberdeen District Council* [1980] 1 WLR 182; *R v Home Secretary, ex parte Jayeanthan* [2000] 1 WLR 354; *R v Soneji* [2006] 1 AC 340. The modern tendency is to decide whether a breach of a procedural requirement renders an action void by reference to: (a) whether the breach has been waived, (b) how material the breach is, and (c) whether any prejudice or risk of prejudice has been caused to the other party by the breach: see the principles stated by Lord Woolf MR in the *Jayeanthan* decision. The fact that the court always has a discretion on whether to make an order quashing the compulsory purchase order means that immaterial or minor breaches of procedural requirements which can cause no significant prejudice to anyone affected are unlikely to lead to a quashing of the order: see paras 2.78 and 2.79.

[189] *English Welsh and Scottish Rly Co v Secretary of State* [2002] EWHC 2641 (Admin).

[190] *Simpsons Motor Sales (London) Ltd v Hendon Corporation* [1964] AC 1088, [1963] 2 WLR 1187; *Grice v Dudley Corporation* [1958] 1 Ch 329, [1957] 3 WLR 314. Cf *R v Carmarthen District Council* (1990) 59 P & CR 379 in relation to the use of the general vesting declaration procedure.

[191] *Enterprise Inns Plc v Secretary of State* (2001) 81 P & CR 236. As explained earlier it is possible to challenge by way of ordinary judicial review proceedings a resolution to make a compulsory purchase order: see para 2.72.

Administrative Court of the Queen's Bench Division of the High Court. Unlike ordinary applications for judicial review it is not necessary for the applicant first to seek and obtain the permission of the court to make the application. The time limits for challenges to the validity of compulsory purchase orders may therefore be summarised as being: (a) a challenge to any administrative action before and as a preliminary to the making of the order may be brought by the ordinary process of judicial review under Part 54 of the Civil Procedure Rules, (b) once the order has been made or prepared in draft by a minister no challenge in the courts to its validity may be brought by judicial review or other proceedings until notice of the confirmation of the order is published, and (c) when notice of the confirmation of the order is published there is a strict six week time limit during which the order may be challenged under the special statutory procedure explained but not by way of judicial review or other procedural process.

2.77   The court hearing an application has power to quash the compulsory purchase order or any provision in it either generally or so far as it affects any property of the applicant. If the order was outside the powers conferred by the empowering Act or was invalid for some similar reason, such as having been made for the wrong purpose or having been made without all relevant considerations taken into account, the court would be likely to quash the order as a whole. On the other hand where there has been a non-compliance with a procedural requirement which affects only the applicant the court might be more inclined to quash the order only as regards the land of the applicant, in effect to remove that land from the order. The power of the court to quash an order or a part of it is stated in different terms in respect of the two grounds of the application. When the ground is that the authorisation to acquire land is not empowered to be granted then there is no further qualification of the power to quash the order. When the application is on the ground that a relevant requirement has not been complied with the court cannot quash the order unless the interests of the applicant have been substantially prejudiced by the non-compliance.

2.78   The court always has a discretion on whether to quash the order in whole or in part when one of the grounds is made out. The discretion derives from the statute which states that the High Court 'may quash' rather than 'shall quash' the order if a ground is made out.[192] This rule follows the general principle that all remedies in administrative law are discretionary. An important consequence of the existence of this discretion is that an investigation must generally be made into what prejudice has been suffered by an applicant whether he relies on the first or the second ground. Consequently the conditions which have to be satisfied by the applicant under the two grounds if he is to obtain an order may not in practice be very different. If an applicant relies on the first ground, for instance by showing that in deciding to make the order the acquiring authority failed to take into account a relevant consideration, the court may refuse to exercise its discretion to quash the order where the applicant has suffered no significant prejudice as a result of the irregularity. An obvious instance of the application of the discretion not to quash the order would be where the consideration not taken into account was something which supported the making of the order. In practice, therefore, the demonstration by the applicant of some prejudice or risk of prejudice to him from the irregularity is relevant to his obtaining an order from the court whichever of the two grounds is relied upon. In one case the court refused to quash an order when notice of the making of the order had not been served on a wife who was a co-owner

---

[192]   *Kent County Council v Secretary of State for the Environment* [1976] 75 LGR 452.

of property with her husband since no prejudice had been shown to have been caused by the error.[193]

A point which not infrequently arises in connection with the exercise of its discretion by the court is whether, if the irregularity which forms the basis of the application had not occurred, the acquiring authority would still have made or prepared in draft the order, or the order would still have been confirmed, in exactly the same way. The general approach by the courts is that if it is wholly clear that the making or preparation in draft or confirmation of the order would have occurred apart from the irregularity the court will in its discretion refuse to quash the order. Indeed this is much the same as saying that in these circumstances the applicant has not shown any prejudice to him.[194] That having been said, the court will not involve itself in speculation on what would have happened in the absence of the irregularity if there is any uncertainty involved so that if there is any significant prospect that the order would not have been made or prepared in draft or confirmed apart from the irregularity it is likely that the court will decide that the order or a part of it should be quashed.[195]   2.79

The result of the quashing of an order as a whole is that the order is taken never to have existed in law. If it wishes to proceed the acquiring authority is, of course, entitled to start the process anew. A quashing of a part of an order, such as the removal of a particular property from it, does not affect the validity of the remainder of the order which may then be put into effect by the acquisition of the remainder of the land within it. Of course in some cases the removal of a particular piece of land from a compulsory order may make the implementation of the remainder of the order difficult or even impossible. If that situation did occur it would be open to the acquiring authority to make a further compulsory purchase order relating only to the land which has been removed from the previous order by the partial quashing of that order. Whether it would be practical for an acquiring authority to start again on the same process of compulsory acquisition would usually depend on the reason which led the court to quash the order in whole or in part. A quashing by reason of a procedural irregularity would not normally prevent the making and confirmation of a new order with the observance of the proper procedure. On the other hand the quashing of an order by reason of it having been made for a wrong or unauthorised purpose would obviously prevent the making of a new order for the same purpose.   2.80

Once an application has been made the court may issue an interim order suspending the operation of the compulsory purchase order or any provision in it, either generally or in so far as it affects any property of the applicant, until the final determination of the proceedings.[196] The result of an interim order is that the acquiring authority may take no further steps to implement the compulsory purchase order, or the relevant part of the order, until the court has reached its final determination. Before it makes an interim order a court will   2.81

---

[193] *George v Secretary of State* (1979) 38 P & CR 609. In another case an order was quashed when the inspector asked questions of local residents on a site visit when objectors were not present because there was a risk of prejudice to the objectors: *Hibernian Property Co Ltd v Secretary of State* (1974) 27 P & CR 197.

[194] *Malloch v Aberdeen Corporation* [1971] 1 WLR 1578. This is a general problem which applies in administrative law. A similar principle applies in New Zealand: see *Wislane v Medical Practitioners Disciplinary Committee* [1973] 1 NZLR 29; *Stininato v Auckland Boxing Association* [1978] 1 NZLR 1.

[195] *Ridge v Baldwin* [1964] AC 40, [1963] 2 WLR 935; *John v Rees* [1970] Ch 345, [1969] 2 WLR 1294; *R (Amin) v Home Secretary* [2003] UKHL 51, [2003] 3 WLR 1169; *Hibernian Property Co Ltd v Secretary of State* (1974) 27 P & CR 197.

[196] Acquisition of Land Act 1981, s 24(1).

wish to be satisfied that there is at any rate some real prospect of the application succeeding. Interim orders are rare since in most cases an acquiring authority faced with an application to the High Court will not wish to take the risk of proceeding further under the compulsory purchase order, for instance by entering the land, until the court has reached its decision. As mentioned there is no screening process for applications and anyone who says he is a person aggrieved may make an application to the court however weak and unmeritorious his case may be. It normally takes some time for a case to be listed for hearing and to be heard and if the acquiring authority believes that the application has no significant prospect of success, and is unwilling to bear the delay and uncertainty involved, it may make an application to the court to strike out the application to quash in the hope that this can be dealt with more quickly than the full proceedings.

2.82   The provisions just described apply to certificates given by a Minister as a part of the procedure for the confirmation of a compulsory purchase order, for example a certificate relating to the giving of exchange land when common land or open space land is being acquired. The validity of such a certificate can be challenged by way of an application to the High Court within the six week period from the giving of the certificate on the ground that any relevant requirement relating to the certificate has not been complied with, that is what has been described as the second ground of challenge.[197] Subject to this statutory right of challenge a certificate cannot be challenged in any legal proceedings.

(J) IMPLEMENTATION OF THE ORDER: NOTICE TO TREAT

1. Introduction

2.83   Once the compulsory purchase order has been confirmed, or made if prepared in draft by a Minister, and has not been successfully challenged in the High Court under the statutory procedure, the acquiring authority may proceed to implement the order. The nature of the procedure is that the order authorises a compulsory purchase of the land, or any of the land, comprised in the order. The acquiring authority is not compelled to acquire the land compulsorily.[198] The authority is entitled to abandon the project altogether or to decide not to acquire some particular area or areas of land within the order or to acquire some land by agreement and some by exercising the powers of compulsion under the order.

2.84   There are two broad procedural courses open to an acquiring authority which wishes to put into effect the authority to acquire land conferred by a compulsory purchase order, the

---

[197] Acquisition of Land Act 1981, s 23(2).
[198] There are suggestions in some older cases that once an acquiring authority has signified an intention to acquire an area of land which it is entitled to acquire it can be compelled by a mandatory order of the court to proceed to acquire that land by serving notice to treat: *R v Hungerford Market Co* (1832) 4 B & Ad 327; *Fotherby v Metropolitan Rly* (1867) LR 2 CP 188; *Morgan v Metropolitan Rly Co* (1868–69) LR 4 CP 97. However, these decisions were at a time when there were suggestions that a notice to treat might of itself create an enforceable contract of sale and before there was a statutory power to withdraw a notice to treat. In practice today there seems little that a landowner can do to enforce the service of a notice to treat (although he may be able to take advantage of the blight provisions in the Town and Country Planning Act 1990) but when a notice to treat has been served the owner can expedite matters by referring the assessment of the compensation to the Lands Tribunal.

notice to treat procedure and the vesting declaration procedure. [199] Both procedures lead to the authority being entitled to enter the land being acquired, to obtain legal title to that land, and lead to a liability on the part of the authority to pay compensation to the dispossessed owner. Some would say that the alternative procedures constitute further and unnecessary complexity within the overall process. The general vesting declaration procedure was intended to be something the use of which would expedite the process of the acquisition of the land. The two procedures are not even wholly separate since the operation of the vesting declaration procedure operates for many purposes as a constructive notice to treat. The statutory provisions on notices to treat go back to the Lands Clauses Consolidation Act 1845 and are now contained in the Compulsory Purchase Act 1965. The newer vesting declaration provisions are contained in the Compulsory Purchase (Vesting Declarations) Act 1981. It is proposed first to describe the notice to treat procedure under this section. The vesting declaration procedure is described in section (q) of this chapter.

2. The Nature and Service of a Notice to Treat

A notice to treat is a notice which gives particulars of the land to which it relates, demands   2.85
particulates of the estate and interest of the recipient of the notice in the land and of the claim to compensation which he makes, and states that the acquiring authority is willing to treat for the purchase of the land and as to compensation.[200] The offer to treat is not an offer to discuss whether the land will be purchased by the acquiring authority since the authority necessarily has power to purchase the land by compulsion and is exercising that power but is primarily an offer to discuss compensation. There is no prescribed form of a notice to treat.[201] It is good practice to describe the land the subject of the notice to treat by reference to a plan annexed to the notice. A notice to treat is given in respect of a particular area of land under the compulsory purchase order and must be given to all persons interested in, or having power to sell and convey or release, the land, so far as known to the acquiring authority after making diligent enquiry. Obviously a notice to treat should be served on every person with a freehold or leasehold interest in the land. Mortgagees and persons with equitable interests should be served including persons holding equitable leases under a specifically enforceable agreement for lease, purchasers under a contract of sale, persons with the benefit of an option to acquire the land and equitable mortgagees.[202] It appears that a

---

[199] It has been explained that some statutes which confer a power of compulsory purchase themselves authorise the acquisition of land usually within a limited and defined area and usually for the purposes of a specific project such as a new railway line: see para 2.5. In such cases no compulsory purchase order is needed to authorise the acquisition of land. Nonetheless the subsequent procedure now to be described involving a notice to treat (or a general vesting declaration: see section (q) of this chapter) must be observed. Of course even when the authority for the compulsory acquisition of land derives from a statute the relevant authority must still decide whether and when and to what extent to exercise that authority.

[200] Compulsory Purchase Act 1965, s 5(2).

[201] In *Hull and Humber Investment Co Ltd v Hull Corporation* [1965] 2 QB 145, [1965] 1 All ER 429, it was conceded that a letter from the District Valuer amounted to a notice to treat. A statement by a Minister that he was prepared to confirm a compulsory purchase order has been held not to amount to a notice to treat: *Bostock Chater & Sons Ltd v Chelmsford Corporation* (1973) 26 P & CR 321.

[202] *Advance Ground Rents v Middlesborough Borough Council* [1986] 2 EGLR 221 (mortgagee); *Martin v London Chatham & Dover Rly* (1865-66) LR 1 Ch App 501 (equitable mortgagee); *Malec v Westminster Council* [2005] RVR 384 (contractual purchaser): a purchaser under a specifically enforceable contract of sale has an equitable interest in the land; *Oppenheimer v Minister of Transport* [1942] 1 KB 242, [1941] 3 All ER 485 (option to acquire land);

person in adverse possession of land should be served with a notice to treat whether or not the period of adverse possession needed to give him a good possessory title has been completed.[203] A notice to treat need not be served on licensees, who do not have a proprietary interest in land, or on persons with a right of pre-emption which is also for this purpose not recognised as an interest in land.[204] A notice to treat need not be served on persons having incorporeal proprietary interests over the land such as easements or the benefit of restrictive covenants. In law such incorporeal interests are not acquired by the acquiring authority but become unenforceable as regards the exercise of statutory powers on the land acquired as a result of the compulsory purchase so giving to the owners of the interests an entitlement to compensation for injurious affection to the land to which the benefit of the interests is annexed.[205] The owner of an interest in land created after the giving of a notice to treat in respect of that land is not entitled to a notice to treat. It is not necessary that all notices to treat in respect of land authorised to be acquired by the compulsory purchase order should be given at the same time. The notice need not relate to the whole of the land of a particular owner and, if necessary, a further notice can be served on the same person or persons so as to cover further land belonging to those persons. It has been explained that as land generally includes an interest in land a notice to treat can probably be given in respect of one interest in an area of land without a notice having to be given to the owners of all other interests. For instance a notice could be given to the freeholder only if the acquiring authority wished to acquire the freehold but not any leasehold interests.[206] The provisions of section 6 of the Acquisition of Land Act 1961 are applied to the service of a notice to treat.[207]

2.86   It is the duty of an acquiring authority to make diligent enquiry to ascertain all persons to whom a notice to treat should be given. Mention has been made of the power of an authority to require persons such as the occupier of land to give information about persons with an interest in the land, a power which can be exercised before or after a compulsory purchase order is made.[208] Where land has registered title information on persons with an interest in it may be obtained in the ordinary way from HM Land Registry. A special procedure is available for acquiring title and obtaining possession of the land where a person with an interest in land cannot be found after diligent enquiry or where a person is absent from the United Kingdom and so cannot discuss compensation with the acquiring authority. It is not possible to give a notice to treat to persons in the first category and, despite modern methods of communication, it may be difficult to give a notice to treat to persons in the second category. In such a case the acquiring authority can have the amount of com-

---

Blamires v Bradford Corporation [1964] Ch 585, [1964] 3 WLR 226 (equitable interest under an agreement for a life tenancy). See section (c) of ch 3 for the categories of persons who are entitled to claim compensation under the seven main heads of compensation.

   [203] *Perry v Clissold* [1907] AC 73 (PC on appeal from HC of Australia). In this case the period of adverse possession needed to create a possessory title had not elapsed at the time of the compulsory purchase.
   [204] *Frank Warr & Co Ltd v London County Council* [1904] 1 KB 713. A right of pre-emption is probably best regarded as not creating an interest in land: see *Pritchard v Briggs* [1980] Ch 338, [1979] 3 WLR 868.
   [205] *Clark v School Board for London* (1874) 9 Ch App 120. The compensation for owners of the benefit of the interest is available under s 10 of the Compulsory Purchase Act 1965. See section (f) of chapter 10.
   [206] See para 2.29. However a contrary view was expressed in the decision of the Lands Tribunal in *Union Rlys Ltd v Kent County Council* [2008] 2 EGLR 183.
   [207] Compulsory Purchase Act 1965, s 30. See n 96. Section 6 of the Acquisition of Land Act 1981 provides a complete code for the service of notices so that some other mode of service such as service on an agent is not permissible: *Fagan v Knowsley Metropolitan Borough Council* (1985) 50 P & CR 363.
   [208] See para 2.38.

pensation determined by the Lands Tribunal at its expense, and can then pay the compensation so assessed into court and execute a deed poll which vests the land in itself.[209]

A special procedure for the acquisition of particular minor interests in land, and for the assessment of compensation in such a case, is provided in the Compulsory Purchase Act 1965.[210] This procedure applies when the land is in the possession of a person having no greater interest than as a tenant for a year or from year to year. No notice to treat is necessary in such a case. This procedure is considered separately in chapter 4.[211]   2.87

3. Time Limits

There are two important time limits relating to the service of notice to treat and actions following the service of that notice. These two limits are in addition to the general limitation period of six years for commencing proceedings to recover sums due under statute prescribed by section 9 of the Limitation Act 1980. This limitation period applies to references to the Lands Tribunal to determine compensation following the service of a notice to treat. The six year period runs from the date of entry by the acquiring authority when a notice to treat has been served and from the date on which the claimant, or a person under whom he derives title, first knew, or could reasonably be expecting to have known, of the vesting of his interest if a general vesting declaration has been made. Limitation of actions is explained under chapter 15 which deals with procedure. The first of the two time limits just mentioned is that the powers of the acquiring authority for the compulsory purchase of the land shall not be exercised after the expiration of three years from the date on which the compulsory purchase order becomes operative.[212] Therefore if a notice to treat is not served within the time limit on the persons on whom it must be served, so far as known to the acquiring authority after making diligent enquiry, the power of the authority to proceed with the compulsory acquisition as against any such person not served in proper time lapses. The only recourse for the authority if it still wishes to acquire all interests in the particular piece of land in question will be to make a further compulsory purchase order and take it through its various procedures with a view to serving a notice to treat under the aegis of that new order. The Act conferring a power of compulsory purchase may exclude or amend this time limit. If the authority to acquire certain land derives directly from an Act which specifies the land, so that no compulsory purchase order will be made or become operative so that there is no three year time limit, the Act may itself contain a time limit for   2.88

---

[209] Compulsory Purchase Act 1965, s 5(3), sch 2. This procedure is described in more detail in section (o) of this chapter.

[210] Section 20 of the Compulsory Purchase Act 1965

[211] See section (i) of ch 4.

[212] Compulsory Purchase Act 1965, s 4. *Advance Ground Rents v Middlesborough Corporation* [1986] 2 EGLR 221. It appears that provided the notice to treat is served within the three years time limit it can in appropriate circumstances be backdated so that it bears an earlier date than the date on which it was served; a notice to treat can also be served after the acquiring authority has taken possession of the land: *Cohen v Haringey* LBC (1981) 42 P & CR 6 (a case in which the owner of land had sold it without the knowledge of the acquiring authority so that the original notice to treat was served on the former owner). If a notice to treat is served within the time limit the acquiring authority can proceed to take possession, for example today by notice of entry under s 11(1) of the Compulsory Purchase Act 1965, after the expiry of the three year period: *Marquis of Salisbury v Great Northern Rly* (1852) 17 QB 840. For notice of entry see section (k) of this chapter. The same time limit applies where the general vesting declaration procedure is used: see section (q) of this chapter.

the service of a notice to treat.[213] Sometimes such an Act provides that the Act itself is to be treated as a compulsory purchase order.

2.89   The second time limit concerns events following the date of service of a notice to treat. The notice to treat ceases to have effect at the end of three years from the date of its service unless: (a) the compensation has been agreed or awarded or has been paid or paid into court, or (b) a general vesting declaration has been executed under the Compulsory Purchase (Vesting Declarations) Act 1981, or (c) the acquiring authority has entered on and taken possession of the land specified in the notice, or (d) the question of compensation has been referred to the Lands Tribunal.[214] The period of three years may be extended with the agreement of the person served with the notice to treat and further successive extensions may be so agreed. It appears that in principle a landowner may be estopped from contending that a notice to treat has lapsed by reason of the three year limit.[215] If a notice to treat lapses under these provisions the power of the acquiring authority to acquire the interest of the person served with the notice terminates. Again in such circumstances the only recourse of the authority will be to make a new compulsory purchase order as regards that interest. If a notice to treat does lapse by reason of the time limit the authority must give notice of that fact to the person on whom the notice was served and to any other person who could have made an agreement to extend the time and the authority becomes liable to pay compensation to any person entitled to such a notice for any loss or expenses occasioned to him by the giving and lapsing of the notice. The amount of the compensation is to be determined by the Lands Tribunal in default of agreement.[216] The type of compensation which might arise could be that for a loss caused by a person being unable to dispose of the land at an advantageous time or a commercial loss where a person was prevented from carrying on his business efficiently, for instance by obtaining contracts to run for a substantial period of time, by reason of the shadow cast over the land by the notice to treat.

4. The Effect of a Notice to Treat

2.90   The effect of a notice to treat is that it signifies the desire and decision of the acquiring authority to acquire a particular piece of land which the authority is authorised by the compulsory purchase order to acquire. The notice creates the right on the part of the acquiring authority to enter the land by giving notice of entry and, upon the determination and payment of the compensation, the right to acquire title to the land. The landowner has a corresponding right to have the compensation determined and paid to him. It was sometimes said that the notice to treat brought about a relationship between the acquiring authority

---

[213] For example, the Crossrail Act 2008 provides in s 6(6) that a notice to treat must be served within five years from the passing of the Act, although the Secretary of State may extend the period in relation to any land for a further period not exceeding five years.

[214] Compulsory Purchase Act 1965, s 5(2A), (2B).

[215] *Oakglade Investments Ltd v Greater Manchester Passenger Transport Executive* [2009] UKUT 20 (LC). Cf *Newbold v Coal Authority* [2012] UKUT 20 (LC), [2013] EWCA Civ 584 (CA), regarding the application of estoppel to areas of public law. The possibility of a time limit being waived also arises in connection with the six year time limit for the making of a reference to the Lands Tribunal to determine the compensation following an entry to the land acquired by the acquiring authority: see *Hillingdon LBC v ARC Ltd (No 2)* [2000] EGLR 97, (2000) 80 P & CR D29, and see ch 15, para 15.41.

[216] Compulsory Purchase Act 1965, s 5(2C), (2D).

and the landowner which was in some ways analogous or similar to that under an ordinary contract for the sale of land.[217] It is doubtful whether this is a good analogy.[218] No equitable interest passes to the acquiring authority; the owner may continue to deal with the land and receive the rents and profits from it; and a notice to treat can be withdrawn in certain circumstances. The relationship between the parties is best considered as a unique relationship brought about by statute. There is nothing to prevent the owner selling the land after he has received a notice to treat and an existing contract of sale of the land is not frustrated.[219] Obviously the right or absence of a right to compensation may influence the price obtained on a sale. The owner remains entitled to receive rent under existing leases.[220] The insurance of the land remains the responsibility of the owner and no estate contract capable of registration or protection on the register under the Land Charges Act 1972 or the Land Registration Act 2002 comes into existence.

The position changes when the amount of the compensation, the purchase price, has been determined by agreement or by the Lands Tribunal. There then come into existence all the elements of an enforceable contract of sale between the parties.[221] The rights of the acquiring authority as the purchaser may then be protected by notice on the registered title of the owner or may be registered as a land charge created by an estate contract if title to the land is not registered. The acquiring authority becomes entitled to enforce the contract by specific performance in the courts and an ordinary transfer of land, as in the completion of a contract of sale, is the normal way in which the acquiring authority gains title if it has followed the notice to treat procedure. There is an alternative statutory procedure under which the acquiring authority can obtain title by paying the compensation into court and executing a deed poll.[222] An acquiring authority may lose its entitlement to proceed to acquire land following the service of a notice to treat if it proposes to acquire the land for a purpose different from that for which the notice to treat was confirmed or it has acted so as to raise the inference that the compulsory purchase was being abandoned.[223]

2.91

---

[217] See, eg *Adams v London and Blackwall Rly Co* (1850) 2 Mac & G 118, per Lord Cottenham; *Haynes v Haynes* 1 DR & SM 426, per Kindersley V-C. at p 450; *Mercer v Liverpool, St Helens and South Lancashire Rly Co* [1903] 1 KB 652.

[218] In *West Midland Baptist (Trust) Association v Birmingham Corporation* [1970] AC 874, [1969] 3 WLR 389 Lord Morris pointed out at p 903: 'A notice to treat does not establish the relation of vendor and purchaser between the acquiring authority and the owner. It does not transfer either the legal or the equitable interest to the acquiring authority'. In *Capital Investments Ltd v Wednesfield UDC* [1965] Ch 774, at p 794 Wilberforce J said that for certain purposes and to a certain extent the notice to treat constitutes the relationship of vendor and purchaser but that it is clear that the notice does not constitute a contract. See also *Cardiff Corporation v Cooke* [1923] 2 Ch 115; *Prasad v Wolverhampton Borough Council* [1983] Ch 333, [1983] 2 WLR 946.

[219] *Cardiff Corporation v Cooke*, above; *Hillingdon Estates Co v Stonefield Estates Ltd* [1952] Ch 627, [1952] 1 All ER 853; *E Johnson & Co (Barbados) Ltd v NSR Ltd* [1996] 3 WLR 583.

[220] *West Midland Baptist (Trust) Association v Birmingham Corporation*, above n 218.

[221] *Harding v Metropolitan Rly Co* (1872) 7 Ch App 154; *Munton v GLC* [1976] 1 WLR 649, [1976] 2 All ER 815; *Prasad v Wolverhampton Borough Council* [1983] Ch 333, [1983] 2 WLR 946. An agreement on the amount of compensation which is 'subject to contract' will not create an enforceable agreement any more than it will do so for any other such agreement relating to the sale of land: see *Munton v GLC* [1976] 1 WLR 649, [1976] 2 All ER 815; *Christos v Secretary of State* [2004] 1 EGLR 5.

[222] Compulsory Purchase Act 1965, s 9. See section (n) of this chapter.

[223] See para 2.75.

(K) ENTRY AND POSSESSION

1. Right to Possession

2.92   It is, of course, open to the acquiring authority to agree the compensation or have it determined and then pay it in order to complete the purchase and take possession of the land. In
many cases the determination of the compensation and the completion of the acquisition
is a long drawn out process and it would be impractical and detrimental to schemes behind
an acquisition if the acquiring authority had to wait in all cases for this process to be brought
to a conclusion before it could enter any of the land which it was authorised to acquire and
so commence its scheme. There is a statutory principle that the authority shall not, except
with the consent of the owners and occupiers of the land, enter any of the land authorised
to be acquired before the compensation has been agreed or determined.[224] The correct practice is that the written consent of every person who has an interest in the land acquired
which entitles him to possession at the time or in the future should be obtained. The statute
refers to the consent of occupiers so that the consent even of licensees should be obtained.
This principle is subject to three important exceptions or qualifications. The principle and
the exceptions now to be described apply to the notice to treat procedure. If the acquiring
authority uses the general vesting declaration procedure, the authority is entitled to enter
the land acquired and take possession on the vesting date as specified in the general vesting
declaration.[225] In a sense the general vesting declaration procedure therefore constitutes a
further wide exception to the statutory principle. In addition persons with only a short
tenancy in the land acquired are not entitled to a notice to treat and the acquiring authority
may take possession as against the owners of such interests before any compensation due to
them has been agreed and paid.[226]

2.93   In many cases entry is today effected before the determination and payment of compensation but any hardship to landowners is mitigated by the duty of an acquiring authority to
estimate the amount of the compensation which will become payable and to make an
advance payment of 90 per cent of that amount.[227] In addition the landowner is entitled to
interest on the compensation, or on the unpaid balance if an advance payment is made,
from the date of entry until the date of payment.[228]

2.94   The first exception is that once the compulsory purchase order has come into operation the
acquiring authority may enter the land for limited purposes. The purposes are for surveying
and taking levels of the land, for probing or boring to ascertain the nature of the soil, and for
setting out the line of the works. Between 3 and 14 days notice of its intention to enter the

---

[224] Compulsory Purchase Act 1965, s 11(4). Consent may be express or may be implied from conduct: *Greenhalge
v Manchester & Birmingham Rly Co* (1838) 3 My & Cr 784. Nor surprisingly a person who has consented to entry
by the acquiring authority cannot normally withdraw his consent: *Knapp v London, Chatham and Dover Rly Co*
(1863) 2 H & C 212.
[225] Compulsory Purchase (Vesting Declarations) Act 1981, s 8(1). See section (q) of this chapter for the vesting
declaration procedure. There is a degree of overlap between the general vesting declaration procedure and the
notice of entry procedure as regards obtaining possession of the land in relation to short tenancies: see para 2.139.
[226] Compulsory Purchase Act, s 20. See section (i) of ch 4.
[227] See ch 15, section (c).
[228] See ch 15, section (d).

land for these purposes must be given by the authority. Compensation has to be paid to the owners or occupiers of the land for any damage caused to them by the exercise of this power and disputed compensation is decided by the Lands Tribunal. This limited power may be exercised before or after service of a notice to treat in respect of the land. [229] The exercise of this power is not itself an exercise of the power of compulsory purchase for the purposes of the three year time limit for the giving of notice to treat. Nor is it an entry or taking possession for the purposes of determining the valuation date for the assessment of compensation.[230]

There is a further general power under section 15 of the Local Government (Miscellaneous Provisions) Act 1976 which entitles a local authority to enter and survey land in connection with a proposal by the authority to acquire compulsorily an interest in the land. There is also a power to enter other land for the purpose of survey. A person interested in the land who suffers damage in consequence of the exercise of this power is entitled to recover compensation for the damage from the local authority, and in the event of dispute the amount of this compensation is also to be determined by the Lands Tribunal.[231] In addition specific powers of entry are given either for the purposes of a compulsory acquisition or more widely by particular legislation dealing with certain areas.[232]

2.95

The second, and most important, exception is that after service of notice to treat in respect of the land the acquiring authority may serve not less than 14 days notice on the owner, lessee and occupier of the land under section 11(1) of the Compulsory Purchase Act 1965 and may then enter on and take possession of the land. It may occur that there is more than one person with an interest in the land being acquired and that only one of those persons is entitled to possession, an obvious instance being when land is let to a tenant. It seems that in order for it to exercise its statutory power of entry and taking possession the acquiring authority must serve notice of entry on everyone with a freehold or leasehold interest in the land as well as on every occupier even though the owners of some interests may not be in occupation or have a current right to occupation. The notice can be served as to a part of the land and possession taken of that part.[233] The notice is usually called a notice of entry. It is often served together with the notice to treat. As well as entitling the acquiring authority to enter and go into possession the notice has other important consequences. Assuming that actual entry is taken pursuant to the notice the date of entry is the valuation date for the purposes of the assessment of compensation. Interest is payable on the compensation from the date of entry until the date of payment of the compensation. Where the notice to treat procedure, rather than the vesting declaration procedure, is used the service of a notice of entry is the usual and frequently used method of obtaining possession of land. The 14

2.96

---

[229] Compulsory Purchase Act 1965, s 11(3).

[230] *Courage Ltd v Kingswood District Council* (1978) 35 P & CR 436.

[231] Local Government (Miscellaneous Provisions) Act 1976, s 15(1) and (5).

[232] See, eg s 324 of the Town and Country Planning Act 1990.

[233] Compulsory Purchase Act 1965, s 11(1). It appears that in certain circumstances a notice of entry may be backdated and served even after entry has been obtained: *Cohen v Haringey LBC* (1981) 42 P & CR 6. See n 211. The power of entry under s 11(1) is not normally available where the land has been specified in a general vesting declaration: Compulsory Purchase (Vesting Declarations) Act 1981, s 8(3). Even so there is no complete dichotomy between the general vesting declaration procedure and the notice to treat procedure as regards obtaining entry to and possession of the land. When a general vesting declaration has been made it is still necessary for the acquiring authority to serve notice to treat and notice of entry in order to gain possession from persons who hold a minor tenancy or a long lease about to expire in the land: see para 2.139.

day minimum time required for notice of entry may be modified by an Act which confers a power to acquire specific land.[234]

2.97   The third exception is a procedure which goes back to the Lands Clauses Consolidation Act 1845 and is now contained in the Compulsory Purchase Act 1965.[235] It is little used since it is complex and it is nearly always preferable for the acquiring authority to rely on the notice of entry procedure. The third procedure requires the acquiring authority to pay a sum of money into court by way of security for the payment of compensation to the owner. The amount to be paid into court is the amount of compensation claimed by the owner or the value of the owner's interest as determined by a surveyor appointed by two justices of the peace. In addition the acquiring authority is required to give further security by giving to the owner a bond (a written guarantee in a deed) for a sum equal to the sum to be paid into court and conditioned for payment to the owner of the compensation as agreed or ultimately determined together with statutory interest. The bond must be with the backing of two sureties. For the purposes of this procedure an owner means any person interested in the land to which entry is to be made or entitled to sell and convey that land who has not consented to entry onto the land. The High Court may order how the money in court is to be paid or applied. It seems that the procedure here described cannot be used until a notice to treat has been served.[236] This procedure may have been useful when there was no other ready means of effecting entry in advance of the determination and payment of compensation particularly where the promoters of the compulsory purchase were commercial undertakings whose financial stability and ability to pay the compensation may have been in doubt. As stated the procedure is of little utility today when a statutory notice of entry can be served and it is used rarely if at all. It is one of the more antiquated aspects of the law of compulsory purchase which is likely to be abandoned if and when there is a comprehensive reform.

2.98   An acquiring authority may make a formal entry onto land but then informally permit the occupier to remain in possession for a limited period. If this occurs the occupier will probably in law retain possession as a licensee of the acquiring authority. There should then be no difficulty in the authority determining the licence in the ordinary way by notice. Care should be taken that the arrangement does not constitute the creation of a new periodic tenancy of some sort by implication of law against the occupier. The acceptance of rent or other periodic payments from an occupier may give rise to the existence of a periodic tenancy by implication of law and, if this occurs, further process will be necessary to determine that tenancy. There are particular risks where the premises are occupied for the purposes of a business since even a periodic tenancy created in these circumstances may attract the protection of Part II of the Landlord and Tenant Act 1954 so that the statutory processes under that Act may need to be employed in order to obtain possession from the tenant. It is obviously in the interests of an acquiring authority to take care that no such situation arises. The prudent course for an acquiring authority may be to delay giving notice of entry or to delay formal entry until possession is in truth needed.

---

[234]   See, eg para 3 of sch 6 to the Crossrail Act 2008 which generally requires that three months notice is given.
[235]   Compulsory Purchase Act 1965, s 11(2), sch 3. Section 25 of the Act contains general provisions as to payments into court.
[236]   *Loosemore v Tiverton & West Devon Rly Co* (1884) 9 App Cas 480, per Lord Watson at p 501.

2. Enforcing the Right

In nearly all cases where an acquiring authority has secured the right to enter the land being 2.99
acquired entry is gained without opposition from any owner or occupier. If the land is
unoccupied the authority may simply make a peaceful entry. Where appropriate some formal act to denote that entry has been taken should be carried out such as changing the locks
or the fixing of a notice to the property.[237] It is important to record the exact date of entry
since this date may have practical consequences such as that it normally fixes the valuation
date and will be the date from which interest becomes payable on unpaid compensation.[238]
If the land is vacant and unoccupied no step is needed save that of a formal entry.[239] Where
under the general law a person is entitled to enter land, such as where a landlord seeks to go
into possession at the end of a tenancy, and if the land is occupied and there is opposition
to the entry, it is usually necessary to seek an order for possession in the County Court. In
the case of a compulsory acquisition the need for such proceedings is removed by a special
procedure now contained in the Compulsory Purchase Act 1965 but which goes back to the
Lands Clauses Consolidation Act 1845.[240] If the owner or occupier or any other person
refuses to give up possession or hinders the acquiring authority in taking possession the
acquiring authority may issue a warrant to the sheriff or an enforcement officer to deliver
possession to it.[241] In practice it is court enforcement officers to whom warrants are directed.
It is the duty of the sheriff or enforcement officer to deliver possession of the land to the
acquiring authority. The costs of the process are recoverable from the person who fails to
give possession. These costs may be deducted from the compensation due to that person or,
if the compensation is insufficient to cover the costs or there is no compensation, then the
costs or the balance of the costs may be recovered by distress on goods on a warrant issued
by magistrates. A distress means the seizure and sale of goods and chattels of a person. Any
sum left over after the sale of the goods and discharge of the costs are to be paid to the person whose goods were seized.[242]

3. Unlawful Entry

An acquiring authority which enters land without statutory authority to do so commits a 2.100
trespass against the landowner. In an appropriate case the owner may claim an injunction

---

[237] In *Pandit v Leicester City Council* (1989) 58 P & CR 305, changing the locks was held to be a sufficient act of
entry even though this occupier who was in hospital at the time subsequently returned to the property for a
period.

[238] See section (c) of ch 4 and section (d) of ch 15.

[239] *Loosemore v Tiverton & West Devon Rly Co* (1884) 9 App Cas 480.

[240] Compulsory Purchase Act 1965, s 13.

[241] The sheriff of a county is the representative of the Crown in that county. The office goes back to Saxon times
(the 'Shirereeve') and is today mainly an honorific position. Enforcement officers are appointed under sch 7 to the
Courts Act 2003. They are often called bailiffs and it is they who, with the assistance of the police if necessary,
normally enforce orders of the court such as taking possession of land and seizure of goods.

[242] If the compensation has been paid into court in accordance with the procedure described in para 2.97 the
court may order the payment out of a sum to the acquiring authority sufficient to cover the costs of obtaining
possession: *Re Schmarr* [1900] 1 Ch 326, at p 331.

to prevent an unlawful entry or may obtain damages for the trespass.[243] The compulsory purchase of an area of land overrides the rights of third parties over that land such as easements to the extent that those rights would prevent or impede the implementation of the purposes of the acquiring authority. Persons whose rights are so overridden may be entitled to compensation under section 10 of the Compulsory Purchase Act 1965 but are not entitled to prevent entry onto the land by the acquiring authority.[244] It is no defence that the authority genuinely believed that in law it had a right to enter the land. Of course instances of unlawful entry will be rare. An authority would be unlikely to seek to take possession of the land before the compulsory purchase order was confirmed or it was otherwise certain of its authority to effect the compulsory purchase or before the expiry of the six weeks allowed for a challenge to the validity of an order.[245] If no challenge is brought under the statutory procedure within this time the order is immune from further legal challenge so that the lawfulness of the entry cannot be challenged by a contention that the compulsory purchase order was void. If the order is being challenged few authorities would wish to try to effect an entry onto the land until the challenge had been dealt with by the court and there is in any event a power of the court to issue an interim order to prevent entry until final determination of the challenge.[246] Nor is an authority likely to enter the land save by way of one of the procedures described above.

2.101   There is a somewhat antiquated statutory procedure, again going back to the Lands Clauses Consolidation Act 1845, which permits the person in possession of the land to obtain a small sum as recompense for an unlawful entry. Should the acquiring authority wilfully enter the land being acquired without the consent of the owners and occupiers before the compensation has been agreed or determined, and without going through one of the specified procedures which allow entry, the acquiring authority shall forfeit to the person in possession £10 and in addition the amount of any damage done to the land. It is only the person in possession who can obtain these sums. The damage to the land means any loss relating to the land (ie injurious affection to it) as opposed to a purely personal or monetary loss.[247] The amount is recoverable as a civil debt. The procedure for recovery of a civil debt is prescribed by the Magistrates Courts Act 1980 under which the court can make an order on a complaint for the payment of money recoverable as a civil debt provided the complaint is made within six months of the time when the matter of complaint arose.[248] There is an appeal to the Crown Court. The requirement that before the penalty is payable the acquiring authority must 'wilfully' have entered the land without complying with the proper procedures may mean that the authority must have acted in deliberate defiance of those procedures or at least without giving any proper consideration to those procedures.

---

[243] See *Fooks v Wilts, Somerset & Weymouth Rly Co* (1846) 5 Hare 199 (injunction refused on grounds that unlawful entry for surveying purposes would not be repeated); *Clark v School Board for London* (1874) 9 LR Ch App 120, per Lord Selborne LC at p 124.

[244] See section (f) of ch 10.

[245] If gaining entry is urgent or a challenge in the High Court is thought to be on specious grounds the acquiring authority may be able to apply for an expedited hearing of the proceedings in the Court or may apply for the proceedings to be struck out.

[246] Acquisition of Land Act 1981, s 24(1).

[247] Compulsory Purchase Act 1965, s 12. The sums as fixed in 1845 have never been altered and would need to be multiplied by about 80 if they were to be expressed in today's depreciated currency.

[248] Magistrates Courts Act 1980, ss 58(1), 127(1).

On the other hand there is in one instance a limited defence of acting in good faith[249] and this may mean that any other similar defence is not generally available.

If the acquiring authority remains in unlawful possession of any of the land after a forfeited 2.102 sum has been adjudged to be due under the above provisions the authority becomes liable to forfeit £25 for every day on which it so remains in possession. In this case the sum forfeited is recoverable by the person in possession of the land in the High Court. In any such proceedings the decision of the Magistrates Court on the complaint to recover the civil debt shall not be conclusive as to the acquiring authority's right of entry. This further right to forfeit a sum also appears to be confined to the person in possession and in this case there is no right to payment of the amount of any further damage done in addition to the sum of £25 per day. There is a limited defence to either of the forms of forfeiture proceedings which is that the acquiring authority has in good faith and without collusion paid the compensation agreed or awarded in respect of the land to a person whom they reasonably believe to be entitled to that compensation or have paid it into court for the benefit of that person or by way of security, even though the person to whom the compensation was paid may not have been legally entitled to it.[250] There seems no reason in principle why a person against whom an unlawful entry has been effected should not bring ordinary proceedings in the courts for damages instead of or in addition to this limited statutory remedy, but if he has obtained the statutory remedy he would, of course, have to give credit in the assessment of damages for any sums recovered under the statutory remedy.

(L) WITHDRAWAL OF A NOTICE TO TREAT

A notice to treat may be withdrawn at any time by agreement between the acquiring author- 2.103 ity and the landowner on such terms as they may agree. Apart from an agreement the acquiring authority may withdraw a notice to treat only in the circumstances provided by statute and subject to the payment of compensation to the landowner for any loss caused to him. The purpose of the legislation is to permit an acquiring authority to withdraw a notice to treat within a limited period after it has had reasonable notice of the amount of compensation which it will have to pay to acquire the land. Pursuant to this aim an acquiring authority is permitted to withdraw a notice to treat in two circumstances.

First, the acquiring authority may withdraw the notice to treat within six weeks after the 2.104 delivery to it of a notice in writing by the owner of the amount of compensation claimed stating the exact nature of the interest in respect of which compensation is claimed, stating details of the compensation claimed, and stating the amounts of compensation claimed under different heads showing how the amount claimed under each head is calculated.[251] This information should give to the acquiring authority the opportunity to assess at least the order of compensation which it is likely to have to pay if it proceeds with the acquisition of the interest in question. Providing that the conditions are satisfied a notice to treat may

---

[249] See para 2.102.
[250] Compulsory Purchase Act 1965, s 12(6).
[251] Land Compensation Act 1961, s 31(1). These are the particulars which the landowner is required to provide to the acquiring authority under s 4(1)(b) of the Act in order to protect his position as to costs if there is a reference to the lands Tribunal. See section (m) of ch 15.

be withdrawn even after the acquiring authority has taken possession of the land. It should be noted that not every claim for compensation brings about the commencement of the six week period. The claim must be one containing some particularity.[252] The effect of the provision is that an acquiring authority may withdraw a notice to treat at any time up until they receive a properly detailed notice of claim and within six weeks after the receipt of such a notice.[253] An acquiring authority which is considering withdrawing a notice to treat can of course ask the claimant to provide further particulars of his claim so as to enable it to decide whether to withdraw the notice.

2.105   Secondly, if the landowner does not deliver a claim as just described the acquiring authority has a right to withdraw the notice to treat within six weeks after the decision of the Lands Tribunal by which the claim for compensation has been finally determined. Obviously upon this determination the authority knows exactly the amount of compensation which it has to pay. Where this second opportunity of withdrawing a notice to treat is relied upon the withdrawal cannot take place after the authority has entered into possession of the land.[254] It often takes a considerable time to obtain a hearing and a decision in the Lands Tribunal especially if a substantial dispute is involved. It would be unusual for an acquiring authority not to have taken possession by the time of a Tribunal decision. In practice this second opportunity to withdraw a notice to treat may therefore be of limited practical usefulness to acquiring authorities. What in practice it may often come to is that an authority will be able to withdraw a notice to treat at any time from the date on which it is given until six weeks after a properly framed claim has been delivered.

2.106   The event which triggers the right to withdraw a notice to treat under the above two sets of circumstances is the action of a claimant or a decision by the Tribunal on the claim for compensation of a claimant. The right to withdraw a notice to treat extends to a notice to treat served on that claimant and to a notice to treat served on any other person interested in the land which is authorised to be acquired and which is the subject of the notice. It is not entirely clear whether there is a right of withdrawal when a claimant has failed to provide full particulars of his claim but the claim has nonetheless been agreed without a decision of the Tribunal. Possibly in such a case there will come a time when it can be said that full particulars of the claim have been delivered to the acquiring authority since otherwise it is difficult to see how there could be agreement on the claim. The point at which such full particulars have been delivered may then be the point at which the six week period for withdrawal of the notice to treat starts to run. On the other hand the service of a notice to treat and agreement on the compensation usually means that a legally enforceable agreement to acquire the land for the amount agreed has come into being so that the withdrawal of a notice to treat may not be possible.[255] Where the circumstances of the second procedure apply, that is where a claimant has failed to deliver a proper notice of claim and where the claim has not been finally determined by the Lands Tribunal or, if it has, where the six weeks for withdrawal have not elapsed, the acquiring authority cannot be compelled to take the land to which the notice to treat relates or to pay compensation for the acquisition of the land.[256]

---

[252]   *Trustees for Methodist Church Purposes v North Tyneside MBC* (1979) 38 P & CR 665.
[253]   Ibid.
[254]   Land Compensation Act 1961, s 31(2).
[255]   See para 2.91.
[256]   Land Compensation Act 1961, s 31(5).

The withdrawal of a notice to treat under either of the above procedures creates a liability on   2.107
the part of the acquiring authority to pay compensation to the claimant and to the owner of
any other interest in the land where a notice to treat has been served on that person and
withdrawn. The compensation is for any loss or expenses caused to the person concerned by
the withdrawal of the notice. There is a qualification in the case of the second procedure for
withdrawal, that is withdrawal after a decision of the Lands Tribunal, in that no compensation is payable for loss and expenses incurred by the owner of an interest after the time when,
in the opinion of the Lands Tribunal, proper notice of claim should have been delivered by
that person.[257] It is uncertain what happens under this qualification if an owner does not
deliver a proper notice of claim in good time but thereafter does deliver such a notice, a situation which could well occur if the claim for compensation is determined by the Lands
Tribunal, if only because the owner will have to provide a proper itemised claim as part of his
case in those proceedings. Possibly the entitlement to compensation may revive in relation to
the period after proper details of the claim have been given. The Lands Tribunal may determine the amount of compensation payable as a result of the withdrawal of a notice to treat.[258]
Any loss or expenses may be included in the claim for compensation if they were occasioned
by the giving and withdrawal of the notice. An obvious example would be the expenses of
obtaining professional advice which a claimant incurred in order to present a proper claim
and, if the matter goes to the Lands Tribunal, the whole of the costs and expenses, if not
recovered by way of an order for costs in his favour, in that Tribunal. Another obvious head
of loss would be that a person could not in practice dispose of his land, or let it, because of
the existence of the notice to treat hanging over his head. The loss of an enhanced purchase
price and the loss of rent would be losses for which compensation could be recovered under
the present provision. Compensation could extend to business losses such as a loss of profits
from a business carried out on the land where new contracts could not be secured because
of the compulsory purchase which was then being carried out.

An empowering Act may exclude a statutory power to withdraw a notice to treat. Enactments   2.108
containing such a provision enacted prior to the Land Compensation Act 1961, and which
referred to the equivalent power of withdrawal contained in the Acquisition of Land
(Assessment of Compensation) Act 1919, are construed as excluding a power of withdrawal
conferred by the Land Compensation Act 1961. A constructive notice to treat which arises
under the general vesting declaration procedure cannot be withdrawn.[259] The use of the
general vesting declaration procedure therefore deprives the acquiring authority of the limited opportunity which it has to withdraw from the acquisition when the notice to treat
procedure is used.

(M) MORTGAGES, RENTCHARGES AND APPORTIONMENT OF RENT

1. Mortgages

The land or interest in land acquired may be subject to a mortgage. As mentioned a mort-   2.109
gagee is entitled to be served with a notice to treat and information on mortgages is one of

---

[257] Ibid, s 31(3).
[258] Ibid, s 31(4).
[259] See section (q) of this chapter.

the items of information which may be required by the acquiring authority under statutory powers prior to or after the making of a compulsory purchase order. There is nothing in principle to prevent the acquiring authority from acquiring the interest of the mortgagor without reference to mortgages but if it does so the mortgage will remain a charge on the land and before making use of the land the authority is likely to have to redeem the mortgage, that is pay to the mortgagee what is due to him. Mortgages may be legal or equitable. Since 2003 there has essentially been only one form of legal mortgage which can be created which is a mortgage created by a charge by deed expressed to be by way of legal mortgage, itself a statutory creation under the Law of Property Act 1925.[260] This is the normal type of mortgage and is often called a legal charge. Equitable mortgages can be created as the mortgage of an equitable interest or by an agreement to create a legal mortgage. In addition an equitable charge may be created without formality simply by the appropriation in some way of the property as security for the discharge of a debt. For present purposes all of these types of mortgage or charge are comprehended within the description of a mortgage. In legal parlance the interest and rights of the mortgagor who continues as the owner of the land subject to the mortgage is often called the equity of redemption.

2.110   It will often not be convenient for the acquiring authority simply to acquire the interest of the mortgagor, the equity of redemption, and then itself deal separately with the mortgagee with a view to discharging the mortgage. Instead, in some cases where the notice to treat procedure is used, the authority may pay the value of the property ignoring the mortgage to the mortgagor and leave it to him to use it to discharge the mortgage before he transfers the land to the authority. If this is not done there are statutory provisions for securing the discharge of the mortgage so enabling the acquiring authority to hold the land free of the mortgage and carry out its project on the land. These provisions vary depending on: (a) whether the value of the land exceeds the outstanding mortgage debt which is secured on the land, and (b) whether the whole or only a part of the land acquired is subject to the mortgage.

2.111   The simplest option open to the acquiring authority is to pay or tender to the mortgagee: (a) the principal sum and any interest due under the mortgage, (b) his costs and charges, for example the legal costs involved in discharging the mortgage, and (c) six months of additional interest. Upon this being done the mortgagee is required to release his interest in the land to the acquiring authority or as the authority directs. In this case the mortgagee is paid what is due to him with an additional half year's interest as a solatium and the acquiring authority holds the land free of the mortgage.[261] The six month period gives the mortgagee a period in which to find an alternative investment for his money.

2.112   A similar but somewhat more complicated course which achieves the same end result is that either the mortgagor has given to the mortgagee six months notice of his intention to redeem the mortgage or the acquiring authority gives notice to the mortgagee that it will pay all principal and interest due at the end of six months from the date of the notice. If either form of notice has been given the acquiring authority may at any time during the six months, or at the end of that period, pay or tender to the mortgagee: (a) the principal sum due and any interest due up to the end of the six months, and (b) his costs and expenses. If

---

[260]   Law of Property Act 1925, s 87(1); Land Registration Act 2002, s 23.
[261]   Compulsory Purchase Act 1965, s 14(2).

this is done the mortgagee is again required to release his interest in the land to the acquiring authority or as it directs and the authority holds the land free of the mortgage.[262]

If, following either of the procedures just described, the mortgagee fails to release his interest in the land or fails to make out a good title, the acquiring authority may pay into court the sums payable to the mortgagee. The acquiring authority, having paid those sums into court, may execute a deed poll describing the land and declaring the circumstances under which, and the names of the parties to whose credit, the payment into court was made. On execution of the deed poll the interest of the mortgagee in the land vests in the acquiring authority and, where the mortgagee was entitled to possession of the land, the acquiring authority become entitled to that possession.[263]

2.113

These powers can be exercised whether or not the acquiring authority has purchased the equity of redemption, that is the interest of the mortgagor, and may be exercised whether or not the mortgagee is a trustee, whether or not the mortgage includes other land in addition to the land being acquired, and whether or not the mortgagee is in possession of the land.[264] Subject to the terms of the mortgage a mortgagee is generally entitled to possession of the mortgaged land whether or not any payments of the mortgage are in arrear although it is rare for mortgagees to exercise this right providing that sums have been duly paid under the mortgage.

2.114

The two methods of dealing with mortgages just described are appropriate when the value of the land acquired exceeds the outstanding mortgage debt. There is a further course available to an acquiring authority where the value of the land is less than the debt, a situation which can arise especially in times of falling land prices. It is this situation which is colloquially described as 'negative equity'. In this situation the compensation for the acquisition of the land is to be settled by agreement between the three parties involved, the mortgagor, the mortgagee and the acquiring authority, and if it is not so settled it is to be determined by the Lands Tribunal. If the amount of the compensation cannot be agreed this procedure therefore cannot be implemented until the conclusion of the proceedings in the Tribunal to determine the amount of the compensation. There is nothing to prevent the acquiring authority taking possession of the land in the meantime under the notice of entry procedure described earlier. Once the amount of the compensation is settled the acquiring authority must pay it to the mortgagee who must then release his interest in the land to the acquiring authority or as it directs. If the mortgagee fails to do so the acquiring authority can pay the amount of the compensation into court and execute a deed poll with the consequences described earlier. Obviously the compensation to be settled in these circumstances is that equal to the value of the land acquired free of the mortgage. In the situation under consideration the mortgagee will not have been paid all of the money due to him under the mortgage arrangement and, notwithstanding the termination of the mortgage, the mortgagee may assert against the mortgagor all rights and remedies under the mortgage and those rights, other than the right to the land, remain in force in respect of so much of the mortgage debt as has not been satisfied by payment to the mortgagee or payment into court. In other words the mortgagor remains liable as a matter of contract to pay to the mortgagee the difference between the value of land and the mortgage debt. How the

2.115

---

[262] Ibid, s 14(3).
[263] Ibid, s 14(4)–(6).
[264] Ibid, s 14(7).

mortgagee exercises this right against a mortgagor who ex hypothesi has received no compensation is of no concern to the acquiring authority.[265]

2.116   The next situation to consider is that which arises when only a part of the land subject to the mortgage is compulsorily acquired. It may be that the value of the land acquired is less than the principal sum and the interest and the costs secured on the value of the whole of the land, and the mortgagee does not consider that the remaining land is sufficient security for the money due or he is not willing to release the part of the land which is being acquired from the mortgage. An example may illustrate the situation. Suppose that a sum of £2 million is secured on an area of land valued at £2.5 million and there is a compulsory acquisition of a part of the land worth £1 million. If the mortgage is discharged as regards the land acquired the remaining land may be worth £1.5 million which would be inadequate security for a debt of £2 million. In these circumstances the value of the land acquired, and any compensation to be paid for loss caused by the severance of the land acquired from the land retained, are to be agreed between the mortgagor, the mortgagee and the acquiring authority. The value and the compensation are to be determined by the Lands Tribunal if not agreed. The acquiring authority can then pay or tender to the mortgagee the amount agreed or determined as the total compensation (£1 million in the above example) and the mortgagee is then required to release his interest in the land to be acquired to the acquiring authority or as it directs. There is the usual provision that if the mortgagee fails to release the land acquired from the mortgage the acquiring authority may pay into court the amount of the compensation and execute a deed poll and the land acquired then becomes vested in the acquiring authority free of the mortgage. A memorandum of what has been paid must be endorsed on the deed creating the mortgage and shall be signed by the mortgagee and a copy furnished, if he so requires, to the mortgagor. When these events have occurred the mortgagee continues to have the same powers and remedies for recovering the mortgage money or the balance of it as against the remaining land comprised in the mortgage as he would have had against the whole of the land originally comprised in the mortgage.[266]

2.117   The last situation to consider is where under the terms of the mortgage deed the payment of the sum secured and thus the redemption of the mortgage cannot occur until a certain date and under the procedures just described the mortgagee is required to accept payment of the principal sum due at an earlier date. The mortgagee can then re-invest the sum paid to him. In such a case the amount payable by the acquiring authority to the mortgagee under the provisions described above shall include both the costs of the re-investment and, if the rate of interest reasonably obtainable on the re-investment is less than the rate of interest under the mortgage deed, it shall also include compensation in respect of the loss sustained by the mortgagee by reason of the lower rate of interest obtainable on a re-investment. The amount of this compensation may be determined by the Lands Tribunal if not agreed.[267] An obvious difficulty in assessing the compensation due to a mortgagee is to know how long the lower rate of interest on a re-investment may last. Possibly the best course is to ask at what rate the amount paid to the mortgagee could be re-invested as a fixed rate for the remaining term of the mortgage. The calculation may be further compli-

---

[265] Ibid, s 15.
[266] Ibid, s 16.
[267] Ibid, s 17.

cated by the fact that, as often happens today, the rate of interest under the mortgage may be liable to fluctuate in accordance with its terms.

In certain circumstances, considered in detail in chapter 15, an acquiring authority may be   2.118
required to make an advance payment of compensation to a landowner on a request for such a payment. If the land is subject to a mortgage, and if the claimant and the mortgagee agree, a payment may be made to the mortgagee either in addition to or in place of the advance payment to the mortgagor. These provisions are an alternative to the provisions here described in that no payment may be made to a mortgagee under the advance payment provisions if a payment has been made to that mortgagee or a notice given to that mortgagee under the provisions just described or an agreement has been made, or the matter has been referred to the Lands Tribunal, under those provisions. If the land being acquired is subject to a mortgage the acquiring authority, if a request for an advance payment is made, should decide whether they wish to operate the procedures here described or the procedures which arise under the advance payment provisions. The payments to a mortgagee under the advance payment provisions are dependent on an agreement between the claimant and the mortgagee so that in the absence of such an agreement the provisions here described may be the only proper recourse for an acquiring authority.

2. Rentcharges

The legislation contains a general provision dealing with rentcharges. A rentcharge arises   2.119
when land is charged, otherwise than under the grant of a lease, with the payment of a periodic sum. A person may charge his land with the payment of an annual or other periodic sum to another person with the result that the other person, the rentchargee, has an interest in the land. No new rentcharges have been able to be created since 1977.[268] The general provisions now to be explained apply to rentcharges which are defined for this purpose as any other payment or encumbrance charged on the land not provided for in the provisions relating to mortgages already described. These provisions therefore do not apply to mortgages which are governed by the provisions just described. A rentchargee is entitled to compensation for his rentcharge over the land acquired and the compensation is to be agreed or determined by the Lands Tribunal. The rentchargee is required to release the rentcharge on payment or tender to him of the compensation. If he fails to do so the acquiring authority can pay the amount of the compensation into court and execute a deed poll which has the effect of extinguishing the rentcharge. Where the acquiring authority purchases a part of land subject to a rentcharge the charge may be apportioned by agreement between the persons concerned and the acquiring authority or the apportionment may be determined by the Lands Tribunal. If the part of the land subject to the rentcharge which is acquired is released from the charge the remaining land becomes charged with the whole of the rentcharge. There is provision for the acquiring authority to affix its seal to a memorandum of the release of the rentcharge on the deed or instrument creating the charge with particulars of the release.[269] Since no new rentcharge can have been created for over 30 years these rules are of diminishing importance.

[268] Rentcharges Act 1977, ss 2, 3, 18(2). There are also provisions for the gradual abolition of existing rentcharges.
[269] Compulsory Purchase Act 1965, s 18.

3. Apportionment of Rent

2.120   An acquiring authority may acquire the reversion in a part of an area of land the whole of which is subject to a lease. The rent payable is then to be apportioned between the land acquired and the residue of the land. The apportionment is to be agreed between the landlord and the tenant and the acquiring authority and, if not agreed, is determined by the Lands Tribunal. Following the apportionment the tenant is liable for only that part of the total rent apportioned to the residue of the land. The lease of the residue of the land remains in being and is subject to all of the terms of the lease of the whole of the land save for the amount of rent payable.[270]

(N) COMPLETION OF THE PURCHASE

2.120   Once the amount of the compensation has been agreed or determined a contract of sale comes into existence between the acquiring authority and the owner of the interest in the land in question. On the compensation being paid or tendered the owner is then bound to complete the purchase in the ordinary way by making out proper title and executing a conveyance or transfer in favour of the acquiring authority. A short form of conveyance of unregistered title is set out in schedule 5 to the Compulsory Purchase Act 1965 but the acquiring authority may use any form of conveyance which it thinks fit. The acquiring authority may enforce its rights by specific performance in the courts.[271] It also has an alternative route which enables it to acquire title. The authority can pay into court the compensation payable to the credit of the parties interested in the land giving, so far as it can, the description of those parties. The authority can then execute a deed poll describing the land and declaring the circumstances of the payment into court. On execution of the deed poll the estate and interest in the land of the parties in question vest absolutely in the acquiring authority. If it has not taken possession the authority then becomes entitled to immediate possession of the land. The High Court may order the distribution of any money paid into court.[272] As explained later where the general vesting declaration procedure is used interests in the land acquired vest in the acquiring authority on the vesting date so that no conveyance or transfer or deed poll is necessary.[273] Whichever procedure is used the acquiring authority should ensure that it becomes registered as the proprietor of the interest acquired in accordance with section 6 of the Land Registration Act 2002.

(O) ABSENT AND UNTRACED OWNERS

2.121   There is a procedure for the assessment, and ultimate possible payment, of compensation when the owner of land or of an interest in land to be acquired is absent or untraceable. The

---

[270] Ibid, s 19.
[271] See para 2.91.
[272] Compulsory Purchase Act 1965, s 9. See section (r) of this chapter for the costs of a conveyance.
[273] See section (q) of this chapter.

provisions apply: (a) where a person cannot be found after diligent enquiry has been made, and (b) where a person is prevented from treating with the acquiring authority by reason of his absence from the United Kingdom. The provisions go back to the Lands Clauses Consolidation Act 1845 and, with modern day international communications, it is plainly less likely than it was that a person will be unable to treat with the acquiring authority because he is outside the country. The provisions apply when the notice to treat procedure is used to acquire land but not when the general vesting declaration procedure is used since under that procedure interests in the land being acquired automatically vest in the acquiring authority and the present provisions are unnecessary.[274]

The procedure is that the compensation payable to such a person is to be determined by the valuation of a surveyor selected from the members of the Lands Tribunal. The acquiring authority must obtain the appointment of this person and must bear all the expenses of and incident to the valuation. The authority must also preserve the valuation and produce it on demand to the owner of the land and to all other persons interested in the land. Having obtained the valuation the acquiring authority must pay into court the amount of the compensation determined to be placed to the credit of the parties interested in the land and must give the descriptions of those persons so far as the authority is in a position to do so. When these steps have been taken the authority may execute a deed poll with a description of the land and a declaration of the circumstances under which, and the names of the person to whose credit, the payment into court was made. The consequence of the execution of the deed poll is that all interests in the land of the parties in respect of whose interest the compensation was paid into court vest absolutely in the acquiring authority and against those persons the authority becomes entitled to immediate possession of the land.

2.122

There is provision entitling any person who claims a part of the money paid into court or claims any interest in the land in question to apply to the High Court which may then order the distribution of the money. The court may make any other order that it thinks fit. The person with an interest in land against whom this procedure has been operated may be dissatisfied with the valuation made of the land by the surveyor appointed by the Lands Tribunal and in that case he may give notice to the acquiring authority requiring the submission to the Tribunal of the question whether the compensation paid into court was sufficient or whether any further sum ought to be paid over or paid into court. If a further sum is awarded by the Tribunal the acquiring authority must pay over that further sum or pay it into court within 14 days of the award. If the Tribunal determines that a further sum ought to be paid the acquiring authority must bear the costs of the new determination. If the Tribunal determines that the compensation paid into court was sufficient the costs of the new determination are in the discretion of the Tribunal.[275] If no order has been made by the court for the payment out of sums paid into court under this provision within 12 years of the payment in the High Court may order that the money be paid out to the acquiring authority. Even so if a person later makes a claim the court may order the authority to pay to that person such amount as it considers just.[276]

2.123

---

[274] Compulsory Purchase (Vesting Declarations) Act 1981, s 10(2). See section (q) of this chapter.
[275] Compulsory Purchase Act 1965, s 5, sch 2.
[276] Local Government (Miscellaneous Provisions) Act 1976, s 29.

(P) MISTAKES BY THE ACQUIRING AUTHORITY

2.125   The acquiring authority may at some stage discover that, having taken possession of land, through mistake or inadvertence it has failed to purchase some interest or right in or affecting the land or has failed to pay compensation for such an interest or right. This situation is most likely to arise in connection with someone who is not in occupation of the land such as the holder of an intermediate tenancy between the freeholder and the tenant in possession or a mortgagee not in possession or the holder of the benefit of a rentcharge. There is a procedure whereby the situation can be rectified. The provisions only apply after the acquiring authority has entered onto the land. In any other case the error can sometimes be rectified by the service of a notice to treat or notice of entry when the identity of the holder of the relevant interest or right is ascertained. In the event of a mistake or inadvertence as just mentioned the authority has the right to remain in possession of the land provided that within six months it pays certain sums to the owner of the interest or right in question.

2.126   The sums to be paid or paid into court are compensation for the right or interest and full compensation for the mesne profits. The period of six months for the payment is six months from the date on which the acquiring authority has notice of the interest or right or, if there is a dispute as to the existence of the interest or right, six months after the interest or right is finally established by law in favour of the claimant.[277] The interest or right may become so established either by the acquiring authority in due course accepting it or as a result of legal proceedings. The legal proceedings may have to be in the ordinary courts or, possibly, as a result of a reference to the Lands Tribunal to determine compensation which enables the Tribunal to determine the entitlement to compensation as well as the amount of the compensation. These provisions apply even if the three year period for the exercise of the power of compulsory purchase running from the date on which the compulsory purchase order became operative has expired.[278] These provisions apply when the notice to treat procedure has been used to acquire land. They are unnecessary when the general vesting declaration procedure has been used since in that case all interests in the land acquired automatically vest in the acquiring authority so that the provisions are excluded if a vesting declaration has been made in respect of an area of land.[279] The procedure described applies only to land within a compulsory purchase order.[280] If an authority enters land not within a compulsory purchase order without lawful authority to do so it will be a trespasser and the ordinary remedies in private law of an injunction and damages will be available against it. It has been said that a claimant can invoke these provisions even though the acquiring authority does not believe that the claimant has a compensatable interest and does not itself wish to invoke the procedure.[281] If the acquiring authority has entered a person's land without observing the appropriate procedures which entitle it to do so, and if the position is not rectified by the procedure here described, a person with an interest affected will be entitled to seek an injunction ordering the removal of the authority and damages for trespass. In some cases, and providing it acts within the three year period permitted for the service of a notice to

---

[277] Compulsory Purchase Act 1965, s 22(1), (3).
[278] Ibid, s 22(2).
[279] Compulsory Purchase (Vesting Declarations) Act 1981, s 10(2). See section (q) of this chapter.
[280] Compulsory Purchase Act 1965, ss 1(3), 22(1).
[281] See *Union Rlys v Kent County Council* [2009] EWCA Civ 363, [2009] RVR 146.

treat stated in section 4 of the Compulsory Purchase Act 1965, an acquiring authority may be able to remedy an error (for example a notice to treat served on a previous owner rather than the current owner) by serving another notice to treat and notice of entry and backdating them.[282]

The compensation payable under this procedure is to be agreed or determined in the same way as if the acquiring authority had proceeded in a regular way, that is had purchased the interest or rights before entering onto the land, or as near to that manner as circumstances admit. The compensation may, therefore, be determined by the Lands Tribunal. The valuation date for the assessment of compensation is the date when the acquiring authority entered onto the land. Any improvements made on the land by the acquiring authority and the construction of the works which are the purpose of the compulsory purchase are to be disregarded in assessing compensation.[283]   2.127

The remaining component which may be payable to the landowner is the mesne profits referred to in the legislation. The expression 'mesne profits' is usually used to mean the sum which a landlord may recover from a tenant who holds over after the termination of the tenancy as a trespasser, and as such is another name for damages for trespass. It is stated that in the present context the expression means the mesne profits or interest which would have accrued to the persons concerned between the entry of the acquiring authority and the time when the compensation is paid so far as such mesne profits or interest may be recoverable in any proceedings.[284] It seems that what is meant by mesne profits or interest is the monetary return which the person holding the interest or right in question would have obtained between the above dates if the acquiring authority had not entered the land. For example, if the person whose interest has been inadvertently omitted from the application of the proper procedure held an intermediate tenancy the mesne profits would be the rent which he would have received in respect of his interest in that tenancy from a sub-tenant during the period just mentioned. The provisions just described are a re-enactment of provisions in the Lands Clauses Consolidation Act 1845 and in some respects the antique language and legal concepts in force in 1845 are preserved in the modern legislation, a technique which is used more than once in the Compulsory Purchase Act 1965.   2.128

(Q) IMPLEMENTATION OF THE ORDER: GENERAL VESTING DECLARATIONS

1. General Provisions

The procedure so far described has been that of the implementation of the powers of compulsory acquisition given by a confirmed compulsory purchase order and by way of service of notices to treat, notices of entry, the assessment of compensation and ultimately the transfer of title to the land to the acquiring authority. There is an alternative, and in many ways more convenient, procedure available to all acquiring authorities with the benefit of a confirmed compulsory purchase order (or the benefit of an authorisation to acquire   2.129

---

[282] *Cohen v Haringey LBC* (1981) 42 P & CR 6. See para 2.88.
[283] Compulsory Purchase Act, s 22(4).
[284] Ibid, s 22(5).

specified land conferred directly by the empowering Act itself) provided by the Compulsory Purchase (Vesting Declarations) Act 1981. The essence of this procedure is that the acquiring authority executes a vesting declaration, called throughout a general vesting declaration, in respect of the land. The effect of the general vesting declaration is that interests in the land vest in the acquiring authority and the authority has the immediate right to enter on and take possession of the land. The rights of mortgagees are not extinguished by the vesting declaration and the acquiring authority must secure the discharge of mortgages as explained in section (m) of this chapter. The rights of persons with third party rights over the land acquired, such as easements, are not destroyed by the vesting declaration but may be overridden so as to entitle the owners of those rights to compensation under section 10 of the Compulsory Purchase Act 1965 as explained in chapter 10. The vesting declaration procedure has advantages over the notice to treat procedure in that

(a) the acquiring authority acquires title to the land at an early stage instead of having to wait until the amount of the compensation is agreed or determined by the Lands Tribunal,

(b) notices to treat need not be served,

(c) notices of entry need not be served in order to obtain possession,

(d) there is no scope for the inadvertent omission of service of a notice to treat in respect of certain interests in the land,

(e) there is no uncertainty over the status of interests created or altered or ended between the date of the notice to treat and the valuation date, and

(f) the valuation date for the assessment of compensation is immediately fixed as the vesting date whether or not there is actual entry on that date.

2.130   Before an acquiring authority can make a general vesting declaration in respect of any land there are certain preliminary matters which must be satisfied. It is necessary that the authority has included in its statutory notice of confirmation of the compulsory purchase order: (a) certain particulars relating to the effect of Parts I and III of the Compulsory Purchase (Vesting Declarations) Act 1981, and (b) a notification to the effect that every person who, if a vesting declaration were executed in respect of all land comprised in the order would be entitled to claim compensation in respect of his land, is invited to give information to the acquiring authority in the prescribed form with respect to his name and address and the land in question. If these particulars have not been included in the notice of confirmation of the compulsory purchase order they may be given in a subsequent notice which complies with the requirements as to publication and service which apply to notices of confirmation of the order. However, such a later notice must be given before notice to treat has been served in respect of the land which will become the subject of the general vesting declaration. The notice must be registered in the register of local land charges. It is also an overriding interest (ie an interest which binds the registered title to the land without protection on the register by notice or other means) for the purposes of the Land Registration Act 2002.[285]

2.131   The rule in section 4 of the Compulsory Purchase Act 1965 that a power of compulsory purchase must be exercised within three years of the date on which a compulsory purchase order becomes operative applies whether the notice to treat or the general vesting declaration procedure is used. Consequently while the general vesting declaration procedure is

---

[285] Compulsory Purchase (Vesting Declarations) Act 1981, s 3. Land Registration Act 2002, sch 1, para 6.

used the declaration must be made within the three year period otherwise the power of compulsory purchase will lapse. The preliminary notification prescribed under section 3 of the Compulsory Purchase (Vesting Declarations) Act 1981 is not itself a sufficient exercise of the power of compulsory purchase to prevent the running of the time limit.[286]

Subject to this preliminary procedure having been carried out the acquiring authority may 2.132 execute a declaration in the prescribed form vesting in itself the land or any part of the land within the confirmed compulsory purchase order to which the vesting relates.[287] The declaration cannot be executed until the expiration of two months from the date of first publication of the notice of confirmation of the order or the subsequent notice which contains the particulars mentioned earlier. Nor can a declaration be executed before the compulsory purchase order has come into operation. A compulsory purchase order comes into operation on the date on which a notice of confirmation is first published so that the two month period just mentioned will usually mean that it is in any event not possible for a declaration to be made before the order has come into operation. Having executed the declaration the authority must serve a notice in the prescribed form specifying the land and stating the effect of the declaration on all occupiers of the land (save for land where there is a short tenancy which is considered later) and on any person who has given information to the acquiring authority pursuant to the invitation in the notice of confirmation described earlier. The date specified in the declaration for the vesting of the land in the acquiring authority must be at least 28 days from the date of completion of the service of these notices. The date so specified is called the vesting date. The acquiring authority can issue a certificate that the service of the notices has been completed which is then conclusive evidence of that fact. A general vesting declaration may be made in respect of all of the land within a confirmed compulsory purchase order or in respect of any part or parts of that land. If a declaration relates to only a part of the land then a subsequent declaration or declarations can be made in respect of other land within the order.[288]

On the vesting date interests in the land specified in the general vesting declaration vest in 2.133 the acquiring authority (subject to short tenancies which are dealt with separately).[289] The vesting date also becomes the valuation date for the assessment of compensation. Since land normally includes an interest in land it seems that a general vesting declaration may be made so as to acquire a particular interest in land, such as only a freehold or only a leasehold interest, without other interests being acquired.[290] Certain encumbrances such as rentcharges are extinguished. In addition on the vesting date the acquiring authority obtains the right to enter upon and take possession of the land. The right to give notice of entry under section 11 of the Compulsory Purchase Act 1965 is therefore not necessary and does not

---

[286] *Co-operative Insurance Society Ltd v Hastings Borough Council* (1993) 91 LGR 608, per Vinelott J, not following the decision of Aldous J in *Westminster City Council v Quereschi* (1990) 60 P & CR 380.

[287] The prescribed form is form 1 in the Compulsory Purchase of Land (Vesting Declarations) Regulations 1990 (SI 1990/497).

[288] Compulsory Purchase of Land (Vesting Declarations) Act 1981, ss 4–6. The prescribed form for stating the effect of the declaration is form 3 in the Compulsory Purchase of Land (Vesting Declarations) Regulations 1990 (SI 1990/497).

[289] Ibid, s 8. See para 2.139 for short tenancies. As stated in para 2.129 the interests of mortgagees in the land and third party interest such as easements are not extinguished by the vesting declaration. The vesting declaration operates as if the acquiring authority had executed a deed poll vesting land in itself under s 9 of the Compulsory Purchase Act 1965.

[290] See para 2.30.

apply to land specified in a general vesting declaration.[291] A number of the provisions of the Compulsory Purchase Act 1965 and the Land Compensation Act 1961 depend upon the service of a notice to treat. Consequently these provisions are applied as if, on the date on which the general vesting declaration was executed, a notice to treat had been served on every person on whom such a notice could have been served under the Compulsory Purchase Act 1965 other than: (a) a person entitled to an interest in land in respect of which a notice to treat had actually been served before the vesting date, and (b) persons entitled to short tenancies as described later. An actual notice to treat served under the Compulsory Purchase Act 1965 may be withdrawn in certain limited circumstances. This power of withdrawal does not apply to the constructive notices to treat just described. The opportunity to withdraw a notice to treat when a particularised claim for compensation is made or when the compensation has been determined by the Lands Tribunal is therefore not available when the general vesting declaration procedure is used. Having made a general vesting declaration in respect of a particular piece of land the acquiring authority cannot avoid its liability to pay compensation to those persons with an interest in the land.[292] When an actual notice to treat has been served the notice lapses unless the acquiring authority takes certain actions, such as an entry onto the land or a reference to the Lands Tribunal, within three years.[293] Since a general vesting declaration operates for the purposes of the Compulsory Purchase Act 1965 as a constructive notice to treat presumably the time limit under that Act applies when a vesting declaration has been made. In principle the validity of a general vesting declaration may be questioned in proceedings for judicial review.[294]

2. Supplementary Provisions

2.134   Where a general vesting declaration is made a number of supplementary provisions apply to the acquisition of the land and the assessment of compensation.

2.135   The general rules for the assessment of compensation are unaffected and apply in the same way as if a notice to treat and notice of entry had been served.[295] An acquiring authority may recover any compensation paid in excess of the proper sum to any party by reason of an encumbrance on the land not disclosed to the authority or because a claimant was not entitled to the interest claimed. Any question of the amount recoverable is to be determined by the Lands Tribunal in the event of dispute but, subject to that, may be recovered by the acquiring authority by proceedings in the ordinary courts.[296]

---

[291] See however para 2.139 for minor tenancies and long tenancies about to expire.
[292] Compulsory Purchase (Vesting Declarations) Act 1981, ss 7–8.
[293] Compulsory Purchase Act 1965, s 5(2A), (2B). See para 2.89.
[294] *R v Carmarthen District Council* (1990) 59 P & CR 379.
[295] Compulsory Purchase (Vesting Declarations) Act 1981, s 10(1).
[296] Ibid, s 11. The provisions of s 11 may not cover all instances of mistakes which result in the payment of money to a claimant which is not properly due to that claimant. For example, the acquiring authority may be under a misapprehension as to certain facts concerning an entitlement to a payment of compensation under r (6) of s 5 of the Land Compensation Act 1961. It is possible that in such cases, as in cases where the notice to treat procedure has been used, recovery of sums paid under a mistake of fact or of law may be recovered under the general law of restitution: see *Kleinwort Benson v Lincoln City Council* [1999] 2 AC 349, [1998] 3 WLR 1095, and Burrows, *The Law of Restitution*, 3rd edn (Oxford, Oxford University Press, 2010), ch 9.

There are provisions in section 22 of the Compulsory Purchase Act 1965 whereby an acquir-   2.136
ing authority can acquire interests omitted by mistake from an acquisition and under section 5 and schedule 2 to that Act whereby the authority can acquire the interests of absent
and untraced owners of land.[297] These provisions are unnecessary when a general vesting
declaration has been made since interests in the land the subject of the declaration are automatically vested in the acquiring authority and the provisions mentioned do not apply
where a vesting declaration has been made.[298] Section 64 of the Law of Property Act 1925
contains various provisions as to the safe custody of documents and to their production
when a person such as a seller of land retains possession of the documents and gives an
undertaking to another person of that person's right to production of the documents.
Where a person retains any documents relating to title after the vesting of land in the
acquiring authority under a vesting declaration he is deemed to have given such an undertaking so that the provisions of section 64 of the Law of Property Act 1925 apply.[299]

The result of land specified in a general vesting declaration having become vested in an   2.137
acquiring authority is that persons may be relieved from liability to make payments in
respect of that land, an example being a tenant under a lease of the land. If a person makes
such payments in error not knowing of the facts which constituted the cessation of his liability he may recover the sum paid from the person to whom it was paid.[300]

If a part of a person's land has been taken as a result of a general vesting declaration and that   2.138
person retains other land there are special provisions, explained elsewhere, whereby that
person can in certain circumstances compel the acquiring authority to acquire the whole of
his land. These provisions are similar to, but not identical to, those which apply where the
notice to treat procedure has been used.[301]

3. Short Tenancies

There are qualifications on the effect of a general vesting declaration when certain short   2.139
tenancies subsist in land specified in the declaration. Two types of tenancy bring about
these consequences. One is a minor tenancy, which means a tenancy for a year or from year
to year or any lesser interest. Weekly or monthly tenancies are examples of lesser interests.
The other type is a long tenancy which is about to expire, which means a tenancy greater
than a minor tenancy but which on the vesting date has a period to run which is not more
than the period, which must be longer than a year, specified for this purpose in the general
vesting declaration for the land in question. When one or other of these two types of tenancy subsists in the land in question there are two consequences.

   (i)   The right of entry conferred by the general vesting declaration is not exercisable
       unless the acquiring authority: (a) serves a notice to treat in respect of the tenancy,
       and (b) serves on every occupier of the land within the tenancy a notice stating that
       at the end of a period specified in the notice, which must be at least 14 days from

---

[297] See sections (o) and (p) of this chapter.
[298] Compulsory Purchase (Vesting Declarations) Act 1981, s 10(2).
[299] Ibid, s 14.
[300] Ibid, s 13.
[301] See section (b) of ch 9.

the service of the notice, the authority intends to enter upon and take possession of the land. The acquiring authority may enter on the land when the period specified has expired. In effect, and as regards the right to enter the land acquired, the general procedure applicable to notices to treat and notices of entry which operates where there is no general vesting declaration is applied to minor tenancies and long tenancies about to expire.[302] To this limited extent persons with minor tenancies may be in a better procedural position when a general vesting declaration has been made than they would otherwise be. If no general vesting declaration is made persons with minor tenancies have no right to receive a notice to treat and are required to give up possession as may be required by the acquiring authority pursuant to section 20 of the Compulsory Purchase Act 1965. A purpose of excluding short tenancies from the general vesting of interests in the acquiring authority on the vesting date may be to permit an authority to wait until such tenancies end in accordance with their term rather than having to acquire them and pay compensation with the vesting date as the valuation date.[303] Certainly this explains the power of the authority to specify a period longer than a year for the purposes of tenancies about to expire.

(ii) All interests in the land save the tenancy vest in the acquiring authority in the ordinary way but that vesting is subject to the tenancy until either the period specified in the notice just mentioned expires or, if it is sooner, the tenancy comes to an end in accordance with its terms. It seems that upon the expiry of the period specified in the notice if the tenancy has not come to an end by that date in accordance with its terms the tenancy simply ends on that date, subject of course to the payment of compensation to the tenant.[304]

If the landlord's interest vests in the acquiring authority pursuant to the general vesting declaration and the authority simply waits until the tenancy comes to an end the interest vested in the acquiring authority is freed from the encumbrance of the tenancy and the acquiring authority may enter the land. The tenancies to which the above provisions apply are equivalent to the types of interest which require the application of special rules for the assessment of compensation by reason of section 20 of the Compulsory Purchase Act 1965.

(R) COSTS OF THE CONVEYANCE

2.140   Where the acquiring authority uses the general vesting declaration procedure the interests in the land acquired vest in the authority at the vesting date. The vesting is by the operation of statute and no conveyance or transfer is necessary. If the land has a registered title or first registration is required the acquiring authority following the vesting date should of course secure the registration of the disposition under the Land Registration Act 2002 so that it becomes the registered proprietor in the ordinary way. If this procedure is not used the acquisition must be completed by a conveyance or transfer of the interests acquired to the acquiring authority as occurs with ordinary purchases of interests in land. Normally the

---

[302] See section (k) of this chapter.
[303] *London Borough of Newham v Benjamin* (1968) 1 WLR 694, [1968] 1 All ER 1195. See para 2.28.
[304] Compulsory Purchase (Vesting Declarations) Act 1981, s 9.

authority cannot insist upon a conveyance or transfer until the compensation has been agreed or determined and they have paid or tendered the amount due to the owner of the interest. Where the interest acquired has a registered title there will be executed a simple transfer in the form issued by HM Land Registry. If the title is unregistered an 'old style' conveyance will be necessary. The authority will then obtain registered title either by virtue of the transfer or by itself effecting a first registration of title following a conveyance of unregistered land. There cannot be a registered title of leases of seven years or less and, unless the vesting declaration procedure has been used, title to the unexpired residue of such a lease will be obtained by an ordinary assignment of the lease.[305]

On an ordinary sale of land each party generally bears its own costs of the process of transfer of title. It is considered that on a compulsory purchase this would be unfair to the landowner who is compelled to sell against his will and by statute the costs of all conveyances (which include a transfer of a registered title) are to be borne by the acquiring authority.[306] One of the purposes of registration of title is that an elaborate investigation of the title of the vendor is not necessary. Conveyances of unregistered land may involve the purchaser being satisfied that there is a good root of title and the costs payable by the acquiring authority include the whole of the costs of this process so far as borne by the vendor.[307] If the costs are not agreed they are subject to assessment by the usual process of assessment of costs in the Senior Courts and are recoverable from the acquiring authority after assessment as if they were payable under an order of the Senior Courts.[308] The costs of the assessment itself are payable by the acquiring authority unless on an assessment one sixth or more of the costs claimed are disallowed in which case the claimant has to pay the costs of the assessment.[309] There is a short form of conveyance of unregistered title set out in schedule 5 to the Compulsory Purchase Act 1965 which may be used but the conveyance can be in any form which the acquiring authority may think fit. If the conveyance is in the form set out in schedule 5, or as near to it as possible, the acquiring authority takes the land free from all rights, interests and estates in it which have been compensated for by the consideration mentioned in the conveyance.[310] 2.141

---

[305] See section (n) of this chapter.
[306] Compulsory Purchase Act 1965, s 23(1).
[307] Ibid, s 23(2).
[308] Ibid, s 23(3), (4). See Pt 47 of the Civil Procedure Rules for the assessment of costs in the courts.
[309] Ibid, s 23(5). The rule is therefore an inducement to reasonable and modest claims for conveyancing costs.
[310] Ibid , s 23(6).

3

General Principles of
the Law of Compensation

3.1   The law of compensation has many detailed rules and complexities but is also subject to a
        number of general principles and concepts which underlie the rules and make them more
        intelligible. Before embarking on the details of the various areas of compensation law and
        of the different heads of compensation it is helpful to examine certain of these general mat-
        ters or principles. There are seven such matters which can be identified and considered. It is
        also useful by way of an introduction to the more detailed rules to take an overview by
        categorising and explaining in outline the nature of the main heads of compensation and to
        explain also in outline the categories of persons who may assert an entitlement to compen-
        sation under these heads.

(A) GENERAL PRINCIPLES

1. The Principle of Equivalence

3.2   The first general matter is the principle which is said to underlie the whole of the law of com-
        pensation, and to provide guidance for the interpretation of the statutory provisions and a
        touchstone by reference to which all claims for compensation can be tested, that is the prin-
        ciple of equivalence. The principle of equivalence is the general, and perhaps obvious, prin-
        ciple that the compensation payable to a person who is deprived of his land in the public
        interest should be equal to the true and actual loss suffered by that person by reason of that
        deprivation, and should be no more and no less than that amount.[1] So viewed the law of com-
        pensation is a series of rules designed to give detailed effect to the principle of equivalence by
        identifying the loss suffered by a landowner and stating how that loss is to be converted into a
        monetary sum which becomes payable by the acquiring authority to the landowner.

        [1] *Director of Buildings and Lands v Shun Fung Ironworks Ltd* [1995] 2 AC 111, [1995] 2 WLR 904, per Lord
        Nicholls at p 125; *Horn v Sunderland Corporation* [1941] 2 KB 26, per Scott LJ at p 49; *Waters v Welsh Development
        Agency* [2004] UKHL 19, [2004] 1 WLR 1304, at para 4; *Transport for London Ltd v Spirerose Ltd* [2009] UKHL 44,
        [2009] 1 WLR 1797, at para 89. The classic definition of the principle of equivalence is that stated by Scott LJ in
        Horn v Sunderland Corporation and is as follows: 'The statutory compensation cannot, and must not, exceed the
        owner's total loss, for, if it does, it will put an unfair burden on the public authority or other promoters who on
        public grounds have been given the power of compulsory acquisition, and it will transgress the principle of equiv-
        alence which is the root of statutory compensation, the principle that the owner shall be paid neither less nor more
        than his loss'. The idea that an owner of land should not receive compensation for a loss which he has not suffered
        is, of course, much older and is a part of the origin of the value to the owner principle and the rule which requires
        the disregard of the scheme of the acquiring authority in valuing the land acquired: see paras 3.10–3.14 of this
        chapter, and see ch 5 and the passage from the judgment of Cockburn CJ in *Stebbing v Metropolitan Board of Works*
        (1870) LR 6 QB 37, cited in para 5.5 of ch 5.

In some ways the law of compensation is similar to the law of damages, both in its purpose   3.3
and in its underlying principle of equivalence. To enter a person's land and to deprive him of
his land against his will is, of course, a civil wrong and gives rise to a claim for damages
against the person involved. The actions of an acquiring authority in entering and taking
land are only lawful because of a specific statutory provision which permits such actions in
the public interest. In general terms compensation can be seen as a sum equivalent to the
damages which would have been payable for the actions of the acquiring authority if those
actions had not been permitted by statute and so had been unlawful.[2] A well known description of the general purpose of damages at common law is that an award of damages seeks to
put the person who has suffered an injury into the same position, so far as money can do so,
as he would have been in had the wrong not been committed against him.[3] The principle of
equivalence suggests that the law of compensation has a similar general purpose. The close-
ness between the concepts of compensation and common law damages is most vivid when
the fifth of the main categories of compensation is examined later in this chapter, that is the
entitlement to compensation for injurious affection caused to land by the execution of works
by an acquiring authority which would amount to a wrongful act in the absence of statutory
authorisation but when no land of the claimant is acquired for those works. In this case the
assessment of compensation is overtly stated in the authorities as something to be carried
out in the same way as the assessment of the damages which would have been payable to a
person whose land was injured if the works had not been lawful because of their statutory
authorisation so that damages would have been payable to the landowner affected.[4]

While the principle of equivalence is undoubtedly important in interpreting the statutory   3.4
law it should not be taken too far. In the end the duty of a court is to find the meaning of
the statutory provisions and to apply that meaning. Parliament is sovereign and it would be
unconstitutional for any court to amend or alter legislation merely because the legislation
was thought not to conform to the principle of equivalence or because the legislation was
thought to have gaps in it.[5] There is a tendency among lawyers who practice in a particular
area of law which is technical and complex to believe that there are specific principles of
statutory interpretation which apply to that area alone. There are not. As has been emphasised in recent high authority the correct approach to legislation is something which is
common to all legislation in all areas and it is hubristic for lawyers in one particular area,
such as taxation or compensation for compulsory purchase, to believe that there are
principles of statutory construction which apply to their particular area alone.[6] Since
2004 specific provisions have been in force which entitle persons whose land has been
acquired compulsorily to receive additional payments over and above their actual loss. This

---

    [2] See *Ricket v Metropolitan Rly Co* (1865) 34 LJ (QB) 257, where Erle CJ compared the principle of compensa-
tion to damages for trespass.
    [3] *Harman v Robinson* (1848) 1 Exch 850; *Livingston v Rawyards Coal Co* (1880) 5 App Cas 25.
    [4] See paras 3.29 and 3.30 and see, eg *Clift v Welsh Office* [1999] 1 WLR 796, [1998] 4 All ER 852.
    [5] *Transport for London Ltd v Spirerose Ltd* [2009] UKHL 44, [2009] 1 WLR 1797, per Lord Collins at para 131.
    [6] *Commissioner of Taxation v Ryan* (2000) 201 CLR 109, per Kirby J at p 146 (HC of Australia), cited by Lord
Walker in *Transport for London Ltd v Spirerose Ltd* [2009] UKHL 44, [2009] 1 WLR 1797, at para 25. See ch 5, para
5.79. This 'hubristic' approach is not confined to statutory construction. The law on when it is permissible to lift
the corporate veil and the separate existence of separate companies has been stated in the clearest general terms by
the Court of Appeal but this has not prevented the Lands Tribunal from recently holding that the general principles are not applicable to claims for compensation: see section (b) of ch 12. This latest excursion into the hubristic
approach may recently have been laid to rest by the decision of the Supreme Court in *Prest v Petrodel Properties Ltd*
[2003] UKSC 34, [2013] 3 WLR 1, in which a similar idea that principles of general law regarding corporate personality did not apply to areas of family law was rejected.

is obviously an express statutory exception to the principle of equivalence. In the years following the Lands Clauses Consolidation Act 1845 it became traditional to add 10 per cent to the value of the land as an additional item of compensation regarded as some recompense to the landowner for the fact that his land was taken from him against his will. This practice was obviously not in accord with the principle of equivalence and was abolished by the Acquisition of Land (Assessment of Compensation) Act 1919.

2. Open Market Value

3.5   The second general matter is the fundamental task which underpins the great majority of assessments of compensation. That matter is the assessment of the open market value of the land acquired. The basic rule for the assessment of compensation is that it shall be equal to the value of the land acquired. The reason is that a person may have a saleable asset, a piece of land, and when he is deprived of that asset against his will he should receive as compensation the sum he would have obtained if he had voluntarily sold his asset on the market at the time it was taken away from him. This basic rule is now embodied in the legislation as rule (2) of section 5 of the Land Compensation Act 1961 and is that the value of land shall be taken to be 'the amount which the land if sold in the open market by a willing seller might be expected to realise'. This statement of the rule at once raises a number of further questions such as the exact date as at which the assessment of the value is to be made, that is that which is usually called the valuation date, and what assumptions are to be made about the circumstances surrounding the notional sale. Both of these questions are considered as part of subsequent general principles in this chapter and are explained in more detail in chapters 4 and 5.

3.6   For the moment it is sufficient to refer to the nature of the notional or hypothetical sale enjoined by the basic rule. It is a sale in the open market so that the land must be taken to have been adequately and properly marketed with such publicity, promotion, and a time for negotiation, as would have attended an actual sale of land of the size and character involved. It is to be assumed that every person who might have an interest in buying the land is a potential bidder in the market. It is important to bear in mind that just as the sale is hypothetical so the parties to it are hypothetical. This point sometimes causes difficulty and confusion. Where the rule refers to a sale by 'a willing seller' it does not mean a sale by the actual owner as the willing seller but rather a sale by some hypothetical person as the willing seller. The assumed seller is an abstraction and is not to be identified with, or given the particular characteristics of, any natural person or company. The dispossessed landowner might have had personal circumstances which would have affected the sale, for instance cash flow problems which could have made him anxious to sell the land or a personal affection for the land which could have made him reluctant to sell it. Such matters are to be disregarded for the purposes of the hypothetical sale and for the purposes of establishing the open market value of the land acquired.[7]

[7] The principle of a hypothetical party to a transaction has been most fully considered and explained in decisions on rent reviews under leases where the purpose is to find the open market rental value of land by way of an assumed or hypothetical letting of the land by a hypothetical willing landlord to a hypothetical willing tenant at the review date. The hypothetical willing landlord has been described as a hypothetical entity and as someone not affected by personal characteristics such as importunate mortgagees. He is someone who wants to let the premises

The statutory formulation of the rule does not refer to a willing buyer. Nonetheless if a sale   3.7
is to be assumed to take place as the rule requires there must also be assumed to be a buyer
who comes to an agreement on the price with the hypothetical seller.[8] That buyer is also an
abstraction, a hypothetical willing buyer, and he is not to be clothed with the characteristics
of any particular actual person or company. He is simply a notional person who is willing
to buy the land at the lowest price which he can negotiate. It is at this point in the process
that actual persons may play a role. If a property is put on the market for sale there might
be a number of real persons who would be interested in bidding for it or trying to reach
agreement on its price. The existence of these persons would constitute the market. The
price which would be agreed for the property would be dictated to a considerable extent by
the number and eagerness of these bidders.[9] The hypothetical willing buyer is the person
who is taken to agree to buy the land and clearly in order to do so he would have to outbid,
or at least offer as much as, any actual persons who would have been in the market and bidding for the land. It may therefore be significant in the valuation process to enquire, or
provide evidence on, whether actual persons might have been interested in buying the land
if it had been on the market and, if so, who these persons would be likely to have been and
what sum they would have been willing to offer. The nature of the hypothetical sale is central to the assessment of compensation and it, and the problems which may be raised by it,
are considered in detail later.[10]

3. The Valuation Date

The third general matter is the valuation date. As with other saleable assets the value of land   3.8
can fluctuate sometimes quite rapidly over short periods of time due to external events and
economic circumstances. It is meaningless to refer to a value of land without specifying the
date for the valuation. The valuation date is the date by reference to which the land is to
be valued. It was established by a decision of the House of Lords that for the purposes of
compulsory purchase valuations the valuation date is generally the date of entry by the
acquiring authority onto the land acquired.[11] This rule was subsequently confirmed by statute as that generally applicable.[12] The rule seems just since the date of the physical expropriation of the land is the date on which an owner who is in possession loses the benefit of

---

at a rent which is appropriate to all the factors which affect the marketability of the premises and the rent: see the
classic formulation of Donaldson J in *Evans (FR) (Leeds) Ltd v English Electric Co Ltd* (1977) 36 P & CR 185, [1978]
1 EGLR 93.

   [8] *Dennis & Robinson Ltd v Kiossos Establishment* (1987) 54 P & CR 382, [1987] 1 EGLR 133, per Dillon LJ (also
a rent review case).

   [9] *Penny's Bay Investment Co Ltd v Director of Lands* (2010) 13 HKCFAR 287 (Ct of Final Appeal, Hong Kong),
per Lord Hoffmann at para 44. It is sometimes said that the whole sale of the property being valued is hypothetical
and the seller and the buyer are hypothetical although the market in which this hypothetical transaction is assumed
to take place is real.

   [10] See sections (b), (c) and (d) of ch 4.

   [11] *West Midland Baptist (Trust) Association Inc v Birmingham City Corporation* [1970] AC 874, [1969] 3 WLR
389.

   [12] Land Compensation Act 1961, s 5A, added by the Planning and Compensation Act 2004. The general rule
applies only to cases where the compensation is based on the value of the land acquired. In the exceptional cases
in which the compensation is based on the cost to the landowner of equivalent reinstatement the cost of that
reinstatement is to be assessed at the first date on which it could reasonably be commenced: see section (a) of
ch 6.

his ownership of the land. If the land has been acquired using the general vesting declaration procedure the date on which the right of entry arises will be the vesting date as specified in the declaration which is the date on which the acquiring authority gains title by virtue of the statutory vesting of title in that authority. If this procedure is used the valuation date is the vesting date. If the notice to treat procedure has been used the date on which the acquiring authority gains title to the land may be substantially later than the date on which it has gained entry following a notice to enter. Notwithstanding this in the case of service of a notice to treat the valuation date is the date of actual entry by the authority. It is possible, though unlikely, that compensation is determined by the Lands Tribunal prior to the date of entry or prior to the vesting date. In that case the date of the hearing is the valuation date.

3.9   The ascertainment of the valuation date is important not only because land prices may be rising or falling. The valuation date also fixes many of the circumstances of the land being valued and circumstances external to the land which may affect its value. The land acquired is normally to be valued in its physical state as at the valuation date. The announcement of proposed new highway facilities or some aspect of changed public policy may affect the value of the land and it may be important to know whether the event in question has happened at the valuation date so that it would be taken into account by the hypothetical willing buyer and other possible bidders in the market. It is a principle of law concerning the valuation of all assets where a hypothetical sale of the asset has to be envisaged that in deciding what price he would pay for the asset the hypothetical willing buyer can only take into account as established facts those events and facts which have happened or exist at the valuation date. The parties are not endowed with foresight of future events. Of course the anticipation of future events where relevant to the valuation of the asset can be taken into account but only as regards events which were reasonably anticipated at the valuation date. The specification of an exact valuation date is essential for the operation of this principle. The exact rules relating to the ascertainment of the valuation date are explained in the next chapter.[13]

4. The Value to the Owner Principle

3.10   Much of what has been explained under the first three matters is common to most areas of the valuation of assets. The fourth general matter or principle is a principle which has been established for the purposes of the law of compensation for compulsory purchase. It is the value to the owner or the value to the seller principle. In its origin the principle is the result of decisions of the courts although its two aspects or consequences have now been put into statutory form. To explain the principle and its two consequences for the purposes of valuing the land acquired it is necessary to go back to the first Act of Parliament which addressed the assessment of compensation on a general or standard basis. It was stated in the Lands Clauses Consolidation Act 1845 that the primary component of compensation was to be the value of the land acquired.[14] Although it was not so stated in the Act that value was soon established as the amount which the land acquired would realise if sold in the open market,

---

[13] See section (e) of ch 4.
[14] Lands Clauses Consolidation Act 1845, s 63.

and this concept of value is now embodied in statute and has been explained as the second fundamental principle considered in this chapter. The amount of the market value of land at a specific date is strongly dependant on the circumstances which exist, or which are to be assumed to exist, at the date of the hypothetical sale which establishes that value. When a compulsory purchase takes place the acquiring authority, be it a central or local government body or a private utility or any other organisation, has a need for the land and a purpose in acquiring the land. The value of the land to its owner or seller, that is to the person from whom it is being acquired, may be significantly different to its value to the purchaser, that is to the acquiring authority which is purchasing it. The need of the acquiring authority to acquire the land and the scheme which the acquiring authority intends to implement may add to the value of the land. In some instances these same factors may reduce the value of the land such as when the land is to be put to a use, say a prison, which creates no value in the land save for that attributable to the need of the body acquiring it or where the land is to be used as part of a new road the prospect of which reduces the value of the land acquired because of environmental effects. Those factors which rest on the need or purposes of the acquiring authority can be said to create a value of the land for that authority and are not a part of the value of the land to the owner. The essence of the value to the owner principle (or value to the seller principle which means the same thing) is that in valuing the land acquired what has to be found is the value to the owner with the result that factors of the nature just mentioned are disregarded. This principle and the reasoning which justifies it are central to the law of compensation and they have generated a series of decided authorities and statutory provisions in which they have been elaborated and applied. It will be necessary to deal subsequently and in detail with the ramifications of the value to the owner principle but at this stage the two main aspects or consequences of the principle may be outlined.

The first main aspect, and that explained next, is what is often described as disregarding the effect on the value of the land acquired of the scheme of the acquiring authority in the valuation process. It became traditional to describe this aspect of the value to the owner principle as 'the Pointe Gourde principle' after a decision of the Privy Council in 1947 in which the principle was applied.[15]   3.11

It is easy to state the apparently simple rule that in valuing the land acquired the effect on value of the need of the acquiring authority for the land and its purpose in acquiring the land are to be disregarded. Such a rule at once raises a series of supplementary questions. It is necessary to know how to determine the exact purpose or scheme of the authority. It is necessary to know whether that which has to be disregarded is confined to physical development of land or extends to other matters such as the acquisition of other land by the acquiring authority or provisions in statutory development plans. It is necessary to know whether that which has to be disregarded is only that which might occur on the land acquired itself or also includes that which might occur on other land. These questions were to some extent answered in the decisions of the courts although the courts tended to avoid some of the difficulties by saying that the extent of the scheme to be disregarded was a matter of fact for the body which decided the amount of the compensation. In due course statute intervened and complex provisions dealing with this aspect of the value to the owner   3.12

---

[15] *Pointe Gourde Quarrying and Transport Co Ltd v Sub-Intendent of Crown Lands* [1947] AC 565.

principle were enacted first in the Town and Country Planning Act 1959 and then in the Land Compensation Act 1961.[16] The latter provisions remain in force.

3.13   A point of particular difficulty which engendered a line of cases was whether, after the enactment of the statutory provisions, there remained some residual or 'common law' principle which could be applied as a supplement to the statutory provisions and the view took hold that such a supplementary principle could be used at least to fill in obvious gaps in the legislation. This last question has now been resolved by a recent decision of the House of Lords which establishes that the statutory provisions are all embracing and that the only function of the value to the owner principle as developed by the courts is as a guide to the interpretation of the relevant statutory provisions.[17] The detailed law relating to this first aspect of the value to the owner principle and the Pointe Gourde principle is explained in ch 5.

3.14   The application of this first aspect of the value to the owner principle in modern circumstances is not without its critics. The application of the principle can be readily justified where the scheme of an acquiring authority reduces the value of land acquired. It would be unfair that a person who is obliged to give up his land in the public interest should then have the value of his land depreciated by the scheme the carrying out of which is a part of that public interest and which justifies the acquisition. The situation where the scheme of the acquiring authority increases the value of the land is more debatable. In the ordinary commercial market where a purchaser has a project which increases the value of land which he needs he will normally have to pay at least a part of that increased value in order to obtain the land for the purposes of his project. The rationale behind a different rule being applied where land is being acquired for a public purpose and in the public interest may be that the additional value of the land is then provided by the public through the scheme and the landowner should not benefit and the public should not suffer from that increased value. This rationale is less readily defensible when the increased value which the land acquired obtains from the existence of the scheme behind its acquisition is brought about not only by the public interest in that scheme being carried out but also by the profit which private persons and companies are likely to make from that scheme. This was the situation in the early days of compulsory purchase where the object of the purchase was often that of a commercial company carrying out a scheme such as the construction of a railway which would both serve the public and provide a profit for its promoters. A similar situation applies today where a compulsory purchase is carried out by a privatised utility company or where there is a major private financial and other involvement in a public project as increasingly occurs. The aspect of the value to the owner principle here being considered is firmly embodied in the law of compensation but the universal nature of its application in modern circumstances is something which might be reconsidered if and when any comprehensive reform of this area of the law is contemplated.

3.15   The second main aspect of the value to the owner principle is that it has brought about that area of compensation known generally as disturbance claims. In the ordinary course of events when a person sells a piece of land he has to bear the burden of such matters as his own removal costs to other premises or, if a business is being carried on at the land, the

---

[16] Land Compensation Act 1961, s 6 and sch 1. Other provisions of the same Act such as s 9 and r (3) of s 5 have their origins in the value to the owner principle.
[17] *Transport for London Ltd v Spirerose Ltd* [2009] UKHL 44, [2009] 1 WLR 1797.

costs of a relocation of the business. A purchaser of the land is unlikely to be concerned with these matters and unlikely to allow them to affect the price he will pay for the land. Where the purchase is compulsory the value to the owner principle has led to the rule that the dispossessed owner, in addition to recovering the value of the land acquired, is entitled to further compensation for items such as those just mentioned. This rule, like the first aspect of the value to the owner principle, emerged from the interpretation which the courts put on the meaning of value in the Lands Clauses Consolidation Act 1845. The availability of this additional compensation became enshrined in statute in the Acquisition of Land (Assessment of Compensation) Act 1919. It is today provided for in rule (6) of section 5 of the Land Compensation Act 1961. Initially the only justification for allowing these additional items of compensation was that the word 'value' as used in the 1845 Act was given an extended meaning because of the value to the owner principle so as to encompass these additional items, and as a result of this historical process the additional or disturbance compensation is still regarded as a part of the value of the land even though the ordinary understanding of value does not include items of the type in question.[18] Compensation for disturbance means compensation for losses caused by the physical dispossession of the landowners from the land such as removal costs to other premises. As will be explained the statutory embodiment of the second aspect of the value to the owner principle also allows compensation to be claimed for other matters not directly based on the value of the land acquired, so that claims can be made for other items of loss which are not due to disturbance in the sense just mentioned. Disturbance or rule (6) compensation is an area of the law of compensation which merits separate and detailed consideration and this is provided in chapter 8. In the light of recent decisions one of the pressing problems in the law of compensation, as it currently stands, is to discern some reasonable limit to the ambit of claims under this head of compensation.

5. The Presumption of Reality

The fifth general matter or principle to consider, and one which flows naturally from the value to the owner principle, is the presumption of reality. This again is a general principle of land valuation. As stated earlier the value of a piece of land at a particular date may be heavily influenced by surrounding events and circumstances external to the land itself. If it is a leasehold interest which is being valued then the likely attitude of the landlord of the premises to ways in which the land may be dealt with could be of considerable importance to the amount which a purchaser of the leasehold interest would pay in order to acquire it. The presumption of reality means that, apart from the hypothesis of a sale of the land being valued and apart from the assumed existence of a hypothetical willing seller and a hypothetical willing buyer, all other surrounding circumstances and events relevant to the value of the land are to be taken as they actually were at the valuation date unless the statutory provisions which govern the valuation provide otherwise expressly or by necessary implication. It follows that where a leasehold interest is being valued the identity of the landlord must be taken to be that of the actual landlord and that there is no justification for assuming the existence of some different or notional landlord who may have a different attitude

3.16

---

[18]   *Hughes v Doncaster Metropolitan Borough Council* [1991] 1 AC 382, [1991] 2 WLR 16.

to the future development or other dealing with the land.[19] A further example of the principle is that, if a piece of land is acquired and there is adjoining it a further piece of land, the owner of which has a particular need for the land in question, in valuing the land acquired the existence of that owner and his special need, and any resultant amount which he would have paid to acquire the land because of that need, are all taken into account.[20]

3.17   There is on the face of it a conflict between the presumption of reality and the first aspect of the value to the owner principle explained earlier.[21] The need of the acquiring authority to obtain the land and the scheme of the acquiring authority are a part of the reality. If they are disregarded for valuation purposes, as is required by the first aspect of the value to the owner principle, then the rule which requires the disregard of these factors can be regarded in terms of legal analysis as an exception to the presumption of reality. It has been said that the presumption of reality and the principle of equivalence amount to much the same thing.[22] Certainly both are wide and general concepts but the principle of equivalence is directed towards the dispossessed landowner obtaining compensation equal to his true and actual loss whereas the presumption of reality is an aspect of the valuation of his land which leads to the principle of equivalence being satisfied.

6. Compensation and Planning

3.18   The sixth general matter is the relationship between the law of compensation and the law of town and country planning. The most important determining factor of the value of an area of land at a particular valuation date may be an expectation that the land can become the subject of a valuable development. Development in this context means a material change in the use of the land or the carrying out of operations on the land. Since the Town and Country Planning Act 1947 this country has been subject to universal planning control the foundation of which is that planning permission is required before it is lawful to carry out development of land. There is, therefore, an inevitable and close linkage between the valuation of land and the law and practice of town and country planning. The compensation code defines carefully what planning permissions are to be taken into account when valuing the land for the purposes of assessing compensation. Any planning permission which exists at the valuation date is to be taken into account. Account may also be taken of any expectation of obtaining a planning permission which exists at the valuation date in the absence of the scheme of the acquiring authority. There is then a series of provisions which require the assumption of the existence of a planning permission at the valuation date even when that permission did not in fact exist.[23] This is a further instance of an express departure from the presumption of reality. The purpose of these provisions, which were first introduced in 1959, appears to be to simplify the valuation process. In practice their existence can lead to complications and disputes. Very recent legislation has in some ways

---

[19] *Trocette Property Co Ltd v Greater London Council* (1974) 28 P & CR 408. The actual decision in this case was affected by the operation of s 9 of the Land Compensation Act 1961 which is examined in section (d) of ch 5. See also *Hoare (VO) v National Trust* [1998] RA 391, at p 415, [1999] 1 EGLR 155.

[20] Such a purchaser is often called a special purchaser and this concept is considered in more detail in section (d) of ch 4.

[21] See paras 3.11–3.13.

[22] *Transport for London Ltd v Spirerose Ltd*, above n 17, per Lord Neuberger at para 52.

[23] Land Compensation Act 1961, ss 14–18, as substituted by the Localism Act 2011.

improved the situation but has also increased its complexity.[24] Chapter 7 is devoted to a consideration of the impact of town and country planning on the assessment of compensation.

Since development and planning are here under discussion this is a convenient point at   3.19
which to introduce a number of expressions used when discussing the value of land for development, namely existing use value, development value and hope value.

(i)   The existing use value of land means the value of land for a continuation of its existing use without any realistic prospect of any significant development of the land. Agricultural or amenity land in a green belt will be likely to have only an existing use value. This value is often taken as the minimum value to be attributed to land which is acquired.[25]

(ii)   The development value of land is its value for some form of development for which planning permission exists. The agricultural land just referred to might be worth £500,000 for a continued agricultural use but might be increased in value to £3 million if it could be developed by building houses on it. In such a situation the expression 'development value' can be used in two senses. It can mean the whole of the value of the land, that is £3 million in the above example. Alternatively it can mean that part of the value of the land in excess of its existing use value which is attributable to the prospect of a particular development being carried out, that is £2.5 million in the above example.

(iii)   When there is a reference to the development value of land in either of the above senses it is usually implicit that there is in existence a planning permission capable of being implemented. In the case of valuations for the purposes of assessing compensation there are circumstances in which a planning permission does not exist, but has to be assumed to exist, and such an assumed permission is normally as valuable as an actual permission. On the other hand it is possible to envisage a situation in which there is no existing or assumed planning permission but there is some reasonable prospect of obtaining a planning permission. A purchaser of land may be willing to pay a price above the existing use value of the land in the hope of obtaining the necessary planning permission which will permit its development. Plainly in such circumstances he is unlikely to be willing to pay as much for the land as he would if there was an actual permission. Equally plainly the amount above the existing use value of the land which a purchaser would be willing to pay depends on his perception of the likelihood of obtaining a permission. To take again the above example of land having an agricultural existing use, if there were a good prospect, but not a certainty, of obtaining planning permission for residential development the value of the land might be increased from £500,000 to £2 million. The land can then be said to have a hope value and, again, the hope value can mean the whole value of the land, the £2 million, or the value in excess of its existing value which is attributable to the hope of obtaining planning permission, that is £1.5 million.[26]

---

[24]   See the Localism Act 2011, s 232.
[25]   The existing use value of land is important to the operation of Pt I of the Land Compensation Act 1973 which provides a measure of compensation for a depreciation in the value of a person's land caused by the use of public works. In assessing that depreciation it is only the existing use value of the land affected, and not its development value, which is taken into account. See section (e) of ch 13.
[26]   See *Mon Tresor v Ministry of Housing and Lands* [2008] 3 EGLR 13 (PC on appeal from Mauritius).

The possibility of some future event which creates a hope value is often the prospect of obtaining a planning permission but in principle any uncertain future event, for example the prospect of development of other land which could increase the value of the land being valued, or the prospect of the release of a restrictive covenant being secured, could be factors which create a hope value.

7. Injurious Affection

3.20   The last general matter is injurious affection. This is a phrase used at important points in the legislation; it is a part of the statutory description of two of the main heads of compensation. The phrase was used in the Lands Clauses Consolidation Act 1845 and has been repeated in modern legislation. The language may seem unusual to modern ears but injurious affection to land means no more than that the land has been adversely affected by some event. In other words the phrase means damage or harm to land.[27] It is used to describe the circumstances in which compensation can sometimes be payable when a piece of land has been harmed by some activity of a public body without that land having been acquired. Two main instances of this occurring are: (a) where a part of a person's land is compulsorily acquired and injurious affection or harm is caused to the retained part of the land by reason of its severance from the part acquired or by reason of the works to be carried out on the land acquired and on other land by the acquiring authority, and (b) where no land is acquired from an owner but his land is injuriously affected by the carrying out of works by an acquiring authority or by the overriding of ancillary rights such as a right of way which would be unlawful if those actions had not had statutory authority. The harm to land which constitutes the injurious affection is nearly always a reduction in its value, either a permanent harm which permanently reduces its capital value, or a temporary harm which reduces its rental value for a period.

(B)   HEADS OF COMPENSATION

3.21   There are a number of main heads under which compensation can be claimed. The first four arise when land of the claimant has been compulsorily acquired. The last three arise when no interest in land of the claimant which entitles him to compensation has been acquired. The seven heads are as follows:

    (i)   Compensation for the value of the land acquired.

    (ii) Compensation for land retained when only a part of the land of the owner has been compulsorily acquired.

    (iii) Disturbance compensation.

---

[27] In *Wildtree Hotels Ltd v Harrow London Borough Council* [2001] 2 AC 1, [2000] 3 WLR 165, Lord Hoffmann said at p 7 that the term 'injuriously affected' connoted 'injuria', that is to say damage which would have been wrongful but for the protection afforded by statutory powers. In *Penny's Bay Investment Co Ltd v Director of Lands* (2010) 13 HKCFAR 287 Lord Hoffmann said at para 34 that injurious affection means 'a diminution in the value of land caused by works authorised by statute which would otherwise have been tortious'.

(iv) Additional statutory compensation payments when land has been compulsorily acquired.

(v) Compensation for injurious affection under section 10 of the Compulsory Purchase Act 1965.

(vi) Disturbance payments under the Land Compensation Act 1973.

(vii) Compensation for depreciation caused by the use of public works under Part I of the Land Compensation Act 1973.

This list is not exhaustive. For example, compensation may be claimed for loss caused by the withdrawal by the acquiring authority of a notice to treat or for damage done to the land by the exercise by the authority of its right to enter and survey the land in advance of a compulsory purchase. These areas of compensation can be considered as ancillary to the main heads and they are explained where appropriate in ensuing chapters.

1. The Land Acquired

The first and primary head of compensation is the open market value of the land acquired   3.22
at the valuation date. The valuation date is generally the date of entry onto the land by the acquiring authority. In general terms the value of the land has to be assessed disregarding the effect on its value of the compulsory acquisition and the scheme or project of the acquiring authority which underlies and justifies the compulsory acquisition. Apart from the disregard of this matter in accordance with the statutory provisions the general rule is that no other matters are to be disregarded and the hypothetical sale of the land which is the basis of the valuation is a sale in which the buyer takes into account all surrounding events which are relevant to the value of the land. This is the application of the presumption of reality described earlier.

The method by which the amount that a hypothetical willing buyer would pay is deter-   3.23
mined is a matter of valuation. Various valuation techniques are used, but the main methods are a valuation by comparables, a valuation by the residual method, and a valuation by reference to anticipated profits which could be made from the continuation or inception of a commercial activity on the land.[28] The underlying principle is that no valuation method is precluded as a matter of law but that in any particular case one method may be preferred as likely to provide a more reliable result than others.

(i) The comparables method requires a consideration of prices paid in transactions on other properties and depends on the reasoning that, after taking account of any relevant differences (for instance differences of time or of location) between those transactions and the hypothetical transaction on the property acquired and being valued, a similar price would be paid for the land acquired. It is the method of valuation generally favoured by valuers since it depends on what has actually happened in the market, rather than on speculation and theory, but of course it is a method of

---

[28] Other valuation techniques are possible. One is the depreciated replacement cost method which means that the value of the property is the cost of replacing that property with a modern building but with deductions to take account of such factors as the age of the building and any obsolete attributes. Esoteric techniques of this nature, for instance 'the contractor's test', are used in valuations for rating purposes where in some instances comparable transactions do not exist because of the nature or use of the property.

valuation which is only possible when satisfactory comparable transactions have occurred. When this method is used the area of dispute between valuers is often that of what adjustments have to be made to the prices paid in the comparable transactions to make them fully appropriate to the hypothetical sale of the property being valued.

(ii) The residual method of valuation may be used when land is being sold for development and there are no satisfactory comparables relating to transactions in such land. This method requires that the value of the land with the development which is anticipated being complete is estimated and the total costs of the development are also estimated. The difference between the two sums, taking account of an element of profit for the developer, is the residual value and it is this residual value which, as the theory runs, would be paid for the land by a prospective developer who would be the hypothetical willing buyer. This method of valuation, although frequently used by valuers, is not popular with tribunals and courts since the components of the valuation process are difficult to prove and small differences in these components or inputs to the process can make a large difference to the ultimate value of the land which is that which has to be assessed.

(iii) The profits method of valuation is self-explanatory in that it assumes that the hypothetical willing buyer will decide how much he will pay for the land by estimating the amount of profits which he believes he can make from a business carried on at the land. This method also involves speculation on matters such as the level of the anticipated income, costs and profits of the business and is less favoured than the comparables method. Nonetheless it is a method of valuation which is popular when valuing properties used or to be used for commercial, leisure and entertainment purposes, for example pubs and restaurants. If the profits method of valuation is used it must be borne firmly in mind that compensation is payable for the value of the land acquired. An analysis of anticipated future profits, such as might be carried out by a hypothetical willing buyer, may be a relevant factor in assessing the open market value of the land, but it is no more than that. The compensation payable as a result of a compulsory purchase of land is for the value of the land acquired not for the loss of the profits of a business.

Sometimes two or more methods of valuation may be used in the hope that the results will confirm and support each other by leading to a similar end result as the value of the land. The whole process of valuation for the purposes of assessing compensation is central to the subject matter of this book and is discussed separately and in more detail in chapter 14. The Appendix to the book contains worked examples of different forms of valuation with an explanation of the process. This first and primary head of compensation, the value of the land acquired, is explained in chapters 4–7.

2. Retained Land

3.24   Turning to the second head of compensation, an acquiring authority may acquire only a part of a person's land for its purposes. An obvious illustration of this situation is where a strip of land is acquired for the purposes of a new road leaving the owner with retained land on both sides of the strip. The land retained may be reduced in value by reason of the acquisition and it has been the law since the Lands Clauses Consolidation Act 1845 that the owner is entitled to compensation for the injurious affection, that is the adverse effect, to his land retained.[29] The injurious affection normally takes one of two forms. The very fact of the severance of the ownership of the land acquired from that of the land retained may reduce the value of the land retained. For instance, the land retained may have been reliant on the land acquired for its access to a public highway. If the access is removed the owner of the land retained may be either without an access to a highway or may have to acquire a new access from some other adjoining owner at a substantial cost to him. Compensation for this type of injurious affection to the land retained is called compensation for severance. The other type of injurious affection to the land retained is that caused by the use or proposed use of the land acquired from the owner and the use or proposed use of other land by the acquiring authority. An instance would be the use of the land acquired for a new road which could reduce the value of the land retained because of the noise and disruption caused by the construction and use of that road. The term 'injurious affection' is sometimes used in this context to mean only an adverse effect on the land retained of this second type although the language of the legislation regards injurious affection as embracing both types of adverse effect.[30]

The assessment of the compensation for injurious affection to land retained is generally carried out by a 'before and after' valuation. What is meant is that the value of the land retained is first assessed as that which it had before the severance from it of the land acquired, and disregarding the acquisition of that land and the scheme of the acquiring authority, and the value of the land retained is then assessed as that which it has after the severance from it of the land acquired and taking into account the scheme of the acquiring authority. The compensation is the amount, if any, by which the second or after value is less than the first or before value. As will be explained valuations of this character may be complex and may involve the concept of marriage value. Marriage value means the additional value which is created when two pieces of land or two separate interests in the same land are merged or married together in one ownership such that the value of the merged land or interests in land is greater than the aggregate of the values of the two areas of land or the two interests in land assessed separately. For example, if plot A is worth £1 million and an adjoining plot B is worth £2 million, if they are merged together (ie the owner of one acquires the other or a third party acquires both) the value of the merged plots may be £3.5 million and not £3 million. The additional £500,000 of value caused by the merger is said to be the marriage value.   3.25

A frequent error which is made in claims for compensation for injurious affection for land retained is that an overall valuation is done. The value of the whole of the land of the owner, the land acquired and the land retained, is assessed as it was prior to the acquisition of the part which is acquired and then the value of the land retained is assessed as it is following the acquisition. The sum which is the difference between these two values is then said to be, in composite terms, the compensation claimed for the value of the land acquired and the compensation for any injurious affection to the land retained. This approach is in principle not acceptable since it conflates together two different heads of compensation which have to be assessed in different ways. It is possible that a valuation carried out in this way will   3.26

---

[29] Lands Clauses Consolidation Act 1845, s 63, now replaced by the Compulsory Purchase Act 1965, s 7.
[30] Compulsory Purchase Act 1965, s 7. A more exact analysis of the statutory language is in ch 9, paras 9.1–9.3.

produce a result for the two heads of compensation together which is the same as it would be if the two heads of compensation were assessed separately and correctly but no confidence can be placed in that result being necessarily correct or as that which would be reached by the application of the statutory language. In other words there may be no absolute rule of law which prevents the two heads of compensation being assessed in this way but if such an assessment is made there is a real danger that it will produce an incorrect result and, although it is simple to carry out the assessment of the two heads of compensation in this way and it has a surface attraction, it is not an accurate or recommended method of proceeding. This head of compensation is explained in chapter 9.

3. Compensation for Disturbance

3.27   The third head of compensation is 'disturbance' compensation. The historical origin of this head of compensation and its nature have been explained earlier in this chapter.[31] Its essence is that it is compensation for losses suffered by the landowner as a result of the acquisition of his land which would not figure in any ordinary assessment of the purchase price of that land and thus in the compensation under the first head. An obvious example is the cost to the owner of acquiring and moving to new premises. Most of the losses under this head can be described as 'disturbance' since they follow from the owner being disturbed in his physical possession of the land acquired. Even so the compensation payable is not confined to the effects of physical disturbance. The amount payable is now governed by the statutory language in rule (6) of section 5 of the Land Compensation Act 1961 which provides compensation for 'disturbance or any other matter not directly based on the value of land'. This formula has been applied by the courts to cover items which have nothing to do with the value of the land such as the costs to a claimant of preparing a claim for compensation and the temporary loss of profits when a business is removed from the land acquired to other premises at which it is restarted. The language of rule (6) is very general and it is difficult to find a clear dividing line between what can and cannot be claimed for compensation under this head. Clearly there must be some causal connection between the loss and the compulsory purchase of the land. Two questions which cause particular difficulty, and which are considered later in some detail, are: (a) when loss incurred prior to the entry by the acquiring authority onto the land acquired may be the subject of rule (6) compensation, and (b) whether the loss caused by the total cessation of a business can be brought within this head of compensation. This latter situation arises where land is acquired and a business is carried on at the land and as a result of the acquisition the business cannot be moved elsewhere and is therefore totally extinguished.[32] This head of compensation is explained in detail in chapter 8.

4. Statutory Additions to the Compensation

3.28   The fourth head of compensation is the current statutory additions to the compensation. When compensation was assessed under the Lands Clauses Consolidation Act 1845 by arbi-

---

[31] See para 3.15 where the origin of this head of compensation is explained as the second of the two aspects of the value to the owner principle.

[32] See section (h) of ch 4 for a discussion of this last situation.

trators and juries it became customary to add on a sum to take account of the fact that the purchase was compulsory. There seemed no logic in this and it was provided by rule (1) in section 2 of the Acquisition of Land (Assessment of Compensation) Act 1919 that there should be no addition or allowance made on account of the acquisition being compulsory. This rule has been continued in rule (1) of section 5 of the Land Compensation Act 1961. The position was to an extent reversed by later legislation which introduced rights to further payments. The further payments are basic loss payments, two varieties of occupier's loss payments, and home loss payments. These amounts are to be added to the compensation which would otherwise be payable. Some of the amounts so payable are worked out by reference to a percentage of the value of the interest acquired or are a sum which is related to the amount of land acquired.[33] This head of compensation is examined in chapter 11.

5. Injurious Affection: Section 10 of the Compulsory Purchase Act 1965

The fifth head of compensation is the most difficult to describe in summary form. Section 68 of the Lands Clauses Consolidation Act 1845 stated that compensation should be available in respect of any land 'which shall have been taken for or injuriously affected by the execution of the works' and for which no compensation had been paid under any other provisions of the Act. This provision was repeated in section 10 of the Compulsory Purchase Act 1965. It was thought for some time that this provision did not entitle an owner to make a reference to the Lands Tribunal in order to claim compensation for the land acquired since there were provisions elsewhere for the assessment of such a claim.[34] More recent authority suggests that the provision may authorise a claim for compensation for land taken.[35] However, that is a procedural question rather than the main question.   3.29

The real issue is what is meant by compensation 'for land injuriously affected by the works' and what are the limitations on a claim for such compensation. The works mean the works or undertaking authorised by the Act which confers the power of compulsory purchase. Following the 1845 Act the courts worked out a series of conditions which had to be satisfied before a claim for compensation for injurious affection could be sustained under this head. The conditions became sometimes known as 'the McCarthy rules' after a decision of the House of Lords in 1867.[36] The essence of the criteria is that compensation may be claimed for an injury to land (ie as opposed to a personal loss or injury) which arises due to the lawful carrying out of the works of the acquiring authority in circumstances where the carrying out of those works would constitute an actionable wrong, usually the commission of the tort of nuisance, if the works had not been authorised by statute. These same criteria are carried forward into the present provision for compensation under this head in section 10 of the Compulsory Purchase Act 1965. Compensation under this head may also be claimed where a right over the land acquired vested in some third party, such as a right of way or an easement of light over the land acquired or the right to enforce a restrictive cov-   3.30

---

[33] Land Compensation Act 1973, ss 29 and 33A–33I, the latter sections having been added by the Planning and Compensation Act 2004.
[34] *Horn v Sunderland Corporation* [1941] 2 KB 36.
[35] *Union Rlys Ltd v Kent County Council* [2009] EWCA Civ 363, [2009] 3 EGLR 68 (CA); [2008] 2 EGLR 153 (LT).
[36] *Metropolitan Board of Works v McCarthy* (1874) LR 7 HL 243.

enant against that land, is overridden by the power given under statute to carry out the works in question. Again this overriding of third party rights may result in an injury to the land to which the third party rights are appurtenant. There was for some time doubt over what link there had to be with a compulsory purchase before a claim could be sustained under section 10. It has now been established that in principle a person whose land has been injuriously affected by works carried out by an authority may recover compensation under section 10 provided the powers given to the authority to carry out the works included a power of compulsory purchase even though the land on which the works were carried out had not been compulsorily acquired and even though the powers of compulsory purchase had never been exercised in relation to any land.[37] This head of compensation is considered in detail in chapter 10.

6. Disturbance Payments

3.31   Turning to the sixth head of compensation, a person who is displaced from land as a result of the compulsory purchase of the land is entitled to compensation under one or more of the first four heads if at the time he had a proprietary interest in the land. It is therefore normally only freeholders, leaseholders, mortgagees, and the holders of equitable proprietary interests, who may claim compensation for the loss of their interest. In English law a person who is in possession of land nearly always falls into one of four categories. He may be the freeholder; he may hold under a lease; he may be a licensee; he may be a trespasser. The first two categories include mortgagees of freehold or leasehold interests. Persons in the first two categories have an entitlement to compensation if displaced (or, in the case of mortgagees, if the mortgage is discharged). Trespassers are by their nature acting unlawfully and have no right to compensation. Prior to 1973 a person lawfully in possession of land as a licensee who was disturbed as a result of the compulsory purchase of the freehold or leasehold interest in the land had no entitlement to compensation. His interest does not bind the acquiring authority since it is not a proprietary interest and he is not entitled to receive a notice to treat.[38]

3.32   This situation was considered to be unfair and today a person lawfully in possession of land, but without a compensatable interest who is displaced from land in consequence of a compulsory purchase of the land, may be entitled to a disturbance payment. The disturbance payment is the aggregate of the reasonable costs of moving from the land and the loss to be suffered by the disturbance of a trade or business carried on at the land by the person displaced. One of the occasions on which this entitlement to compensation is of importance is where the land acquired is owned by a company within a group of companies, so that that company is entitled to compensation for its interest, but a different company within the group is allowed to occupy the land without any formal lease. The company in occupation will normally be a licensee. Apart from the entitlement just described the company in occupation would not be entitled to compensation and no company in the group would be entitled to compensation for disturbance since the company owning the interest in land

---

[37] *Moto Hospitality Ltd v Secretary of State for Transport* [2007] EWCA Civ 764, [2008] 1 WLR 2822. See section (c) of ch 10.

[38] The nature of a proprietary interest in land is explained in ch 2, para 2.27.

was not in occupation and so was not disturbed and the company in occupation which was disturbed had no interest in land which entitled it to make any claim. It is in part this type of situation that the provisions in the Land Compensation Act 1973 regarding disturbance payments were designed to rectify.[39] Disturbance payments in the sense used in this head of compensation must be distinguished from compensation for disturbance under rule (6) of section 5 of the Land Compensation Act 1961 which is the third main head of compensation. The two heads of compensation are mutually exclusive since no claim can be made for a disturbance payment by someone who is entitled to compensation under other provisions and a person who is entitled to compensation under the first three main heads cannot be a mere licensee, that is the main category of persons entitled to disturbance payments. This head of compensation is examined in chapter 12.

7. Depreciation in the Value of Land Caused by the Use of Public Works

The last head of compensation was introduced by the Land Compensation Act 1973 and is   3.33
compensation for the depreciation in the value of an interest in land caused by the use of certain public works. It can occur that a new highway or railway or some other item of public works is constructed near to a person's property with a resultant reduction in the value of the property due to noise or other adverse effects of the scheme. In many cases no land of the person affected is acquired for the purposes of the scheme. Until 1973 a person suffering such a depreciation in the value of his land had no claim to compensation since no interest in his land was acquired and he was not disturbed from land. Nor was there normally a claim under the fifth head of compensation (section 10 of the Compulsory Purchase Act 1965) since the construction of a facility such as a highway was not a wrong in private law where a claim for damages was taken away by the fact that the scheme had statutory authority. The Land Compensation Act 1973 introduced a right to compensation for persons whose interest in land was decreased in value by the use of public works which were highway works, an aerodrome, or any other works provided or used in the exercise of statutory powers.[40] Only certain interests qualify for compensation. Freeholders and tenants with at least three years of the lease to run qualify where the property is occupied as a residence. Interests in other non-residential properties only qualify where the person holding such an interest is in occupation and the land is an agricultural unit or has an annual value which does not exceed a prescribed limit. In other words as regards commercial property persons in occupation of lower value properties are entitled to compensation but persons in occupation of higher value properties are expected to fend for themselves. This head of compensation is examined in chapter 13.[41]

---

[39] Land Compensation Act 1973, ss 37, 38. The existence of connected companies can sometimes raise the question of 'lifting or piercing the corporate veil' as something which may be relevant to the assessment of compensation: see section (b) of ch 12.

[40] Land Compensation Act 1973, Pt 1.

[41] There is a potential for overlap between: (a) a claim for compensation under Pt I of the Land Compensation Act 1973 as here described (depreciation in the value of land caused by the use of public works), (b) compensation for injurious affection to the retained land of a landowner a part of whose land is acquired (under s 7 of the Compulsory Purchase Act 1965 (head 2 above)), and (c) compensation for injurious affection to land caused by the execution of works (as opposed to the use of land) by the acquiring authority under s 10 of the Compulsory Purchase Act 1965 (head 5 above). There are provisions in the 1973 Act which aim to prevent any possibility of double compensation: see section (j) of ch 13.

(C) ENTITLEMENT TO COMPENSATION

3.34   A modern and comprehensive compensation code would state exactly what categories of persons were entitled to claim compensation under the various heads of compensation available. As it is the seven main heads of compensation which have been outlined derive from different statutory sources between 1845 and 2004.[42] In each case the categories of persons entitled to compensation can only be known from the statutory language and in some instances the substantial amount of case law which has followed the original enactments. A full description of the persons entitled to compensation under each head is provided when particular heads of compensation are discussed in later chapters. It is useful at this introductory stage to summarise the categories of persons who are entitled to claim compensation under each head provided of course that any particular person within a category can satisfy the various criteria which have to be satisfied in order to found a claim. In general the person claiming the compensation must own the interest in question at the valuation date although there are qualifications to this principle, such as the rule that an interest created with a view to obtaining compensation or increased compensation may be disregarded, and this subject is explained as the separate heads of compensation are explained in later chapters of the book.

3.35   The first and primary head of compensation is the value of the land acquired. The general principle is that any person is entitled to compensation for his interest in the land acquired if that interest is a proprietary interest and one which confers a present or potential future right to possession of the land. Interests which confer such a right are sometimes called corporeal, as opposed to incorporeal, interests.[43] The nature of a proprietary interest has been explained; in brief terms it means an interest in land which is capable of being enforced not only against the person who as the owner of the land created the interest but also against successors in title of that person.[44] Both legal and equitable interests in the land acquired can create an entitlement to compensation.[45] The following categories of persons are entitled to claim compensation under section 7 of the Compulsory Purchase Act 1965

---

[42] The first three heads of compensation derive originally from s 63 of the Lands Clauses Consolidation Act 1845 and decisions of the court following the enactment of that provision. Certain of the items of compensation in the fifth head were created by provisions inserted into the Land Compensation Act 1973 by the Planning and Compulsory Purchase Act 2004.

[43] See ch 2, para 2.26.

[44] See ch 2, para 2.27.

[45] For those unfamiliar with basic legal concepts a legal interest means an interest in land which the common law recognised as a proprietary interest whereas an equitable interest is a proprietary interest which was recognised by the Courts of Chancery under the general supervision of the Lord Chancellor. The fundamental difference was that a legal interest was binding on all persons who came to own the land affected whereas an equitable interest was binding on all such persons except a purchaser for value of a legal interest in the land without notice of the equitable interest. The importance of this distinction has today become much blurred by the system of registration of interests in land either as land charges, where the title is unregistered, or by notice on the register where the title is registered. For example, leases have been regarded as legal interests since at least the 15th century but the right to enforce a restrictive covenant is an equitable interest which derives from the decision in *Tulk v Moxhay* (1848) 2 Ph 774 in the mid-19th century. The word 'interest' is usually used to describe the types of rights in land which are proprietary rights in the sense just mentioned. Technically freehold and leasehold interests which exist at law are called 'estates' in land and are the only legal estates which can exist (together with certain types of mortgages). All other interests in land are properly called interests and can exist only in equity: see Law of Property Act 1925, s 1. A lucid and comprehensive account of the basic concepts of land law is found in the early chapters of *Megarry & Wade on the Law of Real Property*, 8th edn (London, Sweet and Maxwell, 2012).

(formerly section 63 of the Lands Clauses Consolidation Act 1845) for the acquisition of their interests in land in general accordance with these principles:

(a) Freeholders.
(b) Leaseholders, including sub-leaseholders.
(c) Mortgagees.[46]
(d) Owners of rentcharges.[47]
(e) Beneficiaries under trusts of land.[48]
(f) Owners of equitable interests such as the benefit of a specifically enforceable contract to purchase land or the holder of an option to acquire land.[49]
(g) Persons who have acquired or are in the process of acquiring title by a period of adverse possession.
(h) Persons with an interest in land when rights over that land, such as rights of way, are newly created and compulsorily acquired.[50]

Other proprietary interests do not qualify for compensation under the first head, although   3.36
compensation may be payable to the owners of these interests under other heads. Persons who do not qualify for compensation are mainly the owners of incorporeal interests in land, what are sometimes called third party interests. The following persons come within this category:

(a) The owners of easements over the land acquired such as rights of way.
(b) The owners of the benefit of restrictive covenants over the land acquired.
(c) Licensees.[51] A licence is not a proprietary interest in land.
(d) The owners of a right of pre-emption.[52]

The second head of compensation is compensation for injurious affection to land retained   3.37
by the owner when only a part of his land is acquired. This entitlement derives from section 7 of the Compulsory Purchase Act 1965 (formerly section 63 of the Lands Clauses Consolidation Act 1845). In principle any person who has an interest in the land acquired

---

[46] See section (m) of ch 2 where there is an explanation of the statutory procedure by which an acquiring authority can pay the compensation or a part of it to a mortgagee and secure the discharge of the mortgage.

[47] See section (m) of ch 2.

[48] The claim for compensation will normally be made by the trustees who will hold the compensation received on trust for the beneficiaries.

[49] The reason is that land includes an interest in land and that rights under a contract of sale or an option to acquire land are an interest in land: see *Oppenheimer v Minister of Transport* [1942] 1 KB 242, per Asquith J at pp 249–50; *Soper and Soper v Doncaster Corporation* (1964) 16 P & CR 53. The niceties inherent in the law can be seen from the fact that if a person owns land and has an option to acquire nearby land he is compensated for the value of his option if that land is compulsorily acquired, whereas if that same person has an easement or the benefit of a restrictive covenant over the nearby land his rights are overridden (but not extinguished) by the acquisition of the nearby land and the actions on that land by the acquiring authority, and he must look to a claim for compensation for injurious affection to his land under s 10 of the Compulsory Purchase Act 1965 (ie under the fifth head of compensation: see para 3.30).

[50] This last case involves compensation being payable under s 7 of the Compulsory Purchase Act 1965 for the acquisition of an incorporeal interest. The power to acquire newly created rights only exists where there is a specific statutory provision authorising such an acquisition: see section (c) of ch 2.

[51] See section (a) of ch 12. It was held in *Pennine Raceway Ltd v Pennine Metropolitan Borough Council* [1983] QB 382, [1982] 3 WLR 987, that a licensee was 'a person interested in the land' for the purposes of the right to compensation for the revocation of a planning permission under s 164 of the Town and Country Planning Act 1971.

[52] The owner of a right of pre-emption is probably not entitled to compensation since that right is not regarded as a proprietary interest in land at any rate until it is exercised.

and, as explained in the last two paragraphs, is entitled to claim compensation for the acquisition of that interest can also claim compensation for injurious affection to land retained by him under this second head. The interest of the claimant in the land acquired and in the land retained need not be the same interest.

3.38   The third head of compensation is compensation for disturbance or any other matter not directly based on the value of the land acquired. It derives from decisions following the enactment of the Lands Clauses Consolidation Act 1845 and now has statutory form in rule (6) of section 5 of the Land Compensation Act 1961. Again in principle any person who has an interest in the land acquired and, as explained earlier, is entitled to claim compensation under the first head can also claim compensation for disturbance under rule (6) of section 5 of the Land Compensation Act 1961. A person in possession or occupation of the land acquired as a licensee, and so without a proprietary interest, cannot assert a claim to compensation under rule (6). Such a person may be able to claim a disturbance payment under the sixth head of compensation.

3.39   The fourth head of compensation is that of statutory additions to the compensation and is derived from sections 29 and 30–33I of the Land Compensation Act 1973. The payments are home loss payments, basic loss payments, occupier's loss payments, and occupier's loss payments for agricultural land. The exact persons who can claim these additional payments vary between the three types of payment and are explained when additional statutory payments are described in chapter 11. It is only freeholders and lessees who can claim basic loss payments, occupier's loss payments and occupier's loss payments for agricultural land.

3.40   The fifth head of compensation is compensation for injurious affection under section 10 of the Compulsory Purchase Act 1965. This compensation is available where there is a power to effect a compulsory acquisition of land for a scheme and no land of the claimant is acquired but his land is in some way damaged by the works carried out by the acquiring authority as part of that scheme. The entitlement to compensation goes back to section 68 of the Lands Clauses Consolidation Act 1845 and the conditions which must be satisfied to create a claim to compensation were largely worked out by decisions of the court following the original enactment of this provision. In principle, and provided of course that he can satisfy the necessary conditions, any person with a proprietary interest in the land damaged is entitled to compensation for the damage to his interest.[53] As is explained in chapter 10 it is under this provision that compensation is claimable by persons who have some third party or incorporeal interest in the land acquired which is overridden by the compulsory purchase of that land, for example a right of way over the land or the right to enforce a restrictive covenant against the land. These third party rights over the land acquired do not give an entitlement to compensation under the first head of compensation, the value of the land acquired,[54] but do give a right to compensation for loss to the holders of these interests under section 10 of the Compulsory Purchase Act 1965.

3.41   The sixth head of compensation is disturbance payments under section 37 of the Land Compensation Act 1973. These payments are available to persons who have been disturbed from their lawful possession of the land acquired but who do not have a proprietary interest

---

[53] A person who holds only a licence, and thus not a proprietary interest in the land injuriously affected, is not entitled to compensation under s 10: *Moto Hospitality Ltd v Secretary of State for Transport* [2007] EWCA Civ 764, [2008] 1 WLR 2822.

[54] See para 3.36.

which would entitle them to compensation under the first three heads. It is generally licens-ees who are entitled to compensation under this statutory provision.[55]

The seventh head of compensation is compensation for depreciation in the value of land   3.42
caused by the use of public works in the vicinity of the land. This entitlement to compensa-tion, which does not depend upon a compulsory acquisition of the land of the claimant, was introduced by Part I of the Land Compensation Act 1973. Persons who qualify for compensation must hold what is called 'an owner's interest' which means either the legal fee simple or a tenancy granted or extended for a term of years of which at least three years remain unexpired at the date of the notice of the claim for compensation. Thus only free-holders and certain leaseholders are entitled to compensation under this head.[56]

It has been held that the right to compensation under section 68 of the Land Clauses   3.43
Consolidation Act 1845 (now section 10 of the Compulsory Purchase Act 1965) can be assigned together with the land to which it relates.[57] It seems that in principle other rights to compensation, such as the right to compensation following the service of a notice to treat or the making of a general vesting declaration, can be assigned. An interest in land which is the subject of a notice to treat can be sold and the right to compensation passes to the purchaser.[58]

[55] The nature and status of licences in law and the availability of compensation by way of disturbance payments are described in ch 12.
[56] For a fuller description see ch 13, para 13.17.
[57] *Dawson v Great Northern and City Rly* [1905] 1 KB 260. See ch 10, n 8.
[58] See ch 4, para 4.45.

4

The Value of the Land Acquired

(A) INTRODUCTION

4.1   It is scarcely surprising that when a piece of land is compulsorily acquired the primary component of the compensation due to the dispossessed owner is the value of that land. It is the value of his land that the owner has lost. The legal justification for this head of compensation is section 7 of the Compulsory Purchase Act 1965 which provides that 'regard shall be had . . . to the value of the land to be purchased by the acquiring authority'. This somewhat oblique language, which goes back to the Lands Clauses Consolidation Act 1845,[1] has always been taken to mean that the dispossessed owner is entitled to compensation for the value of the interest in land which is taken from him. A more precise stipulation of this aspect of the law is provided in rule (2) of section 5 of the Land Compensation Act 1961 which states that compensation shall be assessed in accordance with the rule that 'the value of land shall, subject as hereinafter provided, be taken to be the amount which the land if sold in the open market by a willing seller might be expected to realise'. There are important later provisions which qualify or elaborate this rule but it is necessary first to concentrate on the basic rule itself.

4.2   Certain aspects of the rule are apparent from the statutory language. There has to be envisaged an assumed or hypothetical sale of the land in the open market. There is, of course, no actual sale of the land in the market at the relevant time since the land is in reality being acquired by the acquiring authority. The assumed sale is by a willing seller. There is no express reference in rule (2) to a willing buyer. Each of these matters requires further consideration. It is necessary to consider the attributes of a hypothetical sale and the meaning of the sale being in the open market. The concept of a willing seller requires explanation, particularly the principle that the willing seller, like the sale itself, is hypothetical. He is a hypothetical person or corporate body and not a real person. It is necessary to assume a willing buyer in order to make sense of the operation of the basic rule. The willing buyer is also a hypothetical entity. A misunderstanding of these fundamental characteristics of the assumed sale in the market can lead to a wrong result in terms of the value of the land.

4.3   For the purposes of clarity a distinction must be made at the outset between the concepts of 'value' and 'worth'. The value of an asset is in essence the price which would be obtained if that asset was sold in the market. The value in this sense is the highest amount which some person or persons would be willing to pay to acquire the asset if it was being sold. It is something which can be determined largely objectively either by putting the asset on the market and seeing what people will pay or by evidence, usually from experts, of what price

---

[1] Lands Clauses Consolidation Act 1845, s 63.

would be paid for the asset if it was put on the market. The worth of an asset is a subjective concept which depends on the personal views of the owner, so that it may be quite different from the value of the asset as just described. To take a simple example, a person may own a family heirloom, say an item of antique furniture, of which there are other examples in existence so that it is known from recent sales of those other items that if this particular asset was put on the market it would fetch a price of, say, £10,000. However, the owner, because of its personal associations for him and his family, may have no wish to put the item on the market and would be unwilling to accept an offer of it for £10,000. Indeed he may even be unwilling in principle to accept any monetary offer. On the other hand, in the unlikely event that someone was willing to offer a far higher sum than the objective value of the asset which persuaded the owner to consider selling the asset, say £50,000, the owner might be persuaded to sell it at that price but not at any lower price. The worth of the asset can in these circumstances be said to be £50,000, the worth to the owner. The worth is then the subjectively ascertained lowest sum which the owner would insist on receiving before he would part with the asset in question. It is obviously different from the objectively ascertained value of the asset. If someone identifies a family heirloom, which he does not own but wishes for some reason to purchase, the effect may be the same although in this case the result of any negotiations may be influenced by whether the owner had any intention of selling the asset in any event and whether the reason for the interest of the purchaser was known to the owner.[2]

The assessment of the value of land for the purposes of compensation is different from an assessment of worth in the sense just explained. The assessment of the value of land is the determination of its value which, as explained, is in essence the amount which the land would realize if sold in the open market. That having been said the value of land in the sense of its open market value may on occasions be influenced by the worth which certain persons attribute to the land because those perceptions of worth may affect the amount which they are willing to offer to purchase the land. In the *Red Book* publication of the Royal Institution of Chartered Surveyors, referred to later, worth is defined as 'the value of an asset to the owner or a prospective owner, for individual investment or operational objectives'.[3]   4.4

It is sometimes argued that the anchoring of the concept of the value of land to that sum which someone in the market would pay for the land is incompatible with the principle of equivalence, the principle that a person dispossessed of his land should receive as compensation his true and full loss. It is not difficult to identify circumstances in which such a complaint might be made. A person who had lived in a property for a long time, or had some substantial personal attachment to that property and who had no wish to move from it or sell it, might well believe that the open market value of his property was not a full recompense for what he had lost in having to leave the property against his will. A person might have carried out improvements to a property to meet his own individual needs but   4.5

---

[2] In *Raja Vyricherla Narayana Gajapatiraju v Revenue Divisional Officer, Vizigapatam* [1939] AC 302, Lord Romer said at p 312: 'The land, for instance may have for the vendor a sentimental value far in excess of its "market value". But the compensation must not be increased by reason of any such consideration'. Worth to the owner is quite different to the concept of 'value to the owner'. The latter expression connotes a true value but one which is determined leaving out of account the effect on value of certain matters. It is explained in detail in ch 5.

[3] VS 3.4. The *International Valuation Standards 2011*, paras 37 and 38, state that 'Differences between the investment value of an asset and its market value provide the motivation for buyers and sellers to enter the market place'. The *RICS Valuation Professional Standards* (Red Book) (Royal Institution of Chartered Surveyors, 2014) also identifies 'worth' as 'investment value'. See also para 4.19 of this chapter.

finds that the costs of the improvements are not fully reflected in an increased price obtained for the property when put on the market. The owner is then denied the prospect of himself benefiting in further years from the full expense of the works which he has carried out. The compensation received will not take into account what landowners in the positions just described could reasonably regard as a loss to them.

4.6   A further instance of a species of loss which might not be fully reflected in the value of land is the expectation of making a profit in the future from the continuation of a commercial activity on the land. No doubt the anticipated profits would affect the mind of a prospective purchaser and would affect the price which he would pay for the land but that price is not necessarily the same as the present day value of the anticipated stream of future profits. The compensation will be the value of the land and not, if different, the capital value at the valuation date of the anticipated profits from the land. This last situation creates valuation questions of its own and is considered later.[4] The circumstances discussed in this paragraph may be seen as further illustration of the principle that compensation depends on the value of land, in the sense of the price which others would pay for it, rather than the worth of the land to the person who owns it.

4.7   It is possible that some of the items which can in a broad sense be considered to be a loss, but which are not a part of the value of the land and so cannot be a part of the compensation assessed under the present head, may be the subject of disturbance compensation.[5] Items such as removal expenses are recoverable as compensation for disturbance. The idea of worth is therefore not wholly alien to the law of compensation since a part of the worth of a piece of land to its owner may be that by continuing to own it and not disposing of it he avoids disturbance losses such as the costs of selecting and acquiring a new property and the removal costs just mentioned. However, disturbance compensation is a separate head of compensation and its availability does not detract from the general point that under the primary head of compensation, the value of the land acquired, there can be losses to the dispossessed landowner which are not reflected in or relevant to the value of the land assessed in the way in which that value has to be assessed. The absence of compensation for such items is in the end a matter of political or social policy. It would in any event be difficult to arrive at a sum of money which could reimburse a person for some of the losses mentioned, for instance the loss of a personal or sentimental pleasure in being able to continue to live in a much loved family residence, because of the subjective nature of any assessment of such losses.

4.8   This chapter is concerned with the legal principles which govern the assessment of the open market value of the land acquired as the primary component of compensation. There is no clear division between the legal principles and some aspects of the valuation process. Accordingly certain general matters pertinent to value are left for consideration in chapter 14 which covers the subject of valuation in more detail. An example is the well known *Stokes v Cambridge* principle, which is the principle that when the development or use of plot A is dependent on the acquisition of some right, such as a right of access, over plot B the owner of plot A will generally have to pay a part of the development value released by the exercise of the right to the owner of plot B in return for acquiring the right. The values of both plots

---

[4] See section (h) of this chapter.
[5] Disturbance and other compensation under r (6) of s 5 of the Land Compensation Act 1961 is explained in ch 8.

are affected by this situation. The value of plot A is obviously reduced by the fact that a purchaser of it would have to pay a substantial sum to the owner of plot B before he could realise the potential for development and thus the development value of plot A. Where plot B, often a small piece of land, has no value of its own except that of providing the access or other necessary rights to plot A it is sometimes called a ransom strip.[6]

In nearly all cases compensation is paid as a monetary sum. Certainly a determination of the compensation will be expressed as a monetary sum. It is open to the acquiring authority to agree with persons having an interest in the land being acquired that the consideration shall be 'in money or money's worth'.[7] A possible use of this power would be a provision to the landowner of other land in place of the land acquired from him. That other land would then be 'money's worth'.   4.9

It is possible in certain circumstances for an interest in land to have a 'negative value'. What is meant is that if the land were put on the market nobody would be willing to pay anything for it but that if the seller were willing to pay to the buyer a sum of money then a buyer might be found in return for that consideration. There are two obvious sets of circumstances in which this situation could arise. The most frequent situation is where a lease is subject to a rent which has become in excess of the market rent at the time. Rental values may fluctuate and the rental value of the property let may have gone down since either the date on which the lease was granted or the date on which the rent was fixed at a previous rent review. In such a case a buyer would require an inducement to take an assignment of the lease. The amount of money paid to a buyer in these circumstances may be called a negative premium. Another possible set of circumstances leading to the same situation is where land is contaminated and cannot be used until expensive works of decontamination are carried out and where there may arise a statutory liability to carry out such works. In any event, whatever the cause of the existence of a negative value for the purposes of compulsory acquisition, the compensation determined under rule (2) of section 5 of the Land Compensation Act 1961 cannot be a negative figure in the sense that a sum of money has to be paid to the acquiring authority. In the circumstances here considered no sum would be payable by the acquiring authority for the value of the interest acquired under rule (2) of section 5 of the 1961 Act.   4.10

(B) THE OPEN MARKET

The nature of the open market will be known to most people who have sold or bought a property and will be very familiar to those whose professional livelihood is concerned with property transactions. Every day many real transactions take place between sellers and buyers of property of all descriptions. The purpose of the hypothetical sale is to replicate so far as possible the circumstances that would exist if there was an actual sale in the open market of the property being valued so as to arrive at the price which would be paid for that property and thus its value. The theme which emerges from the authorities is that the valuer must assume that the parties to the hypothetical sale, the hypothetical seller and the   4.11

---

[6] See *Stokes v Cambridge Corporation* (1961) 13 P & CR 77, and see ch 14, para 14.12 et seq.
[7] Compulsory Purchase Act 1965, s 3.

hypothetical buyer, act in the same way as reasonable people buying and selling the property would have acted in a real sale. Certain obvious consequences flow from this starting point. It must be assumed that the property has been properly marketed or advertised to the extent that a property of the nature and size and position in question would be marketed or advertised if it was actually being sold. The degree and nature of assumed marketing will depend on the characteristics of the property being valued. The freehold interest in a large new office block in a city centre might be advertised in property publications and perhaps internationally whereas the marketing of a small terraced house might merit no more than a few lines in a local newspaper. At the present time the sale of flats in new blocks being developed in London is advertised in newspapers circulating in cities in the Far East. A reasonable period is to be assumed for negotiation and the preparation and weighing of bids. An expression which encapsulates this process is the 'higgling' of the market.[8]

4.12   The price which would be obtained for a property sold in the market is not normally affected by what the seller proposes to do after leaving the property or how he proposes to use the sum which he receives. It is provided that the amount of the compensation for a compulsory purchase is not to be reduced because the acquiring authority provides residential accommodation under any enactment for the person entitled to the compensation.[9] If a business is being carried on at the property acquired the compensation may be affected by whether the claimant for compensation relocates his business.[10]

4.13   The market in the sense used is not a physical location such as a cattle market; it is an abstract expression meaning the existence of persons who might be interested in buying the type of property being offered and the general circumstances, such as prevailing economic conditions, which affect the thinking of these persons and the sellers of such types of property. Inevitably the market will be influenced by the key factors of supply and demand. Various imprecise descriptions are often applied to the state of the market at any given time by valuers and others, for instance a 'strong' market which means that there are many purchasers wanting to acquire property of a particular type or a 'weak' market which means the opposite. In descriptions of it the market is traditionally judged from the economic viewpoint of sellers or landlords, not buyers or tenants, a method of description which is not confined to the property market.

4.14   The concept of an open market value means that in principle the whole world should be free to bid to acquire the property. The purpose of marketing is to bring the availability of the property to the attention of all those people who would be likely to show an interest in the acquisition of the property. Of course in practice the persons who would be interested in buying a particular property would be limited. The potential purchasers of a large piece of property available for acquisition as an investment or for development might include pension funds and firms of property developers but would be unlikely to include individuals of modest means. In a recent case when land available for industrial development in Hong Kong was to be valued, it was said that the land might produce a lively interest among developers in the area, so that the assumed marketing of it might be directed to persons in

---

[8] An alliterative description of the parties to the hypothetical transaction as 'happy hypothetical higglers' was suggested by Donaldson J in *Evans (FR) Leeds Ltd v English Electric Co Ltd* [1978] 1 EGLR, (1977) 36 P & CR 185.
[9] Land Compensation Act 1973, s 50(1).
[10] This matter is considered in detail in section (h) of this chapter.

that category.[11] In a sophisticated market discreet marketing, possibly to purchasers in a particular category or to no more than a small number, may take place. For the purposes of the hypothetical transaction marketing of any particular asset should be assumed to occur in the way in which it would be undertaken in an actual transaction relating to that asset, that is in such a way as to maximise the value of the asset being sold.

There is no prescribed mode of sale which has to be assumed to take place. The method of sale should be assumed to be that which would be thought likely to result in the highest price and this will vary in accordance with the type of property being notionally sold and valued. Perhaps the most frequent method of selling property is by ordinary advertisement and private negotiation. This is sometimes called a sale by private treaty. In some cases it may be thought that a property would realise the highest price if it was auctioned. In other circumstances a tendering process might be advisable with tenders invited from anyone or from selected persons invited to tender. A seller inviting a tendering process often states that he is not committed to accepting the highest tender. One of the duties of a valuer may be to indicate what mode of selling the property he would think the most appropriate for the property in question.   4.15

The real market in property does not often see a transaction agreed and concluded on a single day. The progress of the sale is much more stately particularly when large commercial properties are the subject of the transaction. A concluded transaction constituting the sale of a property may start with non-binding heads of terms between buyer and seller, that is an agreement on the main elements of the sale such as the price but which is not intended to have binding legal effect, then move to an enforceable formal agreement for sale often including standard terms, before concluding with the completion of the sale by the transfer of title and the payment of the purchase price or the balance of the purchase price if a deposit has been paid at the stage of the formal agreement. Even with sales of modest residential properties a period of several weeks will usually intervene between a meeting of minds on the price of the house and a binding contract of sale while a structural survey and other matters are proceeding, leading to the use of expressions by agents such as 'sold subject to contract'. The law of compensation is focused on a sale at a single and fixed valuation date. The question arises of what part of the transaction is to be taken to have occurred on that specific valuation date. In periods of stable prices a difference in date between heads of terms and ultimate completion of the transaction may not much matter but in times of rapidly moving property values the precise date may be more significant. If price levels are moving with the volatility of, say, 10 per cent per year a three month period over which a transaction takes place could alter the value of a property by 2.5 per cent. The correct answer to the question under discussion is that the hypothetical sale should be assumed to take place on the date at which the parties to it legally bind themselves to the sale so that the value of the property is that prevailing on that day. Where comparable transactions are used as an aid to valuation the 'effective date' of the transaction should be consistent with this approach unless there are special reasons to adopt a different approach. The effective date of a comparable transaction is therefore the date on which the parties to that transaction became legally bound to complete the transaction on the terms agreed. What this means is that if the earlier transaction is used as a guide to the value of the property acquired and   4.16

---

[11] *Penny's Bay Investment Co Ltd v Director of Lands* (2010) 13 HKCFAR 287 (Ct of Final Appeal, Hong Kong), per Lord Hoffmann at para 44.

being valued any adjustment for changes in the value of property, between the date of the comparable transaction and the valuation date for the property acquired, should be assessed over the period from the effective date for the comparable transaction and that valuation date.

4.17   The property valued will usually be a property which would be sold as one unit in the market to one buyer. In some cases a property might be sold in parts to a number of separate buyers with the expectation that the aggregate of the prices of the separate parts would be higher than the price which would be obtained on a sale of the whole property to one buyer. The assessment of value takes account of such a situation. The principle is that the property acquired is taken to be sold on one date by a hypothetical seller who holds the interest in the whole property as acquired by the acquiring authority but that the property can be assumed to be sold by way of a series of sales by that seller to a number of different hypothetical buyers in different lots if that is the way in which a seller would reasonably proceed with the aim of obtaining the highest overall price.[12] If there is some legal constraint to a division of the land at the valuation date then no sales in individual lots of the land acquired can be assumed.[13] However, a purchaser of the whole of the land will consider whether in the future he will be able to sell on the land divided into lots with appropriate consent and the value of the land as a whole may take into account that potential which would be perceived by the hypothetical willing buyer of the whole.[14] What cannot be assumed in circumstances such as those just described is that the hypothetical sales of the separate parts of the land acquired are phased, that is sold at different dates. There is only one valuation date, with a sale or series of hypothetical sales on that date, for the land acquired. Nor can it be assumed that different claimants with different land or interests in land put their land together in order to effect a single sale.

4.18   It is sometimes said, usefully and accurately, that the sale is hypothetical and the parties to the sale are hypothetical but that the market is real. What is meant is that there is no real sale between real parties, only a hypothetical sale between a hypothetical seller and a hypothetical buyer, but the milieu in which they operate is real. There is a real and existing market at the valuation date, and that real market contains real persons who would or might be in competition with the hypothetical buyer if the property had in truth been on the market. In other words the market is real and does not have to be assumed and the hypothetical sale is assumed to take place within that real market.

4.19   The Royal Institution of Chartered Surveyors publishes definitions and descriptions of various concepts involved in the valuation of property, the *RICS Valuation Standards*. This publication is often called the *Red Book*. The current edition defines 'market value' as:

> The estimated amount for which a property should exchange on the date of valuation between a willing buyer and a willing seller in an arm's length transaction after proper marketing wherein the parties had each acted knowledgeably, prudently and without compulsion.

---

[12] *Executors of Lady Fox v Inland Revenue Commissioners* [1994] 2 EGLR 185.

[13] *Maori Trustee v Ministry of Works* [1959] AC 1, [1958] 3 WLR 536. Land in New Zealand acquired by the Government at the valuation date required the consent of the Minister of Maori Affairs under the Land Subdivision of Counties Act 1946 in force in New Zealand before it could be sold in lots.

[14] Ibid. Of course the purchaser would make adjustments to the price he would pay for the whole of the land by reason of the risk of unforeseen costs, other contingencies, and the profit he would require from the transaction.

Subject to certain other matters which are mentioned elsewhere this is clearly a useful description of value and of the process to be carried out by valuers in arriving at value. [15] In previous editions of the *Red Book* that which was defined was 'open market value' as opposed to 'market value' and rule (2) of section 5 of the Land Compensation Act 1961 refers to 'the open market'. It seems unlikely that the inclusion or omission of the adjective 'open' makes any difference to the definition or to the end result of valuations carried out in accordance with the definition. Unless otherwise stated a market is an open market in the sense that anyone interested can be expected to be invited to bid and is entitled to bid for the property. Even so it is logical to assume that the seller adopts the method and extent of marketing which he believes or is advised will maximise the price obtained for the asset, so that if a limited and discreet marketing campaign would be likely in a real sale that sale process should be assumed for the hypothetical sale. [16] The best price reasonably obtainable is to be assessed within the open market although the method of sale which a hypothetical seller will adopt in order best to exploit that market may differ from property to property. It seems that the omission of the word 'open' in the most recent edition of the *Red Book* is in order to bring the definition into conformity with international standards.

(C) THE HYPOTHETICAL PARTIES

It has been said repeatedly in the authorities that the parties to the hypothetical sale are themselves hypothetical or notional. They are a hypothetical willing seller and a hypothetical willing buyer. This rule sometimes causes difficulty and is sometimes forgotten or ignored by valuers and others. The existence and nature of the rule must be explained since its application can affect the valuation process and the end result of the valuation. It is particularly important to note that the seller of the land is hypothetical and is not the actual owner whose land is taken by the acquiring authority. Thus, if the actual owner is the owner of adjoining or nearby land, he is not to be taken to be the hypothetical seller of the land being valued in his capacity as the owner of that land.[17] In English law persons who can own land and persons who are clothed by the law with rights and obligations are either real persons, that is real human beings or groups of human beings, or fictional or artificial persons (in latin *personae fictae*). A fictional person is a creation of the law, usually statutory law. The law states what are fictional persons and what are their attributes which will usually include the capacity to hold and deal in property. The most usual form of fictional persons is limited companies incorporated under the Companies Acts.[18] Fictional persons are

4.20

---

[15] VS 3.2. The *Red Book* concept of market value and the definition of value in r (2) of s 5 of the Land Compensation Act 1961 differ in one important respect which is that the *Red Book* (and the *International Valuation Standards*) in the explanation of value excludes any bid from a special purchaser. In valuations for the purposes of a compensation claim the existence and possible bid of a special purchaser is to be taken into account: see section (d) of this chapter.

[16] There may be occasions on which a property is best marketed by tenders being invited from a selected list of tenderers, as mentioned in para 4.14. However, a negotiation with a single purchaser to whom confidential information is given is not a sale in the open market: *Lynall v IRC* [1972] AC 680.

[17] *Abbey Homesteads Group Ltd v Secretary of State for Transport* [1982] 2 EGLR 198.

[18] See today the Companies Act 2006. A question which may be of importance in some compensation claims is whether it is permissible to ignore the separate existence as separate legal entities of associated companies within the same group of companies. There are only very limited circumstances in which the separate existence of associated companies can be ignored and when this is permissible it is said to be a lifting or piercing of the corporate veil. See section (b) of ch 12.

usually called corporate bodies and some corporate bodies have been created by Royal Charter. The real persons who collectively make up the corporate entity are called corporators, so that the shareholders of a company are its corporators. A corporation which has a number of corporators is called a corporation aggregate and a corporation which has only one corporator is called a corporation sole. In principle any entity can be a corporate body.[19] Local authorities are corporations aggregate and the Crown is a corporation sole. [20] The important fact about the nature of a hypothetical party is that he is not any actual real or fictional person. He is not Mr X or company Y. He is someone, whether real or fictional, who is an abstraction.

4.21   The purpose of envisaging the hypothetical sale as something which takes place between hypothetical parties is that it eliminates the effect on the price agreed for the sale of the individual characteristics or circumstances of particular persons. A particular person or company might have financial or other constraints which influence the price he or it would accept or pay for a property at the valuation date. A person trying to stave off difficulties due to a shortage of credit or due to having 'cash-flow' problems might be desperate to sell a particular property at a certain time to raise cash. The aim of the hypothetical parties rule is to avoid the effect on the value of the property caused by personal matters of this sort. It is said that the disinclination of the vendor to part with his land and the urgent necessity of the purchaser to buy must alike be disregarded.[21] Rent reviews under leases generally involve a hypothetical letting of property which is required in order to find the rental value of the property at the rent review date and a classic definition of the nature of a hypothetical landlord is found in a passage from a judgment of Donaldson J in that context. It is said that a willing lessor is not affected by personal characteristics which may affect actual lessors, such as a cash-flow problem or importunate mortgagees. He is not someone to whom it is a matter of indifference whether he lets the premises on the valuation date, so that he is ready to wait for the market to improve. Nor is he to be taken as someone who is desperate to let at once, as might a person who could only stave off bankruptcy by a quick letting. He is someone who wants to let the premises at a particular time at a rent which is appropriate to all the factors which affect the marketability of premises of the particular category into which they fall, for example geographical location, the extent of the local labour market, the availability of local services and the market rent of competitive premises, that is other premises which would be considered as viable alternatives by a potential tenant.[22] This description may be aptly applied with minor amendments to the notion of a hypothetical willing seller of property. A willing seller has also been described as someone who is prepared to sell the property providing a fair price is obtained in all the circumstances.[23] It does not mean someone who is an anxious seller, that is someone who is prepared to sell at any price and

---

[19] For example it has been said that a Hindu Temple recognised by the law of Tamil Nadu can be a party to proceedings in an English court although it would not itself have legal personality in English law: see *Bumper Development Corporation Ltd v Metropolitan Police Commissioner* [1991] 1 WLR 1362.

[20] Local Government Act 1972, s 2(3); *Willion v Berkley* (1559) 1 Plowd 223, at pp 242, 250.

[21] *Raja Vyricherla Narayana Gajapatiraju v Revenue Divisional Officer, Vizagapatam* [1939] AC 302, per Lord Romer at p 312.

[22] *Evans (FR) Leeds Ltd v English Electric Co Ltd* [1978] 1 EGLR 93, (1977) 36 P & CR 185, per Donaldson J. The judgment of Donaldson J was approved by the Court of Appeal without significant comment. See also *Walton v Commissioners of Inland Revenue* [1996] STC 68, per Peter Gibson LJ at p 83 (a valuation of property for the purposes of capital transfer tax).

[23] *Inland Revenue Commissioners v Clay* [1914] 3 KB 466, per Pickford LJ at p 478.

on any terms. It has also been said that a willing seller is someone who is willing to sell and is deemed to do as well in his sale as a willing seller would reasonably be expected to do.[24]

The definition of value in rule (2) of section 5 of the 1961 Act does not refer to a willing buyer. Nonetheless a buyer has to be assumed to exist since otherwise there could be no hypothetical sale, and that buyer is taken to be a willing buyer.[25] That willing buyer may be regarded as a hypothetical person actively seeking premises to fulfil needs which the premises being valued could fulfil. He will take account of similar factors to those taken into account by the willing seller, and he will also be unaffected by liquidity problems or other personal characteristics which might affect any actual person or corporate body.[26]

4.22

The central characteristic of both of the hypothetical parties is that they act reasonably. The hypothetical seller is a reasonable person who goes about the sale as a prudent man of business would and who negotiates seriously without giving the impression of being over-anxious or unduly reluctant to sell. He is not desperate to sell the property but nor is he someone who will simply refuse to sell or who will put off the sale unless he gets exactly what he desires in terms of price. The hypothetical buyer is also taken to act reasonably and is someone who makes proper enquiries about the property and does not appear over-anxious to buy it.[27] In a sentence both parties are sensible and reasonable people unaffected by personal circumstances and characteristics who wish to reach agreement and do so but each does all that is reasonable to obtain what for him is the most favourable result he can reasonably obtain, that is the highest or lowest price depending on his interest and his viewpoint.

4.23

It does not follow that because both parties to the sale are abstractions they do not have certain characteristics. The purchaser of a large industrial estate or a modern office block is unlikely to be an individual and much more likely to be an institution such as a pension fund or a bank. In such a case the hypothetical buyer can be regarded as such an entity but cannot be a particular named company in this field. What must be left out of account are not the general circumstances which would apply to most possible purchasers of the property in question, but the particular circumstances which might apply to some particular named purchaser. It is obviously the case that the hypothetical seller is someone who holds the whole of the interest in property and all of the rights which he is taken to be selling and who has the capacity to sell that interest and those rights.[28]

4.24

It has been explained that the price which determines the value of the land acquired is that which would be paid for the land by a hypothetical willing buyer. The hypothetical willing buyer is taken to be in competition with those actual persons who would have been in the market for the land and would have bid for it had the land actually been sold at the

4.25

---

[24] *Priestman Collieries Ltd v Northern District Valuation Board* [1950] 2 KB 398, (1949–51) 1 P & CR 131.

[25] *Railtrack Plc v Guinness Ltd* [2003] 1 EGLR 124. This situation was considered by the Court of Appeal in *Dennis & Robinson Ltd v Kiossos Establishment* (1987) 54 P & CR 382, [1987] 1 EGLR 133, in which a rent review clause in a lease referred to a willing landlord but not to a willing tenant. It was held that a willing tenant must be assumed to exist since otherwise there could not be the hypothetical letting necessary for the operation of the rent review clause. The same reasoning applies to the hypothetical sale which establishes the capital value of a property.

[26] *Evans (FR) Leeds Ltd v English Electric Co Ltd*, above n 22.

[27] *Executors of Lady Fox v Inland Revenue Commissioners* [1994] 2 EGLR 185.

[28] The nature of the property sold may mean that certain characteristics have to be attributed to the hypothetical parties. In *Railtrack Plc v Guinness Ltd* [2003] 1 EGLR 124 that which had to be valued was a right of access over railway lines. In these circumstances it was correct to take account of the fact that the hypothetical willing seller would necessarily be a railway company.

valuation date. It follows that the hypothetical willing buyer must offer an amount which exceeds, or is at least equal to, that which any other person would have offered to acquire the property. The difficulty is that when a number of people are bidding against each other to acquire a property in most instances no bidder knows how much his rivals have offered or will offer. The hypothetical seller is in most cases unlikely to tell any of the bidders what others have offered since his interest is to play bidders off against each other and usually his best way of doing so is to leave each of them in the dark as to the bids of his competitors. This might not always be the case and a seller might in some circumstances release information about one bid to another prospective purchaser. The information so released might not be complete and might be part of a process of playing one bidder off against another. All of this is part of the interplay or 'higgling' of the market. Since the hypothetical willing buyer has to make a bid which is at least as high as anyone else in order to acquire the land logic suggests that he might carry out the exercise of estimating what he thinks others are likely to bid and then add a margin to the highest amount which he thinks anyone else would bid in order that he may have a good chance of acquiring the property. Therefore if the view of the valuation experts is that a range of offers for a particular property from real persons who would be in the market would be, say, £1.8 million to £2 million logic suggests that the hypothetical willing buyer, doing the same exercise and receiving the same expert advice, would bid, say, £2.1 million in order to allow himself a margin of 5 per cent with a view to becoming the highest bidder and securing the purchase. In reality this aspect of the logic is not generally followed through and it is assumed that the hypothetical willing buyer offers no more than the highest bid which a real person who was in the market would have offered. The rule which requires that the buyer is a hypothetical entity should be borne particularly in mind when there would be a special purchaser, that is someone with a special interest in acquiring the property, who would bid in the market if the property being valued was offered for sale. The buyer is not the special purchaser, who is a real person, but a hypothetical willing buyer who must of necessity offer as much as the special purchaser would offer in order to acquire the property.

4.26   The process of the valuation of most assets, including interests in land, proceeds by way of a hypothetical transaction between hypothetical parties. Indeed it is difficult to see how the value of a property could be found by any other means unless it was actually exposed to the market. The matters explained in previous paragraphs are therefore common to most valuations of property whether the valuation is required by virtue of statute or by virtue of a contract. As mentioned the principles which govern the nature of the hypothetical sale and the hypothetical parties apply to the frequent case of valuations required to operate rent reviews under leases. Other major statutory instances of the same basic principles are valuations required under Part II of the Landlord and Tenant Act 1954 in order to determine the rent payable under a new tenancy of business premises ordered to be granted by a court.[29] A similar hypothetical transaction occurs as the rating hypothesis for the purposes of determining rateable values, that is an assumed annual letting of the property.[30] There are slight differences in the words used in the governing statute; for instance the Landlord and Tenant Act 1954 refers to a willing lessor but not a willing lessee and the rating hypothesis has no

---

[29] See s 34(1) of the Landlord and Tenant Act 1954 in which it is stated that the rent to be determined by the court is that 'at which, having regard to the terms of the tenancy (other than those relating to rent), the holding might reasonably be expected to be let in the open market by a willing lessor'.
[30] See para 2(1) of sch 6 to the Local Government Finance Act 1988.

reference to a willing lessor. It is doubtful whether any of these nuances makes a difference to the valuation process. What, however, is critical is the terms and circumstances of the hypothetical transaction which are to be assumed and the reference to matters which are to be disregarded. For instance the rating hypothesis requires the assumption of a letting on an annual periodic tenancy and the Landlord and Tenant Act 1954 requires that certain matters are to be left out of account in the valuation such as improvements which have been carried out by a tenant. The most important adjustment in determining the open market value of land for the purposes of compensation is that there has to be a disregard of the effect on value of certain development, or of the prospect of certain development, in the locality attributable to the scheme of the acquiring authority, and this is an important subject of its own dealt with later.[31]

(D) A SPECIAL PURCHASER

The designation of a person as a special purchaser is a valuer's description well known in the market. A special purchaser is a person who wishes to acquire a particular property and has a special reason for doing so which is not shared by the generality of the market. There is no limit to the factors which can give rise to the special reason. A frequent factor is that the purchaser owns adjoining property or some other interest in the property in which he is seeking to buy an interest. An obvious illustration is where plot A is for sale and the owner of adjoining plot B wishes to acquire plot A because it would provide him with a much better access to a public highway than is presently enjoyed by plot B or because he wishes to extend his use into plot A in a way which would not be possible with a different property acquired. Another obvious case is where the freehold of a property is being sold and a tenant has a special reason for acquiring it because of his occupation of the property. A person may be a special purchaser because of some personal wish to acquire the property such as a sentimental attachment felt for the property due to his past association with it.

4.27

The position of a special purchaser in the first two illustrations given in the last paragraph also gives rise to the allied concept of marriage value. The combination of the ownership of plots A and B in one person in the first example may result in a combined value of the two plots which is greater than the aggregate of the value of each of the plots if sold or valued separately. Equally a freehold unencumbered by a lease may have a greater value than the aggregate of the values of the freehold subject to the lease and of the lease.[32] The difference between the value of the two pieces of land, or the two interests in the same piece of land when combined, and the aggregate of the values of the two pieces of land or the two interests when in separate ownerships is said to be the marriage value.

4.28

---

[31] See s 6 and sch 1 to the Land Compensation Act 1961, explained in detail in ch 5.

[32] When the same person acquires the freehold and the leasehold interests in property the two interests are said to merge so as to result in a freehold unencumbered by the lease. Obviously this situation may occur in three ways in that the freeholder may acquire the lease or the leaseholder may acquire the freehold or one person may acquire both of the interests. In the first case the lease is usually said to be surrendered and so to determine by reason of its surrender. In the second and third cases the two interests are said to merge. It is possible to avoid the merging of the two interests by including in the transaction a declaration against merger, that is a statement that no merger is intended. In those circumstances the two interests remain separate but vested in the same person.

4.29   The existence of a known special purchaser for a property is likely to increase the value of that property. The special purchaser may be willing to pay a higher price for the property than would others in the market because of his special reason for wishing to acquire it. Others may be willing to offer higher prices than they otherwise would because of their need to outbid the special purchaser if they are to be the successful purchaser of the property. The effect on value of a special purchaser (or special purchasers) therefore depends on: (a) how strong is the reason of the special purchaser for wishing to acquire the property, and (b) the extent to which his special reason for wishing to acquire the property is known (or believed to be known) to the seller and to others who may be in the market. If there is some particular matter known to a potential purchaser which makes the property of special value to him, but which is not known to the hypothetical seller and is not known generally in the market, the logical conclusion is that that factor and the aspirations of the potential purchaser who knows of it should not affect the open market value of the property. The reason is that the hypothetical willing buyer, who is assumed to buy the property, will not know of the particular factor so that that factor and the position of the person who knows it cannot affect the minds of the hypothetical willing seller and the hypothetical willing buyer and so cannot affect the amount which they agree upon as the purchase price.

4.30   The rule of law is that in valuing land the existence or possible existence of a special purchaser in the market is to be taken into account, and so may in principle increase the value of the land being valued and hypothetically sold, unless there is some provision in the statute or contract which brings about the need for the hypothetical sale which excludes the effect on value of a special purchaser or of some category of special purchaser. There is no exclusion of the existence or effect on value of a special purchaser in rule (2) of section 5 of the Land Compensation Act 1961 or elsewhere in the current compensation legislation.[33] Consequently in valuations for the purpose of assessing compensation the existence and effect of a special purchaser have to be taken into account.

4.31   The principle may be illustrated by a decision of the Court of Appeal in 1914. Under section 25(1) of the Finance (1909–10) Act 1910 the value of land had to be ascertained as the amount which it might be expected to realise if sold at a particular time in the open market by a willing seller. The property being valued was a house which would have sold for £750 as an ordinary private residence. It had next to it a nurses' home the owners of which had a special reason for acquiring the property being hypothetically sold since they could combine it with their nurses' home. The owners of that adjoining property would have been prepared to pay £1,000 for the house. It was held that the existence of the owners of the nurses' home and their position as a special purchaser had to be taken into account with the result that the value of the property, assessed in accordance with the statutory formula, was £1,000.[34]

---

[33] As enacted in 1961 r (3) of s 5 of the Land Compensation Act 1961 required that no account should be taken of 'the special needs of a particular purchaser'. This part of the rule was repealed by the Planning and Compensation Act 1991. The words so removed were in the statutory predecessor of r (3) which was r (3) of s 2 of the Acquisition of Land (Assessment of Compensation) Act 1919. They were included in that Act following the recommendation of the Scott Committee (see ch 1, para 1.11) that the decision of the Court of Appeal in *Inland Revenue Commissioners v Clay* [1914] 3 KB 466 (see para 4.31) should not be applied to the law of compensation.

[34] *Inland Revenue Commissioners v Clay* [1914] 3 KB 466. The legislation was connected with the controversial land tax introduced by the then Chancellor of the Exchequer, Lloyd George. See also *Raja Vyricherla Narayana Gajapatiraja v Revenue Divisional Officer, Vizagapatam* [1939] AC 302 where Lord Romer said at p 312: 'This is implied in the common saying that the value of the land is not to be estimated as its value to the purchaser. But

The correct approach to valuation under the provision in the 1910 Act, and in rule (2) of   4.32
the Land Compensation Act 1961 which is in substance in the same terms, is to be compared with other statutory provisions where the effect on value of a special purchaser is
excluded. An example of a special purchaser mentioned above was that of a tenant in occupation of property who might have a special reason for acquiring the freehold and might
pay a higher value than would some outside purchaser. In section 34(1)(a) of the Landlord
and Tenant Act 1954 it is provided that when the open market rent of business premises is
assessed there shall be disregarded 'any effect on rent of the fact that the tenant has or his
predecessors in tile have been in occupation of the holding'. This provision therefore
excludes the effect on value of the type of special purchaser just mentioned. An excellent
illustration of the existence and the importance of a special purchaser when valuing
property is the early progress of leasehold enfranchisement introduced by the Leasehold
Reform Act 1967. In section 9 of that Act, as originally enacted, the sum which the tenant
was required to pay in order to acquire the freehold of the property was the amount which
that freehold might be expected to realise if sold on the open market by a willing seller.
Since there was no provision excluding the tenant himself from those persons who might
bid in the market for the freehold the position of the tenant as a special purchaser had to be
taken into account and so could increase the value of the freehold above that which it would
have been if the existence of the tenant in the market was excluded.[35] As a result of this
an amendment was introduced with retrospective effect by the Housing Act 1969 which
provided that when applying the statutory hypothesis the tenant and members of his
family were to be taken not to be buying or seeking to buy the freehold. Later legislation in
this area has contained further amendments such that when the tenant claims benefits
under the legislation the marriage value has to be divided equally between landlord and
tenant.

It will, of course, be a matter of evaluating expert valuation evidence to decide in any par-   4.33
ticular case whether a person would be in the market as a special purchaser and how the
existence of that person would affect the value of the land being hypothetically sold. These
matters are referred to again in the chapter on valuation,[36] but one point of principle may
be clarified here. It might be suggested that the existence of a special purchaser would have
only a minimal effect on value because the special purchaser would be willing to pay only a
very small amount above that which the highest other potential purchaser would pay in
order to secure the property. It has been said that this is a fallacy and ignores what is common experience. The 'one small extra bid' theory assumes that when the value of a property
without the existence of a special purchaser has been reached everybody except the special
purchaser will decline to make any further offer. This theory ignores two factors which in
reality occur. One is that the special purchaser does not know how much others are willing
to pay for the property and so cannot make his bid just one step above that of other potential purchasers if he is to be sure of acquiring the property. The other factor is that there may

---

this does not mean that the fact that some particular purchaser might desire the land more than others is to be
disregarded. The wish of a particular purchaser, though not his compulsion, may always be taken into consideration for what it is worth'. See also *Waters v Welsh Development Agency* [2004] UKHL 19, [2004] 1 WLR 1304, per
Lord Brown at p 1341.

   [35]   *Custins v Hearts of Oak Benefits Society* [1969] RVR 58.
   [36]   See ch 14.

well be in the market speculators who will buy the property with a view to selling it on later, at a hoped for profit, to the person in the position of the special purchaser.[37]

(E) THE VALUATION DATE

1. General Principles

4.34   It is not possible to carry out a coherent valuation of land, or indeed of any other asset, without a specified valuation date. The reason is the obvious one that the value of land can and does change over time, sometimes fairly rapidly, so that its value on one date may be significantly different from its value on an earlier or later date which might be only a few months apart from the first date.[38] Values for the type of land being valued may be changing generally due to economic fluctuations or differences in the level of supply and demand for such property. General indices of prices are published by the Government such as the Retail Price Index (RPI) and the Consumer Price Index (CPI), the latter being thought to be a more accurate indicator of general inflation since it does not include changes in the prices of certain items said to be subject to large and temporary fluctuations.[39] Specific indices of land values such as residential property or office rents are prepared by firms of surveyors and commercial organisations, often with a division into localities.[40] There are three general factors which may bring about or contribute to changes in land values over a period of time. They are the effect of general inflation, particular changes in the property market for the type of land in question (including changes in supply and demand), and events which affect the value of a particular property such as the opening of a new road near to it or more general planning or fiscal matters.

4.35   The existence of price fluctuations for land generally is not the only reason for the need to select a specific valuation date. The value of a particular piece of land may be greatly affected by particular external events and circumstances. It may be crucial for valuation purposes to

---

[37] The situation discussed was analysed by Pickford LJ in *Clay v Inland Revenue Commissioners*, above n 33, in which he concluded: 'I do not think that the effect of the needs of a probable purchaser can be confined to the amount of one bid which will take the offer above the bare dwelling-house value. The effect on the market of such a probable purchaser is a matter to be estimated by the referee'. If a property is being sold, or is assumed to be sold, at an auction the situation may be rather different since the special purchaser will then be aware of the next highest bid which he will have to beat. As mentioned in para 4.29 the position may also be different where the special factor which induces a particular purchaser to be willing to pay more than other purchasers in the market is something known only to him and is not known to other potential purchasers or to the hypothetical willing seller or to the hypothetical willing buyer.

[38] The value of other assets such as equities or financial instruments may fluctuate even more rapidly so that when a value is required it may be necessary to specify not only the day but the precise time within the day by reference to which the value is to be ascertained.

[39] The Retail Price Index was first calculated for June 1947. It was sometimes calculated as RPIX, which was an index excluding mortgage interest payments. The Consumer Price Index is less broadly based and excludes, for example, mortgage interest and buildings insurance. The CPI is calculated as the geometric mean of prices whereas the arithmetic mean is used for the RPI and it is this difference which is said to be a main reason for the CPI being generally lower than the RPI. The RPI was rebased at 100 in January 1987 and now stands at over 200. The CPI is now used for purposes such as setting the level of welfare benefit payments.

[40] For example, the office market in Central London is often divided into the City and the West End, sometimes with an intermediate area called 'Mid Town'. Sometimes even smaller geographical areas have their own indices of value such as Victoria or Mayfair within the West End.

know whether some event had occurred before the valuation date or was anticipated at the valuation date. This question can only be answered if a valuation date is specified. It is a truism to say that the hypothetical purchaser in a land transaction cannot be influenced by events of which he knows nothing. One reason why the parties cannot know of an event is that the event is in the future. Another reason might be that at the valuation date an event had occurred and so was known to some people such as the owner of a particular interest in land, but was not known in the market generally, and so cannot have affected the minds of potential purchasers of the asset in the market. An example of such an event might be a decision of the owners of the asset to behave in a certain way or some discovery which had been made, such as the existence of a mineral under the land or a new technological process, but which was not generally known.[41]

It should be stressed that even though an event had not occurred at the valuation date if that event was anticipated then that anticipation may have affected the market. Of course any anticipation may or may not turn out to be the reality as time passes. What is important is not whether that which was anticipated at the valuation date actually occurs or not but rather what was the anticipation of it at the valuation date and how that anticipation would have affected the minds of the persons involved in the hypothetical sale and so would have affected the price which is taken to have been agreed for the property being sold.[42] The subject here being considered is the valuation of land and not the assessment of damages. The different rules which govern these two quite different exercises are of considerable importance and this subject is considered under the next section in this chapter. An exception to the principle that post-valuation date events cannot be taken into account in the valuation process is that regard may be had to comparable transactions which occur after as well as before the valuation date. This is a separate topic and is referred to in chapter 14 on valuation.[43]   4.36

2. Ascertainment of the Date

Until recently the statutory provisions on compensation did not state what was the valuation date. About a century and a half ago in 1868 the question was considered and the rule   4.37

---

[41]   See, eg *Lynall v Inland Revenue Commissioners* [1972] AC 680, [1971] 3 WLR 759. For this reason past financial and operating details of a business carried out on land will not normally be admitted in evidence when that land is being valued unless that information was publicly or generally available: *Cornwall Coast Country Club v Cardgrange Ltd* [1987] 1 EGLR 146 (trading records of Crockfords Casino). See para 4.29 for a consideration of when some particular fact relevant to the amount which he is willing to pay for the land is known to a particular person who might be in the market but is not known to the hypothetical willing seller and is not known in the market generally. There is a full discussion on the subject matter of this paragraph and the relevant authorities in issues 1–3 of volume 13 (2009) of *Landlord and Tenant Review* by Barnes and Bignell.

[42]   A vivid example of this principle is the decision of the Court of Final Appeal in Hong Kong in *Penny's Bay Investment Co Ltd v Director of Lands* (2010) 13 HKCFAR 287, in which the value of land had to be ascertained at a date in 1995 at which it was anticipated that the land would be near to a new container port expected to be built and details of which had been published. In fact the container port project was abandoned a few years after the valuation date and the land became used as an amusement park. It was held that, for the purposes of assessing compensation for injurious affection to the land caused by the removal of its access to the sea pursuant to a scheme of land reclamation, the value of the land at the valuation date had to be assessed taking account of the then anticipated container port project even though by the time the compensation came to be assessed it was known that no container port was ever built.

[43]   See para 14.24 of ch 14.

laid down was that the scheme of the legislation was that every interest was to be valued *'rebus sic stantibus,* just as it was when notice to treat was given'. Thus the date of the giving of notice to treat to the owner of the interest in land acquired became established as the valuation date in respect of that interest.[44] This principle was considered to be the law and was applied for about a century. The question was re-considered by the House of Lords in 1970 in the context of the acquisition of a chapel.[45] The basis of compensation in that case was the cost of equivalent reinstatement under rule (5) of section 5 of the Land Compensation Act 1961.[46] The cost of reinstatement had risen by nearly 60 per cent between the date when notice to treat was served in 1947 and the date when reinstatement became possible in 1961. It was held that the cost of reinstatement should be assessed as that on the date when rein-statement could reasonably have been started. The majority of the House considered that where, as in most cases, rule (2) of section 5 provided the basis of compensation, the valu-ation date for determining the value of the land acquired should be the earlier of the date on which possession of the land was taken by the acquiring authority and the date on which the compensation was assessed by the Lands Tribunal. This became the generally accepted and applied rule.[47] It is possible that the compensation is assessed by the Tribunal before possession is taken since there may be a reference to the Tribunal following the service of notice to treat even though possession has not then been taken. In practice, in the great majority of cases, possession has been taken before compensation is assessed by the Tribunal so that the date of possession became the normal valuation date under rule (2). There would, of course, be great difficulties in selecting a valuation date which was later than the date on which the assessment was carried out since the persons carrying out the valuation would then have to try to guess the state of the market and other events at a future date.

4.38   Statute finally intervened in 2004 when a new section 5A was added to the Land Compensation Act 1961 by the Planning and Compensation Act 2004. Section 5A contains a series of rules on the ascertainment of the valuation date. The rules generally follow those which had been worked out by the courts and, apart perhaps from tidiness, not a great deal seems to have been gained by the enactment of the statutory provision. Nonetheless the statutory rules now constitute the law on the subject of the valuation date when the value of land is to be assessed under rule (2) of section 5 of the Land Compensation Act 1961. The statutory rules govern only the assessment of compensation under rule (2) and do not apply to any other area or head of compensation or its assessment.[48]

[44] *Penny v Penny* (1868) LR 5 Eq 277, per Page-Wood V-C. The expression *'rebus sic stantibus'* is a latin ablative absolute meaning 'as matters stood'. There appears to be some doubt over whether the statement made by Page Wood V-C was correctly reported: see the opinion of Lord Morris in the *West Midland Baptist* decision cited in the next footnote, at pp 906–07.
[45] *West Midland Baptist (Trust) Association v Birmingham Corporation* [1970] AC 874, [1969] 3 WLR 389.
[46] Equivalent reinstatement is explained in section (a) of ch 6.
[47] *W & S (Long Eaton) Ltd v Derbyshire County Council* (1976) 31 P & CR 99 (CA).
[48] The rules as to the valuation date under s 5A do not affect any express provision in any other enactment which requires the valuation of land subject to compulsory acquisition to be made at a particular date and do not affect the valuation of land for purposes other than the compulsory acquisition of that land (even if the valuation is to be made in accordance with the rules in s 5): see s 5A(8). An example of the second category of case is s 4(4)(b) of the Land Compensation Act 1973 relating to compensation payable for the depreciation of the value of land caused by the use of public works where the valuation date is one year after the public works first came into use (see ch 13). The rules do not apply to the assessment of the cost of equivalent reinstatement under r (5) of s 5 of the Land Compensation Act 1961: see section (a) of ch 6. Nor do they apply to the assessment of compensation for severance or injurious affection to the retained land of an owner when only a part of his land is acquired under the second limb of s 7 of the Compulsory Purchase Act 1965 although that compensation is generally assessed by car-rying out valuations of the land at the date of entry onto the land acquired as explained in ch 9.

The statutory rule is that when the land is the subject of a notice to treat the valuation date   4.39
is the earlier of: (a) the date when the acquiring authority enters on and takes possession of
the land, and (b) the date when the assessment is made.[49] When the land is the subject of a
general vesting declaration the valuation date is the earlier of: (a) the vesting date, and (b)
the date when the assessment is made.[50] An acquiring authority has the right to enter and
the possession of the land being acquired on the vesting date by reason of section 8(1) of
the Compulsory Purchase (Vesting Declarations) Act 1981 but of course may not actually
do so until a later date. The valuation date is still the vesting date.[51] It is therefore not totally
accurate to say that the valuation date is always the date when possession is taken by the
acquiring authority. The valuation date may be different from the date of possession: (a)
when compensation is assessed by the Lands Tribunal before possession of the land is taken
by the acquiring authority, and (b) where there is a vesting date under the general vesting
declaration procedure and possession is not taken until a date after the vesting date. It may
be necessary to know what precisely is the date when the assessment is made by the Lands
Tribunal for the purposes of the above rules. The principle is that an assessment of compensation by the Tribunal is treated as being made on the date certified by the Tribunal as either
the last hearing date before it makes its determination or, if the case is to be determined
without an oral hearing, the last date for making written submissions before it makes its
determination.[52]

It is possible that an acquiring authority enters on and takes possession of the land by   4.40
stages. This situation is provided for by the rule that if the authority enters on and takes
possession of part of the land specified in a notice of entry, or in respect of which a payment
into court has been made, the authority is deemed for present purposes to have entered on
and taken possession of the whole of the land on that date.[53]

It may be necessary to define with some precision what exactly amounts to an entry and   4.41
taking possession of land for present purposes. What constitutes entry will depend on the
circumstances of each case but the general principle is that, in the absence of a formal surrender of possession by the owner (for instance through handing over keys),[54] there must
be some physical act in relation to the land done for the purpose of effecting the acquisition
and which, apart from statutory authorisation, would be unlawful as against the landowner.[55] Thus where a contractor had left wagons and other material on the land, by agreement with the owner in advance of beginning the work that he was to carry out for the

[49] Land Compensation Act 1961 (LCA), s 5A(3).
[50] LCA 1961, s 5A(4).
[51] The general vesting declaration procedure is explained in ch 2. The vesting date is defined in ss 2(1) and 4(3) of the 1981 Act.
[52] Land Compensation Act 1961, s 5A(7). The procedure before the Tribunal, including the written representa- tions procedure, is described in ch 15.
[53] Ibid, s 5A(5). Where the notice to treat procedure, rather than the general vesting declaration procedure, is used an acquiring authority may enter the land being acquired by giving notice of entry under s 11 of the Compulsory Purchase Act 1965 or following the payment into court of the amount of the compensation under sch 3 to that Act. It is not necessary to apply the rule relating to entering a part of the land when the general vesting declaration procedure is used since the valuation date is then the vesting date irrespective of whether there is or is not an actual entry onto the land on that date.
[54] See however *Simmonds v Kent County Council* [1990] 1 EGLR 227.
[55] *Esso Petroleum Company Ltd v Secretary of State for Transport* [2008] RVR 351; *Welford v Transport for London* (2008), unreported; *BP Oil UK Ltd v Kent County Council* [2003] RVR 118. In *Pandit v Leicester City Council* (1989) 58 P & CR 305, it was held that there had been entry when the acquiring authority changed the locks of a property while the occupier was in hospital even though the occupier subsequently returned to the property for a period.

acquiring authority, it was held that this did not constitute entry on behalf of the acquiring authority.[56] The mere giving of notice of entry or notice of an intention to enter is not an entry for present purposes. There must be some physical act denoting that entry is made.[57] An acquiring authority is entitled to enter land subject to compulsory purchase for the purpose of surveying and taking levels of the land. This is a preliminary act and does not constitute entry for present purposes.[58]

4.42   Section 5A(2) of the Land Compensation Act 1961 provides that no adjustment is to be made to the valuation in respect of anything which happens after the relevant valuation date. The purpose of this provision is not wholly clear. It may do no more than state the obvious principle that the parties to the hypothetical sale cannot take into account events which occur after the valuation date of which they can have no knowledge. Probably the provision is intended to make it clear that once a valuation has been carried out by reference to the valuation date there can be no question of a subsequent adjustment to the valuation because some later events have occurred which change, or might change, the value of the property. However, this is no more than stating that the property is to be valued at a specific valuation date.

3. Determining the Interest Acquired

4.43   The valuation date determines the date by reference to which prevailing land values are to be ascertained. It also defines the date by reference to which planning assumptions, general surrounding circumstances relevant to the value of the property, and the physical state of the property acquired, are determined. For example, section 14(4)(b) of the Land Compensation Act 1961 requires a consideration of whether planning permission for development could on certain assumptions reasonably be expected to be granted at the valuation date.[59] If the condition of the property deteriorates between the giving of a notice to treat and the valuation date the deteriorated state of the property as at the valuation date must be taken into account unless it was the fault of the acquiring authority.[60]

4.44   It is said that whereas the interests acquired have to be valued as at the valuation date the nature of the interests themselves is to be determined as at the date of the notice to treat.[61]

---

[56]   *Standish v Mayor of Liverpool* (1852) 1 Drew 1, 61 ER 351.

[57]   *Friendly Bar Ltd v Glasgow Corporation* [1972] RVR 475 (LT for Scotland).

[58]   *Burson v Wantage RDC* (1974) 27 P & CR 556. For this power see ch 2, paras 2.94 and 2.95.

[59]   See section (c) of ch 7. This provision was introduced by the Localism Act 2011.

[60]   *West Midland Baptist (Trust) Association v Birmingham Corporation* [1970] AC 874, [1969] 3 WLR 389, per Lord Reid at p 899, overruling *Phoenix Assurance Co v Spooner* [1905] 2 KB 753; *Gately v Central Lancashire New Town Development Corporation* (1984) 48 P & CR 339.

[61]   In the last published edition of *Cripps on the Compulsory Acquisition of Land* (London, Sweet and Maxwell, 1962) it was stated at para 2–058: 'The notice to treat is so far binding that it determines the time at which the value of interests in the land is to be considered for the assessment of the purchase money or compensation'. In *Rugby Joint Water Board v Shaw-Fox* [1973] AC 202, [1972] 2 WLR 757, Lord Pearson said at p 246: 'One can take what is common ground, namely the principle that the nature of the claimant's interest is to be established at the time of (or immediately before or immediately after) the service of the notice to treat'. The principle goes back to *Penny v Penny* (1867) LR 5 Eq 227, and the statement of Page Wood V-C that 'Everyone's interest shall be valued, *rebus sic stantibus*, just as it occurs at the moment when the notice to treat was given'. That last principle has now been abandoned both by reason of the *West Midland Baptist* decision and by reason of s 5A of the Land Compensation Act 1961 insofar as it established a valuation date. In *Penny v Penny* the land acquired was subject to a lease which would endure only as long as the tenants carried on a certain business at the property. It was held that the rever-

Whatever is the significance of this principle as a generality its impact is much diluted by other rules which will now be explained. It is doubtful whether the principle as just stated offers much practical guidance today.

The landowner may sell his interest after receiving a notice to treat and compensation is   4.45
then payable to the purchaser. It is for this reason that an acquiring authority making an advance payment of compensation is required to register the payment as a local land charge so that a purchaser can be made aware of the advance payment which will have effect to reduce the amount of compensation which he will receive.[62] The price paid by the purchaser to acquire the property is not normally relevant to the amount of the compensation which he can claim (save possibly that the sum paid may be comparable if the transaction was an open market sale).[63] Of course the land may have been purchased at an under-value or may even have been acquired as a gift. The giving of a notice to treat after the making of a con-tract to sell land but before completion does not frustrate that contract.[64]

The main practical impact of changes between the notice to treat and the valuation date   4.46
concerns leases. It is said that the grant of a lease after the date of the notice to treat is to be disregarded in assessing compensation so that the new tenant is not entitled to claim com-pensation and the landlord's interest is valued as not subject to the lease.[65] The grant of a lease after receipt of a notice to treat is in practice unlikely. More important is the reduction in the length of the unexpired term or the determination of the lease which may occur after service of the notice to treat but before the valuation date. Clearly the value of the lease, and the corresponding value of the reversion, must be assessed at the valuation date in the light of the unexpired residue of the lease at that date. If the lease has ended by the valuation date it is to be disregarded in the valuation process.[66] It is therefore open to an acquiring

sioner's interest should be valued subject to the lease and that the effect of the acquisition as something which would bring the leases to an end should be left out of account. In the *West Midland Baptist* case, above n 60, Lord Reid regarded the essence of the decision of Page Wood V-C to be that the nature of the interest acquired could not be altered or increased by the giving of the notice to treat or the compulsory acquisition of that interest. It is also possible that there is an error in the exact reporting of what Page Wood V-C said, as was pointed out by Lord Morris in the *West Midland Baptist* case at pp 906–07. The critical question in a case such as *Penny v Penny* is whether the status of the leases is changed by reason of the compulsory acquisition. Today the answer is that the status of the leases is probably prevented from being changed by the operation of s 9 of the Land Compensation Act 1961 (see section (d) of ch 5). This is so whether the matter is looked at as at the date of the notice to treat or as at the valuation date.

[62] See Land Compensation Act 1973, s 52 and see para 15.18 of ch 15.
[63] *Landlink Two Ltd v Sevenoaks District Council* (1986) 51 P & CR 100.
[64] *Hillingdon Estates Co v Stonefield Estates Ltd* (1952) Ch 627, [1952] 1 All ER 853; *E Johnson & Co (Barbados) Ltd v NSR Ltd* [1997] AC 400, [1996] 3 WLR 583 (notice of intended acquisition given under legislation in effect in Barbados, and generally equivalent to a notice to treat). The doctrine of frustration is an aspect of the law of contract which means that a contract may be brought to an end when the substratum of the contract is destroyed by unanticipated supervening events.
[65] *Mercer v Liverpool, St Helen's and South Lancashire Rly Co* [1904] AC 461; *Re Marylebone (Stingo Lane) Improvement Act, ex parte Edwards* (1871) 12 LR Eq 389. It is not easy to reconcile this statement as an inflexible rule with the current general statutory provision in s 4 of the Acquisition of Land Act 1981 to the effect that the creation of an interest is to be left out of account if it was done with a view to obtaining compensation or increased compensation. The grant of a short term tenancy after service of a notice to treat when there was likely to be a delay before entry was required, for instance the renewal of a weekly tenancy of a flat, may be quite reasonable and not done with a view to increasing the compensation. It may be that *Mercer's* case should be regarded today as author-ity for the general principle explained in para 4.47 rather than for any specific proposition related to leases.
[66] *West Midland Baptist (Trust) Association v Birmingham Corporation*, above n 60, per Lord Morris at p 907; *Bradford Property Trust Ltd v Hertfordshire County Council* (1973) 27 P & CR 228; *Holloway v Dover Corporation* [1960] 1 WLR 604, (1960) 11 P & CR 229. In *Runcorn Association Football Club v Warrington and Runcorn Development Corporation* (1983) 45 P & CR 183, a lease had over two years to run at the date of service of a notice

authority to purchase the reversion on a lease and wait until the lease expires or until it is determined by a notice to quit before entering the land, in which case the tenant will have no claim to compensation.[67] A simple example of these rules is a case in which a house was acquired which was subject to a tenancy of a part of it at the date of the notice to treat but where the owner terminated the tenancy by the date on which possession was taken. It was held that the compensation was to be assessed as the value of the property with vacant possession at the valuation date.[68]

4.47   There are two principles which prevent a landowner from carrying out works or creating new interests so as to increase the compensation payable. The first principle, not dependent on a statutory provision, is that it is not competent for an owner of land who has received notice to treat to deal with the land taken, or to deal with other retained land of his which may be injuriously affected, so as to increase the burden of the acquiring authority as regards the compensation payable.[69] It should be noted that this principle refers only to dealings with land after the receipt of a notice to treat. It seems that the principle can embrace the creation of new interest or dealings with existing interests or the carrying out of works or a change of use. The result is that when the principle applies the interest acquired should be valued disregarding the actions which are not competent.

4.48   The second principle is in section 4(2) of the Acquisition of Land Act 1981. This provision states that the Lands Tribunal shall in assessing compensation leave out of account any interest in land created or any works done on land, whether the land acquired or other land, if the creation of the interest or the doing of the works was not reasonably necessary and was undertaken with a view to obtaining compensation or increased compensation. This provision is not anchored to the date of the service of a notice to treat. Otherwise it repeats in different language the substance of what constitutes the first principle.

4.49   A few general explanatory comments may be made on these provisions. It may be that now the underlying principle has been expressed in precise statutory language this is to be taken to be the whole of the law and as something which supervenes any earlier principle built up by the courts.[70] The statutory provision is to be welcomed in that it does not provide for the date of the giving of notice to treat as an arbitrary cut-off point. Actions done to increase compensation before that date should be disregarded as much as actions after that date. The magic of the date of notice to treat as some watershed in the process of acquisition may be overdone. The last matter is that actions carried out reasonably and genuinely in respect of the property, and having nothing to do with the enhancement of compensation, cannot be excluded under either principle. However, the nearer it comes in point of time to the dispossession of the landowner the less likely it is that work to the property will be considered

to treat but only six months to run when possession was taken. It was held that the status of the tenancy was fixed at the date of the notice to treat so that it was not a tenancy subject to s 20 of the Compulsory Purchase Act 1965. There may be some doubt on the correctness of this decision as a matter of principle.

[67] *Newham LBC v Benjamin* [1968] 1 WLR 694. This decision related to a claim under s 20 of the Compulsory Purchase Act 1965 in relation to a short tenancy but the same principle should apply to longer tenancies not subject to s 20.

[68] *Banham v London Borough of Hackney* (1971) 22 P & CR 922.

[69] *Mercer v Liverpool, St Helen's and South Lancashire Rly Co* [1904] AC 461, per Lord Lindley at p 465. The decision concerned the grant of a lease by the owner for building purposes. See n 65.

[70] Certainly this is the approach taken today by the courts in considering the value to the owner principle and its statutory embodiment: see *Transport for London Ltd v Spirerose Ltd* [2009] UKHL 44, [2009] 1 WLR 1797 (see ch 5).

to be reasonable and prudent, and to this extent the date of the service of the notice to treat may be significant since it signifies the definite intention of an acquiring authority to exercise the rights which have been given to it either by the empowering Act or by the authorisation constituted by the confirmation of a compulsory purchase order. Works carried out to keep the property being acquired in a proper state of repair should not normally be left out of account under the statutory or any other principle because of the rule that the property must be valued in its physical state at the valuation date.

One final matter to point out is that if the acquiring authority uses the general vesting declaration procedure, as opposed to serving a notice to treat, certain of the problems discussed in the previous paragraphs disappear. The effect of a general vesting declaration is to vest in the acquiring authority interests in the land the subject of the declaration at the vesting date. The vesting date is also the valuation date. Therefore many of the problems associated with the creation of interests or the carrying out of works between the date of the notice to treat and the date of possession as the valuation date disappear. 4.50

4. Summary

The various rules discussed within this section of the chapter may understandably give rise to some confusion and it may be helpful to attempt to summarise the position in law. 4.51

(i) The property acquired must be valued at the valuation date as explained above, in that it must be valued in accordance with land values prevailing at that date and in its physical condition at that date, and generally in the light of external circumstances relevant to value as prevailing at that date.

(ii) Although there is said to be a general rule that the nature of interests acquired is to be determined as at the date of the notice to treat in practice, and when it comes to leases, the leasehold interest and the reversion on a lease must be valued with the unexpired residue being computed as at the valuation date and, if a lease has ended between the service of notice to treat and the valuation date, no claim can be made for compensation as regards that lease and the reversion must be valued without the encumbrance of such a lease.

(iii) There is a general rule that interests created and works carried out at any time with a view to obtaining compensation or increasing the amount of compensation are to be left out of account in the assessment of compensation.

(iv) Any possible difficulties and doubts which exist and which have been discussed earlier can in the main be avoided if the acquiring authority uses the general vesting declaration procedure since under that procedure the vesting date is the valuation date and interests in the land vest in the acquiring authority at that valuation date.

(F) VALUATION AND DAMAGES

A consideration of the valuation date leads on naturally to an examination of a major cause of confusion in the assessment of compensation which is a failure to distinguish between 4.52

compensation founded on the value of an interest in land and compensation founded on loss or damage to land. This subject is connected with what is sometimes described as the Bwllfa principle following a decision of the House of Lords in 1903.[71] The difficulty is caused by an apparent conflict between two principles. One principle, as described under the previous section of this chapter, is the need for a specific valuation date where land is being valued with the corollary that no account is to be taken in valuing the land of events which occurred after the valuation date. As explained the leaving out of account of post-valuation date events is an inevitable consequence of the method of assessing value by way of a hypothetical sale of the land at a given date with the result that the parties to the hypothetical transaction cannot have taken into account events in the future of which they could not have known. The other principle is that when a court assesses damages payable for a loss in making the assessment the court takes into account all facts and events known to it at the date of making that assessment which are relevant to the amount of the damages.[72] There may appear on the face of it to be a tension between these two principles.

4.53   The situations which may arise can be illustrated by examples. A company might run a hotel in a particular locality which is compulsorily acquired. It might occur that soon after the valuation date a large new infrastructure project is unexpectedly announced in the locality which will take some years to construct. The result might have been to provide substantial business for the hotel over a number of years and thus to increase its value. The effect of this event on the value of the hotel cannot be taken into account because it is something which happened after the valuation date and was not known to the parties who are taken to have agreed the price for the hotel under the hypothetical sale which has to be envisaged to take place at the valuation date. The other example could be the situation where the owners of a valuable seam of coal who were working that coal were required to limit their working by reason of its possible effect on a nearby reservoir. Under the statute, which provides for the restriction on working, the coal owners might be entitled to compensation for the loss or damage caused to them by the restriction. As sometimes happens in the case of a dispute as to compensation the actual assessment of the compensation could occur years after the restriction had taken effect. Since the nature of the compensation is that of providing restitution for a loss or damage suffered events which occurred between the date of the restriction and the date of the assessment of the compensation can in principle be taken into account. One such event might be an unexpected increase in coal prices leading to an increase in the profits which might have been earned if the mining of coal could have continued without restriction, and in those circumstances the compensation assessed should include that attributable to the additional profit lost as a result of the restriction. This last example is akin to the facts of the decision of the House of Lords in the Bwllfa case the name of which has given rise to the description of the Bwllfa principle.[73]

4.54   A further example of a situation which can arise under the compensation code but which is dealt with under the second principle and second method of assessment is where injurious affection to land is caused by some temporary effect which does not involve the acquisition of the land itself. An instance would be the closure of roads around a hotel for a temporary

---

[71]   Bwllfa & Merthyr Dare Steam Collieries (1891) Ltd v Pontypridd Waterworks Co [1903] AC 426.
[72]   As it was put by Harman LJ in Curwen v James [1963] 1 WLR 748, [1963] 2 All ER 619, 'A court should never speculate when it knows'.
[73]   See para 4.52. It was stressed in the Bwllfa case in the opinions in the House of Lords that no land was acquired from the claimants, and it is this which is the crucial factor.

period while road works were being carried out. The owner of the hotel may be entitled to compensation for the injurious affection to his land under section 10 of the Compulsory Purchase Act 1965. By the time that the assessment of his compensation is made the temporary closure of the roads may have ended and the actual loss due to that closure may be known. In such a case it is not necessary to value the land affected at some chosen past valuation date with and without the effect of the road closure but rather the compensation is to be assessed as the real loss due to that closure the amount of which can be accurately known once the closure has occurred and ended.[74]

The reason for the difference in the two methods of assessing compensation lies in the statutory provisions for the assessment. In the case of the compulsory acquisition of land the rule is that the compensation is equal to the value of the land at the valuation date. For reasons just explained such a valuation, made by reference to a hypothetical sale of that land at the valuation date, can only be carried out by leaving out of account events which followed the valuation date and which could not have been known to the parties hypothetically agreeing the price for the land on a sale of it at the valuation date.[75] On the other hand where the compensation is stated to be for loss or damage or injurious affection to land (another name for damage to land) the method of assessing the compensation is akin to the method used for the assessment of damages at common law, for example damages for a breach of contract or the commission of a tort. It is obvious that in assessing common law damages regard should be had to all factors which assist the court in assessing the amount of the damages and are known at the date of that assessment.   4.55

An obvious illustration of this latter principle arises in the case of the assessment of damages for a personal injury. If a person is injured in an accident it may be that at the time of the accident the medical prognosis is that he will make a good recovery. After a few years it may be apparent that this prognosis was optimistic and that his recovery is delayed or that he suffers permanent injury. When a court comes to assess damages for the loss caused by the accident and knows of the true outcome of the medical condition caused by the accident it is plain that the court should take account of the real situation known to it and not assess the damages on some artificial and untrue assumption that the medical condition of the person involved is better than it actually is. A vivid example of this last type of situation is a decision in Australia in a case in which a person was entitled to damages for a loss of earnings brought about by a wrong committed by the defendant. Between the date of the wrongful act and the date when the court had to consider the amount of damages the claimant had been in prison for some time as a result of an event unconnected with the original unlawful act against him. He could not have earned while in prison and it was held that the assessment of the damages for loss of earnings had to take account of this fact. This was so even though, of course, the commission by the claimant of a criminal offence and his imprisonment could not have been anticipated at the date when the original unlawful act against him occurred.[76]   4.56

---

[74] See *Wildtree Hotels Ltd v Harrow London Borough Council* [2001] 2 AC 1, [2000] 3 WLR 165. Compensation payable under s 10 of the Compulsory Purchase Act 1965 is considered in ch 10.

[75] A further illustration of the principles discussed under this section in connection with a claim for the depreciation of the value of land at a certain date caused by the use and anticipated use of public works is *Dhenim v Department of Transport* (1990) 60 P & CR 349. See section (e) of ch 13.

[76] *Lesschke v Jeffs & Faulkner* [1955] *Queensland Weekly Notes* 67, per Hanger J.

4.57 Any conflict between the methods of assessment of compensation is apparent rather than real. No difficulty need arise provided proper attention is paid to the statutory provision which creates the entitlement to compensation. If the statutory entitlement to compensation, or its assessment in any particular case, is dependent on the value of an interest in land at a specified valuation date then the rule is that the value of the interest must be assessed by assuming a sale of the interest at the valuation date with the consequence that events which occur after the valuation date must be left out of account in assessing the value of the interest in land. On the other hand if the statutory entitlement to compensation refers to compensation for loss or damage, or uses some similar phraseology, such that a valuation of land at a particular date is not a necessary or prescribed part of the process of assessment, then in principle events which occur after the date of the event which caused the loss for which compensation is payable can be taken into account in assessing the amount of that loss. This latter situation is sometimes dignified by the name of the Bwllfa principle but it is in truth no more than the application of a general principle which applies to the assessment of damages for loss at common law.

4.58 While the dichotomy between the two methods of assessing compensation, depending on the statutory language which creates the entitlement to compensation is clear, it must not be supposed that where compensation has to be assessed as that payable for some loss or damage, that is the latter category of situation as just discussed, a valuation of land in the traditional sense can play no part. There may be cases in which the only loss or damage suffered by a claimant is the reduction in the value of his land at some given date. In such a case the compensation for the loss or damage to the claimant will be determined by reference to that loss of value involving, as it must, the assessment of the value of land at a given date. Indeed in such cases two valuations of the land as at the same date will often be necessary, one before the event causing the reduction in value and the other after that event. A good example of the assessment of compensation which falls within this last description is the assessment of compensation for damage or injurious affection to the retained land of a landowner where a part of his land has been acquired. This compensation, albeit compensation for damage or injurious affection to the retained land, is normally assessed by comparing the value of the retained land before and after the acquisition by way of two valuations carried out at the valuation date.[77] The important point to bear in mind is that in the latter type of situation, as considered in this paragraph, the compensation for loss or damage is not necessarily and in all cases confined to that which is assessed by ascertaining the capital value of an interest in land at a particular date.

4.59 This chapter is concerned primarily with the assessment of compensation under rule (2) of section 5 of the Land Compensation Act 1961 and this requires an assessment of compensation by way of what has been described as the first method. The interest in land acquired

---

[77] The compensation in such a case is assessed under s 7 of the Compulsory Purchase Act 1965: see ch 9. See also *Wildtree Hotels Ltd v Harrow London Borough Council* [2001] 2 AC 1, [2010] 3 WLR 165, per Lord Hoffmann at p 16. In *Penny's Bay Investment Co v Director of Lands* (2010) 13 HKCFAR 287 (Ct of Final Appeal, Hong Kong) it was held that compensation for injurious affection to land caused by the extinguishment of a right of access to the sea was to be assessed by reference to the value of the land before and after the extinguishment as at the date of extinguishment and leaving out of account future events. As Lord Hoffmann pointed out at para 43 the value of land determined at a relevant date 'obviously cannot be affected by what happened afterwards'. This decision is a stark illustration and application of the correct principle since land was to be valued at a certain date with the anticipation at that date that a container port terminal would be built yet when the reference to the Lands Tribunal was heard it was known that that proposal was subsequently abandoned.

must be valued at the valuation date by way of a hypothetical sale of it at that date taking account only of events known at that date. There are other areas of the law of compensation which require an assessment of compensation by the second method, that is taking account of events which have occurred after the valuation date where those events are relevant to the amount of the loss and the compensation for that loss. One illustration has already been given which is the assessment of compensation for injurious affection under section 10 of the Compulsory Purchase Act 1965 where no land of the claimant has been acquired (indeed in this case there may be no true valuation date). Another example is the assessment of compensation for disturbance, or any other matter not directly based on the value of land, under rule (6) of section 5 of the Land Compensation Act 1961.[78] These are separate heads of compensation and are dealt with later. The central principle to be borne in mind at this stage is that when dealing with the primary component of compensation for the compulsory acquisition of land, which is the value of that land at the valuation date as prescribed by rule (2) of section 5 of the 1961 Act, there is no room for the application of the so-called Bwllfa principle and the valuation must proceed along orthodox lines which involve taking into account in the valuation all facts known, or matters anticipated, as at the valuation date but leaving out of account events which occurred after that date.[79]

(G) THE PRESUMPTION OF REALITY

The principle or presumption of reality has been explained in general terms in chapter 3   4.60
which deals with general principles of the law of compensation.[80] The application of that principle to valuations under rule (2) of section 5 of the Land Compensation Act 1961 is that, apart from the assumption of a sale of the land which is being valued and apart from the assumed existence of a hypothetical willing seller and a hypothetical willing buyer, all other surrounding circumstances and events relevant to the value of the land, and known or anticipated at the valuation date, are to be taken into account as they actually were, or as they were anticipated, at that date unless there is some statutory provision which provides otherwise expressly or by necessary implication. The principle has been stated in the Court of Appeal as being that if the assessment of the value for the purpose of compensation is to be on the basis of ignoring a proven or admitted fact, which would have affected the price of an actual sale in the open market, the use of such a basis must be justified by reference to some specific provision of the legislation.[81] An example of its application was where a leasehold interest in land was being acquired and the attitude of the actual landlord to a possible redevelopment of the premises was relevant to the value of the land being acquired. The Court of Appeal rejected the suggestion that the identity of the actual landlord could be

---

[78] For example, in *Director of Buildings and Lands v Shun Fung Ironworks Ltd* [1995] 2 AC 111, [1995] 2 WLR 904, it was necessary to estimate the profits which might have been made from the operations of a business in future years had it not been extinguished in order to ascertain the compensation for business loss under the terms of the Ordinance being applied and it was held that account could be taken of actual events between the date of the land acquisition and the date of the assessment of the compensation: see per Lord Nicholls at p 131.

[79] It is unfortunate that this principle is not always observed in decisions of first instance: see, eg *Cooke v Secretary of State* [1974] RVR 17 (LT); *Essex County Showground Group Ltd v Essex County Council* [2006] RVR 356 (LT); *China Light and Power v Commissioner of Rating* [1994–95] CPR 618 (LT, Hong Kong).

[80] See ch 3, paras 3.16 and 3.17.

[81] *Trocette Property Co Ltd v Greater London Council* (1974) 28 P & CR 408.

disregarded and replaced by a landlord of some notional or hypothetical character.[82] It should be noted that what was being suggested in this case had nothing to do with the hypothetical parties to the hypothetical transaction which is the foundation of the valuation but rather to the identity of some other party who held an interest in the same land as that in which subsisted the interest of the claimants and the interest which was acquired and was being valued. There are, of course, many surrounding or external circumstances which exist in the real world at the date of the hypothetical sale which may be relevant to what the hypothetical parties would agree and thus to the value of the land. Obvious examples are the existence of transport facilities or the existence of other alternative premises which a purchaser could acquire or public or taxation policies or the general situation and policies as regards town and country planning. All of these matters, and any other similar matters, must be taken for the purposes of the valuation to be as they actually were at the valuation date in the absence of some statutory provision to the contrary.[83]

4.61   There are three important statutory provisions which require or may require a departure from reality and these are dealt with in detail elsewhere.[84] These three main provisions are as follows:

(i)   Under section 6 and schedule 1 to the Land Compensation Act 1961 the effect on the value of the land acquired of development, or the prospect of development, on land other than the land acquired and being valued has to be disregarded in certain circumstances.[85]

(ii)   Under section 9 of the Land Compensation Act 1961 no account is to be taken of any depreciation of the value of the land acquired which is attributable to the fact that an indication has been given that the land is, or is likely, to be acquired by an authority possessing compulsory purchase powers. Any such indication therefore has to be ignored in the valuation process to the extent that it has a depreciatory effect on the value of the land acquired and being valued.[86]

(iii)   In certain circumstances a planning permission is to be assumed to be in force for the benefit of the land being acquired even though there was in reality no such permission.[87]

---

[82]   Ibid. The claimants in this case substantially succeeded on a different ground which is s 9 of the Land Compensation Act 1961. Section 9 is considered in ch 5.

[83]   A good illustration of the operation of the presumption of reality is the decision of the Lands Tribunal in *Urban Edge Group Ltd v London Underground Ltd* [2009] UKUT 103 (LC), [2009] RVR 361. It was argued in that case by the claimant that in valuing the land acquired it had to be assumed, contrary to the reality, that had it not been for the scheme of the acquiring authority other land in the vicinity would have been developed by buildings of a greater height than had actually occurred and that these notional higher buildings should be taken into account in valuing the land acquired. The proposition was that if such higher buildings in the locality could be assumed to exist at the valuation date there would have been a prospect at the valuation date that planning permission could have been obtained for a higher building on the land acquired and being valued. The Tribunal rejected this argument which was backed by no statutory authority. This subject is considered in greater detail in ch 5.

[84]   There are other limited circumstances prescribed by the legislation which require certain other matters to be left out of account in the valuation process. For example, as stated earlier in this chapter (see para 4.48) under s 4(2) of the Acquisition of Land Act 1981 an interest created, or works carried out, must be left out of account in valuing the land acquired if the actions were carried out with a view to obtaining compensation or increased compensation. A further example is that under rule (4) of s 5 of the Land Compensation Act 1961 the effect on value of unlawful uses on the land acquired is to be left out of account if the use increases the value of that land (see section (c) of ch 6).

[85]   See section (d) of ch 5.

[86]   See section (d) of ch 5.

[87]   See section (c) of ch 7.

The exceptions to the presumption of reality, and particularly the first two exceptions just   4.62
mentioned, are closely connected with the so-called Pointe Gourde principle.[88] Indeed the
Pointe Gourde principle, that is in very general terms the principle that the effect on the
value of the land acquired of the scheme which underlies the compulsory acquisition is to
be disregarded, may be analysed in juridical terms as a wide exception to the presumption
of reality.

(H) LAND VALUE AND BUSINESS PROFITS

1. Introduction

A subject which can cause substantial confusion is the relationship between the value of a   4.63
piece of land and the expectation of making a profit from a business carried out or to be
carried out on the land. Whether a piece of land can be used to support a profitable business
operation depends on a variety of factors. The physical condition or the location of the
property may preclude a business use or a particular business use. A property may not have,
or have any hope of obtaining, a planning permission or other consent needed for a business use. However, if no factors such as this preclude a business use at the property, the
essential point to have in mind is that the actual or potential business use of the property is
not something to be regarded as separate from the value of the property but rather is an
inherent component of that value. The expectation of using a property for a particular
business, and of obtaining the profits which the business may generate or continue to generate, is something which contributes to the value of the property; indeed it may be the sole
or predominant factor which confers a value on the property. The primary rule in the
assessment of compensation is that the compensation is to be equal to the value of the land
acquired and that value is the amount which the land would realise if sold in the market at
the valuation date. To speak of the land having a value and the business carried on at the
land having a separate value invites confusion in this particular area of law. There is for
present purposes one value which is the amount which the land with the business would
realise if sold and it is this value which constitutes the primary element of compensation.

It is, of course, correct that not every property which is put to a business use itself generates   4.64
a profit by reason of the specific use to which it is put. A large company may own or lease
an office building used for its administration. The use of that particular office building will
not by itself generate a profit in the same way as would the use of a single shop but of course
the use of the office building can be expected to contribute to the profitability of the company. In such a case the value of the office building will lie in its general capacity for use as
an office and will not be affected by the profitability of the company by which it is used.

All of the above explanation seems apparent. A source of difficulty in valuations for com-   4.65
pensation purposes is that the total compensation has to be assessed by the application of
rules (2) and (6) of section 5 of the Land Compensation Act 1961 and rule (6) may provide
an additional element of compensation for a loss not directly based on the value of land.
The question which sometimes arises is whether compensation for a loss of anticipated

---

[88] See ch 5, paras 5.20–5.22.

profits from a business can be claimed under rule (6) as a sum in addition to the value of the land assessed under rule (2). This important question is addressed below. Compensation claimable under rule (6), often called disturbance compensation, is considered generally in chapter 8 but it is convenient to discuss in this chapter the relationship between claims for the value of the land acquired where a business is carried on at that land and claims under rule (6) which may arise in those circumstances.

4.66   A concept which is often mentioned in the present context is that of goodwill. What this concept means is that a person or company who carries on a business may form contacts with customers and others and may obtain a good reputation in the locality. Contacts may be mainly with customers but can be with others such as suppliers or local authorities or regulatory bodies. The reputation may be built up not only by the provision of goods or services of a high quality but by other acts such as contributions to local community causes. Goodwill has been described as the expectation that an existing custom or clientele built up as part of a business will continue.[89] Goodwill may not be attached to any particular property. For example, a window cleaner could build up a reputation in a locality for reliable and efficient services but have no property except a shed where he keeps his equipment. On the other hand the goodwill of a shop or café may attach itself to the property.

4.67   Goodwill in the sense here used may be a component of the value of a property. A purchaser of the property where a business is carried on with goodwill established will realise that the level of future profits from the business will be enhanced by the goodwill and so might pay more for the property.[90] Whether goodwill increases the value of a property, and the extent to which it does so, will often depend on two matters. The goodwill may be personal to the seller and will not increase the profitability of the business in the hands of a purchaser. If, for example, a person has built up a reputation of providing specialised alternative medical remedies such as acupuncture from a property it is unlikely that a purchaser of the property would be seen by the public and customers as necessarily able to provide exactly the same services. The second matter is what the seller does with his business. The seller may end his business altogether, or start up a similar business in a distant location, in which case the goodwill may be transferred to the purchaser and will increase the value of the property sold. On the other hand the seller may relocate the business to premises in close vicinity to the property sold, in which case he may take his goodwill, in the sense of his established clientele, with him so that a purchaser of the property would pay nothing for it and it will not affect the value of the property sold. The expression 'goodwill' is not generally found in the compensation legislation but it is included in other legislation concerning property values as a possible component of value, an example being Part II of the Landlord and Tenant Act 1954.[91]

---

[89] *Inland Revenue Commissioners v Mercer & Co's Margarine Ltd* [1901] 1 AC 217, per Lord MacNaughten at p 223. The legal concept of goodwill is an old one. In *Crutwell v Lye* (1810) 17 Ves 335, at p 346 Lord Eldon said 'The goodwill, which has been the subject of sale, is nothing more than the probability that old customers will resort to the old place'. Goodwill is often equated with loss of future profits. For instance in the *Shun Fung* decision (considered in detail at para 4.84 et seq) Lord Nicholls at p 131 referred to 'injury to goodwill (loss of profits)'.

[90] Sometimes the value of goodwill is separately assessed (as, eg in *Saglam v Docklands Light Rly Co* [2008] RVR 59) but in strict legal terms it should be regarded as a part of the value of the property assessed under rule (2) of s 5 of the Land Compensation Act 1961.

[91] See Landlord and Tenant Act 1954, s 34(1)(b) which provides that in determining the rental value of premises occupied for the purposes of a business there shall be disregarded 'any goodwill attached to the holding by reason of the carrying on thereat of the business of the tenant (whether by him or by a predecessor of his in that business)'. The draftsman clearly considered that goodwill might attach to a property such that it could increase the

2. The Central Problem

The central problem of valuation is underlain by a cardinal error sometimes made, and an   4.68
error which leads to confusion, which is to believe that for the present purposes when the
land acquired is used for a business purpose the land has one value for which compensation
is payable and that the business, including any goodwill attaching to the business and the
land, has a separate value. It is sometimes suggested that the first value is the compensation
payable under rule (2) and that the second value can be claimed as compensation under
rule (6). This is incorrect in law and in principle. The rule (2) compensation is the amount
which a hypothetical willing purchaser would pay for the property at the valuation date
with the ability to carry on the business, and with the benefit of any goodwill which has
been built up, and which would pass to him on a sale of the property. In other words the
expectation of making a future profit from a business at a property, whether from an existing business or one to be started up, is something which for the purposes of assessing compensation contributes to the value of the property and is not a separate value or separate
sum.

This analysis is amply supported by authority. The question was directly considered in an   4.69
appeal to the Privy Council from New South Wales.[92] The landowners had acquired a piece
of land which they intended to develop and use for the purpose of freezing meat for export.
The land was acquired by the Government of New South Wales and compensation was
determined by a judge and jury as was then the procedure. At the hearing both parties
appear to have accepted that the compensation should be the aggregate of two specific
sums, the market value of the land and the capitalised value of the profits expected to be
made from the business. This approach was encapsulated in a part of the direction of the
Judge to the jury when he said:

> Then you will consider what capital amount fairly represents those savings and those profits and
> you will add that to the amount that you consider fairly represents the market value of the land
> independently of these special questions.

The Privy Council regarded this approach as wholly incorrect. Lord Moulton said:

> Their Lordships are of opinion that this direction is seriously at fault. That which the appellants
> were entitled to receive was compensation not for the business profits or savings which they
> expected to make from the use of the land, but for the value of the land to them. No doubt the
> suitability of the land for the purpose of their special business affected the value of the land to
> them, and the prospective savings and additional profits which it could be shown would probably
> attend the use of the land in their business furnished materials for estimating what was the real
> value of the land to them. But that is a very different thing from saying that they were entitled to
> have the capitalised value of these savings and additional profits added to the market value of the

---

rental value of that property and was a component of the rental value. There is no definition of goodwill in the
1954 Act. Compensation for goodwill was provided for in favour of tenants of business premises on quitting the
premises under Pt I of the Landlord and Tenant Act 1927. There is a reference to goodwill in s 46 of the Land
Compensation Act 1973 in the context of businesses carried on by persons aged 60 or over: see para 4.80.

[92] *Pastoral Finance Association Ltd v The Minister* [1914] AC 1083 at p 1088. The usefulness of this case as a
statement of principle was queried in the Court of Appeal in *Welford v EDF Energy Networks (LPN) Ltd* [2007]
2 EGLR 1, although the basis of the query is not clear. The *Welford* case is considered in para 4.74.

land in estimating their compensation. They were only entitled to have them taken into consideration so far as they may fairly be said to increase the value of the land. Probably the most practical form in which the matter can be put is that they were entitled to that which a prudent man in their position would have been willing to give for the land sooner than fail to obtain it. Now it is evident that no man would pay for land in addition to its market value the capitalised value of the savings and additional profits which he would hope to make by the use of it. He would no doubt reckon out these savings and additional profits as indicating the elements of the value of the land to him, and they would guide him in arriving at the price which he would be willing to pay for the land, but certainly if he were a businessman that price would not be calculated by adding the capitalised savings and additional profits to the market value.

The compensation was assessed under the Public Works Act 1900 in force in New South Wales which contained, as one would expect, provisions identical to those in the Lands Clauses Consolidation Act 1845 in England, so that what was said is in principle applicable to today's legislation in England.[93]

4.70   A similar endorsement of the principles here explained is found in a more recent decision of the Court of Appeal.[94] The claimant had an annual tenancy of agricultural land. It was acquired by the Secretary of State in September 1951. Had it not been for the compulsory acquisition the tenancy could not have been determined until May 1953. The same rules as those currently in force in respect of the assessment of compensation, which were then in the Acquisition of Land (Assessment of Compensation) Act 1919, that is rules (2) and (6) of section 2 of that Act, were to be applied. A question was whether the claimant was entitled to the open market value of his tenancy, which might have been assessed having regard to the profit he could have made from agricultural activities, and in addition to a sum for the loss of anticipated future profits. It was held that he was not so entitled because an assessment of the open market value of the land based on an expectation of future profits meant that that benefit, namely the expectation of those profits, was within the compensation assessed in that way and it would be obvious double counting if there were then a further award of compensation for the capitalised loss of those profits. Lord Evershed MR put the matter as follows:

> Obviously, the profit which this claimant had made in farming these acres is a highly material consideration, because it may well be that a purchaser, who bought the claimant's interest in these 38 acres, would have fixed the price he was prepared to pay on the basis that he, too, would be likely to make such a figure of profit by farming. It is then a matter entirely for the arbitrator to decide what sum should be allowed to compensate for that part of the interest which the claimant must be taken to have willingly sold.

---

[93] The carrying through of the basic provisions of the Lands Clauses Consolidation Act 1845 into the legislation currently in force in England is explained in ch 1, para 1.7. It was suggested by Thomas LJ in *Welford v Energy Networks (LPN) Plc* [2007] 2 EGLR 1 (apparently based on an observation in the Court of Appeal in *Ryde International Plc v London Regional Transport* [2004] 2 EGLR 1) that only limited reliance could be placed on the Privy Council decision in the *Pastoral Finance* case because the exact terms of the legislation in force at the time in New South Wales were not known. Lord Moulton's statement of the law was founded on general principles and not on an analysis of the exact statutory language. In addition it appears that the Court of Appeal was not assisted in either case as it might have been since the statutory provision being applied was s 117 of the Public Works Act 1900 of New South Wales which, as one would have expected, contained precisely the same language as s 63 of the Lands Clauses Consolidation Act 1845 in force in 1914 in England and virtually identical language to s 7 of the Compulsory Purchase Act 1965 in force in England today.
[94] *Watson v Secretary of State for Air* [1954] 3 All ER 582, (1954) 5 P & CR 13. The subsequent decision of the Lands Tribunal in a farm acquisition case in *Valentine v Skelmersdale Development Corporation* (1965) 195 *Estates Gazette* 489 seems erroneous in principle on this matter.

It was suggested by Mr Kekwick that, apart from anything that can be attributed to the land in interest, rule (6) entitles the claimant in addition to say: 'I must also be compensated for disturbance or loss measured by the profit which I can show I did lose during that second year'. But if the figure is properly arrived at under rule (2), it seems to me that any further sum of that nature is necessarily excluded, for otherwise he would be having the same thing twice over. Compensation for disturbance, in the sense of meaning the cost or expense he was put to in actually moving, has already been allowed, and the sum of £76 has been agreed for that; but if rule (2) is construed as I think it ought to be, and if a figure is arrived at to compensate the claimant for that second year of the interest which he has lost, subject, as I have said, to all its incidents under the tenancy agreement, then I think that rule (6) would have no further application.[95]

The same principles have been applied in Scotland.[96] Land was acquired which had the 4.71 potential for residential development. The statutory provisions to be applied were the same as those now in section 5 of the Land Compensation Act 1961. The claimants asserted that they were entitled to compensation under rule (6) for the loss of the profits which they would have earned if they had been allowed to remain on the land and to erect and sell houses. That assertion was rejected. The Lord President of the Court of Session, Lord Clyde, said:

In the first case, head (1) of the claim takes into account the building suitability of the land in question, as r 2 entitles the claimants to do, and it is not now maintained that their claim (3) for prospective future profits could fall under r 2. It obviously could not. Their contention was that it was part of their disturbance claim preserved under r 6. But, in the first place, a claim for prospective profit from an enterprise in the future is not a disturbance claim at all. The typical disturbance claim is for payment in respect of expenditure rendered useless by the compulsory acquisition. It relates to a liability or an expense already incurred at the date of the compulsory acquisition.[97]

Lord Clyde then added:

In the second place, however, the matter can in principle be carried further. To permit the claimants to secure, in addition to the market value of the land at the date of the compulsory acquisition, something additional in respect of the potential profit which they reasonably hoped to make from the land by building houses on it and selling them, is more than the statutes contemplated that they should get. It would give them more than their loss at the date when the compulsory acquisition takes effect. For this is the material date. It was never envisaged that, in addition to the existing value of the land taken, the future profits, which the proprietor might have made out of the land had it not been taken, should also be paid.[98]

In reaching his conclusion Lord Clyde relied on what Lord Moulton had explained in the Privy Council.[99] The Court of Session is the highest civil court with jurisdiction in Scotland alone and in this instance is equivalent to the Court of Appeal in England and Wales.

Finally in this consistent line of authorities the Lands Tribunal has considered the decision 4.72 in the Court of Session.[100] In the case before the Tribunal the land was acquired for the purposes of the Croydon tramway and had on it a number of properties built for occupation by elderly persons. The claimants were compensated in the ordinary way under rule (2)

---

[95] [1954] 3 All ER 582 at p 585.
[96] *McEwing & Sons v Renfrew County Council* 1960 SC 53, (1959) 11 P & CR 306.
[97] Ibid, p 310.
[98] Ibid, p 310.
[99] In the *Pastoral Finance* case, above n 92. See para 4.69.
[100] *Ryde International Plc v London Regional Transport* [2003] RVR 49.The decision of the Tribunal was upheld in the Court of Appeal at [2004] EWCA Civ 232, [2004] 2 EGLR 1.

for the value of the properties sold as a single entity at the valuation date. They claimed in addition under rule (6) the further profit which they said they would have made following the valuation date if they had been left undisturbed on the land and had been able to sell the properties individually at an opportune time. This claim was rejected in law by the Tribunal. The Tribunal concluded that there could be no additional claim under rule (6) for loss of future profits. Apart from the guidance given by a wealth of decided authority the essential reasoning of the decision was that the ordinary rule (2) compensation included the value of any potential which the land acquired had for generating a profit so that to add a claim under rule (6) for the loss of any future anticipated profit would be to give double compensation. In logical and analytical terms this is plainly correct.

4.73   There is powerful support for the reasoning as here explained in the decisions which deal with the nature and assessment of compensation for injurious affection. Injurious affection to land means an adverse effect on land for which compensation is sometimes claimable even though the land is not itself acquired.[101] A primary example of the availability of such compensation is the provision in section 10 of the Compulsory Purchase Act 1965 under which compensation is available in limited circumstances for injurious affection caused to land by the execution of works by an authority with a power of compulsory acquisition.[102] One of the limitations on the availability of that compensation is that the injury or damage must be to the land of the claimant and is not purely a personal or monetary or business loss.[103] It may occur that the injury is to land on which the claimant carries on some business such as that of an hotel and the works of the acquiring authority may adversely affect the running and profitability of that business; for instance the closure of roads near the land may reduce the number of customers who come to the business carried on at the land.[104] The view has consistently been taken that no compensation is payable for the loss of profits as such but that the reduced profits may affect the capital or the rental value of the land and so permit a claim. The point was put succinctly by Buckley LJ in the Court of Appeal in *Argyle Motors (Birkenhead) Ltd v Birkenhead Corporation*,[105] in a passage cited with approval in the House of Lords in *Wildtree Hotels Ltd v Harrow LBC*,[106] where he said 'If [the claimants] can prove that the loss of profitability affected the value of their interest in the land they can recover compensation for the loss of value'. This statement goes to the core of the matter. An expectation of making profits in the future from the use of land is not the value of that land but it may affect the value of that land. An error which is made is to suppose that the capital value of anticipated profits is itself the value of the land for the purposes of rule (2) of section 5 of the Land Compensation Act 1961. What is recoverable as compensation under rule (2) is the value of the land acquired, not the value of a business carried on

---

[101] See ch 3, para 3.20.

[102] This subject is considered in detail in ch 10.

[103] See ch 10, para 10.36 et seq.

[104] Many of the cases over a century and a half relating to the assessment of compensation under s 10 of the Compulsory Purchase Act 1965 (and its predecessor, s 68 of the Lands Clauses Consolidation Act 1845) have rested on a loss of trade and of expected profits from a business carried on at the land affected and thus an effect on the value of that land: see, eg *Ricket v Metropolitan Rly Co* (1865) 5 B & S 149, (1867) LR 2 HL (loss of trade to a public house called 'The Picked Egg' in Camberwell in London); *Wildtree Hotels Ltd v Harrow LBC* [2001] 2 AC 1, [2000] 3 WLR 163 (the leading modern authority on s 10 which involved loss of custom to a hotel as a result of road works in its vicinity and a resultant reduction in the rental value of the hotel).

[105] *Argyle Motors (Birkenhead) Ltd v Birkenhead Corporation* [1975] AC 99, [1973] 2 WLR 187, at p 114. See also per Lord Wilberforce at pp 130–31.

[106] See n 104.

at that land, just as in the injurious affection cases what is recoverable as compensation is a reduction in the value of the land affected and not a loss of profits.

It is sometimes suggested that doubt is thrown on the principles deriving from this line of authorities by the decision of the Court of Appeal in *Welford v EDF Energy (LPN) Ltd.*[107] Land which was about to be developed for commercial purposes had a wayleave to continue the use of underground electrical cables for a period of 15 years compulsorily granted in respect of the land under the Electricity Act 1989 to an electricity operator. The owners and the occupier of the land were entitled to compensation under paragraph 7 of schedule 4 to that Act. Compensation was assessed as the diminution in the value of the land caused by the grant of the wayleave as at the date of its creation. The issue was a claim for additional compensation by way of loss of profits due to the fact that the preparation and inception of the business had been delayed for four years by the grant, partly in the period before the grant and partly in the period after it. The Court of Appeal held that this claim for loss of profits was sustainable under the legislation.   4.74

Paragraph 7 of schedule 4 provided that where a wayleave was granted the owner and occupier of the land could recover compensation from the licence holder of the wayleave. It was also provided that if a person was disturbed in his enjoyment of any land he could recover from the licence holder compensation in respect of that disturbance.[108] The claims allowed seem on the face of it uncontroversial in that the owners of the land were entitled to the diminution in the value of the land caused by the grant of the wayleave and the occupier of the land, who was a different entity, was entitled to compensation for disturbance. A part of the results of its disturbance was obviously the loss due to the fact that the commencement of the business which it wished to carry out was delayed for a number of years. The consideration of these matters was agreed by all parties and the court as something which should proceed as though general principles applicable to the law of compensation applied. In fact the general principles applicable to the law of compensation derived from other legislation altogether. Nonetheless as the court proceeded on this basis the observations in the Court of Appeal are of obvious relevance to the general law.   4.75

The compensation appears to have been founded on the right of the occupier in that case to compensation for disturbance under the above provision. This has nothing to do with the value of land or any diminution in the value of land since the occupier did not own the land. It is also apparent from the decision that the period of the losses for disturbance encompassed in part a period prior to the grant of the wayleave but this is uncontroversial even in respect of the law of disturbance under rule (6) since it is well established that in certain circumstances compensation can be recoverable for losses which occur before the valuation date.[109]   4.76

The difficulty in the *Welford* decision, if there is one, is created by the suggestion that where land is acquired, or land is injuriously affected, a claim for permanent loss of profits can be   4.77

---

[107] *Welford v EDF Energy (LPN) Ltd* [2007] 2 EGLR 1. There is some reference to the *Welford* decision in the subsequent decision of the Lands Tribunal on compensation for electricity wayleaves under sch 7 to the Electricity Act 1989 in *Stynes v Western Power (East Midland) Plc* [2013] UKUT 0214 (LC) at paras 55, 56 and 69. In *National Grid Electricity Transmission Plc v Arnold White Estates Ltd* [2004] EWCA Civ 216 the Court of Appeal refused to apply principles derived from the general law of compensation to the assessment of compensation for the running of an electricity power line over land.

[108] Electricity Act 1989, sch 4, para 7(1), (2).

[109] See section (d) of ch 8.

sustained under the head of disturbance, that is under rule (6) where land is acquired. In fact the decision does not even remotely support such a principle. In the first place the claim was for injurious affection and not for the acquisition of any land (there were separate provisions in the Electricity Act 1989 for the acquisition of land where the ordinary principles of compensation had to be applied). Secondly, it has always been accepted that even when land is acquired a claim for disturbance under what is now rule (6) can be established for a temporary loss of profits caused by the actions of the public authority and that this claim is in addition to the value of any land acquired. There is nothing new in such a claim which goes back to the middle of the nineteenth century in relation to legislation passed before the Lands Clauses Consolidation Act 1845.[110] Thus to the extent that the compensation due under schedule 4 to the Electricity Act 1989 is to be equated to compensation assessed under general principles where there is the acquisition of an interest in land, the claim for the temporary loss of profits over the four years in question in that case would have been recoverable on traditional principles under rule (6). This loss of profits can justly be described as a special or personal loss to the claimant, not normally reflected in the value of his land, and is similar to the traditional claims for loss of profits during a temporary period while a relocation of a business takes place or for the costs of the removal of a business to new premises. On a careful analysis the *Welford* decision is therefore a decision which proceeds in accordance with the general understanding of the ambit of a claim under rule (6), and certainly does not support the suggestion that a wide and general claim may be made under rule (6) for an indefinite loss of future profits whether as a freestanding claim or as a claim additional to the value of land assessed under rule (2). It is clear from the facts of the *Welford* decision that, to the extent that the profitability of the land of the owners of it was affected for the following 15 years by the grant of the wayleave, that loss of profits was reflected in the diminution in the value of their land for which compensation was assessed and paid separately. This method of assessment of the loss is in accordance with general and current principles.

4.78   These authorities amply, and in general consistently, support three simple propositions which are: (a) that the expectation of establishing or continuing to carry on a business at the land acquired, and so of making future profits from that business, is something which may add to the value of the land acquired (indeed in some cases it may be the predominant factor in establishing that value), (b) that the compensation assessed under rule (2) of section 5 of the 1961 Act includes the value attributable to the nature of the business, and to the expectation of future profits from the carrying on of the business, and (c) that if the expectation of future profits is so reflected in the value of the land acquired, as it properly should be, there cannot be any additional claim for the loss of that expectation under rule (6) of section 5.[111]

---

[110] *Jubb v Humber Dock Co* (1846) 9 QB 443. See ch 8, para 8.2 and n 3.

[111] Other decisions in the courts consistent with these propositions are *Collins v Feltham UDC* [1937] 4 All ER 189 and *George Wimpey & Co Ltd v Middlesex County Council* [1938] 3 All ER 781, although in neither case is there any supporting reasoning. There are numerous decisions of the Lands Tribunal where a different valuation approach has been applied, eg *Sceneout Ltd v Centre Manchester Development Corporation* [1995] 2 EGLR 179; *Valentine v Skelmersdale Development Corporation* (1965) 195 *Estates Gazette* 489 (see n 94); *Optical Express (Southern) Ltd v Birmingham City Council* [2005] 2 EGLR 141. Of course the parties may agree that a loss of notional profits represents a diminution in the value of land as was done in connection with a claim under s 107 of the Town and Country Planning Act 1990 for the modification of a mineral planning permission in *MWH Associates v Wrexham County Borough Council* [2013] RVR 112.

3. Relocation of a Business

An owner or tenant of property whose property is acquired is expected to mitigate any   4.79
loss by relocating a business carried out at the property to other property where that is
reasonably practicable. It is important at this point to be clear on what is meant in this
context by the relocation of a business. A business provides goods or services to customers,
often customers in a particular locality. The business is only relocated if in its new location
it continues to serve at any rate a large proportion of its customers at the previous location.
If the business of a café or a book shop at a property in one town was transferred to a property in a town at the other end of the country it would be a case not of relocating the existing business but of starting up a similar but new business with new customers elsewhere.
What is critical in deciding whether a business is relocated is not just the type of business
activity carried on but also the customers or clients to which the goods or services of the
business are provided. If it was only the type of business activity that was relevant a business
of selling newspapers and confectionery outside a railway station in London could be
relocated to a position outside a railway station in Auckland.[112] In principle a person whose
property at which he carries on a business has been compulsorily acquired may either
relocate his business elsewhere, serving wholly or mainly the same customers, or may restart
a new business elsewhere providing services to new customers, or may cease to trade
altogether. Of course there may be a degree of overlap between the first two situations.[113]
The duty to mitigate is that the owner must bring himself within the first category if it
is reasonable and practicable for him to do so. If he fails to relocate his business by adopt-
ing the first of the courses just described when he could reasonably and practically do
so he cannot increase his compensation by his failure to take that course.[114] The duty to

[112] The question of whether the commencement of a business at a location different to that of the land which
has been acquired is in truth the relocation of the same business or the commencement of a different business is a
matter of fact. It will depend upon such circumstances as the similarity of the two businesses, the matter of
whether the same customers will be served from the new location, the distance between the locations, and the time
which it will take to commence the business at the new location. All these matters were considered by the Lands
Tribunal in Hong Kong in *Director of Buildings and Lands v Shun Fung Ironworks Ltd* [1995] 2 AC 111, [1995]
2 WLR 904, in which the proposal was to relocate a business carried on in Hong Kong involving the recovery of
scrap metal from ships to a location in the People's Republic of China at Shunde which was about 70 miles from
the location of the business at Hong Kong. There would have been a substantial time between the cessation of the
business at the land acquired and the commencement of the new business in China. Having considered all these
matters the Lands Tribunal came to the view that the business at Hong Kong had been effectively extinguished and
there was not any relocation of it. The Court of Appeal in Hong Kong reversed this decision but on a further appeal
the Privy Council restored the decision of the Lands Tribunal on the basis that the decision was one of fact and it
was not for an appellate court such as the Court of Appeal to alter a conclusion reached by a Tribunal of first
instance on the basis of its primary findings of fact.

[113] Some businesses have customers not tied to any particular locality. For example a business of constructing
large ships could be relocated to most locations with a suitable frontage to the sea and with adequate labour supplies and supporting infrastructure.

[114] See *Director of Buildings and Lands v Shun Fung Ironworks Ltd*, above n 109, in which Lord Nicholls at p 124
gave general guidance as to the conditions to be satisfied in all claims for compensation. The third condition was
as follows, 'Fairness requires that claims for compensation should satisfy a further, third condition in all cases. The
law expects those who claim recompense to behave reasonably. If a reasonable person in the position of the claimant would have taken steps to eliminate or reduce the loss, and the claimant failed to do so, he cannot fairly expect
to be compensated for the loss or the unreasonable part of it. Likewise if a reasonable person in the position of the
claimant would not have incurred, or would not incur, the expenditure being claimed, fairness does not require
that the authority should be responsible for such expenditure. Expressed in other words, losses or expenditure
incurred unreasonably cannot sensibly be said to be caused by, or be the consequence of, or be due to the resumption. The *Shun Fung* decision is considered in more detail in para 4.84.

mitigate the loss is an aspect of the law applicable to all claims for compensation and damages.[115]

4.80   Where a person aged 60 or more is required to give up possession of land at which he carries on a trade or business by reason of the compulsory acquisition of that land and the annual value of the land exceeds a certain specified limit (fixed by reference to the blight provisions in the Town and Country Planning Act 1990), and he is willing to give certain undertakings to the acquiring authority, the compensation for his interest (or the compensation assessed under section 20 of the Compulsory Purchase Act 1965) is to be assessed on the assumption that it is not reasonably practicable for him to relocate the trade or business.[116] The undertakings required are that the claimant will not dispose of the goodwill of his trade or business and will not for a specified time or within a specified area engage in a trade or business of the same or substantially the same kind. In other words the general duty to mitigate a loss by relocation of a business does not apply. This provision extends to persons aged 60 or more who are partners in a partnership or shareholders in a company. The provision also applies to compensation for disturbance and to disturbance payments under section 37 of the Land Compensation Act 1973. The reference to 'disturbance' may be to a claim made under rule (6) of section 5 of the Land Compensation Act 1961 and, if so, the draftsman may have contemplated that a disturbance claim for loss of goodwill or profits was possible under rule (6). However, these words cannot change the general law and it may be that compensation 'attributable to disturbance', as referred to in section 46(1), means no more than the compensation may be assessed under any head including rule (2) providing that the cause of it was the cessation of the business carried on at the land acquired brought about by the acquisition of that land.

4.81   The course available to, and selected by the dispossessed owner, may affect his compensation. If his property was sold in the no-scheme world the price would reflect the terms of his interest (eg whether a freehold or, if a lease, the duration of the unexpired residue and the rent), the inherent attractions of the property for the business (eg its nearness and convenience to customers), and any goodwill built up. However, if following the compulsory acquisition the business was to be relocated nearby, so keeping most of its customers, the price paid for the property would be affected by: (a) the fact that the goodwill was being transferred to the new premises and so would not be available to the purchaser, and (b) the fact that the property sold and any business carried on at it would have to face new and nearby competitive premises. The compensation payable should have regard to the effect of these factors on the price. This is fair since the dispossessed owner would obtain as compensation the amount he would have obtained for his property if he had sold it voluntarily and relocated his business as he actually does. On the other hand if on a voluntary sale relocation in the sense used above would be impractical, so that the business as carried on by the vendor would end, the price of the property so sold would take account of any goodwill and any unique or special locational advantage which adhered to the property and which would be preserved for the purchaser and would remain unaffected by the sale. The same situation would arise following a compulsory acquisition where relocation of the business is impractical and this again is fair since the owner would then receive as compensation that which he would have obtained for his property and his business with all their

---

[115] See *MacGregor on Damages*, 18th edn (London, Sweet and Maxwell, 2012), ch 7.
[116] Land Compensation Act 1973, s 46.

advantages and goodwill if he had voluntarily sold them and had himself ended his connection with the business. Obviously in such a case the landowner may obtain higher compensation since the property would fetch a higher price but he will lose the benefit of being able to carry on the same business at a new location.

The illustrations in the last two paragraphs explain in general terms the principles which   4.82
apply to the acquisition of a property at which a business is, or is to be, carried on. Each
individual case may be different (for example there could be a partial relocation of a business in the sense used above) and the principles should be applied flexibly in all cases. It will
be observed that this is an area of the law of compensation where a strict dichotomy between
what is called the scheme world and the no-scheme world breaks down. In order to know
the price which would be paid for a property where a business is carried on in the no-
scheme world, and so to assess the compensation under rule (2), it is necessary to know
what is to happen to that business, such as whether and where it is to be relocated, in the
actual or scheme world. The underlying principle is to see what the claimant has done or is
to do about relocating his business following the compulsory acquisition of his property
having regard to his duty to mitigate his loss and then to ask what sum would have been
obtained on a voluntary sale of the property disregarding the compulsory acquisition and
the threat of it but with the same course as regards relocation put into effect by the seller of
the property.[117]

Whereas a claim under rule (6) of section 5 of the 1961 Act cannot be used as an additional   4.83
claim for a loss of anticipated profits when the anticipation of profits has already been
reflected in the rule (2) value, there may still be a role for a rule (6) claim when a business
is relocated. The general nature of rule (6) claims is dealt with in chapter 8 but it is useful
to observe here that when a business is relocated two items of a rule (6) claim which may
arise are a sum for the costs of moving the business from one location to another and a sum
to compensate the owner for a temporary period of reduced business or reduced profits
while the relocation is taking place and in some cases for a period afterwards until the business is fully re-established. These two sums are not a part of the value of the land in the
ordinary sense of value but are sums which arise due to disturbance; that is the physical
removal of a person and his business from his land.[118]

4. The *Shun Fung* Decision

It therefore seems clear on the authorities and as a matter of principle that where a person's   4.84
land on which he carries on a business is compulsorily acquired the expectation of future
profits may figure as something which assists in, or leads to the assessment of, the value of
the land under rule (2) of section 5 of the Land Compensation Act 1961 but that no claim
may be made in respect of those profits under rule (6) either as an addition to the rule (2)
claim or in substitution for that claim. The decision of the Privy Council in *Director of*

---

[117] This formulation of the principle involves the application of s 9 of the Land Compensation Act 1961 which
is explained in ch 5. The concepts of the scheme world and the no-scheme world are further explained and elaborated in ch 5.
[118] An example of a claim for loss of future profits being disallowed under r (6), but a sum for moving expenses
being allowed under that rule, is the decision of the Court of Appeal in *Watson v Secretary of State for Air* [1954]
3 All ER 582, (1954) 5 P & CR 13: see para 4.70.

Buildings and Lands v Shun Fung Ironworks Ltd[119] is sometimes referred to in support of a different view. In that case land in Hong Kong was held under a lease granted by the Crown and was used to break up ships for scrap metal. There was no claim for the value of the land and the only claim was for a loss of expected future profits from the business. The decision of the Privy Council contains important general guidance on how claims for compensation of any sort are to be considered. The decision is not authority for the proposition that in England a person may abandon his primary claim under rule (2) and instead claim compensation for loss of expected profits from his business under rule (6). All compensation claims must be founded on the statutory provisions applicable and the provision applied in the *Shun Fung* case was the specific entitlement to compensation for loss or damage to a business contained in the Lands Resumption Ordinance in force in Hong Kong. That entitlement was to compensation

> on the basis of . . . the amount of loss or damage to a business conducted by a claimant at the date of resumption on the land resumed or in any building erected thereon, due to the removal of the business from that land or building as a result of the resumption.[120]

There is no equivalent provision in English law requiring the compensation to be assessed on the basis of loss or damage to a business. The question of whether there can be a claim for business loss instead of a claim for the value of the land was therefore not in issue between the parties and was not considered by any court in the *Shun Fung* case, up to and including the Privy Council, since it did not arise under the legislation in force in Hong Kong. The Hong Kong legislation stated, in direct contrast to the English legislation, that there could be a direct and separate claim for loss of profits to a business and so it was something which could take the place of a claim for the value of the land acquired. It was such a claim, based on that provision which was with the agreement of both parties accepted as sustainable in principle in all three Courts, through which the *Shun Fung* litigation passed. The *Shun Fung* decision is, of course, important guidance (though, being a decision on appeal from Hong Kong, not binding authority in England and Wales) on questions which were in issue in that case but it is unfortunate that it is sometimes regarded as providing guidance on questions (a) which were not in issue, and (b) the answer to which was agreed by the parties on the basis of legislative provisions which have no parallel in this country.

5. Further Considerations

4.85   While it is reasonably clear that expected future profits from a business carried on at the property acquired are a factor which may contribute to the value of that property, and so are to be reflected in a rule (2) claim and should not in principle be the subject of a claim under rule (6), there remains one point which is perhaps not wholly resolved and which remains arguable. The point can best be explained by an example. A lease of land may be at a full rent and the leasehold interest may have no capital value save to the extent that it

---

[119] *Director of Buildings and Lands v Shun Fung Ironworks Ltd* [1995] 2 AC 111, [1995] 2 WLR 904.
[120] Lands Resumption Ordinance (then the Crown Lands Resumption Ordinance), s 10(2)(d). A resumption of land means a compulsory acquisition of land. In Hong Kong nearly all land is held on lease from the Government (formerly from the British Crown) and on a compulsory acquisition it is considered that the land is resumed by the Crown or the Government as the lessor.

facilitates the expectation of future profits from a business established at the property which an assignee may be able to carry on. Suppose that the expectation of those future profits over the unexpired term of the lease creates a value of £400,000 for the lease, a sum derived by valuers from sales of comparable properties where the expectation of future profits has played a large part in the determination of the value of an interest in land. On the face of it this sum is the compensation assessed under rule (2) and is the totality of the compensation. However it is possible to calculate the capital value of the property attributable to the expectation of a stream of future profits by a discounted cash flow analysis. What in essence this means is that the net profits likely to be earned in each future year are estimated and discounted back to the valuation date at an appropriate discount rate. The aggregate of the discounted profits is then the present capital amount attributed to the expectation of receiving the profits over future years, which includes the value of the leasehold interest if that value has not otherwise been reflected in the analysis. It could be that in the above example this sum is £600,000.

An argument would be that the additional £200,000 is a sum not directly based on the value of land but the loss of it is a loss to the owner of the interest such that that loss can be recovered as compensation under rule (6). While such an argument cannot be ruled out it is very doubtful if it is correct. For one thing it is scarcely consistent with the authorities discussed earlier and if, in accordance with those authorities, the expectation of future profits from a property is a factor in assessing the value of that property it seems scarcely rational then to take a slice of those expected profits and to treat them as not directly based on the value of the land and so as capable of sustaining a further and different claim for compensation. The truer view seems to be that, whether or not the value of the expected profits is wholly transferred in numerical terms to the value of the property assessed under rule (2), the expected profits are still all taken into account in determining that value and a part of them cannot then be used again as the foundation for a different claim under rule (6).   4.86

A further, and probably correct, conceptual way of looking at the matter is to say that the present value of anticipated future profits which can be earned from a business carried on at the property acquired is a part of the subjective worth of the property acquired to its owner but is not a part of the objectively assessed value of the property. Statutory compensation is founded on value not worth. This general aspect of the law of compensation has been discussed earlier.[121]   4.87

Mention was made in the last paragraph of a discounted cash flow analysis. As also there mentioned what such an analysis aims to do is to determine the value at a specified valuation date or base date of a stream of expected future monetary flows. Where the stream is of expected profits each future annual amount may involve an assessment of the gross receipts of a business in the year, and the costs and expenses which will be incurred in earning those receipts, so as to arrive at an estimate of the expected net profits. Each annual sum of expected net profits is then discounted back to the valuation or base date. The discounted sums are aggregated together so as to provide the present value at the valuation or base date of the expectation of obtaining the future profits. Where the business which generates the profits is carried out on a piece of land the question arises of what exactly is the relationship between the result of a discounted cash flow analysis and the value of the land. Clearly the   4.88

---

[121] See paras 4.3–4.6 and see section (a) of ch 14.

result of the analysis will not necessarily dictate the value of the land since that value may be affected by other factors such as the terms of the interest being valued. Even in a simple example, where the land has no value except that attributable to the expectation of making a profit from a business operated on it, the discounted cash flow analysis may not by itself determine the value of the land. The example given earlier is an illustration of this possibility.[122]

4.89   A discounted cash flow analysis is one tool available to a valuer who values a piece of land but there are other potentially more reliable methods of valuation. There could, for instance, be a row of identical shops used for sales of different products. One type of product sold might create a different expectation of profits than would another type. It would not be sensible to suggest that the value of the shops differed according to the product which was being sold and the level of profits anticipated from the business. The value of a particular shop would be much more likely to be determined by the comparables method of valuation which involves looking at what sums were actually paid for such shops in actual transactions. The techniques used by accountants and others in assessing critical factors in a discounted cash flow analysis such as determining the appropriate discount rate may not be the same as the market, or valuers trying to replicate what would occur in the market, would use in valuing an interest in property. Furthermore the elements used in a discounted cash flow analysis, such as the costs of running a business or the rate at which money can be borrowed, may be particular to the actual owner of the land and the business and may not be appropriate for the hypothetical willing buyer or for any persons who might be in the market as competitors to the hypothetical willing buyer. The correct way in which to approach a discounted cash flow analysis is that it may be a useful tool in the valuation of business premises, especially when no other reliable method of valuation is available, but it does not necessarily even in such a case lead inexorably to the correct value of a property or to the amount of a claim under rule (2).[123] The same general comment of course applies to other methods of assessing the value of the right to receive future profits such as the use of a multiplier or a prices/earnings ratio calculation. One of the difficulties in the way of the use of accountancy techniques, as discussed in this paragraph, is that they depend on information on the business and past profitability of the business of the landowner. Yet this information may not be available in the market generally or to the hypothetical willing buyer.[124]

6. Summary

4.90   It may be useful to summarise the situation when compensation is claimed for the acquisition of a property in a case where a business is carried on or can be started at the property. The questions which arise usually relate to cases of an existing business at the property.

   (i)   The expectation that a profit is likely to be made in future years from the business is a factor which is to be taken into account in assessing the value of the land

---

[122] See para 4.85.
[123] The use of discounted cash flow analyses as a valuation technique is considered in section (d) of ch 14.
[124] See *Lynall v IRC* [1972] AC 680, [1971] 3 WLR 759; *Cornwall Coast Country Club v Cardgrange* [1987] 1 EGLR 146.

acquired for the purposes of rule (2) of section 5 of the Land Compensation Act 1961.

(ii) Where any element of goodwill attaches to the property or the business that element is a factor to be taken into account in determining the price which a willing buyer would pay for the property.

(iii) The price which a willing buyer would pay for the property is to be determined taking account of whether, and if so where, the claimant intends to relocate the business after the compulsory acquisition of the property.

(iv) A claimant is bound to mitigate his loss by relocating his business to new premises if it is practical and reasonable for him to do so.

(v) If the business is relocated the claimant is entitled under rule (6) of section 5 to claim compensation for such items as the costs of the relocation and a temporary period of reduced profits while the business is moved and re-established in a new location.

(vi) Save as just indicated no further claim may be made under rule (6) of section 5 in respect of the loss of expected future profits from the business.

(I) THE VALUE OF LEASEHOLD INTERESTS

1. Introduction

In everyday language persons are said to own land but in accurate legal terms what are owned are interests in land. Because of its quality of physical permanence land lends itself to the creation of limited interests. The duration of an interest is said to be the estate or interest held (a freehold or leasehold estate or a life interest) and the status of the interest is said to be the tenure (today freehold or leasehold tenure). What is acquired from a land-owner is therefore properly described as his interest in land, something which may range from a freehold interest which is of permanent duration to a weekly tenancy liable to be ended by a week's notice. The compensation legislation recognises this situation since the word 'land' includes an interest in land.[125] What has to be valued as the primary method of assessing compensation is, therefore, the open market value at the valuation date of the interest in land which has been acquired. When that interest is a leasehold interest what must be sought is the value of the lease.[126] In most cases the acquiring authority will acquire   4.91

---

[125] Section 39(1) of the Land Compensation Act 1961 defines land to mean any corporeal hereditament including a building and including any interest or right in or over land and any right to water. Section 1(3) of the Compulsory Purchase Act 1965 defines land to include anything falling within any definition of that expression in the enactment under which a compulsory purchase is authorised. Schedule 1 of the Interpretation Act 1978 contains a general provision that, subject to any particular provision in an Act, land is taken to include an interest in land. See *Oppenheimer v Minister of Transport* [1942] KB 242, [1941] 3 All ER 485.

[126] The law of landlord and tenant is a complex and specialist subject and is treated in textbooks such as *Woodfall on Landlord and Tenant* and *Hill and Redman's Law of Landlord and Tenant*. The subject has generated its own terminology which must be understood if the valuation of leases is to be understood. There are two essentials for the existence of a leasehold interest in land. The interest must be for a term certain or granted on a periodic basis (periodic tenancies are considered separately below: see para 4.95) and the tenant must be granted the right to exclusive possession of the property leased. A rent is nearly always reserved but is not essential for the existence of a lease. The words 'lease', 'tenancy', 'letting' and 'demise' are used largely interchangeably to describe the transaction. The descriptions of the parties within the pairs of words 'lessee and tenant' and 'lessor and landlord' are of

both the reversionary interest and the leasehold interest but there is normally nothing to prevent the acquisition of only the leasehold interest. If that is done and there is a covenant in the lease against assignment, or against assignment without the consent of the landlord, the acquisition can proceed without any consent by the landlord.[127]

4.92   In principle the value of a lease is determined for the purposes of rule (2) of section 5 of the Land Compensation Act 1961 in the same way as that of the freehold or of any other interest. A hypothetical sale of the lease as at the valuation date is assumed. There are certain characteristics of leases, not shared by freehold interests, which are vital in determining that value. The length of the unexpired residue of the lease is, of course, important (and this illustrates the importance of having an exact valuation date since only then can the exact unexpired residue be known). Equally important is the rent payable under the lease. If the rent payable at the valuation date is equal to what is then the full market rental value of the property (often called a rack rent) the lease may have no capital value in that no purchaser would pay a price or premium to acquire it.[128] Rent review provisions in leases will have an important bearing on the value of a lease. For many decades, following years of high inflation, leases granted at full rents for any duration in excess of five years have normally been subject to rent reviews (usually upwards only) so that the rent can be reviewed and brought up to date at regular intervals with reviews at five yearly intervals being that most frequently included.

4.93   Other provisions of the lease such as restrictions on the use of the premises permitted and obligations for repair may be relevant to value.[129] Provisions on assignment or subletting are also likely to be scrutinised by purchasers and valuers. In the absence of an express provision in the lease to the contrary a tenant is free to assign or sub-let the whole or any part of the property within the lease as he wishes. In practice most leases contain some restriction on assigning or subletting, either an absolute prohibition or a qualified provision to the effect that the tenant must obtain the consent of the landlord before assigning or subletting the property, generally in the case of a qualified provision with a further qualification that

equally interchangeable meaning. When a tenant grants a further lease out of his interest the freeholder is often called 'the head landlord', the intermediate tenant is often called 'the head lessee' or 'the intermediate lessor' and the second tenant is often called 'the sub-tenant' or 'the sub-lessee' or 'the underlessee'. The purchase price paid on the assignment or sale of a lease is often called a 'premium', although the term can equally well mean a capital sum paid for the initial grant of a lease. On occasions, particularly at times of falling rental values, an assignor may pay an assignee a sum for taking an assignment of the lease and so relieving the assignor of future burdens under the lease. Such a sum is sometimes called a reverse premium.

[127]   See section (c) of ch 2 and see *Slipper v Tottenham and Hampstead Junction Rly Co* (1867) LR 4 Eq 112.

[128]   If the rent payable at any time is less than the full or rack rent the difference between the full rent and the rent actually payable is often called the profit rent. For example, if a property is let for five years at a rent of £100,000 per year which is the full rent then obtainable and after two years rental values for property of the kind let have risen by 20% the rack rent becomes £120,000 per year and the profit rent is £20,000 per year. Since the profit rent is expected to continue for a further three years the lease may well have a significant capital value attributable to the benefit of that profit rent over that period. There may be an expectation that rents generally will continue to rise so that the amount of the profit rent will increase over the remaining three years of the lease and that expectation may result in an increase in the value of the lease. It is possible that the rent payable under a lease exceeds the market rent at the time. The property can then be described as 'over rented'. This situation can have implications for valuing the landlord's interest and this is considered in section (c) of the valuation examples discussed in the Appendix.

[129]   The fact that the demised premises are in disrepair and that the tenant is in breach of his repairing covenants may reduce the value of leasehold property and may even reduce its value to nil. It cannot create a negative value in the sense that any sum can be payable to the acquiring authority under r (2) of s 5 of the Land Compensation Act 1961: *Richard Parsons Ltd v Bristol City Council* [2007] 3 EGLR 73. See para 4.10.

consent is not to be unreasonably withheld or delayed.[130] A landlord who unreasonably refuses or delays his consent may be obliged to compensate his tenant for any loss caused to the tenant.[131] When the value of a leasehold interest in land is determined by the use of comparable transactions it is usual for valuers to compare the terms of the leases of the comparable properties with the terms of the lease being valued in order to see whether any adjustments are necessary.[132]

The assessment of the market value of a leasehold interest acquired may be more complex than that of a freehold interest but fundamentally the process is the same. Nonetheless there are certain complexities to be considered which are particular to leasehold interests. These include: (a) periodic tenancies, (b) a right to determine the lease, (c) options to renew the lease, (d) the hope of renewing the lease, (e) the effect of the protection given to tenants of business premises by Part II of the Landlord and Tenant Act 1954, (f) very short leases, and (g) leases of agricultural land. Various forms of statutory protection may affect the value of leases and this is to be taken into account unless expressly excluded for the purposes of the valuation process. The ability of a landlord to give an effective notice to treat so as to end a tenancy of an agricultural holding is restricted by the Agricultural Holdings Act 1986 and this must be taken into account in valuing the interests of the landlord and of the tenant.[133] At one time the security of tenure provided to tenants holding protected tenancies under the Rent Act 1977 was important but few such tenancies remain. Many tenancies of residential premises granted today are assured shorthold tenancies under the Housing Act 1980 and these offer only limited statutory protection to tenants. There has been over recent decades, and in accordance with current economic and social ideas, a marked tendency to leave tenancies to operate in the market in accordance with their contractual terms untrammelled by statutory intervention designed to protect vulnerable tenants. It has become recognised that if owners of properties are subjected to too many restrictions the result is that there may be fewer properties available to be let to tenants who need them.

4.94

2. Periodic Tenancies

Leases are of two types. A lease may be granted for a term certain, for instance 20 years from 1 January 2012, and in that case the exact length of the term and the exact commencement date must be specified in the lease. The other type of lease is a periodic tenancy, for instance an annual or monthly or weekly tenancy. A periodic tenancy continues for the first period and then for successive periods unless and until it is brought to an end at the end of a period by a notice to quit given by either the landlord or the tenant to the other party. The duration of the tenancy is therefore uncertain until a notice to quit is given. The rule for the purposes of assessing compensation is that it is to be assumed that a periodic tenancy is brought to an end following the valuation date at the earliest date on which it could have been brought

4.95

---

[130] See Landlord and Tenant Act 1927, s 19(1), by which a term that consent is not to be unreasonably withheld is implied in qualified provisions against assignment or subletting.

[131] See the Landlord and Tenant Act 1988.

[132] See section (b) of ch 14.

[133] *Rugby Joint Water Board v Shaw-Fox* [1973] AC 202, [1972] 2 WLR 737. See also today the Agricultural Tenancies Act 1995 which has substantially reduced statutory protection for tenancies created after it came into force. This Act provides that the Agricultural Holdings Act 1986 does not apply to tenancies created after 1 September 1995.

to an end by notice to quit given on the valuation date. To take an example, suppose that there is acquired an annual tenancy which runs from 1 May in each year to 30 April in the next year. The rule for the determination of annual periodic tenancies is that they may be brought to an end by a notice to quit which expires on the last day of the year of the tenancy (or on the first day of the next year) and is given at least six months before that date.[134] Therefore if the valuation date was 1 June 2012 a notice to quit given on that date could end the tenancy at the earliest on 30 April 2013. For the purposes of assessing compensation the tenancy must be taken to end on 30 April 2013 and must be valued accordingly.[135]

3. Break Clauses

4.96   A lease for a term certain may contain a right, sometimes called a break clause or an option to determine the lease, which entitles one or other or both parties to determine the lease by notice at a specified date or dates. A minimum length of notice is usually required. Sometimes the right to determine the lease is exercisable without any cause or motive or conditions having to exist and sometimes the right is exercisable only in certain specified circumstances such as that the landlord intends to redevelop the premises. The rules which have been developed concerning compensation in the case of such provisions are as follows. The rules apply in principle whether the valuation being carried out is of the landlord's interest or the tenant's interest.

(i)   If the right to end the lease is exercisable by the landlord, and is not subject to any pre-conditions such as an intention to redevelop the premises, it must be assumed that the lease will come to an end at the earliest date on which it could be brought to an end by a notice given by the landlord at the valuation date.[136] This rule corresponds closely to the rule which operates in the case of a periodic tenancy as stated in the last paragraph.

(ii) If the right to end the lease is exercisable by the landlord but only in specified circumstances or subject to certain conditions, such as an intention by the landlord to redevelop the premises or the grant of a particular planning permission, no automatic assumption should be made that the right can and will be exercised but the lease should be valued on the footing that a purchaser would take account of the possibility of the right to determine the lease becoming exercisable and being exercised before the term date of the lease and would adjust the price he was willing to pay for the lease accordingly.[137] The prospect of the conditions for the determination of the lease being satisfied so that the lease can be determined may then become a significant part of the valuation process.

---

[134] The rule is slightly different from the rule which applies to other forms of periodic tenancy where a notice to quit has to be given so as to expire on the last day of a period of the tenancy and must be of a length at least equal to the period of the tenancy. Consequently in order to end a monthly or weekly tenancy a full month's or week's notice to quit must be given.

[135] *Minister of Transport v Pettitt* (1969) 20 P & CR 344; *Bishopsgate Space Management Ltd v London Underground Ltd* [2004] 2 EGLR 175.

[136] *Bishopsgate Space Management Ltd v London Underground Ltd*, ibid.

[137] The authorities do not cover precisely this situation. However, it would be illogical and unjust that a person whose lease was acquired should be required to have it assumed against him that his lease would be brought to an end by the occurrence of circumstances when that might never be possible.

(iii) If the right to end the lease is that of the tenant alone no assumption should be made that the lease will be determined. The purchaser of the lease would have the same right as the seller of the lease to end it if he thought that to be in his interest. Such a right should, if anything, add to the value of the lease. It would be unrealistic to assume against a purchaser of the lease when it was acquired that it would be brought to an end by him when it might manifestly be against the interests of the tenant for the time being to do so, for example if the rent payable was substantially less than the full market rent at the time.

The rule that a periodic tenancy or a lease with a landlord's break clause is to be assumed to be ended as soon as it could be by notice, although established by authority, is of dubious justification. If such a lease was actually being sold a purchaser of it would form his own view of the prospect of a notice to quit or a notice exercising a break clause actually being given, and would adjust the price he would pay accordingly. There could be circumstances in which the giving of a notice by a landlord under a break clause was improbable. The rent under the lease might be in excess of the market rent in which case it is unlikely that a landlord would give notice to end the lease. Yet the assumption of the lease being ended must operate as regards the valuation of both the landlord's and the tenant's interest. In a case such as that just mentioned the landlord's interest would be depreciated in value by the artificial assumption that the owner of that interest would act as no rational owner would be likely to act. This seems hardly to accord with justice or with the principle of equivalence.[138] A further possible situation is that a purchaser of a periodic tenancy might take the view that the landlord would in practice be unlikely to end that tenancy by a notice to quit, at any rate for some time, perhaps because the tenancy had continued for some time with agreed adjustments to the rent from time to time or was a part of an estate where it was not the general policy of the landlord to end periodic tenancies without good reason. If a price would have been paid in the market for the tenancy founded on such an expectation it does not seem reasonable that the dispossessed tenant should be deprived of compensation determined by reference to the whole of that price.[139] A more rational rule would be that no artificial assumption is made that a landlord's break clause is exercised but instead the prospect of its being exercised shows just one of the factors to be taken into account in assessing compensation for a leasehold interest. The same observation is true as regards the prospect of a notice to quit being given to end a periodic tenancy. The rules here explained do not apply where a disturbance payment to licensees is being assessed under section 38 of the Land Compensation Act 1973 and it seems anomalous that tenants are treated less favourably than licensees.[140]

4.97

---

[138] The principle of equivalence, as a principle which underlies the whole of the law of compensation, is explained in ch 3, paras 3.2–3.4.

[139] As long ago as 1871 Lord Romilly MR pointed to the possible anomaly in *Re Marylebone (Stingo Lane) Improvement Act, ex parte Edwards* (1871) 12 LR Eq 389, where he said at p 391: 'I still retain the opinion which I expressed at the hearing, that it is very hard that a person who has been tenant from year to year (in this case the Petitioner was a weekly tenant) for a great length of time, and is disturbed in his occupation by a railway company, or the like, only gets one year's value. I have had a great number of instances before me in Court, and personally, of persons who have been tenants of property from year to year, and their grandfathers before them, they holding at the present time the same property which their grandfathers formerly did, and I think that a much more liberal compensation ought to be given in those cases'.

[140] In assessing the loss to a person, for the purposes of a disturbance payment, regard must be had to the period for which the land occupied by the claimant might reasonably have been expected to be available for the purposes of his trade or business: Land Compensation Act 1973, s 38(2). See ch 12, paras 12.23 and 12.24.

4. Options to Renew

4.98   Options to renew a subsisting lease cause no valuation complications. The benefit of the option is a part of the interest being hypothetically sold and, depending on its terms, may add significantly to the value of that interest. On occasions leases contain an option to acquire the landlord's interest and obviously such options may also, again depending upon their terms, confer value on the leasehold interest.

5. Hope of Renewal

4.99   An option to renew a lease is an enforceable right, and rights under Part II of the Landlord and Tenant Act 1954 which are described next are enforceable rights, and as such they may be taken into account in valuing the lease. If the lessee has none of these species of rights he may still entertain the hope that he may persuade the landlord to renew the lease when it ends. In an ordinary transaction this hope will pass to a purchaser of the lease and it is something which in principle could affect the price a purchaser would pay to acquire the lease and so its value. The hope might be enhanced if the property let was a part of an estate with a common landlord who had a tradition of looking sympathetically at proposals to renew leases. Despite this reasoning there are strong indications that as a matter of law the hope or expectation of a voluntary renewal of a lease is something which has to be disregarded in assessing compensation for the acquisition of the leasehold interest.[141]

6. Part II of the Landlord and Tenant Act 1954

4.100 Since 1954 leases of property occupied and used for business purposes have enjoyed the protection of Part II of the Landlord and Tenant Act 1954. The substance of the protection is that at the termination of the lease the tenant can apply to the court for an order for the grant to him of a new tenancy. The court must order the grant of a new tenancy unless the landlord can establish certain grounds of opposition of which the most important are an intention by him to demolish the premises or himself to occupy the premises. If certain of the grounds of opposition, including the two just mentioned, are made out so that no new tenancy is granted the tenant is entitled to compensation.[142] Since 1969 it has been possible for the parties to exclude this statutory protection by an agreement made at the time of the grant of the lease.[143] Where a tenancy does not enjoy the statutory protection there is no further explanation needed. This may occur, for example, because the tenant does not occupy the premises or because there has been an agreed exclusion of the protection of the

---

[141] *Minister of Transport v Pettitt* (1968) 67 LGR 499; *Corporation of Glasgow v Lynch* (1903) 11 SLT 263; *Director of Lands v Yin Shuen Enterprises Ltd* [2003] 6 HKCFA 1 (Ct of Final Appeal, Hong Kong), per Lord Millett; *Bishopsgate Space Management Ltd v London Underground Ltd* [2004] 2 EGLR 175; cf *Trocette Property Co Ltd v GLC* (1974) 28 P & CR 408.

[142] A detailed account of the legislation will be found in *Woodfall on Landlord and Tenant,* vol 2 (Sweet and Maxwell).

[143] See the amendments to s 38 of the Landlord and Tenant Act 1954 introduced by the Law of Property Act 1969 and see subsequent further amendments.

Act. However, if a tenancy which is acquired does enjoy the protection of the Act the availability of the rights of tenants under the Act, mainly the ability of the tenant to apply for a new tenancy at the end of the lease, may add to the value of the lease.

As originally enacted the Landlord and Tenant Act 1954 provided that the right to a new   4.101
tenancy should not be taken into account when a leasehold interest was valued for the purposes of assessing compensation.[144] The position was reversed by the Land Compensation Act 1973 and the present law is that where an acquiring authority acquires compulsorily the interest of the landlord in any land subject to a tenancy to which Part II of the Landlord and Tenant Act 1954 applies, or acquires the interest of the tenant in, or takes possession of, such land, the right of the tenant to apply under Part II for the grant of a new tenancy shall be taken into account in assessing the compensation payable in connection with the acquisition of the interest or the taking of possession of the land.[145]

The valuation result is that when land is acquired, which is subject to a tenancy within the   4.102
protection of Part II of the Landlord and Tenant Act 1954, both the landlord's interest and the tenant's interest have to be valued taking into account the rights and obligations of the parties under the Act. The primary right in question is the right of the tenant to apply to the court for an order for the grant of a new tenancy and the corresponding obligation of the landlord is to grant to him the new tenancy if ordered to do so by the court. The right of the tenant is not automatic or absolute. It is dependent on the tenant taking action by making an application to the court within the prescribed time limit.[146] The landlord may be able to resist the grant of a new tenancy on one of the specified grounds. In some cases the court has a discretion on whether to order the grant of a new tenancy such as where the tenant has been persistently late in the payment of rent.[147] Of course in many cases landlords and tenants agree on the terms of a new tenancy so avoiding the need for disputed court proceedings. If the property let is ripe for redevelopment the right to a new tenancy may be of little value since it is likely that the landlord will be able to defeat any application for the grant of a new tenancy at the end of the lease by establishing an intention to redevelop the property.[148] If a new tenancy is granted it will be at the market rent at the time and will be of a duration determined by the court save that it cannot be for a term in excess of 15 years.[149] The court has a discretion as to what shall be the other terms of the new tenancy but the general principle is that the terms will be the same as those of the previous tenancy unless there is good reason for them to be altered.[150]

As well as requiring that rights under the Landlord and Tenant Act 1954 are taken into   4.103
account in valuing the interests acquired the legislation goes on to provide that in assessing the compensation it shall be assumed that neither the acquiring authority nor any other

---

[144] Landlord and Tenant Act 1954, s 39.

[145] Land Compensation Act 1973, s 47(1). The reference to taking possession relates to the procedure under s 20 of the Compulsory Purchase Act 1965 under which the acquiring authority takes possession of land in the possession of a person having no greater interest than as tenant for a year or from year to year. The interest in question is determined rather than being acquired and the person dispossessed is entitled to compensation: see para 4.105 et seq.

[146] Landlord and Tenant Act 1954, s 29.

[147] Landlord and Tenant Act 1954, s 30(1)(a).

[148] Landlord and Tenant Act 1954, s 30(1)(f). The tenant will then in most circumstances have a right to compensation based on a multiple of the rateable value of the property under s 37.

[149] Landlord and Tenant Act 1954, ss 33, 34.

[150] *O'May v City of London Real Property Co Ltd* [1983] 2 AC 726, [1982] 2 WLR 407.

authority possessing compulsory purchase powers has acquired or proposes to acquire any interest in the land.[151] In the absence of this additional provision it would have been open to the acquiring authority to argue that since it had acquired, or proposed to acquire, the property, any application by the tenant for a new tenancy in the near future would be defeated by the acquiring authority as the landlord showing that intention, that is by establishing the ground of opposition to the grant of a new tenancy under section 30(1)(f) of the Landlord and Tenant Act 1954, such that the right of the tenant to a new tenancy would be of little practical value. The above provision excludes such an argument.[152]

4.104 The reference to some other body possessing compulsory purchase powers also being assumed not to have acquired or to propose to acquire any interest in the land is intended to defeat the argument that, if the actual or proposed acquisition of any interest in the land by the acquiring authority is disregarded, some other body with a power of compulsory purchase might have acquired or wished to acquire the land for the same scheme and so would be able to defeat an application for the grant of a new tenancy on the ground of that intention to redevelop. The result again would be that for this reason the right of the tenant to a new tenancy under the 1954 Act would have little value. Because of the additional provision such an argument by the acquiring authority in relation to the value of the tenant's interest is not available. The definition of an authority possessing compulsory purchase powers when used in relation to a transaction, such as a compulsory acquisition of an interest in land, confines that expression to a person or body of persons who could be or could have been authorised to acquire the interest for the purposes of that particular transaction.[153] The acquisition or the prospect of the acquisition of the landlord's interest by an authority with powers of compulsory purchase in order to carry out some other scheme can therefore be taken into account.[154] An instance of where these provisions apply would be where the acquiring authority at the time of the compulsory purchase of the tenant's interest already holds the landlord's interest in the property. The acquiring authority could not then argue that the right of the tenant to apply for a new tenancy under the 1954 Act was of little value because the acquiring authority as the landlord would be able to defeat such an application by establishing its intention to redevelop the property by carrying out the scheme which was the purpose of its acquisition of the tenant's interest.

7. Short Leases

4.105 A further matter to mention under this section of the chapter is that special provisions apply where there is a compulsory purchase of land and a tenant is in possession of the land but has no greater interest than as a tenant for a year or from year to year. The special provisions, which exist for historical reasons, affect both the procedure for obtaining possession of the land and the assessment of the compensation for the dispossessed tenant. The provisions are those in section 20 of the Compulsory Purchase Act 1965.[155]

---

[151] Land Compensation Act 1973, s 47(1).

[152] It is possible that the same result would have been brought above by s 9 of the Land Compensation Act 1961: see ch 5.

[153] Land Compensation Act 1961, s 39(1), applied by Land Compensation Act 1973, s 87(1).

[154] The expression 'transaction' is not defined but the compulsory acquisition of a particular piece of land appears to be a transaction.

[155] Section 20 replaces s 121 of the Lands Clauses Consolidation Act 1845.

The special provisions apply where a person is in possession of the land being acquired and   4.106
his interest is not greater than that of a tenant for a year or from year to year.[156] Persons who
fall within this category are: (a) tenants at will,[157] (b) tenants under annual periodic tenancies (ie tenants from year to year), (c) tenants under periodic tenancies where the period is
less than a year, for example weekly or monthly tenancies, (d) tenants under a tenancy for a
fixed term where the term is for a year or a lesser period, (e) tenants under a tenancy where
the term exceeds a year but where at the time that tenant is required to give up possession
there is less than a year of the term remaining unexpired, (f) tenancies continuing after
their contractual term date under Part II of the Landlord and Tenant Act 1954,[158] and (g)
tenancies which have been determined by the operation of a break clause where the lease is
due to end within a year or less.[159]

Persons in possession of land under a licence, and so with no tenancy at all, are not entitled   4.107
to compensation under the general entitlement to compensation in section 7 of the
Compulsory Purchase Act 1965, or under the special provisions in section 20 of the
Compulsory Purchase Act 1965, but may be entitled to a disturbance payment under
the Land Compensation Act 1973 if they were in lawful possession of the land and were
dispossessed as a result of the compulsory acquisition of the land.[160] If the tenant voluntarily leaves the property without having been required to give up possession he will have
no claim to compensation.[161]

Persons with an interest in land which does fall within section 20 of the Compulsory   4.108
Purchase Act 1965 are entitled to compensation when required to give up possession of the
land and that compensation is in many ways equivalent to the compensation payable to
those with larger interests in land which are acquired. Indeed as a general matter of policy
the assessment of compensation in cases where section 20 applies should follow as far as
possible the methods of assessing compensation in other cases.[162]

---

[156] Compulsory Purchase Act 1965, s 20(1).

[157] Tenancies at will are arrangements which constitute a tenancy but which may be determined at once, at any
time and for any reason, by either the landlord or the tenant. Such tenancies may arise expressly as a result of a
formal agreement or by implication, for example where a tenant is allowed into possession in advance of a lease
being granted to him or where a tenant is allowed to hold over after the end of a tenancy. Tenancies at will, whether
express or implied, are not protected by Pt II of the Landlord and Tenant Act 1954 and of their nature are pre-
carious interests unlikely to have any substantial value: *Wheeler v Mercer* [1957] AC 416, [1956] 3 WLR 841; *Hagee
(London) Ltd v AB Erikson and Larson* [1976] QB 209, [1975] 3 WLR 272.

[158] *London Borough of Newham v Benjamin* [1968] 1 WLR 694, (1968) 19 P & CR 365; *Selborne Gowns Ltd v Ilford
Corporation* (1962) 13 P & CR 350. The decision in *Benjamin's* case was at a time when compensation was to be
assessed without taking account of the rights of tenants under Pt II of the Landlord and Tenant Act 1954. Today
those rights are to be taken into account in assessing compensation whether under s 20 of the Compulsory Purchase
Act 1965 or otherwise: see para 4.100 et seq. However, it is probable that a person whose tenancy continues under
the 1954 Act after the end of its contractual term must claim his compensation, if any, under s 20. The scheme of the
1954 Act is that a tenancy within its protection, that is a tenancy of premises occupied for business purposes, continues after its contractual term date unless determined by some process prescribed under the Act or permitted by
the Act, eg by a landlord's notice to determine the tenancy under s 25 of the Act or by a voluntary surrender.

[159] *Bishopsgate Space Management Ltd v London Underground Ltd* [2004] 2 EGLR 175; *Greenwoods Tyre Services
Ltd v Manchester Corporation* (1972) 23 P & CR 246. It may be that where it has to be assumed that a tenancy
would be brought to an end by a notice operating a break clause at the earliest date on which such a notice given
at the valuation date could end the tenancy (see para 4.96) the end result is a tenancy assumed to have less than a
year to run so that s 20 applies to it.

[160] *Frank Warr & Co v London County Council* [1904] 1 KB 713; *Municipal Freehold Land Co v Metropolitan Rly*
(1883) 1 Cab & El 184. For disturbance payments under ss 37 and 38 of the Land Compensation Act 1973 see ch 12.

[161] *Roberts v Bristol Corporation* (1960) 11 P & CR 205.

[162] *Bishopsgate Space Management Ltd v London Underground Ltd* [2004] 2 EGLR 175.

4.109   Such persons are entitled to compensation for the value of their unexpired term or interest in the land.[163] The value is determined as in the case of other interests and is the amount which the land if sold in the open market by a willing seller might be expected to realise. The valuation date will generally be the date on which the tenant is required to give up possession.[164] If the tenancy is a periodic tenancy the valuation will be subject to the rule, explained earlier, that the interest will be taken to come to an end at the earliest date on which it could have been determined by a notice to quit given at the date on which possession was taken.[165] Tenancies at will are not within the protection of Part II of the Landlord and Tenant Act 1954 but periodic tenancies are in principle entitled to that protection and, as with other tenancies so entitled, the rights available to tenants under that Act are to be taken into account in the assessment of compensation.[166]

4.110   A claimant under section 20 is also entitled to compensation for 'any just allowance which ought to be made to him by an incoming tenant'.[167] This head of compensation goes back to the Lands Clauses Consolidation Act 1845. What is presumably meant is any sums in addition to a purchase price which a person acquiring by an ordinary assignment the residue of the tenancy would have paid to the person dispossessed. Awards under this head of compensation are likely to be rare.

4.111   A claimant is also entitled to compensation for 'any loss or injury he may sustain'.[168] These words also go back to the Lands Clauses Consolidation Act 1845. They are taken today to confer a right to compensation similar to that available to claimants with larger interests under rule (6) of section 5 of the Land Compensation Act 1961, that is compensation for disturbance or any other matter not directly based on the value of land. Thus sums, such as the costs of moving to other premises and the reasonable costs of preparing a claim for compensation, may be included in this head of claim as they can be under rule (6) of section 5 of the 1961 Act.[169]

4.112   Lastly, where possession of only a part of the land subject to the interest which comes within section 20 is acquired by the acquiring authority the claimant is entitled to compensation for the damage done to him by the severing of the part retained from the part of which possession is taken and for other injurious affection to the part retained.[170] This head of compensation is very similar to that provided by the second limb of section 7 of the Compulsory Purchase Act 1965 for persons with larger interests where only a part of their land is acquired and the compensation will be assessed on the same principles as under section 7.[171] An instance of such compensation would be where the works of the acquiring authority reduced the value of the interest of the claimant in the leasehold land within his tenancy

---

[163] Compulsory Purchase Act 1965, s 20(1).

[164] It is not clear whether s 5A of the Land Compensation Act 1961, which contains general provisions on the valuation date as explained in section (e) of this chapter, applies to claims under s 20. It is probable that rr (2)–(4) in s 5 of the Land Compensation Act 1961 apply to the valuation of short leasehold interests under s 20. It was said in *Runcorn Association Football Club Ltd v Warrington and Runcorn Development Corporation* (1983) 45 P & CR 183, that compensation on an equivalent reinstatement basis under r (5) of s 5 of the 1961 Act was not available where compensation has to be assessed under s 20 of the Compulsory Purchase Act 1965.

[165] *Bishopsgate Space Management Ltd v London Underground Ltd*, above n 159. See para 4.95.

[166] See para 4.100 et seq.

[167] Compulsory Purchase Act 1965, s 20(1).

[168] Ibid.

[169] See ch 8.

[170] Compulsory Purchase Act 1965, s 20(2).

[171] See ch 9 for a general explanation of compensation assessed in these circumstances.

retained by him. It had been held that compensation under this head was confined to damage to land within the same tenancy as that of the land of which possession is taken and could not extend to damage to other land of the claimant held under some other tenancy or other form of holding.[172] It appears that the language of section 20(2), as amended by the Planning and compensation Act 1991, permits a claim for compensation for damage to any other interest in land held by the claimant.

If the compensation cannot be agreed it is to be determined by the Lands Tribunal in the ordinary way.[173] 4.113

A tenant may have a tenancy to which Part II of the Landlord and Tenant Act 1954 applies, that is a tenancy of premises which he occupies for the purposes of a business, and may become entitled to compensation under section 20 of the Compulsory Purchase Act 1965 by reason of possession being taken of the land. In such a case the tenant is entitled as compensation to the greater of: (a) the compensation assessed under section 20 as just explained, and (b) the amount of compensation which would have been payable by the landlord to the tenant under section 37 of the 1954 Act if the tenancy had come to an end in circumstances which gave a right to compensation under section 37 and the termination of the tenancy had been the date on which the acquiring authority obtained possession.[174] The compensation payable under section 37 of the Landlord and Tenant Act 1954 is 'the appropriate multiplier' multiplied by either the rateable value of the property or twice the rateable value of the property. The appropriate multiplier is prescribed by statutory instrument and is currently a multiplier of one.[175] In order for the multiplier to be applied to twice the rateable value the property has to have been occupied for the purposes of a business carried on by the occupier, or for those and other purposes, for a period of at least the whole of the 14 years immediately preceding the termination of the tenancy. If there has been a change in the occupier during that period then in order for the higher compensation to be payable the new occupier must have succeeded to the business of the previous occupier.[176] 4.114

When the land being acquired is subject to a short tenancy of the type which falls within section 20 of the Compulsory Purchase Act 1965 it is open to the acquiring authority, if this is consistent with its timing and need for the land, to acquire the landlord's interest and then simply to wait until the tenancy ends, or itself take steps to end the tenancy such as by service of a notice to quit, and then take possession of the land in the same way as any landlord could. If this is done, and the statutory right to possession under section 20 is not exercised, the tenant is not required to give up possession of his land under section 20 and so is not entitled to statutory compensation.[177] The acquiring authority in those 4.115

---

[172] *Worlock v Sodbury RDC* (1961) 12 P & CR 315.

[173] Compulsory Purchase Act 1965, s 20(3). See ch 15 for a general account of the procedure before the Lands Tribunal.

[174] Landlord and Tenant Act 1954, s 39(2).

[175] Ibid, s 37(2); Landlord and Tenant Act 1954 (Appropriate Multiplier) Order 1990 (SI 1990/363).

[176] Ibid, s 37(3). A full account of the provisions and operation of s 37 of the 1954 Act will be found in *Woodfall on Landlord and Tenant*, vol 2.

[177] *Newham London Borough Council v Benjamin* [1968] 1 WLR 694, [1968] 1 All ER 1195; *R v City of London* (1867) LR 2 QB 292, per Blackburn J at p 300; *Syers v Metropolitan Board of Works* (1877) 36 LT 277, per Jessel MR at p 278. Cf *Runcorn Association Football Club v Warrington and Runcorn Development Corporation* (1983) 45 P & CR 183, in which it was held in the Lands Tribunal that where a tenancy had more than a year unexpired at the date of the notice to treat, and so was not a tenancy within s 20 of the Compulsory Purchase Act 1965, it was not open to an acquiring authority which had acquired the landlord's interest to avoid paying compensation simply by waiting until the tenancy ended before taking possession. The general question of the date at which the length of

circumstances would be in no different position from any other person who bought the reversion with a view to taking possession at the end of the lease. If the tenancy is one to which Part II of the Landlord and Tenant Act 1954 applies the acquiring authority will have to go through the procedures under that Act in order to bring the tenancy to an end, for example by serving a notice determining the tenancy under section 25 of that Act, and the tenant will then have the right to take advantage of the procedures under the Act including the right to apply to the court for an order for a new tenancy and the provision for interim continuation under section 64 of the 1954 Act until the disposal of the application by the court. The tenant may then become entitled to compensation under section 37 of the 1954 Act. The time which such procedures will take may not be acceptable to the acquiring authority which needs possession in order to carry out its project and the only available course for the authority then will be to exercise its statutory right to possession under section 20 but with the consequent liability to pay compensation to the dispossessed tenant under that provision.

4.116   A tenant whose tenancy falls within section 20 is not entitled to a notice to treat.[178] The tenant is obliged to give up possession to the acquiring authority when the land is required by them on the payment or tender to him of the compensation.[179] The special legal procedure available to an acquiring authority to enforce its right to possession, explained earlier, is available if the tenant refuses to leave.[180] The difficulty which an acquiring authority may face is where a tenant refuses to give up possession, but where the amount of the compensation has not been agreed or determined, it is difficult to see how in such circumstances the acquiring authority could pay or tender the amount of the compensation since that amount is not known. If there is a dispute as to the amount of the compensation, and it cannot be settled by agreement, the matter has to be determined by the Lands Tribunal and the procedure for determination of compensation before the tribunal may take a considerable time. In the case of longer interests, to which section 20 of the Compulsory Purchase Act 1965 does not apply, there are means by which an acquiring authority can obtain possession in advance of the agreement or determination of the compensation and the best course available to an acquiring authority in the circumstances mentioned may be to use those means notwithstanding their entitlement to possession under section 20. The acquiring authority may serve a notice to treat on other persons with an interest in the land (even though none is strictly required to be served on the tenant) and following the service of a notice to treat a notice of entry may be served and possession acquired by that means under section 11 of the Compulsory Purchase Act 1965. Alternatively the acquiring authority may operate the general vesting declaration procedure which itself creates an entitlement to possession of the whole of the land within the vesting declaration at the vesting date.[181]

4.117   If the claimant for compensation under section 20 has an interest greater than that of a tenant at will the acquiring authority may require him to produce the lease or grant under

---

the unexpired residue of a lease and similar matters have to be judged for valuation purposes is considered in section (e) of this chapter.

[178]   *London Borough of Newham v Benjamin*, ibid.

[179]   Compulsory Purchase Act 1965, s 20(4).

[180]   See ch 2, para 2.99.

[181]   See ch 2, section (p), for a description of the general vesting declaration procedure. Where the tenancy is a minor tenancy, something which is broadly equivalent to the type of tenancy to which s 20 of the Compulsory Purchase Act 1965 applies, a special procedure has to be adopted when a general vesting declaration is made: see ch 2, para 2.139.

which he holds or the best evidence of it in his power. If the lease or grant or the best evidence is not produced within 21 days of the requirement of the acquiring authority the claimant is to be considered to be a tenant holding under a tenancy from year to year and his compensation is to be assessed on that basis.[182]

8. Agricultural Tenancies

The general law on the assessment of compensation for freehold and leasehold land in agricultural use proceeds in accordance with the principles described in this and other chapters. Subject to that there are certain modifications relating to land subject to a tenancy which is of an agricultural holding contained in the Land Compensation Act 1973.[183] They relate to the operation of a notice to quit an agricultural holding where planning permission has been obtained for the non-agricultural use of the land which is the purpose of the acquisition by the acquiring authority. 4.118

Tenants of agricultural holdings enjoy, or have enjoyed, a degree of security of tenure provided by the Agricultural Holdings Act 1986. The tenancy of such a tenant must be determined by notice to quit which cannot have effect for at least 12 months.[184] Nor can a notice to quit have effect save in certain specified circumstances. One of these circumstances is that the land is required for non-agricultural purposes for which planning permission has been granted.[185] When agricultural land is being acquired for some non-agricultural purpose it is likely that the acquiring authority will have obtained planning permission for its scheme prior to the valuation date so that at that date a tenancy of an agricultural holding of the land may have its security of tenure under the Agricultural Holdings Act 1986 reduced because an effective notice to quit can be served on the tenant. This may have the effect of increasing the value of the landlord's interest and reducing the value of the tenant's interest. 4.119

It was held by the House of Lords in *Rugby Joint Water Board v Shaw-Fox*[186] that, in the circumstances just stated, the loss of security of tenure had to be taken into account in valuing the interests in the land. There was no statutory provision which required the disregard of the loss of security of tenure and the Pointe Gourde principle (which it was at that time assumed could have an independent existence outside any statutory provisions) was considered to have no application to the ascertainment of the nature of an interest in land as opposed to the valuation of that interest. This decision is significant in the development of the law on the value to the owner principle and the disregard of the scheme of the acquiring authority.[187] 4.120

The effect of that decision of the House of Lords has been removed by section 48 of the Land Compensation Act 1973. Where the interest of the landlord in an agricultural holding 4.121

---

[182] Compulsory Purchase Act 1965, s 20(5).
[183] An agricultural holding has the same meaning as in s 1 of the Agricultural Holdings Act 1986. It means the aggregate of the land (whether agricultural land or not) comprised in a contract of tenancy which is a contract for an agricultural tenancy, not being a contract under which the land is let to the tenant during his continuance in any office, appointment or employment held under the landlord.
[184] Agricultural Holdings Act 1986, ss 3–5, 25.
[185] Ibid, s 26 and Case B in Pt 1 of sch 3.
[186] *Rugby Joint Water Board v Shaw-Fox* [1973] AC 202, [1972] 2 WLR 737.
[187] See ch 5.

or any part of it is being acquired compulsorily, or where possession is being taken compulsorily, the right of the landlord to serve a notice to quit on the ground that the land is required for non-agricultural use for which planning permission has been obtained is to be disregarded in assessing the compensation for the landlord's interest. This result is brought about by a provision that the right to serve a notice to quit in these circumstances does not apply to the land being acquired by an acquiring authority. A notice to quit already served on the ground stated is to be disregarded. If the tenant has quit the land or a part of it by reason of a notice to quit which is to be disregarded under these provisions it is to be assumed that the tenant has not done so.[188] The same principle applies to the assessment of the value of the tenant's interest in the agricultural holding. The right of the landlord to serve a notice to quit and any notice served on the ground specified is to be disregarded. In this case if the tenant has quit the land by reason of a notice that is taken not to be effective there is no assumption that he has not done so.[189] The disregard of a potential or actual notice to quit applies to compensation assessed for a short tenancy under section 20 of the Compulsory Purchase Act 1965 as it applies to longer tenancies. This is the result of the reference in the legislation to possession being taken of the land as well as to the land being acquired compulsorily. These provisions now have a reducing impact since, by reason of section 4 of the Agricultural Tenancies Act 1995, the Agricultural Holdings Act 1986 does not apply to any new tenancy beginning on or after 1 September 1995.

4.122   Two particular rules apply to the assessment of compensation payable to the tenant of an agricultural holding:

  (a) The compensation is reduced by the amount of any compensation which the acquiring authority is liable to pay to the tenant under section 12 of the Agriculture (Miscellaneous Provisions) Act 1968.[190]

  (b) No account is to be taken of any benefits which accrue to the tenant by reason of additional compensation payable by a landlord for disturbance under section 60(2)(b) of the Agricultural Holdings Act 1986.[191]

4.123   It is possible that the compensation payable to a tenant would be less if the right to serve, or the service of, a notice to quit were disregarded under the provisions described than the compensation would otherwise be. Should this occur the compensation is increased by the amount of the deficiency, that is it is assessed as if the provisions here described did not apply.[192]

4.124   A further element of protection is given to tenants in occupation of agricultural holdings held under short tenancies to which section 20 of the Compulsory Purchase Act 1965 applies, that is an interest no greater than that of a tenant for a year or from year to year.[193]

---

[188] Land Compensation Act 1973, s 48.
[189] Ibid, s 48(3).
[190] Ibid, s 48(5). This provision is to the effect that where an acquiring authority acquires the interest of a tenant in an agricultural holding or takes possession of such a holding then an additional payment may be due to the tenant from the acquiring authority calculated in accordance with s 60(2)(b) of the Agricultural Holdings Act 1986, ie a sum equal to four years rent.
[191] Ibid, s 48(6). This provision is to the effect that where a tenancy of an agricultural holding is terminated by reason of a notice to quit, and the tenant quits the holding, the tenant may be entitled to additional compensation of an amount equal to four years rent of the holding.
[192] Land Compensation Act 1973, s 48(6).
[193] See para 4.105 et seq.

It is open as a matter of principle for an acquiring authority to acquire a landlord's interest in land and then, rather than acquiring the tenant's interest, simply wait until that interest is determined in accordance with the terms of the tenancy, possibly by a notice to quit, and at that point claim possession of the land in its capacity as the landlord. As regards a short tenancy of an agricultural holding an acquiring authority which takes this course may be able to rely on the fact that the land is required for the purposes of its scheme which is a non-agricultural use with planning permission and so to serve an effective notice to quit when that notice to quit would otherwise be ineffective. If that course is taken after the service of a notice to treat on the landlord or the making of a general vesting declaration in respect of the landlord's interest the tenant has an election. He may give up possession to the acquiring authority and elect that section 20 of the Compulsory Purchase Act 1965 shall apply to the acquisition as if the notice to quit had not been served and the acquiring authority had taken possession of the land by serving notice of entry under section 11(1) of the Compulsory Purchase Act 1965. The election must be made on or before the date on which possession is given up to the acquiring authority pursuant to the notice to quit. The election must be made by a notice in writing served on the acquiring authority. [194] Where the notice to quit has been given in respect of a part of an agricultural holding the election may be made in respect of that part. However a tenant of an agricultural holding has a right under section 32 of the Agricultural Holdings Act 1986 to require that a notice to quit part of his holding shall operate as a notice to quit the entire holding. A tenant cannot both give a counter-notice under this provision and make an election under the general provisions here being considered. [195]

The effect of a notice of election made under the above provisions is that compensation   **4.125** becomes payable to the tenant in accordance with section 20 of the Compulsory Purchase Act 1965. That compensation will be assessed disregarding the right of the acquiring authority to serve an effective notice to quit by reason of their scheme for non-agricultural use of the land. On the other hand if he makes an election for section 20 compensation the tenant loses any entitlement which he would otherwise have had to compensation payable to him under the Agricultural Holdings Act 1986 by reason of the notice to quit. [196] Under that Act a tenant who gives up possession following a notice to quit may be entitled to one or two years rent as basic compensation under section 60(3), to a further payment of four years rent to assist in the re-organisation of his affairs under section 60(4), and to compensation, often referred to as 'tenant right', for certain improvements to the land carried out by him. A tenant should therefore consider carefully the impact of the respective rights to compensation, under section 20 of the Compulsory Purchase Act 1965 and under the Agricultural Holdings Act 1986, before he makes his election. The basis of compensation under section 20 of the 1965 Act has been explained earlier. [197]

The election made may relate to a part only of an agricultural holding since the notice to   **4.126** quit related to only that part. The tenant may within two months of service on him of the notice to quit serve notice on the acquiring authority claiming that the remainder of the holding is not reasonably capable of being farmed as an agricultural unit either by itself or in conjunction with other relevant land. If the acquiring authority accepts the notice, or the

---

[194] Land Compensation Act 1973, s 59.
[195] Ibid, s 59(3)–(5).
[196] Ibid, s 59(2)(b).
[197] See para 4.109 et seq.

Lands Tribunal determines that the claim is justified, the tenant may give up possession within 12 months and then section 20 of the Compulsory Purchase Act 1965 will apply as if the acquiring authority had taken possession of that further part of the land compulsorily, so that section 20 compensation can be claimed in respect of that part.[198]

---

[198] Land Compensation Act 1973, s 61.

5

The Effect of the Scheme

(A) THE VALUE TO THE OWNER PRINCIPLE

When a piece of land is sold on the open market the price which it commands is usually   5.1
heavily dependent on the use to which a purchaser can put the land and his need to acquire
the land. In the ordinary course of events the seller can expect to obtain the value attributable to these factors. When land is acquired compulsorily for a particular purpose, and
given that the compensation is the open market value of the land, a question which had to
be answered as the law developed was the extent to which in determining its value the need
of the persons acquiring the land, and the use to which they were to put the land and other
land acquired for the same purpose, should be taken into account in the valuation process.
The result of answering this question has been the nostrum that in valuing the land acquired
for the purposes of assessing compensation it is necessary to disregard the effect on value of
the scheme of the acquiring authority.

In order to explain the current law and the effect of recent decisions on this subject it is   5.2
necessary to describe the development of the rule that the effect of the scheme is to be disregarded. That rule is sometimes described as the Pointe Gourde principle, an expression
derived from a decision of the Privy Council in 1947,[1] but the rule is much older in its origin. The rule has now been subsumed into legislative provisions enacted in 1959 and largely
re-enacted in 1961 but the nature and status of that legislation also cannot be understood
without some considerable reference to the history of the matter.[2] Those who wish only to
proceed to a summary of the law on this complex subject as it stands today may wish to
move directly to section (g) of this chapter.

When general principles governing compulsory purchase and compensation were first   5.3
introduced by the Lands Clauses Consolidation Act 1845 the only guidance given to the
courts by the legislation was the statement that the primary element of the compensation
was the value of the land acquired.[3] Out of this terse language there developed the principle
that in this context 'value' meant what was called value to the owner and not value to the
purchaser, that is to the persons who acquired the land. The expression 'value to the seller'
is sometimes used instead of 'value to the owner' but the import of the two expressions is
the same. It is not self-evident what this principle means. What was envisaged is that the

---

[1] *Pointe Gourde Quarrying and Transport Co Ltd v Sub-Intendant of Crown Lands* [1947] AC 565.
[2] The origin and development of the rule are extensively discussed in the opinions delivered in the House of
Lords in *Transport for London v Spirerose Ltd* [2009] UKHL 44, [2009] 1 WLR 1797, and in *Waters v Welsh
Development Agency* [2004] UKHL 19, [2004] 1 WLR 1304. A valuable survey of the history of the rule is contained
in Appendix D to the final report of the Law Commission, *Towards a Compulsory Purchase Code: (1) Compensation*
(Law Com No 286, 2003).
[3] Lands Clauses Consolidation Act 1845, s 63.

value of the land to its owner irrespective of the needs or scheme of the acquiring authority as the purchaser (in those days often a commercial body such as the promoters of a railway) should determine the compensation payable when that land was acquired compulsorily. In effect this was the market value leaving the scheme out of account. In order to give effect to this purpose it was thought necessary to disregard, when valuing the land, both the need of the acquiring authority to acquire the land for its purposes and the general scheme or project of the acquiring authority which underlay the compulsory acquisition. It might be thought that the effect of such an approach would often be to reduce the value of the land acquired below that which it might have commanded if the need of the acquiring authority and the scheme of that authority which increased the value of the land were taken into account. This will no doubt often be the case but in other cases the scheme of the authority, and the development in the locality which had taken place and was expected to take place in the future due to that scheme, might reduce the value of the land acquired below that which it would otherwise have commanded. The logic of the value to the owner approach requires that such a depreciatory effect in value should also be disregarded.[4]

5.4   The value to the owner principle as it was developed by the courts in the decided cases following the Lands Clauses Consolidation Act 1845 had two major impacts. The first, which may loosely be described as the disregard of the scheme, is the subject matter of this chapter. The second aspect is that which gave rise to the rule that items of compensation which had nothing to do with the value of the land acquired as such, for example the removal expenses of the dispossessed landowner, could be regarded as a part of the value of the land and reclaimed from the acquiring authority. This second aspect of the principle is sometimes described as disturbance compensation. It now has statutory recognition in rule (6) of section 5 of the Land Compensation Act 1961 and is explained as a separate subject in chapter 8.

5.5   The first clear expression of the value to the owner principle in the present context is the decision of the Court of Queen's Bench deciding a case stated by an arbitrator in *Stebbing v Metropolitan Board of Works*.[5] In that case certain churchyards were acquired in order to form a new street and to erect buildings on them. Burial in the churchyards was prohibited. The churchyards had little or no value. The issue was whether they should be valued for compensation purposes having regard to the value which the land had for the development to be carried out by the Metropolitan Board of Works which was acquiring it. It was held that no value attributable to the project of that development was to be taken into account in assessing compensation. Cockburn CJ said:

> When Parliament gives compulsory powers, and provides that compensation shall be made to the person from whom property is taken, for the loss that he sustains, it is intended that he shall be compensated to the extent of that loss; and that his loss shall be tested by what was the value of the thing to him, not by what will be its value to the persons acquiring it.[6]

The Chief Justice provided an illustration of the principle which he was applying.

> Suppose that a right of way exists over land, which prevents it being built upon, and that a public body has powers conferred by statute to apply that land to some purpose inconsistent with the

---

[4] This proposition appears only to have been finally established by the decision of the Privy Council in *Melwood Units Pty Ltd v Commissioner of Main Roads* [1979] AC 426, [1978] 3 WLR 520.
[5] *Stebbing v Metropolitan Board of Works* (1870) LR 6 QB 37.
[6] Ibid, p 42.

right of way, could the owner of the property be admitted to allege that, although he could not apply the land to a profitable purpose, and though he lost nothing by being deprived of it, yet as it would be of some value in the hands of the public body, he was to receive compensation in respect of that value? The answer would be, that as compensation is to be given for the loss which has been sustained, he would be entitled to none because he had suffered no loss. I think the same principle is applicable here.[7]

It must not be supposed that because the value of the land acquired attributable to the project of development of the acquiring authority was to be disregarded all development value was to be disregarded. On the contrary Cockburn CJ had made it clear a few years before the *Stebbing* case that the persons assessing compensation had to consider

5.6

> the real value of the land, and they take into account not only the present purpose to which the land is applied, but also any other more beneficial purpose to which in the course of events at no remote period it may be applied, just as an owner might do if he were bargaining with a purchaser in the market.[8]

Thus the principle as developed became that the landowner was entitled as compensation to the existing use value of his land, and to any development value attributable to a project which could have been carried out, apart from the compulsory acquisition and the scheme of the acquiring authority. All that had to be disregarded was the scheme of the acquiring authority and its particular need for the land. It is possible that the scheme of development of the acquiring authority could, if that authority was not to acquire the land, have been carried out by a private developer and in that case the development value attributable to such a development would be taken into account. For example, a piece of land might have a value in that it might be bought by a developer to erect houses. If a public authority acquired the land in order itself to build houses then the value which the land would have had in a sale in the open market for housing development, apart from the compulsory acquisition by that authority and apart from its particular scheme, would be taken into account.

It is apparent from textbooks published in Victorian times that the principle requiring the disregard of the effect on the value of the land acquired of the scheme of the acquiring authority had become well established. The first edition of *Cripps on Principles of the Law of Compensation* was published in 1881. It was said:

5.7

> The basis on which all compensation for lands required or taken should be assessed, is their value to the owner, and not their value when taken by the promoters. The question is not, what the persons who take the land would gain by taking it; but what the person from whom it is taken will lose, by having it taken from him.[9]

The principle that development value inherent in the land and not created by the compulsory acquisition and the scheme of the acquiring authority is to be taken into account had the authority of the same work. It was said:

> The present value of lands is enhanced by the probability of their more profitable use, and the assessment of compensation should be made on the potential, as well as on the actual value of lands to the owner. When lands used for agriculture are suitable for building purposes, this is

---

[7] Ibid, pp 42–43. This passage may be also regarded as an early statement of the principle of equivalence: see ch 3, paras 3.2–3.4.

[8] *R v Brown* (1867) LR 2 QB 630, at p 631.

[9] Cripps, CA, *Cripps on Principles of the Law of Compensation* (London, Sweet and Maxwell, 1881) at p 144.

necessarily an important element in their value, and a matter for which the owner should be compensated.[10]

5.8   Further authority confirmed the principle that the meaning of value was that of the value to the owner disregarding the effect of the compulsory acquisition and the need and particular scheme of the acquiring authority. In *Re Ossalinsky and Manchester Corporation*[11] Stephen J said:

> When a railway company, or any other person who takes land under compulsory powers, is to pay for that land, you are not to make them, as it were, buy it from themselves; you are not to take the value which, in their hands, it would acquire and make them pay for it as if they had no compulsory power.

5.9   In *Re Gough and Apatria, Silloth and District Joint Water Board*[12] land was acquired to construct a reservoir. It was held that any value which the land had for that purpose, disregarding the compulsory acquisition and the particular scheme of the acquiring authority, should be reflected in its value. Lord Alverstone CJ cited with approval what Wright J had said in the court below, namely that if the site had particular advantages for use as a reservoir, apart from the value created or enhanced by the scheme for appropriating the water to a particular local authority, that value should be taken into consideration.[13] It is said that this is the first decided case in which the expression 'scheme' received judicial approval.

5.10   The most important and influential of the pre-1919 cases may be *Re Lucas and Chesterfield Gas and Water Board*[14] in which again land was acquired to construct a reservoir but in circumstances which made it very unlikely that anyone other than the acquiring authority would either have wanted, or been able, to construct the reservoir. The principle to be applied was expressed as follows by Fletcher Moulton LJ:

> [W]here the special value exists only for the particular purchaser who has obtained powers of compulsory purchase it cannot be taken into consideration in fixing the price, because to do otherwise would be to allow the existence of the scheme to enhance the value of the lands to be purchased under it. But when the special value exists also for other possible purchasers, so that there is, so to speak, a market, real though limited, in which that special value goes towards fixing the market price, the owner is entitled to have this element of value taken into consideration, just as he would be entitled to have the fertility or the aspect of a piece of land capable of being used for agricultural purposes.[15]

It seems that what was meant by 'special value' in this discussion is the particular value of the land attributable to its potential for development for some particular purpose. The question was whether that special value existed apart from the scheme of the acquiring authority, in which case it was to be taken into account in valuing the land, or was due to the scheme of the acquiring authority, or was enhanced by the scheme of the acquiring authority, in which case either the value, or the enhancement of the value, was to be left out of account in valuing the land. Another way of putting the same matter is that, as Vaughan Williams LJ said in the same decision, what should be taken into account is 'the possibility

[10]   Ibid, p 153.
[11]   *Re Ossalinsky and Manchester Corporation* (1883), reported in Browne and Allen, *Law of Compensation*, 2nd edn (1903) at p 659.
[12]   *Re Gough and Apatria, Silloth and District Joint Water Board* [1904] 1 KB 417.
[13]   Ibid, p 422.
[14]   *Re Lucas and Chesterfield Gas and Water Board* [1909] 1 KB 16.
[15]   Ibid, p 31.

and not the realised possibility'. What is meant is that apart from the scheme of the acquiring authority the land might have had a possibility of being developed for a particular purpose and the value of that possibility is to be taken into account but that the acquisition by the acquiring authority for the purposes of their scheme is the 'realised possibility' and any value attributable to that is to be left out of account.

The principle was further developed by decisions of the Privy Council from Canada. *Cedars Rapids Manufacturing and Power Co v Lacoste*[16] in 1914 was an appeal from Quebec relating to acquisitions of land in order to use water power for the generation of electricity. It was held that the proper basis of compensation was the amount for which the land acquired could have been sold had the acquiring authority with its powers not been in existence but including the possibility that the land could still have been sold for the purposes of exploiting water power. Lord Dunedin stated the law in the following way: 5.11

> For the present purpose it may be sufficient to state two brief propositions:- (1) the value to be paid is the value to the owner and as it existed at the date of the taking, not the value to the taker, (2) the value to the owner consists in all advantages which the land possesses, present or future, but it is the present value alone of such advantages that falls to be determined. Where, therefore, the element of value over and above the bare value of the ground itself (commonly spoken of as the agricultural value) consists in adaptability for a certain undertaking . . . the value . . . is merely the price, enhanced above the bare value of the ground which possible intended undertakers would give. That price must be tested by the imaginary market which would have ruled had the land been exposed for sale before any undertakers had secured the powers, or acquired the other subjects which made the undertaking as a whole a realised possibility.[17]

Once again a distinction is drawn between the possibility of development, which is to be taken into account for valuation purposes, and the realised possibility of that development by the acquiring authority and by the implementation of the scheme of the acquiring authority, which is not to be taken into account. Perhaps the most succinct statement of the principle is that of Lord Buckmaster in *Fraser v City of Fraserville*,[18] a further decision on appeal from Quebec relating to land acquired in order to exploit water power, where he said:

> [T]he value to be ascertained is the value to the seller of the property in its actual condition at the time of expropriation for all its existing advantages and with all its possibilities, excluding any advantage due to the carrying out of the scheme for which the property is compulsorily acquired.[19]

In that case the arbitrators had arrived at the amount of the compensation by taking a proportion of the capital value of the expected profits to be made by the undertakers of the electric light undertaking. This was held to be an incorrect approach and inconsistent with the principle as just stated. English law followed the same course as that in *South Eastern Railway Company v LCC*[20] where Eve J at first instance set out six principles governing the assessment of compensation of which the fourth principle was 'increase in value

---

[16] *Cedars Rapids Manufacturing and Power Co v Lacoste* [1914] AC 569.
[17] Ibid, p 576. This passage was described by Lord Scott in *Waters v Welsh Development Agency* [2004] UKHL 19, [2004] 1 WLR 1304, at para 87 as one that in which the principles of compensation, relating in particular to the relevance of the special adaptability or suitability of the land for some particular purpose, have never been more succinctly and clearly expressed. The important *Waters* decision is discussed in para 5.67.
[18] *Fraser v City of Fraserville* [1917] AC 187.
[19] Ibid, p 194.
[20] *South Eastern Rly Co v LCC* [1915] 2 Ch 252, at p 258.

consequent on the execution of the undertaking for or in connection with which the purchase is made must be disregarded'.

5.12   If one pauses at this point in the historical analysis at 1919, prior to the report of the Scott Committee which will be considered next, the law had become tolerably clear as a result of a series of decisions which are summarised above. Different language is used in different judgments and there are different nuances of meaning. Even so the law as it then stood can be stated in a few simple propositions.

    (i)   The value of the land acquired for the purposes of assessing compensation is the value which that land would realise if sold by a willing seller in the open market.

    (ii) In assessing that value the potential of the land for development, that is the possibility that it can be and will be developed, is in principle to be taken into account to the extent that a purchaser would pay a price for that potential or possibility.

    (iii) However, where any value, be it the potential or possibility of development or any other element of value, is due to the particular need of the acquiring authority to acquire the land or to the particular scheme of the authority which underlies and justifies its acquisition, that element of value is to be disregarded.

    (iv) It is possible that the use or development for which the land is being acquired by the acquiring authority is a use or development which could be carried out by persons other than the acquiring authority. In that event any value of the land acquired attributable to that potential use or development by those other persons should in principle be taken into account.

5.13   It is in some ways unfortunate that the rules so established were not left as they were. They form a reasonably simple and coherent framework for the assessment of compensation and one which in broad terms is fair.[21] Nonetheless starting in 1919 there has been a series of legislative interventions, and of judicial explanations of those interventions, and it is of course necessary to state the modern law in the light of that legislation.

(B) THE 1919 ACT

5.14   The report of the Scott Committee (*Second Report of the Committee dealing with the Law and Practice relating to the Acquisition and Valuation of Land for Public Purposes*) at the end

---

[21] These rules do not answer every question which arises on the effect of the scheme and would have needed to be developed and refined by the courts. For instance, it was not clear whether account could be taken in the valuation of the possibility of persons, other than the acquiring authority, competing with that authority for the acquisition of the land even though such other buyers would also need statutory authority in order to put the land to the same purpose as that proposed by the acquiring authority. The view of Fletcher Moulton LJ in the *Lucas* case [1909] 1 KB 16, at pp 31–32 was that this possibility could be taken into account and in the same case at p 25 Vaughan Williams LJ suggested that the acquiring authority could be taken to be in the market as a potential purchaser. There is further discussion of this suggestion in *Sidney v North Eastern Rly Co* [1914] 3 KB 629. The advantage of all such judge-made rules is that they are flexible and can be adapted to meet changing or unforeseen circumstances whereas statutory rules require formal amendment. The question of what exactly was the scheme was a question of fact to be decided by the body which in the event of dispute determined the compensation: see *Fraser v City of Fraserville* [1917] AC 187, per Lord Buckmaster at p 187. The most modern statement of what constitutes the scheme, introduced by the Localism Act 2011 in connection with the assumption of planning permission, provides certain possible answers on the identification of the scheme to be left out of account: see section (c) in ch 7.

of the 1914–18 war addressed a number of questions relating to the development of the law of compensation and not surprisingly the rules just explained as developed by the courts were one of those questions. The report was critical of awards of compensation which took into account theoretical and highly speculative elements of value which had no real existence. In particular the report was critical of the theory that, while the need of the actual acquiring authority and its scheme for the land acquired were to be left out of account, when there was a possibility that other undertakers with statutory powers might bid for the land this competition was a factor affecting value which could be taken into account.[22] The solution of the Committee was to recommend that the land acquired should be valued leaving out of account any increased value which arose by reason of the suitability or adaptability of the land for a purpose to which it could only be applied with statutory powers.

The recommendation of the Committee was implemented by the Acquisition of Land (Assessment of Compensation) Act 1919. Rule (3) of section 2 of that Act excluded from the valuation process the special suitability or adaptability of the land acquired for certain purposes. The rule has now been replaced by rule (3) of section 5 of the Land Compensation Act 1961 and in its present form that rule reads: 5.15

> The special suitability or adaptability of the land for any purpose shall not be taken into account if that purpose is a purpose to which it could be applied only in pursuance of statutory powers, or for which there is no market apart from the requirements of any authority possessing compulsory purchase powers.

As enacted in 1919 and again in 1961 the rule also excluded 'the special needs of a potential purchaser' but these words were repealed by the Planning and Compensation Act 1991. The question of a special purchaser is considered elsewhere.[23]

It seems that the Scott Committee intended that at any rate important aspects of the value to the owner principle should be encapsulated in the new rule. There is powerful support for the proposition that if a wider application had been given by the courts to rule (3) of the 1919 Act much of the subsequent difficulty on the subject of disregarding the scheme might have been avoided. In fact rule (3) of section 2 of the 1919 Act, and its successor, rule (3) of section 5 of the Land Compensation Act 1961, have been narrowly interpreted and there are few reported instances of their application. In these circumstances the limits on the present rule (3) are described more fully elsewhere in this book since the rule has played no substantial part in the development of the value to the owner principle.[24]   5.16

It may nonetheless be useful in explaining the development of the law to state as an illustration one example of the way in which the effect of rule (3) has been limited. In *Batchelor v Kent County Council*[25] land was acquired to construct a roundabout which was needed to serve new residential development proposed in the locality. One question was whether this situation rendered the land acquired especially suitable for the purpose of constructing a roundabout and so for that reason that suitability might have to be left out of account in valuing the land by virtue of rule (3). The Court of Appeal held that the situation was not   5.17

---

[22] See n 17.
[23] See section (b) of ch 6. A purpose of r (3) in this form appears to have been to reverse the decision of the Court of Appeal in *IRC v Clay* [1914] 3 KB 466, that in valuing land the bid of a special purchaser is to be taken into account.
[24] See section (b) of ch 6.
[25] *Batchelor v Kent County Council* (1989) 59 P & CR 357.

one of special suitability since the land acquired was not uniquely suitable for the construction of the roundabout. Mann LJ considered that since there were other possible accesses to the land to be developed residentially the land acquired might be the most suitable land for the purpose of providing an access but that that attribute did not create 'special suitability'. It was said that the adjective 'special' connoted something exceptional in character, quality or degree rather than attributes or qualities shared with other areas of land.[26] What this amounts to is that if the suitability of the land for a particular purpose is to be left out of account by virtue of rule (3) that suitability must be unique to the land in question.

5.18   It is possible that if the courts had been willing to allow to rule (3), following its enactment in 1919, a substantially wider meaning and impact, as it seems likely the Scott Committee intended, that rule could have provided an explicit statutory basis for giving effect to the value to the owner principle as created by judges in the period before 1919. A powerful and detailed analysis in support of just this conclusion is contained in the opinion (dissenting in its reasons but not in its result) of Lord Scott in *Waters v Welsh Development Agency*.[27] Lord Scott believed that a series of decisions of the Court of Appeal and other courts had been wrongly decided in giving the limited meaning which they did to rule (3).[28] The view of Lord Scott was that the issue of disregarding the scheme of the acquiring authority could be resolved by the application of rule (3) with a wider interpretation given to it and by the application of the statutory rules enacted in 1959 and 1961 which are explained below. In this way much of the difficulty associated with what became known as the Pointe Gourde principle could have been avoided. Lord Scott considered, in an observation with which many would agree, that the jurisprudence in the Court of Appeal limiting the effect of rule (3) and creating some supplementary or non-statutory Pointe Gourde rule, had done no favours to landowners or to acquiring authorities.[29] Other members of the Appellate Committee expressed some sympathy with what Lord Scott had said[30] but the view of the majority was that in the light of a long line of authorities which appeared to treat the Pointe Gourde principle as having some existence independent of the statutory provisions, and of other authorities which limited the effect of rule (3), it was too late to set the clock back and, so to speak, to start again. The *Waters* decision was in 2004. It will be explained that only five years later in 2009 the view of Lord Scott, at any rate on the existence of an extra-statutory rule, appears to have been to a large extent vindicated in the recent decision of the House of Lords in *Transport for London v Spirerose*.[31]

---

[26] Ibid, per Mann LJ at p 362. A further example of the restrictive approach which has been taken to r (3) is the *Pointe Gourde* decision considered in paras 5.20 and 5.21.

[27] *Waters v Welsh Development Agency* [2004] UKHL 19, [2004] 1 WLR 1304. This decision is considered more fully in para 5.67.

[28] He considered that both the *Pointe Gourde* decision in the Privy Council and the *Batchelor* decision in the Court of Appeal, mentioned earlier, had been incorrect in this regard.

[29] See para 113 of the *Waters* decision [2004] UKHL 19, [2004] 1 WLR 1304.

[30] Ibid, per Lord Woolf at para 72 and per Lord Brown at para 143.

[31] *Transport for London v Spirerose* [2009] UKHL 44, [2009] 1 WLR 1797. See para 5.71 et seq.

(C) FURTHER DEVELOPMENT OF THE VALUE TO THE OWNER PRINCIPLE

Much discussion and difficulty came to surround the decision of the Privy Council in   5.19
Vyricherla Narayana Gajapatiraju (Raja) v Revenue Divisional Officer, Vizagapatam (usually
called 'the *Indian* case').[32] A harbour authority was developing land as a harbour. Existing
water supplies were malarial and there was a need for a supply of clean water. The land of
the claimant contained a supply of clean water and it was acquired in order for that water
to be used in the continued development of the harbour. The exposition of principle by
Lord Romer suggests that although there was only one possible purchaser of the clean water
supply, which was the harbour authority for its use in the continued construction of the
harbour, any value which adhered to the land acquired due to that need and that project
had to be taken into account. All that had to be left out of account was the fact that compulsory powers of acquisition had been obtained for carrying into effect a particular scheme.[33]
If this decision was based on the value created in the land acquired by the particular use of
it proposed by the acquiring authority then it is in plain contradiction to the previous
development of the value to the owner principle and would deprive that principle of much
of its content.[34] Somewhat unconvincing attempts have been made to rationalise the *Indian*
case in terms of previous and more traditional expressions of principle by saying that on
the facts of the *Indian* case there were two schemes, one for the acquisition of the clean
water supply and another for the harbour construction, and that all that had to be left out
of account was the first scheme. [35] If Lord Scott's solution in *Waters* of regarding the value
to the owner principle as now subsumed in the relevant statutory provisions (including rule
(3) of section 5 of the Land Compensation Act 1961) such difficulties as flow from the
Indian case (where there was no equivalent of rule (3)) disappear.

The other major decision, before the introduction of the current main statutory provisions   5.20
on the subject of the scheme in England, was that of the Privy Council on appeal from
Trinidad and Tobago in *Pointe Gourde Quarrying and Transport Co Ltd v Sub-Intendent of
Crown Lands*.[36] Under an agreement made in 1941 the United Kingdom agreed to let to the
US land for the creation of a US naval base. The claimants owned land which included a
limestone quarry and this was compulsorily acquired to provide stone for the construction
of the naval base. The Tribunal which assessed compensation awarded $86,000 for the value

---

[32] *Vyricherla Narayana Gajapatiraju (Raja) v Revenue Divisional Officer, Vizagapatam* [1939] AC 302. The
Indian legislation was similar to that in force in England at the time except that it contained no equivalent of what
was then r (3) of s 2 in the 1919 Act and is today r (3) in s 5 of the Land Compensation Act 1961.

[33] Ibid, per Lord Romer at pp 319–20.

[34] See *Waters v Welsh Development Agency* [2004] UKHL 19, [2004] 1 WLR 1304, per Lord Nicholls at para 35.
The expression of the value to the owner principle by Lord Romer is perhaps the narrowest possible statement of
that principle since all that it appears to require to be left out of account in the valuation process is the existence
in the acquiring authority of a power to purchase the land by compulsion. The result would be that any increase
in the value of the land acquired due to the scheme which underlay its acquisition, and the need by the authority
for that land in order to implement its scheme, would be taken into account. The approach of Lord Romer was
expressly applied by the Court of Appeal in *Lambe v Secretary of State for War* [1965] 2 QB 612, a decision which
is also important as regards r (3) of s 2 of the Acquisition of Land Act 1919. The *Lambe* decision is considered in
para 6.24 as part of the general explanation of the limited effect which is today accorded to r (3) of s 5 of the Land
Compensation Act 1961.

[35] See *Roads and Traffic Authority (NSW) v Perry* (2001) 116 LGERA 244, per Hodgson JA at p 362 (NSW CA)
and the decision of the Court of Appeal in the *Waters* case [2003] 4 All ER 384, per Carnwath LJ at para 92.

[36] *Pointe Gourde Quarrying and Transport Co Ltd v Sub-Intendent of Crown Lands* [1947] AC 565.

of the quarry, disregarding the special need of the US authorities for the stone for the naval base, and a further $15,000 for the additional value attributable to that need. The issue before the Privy Council was whether the additional $15,000 was properly awarded. It is, of course, this decision which has given rise to the expression 'the Pointe Gourde principle'. In some ways that description of the principle is unfortunate since the principle was in truth one which as an aspect of the value to the owner principle had been in force at least since the 1870s. It may be for this reason that the ratio of the decision has come to be called the 'so-called Pointe Gourde principle'.[37]

5.21   There were two questions before the Privy Council. The first was whether the additional value was excluded by rule (3) of section 11(2) of the Land Acquisition Ordinance of 1941 in force in Trinidad and Tobago which was in the same terms as rule (3) of section 2 of the 1919 Act in England. The decision of the Privy Council was delivered by Lord MacDermott in a short and extempore judgment. It was held that the need of the US authorities was not 'a special suitability or availability of the land for any purpose'. The reason for this conclusion was that 'a purpose' in rule (3) was considered to refer to an actual or potential use of the land itself and did not extend to the use of the products of the land, such as limestone, elsewhere. This part of the decision can be seen as one of a series of decisions which have truncated the potential effect of rule (3) and the limitation as explained by Lord MacDermott has attracted significant later criticism.[38]

Lord MacDermott preferred to conclude that the $15,000 part of the award was not a legitimate element of compensation by reference to the second question before the court which was the operation of the value to the owner principle on the assumption that that principle was not subsumed within rule (3) as, given his view of the limited effect of rule (3), it plainly was not. The record of the argument of counsel contained in the Law Reports does not suggest that this question was argued before the Privy Council. Lord MacDermott referred to *Fraser v City of Fraserville*[39] and to what was said by Eve J at first instance in *South East Railway Co Ltd v LCC*[40] and then stated what he described as the well-settled principle which justified the rejection of $15,000 as a permissible part of the compensation and which was expressed by him in the following brief statement: 'compensation for the compulsory purchase of land cannot include an increase in value which is entirely due to the scheme underlying the acquisition'.[41]

Few would quarrel with this terse expression as a general description of how the value to the owner principle had developed. It has been suggested that one important consequence of the expression of principle of Lord MacDermott in the factual context of the case before him is that it made clear something which had not previously been apparent, namely that where the effect of the scheme of the acquiring authority constituted development on land other than the land acquired, and it was that development or the prospect of it which added value to the land acquired, the value to the owner principle could apply to exclude that ele-

---

[37] An expression used by Lord Neuberger in the *Spirerose* decision [2009] UKHL 44, [2009] 1 WLR 1797, at para 54.
[38] See *Waters v Welsh Development Agency* [2004] UKHL 19, [2004] 1 WLR 1304, per Lord Scott at para 93 and per Lord Brown at para 142. See also ch 6, para 6.23 where the *Pointe Gourde* decision is examined again in the context of the effect today of r (3) of s 5 of the Land Compensation Act 1961.
[39] [1917] AC 187. See para 5.11.
[40] *South East Rly Co Ltd v LCC* [1915] 2 Ch 252. See para 5.11.
[41] [1947] AC 572.

ment of value.[42] What should be held clearly in mind is that the decision in the *Pointe Gourde* case was the latest case in a line of authorities which had then endured for well over half a century and which established the value to the owner principle as a cardinal rule in the assessment of compensation and so did not represent any radically new departure from that principle as it had previously been expressed and applied. Indeed, this is shown by the observation of Lord MacDermott that the rule as he stated it was well-settled.

Following the *Pointe Gourde* decision the next 15 years or so showed little significant devel-   5.22
opment of the value to the owner principle either in English cases or in appeals from the Commonwealth. As far as England is concerned an explanation may be that the Town and Country Planning Act 1947 removed development value as an element of compensation and provided that in general compensation was to be founded on only the existing use value of land. It was unlikely in these circumstances that in assessing compensation the value to the owner principle or the effect of the scheme would play any significant part. This rule was not removed until 1959.

(D) STATUTORY INTERVENTION

The Town and Country Planning Act 1959 re-introduced the principle, which had under-   5.23
lain the assessment of compensation until the Town and Country Planning Act 1947, that the compensation should take account of all the potentialities of the land acquired includ-ing its potential for development. [43] The whole question of the scheme and its effect on value once again became important. It was thought useful at that time to attempt to put the aspect of the value to the owner principle which required the disregard of the scheme into full and detailed statutory form. The legislation was enacted on the assumption that rule (3) in the 1919 Act did not provide an adequate statutory statement of the present aspect of the value to the owner principle. This attempt to do this was made in the Town and Country Planning Act 1959 which contained other statutory interventions, such as the making of assumptions as to planning permission, something else which also became important as a result of the re-introduction into the assessment of compensation of development value.[44]

The five rules contained in section 2 of the Acquisition of Land (Assessment of   5.24
Compensation) Act 1919 remained unaffected by the new legislation. Therefore rule (3) of section 2, which could have been regarded as directed towards the value to the owner prin-ciple, was to operate alongside the new statutory provisions. The Land Compensation Act 1961 re-enacted the statutory provisions in the Town and Country Planning Act 1959 and the rules in section 2 of the 1919 Act. Indeed the preamble to the 1961 Act states that one of its purposes was to consolidate the 1919 Act and certain other enactments relating to the assessment of compensation. The current legislative provisions are therefore those in the Land Compensation Act 1961.

---

[42] Lord Nicholls in *Waters* referred to this aspect of the *Pointe Gourde* decision at para 41 of his opinion. See also per Russell LJ in *Camrose v Basingstoke Corporation* [1966] 1 WLR 1100.

[43] Town and Country Planning Act 1959, s 1.

[44] See Town and Country Planning Act 1959, s 9(2) for the main provisions; these are now in s 14 of the Land Compensation Act 1961 as heavily altered by the Localism Act 2011. See ch 7 where the subject of planning, some-thing of crucial importance to the assessment of compensation in many cases, is considered.

5.25   There are three main areas in which under the provisions of the 1961 Act statutory effect is given to the value to the owner principle. These are: (a) section 6 and schedule 1, (b) section 9, and (c) parts of sections 14 to 17 dealing with statutory assumptions as to planning permission. In addition rule (3) of section 5 of the 1961 Act can be regarded as connected to the value to the owner principle but, because of its historical development and the limited impact which has been attributed to that rule, it is considered separately.[45] These three main areas are now discussed although planning is best examined in detail as a separate subject and this is done in chapter 7. It is the first area, section 6 of the 1961 Act, which is the primary legislative impact of the value to the owner principle.

1. Section 6 of the Land Compensation Act 1961

5.26   Section 6 of the Land Compensation Act 1961 is a provision of substantial verbal complexity. It has been described by eminent judges as designed to postpone to the last moment any expectation of understanding its meaning and as exhibiting the worst aspects of post-war statutory drafting.[46] The easiest way in which to explain the provision is not to make a further attempt to summarise its meaning as a whole but to describe its meaning by a series of five steps in its operation in the hope that at the end of the explanation the meaning, purpose and effect of this item of legislation will become tolerably clear.

5.27   The first step is that section 6 requires the leaving out of account in certain circumstances of any increase or diminution in the value of what is called 'the relevant interest'. The relevant interest is the interest in land which is being compulsorily acquired and so is to be valued.[47] This process is ancillary to, or a qualification of, the primary rule for the assessment of compensation which is rule (2) of section 5 of the 1961 Act and which provides that the value of the relevant interest is the amount which that interest if sold in the open market by a willing seller might be expected to realise. The primary purpose of section 6 is, therefore, that a certain matter or certain matters which would otherwise affect that value are to be left out of account in determining that value.

5.28   The second step is to identify the exact matter the effect of which on the value of the interest acquired has to be left out of account. The matter is certain development which as at the valuation date has been carried out or the prospect at the valuation date of certain development being carried out in the future. Development has the same general meaning as in the planning legislation.[48] It is the carrying out of any building, engineering, mining or other operations in, on, over or under land or the making of a material change in the use of any buildings or other land.[49] For the purposes of the present provision development is given a

---

[45] See ch 6.
[46] See *Camrose v Basingstoke Corporation* [1966] 1 WLR 1100, per Russell LJ at p 1110; *Transport for London v Spirerose Ltd* [2009] UKHL 44, [2009] 1 WLR 1797, per Lord Walker at para 22. In *Davy v Leeds Corporation* in the Court of Appeal [1964] 3 All ER 390 Harman LJ at p 394 called the provisions 'a monstrous legislative morass'. Despite these strictures there had been little difficulty in applying the provisions in s 6. The application of s 9 of the 1961 Act, which is a much shorter and terser provision, has created substantially greater difficulty: see para 5.43 et seq.
[47] Land Compensation Act 1961 (LCA), s 39(2).
[48] LCA 1961, s 39(1).
[49] Town and Country Planning Act 1990, s 55(1).

slightly extended meaning in that it includes the clearing of land.[50] It is important to note at this stage that the only development the effect of which has to be left out of account is development on land other than the land which has been acquired and is being valued. At first sight this might seem curious (and it has led to confusion in the courts which has only recently been corrected by the House of Lords) since the value to the owner principle was directed towards disregarding the scheme of the acquiring authority and that scheme was likely to be carried out at any rate in part on the land acquired from any particular land-owner. The explanation is the policy behind the legislation. If land is acquired for a particular project which adds value to that land it was thought proper that the acquiring authority, which acquires that value, should pay for it in the compensation payable to the dispossessed landowner. This policy is reinforced by the statutory assumption which has to be made that planning permission would be granted such as would permit development of the land acquired from the landowner in accordance with the proposals of the acquiring authority.[51] The matter to be disregarded is therefore development, or the prospect of development, on land other than the land acquired from a particular landowner and which is itself being valued. It is obvious that when a particular piece of land is being valued the existence or prospect of development on other nearby land may increase or decrease the value of the land being acquired. It is that effect on value which has to be left out of account in the valuation process.

It is easy to see how existing development, which is a part of the scheme of the acquiring authority, may increase the value of a particular area of land acquired so that that effect on value may have to be left out of account. An illustration might be the construction of roads or public parks by an urban development corporation which then acquires land on which to construct new housing. The value of the land acquired for housing might be enhanced by the existence of such public facilities. It is equally easy to see that land acquired to build houses on it might be enhanced in value by the prospect of future development by the urban development corporation, or others designed to provide facilities, such as new shops or children's play areas. Where the effect on value of prospective development is to be left out of account then of course questions may need to be asked on how certain that development is and how far in the future it is likely to be before it happens. When the present rules are applied it is frequently described as a case of certain development being left out of account in the valuation process. The more accurate statement in accordance with the statutory language is to say that the effect on the value of the land acquired has to be left out of account. It is doubtful whether any practical difference is caused by this linguistic nicety.

5.29

The third step is to know the area, other than the land being valued, within which certain development or the prospect of certain development has to be left out of account when it affects the value of the relevant interest. Part I of schedule 1 to the 1961 Act prescribes seven such areas in what are called cases.

5.30

(a) The case and area of general application is case 1. This case applies where the acquisition is for purposes involving development of any of the land authorised to be acquired. Where the land is authorised to be acquired by a compulsory purchase order, which will comprise the majority of cases, the land authorised to be acquired means all of the land comprised in that authorisation. In other words it is all of the

---

[50] LCA 1961, s 6(3).
[51] LCA 1961, s 15(1). See ch 7.

land authorised to be acquired by the compulsory purchase order.[52] Therefore, where case 1 applies, the development or the prospect of development which may have to be left out of account must be on any land within the compulsory purchase order. This is an important geographical limitation. Some of the land to be developed within the scheme of the acquiring authority may be outside the geographical ambit of the compulsory purchase order, a situation which may arise when, for example, the acquiring authority owns the land in question or has agreed to buy it so that no compulsory purchase was necessary. As will be explained the courts have had to grapple with problems of this kind. Sometimes the empowering Act itself specifies the land which may be compulsorily acquired, usually where a specific Act provides for a specific project such as the Crossrail project in London. In those circumstances no compulsory purchase order is made. In that event the land authorised to be acquired, and within which the effect of development on value may have to be left out of account, is the whole of the land authorised to be acquired by the Act which is described in the legislation as the special enactment.[53]

(b) Case 2 applies where the land being valued forms part of an area defined in the current development plan as an area of comprehensive development. Such definitions in development plans no longer occur so that case 2 is of no practical significance today.

(c) Case 3 applies where on the date of the service of the notice to treat[54] any of the land acquired forms part of an area designated as the site of a new town under the New Towns Act 1965. The area within which development or the prospect of development may then fall to be left out of account is the area so designated.

(d) Case 3A is an extension of case 3. It applies where at the date of service of the notice to treat any of the land being valued forms part of an area designated as an extension of the site of a new town under the New Towns Act 1965. The area within which development, or the prospect of development, may have to be left out of account is the area designated as the extension of the site of the new town.

(e) Case 4 applies where any of the land being valued forms part of an area defined in the current development plan as an area of town development. This case is again not of importance today since current development plans do not contain definitions of areas of town development.

(f) Case 4A applies where any of the land being valued forms part of an area designated as an urban development area under section 134 of the Local Government, Planning and Land Act 1980. The area within which development or the prospect of development may have to be left out of account is the urban development area. This case may today be of more practical importance.[55]

---

[52] LCA 1961, s 6(3).

[53] For a description of the two methods of specifying the land which may be compulsorily acquired, see para 2.41 of ch 2. See ss 6(3) and 39(1) of the LCA 1961 for the definitions of 'land authorised to be acquired' and 'special enactment'.

[54] In this and in the other cases described a notice to treat includes a notice to treat which is deemed to have been served: LCA 1961, s 39(8). Where the acquisition takes place by way of a general vesting declaration under the Compulsory Purchase (Vesting Declarations) Act 1981 there is no actual notice to treat but there is a constructive (or deemed) notice to treat under s 7(1) of that Act. For the general vesting declaration procedure see section (p) of ch 2.

[55] However, see para 5.38.

(g) Case 4B applies where any of the land being valued forms part of a housing action trust area established under Part III of the Housing Act 1988. The area within which development, or the prospect of development, may have to be left out of account is that area.

The fourth step is to know the circumstances within which development or the prospect of   5.31
development has to be left out of account when it is within the area identified within one of
the cases described under the third step.

(a) Under case 1 development or the prospect of development is to be left out of account if it is development for any of the purposes for which any of the land authorised to be acquired, that is the land within the compulsory purchase order other than the land being valued, is to be acquired. Clearly in order to apply this disregard of development it is necessary to know the purpose or purposes of the land acquisition under the compulsory purchase order. It is at this point that the statutory provisions centre on the scheme of the acquiring authority since the purposes of the acquisition of the land within the compulsory purchase order constitute that scheme.

(b) It is unnecessary to take case 2 any further since current development plans do not contain areas of comprehensive development.

(c) Under case 3 dealing with new towns the development or the prospect of development which has to be left out of account is development which is in the course of the development of the area of the new town as a new town.

(d) Under case 3A the development or the prospect of a development which has to be left out of account is development within the area designated as an extension of the site of the new town which is in the course of the development of that area as part of a new town.

(e) Case 4 is again not of importance today.

(f) Under case 4A the development or the prospect of development which has to be left out of account is development in the course of the development or redevelopment of the urban development area.

(g) Under case 4B the development or the prospect of development which has to be left out of account is development in the course of the development or redevelopment of the housing action trust area.

The fifth and last step is a qualification of the fourth step. By the end of the fourth step it   5.32
has been possible to ascertain the area within which the development or the prospect of
development may have to be left out of account and to ascertain the purpose of the development such that if it was for that purpose it may have to be left out of account. Even so, to
take case 1 as an example, it is not all development or the prospect of all development in the
area of the compulsory purchase order for the purposes of the acquiring authority which
has to be left out of account. Instead the development or the prospect of development will
only be required to be left out of account when that development or the prospect of that
development would not have been likely to be carried out or to exist if the acquiring authority did not propose to acquire any of the land within the compulsory purchase order. In
other words it is only development or the prospect of development which is wholly brought
about by the scheme of the acquiring authority which has to be left out of account in the
valuation process. Other development within the area of the compulsory purchase order,

even if for the purposes of the acquiring authority, must be taken into account in valuing the land if that development would have been likely to occur or to have occurred apart from the proposal of the acquiring authority to acquire land within the compulsory purchase order. The same principle applies to the areas within other cases. Development or the prospect of development within the areas designated, or defined or established as referred to in the other cases, will only be required to be left out of account in the valuation of land acquired if that development would not have been likely to have been carried out or to be carried out in the future apart from the designation or definition or establishment of the areas of land in question.

5.33   Land acquired within an urban development area for the regeneration of that area may be taken as an illustration of the operation of the fifth step. The purpose of the urban development corporation in acquiring the land may be to provide housing development on it as part of that regeneration. The prospect of housing or other development on other land within the urban development area will be left out of account when valuing the land acquired only if that other development would not have been likely to be carried out in the absence of any proposal by the urban development corporation to acquire any of the land within the urban development area. In such a case the prospect of the urban development can be said to be wholly due to the scheme of the acquiring authority. On the other hand if the development of other land within the urban development area would have been likely to be carried out, even if the urban development corporation did not propose to acquire any of the land within the urban development area, then the prospect of the development of that other land will be taken into account in valuing the land acquired. The same principle applies to development within the urban development area which has been carried out by the valuation date. That development on land other than the land acquired will be left out of account in valuing the land acquired only where it was carried out in the course of the development or the redevelopment of the urban development area and where it would not have been likely to have been carried out if the urban development corporation had never proposed to acquire any of the land within the urban development area.

5.34   It can be observed that to some extent the statutory provisions have turned the value to the owner principle, as created by the earlier decisions of the courts, on its head. In those decisions the focus was on disregarding the effect on value of the scheme development to be carried out on the land acquired. The statutory provisions do not apply to development or the prospect of development for the purposes of the scheme on the land acquired and being valued but only to development of other land within the area specified in the third step in the application of those provisions. For instance, if a piece of land is acquired within an urban development area for development as part of a general housing project and apart from the designation of the urban development area no development would have been likely to be carried out within the whole area so designated, it can be assumed that housing development might take place on the particular piece of land acquired and being valued but development and the prospect of development on other land within the urban development area are to be left out of account in valuing the land acquired. The reason that the prospect of housing development on the land acquired can be taken into account in these circumstances in valuing that land is: (a) that a planning permission for that development is to be assumed by virtue of section 15(1) of the Land Compensation Act 1961, and (b) section 6 and schedule 1 in that Act do not require the leaving out of account of development or the prospect of development on the particular area of land acquired and being valued. The end result may be that the land acquired has little if any development value since without the development over the remainder of the urban development area and the infrastructure to be provided within that area no purchaser would pay, or pay much, for the prospect of being able to develop the piece of land acquired in isolation. On the other hand the prospect of developing the particular piece of land acquired and being valued in isolation might have a value particularly if that piece of land was a large one.

The purpose behind these complex statutory provisions can be stated fairly briefly and simply. It is that in valuing land compulsorily acquired no account shall be taken of the effect on the value of that land of any development, or the prospect of any development, on other land which would not have been likely to have been carried out, or to be carried out in the future, apart from the scheme or project or purpose of the acquiring authority which underlies the acquisition. Under the terminology or jargon which has grown up among practitioners this hypothetical situation in which certain development or the prospect of development is disregarded is often called 'the no-scheme world'. There might have been much to be said for either leaving the value to the owner principle to be applied as developed by the courts or stating the statutory rule in some simpler and more general terms as just stated. As it is in carrying out compensation valuations it is necessary to apply the exact statutory language by reference to the various cases under which the principles are stated. A useful and practical way forward may be as follows. When the question arises of whether a particular development should be left out of account it may be useful first to consider the general operation of the rule and its general objective as just stated in this paragraph and as something which underlies the exact statutory provisions. If at this stage it appears that the development in question may have to be left out of account in the valuation of the land acquired by reason of that general rule the second stage is to examine the exact statutory language of section 6 and schedule 1 in the 1961 Act by considering the logical and successive steps which are embodied in the complex statutory language. Of course it is only if the development falls within one or more of the statutory cases as something to be left out of account in the valuation process that that development is disregarded in the valuation process. The general objective of the legislation must always give way to the exact statutory language which has been used. · 5.35

One can understand the wish in 1959 and 1961 to put the judge-made value to the owner principle into precise statutory form despite the complexity of the statutory language which gives effect to this purpose. The main problem to which this attempt has given rise is that the statutory provisions sometimes appear to be less than all embracing. An obvious illustration is that the acquiring authority may have carried out, or may propose to carry out, development on land which they have acquired by agreement and so which was not within the compulsory purchase order made by them. The result is that case 1 does not apply since that case applies only to development on land within the order. There is therefore no statutory provision which in a case of this nature requires the disregard of the effect on value of some development within the scheme of the acquiring authority. The previous loosely defined judge-made expression of the value to the owner principle could embrace circumstances such as those just described. It is the rigidity of the statutory provisions which created the 'lacuna theory' which has troubled the courts in recent years and which may have only recently been laid to rest. These matters are discussed in section (e) of this chapter. · 5.36

2. Special Provisions under Section 6 of the Land Compensation Act 1961

5.37   Certain special provisions apply to case 4A and urban development areas. An increase or diminution in value may have to be left into account even though it is attributable: (a) to any development of land which was carried out before the area was designated as an urban development area, or (b) to any development or prospect of development of land outside the urban development area, or (c) to any development or prospect of development of land by an authority other than the acquiring authority which possesses compulsory purchase powers. An authority possessing compulsory purchase powers is defined to mean, where it occurs otherwise than in relation to a transaction, any person or body of persons who could be or have been authorised to acquire an interest in land compulsorily, and, in relation to any transaction, means any person or body of persons who could be or have been authorised for the purposes for which the transaction is or was effected.[56]

5.38   In addition it is provided that as regards the operation of case 4A the matters mentioned in the last paragraph shall have effect in relation to any increase or diminution in value to be left out of account by virtue of any rule of law relating to the assessment of compensation in respect of a compulsory acquisition as it has effect in relation to any increase or diminution in value to be left out of account by virtue of section 6 of the 1961 Act.[57] This provision suggests that there may be other rules of law, not contained in section 6 but which have broadly the same effect. It has been suggested that this provision is a recognition by Parliament that there is some 'common law' or supplementary rule which can operate in addition to the statutory provisions.[58] That suggestion has now been shown to be generally incorrect.[59] It may be that this provision should now be regarded as applying only to the effect of section 9 of the 1961 Act. Section 9 is considered separately below.

5.39   There are also certain special provisions which apply to the operation of cases 3 and 3A relating to new towns. If a notice to treat as regards an area of land is served after the transfer date cases 3 and 3A do not apply to the assessment of compensation. The transfer date is the date on which, under the relevant statutory provisions relating to the new town, the new town development corporation ceases to act save for the purpose of winding up its affairs. For the purpose of applying this provision regard is to be had to the order which designated the new town in its original form and not as varied.[60] This rule provides a cut-off date for the operation of cases 3 and 3A.

5.40   A further provision relating to new towns applies where, at the time of the service of a notice to treat on land within the area designated as a new town, there is a prospect of development of land within the designated area. In such a case it is immaterial in determining whether the prospect of development falls within case 3 or 3A that the prospective development will or may take place after the transfer date.[61]

---

[56] LCA 1961, s 39(1).
[57] LCA 1961, Sch 1, para 11.
[58] See *Transport for London v Spirerose Ltd* [2009] UKHL 44, [2009] 1 WLR 1797, per Lord Walker at para 30.
[59] See section (f) of this chapter.
[60] LCA 1961, sch 1, paras 5–7.
[61] LCA 1961, sch 1, para 8.

A third provision particular to new towns operates when, before the service of a notice to   5.41
treat, land within the designated area of the new town has been disposed of by an authority
or body such that if the authority or body had been acquiring the land compulsorily case 3
or 3A would have applied. In these circumstances, and when there is a subsequent acquisition of the land by way of service of a notice to treat, cases 3 and 3A do not apply to that
acquisition.[62] What appears to be contemplated is circumstances in which the new town
development corporation disposes of land to another person and then re-acquires it
compulsorily. Cases 3 and 3A do not apply to the assessment of compensation on the re-
acquisition. The reason is that on the first acquisition the purchaser is likely to have paid for
the development value created by the new town and he should receive that value on a re-
acquisition of the land.

3. Section 9 of the Land Compensation Act 1961

Section 9 of the Land Compensation Act 1961 comprises a single sentence but its meaning   5.42
and application have until recently caused nearly as much difficulty as the more elaborate
provisions of section 6 and schedule 1 to the Act. Section 9 is as follows:

> No account shall be taken of any depreciation of the value of the relevant interest that is attribut-
> able to the fact that (whether by way of . . . allocation or other particulars contained in the current
> development plan, or by any other means) an indication has been given that the relevant land is,
> or is likely, to be acquired by an authority possessing compulsory purchase powers.

The words omitted were repealed by the Town and Country Planning Act 1968 as a result
of changes then made to the content of development plans. The relevant land means the
land being acquired and the relevant interest means an interest in the land being acquired
and valued.[63] It is apparent that section 9 is intended to be an application of an aspect of the
value to the owner principle and that it is intended to be complementary to the provisions
in section 6.

If section 9 is read exactly and literally as stated in its language it should cause no difficulty.   5.43
The value to the owner principle requires that the compulsory purchase itself, and proposals for it and the scheme of the acquiring authority underlying that purchase, should be left
out of account in valuing the land acquired. When the value to the owner principle was put
into statutory form the provisions of section 6 of the 1961 Act required the disregard of the
scheme in the sense that the effect on value of much of the development underlying the
scheme was to be left out of account in valuing the land acquired but section 6 says nothing
as to the compulsory purchase order itself or as to the proposals of the acquiring authority
to acquire the land. Section 9 fills this gap in that it requires that any depreciation in the
value of the land acquired due to the actual compulsory purchase, or any proposals for it,
are to be left out of account in the valuation process.[64]

Section 6 of the 1961 Act, when it requires the disregard for valuation purposes of certain   5.44
development or the prospect of certain development within the scheme of the acquiring

---

[62] LCA 1961, sch 1, para 9.
[63] Land Compensation Act 1961, s 39(2).
[64] The substance of s 9, although in a rather different form, was first enacted in s 51(3) of the Town and Country
Planning Act 1947.

authority, requires that disregard to have effect whether the consequence of the development is to increase or to decrease the value of the land acquired. In contrast section 9 requires the leaving out of account of any indication of a compulsory purchase but only to the extent that that indication results in a depreciation in the value of the land acquired. The difference is significant. The reason for the difference is that section 6 applies to development or the prospect of development only on land other than the land being acquired and valued. Section 9 applies to the effect on the value of the land acquired of an indication of a compulsory purchase of that land itself. One of the planning assumptions which has to be made in valuing the land acquired is that planning permission would be granted for development of that land in accordance with the proposals of the acquiring authority.[65] If section 9 had required that there be left out of account any increase in the value of the land acquired due to an indication of its compulsory purchase then its effect might have been seen as taking away with one hand the benefit of the assumed planning permission for development on the land acquired in accordance with the proposals of the acquiring authority which had been given with the other hand. Such a result is avoided by the operation of section 9 being confined to leaving out of account a depreciation in the value of the land acquired. This explanation of the content of section 9 is a further instance of the various provisions within the legislation being intended to operate together in a harmonious fashion.[66]

5.45   That which is required to be left out of account in the valuation process by section 9 is not just the compulsory purchase order, or other provisions such as a specific authorisation of a compulsory purchase of land in an Act of Parliament which authorises the acquisition of the land acquired, but also any indication that that land is, or is likely, to be acquired compulsorily. The reason for section 9 being framed in this way is that if all that had to be left out of account was the actual compulsory purchase order as regards the land being acquired then it could be argued that it was permissible to take into account the fact that the acquiring authority might make some further or different order to acquire the land or that some other acquiring authority might do so for the same purpose. The language of section 9 ensures that the actual compulsory purchase for the purposes of the acquiring authority and any similar proposals for a compulsory purchase for such a purpose are to be left out of account.

5.46   A leading example of the application of section 9, with the meaning as just explained, is the decision of the Court of Appeal in *Trocette Property Co Ltd v Greater London Council.*[67] Compensation was payable for the acquisition by the Greater London Council of a long leasehold interest in a disused cinema where the Council itself was the landlord. The Council had a particular policy as to the use of the land. The claimant contended that the reality of the Council being the landlord should be ignored and that instead an assumption should be made that some different and hypothetical entity, with a different land policy, was the landlord. This conclusion was rejected. However, what was to be left out of account by virtue of section 9 were indications given that the Council proposed to acquire the land for

---

[65] Land Compensation Act 1961, s 15(1). See ch 7, paras 7.12–7.13.
[66] See para 32 of the opinion of Lord Walker in *Transport for London v Spirerose Ltd* [2009] UKHL 44, [2009] 1 WLR 1797.
[67] *Trocette Property Co Ltd v Greater London Council* (1974) 28 P & CR 408. A further example of the application of s 9 is *English Property Corporation v Royal Borough of Kingston upon Thames* (1998) 77 P & CR 1 (on appeal from the decision of the Lands Tribunal at [1997] RVR 99).

the purposes of its road scheme. If those proposals were left out of account then the attitude or policy of the Council as the landlord to a future redevelopment of the property would have changed substantially and with that changed attitude the value of the leasehold interest being acquired would have increased substantially. This decision is a classic instance of the value of the land acquired at the valuation date being depreciated by reason of an indication having been given that the land would be or might be acquired compulsorily and of that depreciation in value having to be left out of account in the valuation process.

There was a considerable period during which the language of section 9 was given an effect which went considerably beyond its ordinary meaning and beyond what was likely to have been its intended effect. The high water mark of this process was the decision of the Court of Appeal in *Jelson v Blaby District Council*.[68] In that case it was proposed that a ring road should be built around Leicester. Residential planning permission was refused on the land being valued since that land was needed for the new road. Land on either side of that land was developed residentially since it was not needed for the road. The road project was later abandoned but permission to develop the land being valued was again refused, this time because of objections to the effect on their amenity from owners of the new houses which had been built on either side of it. The Council was required to purchase the land pursuant to a purchase notice. The issue was whether in valuing the land it should be assumed that a permission for residential development existed at the valuation date. One of the reasons given by Lord Denning MR for holding that such a permission should be taken to exist at the valuation date was the operation of section 9 of the 1961 Act. This decision was sometimes prayed in aid in subsequent cases in favour of the proposition that when an indication had been given in the past that the land acquired was to be acquired compulsorily, and as a result it failed to obtain a planning permission which might otherwise have been granted, section 9 operates so that it can be assumed that such a planning permission would have been granted. Section 9 was applied precisely to this effect by the Lands Tribunal in the *Spirerose* decision at first instance.[69] Any such wide ranging effect of section 9 was rejected by the House of Lords in the *Spirerose* decision.[70] A subsequent attempt to resuscitate the argument for section 9 having the wide effect of allowing a claimant to reconfigure the situation, as regards planning in the years before the valuation date, was made before the Lands Tribunal in *Persimmon Homes v Secretary of State for Transport*,[71] apparently on the footing that section 9 had not been considered or fully considered by the House of Lords in *Spirerose*, but that attempt failed.

5.47

---

[68] *Jelson v Blaby District Council* [1977] 1 WLR 1020.

[69] *Spirerose* [2008] RVR 12. For the facts of the *Spirerose* decision see para 5.71.

[70] *Spirerose* [2009] UKHL 44, [2009] 1 WLR 1797. See para 144 of the opinion of Lord Collins. Some reliance was also placed on *Melwood Units Pty Ltd v Commissioner for Main Roads* [1979] AC 426, [1978] 3 WLR 520, a decision of the Privy Council on appeal from Queensland, in support of the wide meaning of s 9 mentioned. The House of Lords concluded in *Spirerose* that this decision also constituted no authority for the wide meaning. It is apparent that today neither the *Jelson* nor the *Melwood* decisions are to be regarded as establishing any principle of law for the purposes of the general subject here under consideration. The *Melwood* decision did establish that the value to the owner principle could operate to require the disregard of a decrease in the value of the land acquired due to the scheme of the acquiring authority as well as the disregard of an increase in the value of that land due to the scheme. The *Melwood* decision is also an authority to support of the general proposition that in valuing land account may be taken of comparable transactions which occurred after as well as before the valuation date: see ch 14, para 14.24. See also nn 81 and 84. The *Jelson* decision, above n 63, is also of some significance in the development of the so-called Pointe Gourde principle.

[71] *Persimmon Homes v Secretary of State for Transport* [2009] UKUT 126 (LC). In fact s 9 was argued before the House of Lords.

5.48   The decisions so far mentioned on the allegedly wide effect of section 9 centred on the existence, or assumed existence, of a planning permission for the development of the land acquired. If in fact section 9 could be relied upon as something which could reconfigure past events, so as to bring about a notional factual state at the valuation date to be applied for the purposes of the valuation process, then there would be no logical reason to confine that reconfiguration to planning circumstances and events. In *GPE (Hanover Square) Ltd v Transport for London*[72] reversionary interests in land subject to leases had been acquired for the purposes of the London Crossrail scheme. The leases had been granted a few years before the valuation date when there was an indication that the land might be acquired for the purposes of the scheme. It was argued by the claimants that if there had been no indication of the Crossrail scheme the leases would have been granted on terms more favourable to the landlords than those on which they were in fact granted and that, by reason of section 9, it had to be assumed at the valuation date that the leases existed with those more favourable notional terms. In other words what was said was that events prior to the valuation date could be notionally reconfigured or rearranged so as to be taken at the valuation date to be as they would have been, or might have been, if there had never in the past been indication of a likely compulsory acquisition of the land acquired. The Lands Tribunal rejected this argument holding that the leases must be taken to be at the valuation date on the terms as they actually were at that date. The conclusion of the Tribunal was founded primarily on the language of section 9 with reference to the major practical difficulties which would follow if section 9 required a general notional re-arrangement of events and circumstances in the past.[73]

5.49   The meaning and ambit of section 9 of the Land Compensation Act 1961, as a part of the compensation code as a whole, are today clear on the established law. What section 9 requires is that when valuing the land acquired as at the valuation date there is left out of account any indication then existing, or that had been given in the past, that the land is, or is likely, to be acquired by the acquiring authority or any authority possessing compulsory purchase powers so far as that indication results in a depreciation in the value of the land acquired.[74] The land must be valued in its state as it was at the valuation date and with the benefit of any existing or statutorily assumed planning permission as at the valuation date. There is no warrant in section 9 for speculating what other circumstances might have occurred in the period prior to the valuation date in relation to planning or anything else by reason of the fact that an indication had been given in the past that the land might be acquired compulsorily. Interpreted and applied in this way section 9 has a simple purpose and simple effect and its operation should cause little difficulty.

---

[72] *GPE (Hanover Square) Ltd v Transport for London* [2012] UKUT 417 (LC).

[73] The Tribunal also relied on the decision of the House of Lords in *Rugby Joint Water Board v Shaw-Fox* [1973] AC 202, [1972] 2 WLR 757. A good example of the difficulties which could have arisen from the wide meaning of s 9 contended for by the claimants in this case is that apart from a past indication of a possible compulsory purchase the land acquired might have been physically redeveloped in the past. It is difficult to believe that the valuation of the land at the valuation date was intended to take place on the footing that the buildings on it had been demolished and replaced with entirely different buildings at some past date.

[74] It should be noted that the expression 'authority possessing compulsory purchase powers' used in s 9 is defined in s 39(1) of the Land Compensation Act 1961 to mean, when it occurs in relation to a transaction, any person or body of persons who could be or have been authorised to acquire the land compulsorily for the purposes for which the transaction is or was effected. Consequently s 9 does not operate so as to require that there be left out of account an indication or prospect that in the future the land might be acquired by some authority possessing compulsory purchase powers for some different purpose or scheme altogether.

4. Statutory Planning Assumptions

The Town and Country Planning Act 1959 introduced a series of assumptions which were   5.50
to be made in certain circumstances as to the existence of a planning permission for the
benefit of the land acquired. These provisions were repeated in the Land Compensation Act
1961. The provisions have now been radically amended by the Localism Act 2011. The provisions as now in force are treated in detail elsewhere.[75] The only matter which needs to be
mentioned at the moment is that the operation of the former and the current assumptions
depends in certain instances on disregarding the scheme of the acquiring authority and so
can be regarded as a statutory application of the value to the owner principle. For example,
section 14(2) and (4) of the Land Compensation Act 1961, as substituted by the Localism
Act 2011, provide that planning permission is to be assumed to be in force at the valuation
date if it is a permission which could at that date reasonably have been expected to be
granted on an application decided on that date, on the assumption that the scheme of
development underlying the acquisition had been cancelled, and that no action had been
taken by the acquiring authority wholly or mainly for the purposes of the scheme. Plainly
these assumptions are a statutory embodiment of the purpose which underlies the value to
the owner principle.

(E) TWO ERRONEOUS ROUTES

With the new legislation in place in 1959, and then in the current provisions in the Land   5.52
Compensation Act 1961, two important further issues were considered by the courts in a
series of decisions which led to the taking of what have now been recognised as two wrong
and unjustified legal routes. These routes were: (a) the theory of 'the adjusted world', and
(b) the 'lacuna' theory, that is the theory that the judge-made value to the owner principle,
or as it became increasingly to be known, the Pointe Gourde principle, retained a separate
existence as a supplement to the statutory provisions and as something which could be used
to fill or correct obvious gaps or deficiencies in the statutory provisions. In order to understand the modern law it is necessary to summarise these false routes to see how they arose,
and how they have come to be corrected, notably as regards the second route by the recent
decision of the House of Lords in *Transport for London v Spirerose Ltd.*[76]

1. The Adjusted World

The operation of section 6 and schedule 1 in the Land Compensation Act 1961, and the   5.53
operation of the value to the owner principle as summarised in the *Pointe Gourde* decision,
focus on leaving out of account the effect on value of the land acquired of certain actual or
prospective development which would not have occurred or would not occur in the future
apart from what can loosely be described as the scheme of the acquiring authority. A

---

[75] See ch 7.
[76] [2009] UKHL 44, [2009] 1 WLR 1797.

difficulty which emerged is that in some circumstances this negative process can produce something of a vacuum. Schemes such as major infrastructure projects or new towns can be decades in their planning or gestation or progress. For example, land for the current Crossrail scheme in London first began to be safeguarded (ie development on land which might adversely affect the implementation of the Crossrail scheme was first restricted) in 1989. There are still cases in which compensation remains to be agreed or assessed for land acquired to implement the project. The courts started to envisage 'an adjusted world' which could be used for valuation purposes as a method of meeting the perceived difficulty. What was meant is that the valuer not only left out of account development in a locality due to the scheme of the acquiring authority but then went on to ask himself what other development would have been likely to have taken place in that locality over past years if that scheme had never existed. The notional world so built up came to be described as the adjusted world and the land acquired was to be valued at the valuation date as though this notional and adjusted world actually existed around it at that date. The operation of the statutory provisions therefore proceeded through three possible stages. First, the actual world, or the 'scheme world', was considered. Secondly, development or the prospect of development due to the scheme was left out of account although it existed in the real or actual world, so creating a 'no-scheme world'. Thirdly, an adjusted or notional world was built up consisting of what would have been likely to have happened in development and other terms if there had been no scheme. The end of the process was that the valuation was to take place in this final or 'adjusted' world.

5.54   The high water mark of the theory of the adjusted world was the decision of the Court of Appeal in *Myers v Milton Keynes Development Corporation*.[77] Land which was used as a stud farm was acquired for the purposes of the development of Milton Keynes new town. This was an acquisition to which case 3 in schedule 1 to the Land Compensation Act 1961 applied. Therefore the effect on value of the land acquired due to actual or prospective development in the area designated as the site of the new town had to be left out of account. It was said that what had to be imagined was a notional world such as would have been expected in terms of development in rural Buckinghamshire over past years if there had never been any prospect of a new town. In a well known passage which has been subsequently castigated Lord Denning said:

> The valuer must cast aside his knowledge of what has in fact happened in the past eight years due to the scheme. He must ignore the developments which will in all probability take place in the future ten years into the scheme. Instead, he must let his imagination take flight to the clouds. He must conjure up a land of make-believe, where there has not been, nor will be, a brave new town, but where there is to be supposed the old order of things continuing.[78]

The delineation of the adjusted world is a question of fact and may depend on expert evidence. In the *Myers* decision many days of evidence before the Lands Tribunal were taken up by evidence from surveyors and valuers on this abstruse question.

5.55   A further decision to the same effect was *Margate Corporation v Devotwill*[79] where land allocated in a development plan for residential development was acquired to construct a by-pass. The Lands Tribunal had reasoned that if the actual by-pass was to be disregarded there would

[77]   *Myers v Milton Keynes Development Corporation* [1974] 1 WLR 696, [1974] 2 All ER 1096.
[78]   Ibid, p 704.
[79]   *Margate Corporation v Devotwill* [1970] 3 All ER 864, (1970) 22 P & CR 328.

inevitably be the construction of an alternative by-pass on other land which would meet urgent traffic needs and so would have facilitated development for residential purposes on the land acquired. The House of Lords held that the promotion of an alternative route for a by-pass was not to be regarded as an inevitable corollary. Rather there should have been an examination of what other alternative route or routes there might have been and whether they would have been effective and practicable. This again appears to be the process of building up an adjusted world. The difficulties inherent in this approach were recognised in due course and it was provided in the Planning and Compensation Act 1991 that where land was acquired for a highway it was to be assumed for the purposes of planning assumptions under the 1961 Act that 'no highway would be constructed to meet the same or substantially the same need'. The rejection of the adjusted world approach in the particular area of highway acquisitions and planning assumptions was not extended to the generality of compulsory acquisitions or to the assessment of compensation generally. [80]

The adjusted world theory had substantial practical difficulties. Not only was it difficult to know how events might have happened in an area if some major project had never been contemplated, but it was not even possible in some areas such as planning to know the correct time by reference to which the question should be asked. Planning policies and public needs, such as the need for new houses, change over time and when experts peered into the past to ascertain what might have happened in hypothetical circumstances they were uncertain on what date they should concentrate in a world of fluctuating policies and proposals. The result is that the flight to the clouds approach of Lord Denning in *Myers v Milton Keynes Development Corporation* is now regarded as unacceptable.   5.56

The way forward and the modern approach were presaged in *Fletcher Estates (Harlescott) Ltd v Secretary of State* in 2000.[81] In that case the issue was the correct approach to the determination of the content of a certificate of appropriate alternative development under section 17 of the Land Compensation Act 1961. As explained later this is a process under which the local planning authority is to determine what planning permission, if any, would have been granted for development of the land acquired in the absence of the proposals of the acquiring authority for its acquisition.[82] As also mentioned it may be regarded as one of the statutory applications of the value to the owner principle and it could involve some degree of foray into the adjusted world, that is not only the leaving out of account of development which was within the scheme of the acquiring authority, but a consideration of what other development might have been permitted on the land acquired in the absence of that scheme. The claimants asserted that it was proper to ask what development would have been carried out in the locality and over a substantial time in the past if the highway scheme of the acquiring authority, which was the purpose of the acquisition of the land being valued, had never existed and that the content of the statutory certificate should be determined within the context of that notional or adjusted world. The House of Lords rejected this approach, holding that the proper approach was to assume that the scheme of the acquiring authority   5.57

---

[80] A provision to the effect mentioned as regards highways was inserted into the Land Compensation Act 1961, s 14 as s 14(5)–(7) by the Planning and Compensation Act 1991. The relevant provision is now s 14(5)(d) of the Land Compensation Act 1961 as substituted by the Localism Act 2011. For the purpose of an assumed planning permission there is now a more generally applicable provision in s 14(5)(c) of the Land Compensation Act 1961 as substituted by the Localism Act 2011. See ch 7, para 7.29.

[81] *Fletcher Estates (Harlescott) Ltd v Secretary of State* [2002] 2 AC 307, [2000] 2 WLR 438.

[82] See ch 7, paras 7.33 et seq.

had existed but was cancelled at the date by reference to which the planning judgment for the purposes of the statutory certificate had to be made. This approach has been called the cancellation assumption.[83] It avoids a detailed examination of years, perhaps decades, of past hypothetical events. In *Waters v Welsh Development Agency*[84] Lord Brown deplored a version of the value to the owner principle which involved the disregard of the planning history over a much wider area than the land within the compulsory purchase order and dating back many years. He said that it clearly could not be right that the valuer must let his imagination 'take flight to the clouds' as Lord Denning had suggested in *Myers v Milton Keynes Development Corporation*.

5.58   Observations to the same effect have recently been made by the House of Lords in *Transport for London v Spirerose Ltd*[85] in which Lord Neuberger said, after referring to what he described as the so-called Pointe Gourde principle:

> [I]t is, at least generally, inappropriate to invoke the principle for the purpose of speculating what might have happened – see Lord Brown of Eaton-under-Heywood in Waters v. Welsh Development Authority [2004] 1 WLR 1304, para. 148, disapproving what was said by Lord Denning MR in Myers v. Milton Keynes Development Corporation [1974] 1 WLR 696, 704.

5.59   The first erroneous route here under discussion can today be regarded as having ended.[86] When it is necessary to apply the statutory provisions on the value to the owner principle, as explained in section (d) of this chapter, it may be necessary to leave out of account the effect on the value of the land acquired and being valued of development or the prospect of development on other land as specified in those provisions. It may often be necessary to take into account in the valuation process the potential for development of the land acquired and in assessing this aspect of its value the proposed acquisition by the acquiring authority is to be left out of account insofar as it would reduce the value of the land by preventing the implementation of future anticipated development.[87] In assessing the prospect of further development the scheme of the acquiring authority is taken to have been cancelled at a date prior to the valuation date as now specified in section 14 of the Land Compensation Act 1961. It is wrong in principle to investigate what development would or might have happened in the past on the land acquired, or on other land if the scheme of the acquiring authority had never existed, and wrong in principle to value the land acquired with the deemed existence of some assumed notional development which would or might have happened in those hypothetical and notional circumstances.

---

[83] The cancellation assumption has now been given statutory recognition in the provisions and planning assumptions introduced by the Localism Act 2011: see ch 7. In *Urban Edge Group Ltd v London Underground Ltd* [2009] UKUT 103, [2009] RVR 361, the Lands Tribunal refused to speculate on what development might have taken place on land other than the land acquired in the general locality in the years prior to the valuation date if the project of the acquiring authority had never existed. See also the decision of the Tribunal in *Persimmon Homes v Secretary of State for Transport* [2009] UKUT 126, [2010] RVR 11, referred to in para 5.48 in connection with s 9 of the Land Compensation Act 1961.

[84] [2004] UKHL 19, [2004] 1 WLR 1304, at para 148.

[85] [2009] UKHL 44, [2009] 1 WLR 1797, at para 55.

[86] There is a suggestion in some recent decisions of the Lands Tribunal that a process akin to building up an adjusted world in the period prior to the valuation date may be necessary in order to determine claims under r (6) of s 5 of the Land Compensation Act 1961 for compensation for losses incurred prior to the valuation date: see, eg *Pattle v Secretary of State for Transport* [2010] 1 P & CR DG 1. This subject is examined in section (e) of ch 8.

[87] This is the main effect of s 9 of the Land Compensation Act 1961.

2. The Lacuna Theory

An initial and obvious question about the linguistically complex provisions of section 6 and 5.60
schedule 1 in the Land Compensation Act 1961 is exactly what was their overall purpose. They were first enacted in the Town and Country Planning Act 1959 when it became possible to claim compensation for the development value of the land acquired and so at a time when the prospect of obtaining planning permission for such development became in some cases of central importance in the valuation process. The standard answer is that the new statutory provisions, both on disregarding the effect on value of the scheme of the acquiring authority and on the assumption of planning permission in certain circumstances, were needed to meet this new situation. In fact the judge-made value to the owner principle, requiring at least some degree of disregard of the scheme, had been applied for three-quarters of a century up to 1959 during most of which the potential of the land acquired for development had been a component of its value and of the compensation for it. In addition the same principle could be applied to decide what planning permission would have been obtained for the land acquired in the absence of the scheme of the acquiring authority.[88]

It is therefore difficult to see exactly why the new legislation was needed at any rate in such 5.61
a detailed and comprehensive form.[89] Even so the obvious intention was to put the present aspect of the value to the owner principle on a statutory footing, something which may have been intended but without success in rule (3) of section 2 of the Acquisition of Land Act 1919.[90] In introducing the Bill which became the Town and Country Planning Act 1959 the Lord Chancellor said that the provisions in it, which include what is now section 6 of the Land Compensation Act 1961, sought to protect acquiring authorities from paying for the value clearly created by the very scheme for which they were buying the land and that the provisions enunciated and extended the well established principle in compensation that 'value due to the scheme' must be ignored. The legislative provisions clarified matters or altered the previous understanding of the value to the owner principle in three main ways. (a) The exact circumstances in which the effect on the value of the land acquired of development or the prospect of development was to be left out of account, and the exact geographical area within which development or the prospect of development were to be left out of account, were stated. This replaced the view previously taken that the extent of the development to be disregarded was always a question of fact to be determined by the body which assessed the compensation.[91] (b) It was provided that a reduction as well as an increase in the value of the land acquired due to the leaving out of account of the effect on value of development or the prospect of development in the circumstances specified was

[88] In *Melwood Units Pty Ltd v Commissioner of Main Roads* [1979] AC 426, [1978] 3 WLR 520, the Privy Council in an appeal from Queensland found no difficulty in applying the value to the owner principle to the question of what planning permission would have been granted in the absence of the road scheme of the acquiring authority when there were no statutory planning assumptions of the nature contained in the current English legislation.

[89] Some new legislation may have been needed to ensure that the value to the owner principle was applied to land other than the land being acquired and valued but not to that land. See para 5.22.

[90] The other aspect of the value to the owner principle is explained in para 5.4. It had been put into statutory form in r (6) of s 2 of the Acquisition of Land (Assessment of Compensation) Act 1919 (now r (6) of s 5 of the Land Compensation Act 1961). See ch 8.

[91] See, eg *Fraser v City of Fraserville* [1917] AC 187, per Lord Buckmaster at p 194.

covered by the new statutory rules.[92] (c) The leaving out of account of development or the prospect of development due to the scheme of the acquiring authority was to operate only as regards development on land other than the land acquired and being valued and not as regards development on the land acquired. This last rule represents a change in the way in which the value to the owner principle had been formerly understood. For example, in the first case in which that principle clearly appears, *Stebbing v Metropolitan Board of Works*[93] in 1870, the development ignored was development for the purposes of the acquiring authority on the churchyard land acquired.

5.62   It seems fairly clear that the intention behind the legislation as enacted in 1959 and as repeated in 1961 was to put the value to the owner principle into a comprehensive statutory form, with a degree of clarification and a degree of modification to the scope of the principle as operated by the courts, and that the main vehicle for the implementation of this purpose was what is now section 6 and schedule 1 in the Land Compensation Act 1961. The question which required to be answered was whether the statutory provisions were in truth a comprehensive and self-contained statement of the value to the owner principle, or as it came to be called, the Pointe Gourde principle, or there was some residual or supplementary principle which could operate alongside or in addition to the statutory provisions. One would have thought that when Parliament had taken the trouble to enact the principle by provisions in such complex terms, and then subsequently to add to them by introducing from time to time new cases into schedule 1, the answer would be that what was intended was a comprehensive statutory statement of the value to the owner principle. Nonetheless this was not the route of interpretation chosen by the courts at least until recently when the whole matter was revisited by the House of Lords in *Transport for London v Spirerose Ltd.*[94]

5.63   The assumption came to be made that the Pointe Gourde principle might be applied independently of the statutory provisions. For example, in *Rugby Joint Water Board v Shaw-Fox*[95] the issue before the House of Lords was whether the ability of a landlord under an agricultural tenancy to serve a notice to quit free of the restrictions in the Agricultural Holdings Act 1948, which he could only do due to the existence of a planning permission for the reservoir scheme which underlay the acquisition of the land, had to be disregarded because of the Pointe Gourde principle. It was held that there should be no disregard as alleged since the Pointe Gourde principle applied to the ascertainment of the value of an interest in land acquired and not to the ascertainment of the nature of that interest. While this may cut down the scope of the principle, it appears to have been assumed that the Pointe Gourde principle could in other cases be operated within its proper confines outside

---

[92]   The earlier decisions were mainly concerned with disregarding increases in value due to the scheme. It was held in *Melwood Units Pty Ltd v Commissioner of Main Roads* [1979] AC 426, [1978] 3 WLR 520, that the value to the owner principle as developed by the courts was as applicable to the disregard of decreases in value due to the scheme as it was to the disregard of increases in value due to the scheme. It may seem strange that anyone would have thought the contrary. The *Melwood* decision concerned an appeal from Queensland and the acquisition of land for a new road. At that time there were no statutory provisions in Queensland equivalent to s 6 of the Land Compensation Act 1961 so that the decision was founded on the value to the owner principle as developed by the courts in England.

[93]   (1870) LR 6 QB 37.

[94]   [2009] UKHL 44, [2009] 1 WLR 1797.

[95]   *Rugby Joint Water Board v Shaw-Fox* [1973] AC 202, [1972] 2 WLR 757. See also *Davy v Leeds Corporation* [1965] 1 WLR 445, which involved a straightforward application by the House of Lords of the statutory provisions. No member of the Appellate Committee in *Davy* suggested that the value to the owner principle could operate outside the confines of the statutory provisions.

the ambit of the statutory provisions. In *Jelson v Blaby District Council*[96] the Court of Appeal applied the Pointe Gourde principle as an extra-statutory rule along with section 9 of the Land Compensation Act 1961 as one of the reasons for reaching its decision.

There arose a trilogy of cases in which the 'lacuna' theory was specifically enunciated and applied. What this theory means is that the statutory provisions in the 1961 Act are to be applied but if it appears that there is some obvious gap or lacuna in those provisions there is a residual or supplementary Pointe Gourde principle which can be used to plug that gap in the statute. This supplementary principle was sometimes called the common law Pointe Gourde principle to distinguish it from the statutory rules. The expression 'common law' was obviously a misnomer since the whole of the law of compulsory purchase and compensation is statutory. In strict law, to the extent that there could be a principle to work alongside the statutory provisions in section 6 of the 1961 Act and elsewhere, that principle must be a gloss on the meaning of the word 'value' when used in the statutory provisions, and, as has been explained, it was in this way that the value to the owner principle initially arose and was justified.[97]

5.64

The first of the three decisions is *Camrose v Basingstoke Corporation*.[98] Land was acquired at Basingstoke under the Town Development Act 1952 to be developed to meet the needs of overspill population from London. It was agreed that in valuing the land acquired the prospect of development under the overspill scheme had to be left out of account under the statutory provisions where that development was to take place outside the land acquired and being valued. However, as noted earlier, section 6 of the 1961 Act does not apply to the land acquired and being valued in any particular case. Consequently it was argued by the claimants that the land acquired had to be valued with the benefit of the prospect of the town development scheme on that land being taken into account so as to increase its value. The Court of Appeal rejected this submission. It was held that the statutory provisions and the Pointe Gourde principle could operate side by side so that the effect on the value of the land acquired due to the town development scheme on land outside that land was to be left out of account by virtue of section 6 of the 1961 Act and the effect on that value due to the development on the land acquired itself was to be left out of account by virtue of the 'common law' Pointe Gourde principle. In other words the Pointe Gourde principle was to operate as a supplementary principle of law where there was perceived to be an obvious gap in the legislation. The theory, expressed most clearly by Russell LJ[99], was that before the legislation there was some doubt as to whether the value to the owner principle applied to the effect on value of development on land outside the land acquired and being valued, so that the legislation was introduced to make it clear that the principle did so apply, leaving the previous rule unaffected in its application to the effect on value of development on the land being acquired. In a sense this rationalisation regards the statutory provisions as

5.65

---

[96] [1977] 1 WLR 1020. The *Jelson* decision is considered in detail in para 5.48 in the context of s 9 of the Land Compensation Act 1961 to which it is also relevant.

[97] See *Rugby Joint Water Board v Shaw-Fox* [1973] AC 202, [1972] 2 WLR 757, per Lord Pearson at pp 214–15. See section (a) of this chapter. The relevant statutory provision which states that the basis of compensation is the value of the land acquired is today s 7 of the Compulsory Purchase Act 1965 (replacing s 63 of the Lands Clauses Consolidation Act 1845). The whole of the value to the owner principle, the so-called Pointe Gourde principle, and the statutory provisions in s 6 of the Land Compensation Act 1961, may be regarded as a matter of legal analysis as an elaboration of this fundamental statutory rule.

[98] *Camrose v Basingstoke Corporation* [1966] 1 WLR 1100, [1966] 3 All ER 161.

[99] [1966] 1 WLR 1100 at p 1110.

closing a gap in the pre-existing value to the owner or Pointe Gourde principle. On the face of it this decision overrode one of the main purposes of the statutory provisions which was to apply the value to the owner principle to development on land other than the land being valued and to exclude its application to development on the land being valued.[100] It was difficult to understand how the analysis of the Court of Appeal could be consistent with section 15(1) of the Land Compensation Act which provided, and still provides, that planning permission is to be assumed to be in force at the valuation date for development of the land acquired and being valued in accordance with the purposes of the acquiring authority. The result of this decision of the Court of Appeal seemed to be: (a) that planning permission has to be assumed to be in force for the development of the land acquired proposed by the acquiring authority, but (b) the effect on value of that development, or the prospect of it, on the value of the land acquired has to be ignored in assessing compensation. It was difficult to see the rationality in that approach.

5.66   The second of the three cases is the decision of the Court of Appeal in *Wilson v Liverpool City Council*.[101] The facts were that the Council had been trying for some years to assemble a substantial area of land for housing development and had acquired 305 acres by private agreement out of the total of 391 acres required and that planning permission for the whole area had been obtained. A compulsory purchase order was made for 74 acres of the land not acquired by agreement which belonged to the claimant. The question was whether the prospect of development of the 305 acres acquired by agreement was to be taken into account in valuing the land acquired under the order. That prospect of development of that land could not be left out of account by virtue of case 1 in schedule 1 to the Land Compensation Act 1961 since that land was not within the compulsory purchase order. The Court held that the prospect of development of the 305 acres had to be left out of account, notwithstanding that the statutory provisions did not dictate that result, because of the continuing or supplementary Pointe Gourde principle.

5.67   The third decision, and that in which the lacuna theory was most clearly explained, is the decision of the House of Lords in *Waters v Welsh Development Agency*.[102] In the 1990s a barrage was constructed across the mouth of Cardiff Bay in order that an area should become available for regeneration by new development. The scheme had an adverse effect on mudflats in the area and led to the loss of nationally important bird habitats. It was decided to provide a replacement nature reserve and this was done by the Land Authority for Wales (later the Welsh Development Agency) on some 1,000 acres of land about 10 miles along the coast to the east of the barrage. A compulsory purchase order was made for this purpose. It was argued that in assessing the value of the land acquired for the replacement nature reserve the Cardiff Bay barrage scheme had to be taken into account with the possible result that, because of the particular need for replacement land engendered by the construction of that barrage, the land acquired for the nature reserve would be increased in value. There was nothing in the statutory provisions which required the leaving out of account of the

---

[100]   See para 5.61.

[101]   *Wilson v Liverpool City Council* [1971] 1 WLR 302, [1971] 1 All ER 628. A similar problem could arise if two compulsory purchase orders were made for the purpose of putting into effect the same scheme. When valuing land within one order there would be no requirement to leave out of account development or the prospect of development pursuant to the scheme on land within the other order: *Sprinz v Kingston-Upon-Hull City Council* (1975) 30 P & CR 273.

[102]   [2004] UKHL 19, [2004] 1 WLR 1304.

effect on value of the Cardiff Bay barrage development. The House of Lords held that the effect on value of the Cardiff Bay barrage had to be left out of account. The leading opinion to this effect was that of Lord Nicholls who carried out an extensive review of the history and nature of the value to the owner principle. Lord Nicholls observed that despite its late arrival on the scene the expression 'the Pointe Gourde principle' was not a reference to a principle separate and distinct from the 'value to the owner' principle.[103] It was no more than a name given to one aspect of that long established principle. The apparent core of the reasoning of Lord Nicholls in support of the decision of the House was that despite the statutory provisions there existed certain gaping lacunae or gaps in the operation of the value to the owner principle, that two of these had been identified in the *Camrose* and *Wilson* cases, and that the case before the House relating to the Cardiff Bay barrage was a further instance of such a gap. It was in order to close this gap that the effect on value of the land acquired for a nature reserve of the Cardiff Bay barrage scheme was to be left out of account.

In this way, and through this trilogy of cases, the lacuna theory became established, with three lacunae having been identified. It was, of course, possible that other lacunae would be identified. It was never clear how wide the lacuna had to be to justify the intervention of the supplementary Pointe Gourde principle. A further possible event which might have had to be disregarded under the extended application of that supplementary principle was acquisitions of land by the acquiring authority (or by a developer who was in some contractual relationship with the acquiring authority) for the purposes of the overall project of that authority. There is nothing in its statutory provisions which requires the leaving out of account of land acquisitions, as opposed to development or the prospect of development, when considering the effect on the value of the land acquired. The lacuna theory has been described above as the second of two erroneous routes travelled by the Courts. Anyone examining the law following the decision of the House of Lords in *Waters* might have described that theory not as a wrong route but as an established proposition of law which had finally achieved the approval of the House of Lords. Certainly the lacuna theory was something which had its obvious attractions. Nonetheless it is now necessary to state the modern law and to show that the lacuna theory is, at any rate in all probability, an erroneous route and that the statutory provisions are to be regarded as providing a comprehensive statement of the application today of the value to the owner principle.

5.68

(F) THE CURRENT LAW

Before stating the law as it stands today on the subject matter of this chapter it may be useful to summarise the position as it appeared to be following the decision of the House of Lords in *Waters v Welsh Development Agency* in 2004.[104]

5.69

(i) Following the Lands Clauses Consolidation Act 1845 the courts had developed the value to the owner principle as a gloss on the statutory reference in that Act to the compensation being the value of the land acquired. In general terms the value

---

[103] [2004] 1 WLR 1304 at para [42].
[104] *Waters v Welsh Development Agency* [2004] 1 WLR 1304.

to the owner principle meant that any increase or decrease in the value of the land acquired due to the particular need of the acquiring authority to acquire that land, or to the particular scheme of the acquiring authority which underlay or justified that acquisition, was to be disregarded.

(ii) By rule (3) of section 2 of the Acquisition of Land (Assessment of Compensation) Act 1919 (now rule (3) of section 5 of the Land Compensation Act 1961) Parliament probably intended that the value to the owner principle was to be put in whole or in part into statutory form. As a result of subsequent decisions of the courts this provision has been permitted such a limited ambit of operation that its effect on disregarding the scheme is today small.

(iii) The operation of the judge-made value to the owner principle was imprecise and uncertain in a number of respects such as the exact circumstances in which it applied and the exact area of land and events to which it applied.

(iv) By the Town and Country Planning Act 1959 provisions (now mainly repeated in section 6 and section 9 of the Land Compensation Act 1961) were introduced which stated in detailed, and sometimes complicated, terms the value to the owner principle. These provisions specified the circumstances in which that principle was to be applied, the area of land to which it was to be applied, and the events to which it was to be applied, as well as the exact result of its application.

(v) Notwithstanding these statutory provisions the courts subsequently identified a series of what were said to be obvious gaps or lacunae where the statutory provisions did not require the disregard of the effect on the value of the land acquired of aspects of the scheme of the acquiring authority, but where such a disregard would or might have been required by the previous value to the owner principle, a principle which in its present area of application became known as the Pointe Gourde principle.

(vi) In addition, for some time the courts operated a theory under which not only was development or the prospect of development in certain circumstances and on certain land to be left out of account where it had an effect on the value of the land acquired, but also there was to be built up an adjusted world, that is a notional world or situation which would, or might have arisen, or which might arise in the future had the scheme of the acquiring authority never existed at all. This theory had become shown by modern authority to be incorrect.

5.70   The terminology used in discussion of the present subject is sometimes less than exact and it may be useful at this point to attempt a more precise explanation of what exactly is meant by certain phrases. The value to the owner or value to the seller principle is a principle created by the courts following the Lands Clauses Consolidation Act 1845 and in technical terms is a gloss on the word 'value' as used in section 63 of that Act (and as that word is now repeated in very much the same context in section 7 of the Compulsory Purchase Act 1965). The value to the owner principle had two main aspects. One aspect was that certain items of compensation came to be awarded which had nothing to do with the value of land as that concept is normally understood. For example, a temporary loss of profit caused to a landowner while he relocated his business to new premises after the acquisition of his existing premises, became early on to be accepted as an item of compensation.[105] When a person

---

[105] *Jubb v Humber Dock Company* (1846) 9 QB 443.

buys land he would not normally regard the costs of the seller moving his business else-where as a part of the value of the land. To this extent the word 'value' was given an extended meaning which it would not normally bear. The justification for doing so was that the award of the additional amounts as compensation was attributable to the principle that the dispossessed landowner should be compensated for the value to him of the land and not just for its value to a purchaser. This important aspect of the value to the owner principle is now encapsulated in rule (6) of section 5 of the Land Compensation Act 1961 and is dealt with in detail elsewhere.[106] The second main aspect of the value to the owner principle, and that with which this chapter is concerned, is the principle described above as being in gen-eral terms that any increase or decrease in the value of the land acquired due to the particu-lar need of the acquiring authority to acquire that land, or to the particular scheme of the acquiring authority which underlay or justified that acquisition, was to be disregarded. It was this second aspect of the value to the owner principle which became known as the Pointe Gourde principle. Thus the Pointe Gourde principle and the second main aspect of the value to the owner principle mean the same thing.

It was against this background and fluctuating historical development that the whole ques-tion of the value to the owner principle, the Pointe Gourde principle, and the statutory provisions, were considered again by the House of Lords in *Transport for London v Spirerose Ltd*[107] in 2009. The facts of that case were simple. A small area of land containing a single storey 1950s outdated industrial building was acquired in order to construct a part of a new railway in Shoreditch in London. The land had no planning permission relevant to its value, neither an actual permission nor a permission assumed under the statutory provisions.[108] The claimants contended that nonetheless the land acquired must be valued at the valua-tion date as though it had the benefit of a planning permission for a new five storey mixed-use office and residential development. Their contention was based in large part on the application of the Pointe Gourde principle. The claimants succeeded in this contention before the Lands Tribunal which held that such a permission had to be assumed to exist either by reason of the supplementary or 'common law' Pointe Gourde principle or by vir-tue of section 9 of the Land Compensation Act 1961. The claimants also succeeded in the Court of Appeal although the decision of that Court was based rather on matters of 'policy' than on the Pointe Gourde principle as such. The origin of the policy was uncertain but may have been derived from recommendations of the Law Commission published in 2004 but which the Government declined to take forward into legislation.[109] The House of Lords held that no such assumption of planning permission was to be made. The statutory provi-sions in sections 14 to 17 of the Land Compensation Act 1961 provided a comprehensive statement of when a planning permission was to be assumed and none of those statutory assumptions applied in the case before the House. At this stage the decision of the House of Lords may be taken as something which applies to assumptions of planning permission and no more. However, the House took the opportunity to examine again and in some detail the history of the value to the owner principle and the Pointe Gourde principle and, in particu-lar, the relationship of those principles to the statutory provisions in sections 6 and 9 of the

5.71

---

[106] See ch 8.
[107] [2009] UKHL 44, [2009] 1 WLR 1797.
[108] The land had an actual planning permission and assumed planning permission under s 15(1) of the Land Compensation Act 1961 for the construction of a part of the new railway but that added nothing to its value.
[109] Law Commission, *Towards a Compulsory Purchase Code (1): Compensation.* (Law Com No 286, Cm 6071).

Land Compensation Act 1961. Since this decision is the latest, and now the leading, case on the subject it is necessary to state more precisely what the House held.[110]

The leading opinion with its analysis of the subject just mentioned was the opinion of Lord Walker. He stated that the previous statutes including the Town and Country Planning Act 1959 were now consolidated into the Land Compensation Act 1961 and that it had to be recognised that the vigour of the value to the owner principle, or the Pointe Gourde principle, was now channelled and restrained by a much more complex statutory scheme than had previously operated. With this in mind he stated what exactly the Pointe Gourde principle was and what was its status today. His conclusion was as follows: 'In my opinion it [the Pointe Gourde principle] is an imprecise principle, in the nature of a rebuttable presumption, adopted by the Court in the interpretation of statutes concerned with compensation for the compulsory acquisition of land'.[111] Lord Walker approved the description of the Pointe Gourde rule in *Bennion on Statutory Interpretation* as a special interpretive convention which had arisen in relation to the compulsory purchase of land. Lord Collins, delivering the other main opinion, agreed, stating that in his opinion the Pointe Gourde principle was a principle of statutory interpretation, mainly designed and used to explain and amplify the expression 'value'. [112]

5.72   If the value to the owner principle, or Pointe Gourde principle, is today indeed to be regarded as no more than an aid to the interpretation of the statutory provisions it was of course necessary for Lord Walker to consider the trilogy of cases which has been mentioned.

5.73   There is little difficulty in showing that the *Camrose* decision proceeded under a degree of misunderstanding of the purpose of section 6.[113] At the same time as section 6 of the 1961 Act was introduced there was also enacted in the same Act a series of planning assumptions one of which was the assumption that planning permission would be granted in respect of the land acquired such as would permit development in accordance with the proposals of the acquiring authority.[114] It would have been absurd to provide on the one hand, that permission was to be assumed on the land acquired for development as proposed by the acquiring authority, and then on the other hand to provide that any value attributable to that development on the land acquired was to be left out of account. As Lord Walker put it in the *Spirerose* decision it cannot have been the intention that Parliament should snatch back with one hand what it had just given with the other.[115] It seems, therefore, that *Camrose* must today be taken as having been wrongly decided. Equally the reliance on it as justifying and illustrating the lacuna theory by the House of Lords in *Waters* seems to have been a misapprehension of the overall purpose of the statutory provisions. Lord Walker dealt briefly with the *Wilson* decision, saying that it was a marginal case which Parliament may not have foreseen rather than a gaping lacuna.[116]

---

[110] The decision of the House of Lords was the last but one decision of that body sitting as the final appellate court in the United Kingdom after many centuries. It has now of course been replaced by the Supreme Court.

[111] [2009] UKHL 44, [2009] 1 WLR 1797, at para 11.

[112] Ibid, para 128. The passage approved was in *Bennion on Statutory Interpretation*, 5th edn (LexisNexis, 2013) at pp 599–604.

[113] *Camrose (Viscount) v Basingstoke Corpn* [1966] 1 WLR 1100, [1966] 3 All ER 161.

[114] LCA 1961, s 15(1).

[115] *Transport for London v Spirerose Ltd* [2009] UKHL 44, [2009] 1 WLR 1797. See the *Spirerose* decision, per Lord Walker at para 32.

[116] Ibid, para 35.

There remains the decision of the House of Lords in *Waters* in 2004. Lord Walker referred to the summary of section 6 and schedule 1 in the 1961 Act set out by Lord Nicholls in *Waters* but observed that this summary was only for the purpose of deciding whether there were gaps in the statutory code requiring to be filled by the Pointe Gourde principle. Lord Walker's view of the effect of what Lord Nicholls had said on the 'gaping lacuna' theory was as follows: 'Although entitled to the greatest possible respect, this part of his [Lord Nicholls's] opinion cannot, I think, be regarded as essential to the House's decision in Waters'.[117] The decision of any court, including that of the House of Lords or today the Supreme Court, is binding on subsequent courts only if it expresses some principle of law essential to the decision reached. It is apparent from the above citation from what was said by Lord Walker that he did not regard the lacuna theory as essential to the decision of the House in *Waters* so that, in his view, it was not part of the ratio decidendi of that decision and in these circumstances that theory is not binding today on other courts.

As just noted Lord Collins reached a similar conclusion on the Pointe Gourde principle   5.74
being a guide to interpretation and nothing further.[118] All other members of the Appellate Committee, including Lord Collins, agreed with and endorsed what Lord Walker had said.[119] Thus the views expressed by Lord Walker and explained above must now be regarded as the current law on the subject matter of the Pointe Gourde principle and its relation to the statutory provisions as established by a unanimous decision of the House of Lords.

(G) SUMMARY

It would be a bold person who regarded what was said in *Spirerose* as necessarily the last   5.75
word on this subject. Nonetheless it is for the moment the last word on the subject; it is a unanimous decision of the House of Lords; and in our hierarchical system of jurisprudence its reasoning and conclusion state the law as it should now be applied by practitioners and tribunals and courts.[120] The *Spirerose* decision cuts radically across the previous practice

---

[117] Ibid, para 26.

[118] *Transport for London v Spirerose Ltd* [2009] UKHL 44, [2009] 1 WLR 1797, at para. 128.

[119] *Transport for London v Spirerose Ltd* [2009] UKHL 44, [2009] 1 WLR 1797, para 9 (Lord Scott), para 46 (Lord Mance), and para 47 (Lord Neuberger).

[120] *Transport for London v Spirerose Ltd* [2009] UKHL 44, [2009] 1 WLR 1797. Some may feel uncomfortable with a situation in which in 2004 the House of Lords said that there was a supplementary Pointe Gourde principle which could be used to fill gaps in the statutory provisions whereas in 2009 the House of Lords said that there was no such supplementary principle and that the Pointe Gourde principle was a rule of statutory interpretation and no more. It is worth a short excursus in this note to explain how the doctrine of precedent works. It must be clearly understood that it is the second statement of principle which today constitutes the law to be applied. This is the result of the hierarchical system of courts in England and Wales. The effect of the doctrine of precedent or stare decisis is that the ratio decidendi of decisions of the House of Lords (and now of the Supreme Court) bind every other court and tribunal except (now) the Supreme Court which alone may reconsider such decisions. A part of the ratio decidendi of the *Spirerose* decision was the limited scope of the Pointe Gourde principle as a rule of interpretation as just explained. That reasoning was central to the decision of the House since it justified the rejection of some further non-statutory assumption as to the existence of a planning permission such as had been held to exist by the Lands Tribunal and the Court of Appeal. The reasoning was adopted and applied by the House with full knowledge and consideration of what had been said in the previous *Waters* decision. Thus, even if the rationes of the two decisions were different, it is the later ratio or principle as stated in *Spirerose* which must prevail. In fact there is not to be regarded as any conflict between the two rationes. In *Spirerose* Lord Walker considered carefully the reasoning of Lord Nicholls in *Waters* and concluded that the part of Lord Nicholls's reasoning which referred to a non-statutory Pointe Gourde principle was not essential to the decision of the House in *Waters* (see para 5.72

and understanding of the Lands Tribunal in this area of the law.[121] This chapter has of necessity contained a long explanation of the effect of the scheme on value and the present legal position cannot be properly understood without an investigation of what has led up to the present law. Fortunately, despite the long history of the matter and the complexities involved (including the complexities of the statutory language), it is now possible to summarise the law as in force today on the effect of the scheme of the acquiring authority on value when valuing land acquired compulsorily by way of three simple propositions.

(i)   In valuing the land which has been acquired all that has to be left out of account is: (a) any increase or decrease in the value of that land at the valuation date attributable to development or the prospect of development as described in section 6 and schedule 1 in the Land Compensation Act 1961, and (b), as regards a decrease in value, the effect of an indication of the compulsory purchase as provided for in section 9 of that Act.

(ii) The function of the value to the owner principle and the Pointe Gourde principle as developed by the courts is not to supplement or add to or contradict the statutory provisions by way of a separate and free-standing rule but rather to act as an aid to the interpretation of the statutory provisions.

(iii) Where any matters have to be left out of account in the valuation process by reason of the statutory provisions the proper course is to assume that the scheme of the acquiring authority has been cancelled at the relevant date, which will usually be the valuation date, and it is not permissible to enter into a general investigation of what might or might not have happened on the land acquired or other land in the past if there had never been such a scheme.

5.76   The complex and detailed provisions in section 6 and schedule 1 to the Land Compensation Act 1961 apply only where there is a compulsory acquisition of land or of rights over land.[122] The principle that the scheme being carried out by the person acquiring rights may have to be left out of account may apply when compensation has to be assessed under provisions in other legislation such as a wayleave to lay pipes under the Mines (Working Facilities and Support) Act 1966. In such a case in assessing the compensation or the price, and subject to any specific provisions in the legislation in question, the scheme of the person who acquires the rights may have to be disregarded in accordance with the value to the owner principle or the Pointe Gourde principle in the absence of detailed statutory provisions in the legisla-

above). It is for the House of Lords in a later case itself to decide what was the ratio of a previous case and it is evident from what Lord Walker said, with which all other members of the Appellate Committee agreed, that in *Spirerose* the House was concluding that the existence of a supplementary or non-statutory Pointe Gourde principle was not a part of the ratio which led to and justified the decision in *Waters*. Consequently the present position is not that of a later decision of the House of Lords overruling or departing from a previous decision but rather it is a case of a later decision of the House explaining what was or was not the essential basis of a previous decision and then itself stating as the essential basis of its own decision a particular proposition of law. Plainly that later proposition of law is the ratio of the later decision, in this case of the decision in *Spirerose*, and thus in accordance with the doctrine of precedent it constitutes the law binding on all courts and tribunals today.

[121] It is perhaps for this reason that in subsequent decisions the Tribunal appears to have been reluctant to accept the full implication of what was said in the House of Lords. For example, in one case the Tribunal was unaware that the effect of s 9 of the 1961 Act had been fully presented to the House (*Persimmon Homes v Secretary of State for Transport* [2009] UKUT 126 (LC): see para 5.48; *GPE (Hanover Square Ltd) v Transport for London* [2012] UKUT 417 (LC): see para 5.49. In the latter case it was said that the effect of the *Spirerose* decision was confined to questions of the assumption of planning permissions even though Lord Walker expressed his reasoning in much wider terms.

[122] Land Compensation Act 1961, s 5.

tion in question which give effect to that principle. In such a case it may be necessary to ascertain as a matter of fact what is the scheme which is to be left out of account for valuation purposes.[123]

Half a century elapsed between the enactment in 1959 of the main statutory provisions, now in sections 6 and 9 of the Land Compensation Act 1961, and the decision in *Spirerose*. Those of a more speculative frame of mind might enquire as to why it has taken a long series of decisions, and fluctuations in the status and effect attributed to the statutory provisions by the courts, before some clarity and simplicity have now been introduced. One reason may be that in this area courts and practitioners are dealing with a specialised and complex field of law in which special understandings and traditions tend to be built up. A good example of this is the apparent belief of the Lands Tribunal at one stage that the judge-made Pointe Gourde principle was of such significance that it could even to an extent contradict the statutory provisions. This tendency among lawyers in specialised areas is certainly not confined to the law of compulsory purchase and compensation as is shown from a passage from the dissenting judgment of Kirby J in *Commissioner of Taxation v Ryan*,[124] cited by Lord Walker in the *Spirerose* decision.

> It is hubris on the part of specialised lawyers to consider that 'their Act' is special and distinct from general movements in statutory construction which have been such a marked feature of our legal system in recent decades. The Act in question here is not different in this respect. It should be construed, like any other federal statute, to give effect to the ascertained purpose of the Parliament.

It is to be noted that if any such hubris has existed regarding the topic of the Pointe Gourde principle and the disregard of the scheme its effect has now been corrected, and the law put on an altogether simpler and more satisfactory basis as just summarised, by the decision of the House of Lords in *Spirerose*.

5.77

---

[123] *Bocardo SA v Star Energy (UK) Onshore Ltd* [2010] UKSC 35, [2011] 1 AC 380. It was held by a majority in the Supreme Court that there was a statutory scheme under the relevant legislation for the extraction of oil under a licence to extract oil vested in the Crown. If the scheme was disregarded the price payable for the necessary way-leave would be small, assessed in that case as £1,000, as opposed to the very much larger sum which would be represented by a share in the profits to be made from the extraction of the oil. The difficulties of ascertaining what exactly is the scheme for the purposes of the value to the owner principle, in the absence of statutory provisions on the matter, is illustrated by the disagreement in the Supreme Court. There appears to be substantial force in the reasoning of the minority. It is difficult to see why a person who is deprived of rights needed for the extraction of oil under the land of another person should not be compensated by a share of the profits to be made from the extraction of the oil when the conferring of the rights was an essential pre-requisite of that extraction. It is considerations of this nature which raise the question of whether the value to the owner principle and the required disregard of the scheme of the acquiring authority are fair and acceptable in cases where the value of land or of a right over land is increased by that scheme.

[124] *Commissioner of Taxation v Ryan* (2000) 201 CLR 146.

6

Other Valuation Rules

6.1 It is possible to describe the law of compensation under the seven main heads of compensation which are available when land is compulsorily acquired or is damaged by the execution or use of public works.[1] Despite this there are a number of rules which do not fit readily or easily within these heads. This is in part due to the different statutory origins of some of the rules. A convenient way in which to explain these further rules is to collect them into this chapter and to cross-refer to the explanation here given at other points where a particular rule is most likely to affect a particular head of compensation.

6.2 Accordingly the rules explained in this chapter are as follows:

(a) On limited occasions the compensation for land acquired may be assessed not on the basis of the value of the land acquired but on the basis of the cost of equivalent reinstatement elsewhere of the use carried on at that land or at the buildings on that land.

(b) On some occasions the special suitability or adaptability of the land acquired for a particular purpose has to be left out of account in assessing the value of that land.

(c) Any increase in value of the land acquired due to a use of that land which is unlawful may have to be left out of account in assessing the value of that land.

(d) The scheme of the acquiring authority may increase the value of land of the dispossessed landowner other than the land acquired. In certain circumstances an increase in value of that other land may have to be set-off against the compensation payable for the land acquired so as to reduce the amount of that compensation. This process is called taking account of betterment.

(e) A further planning permission may be granted for additional development of the land acquired within 10 years after the acquisition. Further compensation may become payable where this occurs.

(f) A brief account is given of the limited circumstances in which the compensation which would otherwise be payable is to be adjusted by reason of taxation.

The first three of these rules are further rules, rules (3)–(5), contained in section 5 of the Land Compensation Act 1961 and are supplementary to the primary rule, rule (2), examined in chapter 4, that is that compensation is the open market value of the land acquired at the valuation date.

---

[1] See section (b) of ch 3 for a description of these seven heads.

(A) EQUIVALENT REINSTATEMENT (RULE (5))

Equivalent reinstatement means that the cost of reinstatement of the land acquired, or, more accurately, the cost of reinstatement on other land of the buildings or structures on the land acquired, for continued use by the dispossessed landowner for the same purpose as the land acquired may be the basis of compensation. The cost of such a reinstatement is unlikely to be the same as the open market value of the land acquired. In certain limited circumstances compensation may be assessed as the cost of this equivalent reinstatement. The possibility of compensation being assessed on this basis is clearly a departure from the fundamental principle that compensation is to be the value of the land acquired. The availability of compensation assessed on the equivalent reinstatement basis was first created by the Acquisition of Land Act 1919 as a result of the recommendations of the Scott Committee in 1919.[2] It was recognised that in certain circumstances the giving of compensation founded on the market value of the land taken was not fair.[3] The present statutory provision which creates an entitlement to this compensation is rule (5) of section 5 of the Land Compensation Act 1961.

6.3

The legislation in rule (5) provides for strict restrictions on the circumstances in which compensation on the equivalent reinstatement basis will be available. A claimant seeking compensation on this basis has to satisfy four conditions:

6.4

(i)   The land acquired has to be devoted to a purpose of such a nature that there is no general demand or market for that purpose.
(ii) It must be the case that the land would continue to be devoted to the same purpose had it not been for the compulsory acquisition of the land.
(iii) The dispossessed owner must have a bona fide intention to reinstate the use of the land, in effect usually the use of the buildings and structures on the land, in some other place.
(iv) The Lands Tribunal, given that the above three conditions are satisfied, must exercise its discretion to award compensation on the equivalent reinstatement basis.[4]

It is necessary to examine these four conditions in more detail. Rule (5) of section 5 of the Land Compensation Act 1961 appears to contemplate that what is being reinstated on different land to that acquired is a purpose for which the land acquired was used. Land itself cannot be reinstated since it is immovable. It is unlikely that buildings and structures on the land acquired will be reinstated in the sense of being physically transferred to other land. Therefore what is normally envisaged by the cost of the equivalent reinstatement of a purpose is that the dispossessed landowner acquires an interest in other land and, either there are buildings on that other land in which the purpose can be reinstated, or he constructs on the other land the buildings in which the purpose can be reinstated. It appears

---

[2] *Second Report of the Committee Dealing with the Law and Practice relating to the Acquisition of Land for Public Purposes* (Cd 9229, 1918).

[3] See *A and B Taxis Ltd v Secretary of State for Air* [1922] 2 KB 328, per Bankes LJ at pp 336–37 citing a passage from *Cripps on Compensation*, 6th edn (1922) (a decision under the Indemnity Act 1920).

[4] There is, of course, nothing to prevent an acquiring authority agreeing that the compensation shall be assessed on the basis of equivalent reinstatement if it is satisfied that the first three conditions are satisfied and that the case is appropriate for assessment on that basis.

that in principle compensation on the equivalent reinstatement basis is available to the owner of a freehold or a leasehold interest in land.[5] It also seems that when it comes to the application of the conditions which constrain equivalent reinstatement claims the land acquired must be considered as a whole and that it is not possible for compensation to be assessed under rule (5) for a part of the land acquired and on an open market or rule (2) basis for the rest of the land.[6]

6.5   A special rule applies where there is a compulsory acquisition of an interest in a dwelling which has been constructed, or substantially modified, to meet the special needs of a disabled person and where the dwelling is occupied by such a person as his residence immediately before the date on which possession was taken of the dwelling by the acquiring authority or was last so occupied before that date. The owner of the interest may elect that compensation is assessed as if the dwelling were land devoted to a purpose of such a nature that there is no general demand or market for land for that purpose. This assumption brings into play the possibility of a claim for compensation on the equivalent reinstatement basis. It will still be for the claimant to show that the other conditions of a claim are satisfied.[7]

1. Condition 1: No General Demand or Market

6.6   If there is a general demand or a market for the land for the purpose to which it is devoted the landowner will recover compensation equivalent to the price which would be paid for the land in the market and he will be able to use that compensation to buy equivalent other land on which to reinstate the purpose if he so wishes. On the other hand, if there is no general demand or market for land devoted to a particular purpose, the market value of the land may be small or even non-existent so that the compensation will not enable reinstatement of that purpose on other land to take place. It is this last situation to which the provisions for equivalent reinstatement compensation are directed. It seems only fair that a person who in such circumstances is compelled to sell his land should in an appropriate situation obtain compensation which enables him to reinstate on other land or buildings on it activities fulfilling the same purpose as that for which the land acquired was previously used. It is not difficult to think of instances of land devoted to a purpose where equivalent reinstatement compensation would be appropriate in accordance with this principle, and examples are land devoted to religious or charitable purposes, or devoted to use as a particular social or recreational club, or used for carrying on a light railway.[8]

6.7   An initial question is what is meant by a purpose to which land is devoted. A purpose can be looked at narrowly as a particular and limited purpose or can be looked at more widely

---

[5] *Runcorn Association Football Club Ltd v Warrington & Runcorn Development Corporation* (1983) 45 P & CR 183. It was said that equivalent reinstatement compensation could not be awarded to a person who holds only a short tenancy to which s 20 of the Compulsory Purchase Act 1965 applies. See section (i) of ch 4. The length of the tenancy may be a factor relevant to the discretion of the Tribunal to award compensation on the equivalent reinstatement basis. See para 6.12.

[6] *London Diocesan Fund v Stepney Corporation* (1953–54) 4 P & CR 9.

[7] Land Compensation Act 1973, s 45.

[8] See, eg *Zoar Independent Church Trustees v Rochester Corporation* [1975] QB 246, [1974] 3 WLR 417 (church premises); *St John's Wood Working Mens Club v London County Council* (1947) 150 Estates Gazette 213 (club premises); *Edge Hill Light Rly Co v Secretary of State for War* (1956) 6 P & CR 211 (a light railway use).

as a general purpose or use of which the particular purpose to which a piece of land is put is but one type. The aim of the equivalent reinstatement rule is to provide compensation for a person whose land is used for a particular purpose a result of which is that on a sale the price, and thus the ordinary compensation, is limited because of the nature of that purpose. The principle should therefore be that the purpose to be considered when applying the equivalent reinstatement rule is not the narrow and particular purpose to which the land is put but any use, which includes that purpose, to which the land could lawfully be put and so a use to carry on which a purchaser would pay. A purchaser would normally pay a price appropriate for any use to which he could lawfully put the property in accordance with town planning limitations and any other restrictions on use such as a restrictive covenant. Where land is used for a particular and specific purpose it can generally under planning law be used for any other purpose or use: (a) where no material change in the use is involved, or (b) where the new use is within the same use class as the previous use as specified in the Town and Country Planning (Use Classes) Order 1987.[9] It has been held in accordance with this principle that when land was used as a homeopathic clinic the purpose to which it was devoted within the context of the equivalent reinstatement rule was the wider purpose of consulting rooms for medical purposes and not simply the narrow and limited purpose of a homeopathic clinic.[10] However, the principle of considering a general purpose must not be pushed too far. In one case a property was used as a care home for elderly refugees from Poland and Eastern Europe. It was held that, when applying rule (5) and considering whether there was a general demand or market for land for a particular purpose, the purpose to be considered was that of a home for the particular category of persons mentioned and not the general use of premises as an old person's home.[11]

The language of rule (5) makes it clear that the test is not whether there is a general demand or market for the particular land being acquired but whether there is a general demand or market for land for the purpose to which the land acquired was devoted.[12] The adjective 'general' qualifies only the word 'demand' and not the word 'market'. The underlying concept is that there cannot be a market unless supply and demand exist. There may be a general demand for property of a particular nature but no supply in which case the demand will be unsatisfied and there cannot be a market.[13] The question of whether there is a general demand and a market must be judged as a matter of existing fact as at the date by reference to which the compensation (including the question of whether the compensation should be on an equivalent reinstatement basis) falls to be assessed. Here that date is

6.8

[9] Town and Country Planning (Use Classes) Order 1987 (SI 1987/764).
[10] *Manchester Homeopathic Clinic v Manchester Corporation* (1970) 22 P & CR 241. In *Viscount Vaughan v Cardiganshire Water Board* (1968) 14 P & CR 193, a cottage was used as an estate office for the surrounding estate. It was held that in considering a claim for compensation under r (5) what had to be considered was the general purpose to which the property was put, that is property devoted to estate management, and not the limited and specific purpose to which it was put, the management of a particular estate.
[11] *Kolbe House Society v Department of Transport* (1994) 68 P & CR 569. It is difficult to find a clear dividing line between the approaches applied by the Lands Tribunal in the cases referred to in this and in the previous footnote. Planning permission would not normally be required for the use of premises for the care of elderly persons from one part of the world following a previous use for the care of those from another part of the world. For one thing the change would not be a material change in the use of the premises, and the market and potential purchasers in the market would see it in this way.
[12] *Harrison and Hetherington Ltd v Cumbria County Council* (1985) 50 P & CR 396, [1985] 2 EGLR 37 (HL) (no general demand held to exist for land used as a cattle market); *Wilkinson v Middlesbrough Borough Council* (1980) 39 P & CR 12 (general demand held to exist for land used as a veterinary practice).
[13] *Harrison and Hetherington Ltd v Cumbria County Council*, above n 12.

probably the vesting date if the general vesting declaration procedure is used or the date of entry onto the land acquired by the acquiring authority although other dates may be relevant for other aspects of rule (5), such as the date by reference to which the cost of reinstatement has to be assessed. The assessment of compensation is not taken outside the ambit of rule (5) because there is what has been called a 'latent demand', that is a demand which would or might exist in other circumstances at a future date. [14] When considering whether there is a general demand or market for land devoted to a particular purpose a common sense view should be taken of the area in relation to which the question should be addressed. A purpose of rule (5) is to allow compensation on an equivalent reinstatement basis where the property acquired could not be sold or readily sold in the market apart from the compulsory acquisition so that there is no or no substantial market value which could form the basis of the compensation. Accordingly rule (5) should apply if there was no general demand or market for the land in the location which the land occupied even though there might have been a demand or market for land devoted to a purpose of that nature elsewhere. [15] It seems that account may be taken of leasehold transactions in deciding whether a general demand or market exists. [16]

2. Condition 2: Land would Continue to be Devoted to its Purpose

6.9   When deciding whether land would continue to be devoted to a particular purpose if there was no compulsory acquisition it is necessary to consider what would happen in the future and not to concentrate solely on the use to which the land was put at the time of the compulsory acquisition. It is possible that land may be in general terms devoted to a particular purpose in the sense of an intention that that purpose will be resumed in the future even though use for that purpose does not subsist at the time of the compulsory acquisition. There may be some temporary other use at that time. It is said that the language of rule (5) has some elasticity and involves a conception of intention which is a different test from that of de facto use at the date of the acquisition. [17] There are logically two questions under the second condition. The first question is the purpose to which the land was devoted at the date of the acquisition, that date being normally the vesting date if a general vesting declaration is made, or otherwise the date of entry onto the land following a notice to treat. As just stated the use to which the land was devoted at the date of the acquisition may be its general

---

[14] Ibid. In this case land was used as a cattle market. There had been 18 transactions relating to 16 cattle markets over a period of about a quarter of a century. The Lands Tribunal had held that while this did not amount to an existing demand or market for such premises it was evidence of a latent demand which took the case outside r (5). The House of Lords reversed this decision as wrong in principle. See also paras 6.15 and 6.16 for an explanation of the relevant date for certain aspects of the application of r (5).

[15] Cf *Prielipp v Secretary of State* [2002] 3 EGLR 143.

[16] As mentioned in para 6.4 the owner of a leasehold interest which has been compulsorily acquired may be entitled to compensation on an equivalent reinstatement basis in an appropriate case.

[17] *Aston Charities Trust Ltd v Metropolitan Borough of Stepney* [1952] 2 QB 642, [1952] 2 All ER 228. In this case land previously used in connection with church activities had been let in part for storage purposes when it had suffered war damage in 1942 but the owners retained an intention to reinstate the previous use after the war. When the land was acquired in 1946 it was held that for the purposes of r (5) the land was devoted to church purposes and, apart from the acquisition, would have been continued to be devoted to those purposes notwithstanding the temporary interruption to the church activities. Thus the provision embraced both the first and the second questions as identified in this paragraph.

and intended use even though a temporary different use was in place at that time. The second question, which can only be answered when the use to which the land was devoted at the date on the acquisition is ascertained, is whether the land would be continued to be devoted to that use if there was no compulsory acquisition.

Turning to the second question as just identified, it is a question of fact depending on the   6.10
evidence whether the property acquired would continue to be devoted to its purpose at the time of the acquisition but for the compulsory acquisition. It is not necessary that the purpose would be continued in perpetuity or indeed for any particular period. In one case church premises which had had a flourishing congregation in the 1930s had dwindled to 12 members at the time of their deemed acquisition in 1964 but were in fact continued in use for church purposes for a further two years after that date until the roof fell in. The reason for the continued use was that the acquisition was under a purchase notice served under section 129 of the Town and Country Planning Act 1962. The Court of Appeal held that there was no evidence on which the Lands Tribunal could have concluded that the property would not have continued in use for church purposes but for the acquisition. [18]

3. Condition 3: Intention to Reinstate

Whether a bona fide intention to reinstate the land acquired exists is again a question of   6.11
fact. What has to be intended to be reinstated on other land is the purpose to which the land is devoted at the time of the acquisition. The reinstatement of the purpose will generally mean the acquisition of different premises elsewhere. In deciding whether the intention is one of the reinstatement of the purpose to which the premises acquired were devoted relevant considerations will include how far away any new premises will be from the premises acquired, the degree of similarity of the uses of the premises acquired and the new premises, and the degree to which the new premises will be used by the same persons as used the premises acquired. Where it was intended to relocate a church and church centre in premises in London to a location four miles from the property acquired the Court of Appeal held that the Lands Tribunal was entitled to find that an intention of reinstatement was proved.[19] In another case there was held to be an intention to reinstate a church purpose in new premises even though only one person from the congregation at the property acquired would join the congregation worshiping at the new premises. [20] In all cases the conclusion on the question of an intention to reinstate is a matter of fact and degree. A claimant who wishes to claim compensation on an equivalent reinstatement basis in respect of property devoted to a commercial venture should at least demonstrate that the new premises could be run as a commercial venture and should provide some details of the proposed reinstatement. Without such evidence it will be difficult to establish an intention to reinstate.[21] It is doubtful whether the expression 'bona fide' used in rule (5) adds much to the meaning. The

[18] *Zoar Independent Church Trustees v Rochester Corporation* [1975] QB 246, [1974] 3 WLR 417. Section 129 of the Town and Country Planning Act 1962 enabled an owner of land to serve a purchase notice on the local planning authority requiring that authority to purchase the land when it had become incapable of reasonably beneficial use in its existing state. See now s 137 of the Town and Country Planning Act 1990.

[19] *Aston Charities Ltd v Metropolitan Borough of Stepney*, above n 17.

[20] *Zoar Independent Church Trustees v Rochester Corporation*, above n 18.

[21] *Edgehill Light Rly Co v Secretary of State for War* (1956) 6 P & CR 211.

words indicate that the intention to reinstate the purpose must be real and not colourable or fanciful but such a real intention would have to be proved even apart from the use of that expression.

4. Condition 4: Discretion

6.12   If any of the three above conditions is not satisfied the Tribunal cannot assess the compensation on the basis of equivalent reinstatement. If all of the three conditions are satisfied the Tribunal must still exercise its discretion as to whether to award compensation on this basis. All relevant considerations should be taken into account in the exercise of the discretion. In some cases the period during which the property acquired has been devoted to a particular purpose may be relevant and in other instances the length of the period it would take to effect the reinstatement and the likely degree of intensity of the use of the reinstated premises could be relevant. The Tribunal will wish to have regard to the duration of the claimant's interest where that interest is a lease.[22] A major consideration is likely to be the cost of the reinstatement. Before it can properly exercise its discretion the Tribunal needs to know and to weigh up what exactly will constitute the equivalent reinstatement and its cost and it will generally be relevant to compare the amount of the compensation if assessed under rules (2) and (6) of section 5 of the Land Compensation Act 1961 (the value of the land and the compensation for losses due to disturbance) and the amount of the compensation if assessed on the equivalent reinstatement basis under rule (5). [23] It is possible that the Tribunal will exercise its discretion against a rule (5) assessment because of a gross disproportion between the two amounts. It is, of course, unlikely that a landowner would seek to have the compensation assessed as the cost of equivalent reinstatement if that amount was likely to be less than the compensation assessed as the open market value of the land together with a sum for disturbance under rules (2) and (6) of section 5 of the Land Compensation Act 1961.

6.13   Where the property acquired was devoted to a commercial purpose prior to the acquisition a comparison between the value of the business and the cost of equivalent reinstatement is likely to be a relevant factor and may even be a factor of paramount importance in the exercise of the discretion. A cost of reinstatement which is wholly disproportionate to the value of the commercial enterprise is likely to mean that compensation is not awarded on an equivalent reinstatement basis. Even so there is no rule that the equivalent reinstatement basis must be rejected just because the cost of the reinstatement exceeds, or even substantially exceeds, the value of the business. [24] Where the land acquired is devoted to some private or charitable use a comparison of the cost of equivalent reinstatement and the amount of the value of the property acquired will still be relevant but a marked difference between

---

[22] *Runcorn Association Football Club Ltd v Warrington & Runcorn Development Corporation* (1983) 45 P & CR 183; and see para 6.4.

[23] *Harrison and Hetherington v Cumbria County Council* (1985) 50 P & CR 396, [1985] 2 EGLR 37.

[24] *Festiniog Rly Society v Central Electricity Generating Board* (1962) 13 P & CR 248. In this case the Court of Appeal upheld the decision of the Lands Tribunal not to award compensation on the equivalent reinstatement basis when the cost of reinstatement was £180,000 compared to a value of the undertaking of the claimants of £3,000.

the two amounts may be less important. [25] It seems, therefore, that the Tribunal is most likely to exercise its discretion to reject the assessment of compensation on an equivalent reinstatement basis: (a) when the value of the land acquired and the cost of equivalent reinstatement is similar (because there will then be no need to adopt the equivalent reinstatement basis of assessment), and (b) where there is a gross disproportion between the two above sums (especially in the case of premises used commercially). If this analysis is correct the discretion in favour of the equivalent reinstatement basis of assessment is most likely to be exercised where the cost of the reinstatement is greater, but not enormously greater, than the value of the land acquired.

5. Assessment of the Compensation

The compensation is the reasonable cost of equivalent reinstatement. A claimant must always take reasonable steps to minimise his claim in accordance with the general duty of a claimant for compensation of any sort and on any basis to mitigate his loss. [26] Thus the location or size or standard of any replacement building must be reasonable having regard to the nature of the property which has been acquired. It seems that the cost of equivalent reinstatement can include the cost of acquiring an existing building or the cost of acquiring land and constructing on it a new building in place of the building on the property acquired, but with no deduction for the age or obsolescence of the building on the property acquired, although a deduction has been made for a state of disrepair of the property acquired.[27] In this respect the assessment of compensation under rule (5) differs from the depreciated replacement cost method of valuing property where the cost of construction of a new and equivalent building can be used as an indicator of the value of land containing an older building but subject to downwards adjustment for factors such as the age and obsolescence of the building being valued.[28] A claimant may incur losses in addition to the cost of reinstatement, such as removal expenses or a loss of profits, during a move to new premises and compensation can be recovered for such additional losses under rule (6) when the primary assessment of the compensation is under rule (5) just as they can when the primary assessment is under rule (2).[29] Interest is payable under section 11(1) of the Compulsory Purchase Act 1965 on the costs of the reinstatement from the date possession is taken until the cost of the reinstatement, or the last instalment of it, is paid to the claimant.[30]

6.14

[25] In *Sparks (Trustees of East Hunslet Liberal Club) v Leeds City Council* (1977) 34 P & CR 234, a club used for social and recreational purposes was acquired and the cost of equivalent reinstatement was put at £97,832 whereas the acquiring authority estimated the value of the property acquired at about £9,000. The Lands Tribunal had regard to the fact that the purpose of the claimants was not commercial or political and that the premises served a valuable social purpose and allowed the claim in the above sum for the cost of equivalent reinstatement.

[26] *Director of Buildings and Lands v Shun Fung Ironworks Ltd* [1995] 2 AC 111, [1985] 2 WLR 904, per Lord Nicholls at p 126; *Scotia Plastic Binding Ltd v London Development Agency* [2010] UKUT 98 (LC), [2010] RVR 309. See ch 8, para 8.19.

[27] *Trustees of Zetland Lodge of Freemasons v Tamar Bridge Joint Committee* (1961) 12 P & CR 326; *Cunningham v Sunderland County Borough Council* (1963) 14 P & CR 208.

[28] See section (e) of ch 14.

[29] *Eronpark Ltd v Secretary of State for the Environment* [2000] 2 EGLR 165.

[30] *Halstead v Manchester City Council* (1998) 76 P& CR 8. For interest on compensation generally see section (d) of ch 15.

6. Other Matters

6.15   The relevant date for the determination of many of the matters relevant to the fulfilment of the conditions is the date of the acquisition which should be taken as the vesting date if the general vesting declaration procedure has been used or, if a notice to treat has been served, the date on which the acquiring authority enters the land of the claimant. The statutory rules for determining the valuation date are not applicable to compensation on the equivalent reinstatement basis. [31] Whether the land was devoted to a purpose where there was no general demand or market should be determined on the facts as they were on the date just mentioned. It appears that the intention of the claimant to continue that purpose on the land but for the compulsory acquisition should also be determined on the facts as at that date. When it comes to the exercise of the discretion of the Tribunal all relevant matters known at the date of the hearing before the Tribunal should be considered; for example the exact cost of equivalent reinstatement may be known by that date.

6.16   The date by reference to which the cost of equivalent reinstatement should be estimated is the date on which the work of reinstatement might reasonably have been commenced.[32]

6.17   Where a claimant does not itself have funds with which to carry out an equivalent reinstatement, apart from any compensation assessed under rule (5), the intention of that claimant to carry out a reinstatement may necessarily be dependent on the receipt of that compensation. In these circumstances an intention to carry out reinstatement which is conditional in this sense must obviously be sufficient to satisfy the statutory requirements.

(B) SPECIAL SUITABILITY OR ADAPTABILITY OF LAND (RULE (3))

1. Introduction and Background

6.18   Rule (3) of section 5 of the Land Compensation Act 1961 provides that in valuing the land acquired the special suitability or adaptability of that land for any purpose shall not be taken into account if that purpose is a purpose to which the land could be applied only in pursuance of statutory powers or for which there is no market apart from the requirements of any authority possessing compulsory purchase powers. The rule goes back to the Acquisition of Land (Assessment of Compensation) Act 1919. A part of the rule as enacted in the 1961 Act was repealed by the Planning and Compensation Act 1991.

6.19   The structure of rule (3) is that it has a number of components and it is useful to examine its effect by considering the meaning of: (a) the special suitability or adaptability of land for any purpose, (b) a purpose to which land can be applied only in pursuance of statutory powers, and (c) a purpose for which there is no market apart from the requirements of an authority possessing compulsory purchase powers. The first component has to exist if the

---

[31] Section 5A of the Land Compensation Act 1961 applies only to compensation assessed under r (2) of s 5 of that Act.

[32] *West Midland Baptists (Trust) Association (Inc) v Birmingham Corporation* [1970] AC 874, [1969] 3 WLR 389.

rule is to apply. The second and the third components are alternatives. The fundamental requirement for the application of the rule, and that which has attracted the most consideration by the courts, is the first and overall requirement that the land must have a special suitability or adaptability for a purpose.

Rule (3) is described and explained separately in this chapter although it is plain from its language that it has a good deal to do with the wider question of the circumstances in which the scheme or project of an acquiring authority has to be left out of account in valuing the land acquired. The overall subject of the effect of the scheme on valuation is explained in chapter 5 and there is reference in that chapter to the way in which the current law, which requires in certain circumstances the disregard of the scheme of the acquiring authority in valuing the land acquired, has arisen in the context of a narrow view which the courts have taken of the concept of the special suitability or adaptability of land for a purpose within rule (3) of section 5 of the Land Compensation Act 1961. Rule (3) and the statutory rules in sections 6 and 9 of the Land Compensation Act 1961 for the disregard of certain matters in valuing land are best considered separately when the framework of the valuation process is determined even though a broadly similar purpose underlies all three provisions. 6.20

The meaning of rule (3) cannot therefore be understood except in the context of the value to the owner principle.[33] In general terms the main aspect of that principle means that in valuing the land acquired the effect on value of the compulsory acquisition, and of the particular scheme or project of the acquiring authority which underlies that acquisition, is to be disregarded. The value to the owner principle arose by way of a series of decisions mainly in the nineteenth and early twentieth centuries following the Lands Clauses Consolidation Act 1845 which itself contained no express provision stating the principle. The exact extent of the principle was in some ways uncertain when the law of compensation generally was considered by the Committee Dealing with the Law and Practice relating to the Acquisition of Land for Public Purposes in 1918 and was considered in the report of that Committee (the Scott Report). One result of that report was the enactment in rule (3) of section 2 of the Acquisition of Land (Assessment of Compensation) Act 1919 of what is now rule (3) in section 5 of the Land Compensation Act 1961. There is some reason to think that it was intended that that rule as enacted in 1919 should encompass, either wholly or to a considerable extent, the important aspect of the value to the owner principle as just stated. [34] In a compelling analysis Lord Scott of Foscote has explained that rule (3) as enacted in 1919 was the Parliamentary solution to the problems relating to the value to the owner principle as referred to in three important decisions of the Privy Council on that principle between 1909 and 1917. [35] Unfortunately in a series of decisions the courts have attributed a narrow meaning to the concept of the special suitability or adaptability of land for a purpose such that today rule (3) plays only a small part in the law of compensation and almost certainly plays a smaller part than that intended when it was first enacted in 1919. The view of Lord Scott was that by reason of this narrow interpretation the decisions on the meaning of rule 6.21

---

[33] See ch 3, para 3.10 et seq and see section (a) of ch 5.

[34] The value to the owner principle had a further aspect which is that compensation became available for losses caused by the physical disturbance of an owner from his possession of the land acquired and that aspect became r (6) in the series of rules enacted first in 1919 and now contained in s 5 of the Land Compensation Act 1961: see ch 3, para 3.15, and see ch 8 for r (6) and for the assessment of disturbance and other compensation under it.

[35] *Waters v Welsh Development Authority* [2004] UKHL 19, [2004] 1 WLR 1304, at para 89. See section (b) of ch 5.

(3) had taken a wrong turning. Others have shown considerable sympathy for this analysis but the majority view taken by the House of Lords has been that it is too late to put back the clock and that the prevailing narrow interpretation of rule (3) must continue.[36] The cumulative effect of the narrow interpretation given to rule (3) in a series of decisions has led the Law Commission in its report in 2003 to comment that in practice rule (3) appears to have little remaining purpose.[37]

2. Special Suitability or Adaptability

6.22   It seems likely that the concept of the special suitability or adaptability of land for a particular purpose was intended when rule (3) was first enacted, and in accordance with the background to that enactment as just explained, to mean a special value attributable to the scheme of the acquiring authority which was to be left out of account in the valuation process in accordance with principles which had by then been built up by the courts.[38] A good statement of that principle and of the meaning of that special value was that of Fletcher Moulton LJ in *Re Lucas and Chesterfield Gas and Water Board*[39] where he said in 1909:

> Where the special value exists only for the particular purchaser who has obtained powers of compulsory purchase it cannot be taken into consideration in fixing the price, because to do otherwise would be to allow the existence of the scheme to enhance the value of the lands to be purchased under it.

A consideration of the line of authorities on the meaning of rule (3), which establish its present limited meaning, demonstrates how this earlier concept of special suitability or adaptability or special value has been radically cut down. Three important limitations on the concept can be distinguished.

6.23   The first limitation is that the special suitability or adaptability must relate to a purpose which involves a use, actual or potential, of the land itself and not a purpose which is only concerned with the use of the products of the land elsewhere. This limitation was established by the decision of the Privy Council in *Pointe Gourde Quarrying and Transport Company Ltd v Sub-Intendent of Crown Lands*.[40] Land in Trinidad used as a quarry had been acquired in order to provide stone for the construction of a naval base for the United States. The land was valued at $101,000 of which $86,000 was attributable to the quarry as a going concern ignoring the particular project of the construction of the naval base and $15,000 was attributable to the naval base project and the particular need for the stone which arose as a result of that project. Section 11(2) of an Ordinance of 1941 in force in Trinidad contained a provision equivalent to that in rule (3) of section 5 of the Land Compensation Act 1961. It was held that the fact that an additional or special value of $15,000 was attributable to the need for the stone for the naval base did not constitute a special suitability or adapt-

---

[36]   Ibid, per Lord Brown at para 143.

[37]   Law Commission, *Towards a Compulsory Purchase Code: (1) Compensation* (Law Com No 286, 2003). Nonetheless there are instances in the decided cases of the application of r (3). See n 44.

[38]   The words used in the statute are 'suitability or adaptability'. Presumably suitability refers to a use of land in its existing state whereas adaptability refers to a use of land after it has been altered in some way by development or works on it. The same legal principles seem to apply whichever of the two attributes of the land is in question.

[39]   *Re Lucas and Chesterfield Gas and Water Board* [1909] 1 KB 16, at p 31.

[40]   *Pointe Gourde Quarrying and Transport Company Ltd v Sub-Intendent of Crown Lands* [1947] AC 565.

ability of the land for any purpose within the meaning of the statute, the reason being that the purpose in question was the use not of the land but of the products of the land. Where a piece of land has a value which is due wholly or mainly to the use of products of the land itself, such as minerals or peat or agricultural products, it is not easy to see why the use of the land for the purpose of providing that product cannot in an appropriate case be a special suitability or adaptability of the land. In the event the additional $15,000 was disallowed as a part of the compensation on the basis that it was a value attributable to the scheme of the acquiring authority and so in accordance with the general rule that the effect on value of the scheme is to be left out of account in assessing compensation. This, however, is a separate question and raises a separate issue of law.[41] What is not apparent is why a rule which was nowhere expressly stated in the legislation at that time (either that in force in Trinidad or in the equivalent legislation then in force in England and Wales) had to be invoked to justify a result which could have been reached more straightforwardly by the application of an express rule contained in the legislation.

The second limitation is that the special suitability or adaptability of the land for any purpose refers to the quality of the land as opposed to the needs of a particular purchaser. In *Lambe v Secretary of State for War*[42] the freehold of a property was acquired when that property was subject to a lease at a small ground rent. It appeared that on a hypothetical sale of the freehold the tenant might have been willing to pay a higher sum than other persons because he alone could secure the merger of the freehold and leasehold interests and could secure the possible marriage value which would accrue from that merger. It was held that the needs or aspirations of a particular purchaser had nothing to do with the quality of the land and it was to that quality that rule (3) referred when it contained the expression 'special suitability or adaptability of the land'. The Court of Appeal relied on the *Pointe Gourde* decision in reaching its conclusion although the circumstances of the two cases seem very different. The matter of a particular bid from someone in the position of the tenant is a subject which is best considered in the context of a special purchaser and the marriage value which can sometimes be obtained following a purchase of land by a special purchaser. The subject of a special purchaser is separately considered later in this section of the chapter and elsewhere.[43]

6.24

The third limitation is the widest and most important. It is said that if rule (3) is to apply the land being acquired must in effect have a unique suitability for a particular purpose. In *Batchelor v Kent County Council*[44] the land acquired was part of a wider area of land intended for residential development. It was proposed to use the land acquired to construct

6.25

---

[41] The *Pointe Gourde* decision is the origin of the so-called Pointe Gourde principle which has played an important part in land valuation generally in the area of compensation: see ch 5. That principle was not expressly stated in the legislation in force in England and Wales in 1947 but now finds statutory expression mainly in ss 6 and 9 of the Land Compensation Act 1961.

[42] *Lambe v Secretary of State for War* [1955] 2 QB 613, [1955] 2 WLR 1127.

[43] See para 6.28 and for the meaning of marriage value see ch 4, para 4.28.

[44] *Batchelor v Kent County Council* [1990] 1 EGLR 32, (1989) 59 P & CR 357. See also *Persimmon Homes (Wales) Ltd v Rhondda Cynon Taff CBC* [2005] RVR 59. See *Laing Homes Ltd v Eastleigh BC* (1979) 250 EG 350, at p 459, for a decision in which land was held to have a special suitability or adaptability. *Livesey v CGB* [1965] EGD 605, is a further decision in which r (3) was held by the Lands Tribunal to apply. Land was acquired for use as a power station and it was held to have a special suitability or adaptability for that purpose. In *Port of London Authority v Transport for London* [2008] RVR 93, it was held that when an area of airspace over a river was acquired for the construction of a bridge this area of airspace had a special suitability for the purpose of constructing the bridge because of its physical position.

a roundabout which was a part of road improvements needed to serve the general residential development and which would provide an access to that development. The Lands Tribunal assessed the compensation on the basis that the land was the key to the residential development. This conclusion was challenged in the Court of Appeal on the contention that the purpose of constructing the roundabout constituted a special suitability or adaptability of the land so that any increase in value due to that special suitability or adaptability had to be left out of account under rule (3). It was held in that court that the land acquired may have been the most suitable land for the purpose of providing access to the residential land but, since there were other possible accesses to the residential development, the land acquired was not especially suitable for the purpose of providing an access. It was said that 'Most suitable does not correspond with specially suitable'. It is not apparent why land has to be uniquely suitable for a particular purpose for it to be specially suitable for that purpose.[45] It must be remembered that the special suitability or adaptability of land for a particular purpose is not in itself sufficient to result in that special suitability or adaptability being left out of account in the valuation process. One or other of the two further criteria specified in the rule also has to be shown to exist before the special suitability or adaptability of the land is left out of account. This third limitation reduces generally and substantially the circumstances in which rule (3) will be applicable.

3. Application in Pursuance of Statutory Powers

6.26   This component of rule (3) has also been given a strict meaning. In *Ozanne v Hertfordshire County Council*[46] an existing road was to be stopped up and improved for the purposes of proposed nearby housing development. The land acquired was a small strip to the south of the existing road which was to become part of the improved road. The purpose to which the land acquired was to be put, that of road improvement, could be effected without the exercise of statutory powers. Stopping up could not be effected without the use of statutory powers but no stopping up was proposed on the particular piece of land acquired. Consequently it was held that the purpose to which the land acquired was to be applied was not a purpose which could only be effected in pursuance of statutory powers and for that reason rule (3) did not apply in the assessment of compensation for the acquisition.

---

[45] See the cogent criticism of the *Batchelor* decision by Lord Scott in *Waters v Welsh Development Authority* [2004] UKHL 19, [2004] 1 WLR 1304, at paras 113–14. One might have thought that the concept of a piece of land being specially suitable for a particular purpose meant that the land had certain characteristics such as its location, not shared with the generality of land, which rendered it particularly suitable for that purpose. That special suitability could, one would have thought, still exist even though there was some other land which shared the same characteristics and so was, perhaps to a greater or lesser degree, also suitable for the purpose in question. Nonetheless it was the majority view in the *Waters* decision, and so is the law, that this limitation, as also the two earlier limitations explained, are now established law and that it is too late to reconsider them. In the *Waters* decision at first instance before the Lands Tribunal [2001] 1 EGLR 185, it was held that a piece of agricultural land did not have a special suitability or adaptability for the provision of a nature reserve.

[46] *Ozanne v Hertfordshire County Council* [1991] 1 WLR 105, [1991] 1 All ER 769. The *Ozanne* decision was followed by the Lands Tribunal in *Persimmon Homes (Wales) Ltd v Rhondda Cynon Taff CBC* [2005] RVR 59, where it was again held that road improvements could be carried out without the use of statutory powers.

4. Absence of Market

The requirement that for rule (3) to apply there must be no market apart from the require-   6.27
ments of any authority possessing compulsory purchase powers has been mainly considered in relation to the words which were in rule (3) at the time of its enactment, that is 'no
market apart from the special needs of a particular purchaser' but which have since been
repealed. The principle applicable to this part of rule (3) as it remains is that any possible
purchasers can constitute a market and so may prevent rule (3) applying including speculators in the sense of persons who might seek to acquire the land not to use or develop it but
for later disposal by them at a profit.[47] An authority possessing compulsory purchase powers means in relation to a particular transaction where rule (3) has to be applied any person
or body of persons who could be or have been authorised to acquire an interest in land
compulsorily for the purposes for which the transaction is or was effected.[48] A possible
instance in which there would be no market apart from the requirements of the acquiring
authority would be where a particular underground stratum of land was acquired in order
to build an underground railway, or similar project, and where there would be no market
and no purchasers for the land except for the requirements of the acquiring authority who
were promoting the project.[49]

5. Special Purchasers

The nature of a special purchaser and the role of such a purchaser in the valuation of land   6.28
for the purposes of compensation for compulsory purchase are considered elsewhere.[50] A
special purchaser is a person who wishes to acquire a particular property and has a special
reason for doing so which is not shared by the generality of the market. In rule (3) as it was
enacted in 1919, and as it was re-enacted in 1961, the rule applied where the land acquired
had a special suitability or adaptability and there was no market 'apart from the special
needs of a particular purchaser or the requirements of an authority possessing compulsory
purchase powers'. The words 'the special needs of a particular purchaser or' were repealed
by the Planning and Compensation Act 1991. The law today, therefore, is that even where
land has a special suitability or adaptability for a purpose the valuation of it cannot be
brought within rule (3), so that any increase in value due to that special suitability or adaptability is to be left out of account in the valuation process, simply because there is no market
apart from the special needs of a particular purchaser. The general rule is that in principle
where the existence and the needs of a special purchaser would add to the value of land, if
it were hypothetically sold, that additional value has to be taken into account in assessing
the compensation.

[47] See *Barstow v Rothwell UDC* (1971) 22 P & CR 942; *Blandrent Investment Developments Ltd v British Gas
Corporation* [1979] 2 EGLR 18; *Chapman Lowry & Puttick v Chichester District Council* (1984) 47 P & CR 674.

[48] Land Compensation Act 1961, s 39(1).

[49] *Obsidian FG Ltd v Secretary of State for Transport* [2010] UKUT 299 (LC). See ch 2, paras 2.35–2.36 for the
power to acquire a particular stratum of land.

[50] Section (d) of ch 4. A good example of the value of land being increased due to the presence of a special
purchaser is the decision of the Court of Appeal in *Inland Revenue Commissioners v Clay* [1914] 1 KB 339. It is
probable that the inclusion of the provision relating to a special purchaser in r (3) as originally enacted in 1919 (see
below) was to reverse the effect of this decision for the purposes of compensation for compulsory purchase.

(C) UNLAWFUL USES (RULE (4))

1. General Principles

6.29   Rule (4) of section 5 of the Land Compensation Act 1961 provides that any increase in the value of the land acquired shall not be taken into account in valuing that land if it is due to the use of the land acquired or any premises on that land in a manner: (a) which could be restrained by any court, or (b) is contrary to law, or (c) is detrimental to the health of the occupants of the premises or to public health.

6.30   This rule can be a significant restriction on the amount of compensation payable since a hypothetical willing buyer of property may be willing to pay a sum in the hope or expectation of continuing a use even though that use is unlawful. The reason is that if the buyer knows that the land has been used unlawfully for some time without any effective action having been taken to end that use he may well entertain the expectation that following the purchase no action will be taken to prevent him continuing the use.[51] A person may even buy a property in the expectation of instituting a use which is in some way unlawful if experience of other properties shows that no effective action is likely to be taken to prevent any element of unlawfulness involved. The lack of effective action may be because the persons or body entitled to prevent the unlawful use do not know of it or do not think it worthwhile to take enforcement steps. Of course if there is some doubt as to the legality of a use, or some possibility of future enforcement action, a purchaser may make a reduction in the price which he would otherwise be willing to pay for the land. It is to these types of situation that rule (4) is directed. It should be noted that what rule (4) requires to be left out of account is any increase in the value of the land acquired due to an unlawful use. It is possible that an unlawful use decreases the value of land (for example, remediation measures may have to be taken to remove its effects) and in such a case the unlawful use has to be taken into account in accordance with the presumption of reality.

6.31   The underlying rationale of rule (4) is less than apparent. The philosophical basis of compensation is that the dispossessed owner is given compensation which is equivalent to the value of that which he previously owned. This is the well known principle of equivalence which is explained in chapter 3 and which is said to be the underlying feature of the whole of the law of compensation. If a person owns a piece of land and carries out on it a use which is tainted in some way by actual or possible unlawfulness, and in those circumstances a purchaser of the land in a real transaction would pay something for the hope of continuing that use without interruption, then the principle of equivalence suggests that the owner

---

[51] In *Director of Lands v Yin Shuen Enterprises Ltd* [2003] 6 HKCFA 1 (Ct of Final Appeal, Hong Kong) Lord Millett said at para 16: 'Purchasers are often willing to pay more for land than its intrinsic value would justify. Thus the land may be used for an illegal or non-conforming purpose. In a free market purchasers may be willing to buy such land in the hope or expectation that the current use will continue to be tolerated. Such purchasers may be prepared to pay a higher price than would otherwise be justified. On resuming the land, however, the Government obviously ought not to be required to pay compensation on this basis'. The legal arguments in Hong Kong may be rather different from those in England and Wales since in Hong Kong nearly all land is held from the Government (before 1997 from the British Crown) on leases which often contain restrictions on use. Therefore on a resumption (compulsory acquisition) by the Government any unlawful use is a contractual wrong against the acquiring authority. Another question is what exactly is meant by 'intrinsic' value.

of the land, when his land is compulsorily acquired, should receive that amount of value which is attributable to the hope and expectation of the purchaser of being able to continue the use, albeit that the use is in some way unlawful. Unlawfulness when it is relevant to value is not an absolute concept in the sense that no purchaser would attribute any value to the opportunity to continue a use which is unlawful. It is a concept which depends, so far as value is concerned, on the perceptions of a hypothetical willing buyer. The whole of the basis of the law of compensation depends on that same concept. The principle of equivalence depends on that concept. It is therefore arguably contrary to the philosophy of the law of compensation that where an owner of land would, in an ordinary sale of it, receive a sum which is attributable to the hope of continuing an unlawful use he should not receive that same sum when his land is compulsorily acquired. In effect he is deprived in the case of a compulsory acquisition of a part of the value which is in fact inherent and attributable to his land and which could have been realised by him on a sale.

It is often useful to test the nature of legislation by taking a somewhat extreme example.   6.32
One of the reasons which may render a use of land unlawful is that it is in breach of planning control and is amenable to enforcement action, that is action to enforce the planning control. The town and country planning legislation provides that when a use of land has existed in breach of planning control for 10 years no enforcement action may thereafter be taken against it.[52] It is possible to posit a situation of a person who has carried out a use without the necessary planning permission for nine and a half years out of the 10 year period. It may be that the use was well known to the local planning authority and that it had decided to take no enforcement action. A hypothetical willing buyer in these circumstances would realise that there was a high expectation that after six months he would become immune from any enforcement action. Yet the application of rule (4) means that no element of the value of the land attributable to that expectation can be taken into account in valuing the land for the purposes of a compulsory acquisition. It is difficult to justify such a rule on any clear conceptual basis.[53] That having been said, there is a general rule in private law that a person should not be entitled to benefit from his own wrong.[54] A similar principle operates in areas of public law such as planning law.[55]

2. Planning Controls

The most frequent circumstances in which a use of land will be contrary to law are likely   6.33
to be that the use constitutes a breach of planning control, namely that it was a use commenced without planning permission, or a use which is in breach of a condition in a planning permission. An incident of such cases is that after the use has been continued for a certain time, usually 10 years, it becomes immune to planning enforcement action and the question is whether when that happens it remains a use contrary to law for present

---

[52] Town and Country Planning Act 1990, s 171B(3). There is an exception as regards a change of use to a single dwellinghouse where the time limit is four years: see ibid, s 171B(2).

[53] It is possible that the landowner could remedy the difficulty by seeking a certificate of appropriate alternative development under s 17 of the Land Compensation Act 1961: see section (d) of ch 7.

[54] *Alghussein Establishment v Eton College* [1988] 1 WLR 587, [1991] 1 All ER 267 (HL), relating to a provision in an agreement for a lease.

[55] *Welwyn Hatfield Borough Council v Secretary of State* [2011] UKSC 15, [2011] 2 AC 304.

purposes. Under the previous planning law it was held that for some purposes a use which was in breach of planning control remained unlawful for certain planning purposes even though it had become immune from enforcement proceedings because of the period during which it had been carried out.[56] Nonetheless when it came to the operation of rule (4) the use in these circumstances was held not to be contrary to law.[57] Under current planning legislation there is a four year time limit for enforcement action against development constituted by the carrying out of operations and by the change of use of a building to a single dwellinghouse. There is a 10 year time limit for enforcement proceedings against other changes of use.[58] There is within the legislation a procedure under which certificates of the lawfulness of existing or proposed development can be obtained, one of the grounds for the issue of such a certificate being that the development is immune from enforcement action because of the time at which it was carried out. It is provided in the planning legislation that when a certificate is in force the lawfulness of any use or operations specified in the certificate is presumed.[59] In effect when a use is immune from planning enforcement action by reason of these time limits on enforcement action, and a certificate has been obtained, any such use is lawful for the purposes of rule (4). Of course if a use is in breach of planning control, and could be the subject of effective enforcement action by a local planning authority, then it will be a use which is contrary to law within the meaning of rule (4) so that any increase in the value of land by reason of that use is to be disregarded.[60]

6.34   Rule (4) refers to a use of land which is contrary to law. It is well known that in the town and country planning legislation development comprises both operations on land and a material change in the use of land.[61] There is nothing in the Land Compensation Act 1961 which imports this definition of development into the operation of rule (4). The word 'development' is defined in section 39(1) of the 1961 Act by reference to its definition in the planning legislation but rule (4) refers not to development but to the use of land. It might be thought to follow from this reasoning that if the value of land has increased by virtue of a form of physical or operational development, such as the carrying out of building works, which is not itself and as such a change of use, then the use of the building so developed may not be contrary to law so that any increase in the value of the land due to that physical development may not have to be left out of account.

6.35   Such a conclusion would not be generally correct and would be an oversimplification of the situation. Buildings and other structures are erected to be used. Therefore the overall project of erecting a new building or altering an existing building on land involves both the physical works of construction and the use of that new or altered building after the completion of the works. The second element of the project will usually involve a material change in the use of the land and in the absence of a planning permission for that use the new use

---

[56]   *LTSS Print and Supply Services Ltd v Hackney LBC* [1976] QB 663, [1976] 2 WLR 253.
[57]   *Hughes v Doncaster Corporation* [1991] 1 AC 382, [1991] 2 WLR 16.
[58]   Town and Country Planning Act 1990, s 171B. The same time limits apply to breaches of planning control constituted by a breach of a condition to which a planning permission is subject. Other means of enforcement are stop notices (under s 183 of the Town and Country Planning Act 1990), breach of condition notices (under s 187A of that Act) and the obtaining of an injunction (under s 187B of that Act).
[59]   Ibid, ss 191(6), 192(4). The Lands Tribunal, when dealing with the application of r (4), should not regard itself as in all circumstances bound by the result of an application for a certificate of lawful existing use: see *Ullah v Leicester City Council* (1996) 71 P & CR 216.
[60]   *Hall v Sandwell MBC* [2008] RVR 345.
[61]   Town and Country Planning Act 1990, s 55(1).

will be an unlawful use. If a new house were erected without planning permission on land previously used for agriculture the project would be unlawful in two ways in that the construction would be an unlawful building operation and the subsequent use of the building would be an unlawful change in the use of the land from an agricultural use to a residential use. Since the use would be unlawful no account could be taken of it in the valuation of the land by reason of rule (4). It is because of this reasoning that a planning permission to erect a building involves a permission for the operation of constructing the building and a permission to use the building for the purpose specified in the permission or the purpose for which the building was designed. [62] Despite this general reasoning there may be cases of unlawful operational development which do not involve a change in the use of the land. An example would be an extension to a house outside certain limits as permitted by the Town and Country Planning (General Permitted Development) Order 1995 but without planning permission.[63] There would be no change in the use of the planning unit constituted by the existing house and its curtilage and it appears that there is nothing in rule (4) which prevents the value of the extension being taken into account despite the fact that it was an unlawful act in planning terms. Of course in such a case the unlawful works may have little value in the market because of the risk of enforcement action being taken against them within the four year period allowed for enforcement proceedings in relation to residential development.[64]

The position as regards uses in breach of planning control may be summarised in the following way: 6.36

   (a) A use carried out in breach of planning control, whether because the use was commenced without a necessary planning permission, or because the use is in contravention of a condition attached to a planning permission, is unlawful and must be left out of account in valuing the land acquired by reason of rule (4).
   (b) If the use has become immune from enforcement action by reason of the time limit for the service of an enforcement notice having elapsed, usually 10 years from the commencement of the use, the use becomes lawful for present purposes. This is so whether or not a certificate of lawful existing use or development has been obtained.
   (c) Development consisting of operations carried out without planning permission are unlawful in planning terms but there is no specific provision in rule (4) which prevents the value of such development being taken into account. Nonetheless in practice most such development will also involve a change in the use of the land and that change in the use will be unlawful and so must be left out of account under rule (4).

3. Other Reasons for Unlawfulness

Rule (4) refers to a use of land which is contrary to law. There are numerous other restrictions in public law on the use of land for various purposes apart from planning restrictions.   6.37

[62] *Wilson v West Sussex County Council* [1963] 2 QB 764, [1963] 2 WLR 669. See s 75(2), (3) of the Town and Country Planning Act 1990.
[63] Town and Country Planning (General Permitted Development) Order 1995 (SI 1995/418), art 3 and Class A in Pt I of sch 2.
[64] See para 6.33 for limitation periods for the service of an enforcement notice.

Licences or consents are needed for activities on land from the sale of alcohol to the opera-tion of an abattoir or the conducting of marriages. A difference between planning restric-tions and the restrictions under other licences is that planning is concerned primarily with the nature of a use of premises whereas the acceptability of other activities may relate more to the qualifications or attributes of the operator or the exact mode of operation. Even so in many cases the characteristics of the premises may be significant to the grant of a licence and the operation of the control. In principle the same rules should apply to areas of public control of the use of premises other than planning controls as apply to planning restric-tions. If land is being used without a licence, or contrary to the terms of a licence, any value attributable to the use should be left out of account when valuing the land. The Lands Tribunal has held that when land was used as a scrap yard and waste transfer station, some-thing which was lawful in planning terms but which did not have the benefit of a licence required under section 33(1) of the Environmental Protection Act 1990, the absence of the licence did not affect the basic value of the land but could be something which by reason of rule (4) reduced the compensation for disturbance under rule (6) of section 5 of the Land Compensation Act 1961.[65]

6.38   The question of whether an increase in the value of land attributable to a use which is con-trary to law has mainly arisen in the context of uses which are in some way in contravention of an area of public control of the use of property such as planning restrictions or the many other controls of particular uses which today apply. A question which has attracted less attention is whether rule (4) operates as regards a use which is contrary to some aspect of private law such as a contractual provision or a term of a lease or a restrictive covenant. As a matter of language a use which is contrary to some such private law restriction is contrary to law and is something which could be restrained by a court. A court will often issue an injunction to prevent a breach of a restrictive covenant or a breach of a user covenant in a lease. If as a matter of policy it is the law that a person should not obtain by way of compen-sation any value of his land attributable to a use which is contrary to some restriction which binds him there seems no reason of policy to confine that principle to limitations and con-traventions which arise by reason of public law as opposed to by reason of private law. Nor does the statutory language suggest such a limitation of the principle. Nonetheless it has been suggested in the Court of Appeal that rule (4) may be directed to breaches of the gen-eral law such as planning restrictions and not breaches of covenant in a lease.[66]

6.39   The third component of rule (4) is that an increase in the value of land must be left out of account where it is attributable to a use which is detrimental to health. This provision does not require that the use is unlawful, although it may well be. It is not often that this compo-nent of rule (4) will be relevant since a use of property which is detrimental to health is

---

[65] *Taff v Highways Agency* [2009] UKUT 128 (LC). This decision is sometimes cited for the proposition that the absence of a licence, such as a waste disposal licence, does not render a use contrary to law for the purposes of r (4). In fact the decision appears to have proceeded on the footing that the absence of the licence did render the use contrary to law, something which was relevant when it came to the assessment of disturbance compensation under r (6), but that as a matter of fact the absence of the licence did not affect the market value of the land.

[66] *Mean Fiddler Holdings Ltd v Islington LBC* [2003] 2 P & CR 7, per Carnwath LJ at para 6. This decision con-cerned the operation of a restriction in a lease against sharing the use of premises used as a nightclub. As the court said the question of whether r (4) applies to uses in contravention of restrictions such as covenants in leases might have to be determined in due course. It was not determined in the *Mean Fiddler* case since there the claim for compensation was subsequently settled. The general remarks by Lord Millett in *Director of Lands v Yin Shuen Enterprises* [2003] 6 HKCFA 1 (see n 50) were in the context of unlawful uses resulting from a breach of restrictions in leases as opposed to a breach of some aspect of public law.

likely to reduce the value of the property rather than to increase its value. This is not always so and, for example, the use of residential property in overcrowded conditions could result in an increase in the value of that property in times or areas of housing shortage even though the overcrowding was detrimental to the health of the occupants. In this context, in order to show that a use is detrimental to health, it is not necessary to show that there has been any actual harm or illness of the persons involved and it is enough that there is a prospect of such harm or illness caused by the physical state of the property or the activities carried on at the property.[67]

A practical difficulty in the operation of rule (4) is that it may not always be apparent whether a particular use of land is unlawful. This problem can arise where the alleged unlawfulness relates to planning constraints but the difficulty will be even more apparent when the allegation of unlawfulness is of a private or public nuisance and detailed evidence of the nature and effect of the activity on land may be necessary before it can be definitively said whether the use is or is not a wrong. In theory, and faced with such a situation, the Lands Tribunal would have to determine the law and then hear exact evidence on the facts. In practice, when the position is that the Tribunal finds that the alleged unlawfulness of a use is a matter of conjecture, it is likely to conclude that it has not been established that a component of the value of the land attributable to that use should be ignored.[68]   6.40

(D) BETTERMENT

1. The Principle

Betterment is a word the use of which has grown up in the law of compensation to denote a situation in which a person suffers loss to a piece of his land for which he is entitled to compensation and where the actions of the authority which caused the loss also increased the value of other land which he owns. The increase in value of the other land is said to be betterment. The word is not found in the statutory provisions. The question is when the betterment, the increase in the value of the other piece of land, is to be set off against the compensation so as to reduce it or even extinguish it. The answer to the question is that there will only be a set off where there is a specific statutory provision which requires it.   6.41

It is necessary to be precise as to what betterment means in its present usage. It does not normally mean, and should not be taken to mean, any effect on the land for which compensation is being claimed. If the compensation is for the compulsory acquisition of land the land acquired is wholly lost and any possibility of betterment must relate to other land.   6.42

---

[67] *Haq v Eastbourne BC* [2011] UKUT 365 (LC), [2012] RVR 18. In this case compensation due under housing legislation had to be assessed by reference to the rules in s 5 of the Land Compensation Act 1961. The residential premises involved were overcrowded. It was held that this was a use detrimental to the health of the occupants even though there was no actual physical or other harm or injury which the occupants had suffered. The Tribunal carefully considered the meaning of the word 'detrimental' by reference to the law of public health. It is plainly correct that something may be detrimental to the health of a person even though he has not at a particular time suffered any physical or mental harm. For example, smoking is detrimental to health even though at a particular time no illness has yet been suffered by the smoker.

[68] *Bolton v North Dorset District Council* (1997) 74 P & CR 73 (allegation that a use of land for motorcycle scrambling was a public nuisance).

Some of the heads of compensation considered in this book do not involve the acquisition of the land of the claimant. Compensation for injurious affection under section 10 of the Compulsory Purchase Act 1965 and compensation for the depreciation in the value of land caused by the use of public works under Part I of the Land Compensation Act 1973 do not involve any acquisition of land for which compensation is payable. In such cases it is not appropriate to refer to betterment as regards the land affected. The actions of a public authority, such as road works or the use of a road when constructed, may in part cause harm (for example, by increased noise) and in part cause benefit (for example, by an improved access) to the land affected. Both of these effects should be taken into account in assessing the effect on the value of the land affected. These effects should in principle be set off against each other. It is the net loss, the loss taking into account the benefit as well as the harm, which should be the basis of the compensation in such cases. In such a situation there may be no net loss to the land affected in which case there should be no compensation. The word 'betterment' is sometimes used to describe the beneficial effects on a piece of land of the actions of an authority as opposed to the harmful effects on the same land of the same actions. This usage only causes confusion. When there are beneficial effects of this kind they are not betterment to other land, which is to be set off against the compensation, but are an integral part of the assessment of the compensation itself. The critical point is that where betterment is used in its proper sense, that is an increase in value of land of the owner other than the land for which compensation is given, there has to be a deduction from the compensation for the increase in value of the other land only if statute so provides. This section is concerned only with betterment in its generally correct usage as just explained.[69]

6.43   The proposition of law that there can only be a set off against compensation otherwise due by reason of betterment in the above sense if there is statutory authority for the set off is established by the fundamental principle that the whole of the law of compensation is statutory and that, just as any provision for the assessment of compensation must be derived from statute, so any deduction from the compensation so assessed for betterment or anything else must also be derived from statute. It is for this reason that express provisions for a deduction of betterment exist generally in the compensation code and specifically in other legislation.[70] In *London and South Eastern Railway Company v London County*

[69]   The assessment of compensation under s 10 of the Compulsory Purchase Act 1965 is explained in ch 10, para 10.35. Compensation for use of public works is explained in ch 13. The assessment of this last head of compensation is subject to its own betterment provisions. See section (g) of ch 13 for a discussion of betterment in the context of this head of compensation. As there explained the rules for the assessment of this type of compensation mean that for certain purposes betterment has to be considered as a particular beneficial effect on land which may counterbalance other adverse effects on the same land. The correct approach to the concept of betterment is illustrated by the decision of the Court of Final Appeal in Hong Kong in *Penny's Bay Investments Ltd v Director of Lands* (2010) 13 HKCFAR 287. There land was injuriously affected by the extinguishment of its access to the sea as a result of land reclamation in connection with a proposed container port. It was at one time contended by the landowner that any benefit to the land due to the prospect of the container port had to be left out of account because it was 'betterment' and because there was no provision in the legislation for taking account of betterment. The Court of Final Appeal held that the compensation had to be assessed by considering both the beneficial and the detrimental effect of the extinguishment of the access to the sea and the expectation of the container port and associated development: see the declaration of the court as stated by Lord Hoffmann at para 47.

[70]   An example is s 261 of the Highways Act 1980 which provides that in assessing compensation following an acquisition of land by a highway authority the Tribunal shall have regard to the extent to which the remaining contiguous land of the landowner may be benefited by the purpose for which his land is acquired. There is a further specific provision in s 261(1)(b) that when land is acquired to widen a highway there is to be set off against the value of the land acquired any increase in the value of other land of the owner which will accrue by reason of the creation of a frontage to the highway as widened. See para 6.50 for the meaning of the word 'contiguous'. It is

Council[71] land situated on the south side of the Strand in London had a further or return frontage to a street running south from the Strand. A part of the land fronting the Strand was acquired in order to widen that thoroughfare. The result of the road widening was that the retained land which fronted the other street was increased in value because it obtained a direct frontage to the widened Strand. It was argued by the acquiring authority that the betterment, or increase in value due to the scheme, to the retained land should be deducted from the compensation payable for the land acquired. It was held by Eve J, in a decision upheld in the Court of Appeal, that there could be no such deduction for betterment in the absence of an express statutory provision.

2. The Specific Provisions

The general provision which ordains a set off for betterment when land is acquired is that in section 7 of the Land Compensation Act 1961. The provision operates when at the date of the notice to treat the person whose land is acquired is entitled in the same capacity to an interest in land contiguous or adjacent to the land acquired and applies to certain instances of an increase in the value of that interest. If the acquisition is carried out using the general vesting declaration procedure the vesting declaration operates as a constructive notice to treat under section 7(1) of the Compulsory Purchase (Vesting Declarations) Act 1981.   6.44

Put in general terms the increase in value of the other land which has to be deducted from the compensation for the land acquired is any increase due to the scheme which underlies the acquisition. It has been explained in detail in chapter 5 how the principle arose from decisions of the courts following the Lands Clauses Compensation Act 1845 that in valuing the land acquired the effect on the value of that land of the scheme of the acquiring authority had to be left out of account.[72] That principle has now been put into statutory form in the Land Compensation Act 1961 and the provisions of that Act operate as a comprehensive statement of the principle.[73]   6.45

What has to be left out of account, under the principle just described, is the effect on value of development or the prospect of development which falls within one of the seven 'cases' which are set out in schedule 1 to the 1961 Act and which would not have been likely to be carried out if the acquiring authority had not acquired and did not propose to acquire the land being valued.[74] The details and operation of these provisions are described in chapter 5.[75] The same provisions are used for specifying the development or prospect of development which may increase the value of the other land of the owner of the land acquired and   6.46

likely that in s 261 the wider of the two meanings which have been attributed to that word will be applied. See *Esso Petroleum Co Ltd v Secretary of State for Transport* [2008] RVR 351, for the application of s 261. See also *Portsmouth Royal Catholic Diocesan Trustees v Hampshire County Council* (1980) 40 P & CR 579.

[71] *London and South Eastern Rly Co v London County Council* [1915] 2 Ch 252. See ch 9, para 9.43 for a further aspect of this decision.

[72] See section (a) of ch 5.

[73] Land Compensation Act 1961, s 6. See *Transport for London v Spirerose Ltd* [2009] UKHL 44, [2004] 1 WLR 1797, and see ch 5, paras 5.71 et seq.

[74] Ch 5, paras 5.27 et seq.

[75] What is here described is the effect of Case 1 in sch 1 to the Land Compensation Act 1961 which is the case which applies generally to compulsory acquisitions. The remaining cases apply to particular circumstances such as where land is within a designated urban development area (Case 4A).

so will result in that increase having to be deducted from the compensation for the land acquired.[76] There is one important difference which is that when the provisions in section 6 and schedule 1 in the Land Compensation Act 1961 are being applied, so as to leave out of account the effect on the value of the land acquired of the scheme of the acquiring authority, it is development or the prospect of development on land other than the land acquired which has to be left out of account. When the same descriptions of development are used for the betterment provision in section 7 of the Act it is development or the prospect of development on other land and on the land acquired which has to be considered in order to determine whether that development or the prospect of that development increases the value of the other land of the landowner and so may have to be deducted from the compensation.

6.47   An example of what is involved is as follows. Suppose that plots A, B, C and D, all owned by different persons, are acquired in order to construct a housing development. The owner of plot A also owns a piece of land, plot E, in the immediate vicinity. When the value of plot A is being determined for the purposes of assessing compensation the construction, or the prospect of the construction, of the new housing on plots B to D may have to be left out of account insofar as it affects the value of plot A. However, the development or prospect of development of plot A itself for housing does not have to be left out of account (and indeed a planning permission for that housing on plot A is assumed to exist).[77] It may be that plot E is increased in value by the new housing development or the prospect of it, perhaps because of new facilities near it, or a better access to it, or an increased prospect that it itself may be developed at some later date. When considering the effect on the value of plot E for the purposes of the betterment provisions it is the development, or the prospect of the development, on plot A as well as on plots B to D which has to be taken into account. It may be that the value of plot A, ignoring any prospect of development within the scheme, was £200,000. Its value may have become £500,000 when account is taken of the assumed planning permission for housing development on it and the prospect of that development. Therefore, since the prospect of housing development on plot A (though not the prospect of housing development on plots B, C and D) must be taken into account in assessing compensation, the compensation due to the owner of plot A, ignoring any question of a betterment deduction, will be £500,000. There must then be considered the value of plot E and it, like plot A, may have been worth £200,000 prior to there being any prospect of the housing scheme. Its value may have increased to £300,000 by reason of the development, or proposed development, on plots A to D. In those circumstances that additional value of £100,000 will have to be deducted from the compensation of £500,000 payable to the owner of plots A and E for the acquisition from him of plot A. Thus in the end his compensation in the circumstances assumed will be £400,000.

3. Limitations on Betterment Deductions

6.48   There only has to be a deduction from the compensation for betterment if the person whose land is acquired and who is entitled to compensation is also entitled to an interest in other

---

[76] Land Compensation Act 1961, s 7.
[77] Land Compensation Act 1961, s 15(1). See ch 7, paras 7.15 and 7.16.

land 'in the same capacity' as he is entitled to an interest in the land acquired. For these purposes a person entitled to two interests in land is taken to be entitled to them in the same capacity only if he is entitled: (a) to both of them beneficially, or (b) to both of them as trustee of one particular trust, or (c) to both of them as personal representative of one particular person.[78] The interest in the two pieces of land need not be of the same nature or quality or duration. For instance, the betterment provisions will apply if the person claiming compensation owned the freehold of the land acquired but held only a lease of the other land. The relevant increase in value of the other land which must be deducted from the compensation will then, of course, be the increase in the value of his leasehold interest in that land.

The date for determining whether a person owns an interest in the land acquired and the   6.49
other land is the date of the service of notice to treat on him in respect of the land acquired. The provision in section 7 of the Land Compensation Act 1971, which provides for the betterment deduction, was enacted when it was generally thought that the date of the service of the notice to treat was the valuation date for the assessment of compensation. Today when the notice to treat procedure, as opposed to the general vesting declaration procedure, is used there may be a gap between the date of the notice to treat and the valuation date which in those circumstances will be the date of entry onto the land by the acquiring authority. There may also be a considerable period between the initial steps in the promotion of a scheme by the acquiring authority and the date of service of notice to treat. To return to the example used earlier, if the owner of plots A and E had sold plot E prior to the service of notice to treat on him then the enhanced value of plot E attributable to the prospect of the housing development which had been realised by him would not have to be deducted from the compensation payable for plot A. [79] Where the general vesting declaration procedure is used the vesting declaration operates as a constructive notice to treat under section 7(1) of the Compulsory Purchase (Vesting Declarations) Act 1981 so that the date of the making of the vesting declaration is the relevant date for present purposes. The valuations, that is of the land acquired and of any other land of the claimant in order to determine whether there should be a deduction for betterment, will be carried on as at the valuation date which was the date of entry in the case of a notice to treat or the date of the making of the declaration in the case of a general vesting declaration. The valuation process for determining whether land of the claimant has been increased in value will be the same as for the valuation of land acquired and will involve a hypothetical sale by a willing seller to a willing buyer on the valuation date.

The last limitation is that the land which is increased in value by the scheme, such that that   6.50
increase has to be deducted from the compensation payable for the land acquired, has to be contiguous or adjacent to the land acquired. The purpose of this limitation is not entirely easy to understand since fairness suggests that an increase in the value of other land of the dispossessed landowner due to the scheme of the acquiring authority should be deducted from the compensation wherever the other land is situated. The expression 'contiguous' is said to have a strict or a loose meaning. The strict meaning is that one piece of land is only contiguous to another if it touches the other land, that is if they have a common boundary. The looser meaning is that the two pieces of land may be contiguous if they are in the

---

[78]   Ibid, s 39(6).
[79]   See section (d) of ch 4 for the valuation date. The example referred to is in para 6.47.

general vicinity of each other.[80] The looser meaning is the same or similar to the meaning of adjacent and since in the legislation the expressions 'contiguous' and 'adjacent' are used as alternatives it seems that it is intended that 'contiguous' should be applied in its strict sense. Two pieces of land are adjacent to each other when they are in the same general neighbourhood or locality. It is impossible to be more precise than this. The Privy Council refused to interfere with a decision of the Governor of New Zealand when he determined that two administrative areas in the colony were adjacent even though they were separated by about six miles and even though there were other administrative areas between them.[81] Since fairness generally demands that there should be a set off against compensation for betterment it may be anticipated that the courts will give a fairly relaxed meaning to the concept of adjacency within section 7 of the Land Compensation Act 1961. In contrast to the present provisions, and as explained in chapter 9, when a part of a person's land is acquired he may become entitled to compensation for injurious affection to the land which he retains and in that case there is no requirement that the land retained is contiguous or adjacent to the land acquired.

4. Subsequent Acquisitions

6.51   A possible situation is that when a piece of land, plot A, is acquired the compensation has to be reduced under the betterment provisions described because of an increase in the value due to the scheme to plot B which is owned by the same person as plot A, and then plot B is subsequently acquired for the same scheme. In determining the compensation for the acquisition of plot B the normal rule would be that any increase in the value of plot B due to the scheme would have to be left out of account by reason of section 6 and schedule 1 in the Land Compensation Act 1961.[82] Such a result would be unfair since the landowner would then suffer a double reduction for the beneficial effect of the scheme on the value of plot B. The increase in value of plot B would be used to reduce his compensation for plot A and the same increased value of plot B would be used to reduce his compensation for the acquisition of plot B. This result is avoided in that it is provided that, in the circumstances described, section 6 is not to operate so as to require that the effect of the scheme in increasing the value of plot B must be left out of account when plot B is valued for the purposes of the compensation payable for its acquisition.[83]

6.52   A similar situation could arise where plot A was acquired and the owner obtained compensation for injurious affection to plot B because that plot, which he also owned, had been reduced in value by the same scheme.[84] If plot B is subsequently acquired for the purposes of the same scheme the normal rule under section 6 and schedule 1 in the Land Compensation Act 1961 would be that the diminution in its value brought about by the scheme had to be left out of account in assessing the compensation payable for its acquisition. That result would be unfair to the acquiring authority since the landowner would then obtain compen-

---

[80]   *Haynes v King* [1893] 3 Ch 439; *Spillers Ltd v Cardiff Borough Assessment Committee* [1931] 2 KB 21. See n 69 for a provision relating to betterment under highways legislation where the benefited land has to be contiguous to the land acquired if there is to be a set off for betterment.

[81]   *City of Wellington v Borough of Lower Hutt* [1904] AC 773.

[82]   See ch 5.

[83]   Land Compensation Act 1961, s 8(1).

[84]   Ie under s 7 of the Compulsory Purchase Act 1965: see ch 9.

sation for the reduced value of plot B by way of injurious affection, but would obtain the same compensation again when plot B was valued for the purposes of its compulsory acquisition, since the diminution in value would be ignored in the valuation which had to be carried out for that purpose. This result is avoided by the provision that in the circumstances described section 6 is to be taken as not requiring the reduction in the value of plot B due to the scheme to be left out of account when determining its value for the purposes of compensation for its acquisition.[85] To take an example, suppose that plot B was reduced in value from £500,000 to £400,000 by the scheme underlying the acquisition of plot A so that the £100,000 reduction was recoverable by the owner of the two plots as compensation for injurious affection. When it comes to valuing plot B on its subsequent acquisition the reduction in value is not to be left out of account but should be taken into account for the purposes of the valuation with the result that the compensation payable for the acquisition of plot B will be only £400,000.

The valuation provisions explained in the last two paragraphs apply to any subsequent acquisition of land whether the interest acquired by the subsequent acquisition is the same as the interest which was previously taken into account, whether the acquisition extends to the whole of the land in which that interest previously subsisted or only to a part of that land, and where the person entitled to the interest acquired derives title to that interest from the person who at the time of the previous acquisition was entitled to that interest. Where the previous acquisition was by agreement, and if it had been a compulsory acquisition an increase or diminution in value would have fallen to be taken into account, the provisions just described have effect as if the sale had been by way of a compulsory acquisition and the increase or diminution in value had been taken into account accordingly.   6.53

(E) LATER PLANNING DECISIONS

1. Entitlement to Further Compensation

Where a person's interest in land is compulsorily acquired or sold to an authority possessing compulsory purchase powers,[86] that person may become entitled to additional compensation if within 10 years of completion a planning decision is made granting permission for additional development of any of the land in which the interest subsisted. The right to additional compensation arises if the principal amount of the compensation, or the purchase price on a sale, would have been greater if the planning decision had been made before the date of the service of the notice to treat or the date of the making of the contract of sale and the planning permission granted by that decision had been in force at that date.[87]   6.54

---

[85] Land Compensation Act 1961, s 8(2).
[86] For the meaning of this expression, see s 39(1) of the Land Compensation Act 1961.
[87] Ibid, s 23. The provisions for additional compensation have had a chequered history. They were introduced in ss 18–21 of the Town and Country Planning Act 1959 and repeated in the Land Compensation Act 1961. They were then repealed by the Land Commission Act 1967, ss 86, 101 and sch 17 but were re-enacted by the Planning and Compensation Act 1967, s 66 and sch 14. If the acquisition is carried out using the general vesting declaration procedure the vesting declaration operates as a constructive notice to treat under s 7(1) of the Compulsory Purchase (Vesting Declarations) Act 1981 so that the date of the vesting declaration is the relevant date for present purposes.

Any planning permission which is in force at the valuation date will be taken into account in valuing the land acquired. Furthermore a permission is deemed to be in force at the valuation date for development in accordance with the proposals of the acquiring authority.[88] Since the acquiring authority is required to pay as part of the compensation any value of the land acquired attributable to any development which it proposes to carry out on the land acquired it was considered to be fair and logical that if a further permission is obtained for further development on the land acquired in the decade following the acquisition the authority should pay as further compensation any additional value of the land acquired attributable to that further permission and to the development which it authorises. For example, the right to additional compensation could arise where the acquiring authority decided it did not need the land acquired and sold it on for some different form of development.

6.55   In the present provision a planning decision means a decision made on an application under the Town and Country Planning Act 1990. A planning permission means the grant of a permission for development either unconditionally or subject to conditions and either in respect of the land in which the interest acquired subsists taken by itself or in respect of a wider area which includes that land. The date of completion means the date on which the acquisition or sale is completed by the vesting of the interest in land in the acquiring authority.[89] If the general vesting declaration procedure is used the vesting will be on the vesting date specified in the declaration whereas if the notice to treat procedure is used the transfer of title to the acquiring authority may be considerably delayed so affecting the commencement of the 10 year period.[90]

6.56   There is a significant limitation on the entitlement to additional compensation which is that it is not available in the case of a new planning permission which, in the case of a local authority, permits development for the functions for which that authority acquired the land and, in the case of any other acquiring authority, permits development for the project for which that authority acquired the land.[91] In other words new permissions for the scheme which underlay the acquisition do not generally create a right to further compensation.

6.57   When it comes to the meaning of additional development the word development has the same meaning as in the Town and Country Planning Act 1990, namely the carrying out of building, engineering, mining or other operations in, on, over or under land or the making of any material change in the use of any buildings or other land.[92] There are five categories of development which are excluded from being additional development for present purposes, which are as follows:

    (a)   where the acquiring authority is a local authority and acquired the land for the purpose of any of its functions, development for the purposes of the functions for which it acquired the land;

---

[88]   See ch 7 for a general account of actual and deemed planning permissions for the purposes of valuing the land acquired.
[89]   Land Compensation Act 1961, s 29(1), (2).
[90]   See ch 2 for these procedures.
[91]   See para 6.57, and see n 92.
[92]   Land Compensation Act 1961, s 39(1); Town and County Planning Act 1990, s 55(1).

  (b) where the acquiring authority is not a local authority, development for the purposes of the project in connection with which it acquired the interest in land;[93]

  (c) development for which planning permission was in force at the date of notice to treat or of the contract of sale;

  (d) in the case of a compulsory acquisition, development for which it was assumed under sections 14–16 of the Land Compensation Act 1961 that planning permission would be granted; and

  (e) in the case of a sale by agreement, development for which, if the acquisition had been compulsory with a notice to treat served on the date of the contract of sale, an assumption of planning permission would be made under sections 14–16 of the 1961 Act.[94]

In five cases no compensation is payable in respect of a planning decision insofar as it relates to land acquired by the acquiring authority whether compulsorily or by agreement. The five cases are as follows: 6.58

  (a) a decision under section 21A of the Welsh Development Agency Act 1975 (powers of land acquisition);

  (b) a decision under sections 142 or 143 of the Local Government, Planning and Land Act 1980 (acquisitions by urban development corporations and by highway authorities in connection with urban development areas);

  (c) a decision under the New Towns Act 1981 (acquisitions by development corporations and by highway authorities in connection with new town areas);

  (d) where the compulsory purchase order included a decision under section 50 of the Planning (Listed Buildings and Conservation Areas) Act 1990 (minimum compensation where building deliberately allowed to fall into disrepair); and

  (e) a decision under Part I of the Housing and Regeneration Act 2008 (acquisition by the Homes and Communities Agency).[95]

The right to additional compensation is a right personal to the owner whose land has been acquired and does not devolve with any land. For instance, if the person whose land was acquired also owns other land and at some time within the 10 year period prior to the grant of the new planning permission disposes of the other land, the right to the additional compensation remains with the original claimant and does not pass with the other land. If a person dies within the 10 year period, and before the grant of the new planning permission, then the right to compensation upon the grant of that permission for additional development devolves as if the right had been vested in the deceased person immediately before his   6.59

---

[93] It will be a matter of fact in individual cases to ascertain whether the development is for the purpose of the function or project of the acquiring authority. For example, an acquiring authority may acquire land to construct houses with a permission for 20 houses on the land acquired from a particular landowner. If a subsequent planning permission is granted to construct 30 houses on that land the new permission is still probably for the same function or project. In other words the words 'function' and 'project' are probably here intended to have a wide meaning rather than being confined to the details of the proposals of the authority at the time of the acquisition of the land. Support for this approach may be found in *Street's Executors v Secretary of State for Transport* [2011] UKUT 1 (LC), [2011] RVR 167, where land was acquired to construct a motorway service area and within the 10 year period a planning permission was granted to construct a hotel on the land acquired. It was held that no additional compensation could be claimed since the hotel development was a part of the same project as that for which the land had been acquired.

[94] Land Compensation Act 1961, s 29(1).

[95] Ibid, s 23(3).

death. The same rule applies if by reason of some other act or event the right to compensation in respect of additional development, if vested in the original claimant immediately before that act or event, would have vested in some other person. The right to compensation is treated as having devolved as if the right had been vested in the original claimant immediately before that other act or event.[96]

6.60   The assessments of the actual compensation paid and of the compensation which would have been paid, if the new planning permission for additional development had been in force at the date of the notice to treat or at the date of the agreement for sale, are to be carried out by reference to what is called the principal amount of the compensation. The principal amount of the compensation includes not only the amount paid as the value of the land acquired (ie under rule (2) of section 5 of the Land Compensation Act 1961) but also any compensation attributable to disturbance (ie under rule (6) of section 5 of the 1961 Act) or to severance or injurious affection (ie under the second limb of section 7 of the Compulsory Purchase Act 1965).[97] In effect there is to be a complete recalculation of the main heads of compensation on the basis that the new planning decision granting a further planning permission had been in existence when the acquisition of the land or its sale by agreement took place. It should be noted that what creates a possible entitlement to additional compensation is a decision to grant planning permission and not the implementation of that permission by the carrying out of the development permitted. Of course it is the opportunity to carry out further development created by the decision to grant a planning permission which normally adds value to the land the subject of the permission.

6.61   What is contemplated for the purposes of assessing the additional compensation is a new assessment of the compensation at the original valuation date with the single difference that the new decision to grant planning permission on the land acquired is in existence. Land values as at the original valuation date must be applied. All other relevant facts and circumstances and events as at the original valuation date must be taken into account. It would be wrong in principle to carry out the new assessment of the compensation with knowledge of facts and events which had occurred or changed between the original valuation date and the decision to grant a new planning permission except of course for that decision which is taken to be in existence at the valuation date. If the new planning permission covers a wider area of land than the land acquired that may be relevant to the new assessment of compensation. The legislation was enacted at a time when it was believed that the date of the notice to treat was the valuation date. It seems that, just as the original valuation will today have been carried out with the date of entry as the valuation date, so the re-assessment taking into account the new planning permission should be by reference to the same valuation date. This problem will not arise where a general vesting declaration has been made since in that case the declaration operates as a constructive notice to treat and will also be the valuation date.

6.62   There is an exception to the principle as last stated in that at the time of the compulsory acquisition or the sale the person entitled to compensation may have been entitled to an interest in other land, but may have ceased to be entitled to that interest in the whole or a part of the other land, when within the 10 year period there is a decision granting a plan-

---

[96] Ibid, s 23(4).
[97] Ibid, sch 3, para 1. The reference to compensation attributable to disturbance probably includes compensation for any other matter not directly based on the value of land as prescribed in r (6) of s 5 of the 1961 Act.

ning permission for additional development. In these circumstances it would be unreasonable to carry out the comparison between the two amounts of compensation by including compensation for severance or injurious affection in relation to the other land. The reason is that in the type of case being considered the original landowner will have been fully compensated for any reduction in the value of the land retained by him and once he has sold that land he can suffer no further loss in respect of that land. For example, the retained land may have been reduced in value from £400,000 to £350,000 by the acquisition of the land acquired with a planning permission on the land acquired at the time of the acquisition. If the owner then sells the retained land for £350,000 he has been fully compensated for his loss and in the event of the land sold being further reduced in value by a further permission granted for development of the land acquired that loss will fall on the purchaser of the land sold. As stated earlier the right to additional compensation by reason of a new permission on the land acquired is a personal right and does not run with any land. Consequently in these circumstances the assessment of the original, and the new compensation or purchase price, is to exclude any element of compensation attributable to severance or injurious affection.[98]

There is a further exception where at the assessment of the original compensation there was   6.63
a deduction from the compensation which would otherwise have been payable by reason of an increase in the value of other land of the claimant due to the scheme of the acquiring authority, that is a deduction for betterment under section 7 of the Land Compensation Act 1961, or under some other provision to the same effect. When it comes to determining the difference between the original compensation or purchase price and the compensation that would have been payable if the new planning permission had existed it is to be assumed that the circumstances which gave rise to the deduction for betterment did not exist.[99]

To take an example, the land acquired may have been worth £2 million at the valuation date   6.64
but because the owner owned other land which was increased in value by £200,000 by the scheme of the acquiring authority that last amount was deducted from the compensation so resulting in compensation of £1.8 million. If a later planning permission is granted on the land acquired on a new assessment of the compensation taking account of that new permission the value of the land acquired might have been £2.5 million. The claimant will then be entitled to additional compensation of £500,000 not £700,000 since the increased value of the other land of the claimant is to be left out of account both as regards the original assessment of compensation and as regards the new assessment of compensation.

2. The Claim for Further Compensation

It may not be easy for a person whose land has been acquired, and who has received com-   6.65
pensation, to find out whether in the next 10 years a new planning permission is granted for additional development on that land which may entitle him to further compensation. There

[98] Ibid, sch 3, para 2. It is curious that this provision concerns the compensation for severance or injurious affection under the second limb of s 7 of the Compulsory Purchase Act 1965 when it is payable only in respect of land contiguous or adjacent to the land acquired. In fact s 7 refers simply to other land of the dispossessed owner and has no limitation to land which is contiguous or adjacent to the land acquired.
[99] Land Compensation Act 1961, sch 3, para 3. For deductions for betterment see section (d) of this chapter.

is therefore a statutory procedure, described next, which provides for notification to a claimant of a permission for additional development on the land acquired. If the claimant does not take advantage of that procedure he may still claim additional compensation but he must then make his claim within six months of the date of the decision to grant the new permission. If the permission is granted on appeal the six months runs from the date of the appeal decision.[100] There is no prescribed form of claim for the additional compensation.

6.66   The procedure just mentioned is as follows. The person entitled to receive the compensation or purchase price on the acquisition of his land may give to the acquiring authority an address for service. A person who claims under the original claimant, for example a person on whom the right to the additional compensation has devolved on the death of the original claimant, may also give such an address for service. If a planning decision granting permission for additional development is made within the 10 year period the acquiring authority is required to give notice of the decision in the prescribed form to the person who has given them an address for service at that address.[101] The acquiring authority need not give notice if it has reasonable grounds for believing that the person who gave it an address for service is dead or some other act or event has occurred whereby the right to compensation would, if vested in that person immediately before the act or event, have vested in some other person.[102]

6.67   It may occur that an acquiring authority which has been given an address for service ceases to be entitled to an interest in the whole or a part of the land which it has acquired. In that case the acquiring authority is required to notify the local planning authority after which it is the duty of the local planning authority to give notice to the acquiring authority of any planning decision of which the acquiring authority is itself required to give notice to the landowner. The local planning authority must give this notice to the acquiring authority within seven days of the planning decision.[103] The acquiring authority must then of course give notice to the original claimant.

6.68   Where a person has given his address to the acquiring authority, in accordance with these provisions, the time limit for the making by him of a claim for additional compensation is six months from the date on which notice of the planning decision is given to him by the acquiring authority. Again where there is a planning appeal the decision is the decision on that appeal.[104]

---

[100] Ibid, s 24(4). Planning appeals are made under s 78 of the Town and Country Planning Act 1990 and a decision on an appeal includes a decision on an appeal made under s 78(2) of the 1990 Act following a failure of the local planning authority to issue a decision within the prescribed time on an application for planning permission: see Land Compensation Act 1961, s 24(5). The time limits stated in this paragraph and in para 6.68 are limits within which a claim for additional compensation must be made. If a claim is made within the specified time limit and the entitlement of the claimant to additional compensation is not agreed, or the amount is not agreed, there will have to be a reference to the Lands Tribunal to determine these matters. The general six year time limit for claims for the recovery of any sum recoverable by virtue of an entitlement under statute contained in s 9 of the Limitation Act 1980 will apply to that reference. See ch 15, para 15.42 and see *Hillingdon LBC v ARC Ltd (No 1)* [1999] Ch 139, [1938] 3 WLR 754.
[101] Land Compensation Act 1961, s 24(1), (2). The prescribed forms are forms 1 and 2 in the schedule to the Land Compensation (Additional Development) (Forms) Regulations 1992 (SI 1992/271).
[102] Land Compensation Act 1961, s 24(3). See para 6.59 for devolution of the right to additional compensation on the death of the original claimant and in certain other circumstances.
[103] Ibid, s 24(6), (7).
[104] Ibid, s 24(4). See also n 99 for the limitation period for making a reference to the Lands Tribunal.

The amount of the additional compensation is to be determined by the Lands Tribunal if   6.69
not agreed and interest is payable on any additional compensation at the prescribed rate
from the date of the planning decision until payment.[105]

3. Extended Application

In some circumstances a planning permission may be granted otherwise than by way of a   6.70
planning decision made on a planning application. For example, planning permission is
granted automatically for certain types of development by a development order made
under the Town and Country Planning Act 1990 without the need for an application for
planning permission and without any decision of a planning authority to grant permission.
The provisions for additional compensation are extended to cover five such instances of
planning permissions and in these cases the date of the decision is also defined for the purposes of initiating the entitlement to additional compensation. The five cases are as follows:

(a) The first case is a permission granted by a development order and the date of deci-
    sion is when the development is initiated. The main order in force today is the Town
    and Country Planning (General Permitted Development) Order 1995 which as
    amended grants permission for a variety of different forms of development usually
    of a relatively minor nature.[106] It is necessary under this head to specify the initia-
    tion of the development as the date on which a claim to additional compensation
    may arise since there is no decision as such which gives rise to the grant or existence
    of a planning permission.

(b) The second case is a permission granted by an adoption or approval of a simplified
    planning zone scheme and the date of the decision is when the scheme is approved
    or adopted.

(c) The third case is a permission granted by an order designating an enterprise zone
    and the date of the decision is when that designation takes effect.

(d) The fourth case is a permission deemed to be granted by a direction under section
    90 of the Town and Country Planning Act 1990 and the date of decision is when the
    direction is given. Under section 90 when the authorisation of a government depart-
    ment is required for certain development to be carried out by certain bodies, such
    as local authorities or statutory undertakers, the department may when giving the
    authorisation direct that planning permission for the development shall be deemed
    to be granted.

(e) The fifth case is a permission deemed to be granted by a local planning authority
    and the date of decision is the occurrence of the event in consequence of which the
    permission is deemed to be granted.

Notice is required to be given by the acquiring authority of a proposal by it to carry out   6.71
development pursuant to any planning permissions within the above five categories when
the person who originally obtained compensation has given an address for service to the
acquiring authority. If the proposal to carry out the development is by some person other
than the acquiring authority that person should notify the acquiring authority and that

---

[105] Ibid, s 23(5), (6) (applying Pt 1 of the Act). See ch 15, para 15.28, for the prescribed rate of interest.
[106] Town and Country Planning (General Permitted Development) Order 1995 (SI 1995/418).

authority must then give notice to the person who has given his address to it. In the case of a planning permission coming within any of the above categories a claim for compensation must be made within six months of the date of the decision as just specified if no address for service has been given to the acquiring authority or, if an address for service has been given to that authority, within six months of the date on which the acquiring authority gives notice of the proposal to carry out the development. [107]

6.72   The other extension of the provisions is where development is carried out by the Crown. Until 2004 planning permission was not required for development carried out by the Crown so that the provisions for additional compensation could not apply in the ordinary way upon the grant of a planning permission. The extended provision applied where planning permission was not required because the development was initiated by or on behalf of the Crown or the Duchy of Lancaster or the Duchy of Cornwall, or belonged to a government department, or was held in trust for the Crown for the purposes of a government department. Today the Town and Country Planning Act 1990 binds the Crown as it does other persons subject to certain modifications.[108] In general the Crown, which includes government departments, must make an application for planning permission in the ordinary way. The provisions as to the original claimant for compensation giving an address for service to the acquiring authority are again applied and it is the duty of the acquiring authority to give notice in the prescribed form to the person who has given an address for service of the initiation of the development. In the case of Crown development the claim for additional compensation must be made within six months of the time the development is initiated or, where a person has given a notice for service, within six months of the date on which notice has been given to that person of the initiation of the development.[109]

4. Mortgaged Land and Settled Land

6.73   In the operation of the provisions for additional compensation mortgages are ignored. The mortgagor of the land and not the mortgagee is entitled to the additional compensation. The original compensation and the compensation which would have been payable if the new planning permission had been in force are to be assessed as the amounts which would have been payable if the mortgage did not exist.[110]

6.74   Where an interest in land is subject to a settlement within the meaning of the Settled Land Act 1925, or a trust for sale within the meaning of the Law of Property Act 1925, references in the provisions for additional payment to the person entitled to the compensation are to be taken as a reference to the trustees for the time being of the settlement. Any additional compensation payable to the trustees of the settlement shall be applicable by the trustees as if it were proceeds of the sale of the interest which has been acquired or sold to the acquiring authority.[111] Family settlements or strict settlements involved the creation of successive

---

[107] Ibid, s 25.

[108] See Pt XIII of the Town and Country Planning Act 1990 as inserted by s 79(1) of the Planning and Compulsory Purchase Act 2004.

[109] Land Compensation Act 1961, s 26.

[110] Ibid, sch 3, paras 4–6. In most cases the sums secured by the mortgage will have been paid to the mortgagee and the mortgage will have been discharged at the time of the acquisition of the land: see section (m) of ch 2.

[111] Ibid, sch 3, para 7.

limited interests in land. These were once popular but lost their popularity due to taxation disadvantages. It has not been possible to create such settlements since the coming into effect of the Trusts of Land and Appointment of Trustees Act 1996. Since 1 January 1997 all new trusts of land must be trusts for sale.

(F) TAXATION

1. Introduction

There are two questions which need to be considered in connection with compensation and taxation. The first is the incidence of tax on sums received as compensation. This matter is something for the general law of tax and its details are beyond the scope of this book. Nonetheless it is necessary to state a brief and general answer to the question since without that answer it is not possible to understand the answer to the second question. The second question is whether the acquiring authority is entitled to make a deduction from the amount of the compensation assessed and payable by reason of tax matters. As well as these two principal matters a further question which can arise is whether a claim can be made for compensation in respect of an additional tax burden suffered by a landowner as a result of the compulsory acquisition.   6.75

Compensation is of its nature payable in respect of a loss suffered by the claimant. The loss may be the value of the land acquired and of the ability of the owner to realise that value by selling the land in the market. The loss may be injurious affection caused to land retained by the dispossessed landowner. The loss may be a loss of temporary profits where a business previously carried on at the land acquired is located elsewhere. The sums lost, and for the loss of which compensation is payable, might have been subject to tax if they had been realised or received and not lost. Equally the sums received as compensation, equivalent to the sums lost, may or may not be subject to tax. The answer to the question of whether any deduction should be made from the compensation payable by reason of tax liability depends on three matters. (a) If the items lost, for example lost profits, would not have been subject to tax then no question arises of a deduction from the compensation for that item by reason of tax. (b) If the item lost would have been liable to tax and the compensation paid will also be liable to tax in the hands of the recipient then again no deduction from the compensation by reason of tax is justified. For instance, if the lost profits for which compensation is payable were £100,000 and they would have been subject to tax at 20 per cent the claimant would have received a sum of £80,000 after tax if there had been no compulsory purchase and no loss of profits. He would also receive a sum of £80,000 after he had been paid his compensation of £100,000 and had paid £20,000 of tax on it. Clearly in these circumstances the sum paid to him as compensation should be the full £100,000. (c) If the profits would have been subject to tax had they been received but the sum received as compensation would not be subject to tax then there should be a deduction from the compensation paid. If in the last example the full £100,000 was paid as compensation in these circumstances the claimant would be better off since instead of receiving a net sum of £80,000 after tax he would receive and retain a sum of £100,000. What should be done in these circumstances is that the compensation should be reduced to £80,000 so that the claimant is put in the same   6.76

financial position as he would have been in if there had been no compulsory acquisition and no loss of profits. These conclusions can be seen as an application of the principle of equivalence.[112]

6.77   Common law damages, like compensation, are a monetary sum received to compensate a claimant for a loss suffered by him. The principles just explained have been applied so far as tax is concerned when damages are assessed. A principle established by the courts in the context of damages is known as the Gourley principle after the decision of the House of Lords in *British Transport Commission v Gourley*[113] and is that damages are to be paid in full without any deduction for tax unless: (a) the sums lost by the claimant and in respect of which damages are payable would have been subject to tax if they had been received by him, and (b) the damages paid to him would not be subject to tax. If both conditions are satisfied the damages should be reduced by the amount of the tax which would have been payable on the receipts which have been lost. The rule for compensation for a compulsory purchase follows this general principle applicable to damages. One result of the application of the principle is that acquiring authorities before determining the amount of compensation will need to satisfy themselves as to the tax position of a claimant and the application of the general law of taxation.

2. The Main Heads of Compensation

6.78   The disposal of land by the owner to an acquiring authority is a disposal the proceeds of which are liable to capital gains tax, currently at the rate of 28 per cent, under the Taxation of Chargeable Gains Act 1992. Thus, if the only compensation received is the value of the land under rule (2) of section 5 of the Land Compensation Act 1961, the sum received as compensation will in principle be liable to capital gains tax in the hands of the claimant and no deduction should be made by the acquiring authority from the compensation payable by reason of tax. This rule corresponds with the general principle explained earlier. Where the claimant occupied the property acquired as his only or main residence no capital gains tax is payable. The date of the disposal for the purposes of capital gains tax purposes is the date on which the compensation is agreed or determined.[114] Compulsory purchase rollover relief is available if the compensation received is reinvested in land in connection with the replacement of business assets.[115]

6.79   It is possible that the sum received as compensation may contain an amount in respect of disturbance or other compensation under rule (6) of section 5 of the Land Compensation Act 1961. In these circumstances an apportionment of the total compensation received will be made under sections 245(1) and 52(4) of the Taxation of Chargeable Gains Act 1992

---

[112] For the principle of equivalence see section (a) of ch 3.
[113] *British Transport Commission v Gourley* [1956] AC 185, [1956] 2 WLR 41. In *Gourley's* case the claimant was injured in an accident and was awarded the sum of £37,720 as a sum which he would have earned had it not been for the accident. Due to the very high incidence of income tax and surtax at that time the sum which he would have received after tax in respect of such earnings would have been £6,695. The claimant was not liable to tax in respect of the damages paid to him as tax law stood at that time. The House of Lords held that there should be a deduction from the damages of the amount of tax which would have been payable on the earnings had they been received and the award of damages for this item was reduced to £6,695.
[114] Taxation of Chargeable Gains Act 1992, s 246.
[115] Ibid, s 247.

between the amount of compensation for the value of the land and the amount of compensation for disturbance. Only the former sum will be liable to capital gains tax.

If compensation is received for severance or injurious affection to land retained by the claimant under the second limb of section 7 of the Compulsory Purchase Act 1965 then under section 245(2) of the Taxation of Chargeable Gains Act 1992 there is deemed to be a part disposal of the retained land for the purposes of capital gains tax. Again, therefore, and in accordance with the principles explained earlier the whole of the compensation for severance or injurious affection to the retained land should be paid by the acquiring authority without any deduction for tax.

6.80

It remains to mention compensation for disturbance under rule (6) of section 5 of the Land Compensation Act 1965 for matters such as a loss of profits over a temporary period while the business carried on at the land acquired is removed to other premises. As just explained this component of the compensation is not treated as part of the sum received on a disposal of the land and so is disregarded for the purposes of the assessment of capital gains tax.[116] The sums received are likely to be liable to income tax or corporation tax and in these circumstances, and in accordance with the general principle explained, again the whole of the compensation should be paid by the acquiring authority without deduction for tax.[117]

6.81

3. Value Added Tax

Under the Value Added Tax Act 1994 the transfer of an interest in land is a supply of goods or services and value added tax (VAT) can in principle be payable on the purchase price or, in the case of a compulsory acquisition of the land, on the compensation paid for the value of the land. However, the transfer of an interest in land is an exempt supply so that generally no VAT is in practice payable. The owner of the land can waive the right for a transfer of the land to have this exempt status and if this has been done a transfer of the land will attract VAT usually at the standard rate on the price paid or compensation paid on a transfer.[118] Therefore when compensation is paid for the value of land acquired under rule (2) of section 5 of the Land Compensation Act 1961: (a) generally no VAT will be payable by the acquiring authority on the compensation since the supply will be an exempt supply, but (b)

6.82

---

[116] See para 6.79.

[117] *Stoke-on-Trent City Council v Wood Mitchell* [1980] 1 WLR 254. In *West Suffolk County Council v W Rought Ltd* [1957] AC 403, [1956] 3 WLR 589, the House of Lords, following *Gourley's* case, held that where a sum of compensation was payable for a loss of profit, which would have been made on orders lost over a temporary period, there should be a deduction on account of tax from the amount of the compensation for this item. The reason was that the profits would have been taxable if actually received but at that time would not have been taxable as an item of compensation. Thus the two conditions which have to exist for a deduction of tax from damages or compensation in accordance with the principle in *Gourley's* case were satisfied. In the *West Suffolk* case the Inland Revenue had indicated that no tax would be payable on the compensation when received. The situation was different in *Stoke-on-Trent City Council v Wood Mitchell* where it appeared that tax would have been payable on the item of compensation in question so that the Court of Appeal held that no deduction for tax was to be made. This remains the general position today. See also *Pennine Raceway Ltd v Kirklees Metropolitan Borough Council (No 2)* [1989] 1 EGLR 30, in which compensation was payable for an order made under the Town and Country Planning Act 1971 revoking a planning permission and it was held that no deduction should be made from the compensation by reason of tax since the compensation would have been taxable in the hands of the claimant.

[118] Value Added Tax Act 1974, sch 10. The reason for a waiver of the exemption may be that the owner of the property wishes to receive VAT on a disposal which he can then set off against output tax payable by him so as to reduce his overall VAT liability.

VAT will be payable if the exempt supply status of the land has been previously waived. If VAT is payable it becomes payable on any compensation payable under rule (6) as well as the value of the land under rule (2) since technically both components of compensation are a part of the value of the land.[119] If VAT is payable on the compensation this should be taken into account in assessing the sum to be paid to the claimant as an advance payment.[120]

6.83   If compensation is paid under the second limb of section 7 of the Compulsory Purchase Act 1965 for severance or injurious affection to land retained by the claimant no VAT is payable on this component of the compensation since there is no supply of goods or services.

6.84   Under section 33 of the Value Added Tax Act 1994 Her Majesty's Revenue and Customs (HMRC) are required to refund to a local authority and other bodies VAT payable by that body on the supply to it of goods and services (other than supplies for the purpose of a business carried on by the body). Consequently acquiring authorities will normally be able to obtain from HMRC a refund of VAT which they pay on the value of land paid as compensation to a landowner who has waived his exemption from VAT.

6.85   A claimant for compensation under rule (6) is likely to have paid VAT on certain costs and expenses which he includes in his claim such as removal expenses or the expenses of obtaining advice on his claim. In principle compensation should include the VAT paid by the claimant. However, in some cases the claimant may be able to set off the VAT he has paid on the costs and expenses (input tax) against VAT which he is liable to pay to HMRC on the goods and services which he provides as part of his business (output tax). In that case no VAT should be payable as part of the rule (6) compensation since otherwise the claimant would benefit twice, once by receiving the VAT from the acquiring authority and once by his ability to set off the VAT paid on the costs and expenses against his own liability for VAT to HMRC. Consequently it may be necessary in each case to examine the VAT status and position of a claimant for compensation under rule (6). A claimant who has paid VAT on costs and expenses for which he claims compensation will not be able to set it off against output tax payable to HMRC if he does not carry on a business or is not registered for VAT or if his position is such that he is unlikely to have sufficient output tax against which he can set off the VAT paid on the costs and expenses which constitute the rule (6) claim.

6.86   If compensation is assessed on the equivalent reinstatement basis any VAT payable by the claimant on the costs of the reinstatement, that is the acquisition of land or the construction of buildings, should be recoverable as a part of the costs of the reinstatement and so should be payable by the acquiring authority.[121] As with rule (6) compensation no VAT should be payable by the acquiring authority when it appears that the claimant would be able to set off his input tax on the costs and expenses of the reinstatement against output tax which he is liable to pay to HMRC.[122] If it is uncertain whether the claimant will be liable to pay VAT on the costs of the equivalent reinstatement then it is for the claimant to establish on the balance of probabilities that VAT will be so payable by him. If this can be shown on the balance of probabilities then the court should evaluate the risk that the VAT will be payable and award an amount in accordance with that risk. For instance, if there is a 75 per cent risk that VAT will be payable the Tribunal should award 75 per cent of VAT as a part of

---

[119] *Hughes v Doncaster Council* [1991] 1 AC 382, [1991] 2 WLR 16. See section (a) of ch 8.
[120] For advance payments see section (c) of ch 15.
[121] For equivalent reinstatement see section (a) of this chapter.
[122] See para 6.85.

the equivalent reinstatement compensation.[123] This approach follows the general approach adopted by courts when awarding damages or compensation the amount of which depends on hypothetical or future events which cannot be known as a matter of certainty.[124]

4. Compensation for Tax Disadvantage

The fact that a claimant may have to pay tax on the compensation received by him, or on a part of it, cannot in itself be a reason for the amount of that tax being received as additional compensation since the claimant would have had to pay the tax if there had been a sale by him of his land in the ordinary market. Nonetheless a claimant may argue that he has suffered some tax disadvantage by reason of the compulsory acquisition which he would not have borne apart from that acquisition and that he should receive additional compensation for this disadvantage. Any such additional compensation would be payable, if at all, under rule (6) of section 5 of the Land Compensation Act 1961. The decisions of the Lands Tribunal on this question are not wholly consistent and the question may need consideration in the higher courts.

6.87

The leading modern decision, in which the principle was examined in some detail, is *Bishopsgate Parking (No 2) Ltd v Welsh Ministers.*[125] In that case land was acquired and the claimant became liable for capital gains tax in respect of the compensation of £43.5 million. The capital gains tax may have been in the order of £15 million. The claimant contended that it should be awarded compensation for the whole or a part of the tax: (a) because apart from the compulsory acquisition he would have retained the land for a substantial period of time so that any liability to tax would have been postponed, and (b) because if the land had been sold on the market at the valuation date the claimant could have used various means, such as the sale of shares in a company which owned the land rather than a sale of the land, to eliminate or greatly reduce any liability to pay capital gains tax. The Tribunal held as a preliminary issue that in principle a claim for compensation of the nature described could be made under rule (6) of section 5 of the Land Compensation Act 1961 although in practice it was only the claim based on postponement of the capital gains tax liability, rather than its elimination, which could succeed in the circumstances of the case before it and the amount of the claim for the accelerated liability to pay tax would depend on the evidence of what would have been done in the absence of a compulsory acquisition.[126]

6.88

In reaching its decision the Tribunal declined to follow a previous decision of the Tribunal in *Harris v Welsh Development Agency*[127] in which compensation for the acceleration of a liability to pay capital gains tax was refused in principle. The decision in *Harris* was on the footing that the claim relating to capital gains tax could not come within the second

6.89

---

[123] *Scout Association Trust Corp v Secretary of State* [2005] EWCA Civ 980, [2005] RVR 303; *Slot v Guildford Borough Council* [1993] 1 EGLR 213.

[124] *Allied Maples Group Ltd v Simmons & Simmons* [1995] 1 WLR 1602, [1995] 4 All ER 907; *Porter v Secretary of State for Transport* [1996] 3 All ER 693.

[125] *Bishopsgate Parking (No 2) Ltd v Welsh Ministers* [2012] UKUT 22 (LC), [2012] RVR 237.

[126] In *Alfred Golightly & Sons Ltd v Durham County Council* [1981] RVR 229, the Tribunal allowed a claim for an increased liability to development land tax under the Development Land Tax Act 1976 brought about by a compulsory acquisition of a colliery with spoil heaps. This decision is consistent with the decision of the Tribunal in the *Welsh Ministers* case.

[127] *Harris v Welsh Development Agency* [1999] 3 EGLR 207.

component of rule (6) since it would be compensation for a matter directly based on the value of land. It seems to be established today that 'the value of land' in rule (6) means the open market value of the land acquired as stated in rule (2) so that the reason for the decision in the *Harris* case may not be sound.[128]

6.90   The decision in the *Welsh Ministers* case should perhaps be viewed with caution. It is true that an owner of land compulsorily acquired might have retained the land for a considerable time in the absence of the acquisition and so postponed the date of liability to pay capital gains tax. In doing so the owner would also postpone the receipt of the capital value of the land. It is not clear why the owner should receive the value of the land as compensation at the time of the acquisition but be compensated for having to pay CGT on that value at the same time. It seems that the owner is given the benefit under rule (2) of obtaining the value of the land at the time of the acquisition and is then given additional compensation under rule (6) on the hypothesis that he does not receive the value of that land until much later. There is much to be said for compensation being assessed on a single and consistent hypothesis which is that the land is sold at the valuation date and that the price is obtained at the valuation date and any liability to capital gains tax or other similar liabilities also accrue at the valuation date.

6.91   Other methods of avoiding or limiting capital gains tax mooted in the *Welsh Ministers* case seem even more doubtful. For example, the company owning land is compensated for the fact that it has, albeit under compulsion, disposed of its land at a certain date. It appears odd that it can then obtain compensation under rule (6), which is technically a part of the value of the land,[129] on the hypothesis that it has not disposed of the land at all but that shares in a company owning the land have been sold (presumably by someone such as a parent company of the landowning company). If the decision of the Tribunal is pushed to its logical conclusion acquiring authorities in assessing compensation would have to form judgments on how long the owner would have retained the land if it had not been acquired and on the details of what 'tax efficient' methods might have been used at the time of the acquisition to limit liability to tax such as a disposal to a real estate investment trust. It is not explained how such a trust, or other specialised purchaser, is to be equated with the concept of a hypothetical willing purchaser acquiring the land. In practice many compulsory acquisitions are of properties owned and occupied by the claimant as his only or main residence so that no capital gains tax is payable or are of small properties where tax efficient schemes such as debated in the *Welsh Ministers* case would not be realistic. It is not attractive that large commercial landowners who have available accountancy and financial advice may be able to claim additional compensation under rule (6) for the loss of an opportunity to initiate some scheme and so avoid tax while smaller landowners such as the owner of a modest second home or holiday property would not realistically be able to obtain that further compensation. If the principle of the *Welsh Ministers* case is fully applied many landowners may be able to assert a claim under rule (6) founded on an acceleration of the liability to pay

[128] See ch 8, paras 8.21 and 8.22. In the subsequent *Welsh Ministers* case the Tribunal thought that the decision in *Harris* was flawed for this reason. Some might argue that a liability to capital gains tax is something directly based on the capital value of the land acquired since it is a tax which is a percentage of the difference between the value of that land as realised on a disposal and the value of the land at an earlier date. It might be argued that capital gains tax, although based on the value of the land acquired, is not 'directly' based on that value on the valuation date since it is generally a tax exigible on the difference between that value and the price paid for the land or its value at an earlier date.
[129] *Hughes v Doncaster Council* [1991] 1 AC 382, [1991] 2 WLR 16. See section (a) of ch 8.

capital gains tax since many owners will be able to argue that apart from the compulsory acquisition of their property they would have continued to own it for some time and could have postponed their liability to pay capital gains tax for some time.

Once the principle of peering into the future and ascertaining how tax might be avoided or reduced or postponed is accepted the door is opened to substantial difficulties and complications. It has been explained that one way of assisting an assessment of the value of land at the valuation date is to carry out a discounted cash flow analysis of profits which might have been obtained from a business carried out on the land in future years if there had been no compulsory purchase of the land.[130] It would presumably be open to the claimant to argue that in the future he could initiate measures which would have reduced this liability to tax so that the anticipated profits after tax in future years should be increased. It should also be borne in mind that if the land acquired continued to be owned by the landowner so that the liability to pay capital gains tax is postponed the land may increase in value with a resultant liability to pay an increased amount of tax. On the other hand if the interest acquired was a lease at a profit rent with a capital value then if the owner had continued to own the lease with its term date approaching the leasehold interest would be likely to reduce in value so reducing any capital gains tax ultimately payable. It is not at all clear how matters of this sort are to be evaluated in assessing rule (6) claims. The *Welsh Ministers* decision is a further instance of claims being allowed under rule (6) in circumstances to which that rule was probably never intended to apply. The simple answer to claims of the nature here being discussed being asserted under rule (6) may be that future speculative changes in tax liabilities are too remote to be a part of a rule (6) claim.[131]

6.92

---

[130] See section (d) of ch 14.
[131] See section (e) of ch 8 for a discussion on remoteness and claims under r (6).

7

Town and Country Planning

(A) INTRODUCTION

7.1   Town and Country Planning controls originated in parts of England and Wales before the last war but general and uniform planning control was introduced by the Town and Country Planning Act 1947. In its fundamentals the system remains as contained in that Act. Today the greater part of the current legislation is contained in the Town and Country Planning Act 1990. Planning control rests on two essential foundations. The first is the definition of development which is that development means any building, mining, engineering or other operation in or over land or any material change in the use of land.[1] The other foundation is the rule that it is unlawful to carry out development without first obtaining a planning permission which authorises that development.[2] A planning permission must be applied for and an application is either refused or granted by the local planning authority, a grant being nearly always subject to conditions. An appeal against refusal, or against the terms of the conditions, lies to the Secretary of State and is usually decided by an inspector appointed by the Secretary of State after an inquiry, a hearing or the consideration of written representations. The system has many other complications. There is, for example, a specific process of control over buildings listed as of special architectural or historic interest, called listed buildings, and a process of enforcement involving enforcement notices and appeals against them. The whole system is underpinned by national planning guidance issued by the Government and by local development plans.[3] Obviously a full description of the system would take a book of its own. The importance of the system for present purposes is its effect on the value of land and the assessment of compensation.

7.2   When land is valued for the purposes of assessing compensation the principle is that the land is to be valued with all its potentialities including its potential for undergoing development. There was a period of time over a decade between 1948 and 1959 when the basis of compensation was the existing use value of the land but for the last half century the old principle has been restored. The concepts of existing use value, development value and

---

[1] Town and Country Planning Act 1990, s 55(1).
[2] Ibid, s 57(1).
[3] It was the former practice of the Government to issue a series of Circulars covering various areas of planning and development. This process has now been superseded to a large extent by the National Policy Planning Framework published by the Department for Communities and Local Government in March 2012. The nature of development plans has also changed radically from the type of plan first required to be prepared under the Town and Country Planning Act 1947. The movement has been from plans which indicated that specific development was acceptable in prescribed areas but not elsewhere to plans which contain more general and less geographically prescribed policies for development. The former more rigid or 'zoning' system is in force in other jurisdictions such as the Cayman Islands, Hong Kong and the United States. See also para 7.11.

hope value, and the usage of these expressions, have been explained earlier.[4] The importance to the value of land of the existence of a planning permission for development is apparent. To take an illustration, the value of an area of land on the edge of an attractive Cotswold village might be small if its only lawful use was agricultural. The value would be likely to be enormously enhanced if a planning permission was available for residential development on the land. On the other hand policies which seek to prevent the spread of development into open and attractive countryside might suggest that there was little prospect of such a permission being granted.

It must still be borne in mind that while the existence of a planning permission, or even the   7.3
hope of a planning permission, may add enormously to the value of a piece of land it is strictly not the permission which creates the value but the ability to implement that permission by actually carrying out the permitted development. A piece of land might have the burden of a restrictive covenant which prevented any buildings or structures being erected on it. In such a case the grant of planning permission for residential development would not on the face of it increase the value of the land since the implementation of the permission could be prevented by the person with the benefit of, and the ability to enforce, the covenant. Other factors might rob land of all or a part of the value of a planning permission. There might be an easement across the land which would restrict the way in which development could be carried out. The only acceptable access to a public highway might involve the acquisition of land from some other owner who would insist on a share of the development value released by the provision of the access land.

The land value created by a planning permission may be heavily affected by two other   7.4
matters. One matter is the conditions to which the permission is subject. For example, a permission to construct and use large retail shopping units in locations outside a town centre might well be subject to a condition that only specified types of goods could be sold at the premises, the purpose being to protect shopping facilities in the town centre. A second matter is the impact of planning obligations or agreements made between landowners or developers and local planning authorities that may impose financial burdens which have to be observed if the development permitted is to be carried out. Such payments may include payments towards road improvements or other facilities in the area. Conditions must reasonably relate to the development permitted[5] and planning agreements must be executed for planning purposes.

For general valuation purposes the issue is often one of what planning permission does the   7.5
land being valued have, or what planning permission is it to be assumed to have, or what is the hope or expectation of obtaining a valuable planning permission. This issue must be determined before there can be a coherent valuation of the land. In this chapter the issue is explained under four heads:

    (i)   actual planning permissions;
    (ii)   assumed planning permissions;
    (iii) the particular procedure of an assumed planning permission which arises from a certificate of appropriate alternative development; and
    (iv)   the hope of obtaining a planning permission.

---

[4] See ch 3, para 3.19.
[5] *Newbury District Council v Secretary of State for the Environment* [1981] AC 578, [1980] 2 WLR 379.

The law is mainly contained in sections 14–22 of the Land Compensation Act 1961. Some radical changes to the system have recently been made by the Localism Act 2011 and came into effect on 6 April 2012. The law as here described takes into account the amendments made by the Localism Act 2011 but there are important transitional provisions which will preserve the application of the previous provisions for some time.[6] The overall effect of the provisions is now somewhat complicated and this chapter concludes with a summary of law as now in force.

(B) ACTUAL PLANNING PERMISSIONS

7.6   The first head is the most straightforward. Account is to be taken in valuing the land acquired of any planning permission in force at the valuation date.[7] This rule applies to an actual planning permission for development on the land acquired and being valued and to an actual planning permission for development on other land and, of course, to a planning permission which spans the land being valued and other land. The planning permission in question may be unconditional or subject to conditions. A planning permission without express conditions is a rarity today and even in the absence of an express condition to that effect a condition or conditions are implied into a planning permission requiring that the development shall be commenced within a certain period.[8]

7.7   Planning permissions come into existence in three types of case. (a) The general case is that an application is made to the local planning authority which then grants the permission sought. If permission is refused but an appeal to the Secretary of State is successful the permission will be granted by the Secretary of State or by the inspector appointed to determine the appeal. (b) Certain planning permissions are granted automatically by a development order; that is no application for permission is necessary. The Town and Country Planning Act 1990 permits the Secretary of State to make a development order for this purpose and the current order is the Town and Country Planning (General Permitted Development) Order 1995.[9] Twenty-two classes of development are permitted, some of them involving the carrying out of operations on land (often called operational development) and some of them authorising a change in the use of land. Most of the permissions are subject to conditions. A practice has grown up of describing permissions granted on an application, the first of the above types, as 'express permissions', to distinguish them from permissions granted under a development order. (c) Under some statutory provisions a planning permission is deemed to have been granted. An example is that planning permission is deemed to have been granted for certain works required by an enforcement notice.[10] For the purposes of the assessment of compensation land is to be valued with the benefit of any planning permis-

---

[6] The amendments made by the Localism Act 2011 do not apply to compulsory purchase orders made or confirmed by a Minister or confirmed by the authority which made it before 6 April 2012. The former provisions in ss 14–18 of the Land Compensation Act 1961 will therefore continue to apply in many cases for some time when compensation is being assessed. See the Localism Act 2011 (Commencement No 4 and Transitional, Transitory and Saving Provisions) Order 2012 (SI 2012/628), art 18.
[7] Land Compensation Act 1961, s 14(2)(a).
[8] Town and Country Planning Act 1990, s 91(1), (3).
[9] Town and Country Planning (General Permitted Development) Order 1995 (SI 1995/418).
[10] Town and Country Planning Act 1990, s 173(11), (12).

sion in force at the valuation date by whatever process that permission came into being at or before that date.

The expression used in the legislation on compensation is that for it to be taken into account the planning permission must be 'in force' at the valuation date. There are a number of circumstances in which a planning permission may have been granted before the valuation date but is not in force at that date. The most usual case will be where a permission has expired. When granting a planning permission planning authorities are required to specify by condition that the permission will lapse unless the development permitted by it is commenced within a stated time. A planning permission may be a full or an outline planning permission. An outline planning permission means a permission granted with certain matters, called reserved matters, left for subsequent approval by the authority on an application for that purpose.[11] Reserved matters are access, appearance, landscaping, layout, and scale.[12] A permission which is not granted in outline in the above sense is a full permission. The period to be specified for the commencement of the development under a full planning permission is five years although the planning authority may specify a longer or a shorter period. An outline planning permission is to be granted subject to two conditions, the first being that any application for approval of reserved matters must be made within three years and the other being that the development must be commenced within two years of the final approval of reserved matters.[13] Again the planning authority may specify longer or shorter periods. If a permission of either type is granted without the required condition that condition is implied automatically by virtue of the statute with the periods being those just stated. A planning permission where the development has not been started within the required period, or where an application for approval of all reserved matters has not been made within the required period, is not in force for present purposes. Another reason why a planning permission may not be in force at the valuation date is that it has been revoked by the local planning authority or by the Secretary of State.[14] A planning permission once granted cannot be abandoned.[15] A permission may cease to be operable, and so may cease to be in force for present purposes: (a) if a later and inconsistent permission has been granted and has been implemented,[16] or (b) if events disclose that there has opened a new chapter of the planning history of the land in question.[17]

7.8

If development on land has been carried out without planning permission or in breach of a condition attached to a planning permission it is unlawful and any increase in value due to it will normally have to be disregarded by reason of rule (4) of section 5 of the Land Compensation Act 1961.[18]

7.9

The obvious instance of a planning permission being in force at the valuation date is a permission for the development proposed to be carried out by the acquiring authority and which is the justification for the compulsory purchase. Although the existence of a planning permission for the development proposed by the acquiring authority is not a legal

7.10

---

[11] Ibid, s.92.
[12] Town and Country Planning (General Development Procedure) Order 1995 (SI 1995/418), art 1(2).
[13] Town and Country Planning Act 1990, s 92(2).
[14] Ibid, s 97.
[15] *Pioneer Aggregates (UK) Ltd v Secretary of State* [1995] AC 132, [1984] 3 WLR 32.
[16] *Pilkington v Secretary of State* [1973] 1 WLR 1527, (1973) 26 P & CR 508.
[17] *Prosser v Minister of Housing and Local Government* (1968) 67 LGR 109.
[18] See section (c) of ch 6.

requirement for the making or confirmation of a compulsory purchase order it is unusual that in practice an authority will feel justified in making an order unless planning permission for its project exists. In fact whether such a planning permission exists may often make no difference since planning permission is assumed to exist for development of the land acquired in accordance with the proposals of the acquiring authority. This is one of the assumed planning permissions which is considered under the next section of this chapter.

(C) ASSUMED PLANNING PERMISSIONS

1. Introduction

7.11   Until the amendments made by the Localism Act 2011 a series of assumptions as to the existence of a planning permission could be derived under section 16 of the Land Compensation Act 1961 founded on provisions in development plans. Development plans prepared by local planning authorities have been a feature of the planning system since the Town and Country Planning Act 1947. The form and nature of the plans has substantially changed since then. The plans produced under the provisions of the 1947 Act contained 'allocations' of specific land for certain types of development, such as industrial or retail or residential development, and contained the 'definition' of land for certain purposes. Plans produced under later legislation starting in 1968 moved away from this rigid 'zoning' approach in favour of the setting out of general policies on the types of development which might be permitted in various areas and on the circumstances in which different types of development might be permitted in these areas. The assumptions as to planning permission founded on development plans were introduced in 1959 and continued in the Land Compensation Act 1961 but were never substantially amended to accord with the new format and content of development plans. There was an uneasy attempt in decisions of the Lands Tribunal to accommodate the assumptions based on land being allocated or defined for a particular purpose to plans which did not contain allocations or definitions of land in the sense in which these designations were contained in earlier plans. Another defect of the system was that when land was being acquired for a public project, such as a railway, the indication or the proposed use or development of the land on the development plan was likely to be that of a railway so that an assumed planning permission derived from the plan added nothing to the actual planning permission which was likely to exist for the project.

7.12   In these circumstances the Localism Act 2011 has abolished assumptions derived from development plans. Section 16 of the Land Compensation Act 1961 is repealed.[19] This is a welcome modernisation and simplification of the system.

7.13   Until recently it had to be assumed that planning permission would be granted for development of the classes specified in paragraphs 1 and 2 of schedule 3 to the Town and Country Planning Act 1990. The concept of 'third schedule' development goes back to the Town and Country Planning Act 1947 where it was a form of minor development the value of which was not nationalised by that Act.[20] This assumption, contained in section 15(3) and (4) of

---

[19]   This is subject to the transitional provisions mentioned in n 6.
[20]   See para 1.12 of ch 1.

the Land Compensation Act 1961, led to unsatisfactory results,[21] and has now been abolished by the Localism Act 2011 in a further welcome change.

There are today three types of assumed planning permission: 7.14

   (a) Planning permission is to be assumed for development in accordance with the proposals of the acquiring authority.

   (b) Planning permission is to be assumed when at the valuation date and in certain circumstances a planning permission for a particular development could reasonably have been expected to be granted.

   (c) Planning permission is to be assumed for development specified in a certificate of appropriate alternative development.

The third type of assumption is considered separately under the next section of this chapter. The provisions on the second type of assumption have been recently amended by the Localism Act 2011 and can involve an important, but unfortunately complex, investigation of events. The Localism Act 2011 has introduced a further welcome clarification of the nature of a planning assumption. The assumption is either: (a) that the planning permission is in force at the valuation date, or (b) that it is certain at the valuation date that the permission will be granted at the later time at which at the valuation date it could reasonably have been expected to be granted.[22] In the legislation in its previous form the assumptions were that planning permission 'would be granted'. The first two assumptions will now be described.

2. Development Proposed by the Acquiring Authority

In most cases the acquisition of an interest in land is for purposes which involve the carry- 7.15
ing out of proposals of the acquiring authority for development of the land acquired or a part of it. As mentioned earlier very often planning permission for that development is in force at the valuation date so that its existence is taken into account under the general provision that account is taken of actual planning permissions. However, if planning permission for that development is not in force at the valuation date, it is to be assumed that planning permission is in force at that date for the development of the land acquired or part of it in accordance with the proposals of the acquiring authority. It may occur that there is at the valuation date an actual planning permission in force but granted so as not to enure for the benefit of the land and for the benefit of all persons for the time being interested in the land. The general principle is that a planning permission granted does enure for the benefit of the land and for the benefit of all persons for the time being interested in the land but a condition may restrict the implementation of the permission to some particular person or group of persons.[23] Such conditions are infrequent and planning policy is that they should only be imposed in exceptional circumstances. The significance of this matter for present purposes is that if such a personal planning permission does exist for the proposals of the acquiring

---

[21] See *Greenweb Ltd v Wandsworth LBC* [2008] EWCA Civ 910, [2009] 1 WLR 612.

[22] Land Compensation Act 1961, s 14(3)(b).

[23] For the general principle, see s 75(1) of the Town and Country Planning Act 1990. In some cases regulations made under statute provide that a permission enures solely for the benefit of an acquiring authority: see *Roberts v South Gloucestershire District Council* [2002] EWCA Civ 1568, [2003] 1 P & CR 26.

authority it is not taken to be a permission which is in force at the valuation date so that the assumed permission for development in accordance with the proposals of the acquiring authority operates and, of course, operates as a permission without a condition limiting its benefit to a certain person or group of persons.[24]

7.16   There are circumstances in which this assumed planning permission can be of substantial importance in valuing the land acquired. An acquiring authority might acquire land for a purpose, where the development is needed in the public interest such as new housing development, in circumstances in which apart from that particular public purpose no planning permission would exist or would be obtained for such development. In these circumstances permission for the housing development is to be assumed in accordance with the above provision. Clearly it is something which could add substantially to the value of the land acquired. An explanation has been given earlier of a general principle of the law of compensation, known as the value to the owner principle (or sometimes as the Pointe Gourde principle), which in general terms is that the value of land acquired is not to be increased or decreased by reason of the scheme or project of the acquiring authority. This principle is of substantial importance in the law of compensation. The assumption here explained can operate in contradiction to, or as an exception to, this principle since in the type of case just mentioned it is plain that it is the scheme or project of the acquiring authority for development of the land acquired which adds value to that land which it might not have otherwise have had and that that value is to be taken into account. The reason for the assumption is the perception that it is just that where a public authority acquires land for some purpose which is valuable, such as a residential purpose, the authority obtains the value of the development for that purpose so that it should pay to the dispossessed owner the full value of the land for that purpose.[25]

3. Permission Reasonably Expected

7.17   Prior to recent changes in the law the expectation of obtaining a planning permission at the valuation date, and its effect on the value of the land acquired, had been fairly simple to state and to apply. There is a general principle of law that when a court has to assess damages or compensation and a relevant question is whether some event would have happened in the past in hypothetical circumstances, or was likely to happen in the future, the court does not decide on the balance of probabilities whether the event would have happened in

---

[24] Land Compensation Act 1961, s 15. The development permitted is that which is for the proposals of the acquiring authority. It is not possible to pick out a part or parts of those proposals and to assume a permission for that part only. In *Roberts v South Gloucestershire District Council* [2002] EWCA Civ 1568, [2003] 1 P & CR 26, the acquiring authority proposed to construct a road across the land acquired and proposed to extract topsoil and sandstone from the land as a part of the road construction scheme. It was held that the assumed planning permission for the proposals of the authority did not permit the extraction of the materials to be used for some other purpose. See also *Colneway Ltd v Environment Agency* [2004] RVR 37, in which there was an assumed planning permission for a flood alleviation scheme and it was held that the permission did not permit the working of minerals from the land.

[25] See ch 5 for the value to the owner principle, the Pointe Gourde principle, and the general subject of the disregard for valuation purposes of the scheme of the acquiring authority. In *Myers v Milton Keynes Development Corporation* [1974] 1 WLR 694, (1974) 27 P & CR 578, the Lands Tribunal had refused to attribute any value to a planning permission, assumed under s 15 for residential development of the land acquired, on the reasoning that to do so would be in conflict with the Pointe Gourde principle. The Court of Appeal rejected this conclusion.

the past or will happen in the future. Instead the correct approach is for the court to assess the probability that the event would have happened, or that it will happen, and then assess the damages or compensation in accordance with that assessment of probabilities. A good example from the assessment of damages at common law for breach of contract arises when a solicitor has, through his negligent conduct, deprived a client of the advantage of bringing, and succeeding in, legal proceedings, for instance because the solicitor has failed to observe a relevant time limit or limitation period. The court does not decide whether the client, had he been able to commence the proceedings, would or would not have succeeded in them. What the court does is determine the chances of the proceedings having succeeded if they could have been brought. Thus if the proceedings if wholly successful would have resulted in an award of damages of £100,000 and the court assesses the chance of the proceedings having been successful at 80 per cent the damages awarded for the client being deprived of the opportunity to bring the proceedings would be likely to be £80,000. In the same way when a claimant claims damages for personal injury his medical prognosis may be uncertain at the time of the trial. The court will then assess, on the basis of expert medical evidence, the prospect of a further deterioration or complication in his condition and assess the damages in accordance with its view of the prospect of that happening.[26]

These common sense principles have been applied to the question of the expectation at the valuation date of obtaining a planning permission which would increase the value of the land acquired. The prospect of obtaining the permission, ignoring the compulsory purchase and the scheme of the acquiring authority, was estimated and the land was valued at the price which a hypothetical willing purchaser would pay for it with that level of expectation of obtaining the valuable planning permission. For instance, if the land acquired had had a planning permission for a residential development, it might have been worth £600,000 but with only a good expectation of obtaining that permission it would have been worth only £400,000.[27]   7.18

As mentioned this system was simple to explain and not difficult to apply.[28] The law has been complicated by the Localism Act 2011 and the provisions which it has put into effect. The essence of the new and current system is that where there was at the valuation date a reasonable expectation of a particular planning permission being granted, ignoring the compulsory purchase and the scheme of the acquiring authority, there is an assumption that that planning permission is in force. In other words the reasonable expectation is elevated into a certainty. The justification for such an assumption is obscure but it represents the current law. The essence of the new assumption can be stated shortly but the details involve considerable complexity.   7.19

The criterion for the assumption of a planning permission is that on certain assumptions the permission would on the valuation date 'reasonably have been expected to have been granted' on an application decided on that date. What constitutes a reasonable expectation is not stated in the legislation but it seems likely that the test is whether or not on the   7.20

---

[26] See, eg *Kitchen v Royal Air Force Association* [1958] 1 WLR 563; *Allied Maples Group v Simmons & Simmons* [1995] 1 WLR 1602. In the context of valuations for the purpose of assessing compensation in relation to land retained see *Porter v Secretary of State for Transport* [1996] 3 All ER 693, and see the opinion of Lord Walker in *Transport for London v Spirerose Ltd* [2009] UKHL 44, [2009] 1 WLR 1797, at paras 42–44.

[27] See the *Spirerose* decision in the Lands Tribunal at [2008] RVR 12.

[28] The former system will continue to apply for some time for compulsory purchase orders made or confirmed before 6 April 2012: see n 6.

balance of probabilities the planning permission would have been granted in the circumstances postulated. The assumption does not arise if there was an actual planning permission in force for the development at the valuation date. In that event account will be taken of the actual planning permission. The assumed planning permission may be for development of the land being acquired or for development of that land and other land.[29]

7.21   A critical provision is the exact circumstances or assumptions under which the question of the reasonable expectation of the grant of a particular planning permission has to be decided. There are three such assumptions. These are therefore assumptions which have to be made for the purpose of deciding whether a planning permission is to be assumed. Apart from the assumptions, which will now be described, the question is to be decided in the circumstances known to the market at the valuation date, that is all other events and circumstances relevant to the question are to be taken to be as they actually were at the valuation date.[30] To this extent the presumption of reality is retained.

7.22   The first assumption is that the scheme of development underlying the acquisition has been cancelled on what is called the launch date.[31] The valuers are not to imagine that the scheme of the acquiring authority has never existed but rather that it has existed in the past but has been cancelled on the launch date. This may be termed the cancellation assumption.[32] It is therefore necessary to know: (a) what is the underlying scheme, and (b) what is the launch date.

7.23   The current provisions do not define the underlying scheme as such but they do provide certain guidance on how the nature and extent of that scheme are to be ascertained. If there is any dispute as to the scheme it has to be identified by the Lands Tribunal as a matter of fact. This harkens back to the old law on the value to the owner principle (or the Pointe Gourde principle) where it was said that the extent of the scheme was a matter of fact.[33] Any such dispute is likely to arise in the context of a claim for compensation so that in the event of a dispute the Tribunal will have to decide the question of what is the underlying scheme as part of its general function of deciding the compensation due. It may be that in an appropriate case the Tribunal will wish to determine this matter as a preliminary issue in the proceedings.

7.24   The Tribunal is not given its normal untrammelled power to decide questions of fact before it on the evidence but is constrained by further limiting complicated and ancillary rules. The underlying scheme must be determined to be the scheme provided for by the Act, or other instrument, which authorises the compulsory acquisition unless either party shows that the underlying scheme is larger than, although incorporating, the scheme provided for by the Act or other instrument.[34] The reference to the Act authorising the compulsory acquisition presumably applies where a particular scheme is authorised by an Act of Parliament and in most instances no compulsory purchase order is necessary. An example given earlier of this process is the Crossrail Act 2008. In this case the scheme will be the

---

[29] Land Compensation Act 1961, s 14(4)(b).
[30] Ibid, s 14(2)(b).
[31] Ibid, s 14(5)(a).
[32] The genesis of the cancellation assumption may be the opinion of Lord Hope in *Fletcher Estates (Harlescott) Ltd v Secretary of State* [2002] 2 AC 307, [2002] 2 WLR 438.
[33] See ch 5, para 5.13, n 17 and see, eg *Wilson v Liverpool City Council* [1971] 1 WLR 302, [1971] 1 All ER 628, discussed in ch 5, para 5.66.
[34] Land Compensation Act 1961, s 14(8)(a).

whole of the Crossrail project as authorised by the Act. The reference to the acquisition being authorised by another instrument is presumably to the more general case where an Act gives a general power of compulsory purchase for certain purposes, such as highways or housing, but a specific compulsory purchase order has to be made which authorises the acquisition of a particular area or areas of land. The legislation seems to mean no more than the obvious proposition that in identifying the ambit of the scheme it is necessary to consider the terms of the compulsory purchase order authorising the acquisition of the land being valued as opposed to the terms of the Act which permits the making of the compulsory purchase order. There is then another limitation. There is no restriction on the ability of the claimant to adduce evidence of what is the underlying scheme. However, if the acquiring authority wishes to adduce evidence of what is the scheme it may only do so if either: (a) the evidence is in support of a scheme being larger than that provided for by the Act or other instrument which authorises the compulsory acquisition and the alleged larger scheme is one which is identified in the instrument which authorises the compulsory acquisition and any documents published with it, or (b) there is agreement that evidence of the larger scheme may be adduced, or (c) there are special circumstances.[35]

It is necessary to know what exactly is the launch date since it is on that date that the scheme underlying the acquisition is taken to be cancelled. The launch date is one of three dates depending on the administrative process adopted for the compulsory acquisition:[36]   **7.25**

(i)   The usual case will be when the compulsory acquisition is authorised by a compulsory purchase order. In that case notice of the confirmation or making of the order has to be given by advertisement in local newspapers and other means. The order is confirmed by a Minister if it has been made by a local authority. If it has been prepared in draft by a Minister the process is that it is ultimately made by that Minister. In these cases the launch date is the date of first publication of the notice of the confirmation or making of the order.[37] The launch date is a date which is intermediate in the total process of the compulsory purchase. Some time may elapse after the notice of confirmation before the acquiring authority serves notice to treat or makes a general vesting declaration.

(ii) It may be that the acquisition is authorised by another order, for example an order made under the Transport and Works Act 1992.[38] In that case a notice has to be published or served in connection with the acquisition. The launch date is the date of the first publication or service of the requisite notice.

(iii) If the acquisition is authorised by a special enactment other than an order of one of the above types the launch date is the date of first publication of the notice in accordance with any Standing Order of either House of Parliament in relation to private Bills.

The second assumption is that no action has been taken by the acquiring authority wholly or mainly for the purposes of the underlying scheme. The actions which are to be disregarded include any development or works or any acquisition of land.[39] This is an important   **7.26**

[35] Ibid, s 14(8)(b).
[36] Ibid, s 14(6).
[37] See section (e) of ch 2.
[38] For such orders, see section (b) of ch 2.
[39] Land Compensation Act 1961, s 14(5)(b).

assumption. It means, for instance, that when the expectation of a planning permission is assessed the fact that the acquiring authority has acquired land in the area for the purposes of its scheme is to be disregarded. That which has to be disregarded involves works as well as development so that certain actions not within the ordinary definition of development such as clearance works have to be disregarded. Even so that which has to be disregarded is limited. It may occur that other persons, for example developers hoping to co-operate with the acquiring authority, have acquired land prior to the valuation date and these land acquisitions are not to be disregarded in assessing the expectation of a planning permission being granted on the land being acquired or that land together with other land. Equally development or works carried out by developers, or persons other than the acquiring authority, for the purposes of the underlying scheme is not to be disregarded for the purposes of deciding what is the expectation of a particular planning permission being granted. This second assumption is not anchored to the launch date. Actions of the acquiring authority at any time in the past are to be disregarded if made wholly or mainly for the purposes of the underlying scheme.

7.27   As well as being complicated the new legislation can be accused in one respect of being lacking in rigour. It is one thing, and it is no doubt generally sensible, that in considering the expectation at the valuation date of a planning permission being granted actions taken for the purposes of the scheme of the acquiring authority are left out of account. In practice actions for the purposes of that scheme are not infrequently taken by other persons such as developers who are acting under arrangements made with the acquiring authority. This is particularly so today where schemes of regeneration and major development are often the subject of co-operation between public and private bodies. A more rigorous drafting of the new legislation might have led to all actions carried out for the purposes of the underlying scheme being left out of account.

7.28   The third assumption is that there is no prospect of the same scheme, or any project to meet the same or substantially the same need, being carried out in the exercise of a statutory function or by the exercise of compulsory purchase powers.[40] This provision is needed to combat the view that if a particular scheme of the acquiring authority is to be assumed to be cancelled there would be an expectation that some further and similar scheme would come forward to meet the same need or much the same need. In the absence of this assumption it might be argued that there was little expectation of a planning permission for development being granted at the valuation date on the land being valued since that development might frustrate the anticipated further scheme or project. Clearly an assumption of the present nature is required if the expectation of a planning permission in the 'cancelled scheme' world is to have its intended effect. It is helpful that a general provision of this nature is set out expressly in the statutory provisions.

7.29   The third assumption is further elaborated in the case of acquisitions for highway purposes. If the underlying scheme was for, or in connection with, the construction of a highway the assumption is that no highway will be constructed to meet the same or substantially the same need as the highway scheme would have been constructed to meet. The construction of a highway here includes the alteration or improvement of a highway.[41] This provision

---

[40] Ibid, s 14(5)(c).
[41] Ibid, s 14(5)(d). In the former legislation a provision to a similar effect relating to highway acquisitions was introduced in 1991 by the Planning and Compensation Act 1991: see ch 5, para 5.55, n 75. The present provision,

appears to apply the generality of the third assumption to the particular circumstances of an acquisition of land for highway purposes.

The assumption of the grant of a planning permission so far explained is an assumption that in the circumstances stated a planning permission for a particular development is in force at the valuation date. The assumption is extended to a future situation and operates where in the same circumstances it could reasonably be expected at the valuation date that a planning permission for that development would be granted at a time later than the valuation date. In this situation the statutory assumption is that it is certain at the valuation date that planning permission for that development would be granted at the later time.[42] There may be many circumstances which result in the planning permission being one which could be expected to be granted at a future time such as, for example, the need for a new road to serve the development which was expected to be built and open for traffic at a future date. The effect of this further assumption is that the land being valued has the certainty that permission will be granted at the determined future time so that any additional value attributable to the prospect of implementing the permission is likely to have to be deferred. A piece of land with a planning permission for a valuable development assumed to be in force may have one value but the same piece of land with the certainty of a planning permission being granted in, say, two years time may have a lesser value. There is a limit to the certainty created. The local planning authority may certify that planning permission would be granted if and when some future uncertain event occurs, for instance when a new public sewer is laid. The only assumption of a planning permission can then be that it will be granted if an uncertain event happens at an uncertain time. These elements of uncertainty would have to be reflected in the valuation of the land acquired. 7.30

Certain general comments may be made about the statutory assumption introduced by the Localism Act 2011. Despite the complicated provisions relating to the ascertainment of the underlying scheme and the launch date the legislation sets itself squarely against any re-configuration of past events. The scheme is taken to have been cancelled at the launch date. There is no question of an investigation of hypothetical events which might have happened before that date. It might be that had the scheme of the acquiring authority never existed at all various forms of development might have occurred in its stead which, had they occurred, would have influenced the prospect of obtaining planning permission on the land acquired at the valuation date. There is to be no investigation of such hypothetical circumstances in the past. This is the effect of the cancellation assumption. Here legislative clarity removes what has previously been an area of doubt and difficulty. 7.31

The other comment is that of the difficultly in knowing what, rationally and in policy terms, can justify the transformation of a reasonable expectation, say a 50–60 per cent hope, of obtaining a planning permission into the assumption that a planning permission would certainly be granted. In the real world land often has a good expectation of obtaining a planning permission with the result that that expectation increases its value but its value is still less than it would be if a planning permission existed or was assumed to be granted as a matter of certainty. Such a normal and established practice by valuers in establishing the value of land is applied in valuation situations generally such as in rent reviews or in valuing 7.32

like its statutory predecessor, reverses the effect of the decision of the House of Lords in *Margate Corporation v Devotwill Investments* [1970] 3 All ER 864, (1971) 22 P & CR 388.

[42] Ibid, s 14(3), (4), (5)(iii).

land the subject of an option. It is perhaps not wholly a step forward to abandon this ratio-nal and normal practice in the special field of compensation valuations and planning per-missions. If a piece of land compulsorily acquired would have had a reasonable expectation of obtaining a planning permission ignoring the scheme of the acquiring authority it is difficult to understand why it is not valued for compensation purposes with just that expec-tation and not with the artificial additional value attributable to a certainty of the permis-sion being granted which the land does not have, and would not have had, even if there had never been an underlying scheme behind the compulsory acquisition. The illogicality, as well as the complicated nature of the new assumption, is obvious.[43]

(D) CERTIFICATES OF APPROPRIATE ALTERNATIVE DEVELOPMENT

7.33   What the landowner and the acquiring authority will often want to know is what would be the attitude of the local planning authority to an application for planning permission if the scheme did not exist. To know this would be useful in order to see whether, disregarding the scheme, there is development for which on the valuation date planning permission might reasonably have been expected to be granted so as to create the statutory assumption that planning permission for that development is in force at that date as discussed under the last section of this chapter. Yet under the general law local planning authorities cannot decide planning applications in hypothetical circumstances and if there is a dispute as to what permission might have been granted in the hypothetical circumstances of a cancellation of the scheme that dispute would have to be resolved by the Lands Tribunal as part of its assessment of a compensation claim.

7.34   In these circumstances there exists a special statutory procedure under which the local planning authority can be asked to decide whether planning permission would have been granted for a particular development if the scheme of development of the acquiring author-ity had been cancelled. The development the subject of such a decision of the local planning authority is a form of appropriate alternative development and the decision of the local planning authority is called a certificate of appropriate alternative development. In general parlance such certificates are sometimes described as section 17 certificates since the proce-dure for the application for and the giving of such certificates is within section 17 of the Land Compensation Act 1961. As is explained later the effect of a certificate is that planning permission for the development certified as appropriate alternative development is assumed

---

[43] See also paras 7.18, 7.19 and 7.60 where a similar point is considered. Lord Neuberger put the point more strongly in *Transport for London Ltd v Spirerose Ltd* [2009] UKHL, [2009] 1 WLR 1797, at para 62 where he said that there was a 'logical incoherence' in a 51% prospect of obtaining a planning permission being translated into a 100% prospect. The unfairness to acquiring authorities is obvious. If a compulsory purchase order was con-firmed on 5 April 2012 a 51% prospect of obtaining a permission will be valued as what it was, a 51% prospect. If the order was confirmed on 6 April 2012 then the prospect of obtaining the permission will have to be assumed to be 100% since the permission will be assumed to be in force. The change is important in monetary terms. For instance, on the facts of the *Spirerose* case the new and artificial assumption would increase the compensation by 50% (see para 7.18). It may be that when a comprehensive reform of the law of compensation is produced the complications and difficulties of some of these recent changes in the Localism Act 2011 will be one of the matters to be replaced by simpler and more straightforward rules which can be added to the more welcome aspects of the changes.

to be in force at the valuation date. A certificate which states that there is no appropriate alternative development is sometimes referred to as a nil certificate.

The purpose and effect of certificates is to establish what development value, if any, the land acquired would have had in the absence of the scheme underlying the acquisition. From 1948 until 1959 the basis of compensation was the existing use value of the land acquired so that the prospect of development and the need for planning permission for development did not play a central part in the assessment of compensation. The present machinery for obtaining a certificate of appropriate alternative development was first introduced in the Town and Country Planning Act 1959 which reinstated the value of the prospect of development as a possible component of compensation. The procedure was continued in the Land Compensation Act 1961 and has recently been altered in significant ways by the Localism Act 2011 although the main structure and effect of the machinery remains as it was. The procedure which will now be described is that applicable to acquisitions under compulsory purchase orders confirmed on or after 6 April 2012. The former procedure continues to apply to orders confirmed before that date.[44]   7.35

In describing the system of certificates of appropriate alternative development it is necessary to consider: (a) the making of an application for a certificate, (b) the making of decisions on applications, (c) appeals, and (d) the effect of a certificate.   7.36

1. Applications for Certificates

An application for a certificate of appropriate alternative development may be made to the local planning authority where an interest in land is proposed to be acquired by an authority possessing compulsory purchase powers and may be made by either of the parties directly concerned.[45] There is no prescribed form of application but, as explained later, an application must contain certain material. Each of these components of the rule has a statutory definition. An authority possessing compulsory purchase powers, where as here that expression is used in relation to a transaction such as the proposed acquisition of an interest in land, means any person or body of persons who could be or have been authorised to acquire the interest compulsorily. In other words the expression means the acquiring authority.[46]   7.37

An interest is proposed to be acquired by the acquiring authority in three circumstances.[47] The first of the circumstances is that for the purposes of the compulsory acquisition of the land in which the interest subsists a notice has been published or served as required by an Act of Parliament or, as regards private Bills, by any Standing Order of either House of Parliament. The usual situation in which this will occur is where a compulsory purchase order is made by an acquiring authority and notice of the making of the order is published in local newspapers, affixed to an object near the land to be acquired, and served on owners,   7.38

---

[44] See n 6. A further amendment to the law introduced by the Localism Act 2011 is the new s 17(10) of the Land Compensation Act 1961 which provides that in assessing compensation account can be taken of costs reasonably incurred in connection with the issue of a certificate.

[45] Land Compensation Act 1961, s 17(1).

[46] Ibid, s 39(1).

[47] Ibid, s 22(2).

lessees, tenants and occupiers of the land, as required by the Acquisition of Land Act 1981. The second of the circumstances is that a person has given notice to an authority requiring that his interest in land be acquired and the authority is deemed to have served a notice to treat in respect of that interest. Such a situation could arise, for example, under Part VI of the Town and Country Planning Act 1990 when a person is refused planning permission and claims that his land has become incapable of reasonably beneficial use. That person may then serve a purchase notice on the relevant public authority. If the authority accepts that the conditions for the service of the purchase notice are satisfied it is deemed to have served a notice to treat in respect of the interest in land. A further example is where a blight notice has been served and accepted also under Part VI of the Town and Country Planning Act 1990. The third of the circumstances is where an offer in writing has been made by the acquiring authority to negotiate for the purchase of the land.

7.39   The last expression, the parties directly concerned, means the acquiring authority and any person entitled to the interest in land proposed to be acquired.[48]

7.40   The above provisions prescribe the earliest date on which an application for a certificate can be made. No date is prescribed as the latest date on which such an application can be made although in practice an application would be purposeless once the amount of the compensation has been decided either by the Lands Tribunal or by a binding agreement between the parties. There is one further limitation which applies where a notice to treat (including a constructive notice to treat) under section 7 of the Compulsory Purchase (Vesting Declarations) Act 1981 has been served in respect of an interest or an agreement has been made for the sale of the interest to the acquiring authority. Such agreements not infrequently provide that the price to be paid for the land is that amount which would have been payable had there been a compulsory acquisition. The limitation arises when, following one of these events, a reference has been made to the Lands Tribunal to determine the amount of the compensation. If notice to treat has been served a reference may be made to the Tribunal to determine the compensation. Up until a reference is made an application for a certificate of appropriate alternative development may be made by either party and as a matter of right in the circumstances described above. Once a reference has been made to the Tribunal no application for a certificate may be made by either of the parties directly concerned except: (a) with the consent in writing of the other party directly concerned, or (b) with the permission of the Tribunal.[49] In the event of dispute the Tribunal therefore has a discretion as to whether to permit the making of an application for a certificate. If the reference is at an early stage, and it appears that matters may usefully be decided by the local planning authority on an application for a certificate made to that authority, the Tribunal is likely to permit the making of such an application. On the other hand, if proceedings under the reference are much advanced and the parties are in a position to litigate before the Tribunal the question of the expectation of the grant of a planning permission, it may well be that the Tribunal will feel that rather than go through the procedure of a separate application to the local planning authority for a certificate of appropriate alternative development the Tribunal itself would be better placed to decide planning issues and in such a case may refuse its permission. In one case the Tribunal refused permission to an acquiring authority to apply for a second certificate when an earlier certificate existed. The purpose

---

[48]   Ibid, s 22(1).
[49]   Ibid, s 17(2).

of the authority was to obtain a more limited form of certified development. A second certificate, even if obtained in the terms sought, would have served no useful purpose since nothing in it could have removed the assumption that planning permission was in force at the valuation date for the development certified in the first certificate.[50] In deciding whether to give its consent the Tribunal will be aware that under current provisions it can hear and determine an appeal from the decision of the local planning authority on an application for a certificate.

An application for a certificate must be for a certificate which is to contain a form of what   7.41
is called 'the applicable statement'. The applicable statement is a statement for the purposes of section 14 of the 1961 Act. As will be explained a certificate of appropriate alternative development may result under section 14 in there being an assumed planning permission for a particular development or may result in there being no appropriate alternative development in relation to the land acquired. There are two forms of applicable statement which may be contained in a certificate. (a) The first form is that in the opinion of the local planning authority there is development that is appropriate alternative development in relation to the acquisition. (b) The second form is that in the opinion of the authority there is no development that is appropriate alternative development in relation to the acquisition.

Accordingly the application for a certificate must itself contain one of the two forms of   7.42
applicable statement, that is either that in the applicant's opinion there is development that, for the purposes of section 14, is appropriate alternative development in relation to the acquisition concerned or that in the applicant's opinion there is no development that, for the purposes of section 14, is appropriate alternative development in relation to the acquisition concerned. If the first of these opinions is stated to be that of the applicant then the application must specify each description of the development that in the applicant's opinion is appropriate alternative development and the reasons of the applicant for holding that opinion. An applicant may specify two or more forms of development which in his opinion is appropriate alternative development. In all cases an application for a certificate must be accompanied by a statement specifying the date on which a copy of the application has been or will be served on the other party directly concerned.[51] Although applications for certificates can be made by either a landowner or an acquiring authority in practice most applications are made by landowners who wish to increase their compensation by securing the assumption of a planning permission. It can of course occur that the acquiring authority and the local planning authority is the same body so that the decision on an application for a certificate has to be made by a public authority which is itself affected financially by the effect of its decision. An acquiring authority might decide to apply for a certificate that there is no appropriate alternative development on the land being acquired in order to settle the question of development value at an early stage. More than one application for a certificate may be made since it is possible that both parties will apply for a certificate. Even if a certificate has been issued a further application for a second certificate can be made (with the consent of the Tribunal when its consent to an application is needed).[52]

Where the acquiring authority proposes to acquire an interest in land of a person who is   7.43
absent from the United Kingdom or cannot be found there was a procedure under section

[50] *Kingsley v Highways Agency* [2011] 1 EGLR 151. The effect of a certificate is described in paras 7.54 and 7.55.
[51] Land Compensation Act 1961, s 17(3).
[52] *Kingsley v Highways Agency* [2011] 1 EGLR 151. See n 68.

58 of the Lands Clauses Consolidation Act 1845, now replaced by a procedure under schedule 2 to the Compulsory Purchase Act 1965, under which the compensation may be determined by a surveyor appointed by the Lands Tribunal. The surveyor is entitled to apply to the local planning authority for a certificate of appropriate alternative development and the provisions for the application for, and the determination of, such applications and the grant of certificates, including an appeal against a determination, apply as in other cases.[53] On receipt of the certificate the surveyor must serve copies of the certificate on both the parties directly concerned.[54]

2. The Decision of the Local Planning Authority

7.44   Turning to the matter of the decision by a local planning authority on an application made to it for a certificate, no certificate may be issued before the end of 22 days beginning with the date specified as that on which a copy of the application has been served on the other party without the agreement of that other party.[55]

7.45   The function of the local planning authority on receiving an application for a certificate is to identify every description of development which in its opinion is appropriate alternative development. In doing so the authority may conclude that a particular description of development is appropriate alternative development, and so should be certified as such, even though that development is not specified in the application. At this point the local planning authority must apply for the purposes of its decision the definition of appropriate alternative development in section 14 of the 1961 Act as amended by the Localism Act 2011. This definition has been explained in detail earlier. In essence it is development for which planning permission could at the valuation date reasonably have been expected to be granted on an application decided on that date or at a time after that date on certain specified assumptions. The critical assumption is that the scheme of development underlying the acquisition had been cancelled on the launch date. The whole of the specified assumptions and the meaning of the launch date have also been explained earlier.[56] It is generally considered under planning law that if an application is made for planning permission it is not for an applicant for permission to show that permission should be granted but for a local planning authority to show that there is a sound reason for refusing planning permission if that is to be its decision. An application for a certificate should be considered by the authority which receives it with this principle in mind.

7.46   The valuation date will normally be the date of entry into possession of the land by the acquiring authority or the vesting date if there has been a general vesting declaration. Of course the acquiring authority may take possession on the vesting date. It is possible, in accordance with the rules mentioned above, that an application may be received by a local

---

[53] Land Compensation Act 1961, s 19(1). The appointment by the Lands Tribunal is made under s 1(6) of the Lands Tribunal Act 1949. The application must be accompanied by one of the statements required by s 17(3)(a) or (b) of the Land Compensation Act 1961: s 19(3): see paras 7.41 and 7.42. The application must also be accompanied by a statement specifying a date on which a copy of the application has been or will be served on each of the parties directly concerned: s 19(3).

[54] Land Compensation Act 1961, s 19(3).

[55] Ibid, s 17(4).

[56] See s 14(4), (5) of the Land Compensation Act 1961 and see para 7.20 et seq.

planning authority substantially in advance of the valuation date.[57] It seems that in such circumstances the authority must either postpone its decision until the valuation date, so that all circumstances known at the valuation date which it is bound to take into account can be considered by it, or issue a decision doing its best to apply what it believes will be relevant circumstances at the valuation date. A difficulty in postponement is that the authority is required to determine an application for a certificate within two months of the receipt of an application although this period can be extended by consent. This situation and its potential difficulties do not appear to have been specifically considered by the draftsman of the provisions in the Localism Act 2011. Any potential difficulty may be reduced by the fact that in practice applications for certificates are rarely made until the progress of compulsory acquisition is fairly advanced.

The certificate as issued by the local planning authority must contain one or other of the two applicable statements described earlier. If the applicable statement is that there is development that is appropriate alternative development in relation to the acquisition then the certificate must also identify every description of development that in the opinion of the local planning authority is alternative appropriate development. In these circumstances the certificate must also give a general indication of any conditions to which planning permission for the development could reasonably have been expected to be subject and of when the permission could reasonably have been expected to be granted if that would be at a date after the valuation date.[58] Clearly the local planning authority may specify any number of descriptions of development for this purpose. In practice it is likely that there is one form of appropriate alternative development which the landowner contends should be specified and the certificate, if it specifies any description of development as appropriate, is likely to relate to that form of development or some variety of it. Even so it is open to the local planning authority to certify any form of development as appropriate alternative development and that development could, in principle, be quite different to that referred to in the application for a certificate. 7.47

It is not specified in the legislation how general or particular the description of the appropriate alternative development in the certificate need be. The purpose of a certificate is to assist in the valuation of the land acquired and thus the assessment of compensation and the value of an expectation of a particular form of development on land may vary according to what details are known of the development certified as that which is or will be permitted. For instance, residential development on an area of land may take many forms and the value of the land may depend upon which form is appropriate. It would be a sensible practice if local planning authorities, in specifying a description of development, could make it clear, either in the description itself or in the conditions which the authority says would be likely to be imposed, what form of development within any general description would be permitted. An illustration of such a process, in the circumstances just mentioned, would be the description of the respective development itself or conditions which limited 7.48

---

[57] See para 7.38. A considerable time may elapse between the publication of notice of the making of a compulsory purchase order and the making of a general vesting declaration or entry onto the land following the service of a notice to treat which determines the valuation date.

[58] Land Compensation Act 1961, s 17(5)(b)(i), (ii). If the certificate is equivocal in its terms it may have to be construed as meaning not that planning permission could reasonably have been expected to be granted, as stated in s 14(4) of the Land Compensation Act 1961, but as a statement that planning permission might have been granted. In that case the purported certificate will not bring about the assumption that a planning permission was in force at the valuation date: *Kingsley v Highways Agency* [2011] 1 EGLR 151.

the number of dwellings which might be permitted on the land acquired, the form and scale of such dwellings and their configuration, and which stated any other matters such as access or road layout which were important. Actual applications for planning permission are nearly always accompanied by plans which describe in some detail the development for which permission is sought and it is frequent practice that local planning authorities, if they grant permission, grant it in terms that the development shall be carried out in accordance with the plans submitted.[59] That process cannot normally be followed where the application is for a certificate of appropriate alternative development since normally no plans of the development will be submitted with the application. In that event it is all the more important that the local planning authority should, by way of their description of the development and by way of their description of conditions which could reasonably have been expected to be imposed, indicate in reasonable detail the form of development which they regard as appropriate alternative development. In doing so they will fulfil the purpose of certificates which is to assist in assessing the value of the land acquired in the hypothetical world of the underlying scheme of the acquiring authority having been cancelled.

7.49   In addition to specifying every description of development considered to be appropriate alternative development, and specifying likely conditions and the likely timing of a grant of permission, the local planning authority must give a general indication of any pre-condition for granting the permission that could reasonably have been expected to be met.[60] An example which is given, which will be the primary example of such a pre-condition, is entry into an obligation. It is frequent practice that, certainly in relation to substantial developments, local planning authorities will not grant permission until the owner of the land has entered into a planning obligation. Such an obligation may relate to many matters, including the making of contributions to the local planning authority or others to be used towards such matters as highway improvements or the provision of other facilities such as educational facilities, which are needed before the development can properly proceed. The content of such planning obligations may obviously affect the value of land which obtains a planning permission but subject to such obligations. It is reasonable that this situation should be reproduced in the hypothetical world of development which is specified as appropriate alternative development following the cancellation of the underlying scheme of the acquiring authority. This purpose can be achieved by the local planning authority when issuing a certificate indicating the type of planning obligation which it would have expected to have been entered into by the landowner prior to the issue of a permission.

7.50   The other type of applicable statement which may be contained in a certificate is that in the opinion of the local planning authority there is no development that is appropriate alternative development in relation to the acquisition. In this case it is sufficient for the authority simply to issue a certificate containing such a statement without further elaboration. Where an actual application is made for planning permission and is refused the local planning

---

[59] The form of an application for planning permission and the documents which must accompany an application are prescribed by art 6 of the Town and Country Planning (Development Mandatory Procedure) England Order 290 (SI 2010/2184). In certain cases the application must be accompanied by a design and access statement as required by art 8 of the Order.

[60] Land Compensation Act 1961, s 17(5)(b)(iii). A more uniform and rational system of requiring developers to make contributions to infrastructure needed to support the development is gradually being introduced by local planning authorities by way of the community infrastructure levy introduced by the Planning Act 2008: see the Community Infrastructure Levy Regulations 2010 (SI 2010/948).

authority must specify its reasons for refusal.[61] Such reasons are not necessary where a certificate with this type of applicable statement, what is often called a nil certificate, is issued. There is, of course, nothing to prevent the local planning authority indicating its reasons for issuing a nil certificate if it wishes, and to do so may be helpful to the parties in assessing compensation and will be helpful if there is any appeal against the issue of the certificate.

When the authority issues a certificate containing either type of applicable statement to one of the parties directly concerned a copy must be served by the authority on the other party.[62]   7.51

3. Appeals

Formerly there was a right of appeal against the issue of a certificate to the Secretary of State and appeals were determined, usually by an inspector appointed by the Secretary of State, in much the same way as ordinary planning appeals under section 78 of the Town and Country Planning Act 1990. A new system of appeals has been introduced by the Localism Act 2011. Appeals are now to the Lands Tribunal and may be made by the person interested in the land or by the acquiring authority.[63] The Tribunal must consider the matter to which the certificate relates as if the application for a certificate had been made to the Tribunal in the first instance. In other words the appeal is a hearing *de novo* at which new evidence may be adduced and at which neither party is confined to what was put before the local planning authority.[64] It is of course open to the Tribunal to give such weight as it thinks proper to the decision of the local planning authority. Such decisions are often preceded by a report from planning officers and the content of such a report, and its recommendation, may be of assistance to the Tribunal.   7.52

The Tribunal must deal with the appeal by either confirming the certificate as issued or varying it or cancelling it and issuing a different certificate in its place.[65] If the Tribunal does not confirm the certificate as issued by the local planning authority its decision on whether to vary the certificate, or to issue a new certificate, is likely to depend on the extent to which the Tribunal disagrees with the decision of the local planning authority and on the practicability of expressing its disagreement with any aspect of the certificate by a simple variation. The Tribunal is likely to deal with an appeal against the issue of a certificate as a separate matter before coming on to the determination of the compensation since the valuations of the parties cannot normally be prepared in final form until the result of the appeal and thus the content of the certificate are known. Of course a decision on the appeal may mean that the compensation can be settled without further proceedings in the Tribunal. Even so there may be cases in which the appeal against the issue of a certificate can be conveniently dealt with as a part of a reference for the determination of compensation. An   7.53

[61] Town and Country Planning (Development Management Procedure) (England) Order 2010 (SI 2010/2184), art 31(1)(b) Order 1995 (SI 1995/419), art 22(1)(c).
[62] Land Compensation Act 1961, s 17(9).
[63] Ibid, s 18(1), as substituted by the Localism Act 2011.
[64] Ibid, s 18(2). This rule mirrors the rule in ordinary planning appeals that the Secretary of State who determines an appeal may deal with the application for planning permission as if it had been made to him in the first instance: Town and Country Planning Act 1990, s 79(1). An appeal by way of a complete rehearing is to be contrasted with most appeals to the Court of Appeal which under the Civil Procedure Rules, r 52.11, are normally confined to a review of the decision of the lower court so that, eg, new evidence will not normally be heard.
[65] Land Compensation Act 1961, s 18(2).

appeal may be brought to the Tribunal if the local planning authority has failed to issue a certificate within the prescribed time period of two months or within any extended period agreed on by the parties.[66]

4. The Effect of a Certificate

7.54   The next matter to explain is the effect of a certificate. If a certificate does identify some description of development as appropriate alternative development then planning permission for that development is assumed to be in force at the valuation date or it is assumed at the valuation date that such a permission is certain to be granted at the later time specified as that when it could reasonably have been expected to be granted.[67] Where the certificate indicates conditions to which a planning permission would be subject, or pre-conditions which would have to be met, these matters apply to the assumed planning permission. It seems that when a certificate is issued, which identifies one or more descriptions of development as appropriate alternative development, planning permission for the description of development or developments so identified is assumed but no other investigation can take place as to whether a permission would reasonably have been expected to be granted at the valuation date so as to create an assumption that such a permission for that further development was in force at the valuation date.[68] It seems therefore that a claimant, who has obtained a positive certificate relating to a form of development, cannot then contend before the Lands Tribunal that permission could reasonably be expected to be granted at the valuation date on the assumptions specified in section 14 for some other and more valuable form of development. In other words the obtaining of a certificate from the local planning authority and proceedings before the Tribunal are alternative, but not cumulative, methods of gaining the assumption that a permission for appropriate alternative development is in force at the valuation date. It is possible that more than one application is made and that two or more certificates are issued identifying different forms of development. In that event an assumption would have to be made that planning permission was in force at the valuation date for both forms of development. Nothing stated in one certificate could permit or qualify the assumed existence or effect of the planning permission which arose from the other certificate.[69]

7.55   If a certificate is issued with a statement that in the opinion of the local planning authority there is no development that is appropriate alternative development in relation to the acquisition (ie a 'nil certificate') then there is no appropriate alternative development of any description which can bring about the assumption that a planning permission for such

---

[66]   Ibid, s 18(3).
[67]   Ibid, s 17(6).
[68]   Ibid, s 17(6)(a).
[69]   *Kingsley v Highways Agency* [2011] 1 EGLR 150. In this case the permission of the Lands Tribunal was needed for an application to be made for a second certificate since a reference had been made to the Tribunal. Permission was refused when a second certificate was being sought by the acquiring authority relating to a more limited form of development than that already certified in an earlier certificate. A second certificate in these terms would have been purposeless since it could not have removed or qualified the effect of the first certificate or of the planning permission which had to be assumed as a result of the first certificate. The situation might have been different if the second application had been by a claimant who sought certification of a different or more valuable form of development than that identified in the first certificate.

development is in force at the valuation date or is at that date certain to be granted at a future date.[70] Thus the issue of either a positive or a nil certificate settles the question of whether there can be an assumption, and if so what assumption, of appropriate alternative development and the matter cannot be raised again by a claimant before the Lands Tribunal (except by way of an appeal against the determination of the local planning authority). It appears, however, that a claimant can still assert that there was a hope at the valuation date of obtaining a planning permission and that the land had some hope value consequent upon that hope.

(E) HOPE OF OBTAINING PLANNING PERMISSION

Prior to the amendments effected by the Localism Act 2011 the general situation relating to   7.56
planning permission on the land acquired could be stated in fairly simple terms. The land acquired on the valuation date either had an existing planning permission or had the benefit of an assumed planning permission created under a statutory assumption or by virtue of a certificate of appropriate alternative development which itself resulted in an assumed planning permission. In addition any hope or expectation of a planning permission which would have existed at the valuation date, apart from the compulsory purchase and the scheme of the acquiring authority, could be taken into account but its effect on value depended on the strength of the hope, that is what was important was the additional value which the market would attribute to the perceived hope. The amount of this additional value could vary from a sum close to the value under an actual planning permission where the expectation of obtaining the permission was very high to a small sum (if any sum at all) where the expectation was poor.

It is still necessary to take into account the prospect at the valuation date of planning per-   7.57
mission being granted at that date or later for development on the land acquired or on other land. This prospect is to be taken into account in addition to any planning permission which exists at that date or is assumed to exist under the statutory assumptions including an assumption resulting from a certificate of appropriate alternative development. The prospect of a permission being granted must be judged in the circumstances known to the market at the valuation date subject to the three assumptions which are the same as those which have been described earlier, namely in general terms that the scheme underlying the acquisition has been cancelled on the launch date, that no action has been taken by the acquiring authority for the purposes of the scheme, and that there is no prospect of the same scheme or a similar scheme to meet the same need being carried out as an exercise of statutory functions.[71]

---

[70] Land Compensation Act 1961, s 17(7). Presumably if there were two certificates, a positive certificate and a nil certificate, the nil certificate could not override the effect of the positive certificate. See n 69.

[71] Ibid, s 14(2)(b) which states that account may be taken of the prospect at the valuation date of planning permission being granted on or after that date for development which is not appropriate alternative development, ie is not development pursuant to a planning permission which is to be assumed to exist. See paras 7.21 et seq for the three assumptions. It seems that the issue of a 'nil' certificate by the local planning authority or the Lands Tribunal on appeal does not prevent it being asserted that there was still some prospect of a particular planning permission being granted since the effect of such a certificate relates only to appropriate alternative development, ie to the existence of an assumed planning permission.

7.58   These provisions can, of course, be applied without great difficulty and on the basis of expert evidence. In the event of dispute the level of the expectation of planning permission and its effect on value will be determined by the Lands Tribunal. The Tribunal will also be bound, in the event of dispute, to determine what precisely is to be taken to be the underlying scheme for the purposes of the three assumptions just mentioned in accordance with the statutory provisions as to how that underlying scheme is to be identified by the Tribunal. Nonetheless certain points should be noted.

7.59   First, if the expectation of the planning permission exceeds 50 per cent, that is that it is established on the balance of probabilities, then the statutory assumption as to that planning permission being in force at the valuation date described earlier will operate and it is to be assumed as a matter of certainty that the permission is in force at the valuation date or would be granted at a later date.[72] If that level of expectation can be established then there is no need to have recourse to an examination of what value would be added to the land by the expectation of the permission in accordance with the strength of that expectation. An assumed planning permission is as good in valuation terms as an actual planning permission. In other words the position of a claimant will be: (a) that he can seek to establish that there is at the valuation date an expectation greater than 50 per cent of the permission in question being granted, in which case the permission becomes a certainty, or (b) that if he cannot establish this level of expectation then he can still assert a level of expectation which is less than 51 per cent and can attribute a value to the property in accordance with that lower expectation.

7.60   This leads to the second matter to note. When land is sold in the market and there is no actual planning permission (and in the case of a compulsory purchase no assumed certain planning permission) in all, or nearly all, cases the market assesses the probability of a permission being granted and confers a value on the property in accordance with the level of that probability. It is not easy to see why this process is not applied to a valuation for the purposes of compulsory purchase, as indeed it was prior to the alterations made by the Localism Act 2011. [73] Those amendments bring about a curious situation in which, to take an extreme example, where land has at the valuation date and in the absence of the scheme of the acquiring authority a 51 per cent expectation of obtaining planning permission for a particular development the land obtains 100 per cent of the development value attributable to the assumed existence of that planning permission but where in the same circumstances land has only a 49 per cent prospect of obtaining permission for that development the question to be asked is what value the market would attribute to that 49 per cent. Many would believe that this involves a degree of artificiality since it may involve a precise assessment of the arithmetical chances of obtaining a planning permission, a process which in the uncertain and discretionary world of town and country planning itself has a high degree of unreality within it. This is a situation which Lord Walker in the House of Lords in the *Spirerose* decision described as not satisfactory and which Lord Neuberger, perhaps more trenchantly, described as embodying a logical incoherence.[74] The approach contained in the amendments effected by the Localism Act 2011 also transgress the ordinary rule, in the assessment of damages or compensation for a loss in English law, that when the amount of the loss

---

[72] See paras 7.20–7.30.

[73] See s 14(3) of the Land Compensation Act 1961 prior to the amendments made by the Localism Act 2011 and see *Transport for London v Spirerose Ltd* [2009] UKHL 44, [2009] 1 WLR 1797.

[74] See *Transport for London v Spirerose Ltd* [2009] UKHL 44, [2009] 1 WLR 1797, at paras 38 and 62.

depends upon some uncertain future event the court normally assesses the prospect of that event occurring and determines the monetary amount payable to a claimant in accordance with that prospect.[75] In any event, whether incoherent or not, the law as described under this section is now applicable unless and until there is a comprehensive review of the law of compulsory purchase and compensation.

(F) SUMMARY

Under the system of law in force prior to the Localism Act 2011 the law on planning permis-   7.61
sions relevant to the value of the land acquired was reasonably simple and straightforward. Account was to be taken in the valuation process of three types of planning permission at the valuation date. (a) Any actual planning permission was to be taken into account. (b) Any planning permission required to be assumed was to be taken into account. An assumed permission was as good in valuation terms as an actual permission. (c) In addition account was to be taken of the prospect at the valuation date of obtaining a planning permission in the absence of the scheme of the acquiring authority. The strength of that prospect was to be assessed and the land valued as the amount it would realise in a sale in the market in the light of the prospect of that planning permission being granted.

As a result of the changes effected by the Localism Act 2011 the law has become in some   7.62
ways significantly more complex and more difficult to describe, something which is in part due to the nature of the language in which the new section 14 of the Land Compensation Act 1961 is expressed. On the other hand the 2011 Act has introduced a number of alterations and changes which have clarified the system and removed elements of it which were unnecessary, or positively harmful, in today's circumstances. It may be of assistance to conclude this chapter by summarising the law as it now stands in a few brief and necessarily simplified propositions:

(i)   Account may be taken in valuing the land acquired of any planning permission actually in force at the valuation date.

(ii)   In addition account may be taken of three forms of assumed planning permission. An assumed planning permission must be taken either to be in force at the valuation date or as certain at that date to be granted at some future time. Development for which planning permission is to be assumed is called appropriate alternative development.

(iii)   The first form of assumed planning permission is a permission for development of the land acquired in accordance with the proposals of the acquiring authority.

(iv)   The second form of assumed planning permission is permission for development which at the valuation date, and in the circumstances of the market at that date, could reasonably have been expected to be granted on three specified assumptions. The expression 'reasonably have been expected to be granted' means that the permission was likely to be granted on the balance of probabilities. Therefore a permission which had, say, a 60 per cent prospect of being granted is elevated to

---

[75] See para 7.17 and see *Porter v Secretary of State for Transport* [1996] 3 All ER 693 (a decision on compensation for damage to retained land under s 7 of the Compulsory Purchase Act 1965, approved as correct in principle by the House of Lords in *Spirerose*). See ch 9 for claims under s 7 of the Compulsory Purchase Act 1965.

the status of a permission in force at the valuation date or a permission certain at the valuation date to be granted at a future time.

(v)   The three specified assumptions are: (a) that the scheme underlying the acquisition has been cancelled, (b) that no action has been taken by the acquiring authority wholly or mainly for the purposes of the scheme, and (c) that there is no prospect of the same or a similar scheme being carried out in the exercise of a statutory function or by the exercise of compulsory purchase powers.

(vi)   The third form of assumed planning permission is a permission for development certified by a local planning authority on an application to it, or by the Lands Tribunal on an appeal from a determination of a local planning authority, as development for which planning permission could on the valuation date reasonably have been expected to be granted in the situation in the market on that date and on the three specified assumptions just described. Again a permission is reasonably expected to be granted if it is likely to be granted on the balance of probabilities so that a permission with a prospect in excess of 50 per cent of being granted becomes a permission which is either assumed to be in force at the valuation date, or is assumed to be certain at the valuation date to be granted at a future time.

(vii)   If a planning permission for development is not actually in force at the valuation date, and is not to be assumed to be in force at that date or certain at that date to be granted at a future time, then the prospect or hope at the valuation date of permission for that development being granted may still be taken into account. The prospect of the planning permission being granted is to be assessed in the circumstances of the market at the valuation date and on the three specified assumptions as described above. If the prospect of the permission being granted exceeds 50 per cent then the permission will be assumed to be in force as described in sub-paragraphs (iv) or (vi) so that the level of the prospect need not be further assessed. If the prospect of the permission being granted is 50 per cent or less it will be necessary to assess the level of the prospect and to value the land acquired accordingly.

8

Rule (6) Compensation

(A) INTRODUCTION

Compensation payable under rule (6) of section 5 of the Land Compensation Act 1961 is   8.1
an important head of compensation but it cannot be understood except in its historical
context. This has been explained elsewhere[1] but it is necessary to mention it again in outline
for the purposes of this chapter. The Lands Clauses Consolidation Act 1845 stated in section 63 that the basis of compensation was the value of the land acquired. The concept of
value was not defined but it was soon established that it meant the price which could be
obtained for the land on a sale in the open market. However, an additional rule arose which
was that value meant the value to the owner and not the value to the authority acquiring the
land.[2] An aspect of the value of land to its owner is that he can benefit from the continued
ownership of it and avoid the costs of moving elsewhere or similar costs or losses which will
be incurred if he sells the land. The theory emerged that when the owner was disturbed
from his land, compulsorily and against his will, he should be compensated for a part of the
loss which he suffered such as his removal expenses and similar costs or losses caused by the
disturbance and the avoidance of which could be regarded as a part of the value of the land
to him. Such an element of value is not of course a value to a purchaser or a value which
could be realised in the market but it can be regarded as part of the value to the owner as
that concept came to be understood.

This compensation for additional loss to the dispossessed owner, as a component of the   8.2
value to the owner, became recognised as a separate head of compensation and became
described as compensation for disturbance or disturbance compensation. In an early case
in 1846 compensation for a temporary loss of profits after he moved to new premises was
allowed to a brewer whose land had been acquired by compulsion.[3] The principle of disturbance compensation gained statutory recognition in rule (6) of section 2 of the Acquisition
of Land (Assessment of Compensation) Act 1919 and is today embodied in rule (6) of section 5 of the Land Compensation Act 1961.

The language of rule (6) reflects its history. It might have been expected that the rule would   8.3
have stated in straightforward terms that compensation was recoverable for disturbance
and other similar losses and that disturbance meant the fact that a person was disturbed
from the physical possession of land in which he held an interest. In fact rule (6) does not

---

[1] See ch 3, para 3.15.

[2] Chapter 3, paras 3.10 et seq. An early statement of the value to the owner principle is in *Stebbing v Metropolitan Board of Works* (1870) LR 6 QB 37, where Cockburn CJ said: 'His loss [ie the loss to the dispossessed landowner] shall be tested by what was the value of the thing to him, not by what will be its value to the person acquiring it'.

[3] *Jubb v Humber Dock Co* (1846) 9 QB 443 (a decision on the language of a private Act passed shortly before the Lands Clauses Consolidation Act 1845).

state what is meant by disturbance and, far from specifying an entitlement to compensation, merely states that the provisions of a previous rule, rule (2), shall not affect the assessment of compensation for disturbance. Rule (6) is as follows:

> The provisions of rule (2) shall not affect the assessment of compensation for disturbance or any other matter not directly based on the value of land.

As stated by Lord Alness in *Venables v Department of Agriculture for Scotland*[4] rule (6) confers no new rights although it manifestly purports to save existing rights.

8.4   The nature and purpose of rule (6) were explained by Scott LJ in *Horn v Sunderland Corporation*.[5] He said that the rule had been inserted into the legislation in 1919 for two purposes. The first and general purpose was to prevent misconception as to the scope of the alteration effected by rule (2) in the previous judicial basis for ascertaining the market value to the owner of the land sold, and the second, and more particular purpose, was to forestall the argument that a willing seller must in law be presumed to have moved out voluntarily to give vacant possession to the buyer. In other words when rule (2) requires the assumption of a hypothetical willing seller in order that the value of the land as the primary component of compensation can be determined it does not require it to be assumed, contrary to the reality, that the actual landowner, who is dispossessed of his land against his will, was a voluntary seller. The result of this explanation is that rule (6) was not introduced in order to provide a new or separate head of compensation but rather to make it clear that compensation which was previously payable for items such as the removal costs of a dispossessed landowner remained payable notwithstanding the enactment of rule (2). Thus, as Scott LJ put it, compensation for disturbance stood where it did before the Act of 1919. This observation is as true in principle today as it was when *Horn v Sunderland Corporation* was decided in 1941. Nonetheless there has grown up over recent decades a body of law which explains somewhat more precisely the items of loss which may be brought within a claim under rule (6).

8.5   The result of the historical and juridical origins of rule (6) is that compensation which is assessed under that rule is strictly not a separate head of compensation. It is a part of the value of the land as that expression was used in section 63 of the Lands Clauses Consolidation Act 1845 and as it is used today in section 7 of the Compulsory Purchase Act 1965 (which replaced section 63 with only minor modifications). The courts have always adhered to this analysis. Prior to the embodying of compensation for disturbance losses in a separate rule or provision it had been held that the compensation so assessed was a part of the consideration for the sale and so was liable to *ad valorem* stamp duty.[6] In *Horn v Sunderland Corporation*[7] Lord Greene MR said that it was a mistake to construe rules (2) and (6) as though they conferred two separate and independent rights, one to receive the market value of the land and the other to receive compensation for disturbance, each of which must be ascertained in isolation. In *M'Ardle v Glasgow Corporation*[8] Lord Clyde said in the Court of Session:

---

[4] *Venables v Department of Agriculture for Scotland* 1932 SC 573, at p 579.

[5] *Horn v Sunderland Corporation* [1941] 2 KB 26, at pp 40–41. As the Chairman of the Committee which produced a report in 1918 which resulted in s 2 of the Acquisition of Land (Assessment of Compensation) Act 1919 Scott LJ, then Sir Leslie Scott, was in a particularly good position to explain these matters.

[6] *Commissioners of Inland Revenue v Glasgow and South-Western Rly Co* (1887) 12 App Cas 315. The jury had assessed the compensation by way of separate sums for the value of the land and for loss of a business.

[7] [1941] 2 KB 26, at pp 34–35.

[8] *M'Ardle v Glasgow Corporation* 1972 SC 41, at pp 47–48. The Court was considering provisions in the Land

But the fact is that nowhere in this series of statutory provisions since 1845 is a disturbance claim treated as something separate and distinct from the rest of the claim. It is an element in the total computation of the compensation. The distinction which the acquiring authority seek to make between a disturbance claim and a claim for the value of the land is thus a false distinction. They are both elements in the value of the relevant interest within the meaning of that phrase in this series of Acts of Parliament.

In *Hughes v Doncaster Council*[9] Lord Bridge pointed out that the elements of compensation under rule (2) and rule (6) were inseparable parts of a single value in that together they made up the value of the land to the owner.

Given this learning it might be asked why compensation under rule (6), or disturbance compensation as it is more often (though not wholly accurately)[10] known, should be treated as a separate head of compensation in this book and explained separately in this chapter. The reason is that despite the legal theory that any item of compensation allowed under rule (6) is a part of the value of the land: (a) in reality the sums which constitute claims under rule (6) would not be regarded as a part of the value of the land in the ordinary understanding of that concept, and (b) in practice it is inevitable that items of claim under rule (6) are nearly always assessed separately. As Lord Bridge recognised in *Hughes v Doncaster Council* 'compensation in respect of the market value of land acquired and compensation for disturbance must in practice be separately assessed'.[11] A typical item which falls within rule (6) is the cost to a dispossessed landowner in occupation of the land, whether the property is residential or commercial, of moving himself and his effects and his business to alternative premises. Such a cost is not within the meaning of the value of the land acquired as ordinarily understood in the sense that the price which a purchaser would pay for that property would normally be unaffected by the cost to the owner of moving. Consequently the cost in question is assessed separately.

8.6

Compensation for disturbance under rule (6) must not be confused with disturbance payments which may be claimed under section 37 of the Land Compensation Act 1973 when a person is disturbed in his lawful possession of land but does not hold an interest in that land which entitles him to compensation under other provisions such as rule (6) of section 5 of the Land Compensation Act 1961. Disturbance payments are explained in chapter 12. In many instances the type of loss for which compensation can be recovered may be similar, for instance the cost of moving a business to new premises. Nonetheless there are two important differences between the two heads of compensation. (a) Compensation under rule (6) depends on the claimant having a legal or equitable interest in the land acquired which entitles him to compensation for the value of that interest. As explained compensation under rule (6) is regarded as a part of that value. A disturbance payment under the Land Compensation Act 1973 is only available to persons such as licensees who do not have an interest in the land acquired which entitles them to compensation for the value of their interest. (b) The assessment of a disturbance payment under the 1973 Act proceeds on a somewhat different basis to the assessment of compensation under rules (2) and (6) of the

8.7

Compensation (Scotland) Act 1963 which were the same as the rules applicable in England and Wales in the Land Compensation Act 1961.

[9] *Hughes v Doncaster Council* [1991] 1 AC 382, [1991] 2 WLR 16, at p 392.
[10] See para 8.8.
[11] [1991] 1 AC 382, [1991] 2 WLR 16, at p 392.

1961 Act. The amalgamation of these different heads of compensation may be a fruitful subject for law reform but at present the differences must be noted and applied.

(B) THE COMPONENTS OF RULE (6)

8.8   Rule (6) has two components which are compensation for disturbance and compensation for any other matter not directly based on the value of land. It is because of this second component of the rule that it is inaccurate to describe all claims under rule (6) as disturbance claims. In this chapter the expression 'disturbance claim' is confined to claims under the first component of rule (6). Disturbance means that a person is disturbed in his physical possession and occupation of land. Consequently compensation within the first component is confined to claims by those persons who prior to the compulsory acquisition were in occupation of the land and were disturbed from it. Therefore a person who is not in occupation of the land by virtue of an interest which he holds in it, whether because he has granted a tenancy or for other reasons, is not entitled to disturbance compensation. Compensation under the second component of rule (6) extends more widely. The loss for which compensation may be claimed does not in this case depend upon the claimant being in possession or occupation of the land acquired. As will become clear a variety of items can be brought within the second component, including the costs reasonably incurred by a claimant in formulating his claim for compensation in order to engage in discussions with the acquiring authority and prior to any reference to the Lands Tribunal (often called 'pre-reference costs'). Indeed it is at present difficult in principle to discern any clear limitation on the losses which may be brought within the second component of rule (6), save that the matter for which compensation is claimed must not be directly based on the value of land, and that there must be a sufficient causal connection between the loss for which compensation is claimed and the compulsory acquisition of the land in which the claimant has an interest.[12]

8.9   It should also be borne in mind that despite the wide language of rule (6), and especially of its second component, the rule does not override the principle that it is only a person who has a proprietary interest in the land acquired who is in principle entitled to compensation at all for the compulsory acquisition. A person is not entitled to compensation under rule (6) simply because he has been disturbed from land or because he has suffered some loss not directly based on the value of land unless he can first anchor his claim to that of the acquisition from him of a proprietary interest in the land. It is because of the possible harshness of this principle in some cases that since 1973 compensation known as a disturbance payment has been available in certain circumstances to persons in lawful possession of land but without an interest which entitles them to compensation and it is this separate entitlement to compensation which is considered in chapter 12.[13]

[12] The matter of general limitations on claims under r (6) is considered in section (e) of this chapter.
[13] See para 8.7. The best example of a person who may be disturbed from his possession of land, but who does not have any claim to compensation under s 7 of the Compulsory Purchase Act 1965 and the rules in s 5 of the Land Compensation Act 1961, is that of a licensee who does not have a proprietary interest in land: see *Warr (Frank) & Co Ltd v London County Council* [1904] 1 KB 713, and see ch 12, paras 12.2–12.5, for a discussion on the nature of licences. The nature of a proprietary interest in land is explained in ch 2, para 2.27.

There are certain general problems which arise from the language and operation of rule (6)   8.10
and these are considered in section (e) of this chapter or elsewhere in the book where they
are relevant. The main problems are: (a) what are the limits to a claim under rule (6) especially when the claim is founded on the wide and general language of the second component of the rule, (b) what exactly is meant by the words 'not directly based on the value of
land', (c) whether and to what extent claims may be brought under rule (6) for losses which
have been incurred prior to the date of the physical dispossession of the owner from the
land, and (d) the relationship between rule (6) and rule (2), particularly as regards losses to
a business carried on at the land acquired.[14]

(C) DISTURBANCE COMPENSATION

1. General

Compensation for disturbance is compensation for losses suffered by the landowner as a   8.11
result of being physically dispossessed of the property acquired. Accordingly it is only available where the claimant was in occupation of the property acquired prior to the acquisition,
and at the date of the acquisition of the property, and where the loss is caused by the acquisition of the property by the acquiring authority.[15] Disturbance compensation is in principle available whatever is the proprietary interest in land which entitles the claimant to
general compensation for the acquisition of that interest. It may be a freehold or a leasehold
interest and may be an equitable interest such as the benefit of an equitable lease.[16]

The basis of the assessment of compensation under rule (2) may preclude a claim for dis-   8.12
turbance compensation under rule (6). If the open market value of the land acquired is its
value for development there can generally be no claim for disturbance compensation since
the development of the land would itself mean that the owner would have to give up possession. It would be illogical and inconsistent to allow a claimant to obtain compensation
for being dispossessed from land when the value of the land, for which he is compensated
under rule (2), would itself involve him having to give up possession.[17] The rule was stated
by Dixon CJ and Kitto J in the High Court of Australia to be that if the land is valued on the

---

[14] The first three of these matters are considered later in this chapter. The fourth matter is of relevance to the
assessment of the primary head of compensation, the value of the land acquired determined under r (2) of s 5 of
the Land Compensation Act 1961, and is examined separately in section (h) of ch 4.

[15] *Wrexham Maelor Borough Council v MacDougall* (1995) 69 P & CR 109, at p 128; *Kovacs v Birmingham City
Council* (1984) 272 *Estates Gazette* 437. In *McTaggart v Bristol and West Building Society and Avon County Council*
(1985) 49 P & CR 184, a mortgagor who had defaulted on his payments under the mortgage gave up possession to
the mortgagee following a possession order made in the County Court. Thereafter there was a deemed compulsory
acquisition by reason of the service of a blight notice under planning legislation which was accepted by the local
authority. It was held that the mortgagor could not claim from the acquiring authority the interest payable by him
up until the transfer of title to the acquiring authority under r (6). His dispossession from the land was caused by
the order of the County Court not by the deemed compulsory acquisition.

[16] An equitable lease arises where there is a specifically enforceable agreement for a lease which has not been
completed by the grant of the lease under the doctrine in *Walsh v Lonsdale* (1882) 21 Ch D 9. In addition where
there is a registrable disposition of an interest in land with registered title, which includes leases for terms in excess
of seven years, the grantee has only an equitable interest until the disposal is registered at HM Land Registry: see
Land Registration Act 2002, s 27(1).

[17] *Horn v Sunderland Corporation* [1941] 2 KB 26.

basis of its suitability for some more profitable form of use than its existing use there can be no justification for making an addition to the value so ascertained because of disturbance. There would be an obvious inconsistency in awarding disturbance compensation in such a case. Accordingly compensation for loss to a business was refused.[18]

2. Remoteness and Mitigation

8.13   Some general attempts have been made to state what are the limits on compensation for disturbance. In *Harvey v Crawley Development Corporation*[19] the claimant was held to be entitled to compensation under rule (6) for the costs of acquiring a new house when her existing property had been compulsorily acquired. The costs included legal and surveyor's costs and travelling expenses. It was stated that the authorities established that any loss sustained by a dispossessed owner which flows from a compulsory acquisition may properly be regarded as the subject of compensation for disturbance, provided, first, that it is not too remote and, secondly, that it is the natural and reasonable consequence of the dispossession of the owner.

8.14   A fuller attempt to state the general limitations on disturbance compensation was made by Lord Nicholls in *Director of Buildings and Lands v Shun Fung Ironworks Ltd.*[20] This decision of the Privy Council was on appeal from the courts in Hong Kong where the legislation being applied was significantly different from that in force in England. The critical provision was section 10 of the Crown Lands Resumption Ordinance which provided that the Lands Tribunal should determine the compensation payable on the basis of, inter alia,

> the amount of loss or damage to a business conducted by a claimant at the date of resumption on the land resumed or in any building erected thereon, due to the removal of the business from that land or building as a result of the resumption.

Nonetheless Lord Nicholls proceeded to state as useful guidelines to the general assessment of fair and adequate compensation of any kind three conditions which must be satisfied.[21] The first condition was that there must be a causal connection between the compulsory acquisition and the loss in question. The second condition was that the loss must not be too remote if it was to qualify for compensation. The third condition was that persons claiming compensation were expected to behave reasonably and to take steps to eliminate or reduce the loss. The third condition is therefore a statement of the general principle of mitigation which applies to the assessment of damages at common law. While these are no doubt useful general guidelines their very generality means that they cannot produce an automatic answer on the acceptability of all claims for disturbance compensation. In particular it must always be remembered that if a claim is to come within rule (6) of section 5 of the

---

[18]   *Australia v Milledge* (1953) 4 P & CR 135, 26 ALJ 621.
[19]   *Harvey v Crawley Development Corporation* [1957] 1 QB 485, per Romer LJ at p 494.
[20]   *Director of Buildings and Lands v Shun Fung Ironworks Ltd* [1995] 2 AC 111, [1995] 2 WLR 904, at p 126.
[21]   The three conditions or tests stated by Lord Nicholls were expressed and intended to apply to all forms of statutory compensation arising out of the compulsory acquisition of land even though the only claim before the court, and the only head of claim in issue between the parties, was a claim founded on a statutory provision in force in Hong Kong which had no exact equivalent in England. The nearest equivalent is r (6) and it is perhaps for this reason that the three conditions have generally been considered in the context of claims under r (6). See also ch 4, para 4.84.

Land Compensation Act 1961 that claim must be capable of being brought within the language of that provision whether or not it would otherwise be sustainable in accordance with the three general principles just mentioned. The guidelines suggested by Lord Nicholls have been applied by the Lands Tribunal in allowing certain claims under the second component of rule (6) and the general problem which arises of finding a coherent limitation on the extent of such claims is examined later in this chapter. It is in connection with the second component of rule (6) that the problem of drawing a coherent line between losses, which may and may not be recoverable, has proved to be most acute. It is arguable that reliance on Lord Nicholls's guidelines as though they were themselves statutory provisions has opened the gates to claims under rule (6), and especially under its second component, which are unacceptably wide.[22]

A particular difficulty is that of knowing the test which is to be applied in order to determine whether a particular loss is too remote. Questions of remoteness have long troubled the courts in assessing damages in the law of torts. A test which was once applied was that the loss in question had to be a direct consequence of the tortious act if damages were to be recoverable.[23] This test as stated by the Court of Appeal was said by Viscount Simonds in *Overseas Tankship (UK) v Morts Dock and Engineering Co (The Wagon Mound)*[24] in the Privy Council to be something which led to never-ending and insoluble problems of causation. The test of remoteness stated in *The Wagon Mound* was one of foreseeability in that damages might be recovered when a tort had been committed if the loss in question was of a kind which was reasonably foreseeable by the tortfeasor at the date of the commission of the tort. Later authorities have shown that even this test has to be heavily qualified if it is to offer a satisfactory general rule.[25]

8.15

It may be that the test of foreseeability is one guide to questions of remoteness when compensation is claimed under rule (6) whether for disturbance or for matters under the second component of that rule. Nonetheless the test is far from one which can provide a universal answer to problems of remoteness. To the extent that the test can be applied to claims under the first component of rule (6) the question would be whether a particular loss claimed under that rule was reasonably foreseeable by the acquiring authority at the date of dispossession of the claimant as loss of a kind which was likely to result from the dispossession. However this use of the foreseeability test as the criterion for distinguishing between losses which are or are not too remote breaks down when it is borne in mind that in principle losses may be recovered under rule (6) where they occur prior to the date of

8.16

---

[22] See section (e), paras 8.43 et seq.

[23] *Re Polemis* [1921] 3 KB 560.

[24] *Overseas Tankship (UK) v Morts Dock and Engineering Co (The Wagon Mound)* [1961] AC 388, [1961] 2 WLR 126. This well known decision is usually referred to as *The Wagon Mound (No 1)*. It concerns the recovery of damages for negligence when a ship was damaged by a fire following the discharge of oil from another ship in Sydney Harbour in Australia. For the principles concerning remoteness of damage where the injury is to land see *Cambridge Water Co Ltd v Eastern Counties Leather Plc* [1994] 2 AC 264, [1994] 2 WLR 53.

[25] See generally *Charlesworth & Percy on Negligence*, 12th edn (London, Sweet and Maxwell, 2013), ch 5. In *Khurami v Transport for London* [2012] RVR 42, the costs of a relocation was disallowed as too remote when the claimant had acquired new premises and then had to sell them as they were too expensive. It was held that the claimant had not behaved as a reasonable businessman would behave. The subject of remoteness of damage is also relevant to claims for compensation for injurious affection under s 10 of the Compulsory Purchase Act 1965 where similar problems arise of knowing when a loss is too remote to give rise to a right to compensation: see ch 10, para 10.53.

dispossession.[26] An example of such a loss which is caused by the dispossession of the land-owner is the cost of moving to new premises when the owner moves a short time in advance of the day on which he was due to be dispossessed. A claim for such a loss is recoverable, as explained in more detail in section (e) of this chapter, but as the loss was incurred prior to the date of dispossession it cannot be said to have been foreseeable on that date. A further illustration of the difficulty in using foreseeability as a test of remoteness is *Harvey v Crawley Development Corporation*[27] referred to earlier. Denning LJ was willing to allow the legal and professional costs of acquiring a new house as part of the disturbance compensation pay-able to someone who was dispossessed of an existing house in which she lived. Although this was not mentioned the owner-occupier of a commercial property should be entitled to compensation for the costs and expenses of buying a new property in the same way. Denning LJ then added that if a person owned a house as an investment, and then chose to use the compensation payable to him for its acquisition to buy a further house as an investment, he would not be entitled to the legal costs of acquiring the further property. It is difficult to see why in one case the loss is too remote and in the other case it is not too remote. Of course as the claimant in respect of a house or other property owned as an investment and let to tenants would not be himself disturbed in his possession of the property he would have to frame his claim under the second component of rule (6). This particular anomalous situa-tion, brought about in part by the imprecise nature of the concept of remoteness, has now been recognised to be unsatisfactory and has been remedied by statute as is explained in the next paragraph.[28]

8.17   It is apparent from the principles and authorities discussed that a person who is dispos-sessed from land is entitled as part of his compensation to the reasonable expenses of relo-cating himself to other premises including the costs and expenses incurred in acquiring the other premises. This is so whatever the purpose for which he occupies the land acquired, whether it be a residential, or commercial or other purpose. However, as with all claims for disturbance compensation, that is compensation under the first component of rule (6), the person who claims an item of compensation under this head must have been in occupation of the land prior to and at the date of the acquisition. There is in force a further statutory rule which may entitle a person to compensation for charges and expenses in acquiring a different property even when he was not in occupation of the property acquired. Under section 10A of the Land Compensation Act 1961, as inserted by the Planning and Compensation Act 1991, a person whose interest in land is acquired but who was not in occupation of that land and who then incurs incidental charges or expenses in acquiring within the period of one year beginning with the date of entry to the land acquired an inter-est in other land in the United Kingdom is entitled to the charges and expenses in question as part of his compensation as he would be if he had been in occupation of the land acquired. It is not necessary that the other property is of the same character as that acquired or is acquired as a replacement investment. The overall position therefore is that a person

---

[26] This rule is examined in section (e) of this chapter in connection with general limitations on claims to com-pensation under r (6). See that section also for a consideration of the test of remoteness as a possible limitation on the wider ambit currently allowed to claims under the second component of r (6) when the owner is not physically dispossessed of his property, or his loss does not flow from physical dispossession, so that the owner cannot claim compensation under the first component of r (6). In such cases, subject to any question of remoteness, the owner might pursue his claim under the second component of the rule.

[27] [1957] 1 KB 485. See para 8.13.

[28] See now s 10A of the Land Compensation Act 1961.

physically disturbed from possession of his land is entitled as part of his disturbance compensation to the reasonable charges and expenses in acquiring a new property at which to establish himself and a person who holds an interest in a property as an investment is also entitled to the reasonable charges and expenses of acquiring a different property providing he acts promptly in doing so. It is convenient to mention section 10A at this point since the recovery of the expenses of acquiring a different property is under consideration but the claim under this section is not strictly a disturbance claim as defined in this chapter since the claimant has not been disturbed in his occupation of the property acquired.

Where a claimant carries on a business at the land acquired and his business is extinguished he may be entitled to compensation under rule (2) of section 5 of the Land Compensation Act 1961 for the value of the land which would have been created by the expectation of future profits to be earned from the land if he had sold the land at the valuation date. In such a case the owner may in principle be entitled to compensation under rule (6) for costs such as redundancy payments which he would not have had to pay if the land had been sold with the business on it.[29]   8.18

The third of the three guidelines mentioned by Lord Nicholls in the *Shun Fung* decision was that a claimant for compensation must mitigate his loss. This is a rule which, as mentioned, is applicable generally to claims for damages at common law. It has been said, reflecting the principles which apply to common law damages, that there are certain rules in the application of this principle in compensation cases. The first is that the claimant must take all reasonable steps to mitigate his loss with the result that he cannot recover compensation for any loss which he could have avoided. The second rule is that where the claimant does take reasonable steps to mitigate his loss he can recover as compensation the costs and expenses incurred in the process of mitigation. The third rule is that where the claimant does take proper steps to mitigate the loss to him the compensation which he can obtain is that which is consequent upon his loss having regard to the mitigating steps which he has taken. It is sometimes said that the first rule means that the claimant cannot recover for an avoidable loss, the second rule means that the claimant can recover the expenses incurred in reasonable attempts to avoid a loss, and the third is that the claimant cannot recover for loss which he has, by taking proper steps in mitigation, avoided.[30] An illustration of the duty to mitigate a loss is that where he removes his business to new premises the claimant must move the business to the most suitable premises which are available to him and will not be entitled to recover costs which are consequent upon a removal to less suitable property.[31] Of course the duty of a claimant to move his business to suitable new premises, where that can reasonably be done, is itself an aspect of the duty to mitigate the loss which flows from the compulsory purchase.[32] In accordance with general principles it will be for an acquiring authority, which contends that a loss was unreasonably incurred and could have been mitigated so as to be in whole or in part avoided, to prove that that is so.[33]   8.19

---

[29] See section (h) of ch 4 for the relationship between the value of land and the expectation of future profits from a business carried on at the land.

[30] *Scotia Plastic Binding Ltd v London Development Agency* [2010] UKUT 98 (LC), [2010] RVR 307; *Appleby & Ireland v Hampshire County Council* [1978] RVR 156.

[31] *Scotia Plastic Binding Ltd v London Development Agency*, ibid.

[32] See section (h) of ch 4 for a discussion of the relationship between losses when a business cannot be moved to alternative premises, and so is extinguished, and claims for compensation under rr (2) and (6) of s 5 of the Land Compensation Act 1961.

[33] *Bede Distributors Ltd v Newcastle Corporation* (1973) 26 P & CR 298.

(D) THE SECOND COMPONENT OF RULE (6)

8.20   The second component of rule (6) allows compensation for 'any other matter not directly based on the value of land'. It is apparent that any loss which may be recovered under this second component does not depend on the claimant having been in occupation of the land prior to the compulsory acquisition. Of course, a claim under the second component is not precluded where the claimant has been in occupation of the land but in such a case the claim will relate to losses not consequential upon his being removed from the occupation of the land. When the language of rule (6) refers to 'any other matter' this is presumably intended to be equivalent to any other loss arising from a matter not directly based on the value of land.

1. The Value of Land

8.21   The first question which arises on the meaning of the second component is what is meant by 'the value of land' within the words 'not directly based on the value of land'. In general terms land may have a capital value or a rental value. An interest in land has a capital value if it can be sold for a capital sum. Clearly the freehold interest in an area of land can generally be sold for a capital sum. A leasehold interest in land may also be saleable for a capital sum if the rental payable under the lease is less than the full open market rental value at the time of the sale. The rental value of land is the periodic return by way of rent which can be obtained from a letting of it. The rental value is usually assessed as an annual sum although it may, of course, be expressed on some other basis such as a monthly or weekly rental value. For the purposes of land valuation generally, and for certain purposes relating to the assessment of compensation, the value of land may mean either its capital value or its rental value. In the leading modern authority on the assessment of compensation for injurious affection under section 10 of the Compulsory Purchase Act 1965 it was held that injurious affection, in the sense of damage to land, could include damage by way of a reduced rental value over a period of time as well as damage by way of a reduced capital value.[34]

8.22   The question therefore arises, as regards the language of the second limb of rule (6), whether that which is precluded as an item of compensation is any matter which is directly based on the rental value as well as on the capital value of the land acquired. The view which has recently prevailed certainly in the Lands Tribunal is that the expression 'the value of land' as used in rule (6) means the same as the capital value of land which is referred to in rule (2) and so means the amount which the land if sold on the open market by a willing seller might be expected to realise.[35] There is support for this view in the fact that the words 'the value of land' are used in rule (2) and in rule (6) so that it might have been intended that they meant the same thing wherever used within the whole of section 5 of the Land

---

[34] *Wildtree Hotels Ltd v Harrow LBC* [2001] 2 AC 1, [2000] 3 WLR 163. See also *Ford v Metropolitan and Metropolitan District Rly Co* (1886) 17 QBD 12, per Bowen LJ at p 28.

[35] *Pattle v Secretary of State for Transport* [2001] 1 P & CR DG 1, [2009] RVR 328; *Bishopsgate Parking (No 2) Ltd v Welsh Ministers* [2012] UKUT 22 (LC), [2012] RVR 237, at para 104; *Ryde International Plc v London Regional Transport* [2004] RVR 60, at para 25 (CA).

Compensation Act 1961. In addition the purpose of rule (6) is to provide for elements of compensation which are in addition to the basic element of compensation which is the open market capital value of the land acquired as assessed under rule (2). It might therefore be concluded that the purpose of excluding from compensation under rule (6) matters directly based on the value of land was to exclude from rule (6) compensation any matter which would be subsumed within the primary claim for compensation under rule (2).[36] While this matter has still to be fully considered in the higher courts it does seem a good and sensible working rule for present purposes to conclude that all that is excluded by the final words of rule (6) is matters directly based on the capital value of the land as ascertained under rule (2). The result is that in principle there is nothing to prevent a claim under rule (6) which is founded on some loss of rental value at or over some particular period.[37]

2. Pre-reference Costs

An important head of claim which often arises under the second limb of rule (6) is a claim   8.23
for the costs and expenses incurred by a claimant in taking advice on his claim, formulating it, and presenting and discussing it with the representatives of the acquiring authority in order that an agreement can, if possible, be reached on the amount of the compensation. Indeed, a notice to treat which is a part of many compulsory acquisitions is, as its name states, a notice that the landowner is required to treat or discuss the matter of compensation with the acquiring authority. A general vesting declaration operates as a constructive notice to treat. Claims for such costs and expenses, provided they have been reasonably incurred, are recoverable under the second limb of rule (6) as an item of compensation.[38] This item of claim is often described as pre-reference costs in the sense that they are costs incurred by a claimant prior to any reference to the Lands Tribunal. In large cases the amount of pre-reference costs can be substantial and can include, as well as the costs of legal advice, the costs of obtaining advice from other professional persons such as surveyors, planners, accountants and architects. A claimant may have incurred pre-reference losses by reason of time of its employees having to be deployed in providing information and in formulating the claim. It seems that in principle such items can be recovered as pre-reference costs under rule (6) since, had there not been the need to spend time in preparing the claim, the time of employees could have been devoted to the general business of the company.

It must be borne in mind that pre-reference costs are an item of compensation not the costs   8.24
of legal proceedings. If the claim is submitted to the Lands Tribunal by way of a reference the incidence of costs from the making of the reference to the Tribunal will be a matter for the Tribunal itself. The distinction between pre-reference costs and the costs of a reference

---

[36] See the general explanation of the purpose of r (6) given by Scott LJ in *Horn v Sunderland Corporation* [1941] 2 KB 26, at pp 40–41, and see para 8.4.

[37] Such a claim was allowed in *Pattle v Secretary of State for Transport*, above n 35. See para 8.46.

[38] *London County Council v Tobin* [1959] 1 WLR 354. In that case the claim for compensation under this head was in respect of legal advice and the advice of an accountant taken in preparing the claim, costs which came in total to just over £26. *Lee v Minister of Transport* [1966] 1 QB 111. Account is to be taken in assessing compensation of any expenses reasonably incurred in connection with the issue of a certificate of appropriate alternative development under s 17 of the Land Compensation Act 1961: see s 17(10) of that Act as substituted by the Localism Act 2011. See section (d) of ch 7 for these certificates.

to the Tribunal is important for a number of reasons. Since pre-reference costs are an item of compensation then, provided they are reasonable in amount, they can be recovered as a matter of right as a part of the total compensation. The costs of a reference to the Tribunal are different since they are always in the discretion of the Tribunal itself. Interest is payable on pre-reference costs as a part of the compensation from the date of entry (or, where a general vesting declaration has been made, from the vesting date) up until the date on which the costs are recovered as a part of the compensation and this again is a matter of right. A final distinction is that experience shows that even when a party obtains an order for the costs of any legal proceedings on the standard basis of assessment, including a claim before the Tribunal in his favour, in the end because of processes of discussion, and if necessary formal assessment, the amount which he recovers is generally significantly less than the total amount which he expends on lawyers and others in presenting and fighting his claim before the Tribunal.[39]

8.25   There is a possible particular difficulty with the assessment of pre-reference costs as an item of compensation if the claim is heard before the Lands Tribunal. It is for the claimant to prove this item of loss and claim for compensation as it is for any other item. If the matter is in dispute as to its detail then the claimant will have to show what was the work done for him for the costs of which he makes a claim and must show that the amount claimed was reasonable. In respect of legal fees which often take up a significant part of pre-reference costs this may be difficult in proceedings before the Tribunal because it might involve disclosing to the acquiring authority some details of the work which was done by lawyers on behalf of the claimant; yet this is something which in the ordinary way is privileged from disclosure and is something which is confidential to the claimant and something the disclosure of which could cause disadvantage or embarrassment to him in the proceedings. Generally this difficulty can be avoided in that a claimant may have to disclose only the number of hours work which have been done for him and the hourly rate charged and the substance or nature of the work in order to sustain his claim.

3. Other Losses

8.26   There appear to be no general or clearly expressed limits on the ambit of claims under the second limb of rule (6) save for the statutory language itself which, as interpreted, means that a claim cannot exist in relation to a matter which is based directly on the capital value of the land acquired and save for the general limitations referred to by Lord Nicholls in the *Shun Fung* decision.[40] The wide ambit of possible claims can be seen from the decision of the Court of Appeal in *Wrexham Maelor Borough Council v MacDougall*.[41] In that case the claimant held the unexpired residue of a five year lease of premises from which two compa-

---

[39] See section (m) of ch 15 for costs before the Lands Tribunal. There is today a substantial case for saying that in general the costs of a successful claimant before the Lands Tribunal should be on the indemnity rather than on the standard basis in which case it is more likely that a claimant with an order for costs in his favour will obtain the whole or nearly the whole of his expenses of the proceedings by way of costs: see ch 15, para 15.132, where this matter is further discussed and the distinction between costs on the standard basis and on the indemnity basis is explained.

[40] See para 8.14. The question of possible general limits to claims under the second component of r (6) is examined in section (e) of this chapter.

[41] *Wrexham Maelor Borough Council v MacDougall* (1995) 69 P & CR 109.

nies carried out insurance business. He and his wife owned all of the shares in the two companies. The Lands Tribunal awarded compensation of (a) £9,000 for the value of the claimant's lease, (b) £263,000 as a disturbance payment to the companies under section 37 of the Land Compensation Act 1973 (the two companies carrying on the business who made this claim held no interest in the land which qualified for compensation so that the only available compensation was that of a disturbance payment under the 1973 Act), and (c) £61,068 to the claimant by reason of the losses which he suffered as a result of a service contract which existed between him and the companies becoming no longer operable following the compulsory acquisition. This third claim was under the second component of rule (6). The claim was a purely personal and economic claim and had nothing to do with the value of the land acquired which under the first head of claim had given rise to compensation of £9,000. It was held that the loss to the claimant was not too remote and that under the second component of rule (6), in contrast to the first limb, it was not necessary that the claimant should have been in occupation of the land acquired.[42]

It should be borne in mind in considering this decision that, although the successful claim under rule (6) was for a purely personal and economic loss to the claimant, in effect a loss of an anticipated future income, the ability of the claimant to bring that claim under section 7 of the Compulsory Purchase Act 1965 and rule (6) depended on his owning a leasehold interest in the land. The value of his leasehold interest in the land acquired was not affected by the terms of his personal contract with the two insurance companies which he and his wife controlled. If there had been someone else who had had a similar service contract with the companies but had held no interest in the land acquired that person, albeit that he had suffered the same economic loss, would have had no claim for compensation against the acquiring authority. Equally if the income from the contracts had been relevant to the value of the leasehold interest in the land that income might have increased the value of that interest and the claim for the value of that interest under rule (2) of section 5 of the 1961 Act and would not then have been the foundation of a claim under rule (6). The decision in the *Wrexham Maelor* case perhaps reaches towards the limit of that which is recoverable under the second component of rule (6).   8.27

Decisions of the Lands Tribunal suggest that in principle a claim may lie under the second component of rule (6) for compensation for certain forms of tax liability or disadvantage which may be caused by a compulsory acquisition of land.[43] It has also been suggested that where the result of the compulsory acquisition is that the landlord is relieved of some liability, such as a duty to repair property which is in disrepair under a repairing covenant in a lease, and this factor is not reflected in a reduction in compensation under rule (2) the gain to the claimant may have to be taken into account in assessing any compensation due under rule (6).[44]   8.28

---

[42] A similar result occurred in the decision of the Lands Tribunal for Northern Ireland, applying the same statutory language, in *Maxol Oil Ltd v Department of the Environment for Northern Ireland* [2005] RVR 97, in which a sum was awarded for loss of income under a solus agreement. The Tribunal followed and applied what was said in the *Wrexham Maelor* decision.

[43] *Bishopsgate Parking (No 2) Ltd v Welsh Ministers* [2012] UKUT 22 (LC), [2012] RVR 237. This subject is fully explained in section (f) of ch 6.

[44] *Richard Parsons Ltd v Bristol City Council* [2007] 3 EGLR 73.

(E) LIMITATIONS ON RULE (6) CLAIMS

8.29   It is intended in this section of the chapter to deal with possible limitations on rule (6) claims and other general matters relating to the ambit of such claims. The overriding difficulty is that the terse language of rule (6), and especially of the second component of that rule, does not introduce any limitations save that under the first component a claim can only be made by a person who has been disturbed from physical possession of land and under the second component the loss in question for which compensation is claimed must not be something which is directly based on the capital value of the land acquired. Such other limitations on the width of claims, as may exist, derive from decisions of the courts or from the common sense conclusion that there must be some reasonable limit on sums which can be claimed. The various limitations, some of which have been referred to previously, are here gathered together.

1. Occupation

8.30   As already mentioned a person can only make a claim for disturbance under the first component of rule (6) if he has been disturbed from his occupation of the land. The criterion is sometimes described as occupation and sometimes as physical possession but the meaning is the same.[45]

2. The Value of Land

8.31   It has also been mentioned that, by virtue of the language of the second component of rule (6), a claim cannot be made under that component for any loss which is directly based on the value of land. In this context the expression 'value of land' probably means the value of the land as determined under rule (2), that is its capital value which is the basis of compensation under rule (2).[46] It is sometimes said that a permanent loss of future anticipated profits from a business carried out on the land acquired, but which has been extinguished by the compulsory acquisition of that land, can be claimed as the subject matter of compensation under rule (6). The anticipation of future profits may better be regarded as a component of the capital value of the land and so as something which is relevant to, or even establishes, the compensation recoverable under rule (2) and as something which in some cases may provide the best guide to that value. As such the loss of the anticipated profits is a matter directly based on the capital value of the land acquired and for that reason cannot figure as a claim under rule (6). This subject is more fully covered in section (h) of chapter 4. The better view of the linguistic structure of rule (6) may be that any loss attributable to disturbance, and any loss attributable to any other matter, must both satisfy the criterion that they are not directly based on the value of the land acquired. Such an interpretation is necessary to prevent any overlap between claims under rule (2) and claims under either component of rule (6).

[45] See para 8.11.
[46] See para 8.21.

3. Facts at the Date of the Hearing

The general approach in assessing compensation for the value of an interest in land is to   8.32
determine the valuation date and then to determine the value of the interest as at that date.
This process does not permit the taking into account of events following the valuation date
since those events could not have been known to the hypothetical parties who sold and
bought the interest at the valuation date.[47] However, this situation must be distinguished
from a situation in which what is being assessed is not the value of the land at a particular
date but rather the amount of loss suffered by a claimant which is likely to have nothing to
do with the value of land as such. In these latter circumstances the general rule which
applies to the assessment of damages is applied to this aspect of the law of compensation so
that the body which has to determine the compensation is entitled, and indeed bound, to
have regard to all relevant facts and events which have occurred at the date of the hearing in
order to ascertain the true loss.[48] The principle that all relevant facts and matters existing at
the date of the hearing, at which the compensation for a loss which is not the value of land
is assessed, must be taken into account is sometimes called the Bwllfa principle after the
decision of the House of Lords in *Bwllfa and Merthyr Dare Steam Collieries (1891) Ltd v
Pontypridd Waterworks Company*.[49] The principle so stated is an aspect of the general law of
damages. This rule has been applied as regards claims for disturbance and similar compensation.[50]

4. Claims Relating to Retained Land

It is sometimes suggested that a claim may be brought under rule (6) for compensation for   8.33
loss to land of the owner which is retained by him and is not a part of the land acquired.[51]
Such suggestions are misconceived for a number of reasons.

First, the payment of compensation under rule (6) derives its validity from section 7 of the   8.34
Compulsory Purchase Act 1965 in that it is a part of the value of the land acquired. Section
7 of the 1965 Act provides for two separate entitlements to compensation. One is compensation for the value of the land acquired. The other is compensation for injurious affection

---

[47] See section (f) of ch 4.
[48] Ibid, see, eg *Lesschke v Jeffs & Faulkner* [1955] *Queensland Weekly Notes* 67.
[49] *Bwllfa and Merthyr Dare Steam Collieries (1891) Ltd v Pontypridd Waterworks Co* [1903] AC 426. The facts of
this decision are explained in ch 4, para 4.53.
[50] *Director of Buildings and Lands v Shun Fung Ironworks Ltd* [1995] 2 AC 111, [1995] 2 WLR 904, per Lord
Nicholls at p 133. In that case compensation was estimated under the terms of an Ordinance in force in Hong Kong
as the present value of a stream of future profits and one of the issues was the discount rate to be applied in carrying out this exercise. Lord Nicholls observed that the ascertainment of the discount rate was heavily dependent on
the risks of the future profits actually being obtained and that when the Tribunal gave its judgment, after five years
during which future profits might have been earned had passed, it was no longer necessary to speculate on what
risks might have assailed the claimant in running its business in those years and the Tribunal was in a position to
know that there had been no untoward happenings which would have substantially deprived the claimant of its
profits over at any rate those initial years. See ch 14, paras 14.71 et seq, for a discussion on the use of discounted
cash flow methodology in estimating the present day value of an expected stream of future profits. See also *Wicham
Growers v Southern Water* [1997] 1 EGLR 175.
[51] See *Pattle v Secretary of State for Transport* [2010] 1 P & CR DG 1 (see para 8.46); *Brickell v Shaftesbury* (1955)
5 P & CR 174; *Tamplin's Brewery v Brighton CBC* (1971) 22 P & CR 746.

to other land of the dispossessed owner, that is his retained land. Since claims under rule (6) are a part of the first entitlement it is contrary to the form and structure of the underlying legislation to allow under rule (6) claims which are in truth a part of the second and separate entitlement to compensation.

8.35   Secondly, authority in the House of Lords establishes that any sum payable under rule (6) is a part of the value of the land acquired.[52] Consequently a claim under that rule cannot relate to land retained by the owner since any sum awarded on such a claim will not be a part of the value of the land acquired.

8.36   Thirdly, rule (6) does not introduce a new head of claim but merely preserves claims which prior to the Acquisition of Land (Assessment of Compensation) Act 1919 would have been payable. Obviously before the introduction of these rules in 1919, the rules which now constitute section 5 of the Land Compensation Act 1961, no claim could have been made for injurious affection to retained land as part of the value of the land acquired so that no claim for such injurious affection can today be made under rule (6).

8.37   Fourthly, claims in relation to land retained are claims for injurious affection to that land which are normally damage to the land as opposed to personal or monetary claims such as can be made under rule (6). This difference also makes it impractical to apply the method of assessing rule (6) claims to claims concerning land retained.

5. Pre-acquisition Losses

8.38   Rule (6) does not state the date at which a loss to a claimant must have occurred if it is to become the subject of compensation. Since a loss can clearly be compensatable only if it has been caused by the compulsory acquisition it might be thought that it was only losses which occurred following the acquisition which could attract compensation. Any such limitation would come up against the difficulties: (a) that a compulsory acquisition of land is an ongoing process which can take a considerable time and go through several stages so that it is not clear what exactly is the date of the acquisition, and (b) there may be circumstances in which a person suffers losses or reasonably incurs expenses prior to the moment when he is bound to leave the land acquired. For instance, if a person receives a notice to treat and then takes an opportunity which presents itself to move to alternative premises before the date on which he is actually required to leave the property acquired, it would seem unsatisfactory and unfair if he was denied compensation under rule (6) for the expenses of the move simply because he could have waited until a notice of entry was served on him and he was obliged to move. Indeed if the amount of a loss to the landowner can be reduced by a timely move, or other action prior to the date on which the landowner is bound to leave the land acquired, a failure to reduce the loss in this way could be categorised as a failure by a claimant to take all reasonable steps to mitigate his loss.[53] It may even be reasonable for a person to move to new premises before a notice to treat has been served on him or before a general vesting declaration has been made which includes his property.

---

[52]   *Hughes v Doncaster Council* [1991] 1 AC 382, [1991] 2 WLR 16. See para 8.5. Lord Wilberforce stated in *Argyle Motors v Birkenhead Corporation* [1975] AC 99 at p 133 that the rules in s5 of the Land Compensation Act 1961 (including rule (6)) had nothing to do with the assessment of compensation for injurious affection.
[53]   For the duty to mitigate losses, see para 8.19.

There was at one time a considerable line of decisions in the Lands Tribunal to the effect   8.39
that the only losses which could qualify for compensation under rule (6) were those which
occurred after the acquisition.[54] There were general observations in decisions of the Court
of Appeal stating that losses were compensatable under rule (6) only if they were the consequence of dispossession of the owner, something which suggested that a loss which
occurred before the date of physical dispossession (or possibly before the date of the notice
to treat) would not be compensatable.[55] While these decisions could suggest that it is only
losses incurred after the acquisition which can qualify for compensation it is not apparent
what is for these purposes to be taken as the date of the acquisition. One possibility is that
the date of the service of the notice to treat is the critical point (or the vesting date where
there is a general vesting declaration which operates as a constructive notice to treat given
on the vesting date) and another possibility is that the date of physical possession is the
critical point.[56] Other dates might be suggested as the date of the acquisition such as the
date of the confirmation of a compulsory purchase order which authorises a compulsory
acquisition. This view of the right to compensation corresponded with the rule in regard to
damages at common law which is that damages cannot be recovered for a loss which has
occurred before the accrual of a cause of action.[57]

A different view of the issue was taken by the Scottish courts applying equivalent legislation   8.40
in Scotland. The Scottish Lands Tribunal refused to follow the line of decisions in the
English Lands Tribunal and refused to accept the view that loss, injury or expense reasonably incurred prior to the date of a notice or deemed notice to treat was not to be compensated. It was said that the statutory language was apt to embrace prior loss provided always
that the loss was naturally and reasonably incurred and could truly be described as loss or
expenditure incurred through the claimant being deprived of his land as opposed to something extraneous or due to some independent business decision of his own.[58] The reasoning
of the Scottish Lands Tribunal was approved by the Court of Session in *Aberdeen City
District Council v Sim*.[59] The reasoning of the Court was that the principle that a loss had to
be consequent upon the compulsory acquisition referred to consequence in a causal sense
rather than in a temporal sense.

---

[54]   *Webb v Stockport Corporation* (1962) 13 P & CR 339; *GE Widden & Co Ltd v Kensington and Chelsea LBC*
(1970) 10 RVR 130; *Bostock, Chater & Sons Ltd v Chelmsford Corporation* (1973) 26 P & CR 321; *Walters, Brett and
Park v South Glamorgan County Council* (1976) 32 P & CR 111; *Bloom (Kosher) & Sons Ltd v Tower Hamlets LBC*
(1977) 35 P & CR 423. In the last of these cases Mr Wellings QC, giving the decision of the Tribunal, stated: 'I cannot accept that a loss is consequent upon an acquisition if it is incurred before there is an acquisition . . . loss which
precedes an acquisition cannot, in my view, be regarded as a consequence of it'.
[55]   In *Harvey v Crawley Development Corporation* [1957] 1 QB 485, [1957] 2 WLR 332, Romer LJ said at
p 494 that a loss only came within the ambit of r (6) if it was 'the natural and reasonable consequence of the dispossession of the owner'. In *Bailey v Derby Corporation* [1965] 1 WLR 213, [1965] 1 All ER 443, Lord Denning MR
said at p 219, having cited the above passage from Romer LJ in the *Crawley Corporation* case: 'You must first ascertain the value of the land. That must be taken as at the date of the notice to treat. Next, you must ascertain the
compensation for disturbance, as it is called. That must be ascertained by looking at what has in fact happened
since the notice to treat'. Here Lord Denning appears to have regarded the date of the notice to treat as the date of
the acquisition.
[56]   See previous note.
[57]   *Prince v Moulton* (1697) 1 Ld Raym 248 (where the wrong alleged was causing a meadow to overflow on
3 August damages could not be claimed for loss of profit in the period 2 July to 3 August).
[58]   *Smith v Strathclyde Regional Council* (1981) 42 P & CR 397.
[59]   *Aberdeen City District Council v Sim* (1982) 264 EG 621. The Court of Session in Scotland is equivalent to the
Court of Appeal in England and Wales.

8.41   The issue came before the Court of Appeal in England in *Prasad v Wolverhampton Borough Council*[60] in connection with a claim for a disturbance payment under section 37 of the Land Compensation Act 1973. Disturbance payments are available when a person without an interest in land which would entitle him to compensation under any other provision is displaced from land of which he is in lawful possession 'in consequence of the acquisition of the land' by an acquiring authority.[61] The claimants moved from their house, used in part as a doctor's surgery, a short time before a notice to treat was served on them. One of the items for which a disturbance payment can be claimed is the reasonable expenses of the person displaced in moving from the land from which he is displaced.[62] The Court of Appeal adopted the same view as in the Scottish authorities and found that the removal costs were recoverable. As Fox LJ pointed out the service of a notice to treat is no more the acquisition of the land than is the compulsory purchase order. The removal costs could be in consequence of the acquisition of land even though they preceded the service of a notice to treat and preceded the date on which the owner became legally bound to give up possession of the land acquired. The decision is in formal terms one on the language of section 37 of the Land Compensation Act 1973 and not on rule (6) of section 5 of the Land Compensation Act 1961 but the reasoning of the Court is applicable to claims under rule (6). Indeed the position of a claimant who claims compensation for disturbance under rule (6) for costs incurred at a time before he is physically dispossessed may be stronger than that of a claimant under section 37 since rule (6) says nothing about the loss having to be 'consequent' on the acquisition of the land.

8.42   The issue was further considered by the Privy Council in *Director of Buildings and Lands v Shun Fung Ironworks Ltd.*[63] That decision was an appeal from Hong Kong and concerned the acquisition (or, as called in Hong Kong, the resumption) for the purposes of a new town of land used for breaking up ships for scrap. The threat of a resumption started in November 1981 whereas the actual resumption occurred on 30 July 1986. In the intervening period, there called the shadow period, the landowners suffered a loss of profit which they might have otherwise made because of their inability to secure long term contracts as a result of the threatened or impending resumption. Section 10 of the Crown Lands Resumption Ordinance provided that compensation should be payable for the amount of loss or damage to a business 'as a result of the resumption'. The date of the resumption was clear in this case since it was provided by the terms of the Ordinance that it was a specific date on which there was a reverter of the land to the Crown, in that case 30 July 1986. The issue was whether the loss during the shadow period could be said to be a loss which was as a result of the resumption when it occurred before the date of the resumption. The Privy Council held by a majority that the loss of profits during the shadow period was recoverable as compensation under the terms of the legislation. The principle was said to be that a loss sustained post-scheme and pre-resumption will not fail for lack of causal connection by reason only that the loss arose before the resumption 'providing it arose in anticipation of resumption and because of the threat which the resumption presented'.[64] It was said that the Scottish decisions and the decision in *Prasad* were correct. Although this decision of the

[60]   *Prasad v Wolverhampton Borough Council* [1983] Ch 353, [1983] 2 WLR 946.
[61]   See ch 12 for disturbance payments.
[62]   Land Compensation Act 1973, s 38(1)(a).
[63]   [1995] 2 AC 111, [1995] 2 WLR 904.
[64]   See per Lord Nicholls, at pp 137–38.

Privy Council is not binding on any court in England and Wales it seems clear from the tenor of this decision, as well as from what was said in *Prasad*, that in principle a loss which is sustained prior to the actual dispossession of the landowner from his land may be recoverable as a loss which comes within the meaning of the word 'disturbance', or within the words 'any other matter not directly based on the value of land', as used in rule (6) of section 5 of the Land Compensation Act 1961. Given that this is so it seems unlikely that there is some earlier cut-off date within the compulsory purchase procedure such as the date of the service of a notice to treat or the date of the making of a general vesting declaration which is a date before which in principle no costs or losses incurred can qualify for compensation under rule (6). The scope which this principle opens for claims under rule (6) is further widened by the fact that 'the value of land', as referred to in the rule, probably means the capital value of the land acquired so that a claim can be made for a loss of the rental value of the land in a period prior to the dispossession of the owner.[65]

6. General Limitation on Claims

The terse language of rule (6) inevitably gives rise to the question of what general limits   8.43
there are on losses, not directly based on the value of the land acquired, which may be
brought within one or other of the two components of rule (6).

As mentioned when discussing the first component of rule (6) a general attempt was made   8.44
by Lord Nicholls in the *Shun Fung*[66] decision to state certain general rules which governed
the assessment of compensation. Although spoken in the context of a decision which concerned loss of profits to a business the rules purport to be generally applicable to all types of claim for compensation. It was said as useful guidelines that there were three conditions which needed to be satisfied if there was to be fair and adequate compensation. The first condition was that there must be a causal connection between the acquisition and the loss in question. The second condition was that the loss must not be too remote if it is to qualify for compensation. The third condition was that a claimant must have taken steps to eliminate or reduce his loss so that if he has failed to do so he cannot fairly expect to be compensated for the loss or for the part of it which should have been mitigated. Certain general observations may be made on these guidelines. They are of a very general nature and are expressly stated to apply to all claims for compensation and not just to claims for compensation for disturbance of similar claims. For example, the third condition, the duty to mitigate, is something which is common to claims for compensation and claims for damages and it can hardly be doubted that the general law on mitigation of damages should be applied within the field of compensation. The general guidelines were given in the context of a particular claim for loss of profits under an Ordinance in force in Hong Kong which specifically provided that compensation was available for 'the amount of loss or damage to a business conducted by a claimant at the date of resumption on the land resumed'.[67] There is no equivalent specific provision in force in England and Wales. Rule (6) states that compensation may be available for disturbance and may be available for any other matter not

---

[65] See paras 8.21, 8.22. Such a claim was allowed in *Pattle v Secretary of State for Transport* [2010] 1 P & CR DG 1, as explained in para 8.46.

[66] See [1995] 2 AC 111, at p 126. See para 8.14.

[67] Crown Lands Resumption Ordinance (now the Lands Resumption Ordinance), s 10(1)(d).

directly based on the value of land. It follows that in this country a claim for compensation founded on rule (6) must be brought within one or other of these heads. Although they have sometimes been treated as such it is plain that the guidelines of Lord Nicholls do not purport to create, and certainly do not create, some universal panacea which solves the problems attendant on particular claims for compensation. Nor do they in themselves answer an important question as to the correct limits of rule (6) claims which is now considered. The question can best be approached by referring to two modern decisions of the Lands Tribunal on the application of rule (6).

8.45   In *Ryde International Plc v London Regional Transport*[68] a claim under rule (6) was allowed in the Tribunal in reliance on the three conditions of Lord Nicholls. In that case a developer of properties for occupation by old persons had its land compulsorily acquired in 1997 for the purposes of a tram link scheme. It was agreed that had it not been for the blighting effect of the scheme the owner would have been able to sell its properties in 1993. It was held that the claimant was entitled to compensation under rule (6) for the holding costs of the property (eg insurance costs and maintenance costs) over the years 1993–97. The calculation of the claim involved considering interest on the capital value of the property over the period 1993–97.

8.46   A more recent decision of the Tribunal, *Pattle v Secretary of State for Transport*,[69] shows the width to which it may be that claims can extend by reason of the application of the three conditions of Lord Nicholls. In the *Pattle* case an area of land, only about a 30th of the total holding of the owners, was acquired for the purposes of the Channel Tunnel Rail Link. The land was used as a joinery business. It had a planning permission granted in 1995, about seven years before the valuation date, for redevelopment by way of 20 new units to be used for commercial purposes. The redevelopment did not take place due to the uncertainties associated with the railway project and instead a rent was obtained by the owners from letting the existing units on the land. There was a claim under rule (6) for the loss alleged to have been suffered in respect of the whole of the land (not just in respect of the part acquired) by reason of the redevelopment scheme not having proceeded, and the Tribunal held that in principle such a claim under rule (6) was sustainable in law. This was held as a result of a preliminary issue and the quantification of the claim was never litigated.

8.47   There are major difficulties in allowing the very wide ambit of rule (6) claims as contemplated in the decisions of the Lands Tribunal just summarised. The fundamental difficulty is that of knowing where to draw the line between what is and is not acceptable as a claim. Many wide claims will relate to a period prior to the acquisition of the land. If claims such as that in *Pattle* are generally allowed under rule (6) it becomes necessary to cast back perhaps for many years into a hypothetical world of what would or might have happened if there had never been any proposals for the scheme of the acquiring authority which ultimately crystallised into a compulsory acquisition and the Tribunal will have to decide what might or would have happened in that hypothetical world. For example, if there had never been proposals for a particular public scheme a piece of land might have been redeveloped at some date in the past so that the landowner can say that he has lost the development value of the land, that is lost the sum which he would have obtained if the land could have been sold for the redevelopment or the profit which he could have made had he redevel-

---

[68]   *Ryde International Plc v London Regional Transport* [2001] 1 EGLR 101.
[69]   *Pattle v Secretary of State for Transport* [2010] 1 P & CR DG 1.

oped the land himself. Apart from the scheme of the acquiring authority interests may have been created in the land different from those which actually existed at the valuation date, so that the claimant could say that he had lost the benefit of those non-existent interests. The process is unending and there seems no logical limit to the type of case which might succeed under rule (6). The rule is in effect being transposed into a general principle that an owner whose land is compulsorily acquired is entitled to compensation for any losses he may have suffered at any time in the past by reason of the scheme of the acquiring authority or the possibility of a compulsory purchase of his land. Rule (6) was enacted in order to put into statutory form the rule which had grown up from decisions of the courts which allowed ancillary items of loss, for instance removal expenses, which were not a part of the open market value of the land as the concept of value was generally understood.[70] It is difficult to believe that it was ever intended to embrace such speculative and potentially large claims as might be brought within it in accordance with recent decisions of the Lands Tribunal purporting to rely upon the wide general guidance given by Lord Nicholls in *Shun Fung*.

There are major theoretical and practical reasons why some more reasonable limitation on rule (6) claims may have to be established if not by the Lands Tribunal then by the higher courts.   8.48

(i)   The process of such claims as were allowed in *Pattle* appears to be one of going back for years into the past prior to the valuation date, imagining that there had never been any scheme of the acquiring authority, and then building up an adjusted world of what might have happened to the land acquired in the absence of such a scheme. This appears to be very close to the process of a 'flight to the clouds' which was at one time an accepted way of applying the Pointe Gourde principle but has now been repeatedly condemned on high authority as unacceptable in law and practice.[71] The law over recent years has increasingly favoured the cancellation assumption for the purposes of assessing compensation, namely the assumption that the scheme of the acquiring authority existed up until it was cancelled at a date at or shortly before the compulsory acquisition.[72] The almost limitless application of rule (6) seems to envisage an investigation of facts which may have to go on in relation to a period over a decade prior to the valuation date. An example is the Crossrail Act 2008 where compensation claims are still being considered and may not even yet have got before the Tribunal whereas the first indication of the London Crossrail scheme goes back well over a decade.[73] There seems no alternative to such a process if claims such as that allowed in *Pattle* and *Ryde* are to continue to find favour.

[70]   See section (a) of this chapter.
[71]   See ch 5, paras 5.53 et seq and see, eg *Waters v Welsh Development Agency* [2004] UKHL 19, [2004] 1 WLR 1304, per Lord Brown.
[72]   The cancellation assumption has been used as one of the foundations of the amendments to the law on the making of planning assumptions introduced by the Localism Act 2011: see ch 7, paras 7.22 et seq. The Lands Tribunal has recently set its fact against allowing s 9 of the Land Compensation Act 1961 to be used as a means of investigating what might have happened in hypothetical circumstances years before the valuation date when assessing the value of the land acquired under r (2) of s 5 of the Land Compensation Act 1961: *GPE (Hanover Square) Ltd v Transport for London* [2012] UKUT 417 (LC): and see ch 5, para 5.49.
[73]   The Crossrail scheme is the largest current civil engineering project in Europe. It is due to be completed in 2018. There are tentative suggestions that the present scheme may be succeeded by 'Crossrail 2' running between Hackney and Chelsea under central London. If the wide approach to r (6) claims favoured by the Lands Tribunal in *Pattle* is generally adopted it may soon be necessary to imagine what hypothetical events may or may not be occurring in the absence of Crossrail 2 since this speculation may become relevant if and when property is acquired for that scheme.

(ii)   What claims of the nature here under discussion often amount to is that land has been in some way blighted in the past by the scheme of the acquiring authority in the sense that it could not have been dealt with or disposed of as it might otherwise have been. There are provisions in Part VI of the Town and Country Planning Act 1990 for compensation for blight available under certain limited circumstances. It seems strange that when land is compulsorily acquired there should be a wholesale remedy for blight prior to the valuation date not provided by Parliament in the specific provisions which do provide compensation for blight. Furthermore the land of many persons may be blighted, or otherwise affected by a prospective public scheme, but if the land of those persons is not in the end acquired they will not obtain any compensation whereas when a person's land is compulsorily acquired he obtains compensation under rule (6) for the past blight.[74]

(iii) Neither the Privy Council in the *Shun Fung* decision nor the Lands Tribunal in the *Ryde* and *Pattle* decisions had before them the benefit of the decision of the House of Lords in *Transport for London v Spirerose Ltd*[75] which explained the current day effect and purpose of the Pointe Gourde principle. Lord Nicholls in his decision in *Shun Fung* on pre-acquisition losses relied considerably on the effect of the Pointe Gourde principle. A central aspect of the decision of the House in *Spirerose* was that the Pointe Gourde principle could not be used so as to investigate whether in the absence of the scheme of the acquiring authority a planning permission might have been granted for development of the land acquired and which was not granted because of the existence of the scheme. It is not easy to see why if this rule applies to the question of whether a planning permission might have been granted in the past in the absence of the scheme it should not apply to the question of whether other events relevant to the value of the land and to the loss to the claimant might or might not have occurred in the absence of the scheme in the pre-acquisition period. If the *Spirerose* decision and its analysis and re-statement in it of the status and effect of the Pointe Gourde principle today applies generally, as it was surely intended to, then it is difficult to see how decisions such as the two decisions of the Lands Tribunal discussed earlier can be reconciled with what the House of Lords recently said.

(iv)   It is a general principle of law that when it is necessary to investigate past events in hypothetical circumstances in order to quantify an amount of damages or compensation what has to be considered is the probability of those events having happened.[76] It therefore appears that in order for rule (6) claims of the wide nature under discussion to be allowed what should be considered is not whether past events, such as a redevelopment of the property or the creation of different interests in the property or the sale of the property, would have happened in the past as a matter of certainty but rather the probability of these events having happened with a consequent reduction in the quantum of compensation to represent the degree of probability. This creates a further complexity and difficulty in the supposed function of the Lands Tribunal in flying to the clouds in deciding claims of this nature.

---

[74] These considerations were mentioned by Lord Nicholls in *Shun Fung* but were not regarded as preventing the wide formulation of the boundaries of acceptable compensation which he put forward. The same matters were also considered in the powerful dissenting opinions of Lord Slynn and Lord Mustill at [1995] 2 AC 111, at p 143.

[75] [2009] UKHL 44, [2009] 1 WLR 1797.

[76] *Porter v Secretary of State for Transport* [1996] 3 All ER 693, approved by the House of Lords in *Spirerose*, above n 75.

It is perhaps plain that the law on the boundaries of claims under rule (6) is in a state which 8.49
is both uncertain and unsatisfactory at the present day. There may in truth be only three
ways forward in order to introduce a degree of reality and reasonable limitations into this
subject. One is that the matter should be considered by the higher courts in order that some
clearer rules can be articulated as to what is the true ambit of rule (6) claims where they
relate to pre-acquisition losses or events. This may require some modification or qualification of the very general guidelines suggested by Lord Nicholls in *Shun Fung*. There may be
no great difficulty in revisiting the guidelines in the light of later experience since they are
guidelines only and, of course, being contained in a decision of the Privy Council, are not
binding as a matter of precedent on any English court.

The second possibility is that the principle that a loss must not be too remote if it is to 8.50
qualify for compensation can be invoked in order to create a realistic limitation on the
width of claims. Of course the difficulty with remoteness as a tool for containing claims is
that it is very difficult to establish a criterion which provides clear guidance as to when a loss
is or is not too remote. The general principles which have been worked out in connection
with remoteness of damage in claims for common law damages for breaches of contract
and torts are unlikely to offer useful guidance in the context of compensation claims and
losses which have occurred prior to the date of acquisition.

The rule as to remoteness of damage in tort is based on the foreseeability of a particular 8.51
type of loss as something likely to be caused by the tort with foreseeability judged as at the
date of the commission of the tort. [77] This principle might offer the closest analogy for judging remoteness where that is necessary in the context of statutory compensation for the
compulsory acquisition of land since that acquisition can for some purposes be analysed as
the commission of an act which would be a wrong in civil law apart from its statutory
authorisation.[78] The difficulty, as pointed out earlier, is that the main problems under rule
(6) relate to losses which have allegedly been incurred prior to the acquisition and it is
therefore difficult to gain much assistance from what was foreseeable at the date of the
acquisition.[79] One is therefore left with only the subjective view of the Lands Tribunal on
whether a loss is or is not too remote with no coherent guiding principle to assist that decision.[80] Nonetheless it may be possible to scrutinise and limit claims of the broad nature as
held to be valid in *Pattle*, or even wider claims, by the criterion of remoteness.

A third way forward may be to refine the nature of causation as a criterion of the validity of 8.52
claims under rule (6). It seems clear that a claim for compensation for a loss under rule (6)
may be established on the basis that it was caused by a compulsory acquisition of land even
though the loss was incurred prior to the acquisition (whatever precisely is taken in this
context to be the date of the acquisition). What in truth this rule generally means is that the

---

[77] *The Wagon Mound (No 1)* [1961] AC 388, [1961] 2 WLR 126. See para 8.15.
[78] See ch 3, para 3.3.
[79] See para 8.16.
[80] For example, in *Wrexham Maelor Borough Council v MacDougall* (1995) 69 P & CR 109 (the facts of which
are given in para 8.26) the Court of Appeal confined itself to stating that it was open to the Lands Tribunal to
conclude that the claim under the second limb of r (6) was not too remote in law without enunciating any principle which governed the issue of remoteness. A similar problem arises in connection with claims for compensation for injurious affection under s 10 of the Compulsory Purchase Act 1965 where the courts have again said that
the damage to the land affected must not be too remote but have not stated any clearly applicable principle for
determining when a loss is or is not too remote to qualify for compensation: see ch 10, para 10.53, and *Moto
Hospitality Ltd v Secretary of State for Transport* [2007] EWCA Civ 764, [2003] 1 WLR 2822.

loss was caused not by the acquisition but by the prospect of the acquisition. A purist view of causation suggests that a loss can be said to be caused by the prospect of an acquisition if on the balance of probabilities that loss would not have occurred apart from that prospect of the acquisition.[81] However, such an approach opens the doors almost limitlessly for claims for events which have happened, or for losses caused because an event has not happened, at any time in the past from the date when the scheme which underlies the acquisition first appeared. It may therefore be possible to provide a more realistic limit on the availability of claims under rule (6) for loss caused by pre-acquisition events if a more stringent approach to causation is adopted in relation to such events, possibly a rule that an event, or the absence of an event, which leads to a loss is for present purposes only caused by the compulsory acquisition if it occurred when the prospect of the acquisition was imminent and the loss was an inevitable, or nearly inevitable, result of the proposed acquisition.[82] After all if a loss can be said to be caused by a compulsory acquisition when the loss occurred before the acquisition, and is in truth a loss caused by the prospect of the acquisition, it needs little further elaboration to curtail the well-nigh boundless nature of claims opened by this principle by the introduction of a more stringent criterion of causation.

[81] It may be that even this approach is flawed since the occurrence of past hypothetical events usually has to be assessed as that of the strength of their probability rather than on the balance of probabilities when matters of damages or compensation are in issue: see para 8.48(iv).

[82] In relation to home loss payments under s 29 of the Land Compensation Act 1973 there is a statutory rule in s 29(3) that a person can claim a payment even if he leaves a dwelling before he is required to do so by the acquiring authority but only where occupation is given up on or after the date on which the authority were authorised to acquire the interest of that person, that date usually being the date of the confirmation or making of a compulsory purchase order: see ch 11, para 11.35.

9

Acquisition of a Part of Land

(A) THE LEGISLATION

It happens not infrequently that an acquiring authority needs to acquire not the whole but   9.1
only a part of the land of a particular landowner. Here a part of the land means a part in the
geographical sense. The question of the acquisition of one interest only in an area of land,
for example the acquisition of a leasehold interest but not the freehold, is considered elsewhere.[1] It has always been recognised that when a person is left with only a part of the land
which he owns or in which he has an interest he may suffer a loss in connection with the
land which he retains and that he should be compensated for this loss separately and in
addition to being compensated for the value of the land which is acquired from him. The
basic legal provision which provides for this element of compensation has remained largely
unchanged since the Lands Clauses Consolidation Act 1845. Section 63 of that Act has been
replaced in slightly modernised language by section 7 of the Compulsory Purchase Act 1965
which is the legislation currently in force. Section 7 provides:

> In assessing the compensation to be paid by the acquiring authority under this Act regard shall be
> had not only to the value of the land to be purchased by the acquiring authority, but also to the
> damage, if any, to be sustained by the owner of the land by reason of the severing of the land pur-
> chased from the other land of the owner, or otherwise injuriously affecting that other land by the
> exercise of the powers conferred by this or the special Act.

The words which start with 'but also' are sometimes referred to as the second limb of section 7 and it is the operation of this second limb which is the main subject matter of this
chapter. The other topic of general importance covered is the opportunity for a landowner,
a part of whose land is acquired, to compel the acquiring authority to purchase the whole
of his land. The second limb of section 7 itself has two parts: damage caused by severance
and damage caused by some other form of injurious affection.

Attention should be paid to the structure of the statutory language. Compensation payable   9.2
is for damage to be sustained by the owner of the land acquired. In referring to damage the
provision is in contrast to the first limb of the same section where, when referring to the
compensation for the land acquired, the basis of compensation is said to be the value of that
land. In practice, under a claim for compensation relating to retained land, it is the reduction in the value of that land which constitutes the damage and thus the compensation.
Damage sustained by the owner of the land does not encompass any personal loss or other
loss which is not damage to the retained land itself. The statutory language also refers to
damage 'to be sustained'. This element of futurity does no more than recognise that the

---

[1] See section (c) of ch 2.

damage to the retained land is often likely to be experienced in the future as a result of the activities of the acquiring authority. In reality the value of the retained land will be reduced in value at the date of the acquisition of the land acquired by reason of the anticipated activities of the acquiring authority and it is this reduction in value at the date of the acquisition which constitutes the compensation.[2]

9.3   A further aspect of the statutory language to be noted is that there are two distinct forms of damage which may give rise to a right to compensation. The first form of damage is that caused by the severing of the land acquired from the retained land. The second form of damage is that the retained land is otherwise injuriously affected by the exercise of the powers conferred by the Compulsory Purchase Act 1965 or the special Act.[3] Injurious affection is a somewhat antiquated term taken from the Lands Clauses Consolidation Act 1845, which means no more than damage to land so that the underlying right to compensation is for compensation for damage to land.[4] Although section 7 of the Compulsory Purchase Act 1965 refers to 'damage' to be sustained, that damage has to arise by reason of injurious affection, and injurious affection normally connotes a diminution in the value of the land affected.[5]

9.4   The severance of the land acquired from the retained land may be a physical severance in that a part of a single parcel or area of land is acquired. Following the acquisition and the severance the land acquired and the retained land will be in separate ownership but contiguous in that they will have a common boundary. Severance of this sort is not necessary for a claim for compensation to be sustained in respect of the retained land. The retained land may be some distance from the land acquired. There is no limitation in the legislation such as that the retained land must be 'contiguous' or 'adjacent' to the land acquired so that in principle the two pieces of land may be any distance from each other.[6] Section 7 simply refers to 'the other land of the owner' without stating where that other land has to be located. The essential fact which must be present if a claim is to be sustained under section 7 is that the claimant is the owner of an interest in both the land acquired and the retained land. The severance must be a severance of ownership and may or may not also be a physical or geographical severance in the sense that a part of a single plot of land is acquired. Land normally means an interest in land and it is not a necessary condition of a claim that

---

[2] *Sisters of Charity v Rockingham* [1922] 2 AC 315. This principle may be contrasted to the rule applicable to claims for the reduction in value caused to persons by the use of public works where no land of the owner is acquired and where compensation is payable under Pt I of the Land Compensation Act 1973. In that case the reduction in value has to be assessed as at a date, called the first claim date, which is one year after the public works have been first brought into use: see ch 13.

[3] The language is in fact arguably ungrammatical. 'Severing' is apparently used as a noun whereas 'injuriously affecting' is a participle. The section would have been better phrased if it had read 'or by some other form of injurious affection caused to that other land by'. The infelicitous language goes back to the Lands Clauses Consolidation Act 1845 and, although there was some modernisation of the language when s 63 of that Act was replaced by s 7 of the Compulsory Purchase Act 1965, no opportunity was taken to remedy this possible deficiency. It does not seem that the effect or the operation of s 7 has been affected by this matter.

[4] See ch 3, para 3.20. See also ch 10, para 10.13.

[5] *Penny's Bay Investment Co Ltd v Director of Lands* (2010) 13 HKCFAR 287 (Ct of Final Appeal, Hong Kong), per Lord Hoffmann at para 34 citing *Re Penny and South Eastern Railway Co* (1857) 7 E&B 660, at p 669. It follows that if no diminution in the value of the retained land can be shown a claim under s 7 will not normally succeed: *Frederick Powell & Son v Devon County Council* (1979) 50 EG 659. See also n 67.

[6] In *Cowper Essex v Acton London Board* (1889) 14 App Cas 153, the land acquired was separated from the retained land by a railway line. See also *Holditch v Canadian Northern Ontario Rly* [1916] 1 AC 536. Cf the language used in other legislation such as s 7 of the Land Compensation Act 1961 which refers to land 'contiguous or adjacent' to the land acquired when providing for the effect of 'betterment': see ch 6, para 6.50.

the owner of the two pieces of land has the same interest in both of them.[7] If a person's freehold land is acquired he can in principle claim compensation for the severance of his freehold interest in that land from a leasehold interest held by him in other land, and of course vice versa. It is not necessary that the claimant is in occupation of both or either of the areas of land acquired and retained.

Damage by severance therefore means damage caused to the common owner by reason of the severance or separation of the ownership of the land acquired and the retained land. Many examples of such damage can be found. The retained land may have relied on the land acquired as a means of access or of convenient access to a public highway prior to the severance so that the retained land is obviously reduced in value if it is not possible to secure an alternative highway access or a new access has to be obtained at a cost from a different owner. The land acquired may have had an amenity value to the retained land such as a part of a garden or a buffer against unsightly development so that the retained land is reduced in value by reason of the loss of the amenity. There may be a commercial connection between the two areas of land, for instance where a business carried on at the retained land relied on the land acquired for providing parking or storage space. The reduction in the commercial value of the retained land will then form the basis of the claim for compensation under the second limb of section 7. While the damage for which compensation is payable must be damage to land, and not to a business, the fact that the usefulness of a piece of land for a particular business use is reduced may reduce the value of the land and so result in damage to the land.[8] The word used in section 7 of the Compulsory Purchase Act 1965 is 'severing' and the expression 'severance compensation' is frequently used to describe the type of damage here identified or, more loosely, any kind of damage under the second limb of section 7. It should be remembered that, as stated earlier, when the land acquired is severed from the retained land there is not a physical severance in the way in which the head of Charles I was severed from his body. Land is an immovable asset and the land acquired will remain next to or near to the retained land. What is severed is the common ownership of the two areas of land since the ownership of the land acquired passes to the acquiring authority.

9.5

The other form of damage, injurious affection, has nothing to do with severance as such. It simply means that the retained land is injuriously affected, that is damaged, by the exercise of the powers conferred on the acquiring authority. These powers must derive from the Compulsory Purchase Act 1965 or the special Act. The special Act means the compulsory purchase order and the enactment under which the compulsory purchase is authorised,[9] that is the Act which conferred on the acquiring authority its power to effect the compulsory purchase, often called the empowering Act. In general terms what this phraseology amounts to is that the dispossessed landowner is entitled to compensation for any reduction in the value of his retained land attributable to the works which the acquiring authority has carried out, or which it intends to carry out, pursuant to its statutory powers on the

9.6

---

[7] Land is stated in s 1(3) of the Compulsory Purchase Act 1965 to include anything within any definition of that expression in the enactment under which the purchase is authorised. Many statutes when conferring a power of compulsory purchase define land to include an interest in land. Land is so defined in sch 1 to the Interpretation Act 1978. In *Holt v Gas, Light and Coke Co* (1872) LR 7 QB 728, the land acquired and the land retained, which had been reduced in value by the severance, were held under different leases.

[8] See section (h) of ch 4 and see n 75 to para 9.40. See also ch 10, para 10.42.

[9] Compulsory Purchase Act 1965, s 1(2).

land acquired from him or on other land.[10] An obvious example of this form of damage would be where the acquiring authority acquired a part of a property on which to build a part of a new road and the retained land of the owner was reduced in value by the construction and use, or the prospect of the construction and use, of the new road with its attendant noise or other pollution. The compensation extends to the effect of both the execution and the use of the works.[11] It should, however, be pointed out that while it is the exercise of the powers of the acquiring authority by carrying out works which usually gives rise to a claim under section 7 the damage can, in principle, be that caused by the exercise of any of the powers of the acquiring authority under the empowering legislation.

9.7   It is sometimes suggested that compensation for the effect of a compulsory acquisition on retained land of the landowner can be claimed under rule (6) of section 5 of the Land Compensation Act 1961, presumably on the footing that the compensation is for a matter not directly based on the value of the land acquired.[12] Such a suggestion is incorrect in law. Compensation for the value of the land acquired is payable under the first limb of section 7 of the Compulsory Purchase Act 1965. Compensation under rule (6) is a part of the value of the land acquired and the entitlement to that compensation as a part of the value of the land acquired arose from judicial exegesis of the first limb of section 7 (when it was the first limb of section 63 of the Lands Clauses Consolidation Act 1845) and subsequently from statutory provisions intended to give effect to that exegesis.[13] The entitlement to compensation for injurious affection to other land of the landowner which he retains is governed wholly by the second limb of section 7 of the Compulsory Purchase Act 1965 (formerly the second limb of section 63 of the Lands Clauses Consolidation Act 1845). The statutory rules which apply to the assessment of compensation for the land acquired contained in the Land Compensation Act 1961 do not apply to claims for compensation for injurious affection to the retained land. The distinction which must be drawn between the second limb of section 7 of the Compulsory Purchase Act 1965, which relates wholly to the retained land, and rule (6) of section 5 of the Land Compensation Act 1961, which relates wholly to the land acquired, is considered more fully in section (e) of chapter 8.[14]

9.8   A question which is sometimes asked is why a person a part of whose land is acquired is treated in what appears to be a particularly favourable fashion. Suppose that person A has the whole of his land acquired for the building of a new road. He receives compensation equal to the value of his land and, because of the rule that in general the effect on the value of his land of the scheme of the acquiring authority is left out of account, he obtains an amount of compensation which disregards any reduction in the value of his land due to the road. Person B has a part of his land acquired for the new road. He receives as compensa-

[10] The exact area or location of the land on which the works of the acquiring authority can give rise to a claim for compensation has been modified since the legislation was first enacted in 1845 but is still subject to some degree of doubt in law. This subject is considered more fully later: see section (e) of this chapter.

[11] This is to be compared with compensation due under Pt I of the Land Compensation Act 1973 where it is only the effect of the use of the works which gives an entitlement to compensation: see section (b) of ch 13.

[12] See ch 8 for r (6) compensation. Decisions of the Lands Tribunal which suggest that claims in respect of the land retained may be made under r (6) are: *Pattle v Secretary of State for Transport* [2010] 1 P & CR DG 1; *Brickell v Shaftesbury* (1955) 5 P & CR 174; *Tamplin's Brewery v Brighton CBC* (1971) 22 P & CR 746.

[13] The original statutory provision was r (6) of s 2 of the Acquisition of Land (Assessment of Compensation) Act 1919, now replaced by r (6) of the Land Compensation Act 1961. See section (a) of ch 8 for a full explanation of the origin and purpose of r (6).

[14] See also para 9.14 and see *English Property Co v Kingston upon Thames London Borough Council* (1998) 77 P & CR 1; *Argyle Motors v Birkenhead Corporation* [1975] AC 99, per Lord Wilberforce at p 133.

tion: (a) the value of the land acquired disregarding the effect on its value of the road, and (b) the amount of any reduction in the value of his retained land due to the road works in accordance with the provisions discussed in this chapter. Person C has no land acquired for the new road but finds that the road reduces the value of his land. He receives no compensation under the main statutory provisions for compensation. There is an apparent injustice or anomaly in this situation. Until 1973 there was nothing to mitigate the anomaly. Someone in the position of person C may now be able to obtain compensation for the effect of the new road under Part I of the Land Compensation Act 1973 but there are limits on that right. For instance, properties in commercial use are excluded from any entitlement to compensation under the 1973 Act where their value exceeds a certain limit.[15]

(B) COMPELLING PURCHASE OF THE WHOLE

There are two separate procedures under which a person, a part of whose land is being acquired, can require the acquiring authority to acquire the whole of his land. The first procedure applies only where the acquiring authority exercises its power of acquisition by serving a notice to treat. The second procedure applies where the authority exercises its power by making a general vesting declaration.[16] The first procedure is contained in section 8 of the Compulsory Purchase Act 1965. The second procedure is in schedule 1 to the Compulsory Purchase (Vesting Declarations) Act 1981.[17] It is a matter of regret that what is substantially the same rule is bifurcated into two separate sets of provisions. The law is further complicated by a separate set of provisions which apply only when agricultural land is acquired. It is proposed first to describe the procedure applicable when a notice to treat has been served.

9.9

1. The General Rule: Notices to Treat

The general impact of section 8 of the Compulsory Purchase Act 1965 is that when an acquiring authority seeks to acquire a part of a person's land by serving a notice to treat that person if he wishes can compel the authority to acquire the whole of his land unless the part can be acquired without substantial detriment to the remainder. Sometimes the empowering legislation which confers power for the acquisition of the land contains its own provisions which are to the same general effect as section 8 of the 1965 Act.

9.10

The right of the landowner to require the acquisition of the whole of his land arises: (a) where the acquiring authority proposes to acquire a part of a house, building or manufactory, and

9.11

---

[15] See ch 13 for Pt I of the Land Compensation Act 1973. It is possible that in limited circumstances a person in the position of person C can claim compensation for injurious affection caused to his land by the execution (but not the use) of the works of the acquiring authority under s 10 of the Compulsory Purchase Act 1965: see ch 10.

[16] The two procedures are described in sections (j) and (q) of ch 2.

[17] Section 8 of the Compulsory Purchase Act 1965 is not on the face of it restricted in its operation. However, para 2(3) of sch 1 to the Compulsory Purchase (Vesting Declarations) Act 1981 states that s 8 does not apply to land in respect of which a general vesting declaration is made. The second procedure continues to make use of some of the antiquated phraseology of the first procedure which goes back to the Lands Clauses Consolidation Act 1845.

(b) where the acquiring authority proposes to acquire a part of a park or garden belonging to a house. In the first case the owner can compel the acquisition of the whole of the house, building or manufactory unless the part proposed to be acquired can be taken without material detriment to the whole building. A test which has been applied in deciding whether there is material detriment is to ask whether, on part of the property being taken, the remainder of the property would be less useful or less valuable in some significant degree.[18] The fact that the owner will receive compensation under section 7 of the Compulsory Purchase Act 1965 for any damage to the part of his land which he retains by reason of its severance from the part acquired cannot in itself mean that there can be no material detriment since otherwise it might rarely be possible to show material detriment. In the second case, where a part of a park or garden belonging to a house is proposed to be acquired, the owner of the house can compel the acquisition of the whole park or garden unless the part proposed to be acquired can be taken without seriously affecting the amenity or convenience of the house.[19] In order for these provisions to apply the same person must own the part of the property which the acquiring authority proposes to acquire and the remainder of the property which that person requires that authority to acquire. The provisions will not therefore apply if the part proposed to be acquired is owned by one company and the remainder of the property is owned by an associated company. Nor will the provisions apply if a part of a property is owned by trustees on behalf of a beneficiary who owns the remainder of the property.

9.12   The detriment or damage to a building caused by the taking of a part of a person's land, or the effect on the convenience of a house caused by the taking of a part of its park or garden, may arise simply from the fact that the ownership of the part of the land acquired and the part of the retained land are severed from each other. However, in many cases the detriment or damage or effect may be due wholly or mainly to the use of the part of the land acquired as proposed by the acquiring authority. If a part of a garden is taken to construct a part of a road it is the proposed use of the land taken and other land as a road which is most likely to harm the nearby house. It is therefore provided that in judging whether there is material detriment or damage to a building or a serious effect on the amenity or convenience of a house account is to be taken not only of the effect of the severance of the land acquired from the retained land but also the use proposed for the land acquired and, where the land acquired is to be the subject of works or purposes which extend also to other land, account is to be taken of the effect of the whole of the works and of the use to be made of other land as well as the works and the use proposed on the land acquired.[20]

9.13   The reference to 'house, building or manufactory' goes back to section 92 of the Lands Clauses Consolidation Act 1845 although that section simply provided that a person could require that the whole of his land was acquired without his having to show that the taking of only a part would cause material detriment to the property. There is a substantial amount of learning and authority on the meaning of the above words. The general tendency has been to attribute a very wide meaning to the concept of a house but to narrow the understanding of what is meant by a building. A house includes all that which would pass on a conveyance of a house including a garden and general curtilage.[21] Thus a private access way

---

[18]   *Ravenseft Properties Ltd v Hillingdon LBC* (1969) 20 P & CR 483.
[19]   Compulsory Purchase Act 1965, s 8(1).
[20]   Land Compensation Act 1973, s 58(1). A similar principle applies when assessing compensation for injurious affection to the land retained: see section (e) of this chapter.
[21]   *Grosvenor v Hampstead Junction Rly* (1857) 26 LJ Ch 731; *King v Wycombe Rly Co* (1860) 29 LJ Ch 462.

to a house or a courtyard is a part of the house for present purposes.[22] On the other hand a piece of land of six and a quarter acres used for grazing horses and cows and separated from the house by a public highway was held not to be a part of the house.[23] The word 'house' is not confined to buildings used exclusively or primarily for residential purposes but can include a shop or an inn.[24] Thus premises used for business purposes may be a house and a house may even include a hospital.[25] A warehouse may be a house for present purposes,[26] as may a church.[27] It has been said that the meaning of the word 'house' in the statute is that attributed to the words in *Coke upon Littleton*.[28] It has also been said that each of these descriptions, house, building and manufactory, is different from the others[29] although the modern tendency has been to accept that a property comes somewhere within the ambit of the section without it being necessary to determine which of the descriptions is most apposite to cover it. A manufactory is what would today be called a factory or industrial premises. If a part of the building is used for manufacturing purposes the whole building can constitute a manufactory.[30] While the word 'house' has been given a wide and liberal meaning to include, for example, property used as a shop which would not be called a house in ordinary parlance, the word 'building' has been construed more strictly as meaning something which is of the nature of a house.[31] It must be borne in mind that the decisions on the meaning of a building are under section 92 of the Lands Clauses Consolidation Act 1845 where the expression used was 'any house or other building'. The omission of the word 'other' in section 8(1)(a) of the Compulsory Purchase Act 1965 may indicate that a less restricted meaning should now be given to the word 'building'.

There is also some learning on what is meant by a park or a garden. The land in question must belong to a house so that a wholly separate area used as a recreation ground or as allotments would not be included. One judicial definition of a garden is that it is a substantially homogenous area, substantially devoted to the growing of fruits, flowers and vegetables.[32] An ordinary garden area which is a part of the curtilage of a house is clearly a garden for present purposes but a further area of rough pasture severed from the garden by a fence and a gate has been held not to be a part of a garden.[33] The nature of a park is that it is a substantial piece of land attached to or surrounding a country house or mansion.[34]

9.14

---

[22] *Caledonian Rly Co v Turcan* [1898] AC 256.
[23] *Steele v Midland Rly Co* (1866) 1 Ch App 275.
[24] *Richards v Swansea Improvement and Tramway Co* (1878) 9 Ch D 425, per James LJ at pp 431–32.
[25] *Ravenseft Properties Ltd v Hillingdon LBC* (1968) 20 P & CR 483; *Governors of St Thomas's Hospital v Charing Cross Rly Co* (1861) 1 J & H 400.
[26] *Caledonian Rly Co v Turcan*, above n 22; *Siegenburgh v Metropolitan District Rly* (1883) 49 LT 554.
[27] *London Transport Executive v Congregational Union of England and Wales* (1978) 37 P & CR 155.
[28] *Barnes v Southsea Rly Co* (1884) 27 Ch D 536, per Bacon V-C.
[29] *Richards v Swansea Improvement and Tramways Co*, above n 24, per Bowen LJ.
[30] *Brook v Manchester, Sheffield and Lincolnshire Rly Co* [1895] 2 Ch 571.
[31] See, eg *Regents Canal and Dock Co v London County Council* [1912] 1 Ch 583 (the canal and undertaking of a company held not to be within the words 'house or other building or manufactory' in s 92 of the Lands Clauses Consolidation Act 1845); *Richards v Swansea Improvement and Tramways Co*, above n 24.
[32] *Bomford v Osborne (Inspector of Taxes)* [1942] AC 14, [1941] 2 All ER 424, per Lord Wright at p 40.
[33] *Methuen-Campbell v Walters* [1979] 1 QB 523, [1979] 2 WLR 113, a decision on the meaning of the word 'garden' in s 2(3) of the Leasehold Reform Act 1967.
[34] *R v Bradford* [1908] 1 KB 365 (field of 30 acres attached to a house); *Pease v Courtney* [1904] 2 Ch 503 (35 acres attached to a house); *White and Collins v Minister of Health* [1939] 2 KB 838 (compulsory purchase order quashed when it purported to authorise the acquisition of 23 acres of an area of 35 acres which surrounded a large house in Yorkshire since the empowering Act prohibited the acquisition of any land which formed part of any park or garden).

9.15   It is unfortunate that the legislation does not simply state that the owner of any property of which a part is acquired can require that the whole of his land is acquired when the taking of a part would cause material detriment to the part not acquired. As it is most types of structures will fall somewhere within the description of a house or a building or a manufactory especially if a wide and normal meaning is allowed to the word 'building'. On the other hand they may well be open areas which are not a park or garden to which section 8(1) will not apply. [35]

9.16   No method is prescribed by section 8 of the 1965 Act for informing the acquiring authority that a landowner requires that the whole of his land should be acquired. Obviously some notification must be given to the acquiring authority. It is not even stated whether the notification has to be in writing as opposed to merely oral. In practice an owner who has received a notice to treat and who wishes to invoke section 8(1) would be well advised to state clearly and in writing to the acquiring authority that he requires the whole of his land to be acquired. Nor does section 8(1) state when the notification by the owner has to be given. The notification cannot be given before a notice to treat has been served since until then it is not known whether the acquiring authority will proceed by way of the notice to treat procedure, or by way of a general vesting declaration, and if the latter course is taken section 8 of the Compulsory Purchase Act will not apply. [36] It appears that the notification must be given prior to entry by the acquiring authority. [37] It should be noted that in the case of a park or garden belonging to a house what the acquiring authority can be required to purchase is the whole of the park or garden and not the house to which it belongs. It should also be noted that where an authority proposes to acquire a part of a house, building or manufactory what it can be required to purchase under section 8 of the Compulsory Purchase Act 1965 is the whole of the remainder of the house, building or manufactory. This provision does not entitle the landowner to require the purchase of some further part of the building or of the park or garden as opposed to the whole of it. As will be explained the law on this last matter is significantly different where the acquiring authority uses the general vesting declaration procedure to acquire land.

9.17   If there is a dispute on whether there is material detriment to the retained part of the building caused by the taking of a part of it or a serious effect on the amenity or convenience of a house caused by the taking of a part of its park or garden, that is a dispute on whether the acquiring authority can be required to take the whole, that issue is decided by the Lands Tribunal. [38] Of course if the Tribunal decides that there is material detriment, or a serious effect on amenity or convenience, the whole of the building or the whole of the park or garden must be acquired and the compensation will be the value of the whole. It seems that the acquiring authority is bound to acquire the whole of the land of the owner if the

---

[35] An example of structures which were held not to be within any part of this description was the canal and enterprise of the Regents Canal and Dock Company: see n 31 above. If the open land is agricultural land it may be possible to compel the purchase of the whole of it under provisions in the Land Compensation Act 1973 explained later in this section of the chapter.

[36] See para 9.9. The equivalent procedure when a general vesting declaration is used does prescribe a time limit of 28 days for the giving of a notice by a landowner: see para 9.19.

[37] *Glasshouse Properties Ltd v Department of Transport* (1993) 66 P & CR 285.

[38] Compulsory Purchase Act 1965, s 8(1). The statute states that the whole of the land required by the landowner shall be acquired unless the Lands Tribunal determines that there is no material detriment or serious effect so that an acquiring authority which is unwilling to acquire the whole of an owner's land has the burden of obtaining a determination from the Tribunal.

Tribunal so rules even though there was no power under the compulsory purchase order or the empowering Act to do so. If the Tribunal decides that there is no material detriment, or no serious effect on amenity or convenience, then the acquiring authority continues to acquire only the part of the building or of the park or garden as it proposes, but compensation will be payable in the ordinary way for the value of the land acquired and for any damage caused to the retained land as a result of its severance from the land acquired, or as a result of the exercise of its powers by the acquiring authority.

2. The General Rule: General Vesting Declarations

The procedure which applies when a general vesting declaration is made is in its essentials the same as when a notice to treat has been served although significant differences do appear.

9.18

The procedure again applies to a proposal, in this instance made by a general vesting declaration, to acquire a part only of a house, building or manufactory or a part only of a park or garden belonging to a house.[39] The meaning of these expressions has been explained. They extend to most, although not to all, proposals to acquire a part of the land of a landowner. A person who receives a notice explaining that his land is within a general vesting declaration and the effect of the declaration may give notice to the acquiring authority within 28 days requiring the authority to acquire the whole of his interest in the land.[40]

9.19

The immediate effect of a notice given by the landowner is that until his notice has been dealt with, under the provisions now to be described, the general vesting declaration does not vest in the acquiring authority the interest the subject of the notice nor does it entitle the acquiring authority to enter into and take possession of the land within that interest, that is the powers which would otherwise exist under section 8 of the Compulsory Purchase (Vesting Declarations) Act 1981 are suspended.[41]

9.20

The acquiring authority then has three months to take one of three courses. First, it may serve on the owner a notice withdrawing the notice to treat which has been deemed to be served by the making of the general vesting declaration. The result is that there is no vesting of the land in the acquiring authority and the authority has no entitlement to possession of the land in question. In effect the compulsory purchase is withdrawn as regards the land of the owner concerned.[42]

9.21

The second course available to the acquiring authority is to agree that it will acquire the whole of the land of the landowner. In that case the general vesting declaration and the compulsory purchase order have effect as if the whole of the land of the owner was to be acquired. This effect occurs even if the compulsory purchase order could not have authorised the acquisition of the whole of the land, for example if the balance of the land of the

9.22

---

[39] Compulsory Purchase (Vesting Declarations) Act 1981, sch 1, para 2(1).
[40] Ibid, para 2(2). The notice of the making of the general vesting declaration is under s 6 of the Compulsory Purchase (Vesting Declarations) Act 1981. This time limit is to be contrasted with the procedure when a notice to treat is served when there is no statutory time limit for the giving of a notice requiring the acquisition of the whole of a property.
[41] Ibid, para 3.
[42] Ibid, para 4(1)(a), (6).

owner was not required for the purposes of the scheme of the acquiring authority. In this case the landowner therefore achieves that which he seeks by his notice to the acquiring authority.[43]

9.23   The third course available to the acquiring authority is to refer the notice of objection to severance to the Lands Tribunal and to notify the landowner that a notice has been so referred. This is a course which will be taken by the acquiring authority if it is not willing either to abandon the acquisition of all land from the landowner in question or to acquire the whole of the land of that landowner. The consequences of this course are considered below.

9.24   There is a sanction on the acquiring authority in that if it does not within the three months permitted take one or other of the three courses available to it then it is deemed to have taken the first course and is deemed to have withdrawn the notice to treat deemed to have been served on the landowner in respect of the whole of his interest in the land which the authority proposed to acquire from him.[44]

9.25   It is at this stage of the process that the difference between the notice to treat procedure and the general vesting declaration procedure most starkly emerges in the context of the provisions here being explained. The third course open to the acquiring authority that receives a notice of objection to severance from the landowner is to refer the notice to the Lands Tribunal and to notify the landowner that the notice has been so referred.[45] The Tribunal then has two courses which it can make. It can determine that there will be no material detriment to the house, building or manufactory, or that in the case of a park or garden there will be no serious effect on the amenity or inconvenience of the house if only a part of the land of the owner was acquired. In that event the suspension on the operation of the general vesting declaration and on the further progress of the compulsory acquisition ends and the acquisition remains one of taking only the part of the land of the landowner which is within the proposals of the acquiring authority.[46] In reaching its determination on this question the Tribunal is required to take into account not only the effect of the severance but also the effect of the use to be made of the part proposed to be acquired and of other land by the acquiring authority. This repeats the rule in relation to cases where the notice to treat procedure has been used.[47]

9.26   The second course is as follows. The Tribunal, if it makes a determination that there will be material detriment to the house, building or manufactory or serious effect to the amenity or convenience of the house, must go on to determine the area of the total land of the landowner (which may be the whole or a part of that land) which the acquiring authority 'ought to be required to take'. No guidance is given as to how the Tribunal is to determine this question. It seems that the Tribunal must alight upon either the whole of the land of the landowner, or a part of that land which the acquiring authority does not propose to acquire, as the land which ought to be acquired. In any event the effect of such a determination is that the general vesting declaration has effect in relation to the area so determined by the Tribunal as though that area had been comprised in the general vesting declaration and as

---

[43]   Ibid, para 4(1)(b).
[44]   Ibid, para 5.
[45]   Ibid, para 4(1)(c).
[46]   Ibid, para 8(1).
[47]   Ibid, para 8(2). See s 58 of the Land Compensation Act 1973.

though the acquiring authority could have been authorised to acquire the interest of the owner in that area.[48]

If the landowner has been served with a notice stating the effect of the general vesting dec-   9.27
laration and does not serve a notice objecting to the acquisition of only a part of his land within the 28 days prescribed for such a notice he loses his right to object to the acquisition of a part only of his land. If he was not served with such a notice as is required under section 6 of the Compulsory Purchase (Vesting Declarations) Act 1981 he may still serve a notice of objection within 28 days from the date on which he first had notice of the execution of the general vesting declaration and that notice of objection given by him may have effect. The result of a late notice is that the matter may still be referred by the acquiring authority to the Lands Tribunal who may still make a determination of the nature explained above.[49]

3. Agricultural Land

Persons who have an interest in agricultural land greater than that of the tenant for a year   9.28
or from year to year have an additional right to require the acquiring authority in certain circumstances to acquire further land.[50] The right is additional in the sense that it is without prejudice to the rights conferred by section 8 of the Compulsory Purchase Act 1965 and schedule 1 to the Compulsory Purchase (Vesting Declarations) Act 1981, which have been described earlier,[51] so that it is possible that a person could bring himself within and take advantage of either provision. On the other hand agricultural land will not generally fit easily into the description of a house, building or manufactory or a park or garden belonging to a house to which the provisions described earlier apply. The right arises where a person served with a notice to treat in respect of agricultural land has an interest, again greater than that of a tenant for a year or from year to year, in other agricultural land which is comprised in the same agricultural unit. Agricultural land has the same meaning as in section 109 of the Agriculture Act 1947 and agricultural unit has the same meaning as in section 171(1) of the Town and Country Planning Act 1990.[52] The person on whom the notice to treat is served is called the claimant. The claimant has two months from the service of the notice to treat on him to serve a counter-notice on the acquiring authority. A counter-notice is a claim that the other agricultural land in the unit is not reasonably capable of being farmed, either by itself or with other relevant land, as a separate agricultural unit and it requires the acquiring authority to purchase the interest of the claimant in the whole of the other land in the unit. Other relevant land for the purposes of the claim means: (a) land comprised in the same agricultural unit as that to which the notice to treat relates but in which the interest of the claimant is not greater than that of a tenant for a year or year to year, and (b) land comprised in any other agricultural unit occupied by the claimant in respect of which he does have an interest greater than that of a tenant for a year or from year to year.

---

[48] Ibid, para 9(1).
[49] Ibid, para 10.
[50] Land Compensation Act 1973, s 53.
[51] See para 9.10 et seq.
[52] Ibid, s 87(1). An agricultural unit means land which is occupied as a unit for agricultural purposes and includes any dwellinghouse occupied by the same person for the purposes of farming the land.

9.29   It is possible that the acquiring authority has served a notice to treat in respect of other agricultural land in the unit or other relevant land as defined. In that case, and until that notice to treat is withdrawn, the land the subject of that notice to treat is taken not to form part of the agricultural unit or the other relevant land. The above provisions apply whether a notice to treat is an actual notice or is a notice to treat deemed to have been served by reason of the making by the acquiring authority of a general vesting declaration.[53] The claimant is required within the two months allowed for the service of a counter-notice to serve a copy of the notice on any other person with an interest in the land to which the counter-notice relates, but a failure to comply with this requirement does not invalidate the counter-notice.[54]

9.30   A counter-notice may become valid in two ways. The acquiring authority may agree within two months of its service to accept it as valid. If that does not occur either party may, after the expiry of the two months, refer the counter-notice to the Lands Tribunal which will then decide whether the claim that the other land is not reasonably capable of being farmed as a separate agricultural unit is justified. If the counter-notice does become valid the acquiring authority is deemed to be authorised to acquire the land to which the counter-notice relates and to have served a notice to treat relating to that land on the date of the service of the original notice to treat. The deemed notice to treat cannot be withdrawn. The compensation payable in respect of the acquisition of the land the subject of the counter-notice is determined in accordance with certain assumptions which are prescribed for the purposes of claims for compensation for the effect on land of the use of public works under Part I of the Land Compensation Act 1973. The general effect of the assumptions is that it is assumed that planning permission would not be granted for development of the land.[55] The acquiring authority may become entitled to a lease of the land under these provisions but not of the reversion on the lease. If so the authority must offer to surrender the lease to the lessor on terms which it considers reasonable. Either party may refer the question of the reasonableness of the terms to the Lands Tribunal. If the Tribunal then determines the reasonable terms the lessor is deemed to have accepted the surrender. Should the lessor refuse to accept the surrender the acquiring authority may pay into court the sum determined as reasonable.[56] In addition the acquiring authority has power to farm the land.[57] The claimant is entitled to withdraw his counter-notice at any time up to and within six months after the compensation is determined in which case the deemed notice to treat created by the valid counter-notice is taken to be withdrawn.[58]

9.31   A very similar procedure is available where a person with a short tenancy, that is an interest no greater than as a tenant for a year or from year to year, is in occupation of an agricultural holding (as defined in section 1 of the Agricultural Holdings Act 1986) and is served with a notice of entry under section 11 of the Compulsory Purchase Act 1965 which relates to only a part of the holding. The tenant has two months in which to give a counter-notice claiming that the remainder of the holding is not reasonably capable of being farmed by itself or with

---

[53]   See s 7 of the Compulsory Purchase (Vesting Declarations) Act 1981. See section (q) of ch 2.
[54]   Land Compensation Act 1973, s 53(2).
[55]   Ibid, ss 54(5), 5(2)–(4). See paras 13.37 and 13.38 of ch 13.
[56]   Ibid, s 54(7). The provisions of s 9(2) and (5) of the Compulsory Purchase Act 1965 apply so that the sum is placed to the credit of the persons interested in the land and the High Court may order the distribution of the money in court as it thinks fit.
[57]   Ibid, s 54(8).
[58]   Ibid, s 54.

other relevant land as a separate agricultural unit and electing that the notice of entry shall relate to the entire holding.[59] A tenant with a short tenancy is generally not entitled to a notice to treat. The same procedure is applied where the acquiring authority acts so as to take possession of a part of an agricultural holding vested in a tenant with a short tenancy under the alternative procedures available for taking possession: (a) by making a general vesting declaration, or (b) by paying compensation to the tenant under schedule 3 to the Compulsory Purchase Act 1965.[60]

A counter-notice given following a notice of entry becomes valid if the acquiring authority accepts it within two months of its service or either party refers it to the Lands Tribunal which then determines that the notice is justified. The result of a valid counter-notice is that if the tenant has given up possession of the whole of the agricultural holding to the acquiring authority within a year of the acceptance or determination of the validity of the notice the notice of entry is deemed to have extended to the whole of the holding and the acquiring authority is deemed to have taken possession of the whole in pursuance of the notice.[61] If the acquiring authority has not been authorised to acquire the landlord's interest in the land specified in the counter-notice then on taking possession of that land the authority shall give up possession of it to the landlord, and the landlord shall take possession of the land, and the tenancy shall be treated as terminated on that date. Any rights or liabilities of the landlord against or to the tenant arising from the termination of the tenancy, whether under the tenancy or under the Agricultural Holdings Act 1986, become those of the acquiring authority.[62] Any increase in the value of the land due to the landlord taking possession under these provisions shall be deducted from any compensation payable to the landlord for the acquisition of his interest in the remainder of the holding.[63] Where a tenancy is terminated in the circumstances just described the landlord's right to compensation for deterioration of the holding under section 72 of the Agricultural Holdings Act 1986 shall have effect as if the landlord's notice of intention to claim compensation was to be served on the acquiring authority and was to be so served within three months after the determination of the tenancy.[64]

9.32

4. Acquisitions which Divide the Land of a Landowner

There is a further provision which in limited circumstances gives a landowner, a part of whose land is acquired, a right to require that the whole of his land is taken by the acquiring authority. The provision applies only to land which is not situated in a town and is not built upon.[65] It applies when the works of the acquiring authority, that is the works or

9.33

[59] Ibid, s 55.
[60] Ibid, s 57. See section (q) of ch 2 for general vesting declarations under the Compulsory Purchase (Vesting Declarations) Act 1981 and see para 2.97 of ch 2 for the procedure, rarely used today, under sch 3 to the Compulsory Purchase Act 1965. The procedure under s 55 of the Land Compensation Act 1973 is also applied, with any necessary modifications, to notices under sch 6 to the New Towns Act 1981 and s 584 of the Housing Act 1985.
[61] Land Compensation Act 1973, s 56(2).
[62] Ibid, s 56(3).
[63] Ibid, s 56(3)(e).
[64] Ibid, s 56(4).
[65] Land situated within a town has been said to be 'land surrounded by continuous houses, or covered by continuous houses': see *Lord Carrington v Wycombe Rly Co* (1868) 3 Ch App 377, per Lord Cairns LJ at p 383. Land has been said to be 'built upon' if it is covered with continuous buildings eodem modo as the solum of the town':

undertaking authorised by the empowering Act, cut through and divide the land of the owner. If the land left on either or both sides of the land taken is less than half an acre the owner can require the authority to purchase that land as well as the land which is compulsorily acquired. There is a qualification in that if the owner has other land adjoining the land left on a side of the works, and that other land can be conveniently thrown into the land left so as to be conveniently occupied with it, the right to require the land left to be taken by the acquiring authority does not arise. In circumstances in which this qualification applies the owner can require the acquiring authority to carry out works of removing fences, levelling the sites and putting soil on the sites in a satisfactory and workmanlike manner.[66]

9.34   It may occur that the Act which confers the power of compulsory purchase has provisions under which the acquiring authority can be required to provide a communication, such as a bridge or a culvert, between two pieces of land of an owner when his land has been divided by the works. Acts which authorised the construction of railway lines sometimes contained such a provision. In such a case, and in certain circumstances, the acquiring authority can require the owner to sell to it a piece of land on one or both sides of the land acquired instead of the authority having to build the communication across the land acquired. The circumstances are that the land left on one or both sides is less than half an acre, or if greater in size its value is less than the cost of constructing the communication, and the owner does not have other land adjoining the land left. Any dispute as to the value of the land left or the expense of making a communication between two areas of land is to be decided by the Lands Tribunal.[67]

(C) ASSESSING COMPENSATION: THE METHODOLOGY

1. General Considerations

9.35   The compensation which is provided for in the second limb of section 7 of the Compulsory Purchase Act 1965 is compensation for damage. The damage is, of course, to the retained land. As explained earlier the damage is of one or both of two types, the first type being due to injurious affection caused by the severance of the land purchased from the retained land and the other type being some other form of injurious affection to the retained land caused by the exercise of the powers of the acquiring authority. In other words the damage in question, if compensation is to be available for that damage, must be a form of injurious affection to the retained land. Injurious affection is an expression which itself means damage to land and normally that damage is a reduction in the value of the land. It follows that a claim for compensation under section 7 of the 1965 Act must relate to damage to the retained land and that that damage will normally be measured by a reduction in the value of the retained land.[68] Damage which is personal to the owner of the retained land, or which

---

ibid at p 384. See also *Directors of the London and South Western Rly Co v Blackmore* (1870) LR 4 HL 610, per Lord Hatherley at pp 615–16; *Falkner v Somerset and Dorset Rly Co* (1873) LR 16 Eq 458.

[66] Compulsory Purchase Act 1965, s 8(2).

[67] Ibid, s 8(3).

[68] In *Duke of Buccleuch v Metropolitan Board of Works* (1872) 5 LR HL 418, at p 460 Lord Chelmsford equated

relates only to some business or other activity on the retained land without being damage to the land itself, is not something for which compensation can be claimed under section 7. Of course if a business is carried on at the retained land the severance from that land of the land acquired may affect the profitability of the business (or may even cause the cessation of the business) and this may damage the retained land by reducing its value.[69]

The rules set out in section 5 of the Land Compensation Act 1961 are not applicable to the assessment of compensation for damage to the retained land. It is true that section 5 is introduced by the statement that compensation in respect of any compulsory acquisition shall be assessed in accordance with the six rules set out and that compensation for damage to retained land can be said to be an item of compensation in respect of a compulsory acquisition. However, provisions within the rules are not apt to apply to compensation under section 7 of the 1965 Act. The provision for compensation for equivalent reinstatement under rule (5) is not apposite to a claim under section 7 of the 1965 Act, nor is compensation under rule (6) for disturbance and for other matters not directly based on the value of land.[70] Furthermore section 5 concludes with the words that the following provisions of Part II of the 1961 Act are to have effect with respect to the assessment of compensation and certain of those provisions, notably the requirement of disregarding certain actual or prospective development in the valuation process contained in section 6, do not fit with an assessment of compensation under section 7 of the Compulsory Purchase Act 1965. It has been held that section 9, which is also within Part II of the 1961 Act, does not apply to claims concerning compensation for retained land.[71] In historical and analytical terms the rules in section 5 of the Land Compensation Act 1961 and the provisions in the remainder of Part II of that Act govern the ascertainment of the value of the land acquired which is the compensation prescribed as that available for the acquisition of that land under the first limb of section 7 of the Compulsory Purchase Act 1965. Compensation in relation to the retained land is compensation for injurious affection prescribed by the second limb of section 7 of the 1965 Act and is unaffected by the rules in section 5 of the Land Compensation Act 1961 and the further provisions in that Act which amplify those rules.   9.36

On the other hand, since compensation for injurious affection under section 7 of the 1965 Act is dependent on a diminution in the value of the retained land, then plainly valuations   9.37

the expression 'injuriously affected' with 'depreciated in value'. Coming forward well over a century Lord Hoffmann in *Penny's Bay Investment Co Ltd v Director of Lands* (2010) 13 HKCFAR 287 (Ct of Final Appeal, Hong Kong) said at para 34 that injurious affection meant 'a diminution in the value of land caused by works authorised by statute which would otherwise have been tortious'. See also *Halliday v Brecklands District Council* [2012] UKUT 193 (LC), [2012] 3 EGLR 95, in which it was said in the Lands Tribunal at para 16 that 'under s 63 or s 7 the basis of compensation for injurious affection is the diminution in the value of the retained land of the claimant'. The principle which emerges is that the damage or injurious affection must be damage to the retained land as land and that that damage will be measured by a reduction in the value of that land. See also n 5.

[69] See para 9.40 and see section (h) of ch 4 where this proposition is fully explained.

[70] See para 9.7 and see section (e) of ch 8 where this last point relating to r (6) is explained in greater detail.

[71] *English Property Co v Kingston upon Thames London Borough Council* (1998) 77 P & CR 1. In dealing with a different provision for compensation for injurious affection to land, that in s 10 of the Compulsory Purchase Act 1965, Lord Wilberforce said in *Argyle Motors (Birkenhead) Ltd v Birkenhead Corporation* [1975] AC 99, [1973] 2 WLR 487, at p 133: 'That Act [the Land Compensation Act 1961], and in particular the principles of compensation laid down by it in the well known six rules in section 5, relates to the acquisition of land and not to injurious affection or damage at all'. This last statement of law is as applicable to the second limb of s 7 of the 1965 Act as it is to s 10 of that Act. It is implicit in the passage from the decision of Mr Wellings QC in *Abbey Homesteads Group Ltd v Secretary of State for Transport* [1982] 2 EGLR 198, cited in para 9.46, that Mr Wellings considered that s 5 and the ensuing provisions in Pt II of the Land Compensation Act 1961 had nothing to do with the assessment of compensation for injurious affection to retained land.

on different bases of that land have to be carried out in order to assess the compensation. In those circumstances a valuation of the retained land will proceed on the ordinary principle which is that the value of the land is that sum which would be obtained if the land was put on the open market with a view to its sale by a hypothetical willing seller to a hypothetical willing buyer in the ordinary way. One consequence of this principle is that in carrying out the two valuations of the retained land in order to assess the diminution in value it is only facts and matters known or reasonably anticipated at the valuation date which may be taken into account, this being a further rule applicable generally to valuations of land.

9.38   Nor do the rules as to the valuation date now contained in section 5A of the Land Compensation Act 1961 apply to the assessment of compensation in respect of damage to the retained land. Nonetheless that damage, constituted by a diminution in the value of the retained land, has to be assessed as at a certain date since a valuation of land cannot coherently take place save by reference to a specified valuation date. That valuation date must, at any rate in ordinary circumstances, be the same valuation date as that applicable to the assessment of compensation in respect of the land acquired. That valuation date will generally be the date of entry onto the land acquired by the acquiring authority.[72]

2. The Correct Methodology

9.39   The general considerations of law which govern claims for compensation relating to retained land under the second limb of section 7 of the Compulsory Purchase Act 1965 may therefore be summarised as being: (a) that the compensation is for damage to the retained land caused by injurious affection which may take the form of severance or some other form of injurious affection, (b) that the damage caused by injurious affection takes the form of a reduction in the value of the retained land, (c) that the rules in section 5, and in the remainder of the provisions in Part II of the Land Compensation Act 1961, do not apply to claims for compensation in respect of retained land, and (d) that although no statutory valuation date is specified a reduction in the value of the retained land will normally be carried out by way of valuations as at the date of entry onto the land acquired or at the vesting date if a general vesting declaration is made. With these general considerations in mind the methodology which should normally be adopted in order to determine the compensation in respect of the retained land can be readily stated. The methodology requires two valuations to be made as at the same date. It is necessary first to ascertain the value of the retained land prior to its severance from the land acquired. This value will be assessed without regard to the scheme of the acquiring authority and without regard to the works or the likelihood of works or other actions to be carried out by the acquiring authority in the exercise of the powers conferred by the empowering Act.[73] The other valuation is the value

---

[72] The determination of the valuation date is explained in section (e) of ch 4.
[73] See, eg *Melwood Units Pty Ltd v Commissioner of Main Roads* [1979] AC 426, [1978] 3 WLR 520. It is sometimes asked whether the Pointe Gourde principle applies to the assessment of compensation for injurious affection to retained land. The answer is that as such it does not since the Pointe Gourde principle is an aspect of the value to the owner rule and that rule applies to the assessment of the value of the land acquired: see ch 5. However, it is a matter of common sense that if the retained land has to be valued before and after the acquisition of the land acquired in order to determine the reduction in its value caused by that acquisition then the before value must be a value of the retained land disregarding the acquisition and the scheme of the acquiring authority which undertook that acquisition. This last proposition is derived from the nature of the assessment of the damage by injurious affection and not from any extraneous principle.

of the retained land following the severance of that land from the land acquired, and taking account of that severance and taking account of works or other actions carried out or to be carried out by the acquiring authority in the exercise of the powers conferred by the empowering Act. The two values should then be compared and the compensation due under section 7 of the 1965 Act in relation to the retained land will be the difference between these two values assuming, as will often be the case, that the second value is lower than the first value.[74]

An assessment of compensation due under section 7 of the 1965 Act, by way of this methodology, has regard to the statutory language in that it results in compensation which is the damage to the retained land in the sense of injurious affection to that land and is not merely a personal or commercial loss unrelated to the value of land. It has been explained earlier that the use, or the prospect of the use, or the continuation of the use, of land for a business or commercial purpose may add value to that land and this of course may be taken into account in the assessments of the value of the retained land. Nonetheless the compensation is for damage to the land by way of a form of injurious affection and is not damage for a business loss. Compensation for injurious affection to land by the execution of works by the acquiring authority is also claimable in certain circumstances under section 10 of the Compulsory Purchase Act 1965.[75] In that context it has been made clear that injurious affection means damage to the land and not personal damage or a commercial loss as such although it is also clear that when the damage to land is assessed by way of a reduction in its value (whether capital value or rental value) any potential to use or continue the use of the land for business purposes may be one of the factors which determines or contributes to the value of the land.[76]

Although the framework of the required valuations in the assessment of a claim under section 7 is clear in practice that framework is sometimes ignored. In particular there has grown up a practice, perhaps thought convenient, of carrying out what may be called an 'overall before and after' valuation process.[77] What is meant by this process is that the value of the land acquired and the retained land is ascertained as the value of a single area of land

9.40

9.41

[74] An early example of the operation of this process is the decision of the House of Lords in *Duke of Buccleuch v Metropolitan Board of Works* (1872) 5 LR HL 418. During the 1860s the embankment on the north bank of the Thames from Westminster to Blackfriars was constructed. The tenant from the Crown of a large house previously had direct access to the river. Land was taken from him for the construction of the embankment and roadway and the value of the leasehold interest in the retained land was reduced. It was held that the tenant was entitled to compensation under the second limb of s 63 of the Lands Clauses Consolidation Act 1845 and that the compensation was properly assessed as the diminution in the value of the leasehold interest by reason of the loss of river frontage and by reason of the effect on amenity of the new road adjoining the property. A further early decision of the House of Lords is *Cowper Essex v Acton Local Board* (1889) 14 App Cas 153, in which the claimant owned land laid out as a building estate a part of which was acquired for use as a sewage farm. Compensation was awarded for the reduction in the value of the retained building estate land caused by the sewage farm.
[75] See ch 10.
[76] See *Argyle Motors (Birkenhead) Ltd v Birkenhead Corporation* [1975] AC 99, [1973] 2 WLR 487, per Lord Wilberforce at pp 130–31 (and see per Buckley LJ in the Court of Appeal at p 114); *Wildtree Hotels Ltd v Harrow LBC* [2001] 2 AC 1, [2003] 3 WLR 165, per Lord Hoffmann at pp 17–18; *Moto Hospitality Ltd v Secretary of State for Transport* EWCA Civ 764, [2008] 1 WLR 2822, per Carnwath LJ at paras 73–74. For a general discussion on the relationship between the value of land and the anticipated future profits which may be earned from a business carried out, or to be carried out, on the land see section (h) of ch 4. Obviously the injurious affection to the retained land may be direct and physical, such as in *Countess of Malmesbury v Secretary of State for Transport* [1982] 2 EGLR 188, where road works affecting the water table of the retained land caused subsidence, or an effect on the amenity of the retained land such as noise from a new road.
[77] See, eg *RA Vine (Engineering) Ltd v Havant Borough Council* [1989] 2 EGLR 15.

comprising both components prior to the severance of the land acquired from the retained land and ignoring the scheme of the acquiring authority. This can be called the overall before value. Then a similar valuation is carried out of the retained land alone after the severance from it of the land acquired and taking account of the scheme of the acquiring authority. This can be called the after value. The difference between the two values is then taken as the total compensation payable under rule (2) of section 5 of the 1961 Act for the land acquired and under the second limb of section 7 of the 1965 Act in relation to the retained land. This is in a sense a simple process and in some cases it can give a result which is certainly not unjust as the total compensation payable to the landowner who is dispossessed of a part of his land and retains the remainder. However, it is not the process required by the statutory provisions and it is not legally correct. The correct method of proceeding is to carry out the two separate valuations as just explained, that is a valuation of the retained land alone prior to the severance and ignoring the scheme of the acquiring authority, and then a valuation of the retained land alone after the severance and taking into account the scheme of the acquiring authority. This process may also be described as a before and after valuation process in the sense that it is two valuations of the same land on the same date but in a 'before' and 'after' situation. The crucial difference between this correct process and the perhaps simplified but incorrect process, described earlier in this paragraph, is that the correct process concentrates solely on the retained land and the value of the retained land by itself in the two different situations which underlie the two valuations.[78]

9.42   The primary reason why the compensation in respect of the retained land should be calculated in the way just described is that to do so is consistent with the language of section 7 of the Compulsory Purchase Act 1965 which contemplates that the compensation for the land acquired and the compensation in respect of the retained land shall be considered separately and on different bases. The basis of the compensation for the land acquired is the value of that land while the basis of the compensation in respect of the retained land is the damage caused to the owner of that land by two forms of injurious affection to it. To elide together the two forms of compensation is to fail to apply that which the legislation clearly and expressly states. The decided cases also strongly indicate that the separate valuation methodology of assessing section 7 claims in relation to retained land as described above is correct in law. It is therefore necessary to consider these authorities.

9.43   A leading decision of Eve J and of the Court of Appeal on this subject relied on in subsequent decisions is *South Eastern Railway Company v London County Council*.[79] The claimants owned property on the south side of the Strand in London and owned further property at the rear of the first property along a road called Craven Street running south from the Strand. The first property was acquired in order to widen the Strand. The result of the acquisition was that the second property, that in Craven Street to the rear of the first property, became a property which itself fronted onto the Strand and was substantially increased in value for that reason. The London County Council, as the acquiring authority, contended that the compensation payable for the acquisition of the Strand property should be calculated by taking the value of the two properties together before and, so far as still held

---

[78] It is of course possible that the simplified and the correct processes will lead to the same numerical result but this is not necessarily the case. See paras 9.58–9.59 where a somewhat simplified example is used to explain the application of the correct methodology. In the *Abbey Homesteads* decision, referred to in detail in para 9.45, the two valuations presented by the claimants using the two different processes did produce the same numerical result.

[79] *South Eastern Rly Co v London County Council* [1915] 2 Ch 252.

by the claimants, after the acquisition and finding the overall difference. The purpose of the Council was, of course, to bring the retained property at Craven Street into the equation so that the betterment to it could be used to reduce the overall compensation. The courts rejected this process as something which had no statutory warrant. The compensation due was the open market value of the land fronting the Strand which was that which was acquired. If there had been a reduction in the value of the retained land by reason of its severance from the land fronting the Strand that reduction would have been the basis of a further claim for compensation. As it was there was an increase in the value of the retained land so that no such compensation claim could be made. What was wrong in law was to lump together the two areas of land and to carry out some species of overall before and after valuation exercise. What the acquiring authority was seeking to do was in effect to deduct from the compensation for the land acquired an increase in the value of the retained land brought about by their scheme. Such a process is termed a reduction in the compensation by reason of 'betterment'. The decision of Eve J, affirmed in the Court of Appeal, is an important authority which, as well as its significance in the present context, shows that there is to be no reduction for betterment in the absence of a specific statutory authority for such a reduction.[80]

The decision of the Court of Appeal in *Hoveringham Gravels v Chiltern District Council*[81] is   9.44 to the same effect. The facts of the case are complicated but it suffices for present purposes to say that two adjoining pieces of land, the front land and the back land, were acquired from the owner at the same time by two different authorities. The decision of the Court of Appeal concerned the valuation of the back land. The claimants contended for a before and after type valuation exercise, that is with the compensation for the back land being calculated as the difference in value between: (a) the value of the back land (the land acquired), and the front land (the retained land), taken together as they were before the acquisition of the back land, and (b) the value of the front land (the retained land) after that acquisition. The decision of the Court of Appeal was complicated by the existence of a certificate of appropriate alternative development under section 17 of the Land Compensation Act 1961, but that point is not relevant for present purposes.[82] The point of central importance to the present subject is that the Court held that when assessing the compensation for the back land as the land acquired it was necessary to find the value of that land and then to consider whether there had been any reduction in the value of the front land as the retained land due to its severance from the back land, that is precisely the approach which is being explained in this chapter. The decision of the court followed a consideration of section 7 of the Compulsory Purchase Act 1965 and the relevant authorities including the often cited decision of Scott LJ in *Horn v Sunderland Corporation*.[83] Scott LJ was the chairman of the committee which produced the report which led to the modern statutory rules on the assessment of the value of the land acquired, now in section 5 of the Land Compensation Act 1961.[84] Roskill LJ said:

---

[80] Betterment is examined in section (d) of ch 6. There is today a general provision in s 7 of the Land Compensation Act 1961 for the making of a reduction from the compensation due for the land acquired by reason of an increase in the value of other land of the claimant brought about by the scheme of the acquiring authority.

[81] *Hoveringham Gravels v Chiltern District Council* (1978) 35 P & CR 295.

[82] See section (d) of ch 7 for certificates of appropriate alternative development.

[83] *Horn v Sunderland Corporation* [1941] 2 KB 26.

[84] Scott Committee, *Second Report of the Committee Dealing with the Law and Practice Relating to the Acquisition of Land for Public Purposes* (Cd 9229, 1918).

It was argued that section 7 enabled severance loss to the back land to be additionally recovered as well as the market value of the front land. With all respect to the ingenuity of the argument (which seems not to have been advanced before the Lands Tribunal – there is certainly no reference to it in their decision), we think that it breaks down as a matter of the construction of the section. In construing the words 'by reason of the severing of the land purchased', the later words 'or otherwise injuriously affecting the other land' cannot be ignored. It seems to us that the section on its true construction is envisaging an additional head of compensation for the owner of the land taken by reason of other retained land of his being less valuable to him through that retained land being severed from or otherwise injuriously affected by the compulsory acquisition of the land taken. We arrive at that conclusion solely as a matter of the construction of the section, but we think that consideration of the earlier legislation and Scott LJ's judgment in *Horn v. Sunderland Corporation* which was concerned with that earlier legislation, supports our view. Section 7 is the legislative successor of section 63 of the Lands Clauses Consolidation Act 1845 (as amended). Its text and that of section 49 of the same Act will be found discussed in Scott LJ's judgment. It is true that the former section 63 and the present section 7 are not quite textually identical, but we cannot believe that section 7, when enacted in 1965, was intended to effect so drastic a change in the law as would be involved if we were to accept this part of Mr Glidewell's argument.[85]

9.45   Obviously this decision of the Court of Appeal supports the explanation of the correct valuation process described earlier. The case was remitted to the Lands Tribunal for further consideration and when so considered separate valuations were carried out of the back land and the front land. In each case the valuations proceeded along the lines just indicated. When the compensation for the acquisition of the back land was being determined that compensation amounted to: (a) its open market value looked at by itself, and (b) the reduction in value of the front land by reason of its severance from the back land. When the compensation for the acquisition of the front land was being determined that determination proceeded in the same way, namely: (a) by assessing the open market value of the front land looked at by itself, and (b) by determining any reduction in the value of the back land as a result of its severance from the front land.[86] The complicated and unusual facts of the *Hoveringham* case and the symmetry of the analyses therefore illustrate fairly vividly the correctness of the approach in law to the valuation of compensation under the second limb of section 7 of the 1965 Act explained earlier.

9.46   The guidance from the Court of Appeal on the law in this area appears to be clear. That guidance has been put into effect by the Lands Tribunal. In *Abbey Homesteads Group Ltd v Secretary of State for Transport*[87] a strip of land to the south of Witney was acquired from the claimants in order to construct the Witney by-pass. The claimants owned substantial other land on both sides of the strip of land acquired. In the Lands Tribunal the claimants presented two valuations, one on the basis of separate values of the land acquired and the retained land and one on the overall before and after approach discussed earlier, that is valuing both areas of land together before the acquisition and then valuing the area of retained land after the acquisition.[88] The acquiring authority provided only one valuation which was on what has been described as the overall before and after approach, that is on the same basis as the second valuation of the claimants. A fundamental issue to be decided

---

[85]   Ibid, pp 305–06.
[86]   (1980) 39 P & CR 414.
[87]   *Abbey Homesteads Group Ltd v Secretary of State for Transport* [1982] 2 EGLR 198. See also *Cooke v Secretary of State* (1974) 27 P & CR 234.
[88]   See para 9.41.

by the Tribunal was, therefore, whether the overall before and after approach which under-lay two of the three valuations before the Tribunal was permissible in law. The Tribunal addressed this issue squarely, considering the legislation and the two decisions of the Court of the Court of Appeal just mentioned. It was concluded that the valuations put before the Tribunal on the overall before and after basis were produced on a wrong legal premise. The Member deciding the case (Mr Wellings QC) said:

> Mr Graham answered this question in the affirmative, but Mr Rich submitted that the decision of the Court of Appeal in *Hoveringham Gravels v Chiltern District Council* (1977) 35 P & CR 295 supported the contrary view. Because the red land [the land acquired] could not be developed by itself, it was right, he said, to value the entirety of the land and apportion its value to the several parts: that is to say, to assess the totality of the loss and apportion it to the relevant statutory provisions: namely, rule (2) of section 5 of the Act of 1961 and section 7 of the Act of 1965. That course had the merit that it avoided a whole host of problems, which otherwise would have to be considered.
>
> It appears to me that even before rule (2) was introduced (in the Acquisition of Land (Assessment of Compensation) Act 1919), that is to say at a time where market value was not necessarily in all cases the measure of compensation for land acquired, a separate assessment of compensation for land acquired was as a matter of law required and that compensation was not to be ascertained by deducting the value of what was left to the owner after the acquisition from the aggregate value of the entirety immediately prior to the acquisition: see per Eve J in *South Eastern Railway v London County Council* [1915] 2 Ch D 252, at p 260, that judgment having been approved by the Court of Appeal, ibid, at p 260. In my opinion, sections 5, 6, 7, 14–16, 17, 18 and 22 of the Land Compensation Act 1961, and the observations per curiam in the Court of Appeal in the *Hoveringham Gravels* case, supra, at pp 301 and 303, all lead to the conclusion that land acquired must be valued for the purposes of compensation separately from other land retained by the owner. See also the decision of the Lands Tribunal (J H Emlyn Jones MBE FRICS), to similar effect, in *Turris Investments v Central Electricity Generating Board* (REF/31/1980). It follows that in the present case, Mr Westoby's valuation 2 and the district valuer's valuation are based on a wrong legal premise. The district valuer of course had no alternative valuation.[89]

The approach adopted by the Lands Tribunal under the modern law is therefore not in any doubt. It will be seen from the report of the decision that when he came to the actual valuation Mr Wellings did carry out separate valuations of the land acquired and the retained land. As regards the land acquired he simply took the open market value of it. As regards the retained land he considered the value of it as it was before the acquisition and the value of it as it became after the acquisition and awarded as compensation the difference between those two values. It is important to note that in this decision Mr Wellings was not saying that as a matter of valuation judgment he preferred one valuation technique to another. He was rejecting the type of valuation technique described here as an overall before and after valuation as something which was not in accordance with the statutory provisions which constitute the compensation code.   9.47

The correct method in law of assessing claims for severance or injurious affection to land, as described above, has very recently been upheld and reiterated by the Court of Final Appeal in Hong Kong in *Penny's Bay Investment Company Ltd v Director of Lands*.[90] In that case the claimants held a long lease of land fronting the sea at Lantau Island in Hong Kong which was used by them as a shipyard. They had enjoyed what were described as marine   9.48

---

[89] [1982] 2 EGLR 198 at p 211.
[90] *Penny's Bay Investment Company Ltd v Director of Lands* (2010) 13 HKCFAR 287.

rights, that is the right of passage or access between the land and the open sea. The marine rights were extinguished under the Foreshore and Sea-bed Reclamations Ordinance in order for a part of the sea to be reclaimed and a container port constructed. The claimants were entitled to compensation for injurious affection under the terms of the Ordinance. The situation was not quite the same as that the subject of the English authorities summarised above. It was not a case of a person owning areas A and B and having area A compulsorily acquired. Rather it was a case of a person owning area A with valuable ancillary rights, the marine rights, and having those rights compulsorily taken from him. The situation was therefore more akin to claims for compensation under section 10 of the Compulsory Purchase Act 1965 than to claims under the second limb of s 7 of that Act but it still offers valuable guidance on the correct method of assessing claims for compensation for injurious affection to land, a process which is common to section 10 claims and section 7 claims.

9.49   In the Lands Tribunal in Hong Kong the case for the Government as the compensating authority, which found favour with the Lands Tribunal, was that the compensation should be assessed as though it were a claim in tort and by simply considering the damage to the land of the claimants rather than by two valuations as at the date of extinguishment (which was the valuation date), one being the value of the land prior to the extinguishment of the marine rights and the other being the value of the land after that extinguishment. Lord Hoffmann, delivering the main judgment in the Court of Final Appeal, rejected this approach and said that the correct method of assessing the compensation for injurious affection was by the traditional means as explained above and as upheld in the English courts.[91] The correct approach in law, as just explained, has therefore been upheld by high recent authority (though not of course authority binding in England) in a situation not substantially different in conceptual terms from that under consideration in this chapter.

9.50   There is a further significant reason, presaged by the decision in *South East Railway Company v London County Council*,[92] why an overall before and after valuation is unlikely to be in accordance with the statutory provisions. When a person whose land is acquired is also the owner of land contiguous or adjacent to the land acquired, that is retained land, the amount of any increase in the value of that retained land due to development or the prospect of development attributable to the scheme of the acquiring authority has to be deducted from the compensation for the land acquired. This process is usually called taking account of 'betterment' and is dealt with separately elsewhere.[93] If a permissible general method of assessing compensation was to take the overall value of the whole of the land of the claimant, the land acquired and the other contiguous and adjacent land not acquired, before the acquisition and then to take away from it the value of the contiguous or adjacent land alone after the acquisition then that process would itself take account of any betterment to the contiguous or adjacent land and in those circumstances it seems unlikely that there would be any need for separate provisions relating specifically to damage to the retained land (the second limb of section 7 of the Compulsory Purchase Act 1965) and to an increase in the value of the retained land (section 7 of the Land Compensation Act 1961). It is more consistent with the underlying scheme of the legislation to conclude that separate assessments and valuations are required: (a) of any diminution in the value of the

---

[91] *Penny's Bay Investment Co Ltd v Director of Lands* (2010) 13 HKCFAR 287 at para 35 et seq.
[92] *South East Rly Co v London County Council* [1915] 2 Ch 251.
[93] Land Compensation Act 1961, s 7. The betterment provisions are explained in section (d) of ch 6.

retained land due to the compulsory purchase and the scheme of the acquiring authority, and (b) of the value of the land acquired disregarding the compulsory purchase and the scheme of the acquiring authority.[94]

A strong case can therefore be made out that when a claim for compensation under section 7 of the 1965 Act in respect of retained land falls to be assessed the method of assessment should be by way of before and after valuations of the retained land alone as set out earlier. This proposition accords with the language of section 7, accords with the guidance derived from decisions of the Court of Appeal, and accords with the analysis and decision of Mr Wellings in the *Abbey Homesteads* decision. That having been said, while the statutory provisions state the basis of compensation they do not, of course, in themselves prescribe a single method of valuation which must be adopted in order to arrive at the amount of that compensation. Nonetheless it is difficult to envisage how an 'overall before and after' valuation, taking together both the acquired land and the retained land, as described, could accord with the statutory provisions and it is not easy to see how any valuation process which did not adhere to, or at least closely follow, the process of a 'before and after' valuation of the retained land alone could properly accord with the statutory provisions and with their intent.[95]

9.51

In summary, therefore, a valuation of which the purpose is to assess compensation in respect of the retained land in accordance with the second limb of section 7 of the Compulsory Purchase Act 1965 should normally proceed by way of two valuations carried out as at the same valuation date, normally the same valuation date as for the purposes of assessing compensation for the land acquired, those valuations being: (a) a valuation of the retained land by itself prior to its severance from the land acquired and ignoring the scheme of the acquiring authority, and (b) a valuation of the retained land by itself following the severance of that land from the land acquired and taking into account the scheme of the acquiring authority. The compensation will then be the amount, if any, by which the second valuation is lower than the first valuation. Anyone who wishes to put forward an assessment of compensation under the second limb of section 7 by way of some other valuation method or process would have the burden of showing that that other method or process does accord with the statutory provisions in section 7 and with their purpose.

9.52

(D) ASSESSING COMPENSATION: APPLYING THE METHODOLOGY

Once the correct methodology has been established its application by way of carrying out the before and after valuations of the retained land alone should be rigorous and precise. It is necessary to be clear on the exact assumptions to be made for the purposes of each of

9.53

---

[94] It could be argued that the overall before and after method of assessing compensation was only possible where there was a claim for damage to the retained land so that the betterment provisions would still be necessary where no such claim was made.

[95] See, however, *Pattle v Secretary of State for Transport* [2009] UKUT 141, [2010] 1 P & CR D61, where, in relation to preliminary issues and without any valuations before it, the Lands Tribunal expressed itself as unwilling to say that an overall before and after valuation approach could never be used as a matter of law. See also *ADP&E Farmers v Department of Transport* [1988] 1 EGLR 209. Neither decision of the Tribunal contains any analysis of the reasoning and authorities set out in this section of this chapter.

these valuations. Rule (2) of section 5 of the Land Compensation Act 1961, which defines the meaning of the value of land, is not incorporated as such into the valuations needed for present purposes but the underlying principles of valuation, such as the assumption of a hypothetical sale of the asset being valued by a hypothetical willing seller to a hypothetical willing buyer, apply to all land valuations unless some other method is prescribed.

9.54   The before valuation is a valuation which depends on the sale by a hypothetical willing seller to a hypothetical willing buyer of the retained land by itself at the valuation date. The seller is not the claimant who actually owns the retained land but a hypothetical entity, this being a characteristic of all valuations of land carried out for the purposes of assessing compensation.[96] In this case there is no statutory definition of what is the nature or extent of the scheme to be disregarded (as there is in section 14(8) of the Land Compensation Act 1961 as recently introduced by the Localism Act 2011). A valuer must therefore form a judgement as a matter of fact on what is the scheme to be disregarded. If the scheme is a specific project such as a new road or railway, or an extension to an airport or the creation of a nature reserve, there will be no difficulty in identifying what is to be disregarded. The judgement on this question may be less easy when the scheme is more diffuse such as a new town or a wide ranging project of urban regeneration or a project which is consequential upon some other project. All surrounding circumstances are to be taken to be as they actually would be if the scheme of the acquiring authority, including its proposal to acquire land from the claimant, were disregarded. It follows that one important fact to be taken into account in the before valuation is that the claimant owns the land which is being acquired from him. That fact may sometimes put him in the position of a special purchaser for the purposes of a hypothetical sale of the retained land.[97] If the retained land was sold by itself the owner of the land acquired might have a special interest in acquiring it so that he could become the owner of both pieces of land (as he in fact was and as would have remained the case if there had been no compulsory purchase). In addition there may be a marriage value to be gained in the hands of the claimant as the owner of the land acquired seeking to acquire the retained land and to join it to the land acquired and this should be reflected in the before value of the retained and. While the owner of the land acquired could therefore be envisaged as the person who would be likely to make the highest bid in the market for the retained land in the end the successful bidder must be taken to be the hypothetical willing buyer. Thus the hypothetical willing buyer would have to offer at least as much as the claimant for the retained land in order that he should become the successful buyer. The hypothetical willing buyer may calculate this amount by himself estimating how much the claimant would be likely to offer and then at least equalling that amount in his own bid.[98]

9.55   The assessment of the before value must be consistent with the assessment of the valuation of the land acquired. Therefore, if the land acquired is valued on the basis of some development of it which would have occurred in the absence of the scheme of the acquiring authority, the before value of the retained land should also be assessed on the footing that that

---

[96] See section (c) of ch 4.
[97] See section (d) of ch 4 for the nature of a special purchaser.
[98] It is possible that the claimant has some particular knowledge of the retained land or its potential not known to the market as a whole. In such a case any additional value of the retained land attributable to that knowledge should not be reflected in the before value of the retained land since it is something not known to the market as a whole and not known to the hypothetical willing buyer.

development would proceed.[99] It has been suggested that the retained land must be valued as at the date of entry in its actual physical condition as at the date of notice to treat, said to be the normal rule,[100] but the normal rule today for the valuation of the land acquired is that it is valued in its physical condition not at the date of notice to treat but at the valuation date.[101]

The value of the retained land in the before value situation may depend on the prospect of its development in the absence of the scheme of the acquiring authority. That prospect may in turn depend on the prospect of obtaining the planning permission necessary for a particular development. When it comes to the planning situation as regards the land acquired there is a complex system of planning assumptions which have to be applied including the possibility of obtaining a certificate of appropriate alternative development.[102] No such statutory assumptions apply to the valuation of the retained land. If that land has an existing planning permission which may be implemented then of course that permission can be taken into account in its valuation. If the retained land has only a prospect or hope of obtaining planning permission the strength of that prospect must be assessed in valuing that land in the same way as the strength of a prospect of obtaining planning permission is assessed in valuing any land.[103]

9.56

Since the assessment of compensation is proceeding by way of two valuations of land, and since the valuation date is normally the same date as that for the valuation of the land acquired, it should follow in accordance with normal principles that the valuation should proceed on the basis of known and anticipated facts as at the valuation date and not by way of taking into account subsequent events which cannot have been known to the parties to the hypothetical transaction at the valuation date. Nonetheless it has been held in the Lands Tribunal[104] that, in accordance with the Bwllfa principle, events after the valuation date can be taken into account such as the obtaining of a planning permission for the retained land years after the date of acquisition of the land acquired. In dealing with this matter the Court of Appeal did not dissent from what had been said in the Lands Tribunal but declined to treat it as a matter of law.[105] The meaning and application of the Bwllfa principle and its relation to the assessment of compensation is explained elsewhere.[106] The better view in accordance with general principle is that valuations for the purposes of assessing compensation under the second limb of section 7 of the Compulsory Purchase Act 1965 should proceed on orthodox principles so that account can be taken only of matters known or anticipated as at the valuation date. This proposition is in accordance with modern authority on the assessment of compensation for injurious affection.[107]

9.57

[99] *RA Vine (Engineering) Ltd v Havant Borough Council* [1989] 2 EGLR 15, applying the principle applicable to disturbance compensation as stated in *Horn v Sunderland Corporation* [1941] 2 KB 26, [1941] 1 All ER 480. See ch 8, para 8.12.
[100] *English Property Corporation v Royal Borough of Kingston and Totnes* (1999) 77 P & CR 1, per Morritt LJ at p 11.
[101] See ch 4, para 4.43.
[102] See sections (c) and (d) of ch 7.
[103] *Porter v Secretary of State for Transport* [1996] 3 All ER 693, approved by the House of Lords in *Transport for London v Spirerose Ltd* [2009] UKHL 44, [2009] 1 WLR 1797.
[104] *Waterworth v Bolton Metropolitan Borough Council* (1979) 37 P & CR 104.
[105] *Bolton Metropolitan Borough Council v Waterworth* (1981) 42 P & CR 289, per Sir Patrick Browne at p 299.
[106] See section (d) of ch 4.
[107] The correct statement of the law is as stated by Lord Hoffmann in *Penny's Bay Investment Co Ltd v Director of Lands* (2010) 13 HKCFAR (Ct of Final Appeal, Hong Kong) 287 at para 43 where he said: 'As the measure of

9.58   The process may appear complex but it is not unreasonably so if it is kept clearly in mind: (a) that the hypothetical sale of the retained land which establishes its value is a sale of that land alone with the land acquired in different ownership, and (b) that the sale is between hypothetical persons and not any actual persons. The process can perhaps best be explained by an example. A person might own a large house within 4 acres of grounds worth £5 million in all. The acquiring authority acquires 1 acre of the grounds in order to include that land in a new road. The claimant is then entitled as compensation to: (a) the value of the land acquired ignoring the scheme of the acquiring authority, and (b) a sum for the damage by injurious affection to the retained land of 3 acres. The second head of compensation requires the carrying out of a before and an after valuation of the retained land as explained. The before value of the retained land will be the amount which that land would realise if sold by itself by a hypothetical willing seller to a hypothetical willing buyer on the valuation date ignoring the road scheme and assuming that the claimant was and would remain the owner of the 1 acre of land which was to be acquired. It may be that in these circumstances a person unconnected with either piece of land would offer £4 million for the retained land to use it as a house with reduced grounds. However, the claimant as the owner of the land to be acquired might offer more, say £4.5 million, because of his special position as the owner of the adjoining land and because after the sale he would acquire an asset worth £5 million in all. The reasoning of the hypothetical willing seller of the retained land and the claimant might be that by combining the two areas of land there would be a gain or marriage value of £1 million and that this sum should be shared equally between them, something which would be achieved if the sale of the house and its 3 acres were to the claimant at a price of £4.5 million. The hypothetical willing buyer of the retained land would carry out a similar calculation and, having estimated that the claimant would offer £4.5 million for the retained land, would himself make an offer of at least this sum in order to acquire the retained land. The before value of the retained land in these circumstances is therefore £4.5 million.[108]

9.59   The next step is to carry out the after valuation of the retained land. Again a sale by a hypothetical willing seller to a hypothetical willing buyer of the retained land by itself on the valuation date is envisaged. The important difference between this sale and the sale for the purposes of the before valuation is that, for the purposes of the after valuation, the acquiring authority is taken to have acquired the land which they need and to be about to carry out their scheme on it and on other land. If the house with its 3 acres of land were sold with the 1 acre acquired and a new road to be built passing the land the price might be £3.5 million. There would then be no question of the claimant himself offering to buy the retained land by reason of his ownership of the area of land acquired since for the purposes of the after valuation that area is taken to be owned by the acquiring authority pursuant to its

compensation [for injurious affection] is the difference between the respective values of the land with and without access to the sea on 5 May 1995, Cheung JA must be right in saying that nothing which happened after that date can affect the valuation. The value of a property means the price which it would have fetched on a sale in the open market between a willing seller and a willing purchaser on the relevant date. That obviously cannot be affected by what happened afterwards'. The *Waterworth* decision of the Lands Tribunal must therefore be treated as out of accord with principle and authority and as wrong in law.

    [108] The valuations are somewhat simplified for the purposes of this example, but the underlying process and reasoning are clear. For example, the bargaining strengths of the hypothetical seller and the hypothetical buyer might for some reason not be entirely equal so that a valuer might conclude that the division of the marriage value between them would not be on a wholly equal basis.

compulsory purchase. On occasions acquiring authorities carry out, or obligate themselves to carry out, works which will remove or reduce the damage to the retained land, called accommodation works. For instance in the present example the acquiring authority might undertake to build a bank or screen on the retained land so as to reduce the visual and acoustic effect of the new road. The effect of such accommodation works should of course be taken into account in assessing the after value of the retained land.

The compensation for the retained land is then the amount by which the after value is less   9.60
than the before value and in the above example this is £1 million. The total compensation payable to the claimant will be: (a) the value of the land acquired disregarding the road project, and (b) the £1 million just mentioned in respect of the retained land.[109]

(E) LOCATION OF THE WORKS

Section 7 of the Compulsory Purchase Act 1965 states that compensation is recoverable for   9.61
injurious affection to the retained land of the landowner caused 'by the exercise of the powers conferred by this or the special Act'. The usual case of the exercise of powers by an acquiring authority so as to cause injurious affection is the carrying out by it of works, although this is not necessarily the only form of the exercise of powers which causes injurious affection to the retained land.[110] Section 7 does not state that the exercise of the powers has to be on or in relation to any particular area of land. For example, if a part of an owner's land is acquired in order to build a new road across it the injurious affection to the retained land of the owner may be caused in part by the construction of the road and its use on the land acquired and in part, and probably to a greater extent, by that construction and use on other land which is not acquired from the owner.

The same or much the same language as is now in section 7 of the 1965 Act was formerly   9.62
contained in section 63 of the Lands Clauses Consolidation Act 1845. It was held in a series of cases under that Act that compensation for injurious affection to the retained land of the owner could be recovered only in respect of the damage to the retained land which was attributable to the activities of the acquiring authority in the exercise of its powers on the particular area of land acquired from him. No compensation could be recovered for damage caused by activities on other land such as land acquired from other persons.[111]

---

[109] If the value of the land acquired, disregarding the effect on its value of the road scheme of the acquiring authority, was £0.5 million then the total compensation (ignoring any possible claim under r (6) of s 5 of the Land Compensation Act 1961) would be £1.5 million. This result would be the same as if the claims for the value of the land acquired (under r (2) of s 5 of the 1961 Act) and for injurious affection to the retained land (under the second limb of s 7 of the 1965 Act) has been assessed by the overall before and after value process described in para 9.41 et seq. The whole of the land would be worth £5 million before the acquisition and the retained land would be worth £3.5 million after the acquisition, resulting in compensation of £1.5 million as the difference between the two sums, and so the same compensation as in the example. However, in many cases the figures may not be as neat and rounded as in the example given and it is by no means certain that the result of an overall before and after process would be the same as separate assessments of the two claims. This is one of the reasons why the correct process is as described in this and the last section of this chapter.

[110] See para 9.6.

[111] *Re Stockport, Timperley and Altrincham Rly Co* (1864) 33 LJQB 251; *Cowper Essex v Acton Local Board* (1889) 14 App Cas 153; *Duke of Buccleuch v Metropolitan Board of Works* (1879) LR 5 HL 418; *Sisters of Charity of Rockingham v The King* [1922] 2 AC 315. The limitation imposed by these decisions was not contained in the language of the legislation.

9.63   This matter was considered by the Court of Appeal in *Edwards v Minister of Transport*[112] at a time when the Lands Clauses Consolidation Act 1845 remained the legislation in force. In that case the claimant owned a house and adjoining land of about 4.5 acres in extent. The acquiring authority acquired a small area of 340 square yards of the land to include it in a new trunk road passing the property. Having considered the older authorities the Court held that the compensation payable to the claimant was confined to that for the damage to his property caused by the use of the new road on the 340 square yards acquired from him and the compensation did not extend to the greater damage caused to the property by the use of the remainder of the new road.[113] The same principle applied to section 7 of the Compulsory Purchase Act 1965 when that came into force.

9.64   The principle as so established was considered to be less than satisfactory and the law was altered by section 44 of the Land Compensation Act 1973. Section 44(1) provides that where land is acquired from an owner, for the purpose of works which are to be situated partly on that land and partly elsewhere, compensation for injurious affection to retained land by that owner shall be assessed by reference to the whole of the works and not only the part of the works situated on the land acquired from him.[114] Clearly in the majority of cases the principle stated in the *Edwards* decision is reversed by this provision. If the provision had been in force at the time of the acquisition in the *Edwards* case the compensation for the injurious affection to the retained house and grounds of the claimant would have been assessed by reference to the effect of the road works carried out or to be carried out by the acquiring authority over the whole length of that road and not just by reference to the small part of it carried out on the 340 square yards acquired from the claimant. On the figures determined in that case the compensation would have been £4,000 and not £1,600.[115]

9.65   Despite the alteration in the law effected by the Land Compensation Act 1973 there remains a doubt as to the ambit of the entitlement to compensation in certain possible though limited cases. It is possible to distinguish three categories of case in which a part only of a person's land is acquired and works are carried out by the acquiring authority which injuriously affect the retained land of that person. (a) The first category is where the works of the acquiring authority are situated wholly on the land acquired from the claimant. (b) The second category of case is where the works of the acquiring authority are situated partly on the land acquired from the claimant and partly on other land. (c) The third category of case is where no works of the acquiring authority are situated on the land acquired from that claimant but all works are carried out on other land.

9.66   The first category of case presents no possible difficulty. Both before the alteration of the law in 1973 and afterwards the claimant will be entitled to compensation for the injurious

---

[112]   *Edwards v Minister of Transport* [1964] 2 QB 134, [1964] 2 WLR 515.

[113]   An obvious difficulty in applying this principle is how to determine in a case such as the *Edwards* case the damage caused to the retained land by the works on the land acquired from the claimant as opposed to the whole damage caused by the whole road scheme. In that case the whole damage to the retained land was determined at £4,000 whereas the parties agreed (by a process which Harman LJ described as 'some alchemy') that the damage caused to the retained land by the new road on the 340 square yards acquired from the claimant was £1,600.

[114]   It should be noted that s 44(1) only operates as regards injurious affection caused to the land retained by the owner by reason of works. It is possible that in some circumstances injurious affection could be caused by some other form of the exercise of statutory powers by the acquiring authority: see the concluding words of s 7 of the Compulsory Purchase Act 1965 (set out in para 9.1) and see para 9.6.

[115]   See n 113.

affection to his retained land caused by the works carried out on the land acquired from him. In this case there are no other works.

Nor can there be any doubt in the second category of case. This category of case falls   9.67
squarely within that which is stated in section 44(1) of the Land Compensation Act 1973 in that the works of the acquiring authority are situated partly on the land acquired from the claimant and partly on other land. The claimant will be entitled to compensation for injurious affection to his retained land caused by the whole of those works. It should be noted that in this type of case it is not necessary for a claim for compensation to succeed that any injurious affection is caused by the works carried out on the land acquired from the claimant as opposed to the works carried out elsewhere. All that is necessary is that there are works carried out by the acquiring authority under the powers conferred on it by the empowering Act which are partly situated on the land acquired and partly situated elsewhere. Thus compensation may be claimed for injurious affection to the retained land even though the whole of that injurious affection is caused by works on land other than the land acquired from the claimant. An example of what is here being discussed would be where a stratum of land under the ground was acquired for the purpose of building a tunnel as part of a railway project and injurious affection was caused to the remainder of the land, perhaps to a building on it, not by the works of constructing and using the tunnel, but by other works which are part of the project towards which the tunnel contributes. For instance, a new station entrance might be built near to the building underneath which the stratum was taken for the tunnel and this might adversely affect that building by reason of noise, congestion or other effects. In such a case there would be works situated partly on the land acquired, that is the tunnel, and works partly on the remainder of the project. If the works on the remainder of the project caused injurious affection to the retained building of the claimant then he would be entitled to compensation for that injurious affection. While this may be a somewhat specialised instance it illustrates one possible operation of the second category of case.

It is the third category of case which raises some doubt.[116] It is possible that an acquiring   9.68
authority acquires a part of an owner's land for its overall project but does not carry out any works on that land although it may carry out extensive works on other land. An instance might be where the land acquired was used purely as an access route, or as a parking or open storage area, for the main project so that no works were actually carried out on it. The possible difficulty in such a case is that section 44(1) applies only where land is acquired from an owner for the purpose of works which are to be situated partly on that land and partly elsewhere. In the circumstances just postulated that provision would not apply since there would be no works situated on the land acquired from the particular owner. However, section 44(1) of the 1973 Act does not repeal section 7 of the Compulsory Purchase Act 1965, which remains the primary statute conferring an entitlement to compensation for injurious affection to retained land, but only introduces a gloss or alteration to it. It can therefore be argued that, in a case where section 44(1) does not apply such as in the third category of case here under consideration, section 7 of the 1965 Act has to apply in the way in which it was interpreted and applied by the Court of Appeal in the *Edwards* case. The consequence of this chain of reasoning is that in the third category of case the claimant would obtain no compensation for injurious affection to his retained land since: (a) section 44(1) of the

---

[116] See *Tollgate Hotels Ltd v Secretary of State for Transport* [2006] RVR 315, per Judge Rich QC.

1973 Act does not apply, and (b) section 7 of the 1965 Act, as interpreted in the *Edwards* case and earlier decisions and as unaffected by section 44(1), does not give an entitlement to compensation for injurious affection caused by works on land other than the land acquired.

9.69   A degree of further force is added to the argument explained in the last paragraph by provisions in section 8 of Part I of the Land Compensation Act 1973. Part I of that Act provides for compensation for the depreciation of an interest in a person's land caused by the use of public works when no land is acquired from that person.[117] Section 8(2) provides that where a person is entitled to compensation under section 7 of the Compulsory Purchase Act 1965, in the circumstances considered generally in this chapter, he cannot then make a claim under Part I of the 1973 Act. The purpose, of course, is to avoid any possibility of double compensation. However section 8(5) of Part I of the 1973 Act states that this exclusion of compensation under Part I of that Act shall not preclude the payment of compensation under that Part where compensation for injurious affection falls to be assessed otherwise than in accordance with section 44 of the 1973 Act. The suggestion made is that where compensation under section 7 of the 1965 Act is to be determined otherwise than in accordance with section 44 of the 1973 Act, that is where it is a case in which works are carried out by the acquiring authority which injuriously affect retained land of the claimant but those works are not carried out in part on the land acquired from the claimant and in part elsewhere, a claim for compensation may still be made under Part I of the 1973 Act. The reason for this provision in section 8(5) of the 1973 Act, it is suggested, is that in the type of case where section 44(1) of the 1973 Act does not apply, that is the third category of case as described above, no claim is available under section 7 of the 1965 Act for compensation for injurious affection so that a claim can be sustained under Part I of the 1973 Act without any risk of double compensation.

9.70   There is obvious force in the arguments and reasoning just outlined. On the other hand it can be said that the plain intention of Parliament in enacting the 1973 Act was that a person, a part of whose land was acquired and whose retained land was injuriously affected by the works of the acquiring authority, should be entitled to compensation under the 1965 Act. If that is so the legislation in section 44 of the 1973 Act may have impliedly altered as a whole the limitation on the ambit of compensation for injurious affection under section 7 of the 1965 Act as that limitation was stated in the *Edwards* decision. The most that can be said at present is that the availability of compensation under section 7 of the 1965 Act in the third category of case identified in this explanation is in a degree of doubt. The tidy conclusion would certainly be that where a part of an owner's land was acquired and injurious affection was caused to the retained land by the works of the acquiring authority, whether situated wholly on the land acquired or partly on that land and partly on other land or wholly on other land, compensation for that injurious affection should be available under section 7 of the Compulsory Purchase Act 1965. That would leave compensation to be available for the depreciation in value of an interest in land caused by the use of public works in a case where no land of a claimant was acquired to be covered by Part I of the Land Compensation Act 1973, with the particular limitations on the entitlement to compensation in that Act, and with different rules for its assessment, as compared to the entitlement to compensation under section 7 of the Compulsory Purchase Act 1965. If it is correct that there can be no claim under section 7 of the Compulsory Purchase Act 1965 in respect of

---

[117] See section (j) of ch 13.

injurious affection to retained land caused by works carried out wholly on land other than the land acquired then presumably a claim for compensation for the depreciation of the value of the retained land could be made under Part I of the Land Compensation Act 1973. Claims under Part I of the 1973 Act are limited in various ways as explained in chapter 13. A claim under Part I of the 1973 Act: (a) is only available to persons with certain interests in land, (b) can be made only for loss caused by the use, as opposed to the execution, of public works, and (c) cannot generally be made until the public works have been in use for one year. What has here been described as the third category of case may not very frequently occur but if and when it does the law remains in some degree of doubt. That doubt having been noted the better, fairer and tidier view is that section 7 of the Compulsory Purchase Act applies to all three categories of case as just identified. That result can be achieved if section 44(1) of the Land Compensation Act 1973 is interpreted perhaps boldly and purposively as impliedly removing in its entirety the limitation on the operation of section 7 held to exist in decisions which culminated in *Edwards v Minister of Transport*.[118]

(F) SUMMARY

The main rules which govern the entitlement of a landowner to compensation when a part, but not the whole, of his land is compulsorily acquired may be summarised in the following way.   9.71

(i)   In principle in such a situation the landowner is entitled not only to compensation for the open market value of the land acquired from him but also to compensation for damage caused to him in relation to his retained land by reason of its severance from the land acquired, or by reason of any other form of injurious affection to it caused by the exercise by the acquiring authority of the powers conferred on them by the empowering Act. This is the effect of section 7 of the Compulsory Purchase Act 1965.

(ii)   The claim for compensation may arise out of a diminution in the value of the retained land caused solely by the fact that the ownership of it is severed from that of the land acquired and irrespective of any works to be carried out by the acquiring authority on the land acquired or elsewhere. In such a case the compensation may be described as compensation for severance.

(iii)   A frequent further case of a claim for compensation under this provision is where the acquiring authority carries out works on the land acquired and on other land which cause injurious affection to the retained land. However, in principle a claim for compensation for injurious affection is also sustainable where it is some other action of the acquiring authority, that is other than the carrying out of works, on the land acquired which causes the injurious affection.

(iv)   Where the injurious affection is caused by works carried out by the acquiring authority wholly on the land acquired or in part on that land and in part on other

---

[118] *Edwards v Minister of Transport* [1964] 2 QB 134, [1964] 2 WLR 515. In an obiter observation Carnwath LJ suggested in *Moto Hospitality Ltd v Secretary of State for Transport* [2007] EWCA Civ 764, [2008] 1 WLR 2822, at para 54 that if the *Edwards* decision came before the courts today it would be likely to be decided differently. In *Stynes v Western Power (East Midlands) Plc* [2013] UKUT 0214 (LC), the Lands Tribunal found it unnecessary to adjudicate on whether the view of the Court of Appeal in *Edwards* or in *Moto* was to be preferred.

land there is no doubt as to the entitlement of the owner to compensation for the injurious affection caused by those works to his retained land.

(v)   There remains some doubt as to whether, in the circumstances here considered, a landowner is entitled to compensation for injurious affection to his retained land when that injurious affection is caused by works of the acquiring authority which are carried out wholly on land other than the land acquired from that landowner. If a landowner is not entitled to compensation in these circumstances he may have a claim for compensation under Part I of the Land Compensation Act 1973 if his retained land is reduced in value by the use of public works carried out by the acquiring authority on other land.

(vi)   In any of the cases mentioned where compensation is claimable the correct method of assessing the compensation is to carry out a 'before and after' valuation. What is meant is that the value of the retained land is assessed by way of a notional sale of that land in the market by a hypothetical willing seller to a hypothetical willing buyer in the circumstances which existed prior to the acquisition of the land acquired by the acquiring authority and ignoring the scheme of the acquiring authority, this being the before value. A similar valuation is carried out of the retained land after its severance from the land acquired and taking into account the scheme of the acquiring authority including the works to be carried out by that authority, this being the after value. Both valuations should normally be carried out as at the date which is the valuation date for assessing compensation for the land acquired. The compensation due under section 7 of the Compulsory Purchase Act 1965 is the amount, if any, by which the before value exceeds the after value.

10

Compensation for Injurious Affection under Section 10 of the Compulsory Purchase Act 1965

(A) INTRODUCTION

It has been explained that the structure of compensation claims goes back to the provisions of the Lands Clauses Consolidation Act 1845.[1] The general entitlement to compensation today rests on section 7 of the Compulsory Purchase Act 1965 which repeats, with small adaptations to modern language, section 63 of the 1845 Act. The 1845 Act provided for two categories of compensation in respect of land compulsorily acquired: (a) compensation for the value of the land acquired, and (b) compensation for damage by reason of injurious affection to any other land of a dispossessed owner, his retained land, as a consequence of the severance of the land acquired from the land retained.[2] Where a person had land which was in some way injuriously affected by the compulsory purchase of land which he did not own and by the works of the acquiring authority there were no provisions which in clear and express terms provided compensation to him for the damage to his land.

10.1

What was contained in the Lands Clauses Consolidation Act 1845 was section 68 which provided that a person entitled to compensation in respect of any land 'which shall have been taken for or injuriously affected by the execution of the works' and for which the promoters of the undertaking had not made satisfaction under the 1845 Act or under the Act which authorised the works could have his compensation (if it exceeded £50) determined by arbitration or by a jury. On the face of it this was a procedural provision which specified the means of assessing a claim which could be made under other provisions of the 1845 Act or of the Act which authorised the works. There was other provision in the 1845 Act which conferred a substantive right to compensation for land taken, or for injurious affection to land retained by a person a part of whose land had been taken, as mentioned in the last paragraph.

10.2

It was possible to attribute two meanings to section 68 of the 1845 Act. One possible meaning as just mentioned, and that which perhaps most naturally flowed from its language, was that it was procedural only in its impact and provided a further means of obtaining compensation for land acquired, or for injurious affection to land retained where part of a landowner's land was taken, the payment of which was ordained under other provisions of the legislation. It seemed difficult to believe that this was the only intention behind the

10.3

---

[1] See ch 1, para 1.7.
[2] Lands Clauses Consolidation Act 1845, s 63.

enactment of section 68 since adequate means existed under other provisions in the 1845 Act for the assessment of compensation in the event of dispute. On the other hand if section 68 had a different meaning, so that its purpose was to confer a separate substantive right to compensation available in circumstances not covered by other provisions, then the language of section 68 gave little clue as to the circumstances in which such compensation was separately available. As will be explained, the courts grappled with this obscurity in the legislative language and intent by interpreting section 68 to mean that a separate head of possible compensation was created by that provision but in doing so the courts limited the circumstances in which compensation could be claimed under that head by establishing a number of conditions which had to be satisfied before a claimant could obtain compensation.[3] The separate head of compensation permitted in certain circumstances a claim for compensation by the owner of land injuriously affected or damaged by works carried out by an acquiring authority even though none of his land was acquired by the authority.

10.4   The result of this process was that with the passing of the decades following its enactment section 68 of the 1845 Act came to bear a meaning which owed little to its terse and unhelpful language. In a well known passage Lord Wilberforce in 1975, more than a century after section 68 was enacted, said:

> The relevant section of the Act of 1845 (section 68) has, over a hundred years, received through a number of decisions, some in this House, and by no means easy to reconcile, an interpretation which fixes upon it a meaning having little perceptible relation to the words used. This represents a century of judicial effort to keep the primitive wording – which itself has an earlier history – in some sort of accord with the realities of the industrial age. [4]

This interpretation now falls to be employed in the computer age.

10.5   It is perhaps unfortunate that when section 68 of the 1845 Act was re-enacted as section 10 of the Compulsory Purchase Act 1965 the opportunity was not taken to state in explicit modern form the exact circumstances in which a claim for compensation could be made for injurious affection to land caused by the execution of works on other land under statutory powers where no land was acquired from the claimant. Instead the legislature confined itself to repeating section 68 in slightly modernised language, removing the £50 minimum limit, and stating that section 10(1) was to have the same meaning as the courts had attributed to section 68. The legislation currently in force, section 10(1) of the 1965 Act, states:

> If any person claims compensation in respect of any land, which has been taken for or injuriously affected by the execution of the works, and for which the acquiring authority have not made satisfaction under the provisions of this Act or of the special Act, any dispute arising in relation to the compensation shall be referred to and determined by the Upper Tribunal.

Section 10(2) states that section 10(1) shall be construed as affording in all cases a right to compensation for injurious affection to land which is the same as the right which section 68 of the 1845 Act has been construed as affording where the amount claimed exceeded £50.[5]

---

[3] Five conditions were established and these are considered in section (d) of this chapter.

[4] *Argyle Motors (Birkenhead) Ltd v Birkenhead Corporation* [1975] AC 99, [1973] 2 WLR 487, at p 129. Expressions of judicial difficulty are far from new. Within two or so decades of the enactment of s 68 the Lord Chancellor, Lord Chelmsford, said in *Ricket v Metropolitan Rly Co* (1867) 2 LR HL 175, at p 189: 'It appears to me to be a hopeless task to attempt to reconcile the cases upon the subject. I must endeavour, by an examination of them, to determine which, in my judgment, are most in accordance with principle'.

[5] Under the Lands Clauses Consolidation Act 1845 a claim for £50 or less was settled by two justices under s 22

Before coming to the substance of section 10, and for purposes of clarity, it is necessary to   10.6
distinguish between the three situations within the law of compensation as a whole in
which compensation may be claimed for some loss or damage to land when that particular
land is not compulsorily acquired from the claimant or the claimant is not disturbed in his
possession of that land by its compulsory acquisition.

(i) When only a part of a person's land is acquired that person may be entitled to
     compensation under section 7 of the Compulsory Purchase Act 1965 for injurious
     affection to the land retained by him. This right to compensation is explained in
     chapter 9.

(ii) A person may be entitled to compensation for a reduction in the value of his land
      caused by the use of public works even though no land is acquired from him. This
      is a right to compensation introduced by Part I of the Land Compensation Act 1973.
      It is unlikely that it will overlap with the subject matter of this chapter since there
      are important differences between the two entitlements to compensation and there
      are provisions which prevent the receipt of double compensation. The right to com-
      pensation under the 1973 Act is explained in chapter 13.[6]

(iii) There is a right to compensation under section 10 of the Compulsory Purchase Act
       1965 for injurious affection to a person's land caused by the execution of works by
       an acquiring authority even though no land is acquired from that person. That right
       is the subject matter of this chapter. As will be explained it is a right which is hedged
       with substantial conditions and limitations. As with most heads of compensation
       (including those in sub-paragraphs (i) and (ii) above) a person who claims com-
       pensation for injurious affection to his land under section 10, must hold a proprie-
       tary interest in land.[7] A person who holds a short tenancy, whose compensation for
       the value of his interest and other matters is determined under section 20 of the
       Compulsory Purchase Act 1965, is entitled to claim compensation for injurious
       affection under section 10.[8]

(B) OUTLINE OF THE ENTITLEMENT TO COMPENSATION

Before coming to the details of the entitlement to compensation under this head it is useful   10.7
to explain in outline the two main areas within which, as a result of the meaning attributed
to section 68 of the 1845 Act and now section 10 of the Compulsory Purchase Act 1965,
compensation is available where it is not available under any other statutory provision.

---

of that Act.

[6] One of the main reasons that there is unlikely to be an overlap is that compensation under s 10 is confined to
the effect on the land of the claimant of the execution (as opposed to the use) of works by the acquiring authority
whereas compensation under Pt I of the Land Compensation Act 1973 is confined to the effect of the use of public
works.

[7] A licensee is therefore not entitled to claim under s 10: see *Moto Hospitality Ltd v Secretary of State for Transport*
[2007] EWCA Civ 764, [2008] 1 WLR 2822, at para 2. For the nature of proprietary interests see para 2.27 of ch 2.
The general question of the nature of interests in land which can found a claim for compensation is explained in
section (c) of ch 3.

[8] *R v Middlesex Sheriff, Re Somers and Metropolitan Rly* (1862) 31 LJQB 261. It appears that where a person who
has a claim for compensation under s 10 transfers the land which has been injuriously affected the benefit of the
claim may be assigned with the land: *Dawson v Great Northern and City Rly* [1905] 1 KB 260.

10.8   The first area is where a person's land is in some way damaged, that is injuriously affected, by the execution of works by a public authority even though no land of his is compulsorily acquired. In these circumstances the essence of the right to compensation under this head is that the works carried out by the public authority are authorised by statute, and for that reason cannot be a civil wrong such as a tort against the owners of any land in the vicinity of the works, but that those works would be a civil wrong against the owner of the land who claims compensation had there not been statutory authorisation so that, in the absence of the statutory authorisation, the owner of the land would have had a remedy at common law against those who carried out the works.[9] In other words the situation contemplated is that a public authority has a statutory power to carry out works and so cannot be liable for ordinary civil wrongs or torts which it would otherwise commit by carrying out the works but should in those circumstances be required to pay compensation to persons whose land is damaged by its works and who would have had a right to damages if the works had been carried out by some other body without statutory authorisation. The justice of this situation is apparent and the motives of the courts in interpreting and applying section 68 so as to cover a situation of this sort, and to provide compensation in a situation of this sort, are readily understandable.

10.9   The second area in which compensation is recoverable under this head relates to what are often called third party rights. Third party rights is an imprecise expression which means that a person has proprietary rights over land which are not a corporeal interest in the sense of giving him a right to possession of the land.[10] The rights are sometimes described as *iura in re aliena*. Primary examples of this category of interest are an easement, such as a right of way, over the land of some other person or the benefit of a restrictive covenant which entitles a person to prevent the owner of other land using or developing it in some way. Such rights arise generally as a result of an express or implied term in a contract or a conveyance of land and are proprietary rights, as opposed to being merely contractual rights, because they are in principle enforceable not only against the owner of the land who was the other party to the contract or conveyance which created the rights but also against all other persons who come to hold an interest in the land burdened by the right or restriction.[11] Where there is a compulsory acquisition of the land over which these third party rights exist the effect of the acquisition is to extinguish or override the third party rights at any rate to the extent to which they prevent the scheme of the acquiring authority which underlies the compulsory acquisition.[12] There is the same consequence if land is acquired by agreement

---

[9]   At common law (that is apart from any specific statutory provision) a person who suffers or may suffer a wrong, such as the commission of the tort of nuisance to his property, may be entitled to: (a) an injunction to prevent the wrong or the continuation of the wrong, and (b) damages for the loss caused to him by the wrong. An injunction is a discretionary remedy in that a court may or may not order it in any particular case. The right to damages for loss caused by the wrong is an entitlement as of right and is not dependent on the discretion of the court.

[10]   See ch 2, para 2.26 for the distinction between corporeal and incorporeal interests in land.

[11]   See ch 2, para 2.27.

[12]   *Kirby v School Board for Harrogate* [1896] 1 Ch 437. See further paras 10.55 and 10.56. In some cases the empowering statute contains an express provision that rights, or certain rights such as rights of way, over the land acquired are extinguished: see, eg s 236 of the Town and Country Planning Act 1990. There is a general provision for the overriding of third party rights in s 237 of the same Act which operates when development is carried out in accordance with a planning permission by a local planning authority or a successor in title of that authority and where the land has been acquired or appropriated by the authority for planning purposes. Persons whose rights are overridden pursuant to this provision are entitled to compensation assessed under s 10 or s 7 of the Compulsory Purchase Act 1965.

by an authority in order to carry on a scheme under statutory powers. It would be unjust if the owner of the third party rights in this situation had his rights permanently or temporarily extinguished or overridden but was entitled to no compensation from the acquiring authority for the loss which was suffered by him. Section 68 of the 1845 Act, and now section 10 of the Compulsory Purchase Act 1965, have been interpreted as a provision which provides an entitlement to compensation to persons who lose the right to enforce their third party rights in these circumstances. Again one can readily understand the motives of the courts which attributed to section 68 of the 1845 Act this effect which is not immediately apparent from its linguistic form.

(C) THE GENERAL AMBIT OF SECTION 10

Assuming, as was soon established, that section 68 of the Lands Clauses Consolidation Act   10.10
1845, and now section 10 of the Compulsory Purchase Act 1965, have more than a procedural effect, it is necessary to consider the language by which section 10 provides a substantive and separate right to compensation. The language of section 10 states that compensation is payable: (a) in respect of land, or an interest in land, which has been taken for the execution of the works, and (b) in respect of land, or an interest in land, which has been injuriously affected by the execution of the works. The works mean the works of whatever nature authorised by the Act under which the compulsory purchase is authorised.[13] Before coming to the critical question of the five conditions which have to be satisfied before a specific claim to compensation can succeed under section 10 it is necessary to explain two initial matters concerning the ambit of the provision. The first initial matter is what is the meaning and effect of the reference in section 10(1) to land which has been taken. The second initial matter is what link has to exist between a compulsory purchase of land and injurious affection to the land of the claimant caused by the works of the acquiring authority before a claim for compensation for that injurious affection can arise.

1. The Reference to Land Taken

It is difficult to see what is the significance or purpose of the provision in section 10 of the   10.11
1965 Act that compensation may be claimed for 'land which has been taken'. Compensation for land taken, equal to the value of that land, is provided for by section 7 of the Compulsory Purchase Act 1965 and if the compensation is not agreed the amount of it may be settled by the Lands Tribunal under its powers in section 1 of the Land Compensation Act 1961 or section 6 of the Compulsory Purchase Act 1965.[14] The Lands Clauses Consolidation Act 1845 provided in section 63 for compensation equal to the value of the land taken and contained statutory provisions for the determination of the amount of the compensation by magistrates, by a surveyor appointed by magistrates, by arbitration or by a jury.[15] The

---

[13] Compulsory Purchase Act 1965, s 1(2), (4).
[14] References in these provisions to the Lands Tribunal were amended to the Upper Tribunal by the Tribunals, Courts and Enforcement Act 2007.
[15] Section 21 et seq of the Lands Clauses Consolidation Act 1845.

structure of the legislation leaves little room for a further provision in section 10 of the 1965 Act that there shall be a claim for compensation for the land taken.

10.12   In early cases there are indications that section 68 of the 1845 Act could be used to seek a determination of the compensation for land taken.[16] In *Horn v Sunderland Corporation*[17] Scott LJ set out a survey of the main provisions then in force governing the assessment of compensation and suggested that the words 'taken for' in section 68 may have been inserted by way of a clerical error. He said that it was notorious that section 68 had always been considered as a provision which applied only to land not taken with the lands taken. More recently the Lands Tribunal has held that when section 10 of the 1965 Act refers to a dispute arising in relation to the compensation being referred to the Tribunal it includes a dispute relating to the value of an interest in land compulsorily acquired.[18] When this decision came before the Court of Appeal that Court did not find it necessary to decide the point.[19] The position therefore appears to be that while section 10 does not provide for compensation for land acquired on any basis other than that provided for elsewhere in the legislation it may be that reliance can be placed on section 10 as a provision which confers jurisdiction on the Lands Tribunal to determine the amount of the compensation for land acquired. Since there are other provisions in the legislation which confer this jurisdiction on the Tribunal it will be rare that reliance need be placed on section 10 for this purpose even if such reliance is possible.[20] It seems, therefore, that as regards land compulsorily acquired section 10 has at most a procedural significance.

2. The Link to Compulsory Purchase

10.13   It is, of course, the second category of compensation provided for in section 10, compensation in respect of land or an interest in land injuriously affected by the execution of the works carried out by the acquiring authority, which constitutes an important and separate

---

[16] *Adams v London and Blackpool Rly Co* (1850) 2 Mac & G 118; see *Union Rlys (North) Ltd v Kent County Council* [2008] 2 EGLR 183 (Lands Tribunal) for a review of the earlier authorities. In *Tiverton & North Devon Rly Co v Loosemore* (1884) 9 App Cas 480, Lord Blackburn at p 498 suggested that s 68 of the 1845 Act could be used to compel an assessment of the price for land taken but that recourse could also be had to earlier sections of the Act for that purpose (eg s 21 et seq). In *Wildtree Hotels v Harrow LBC* [2001] 2 AC 1, [2009] 3 WLR 163, Lord Hoffmann said at p 7 that s 10 of the Compulsory Purchase Act 1965 gave a right to compensation to someone whose land has been injuriously affected by the execution of the works. He said that if land was taken the compensation for injurious affection of his remaining land was calculated on different principles under s 7 of the 1965 Act. This observation suggests that Lord Hoffmann, like Scott LJ in *Horn v Sunderland Corporation* [1941] 2 KB 26, [1941] 1 All ER 480, at pp 42–43, thought that s 10 had nothing to do with compensation for land taken. It may be noted that s 10(2) does not refer to land taken.

[17] *Horn v Sunderland Corporation* [1941] 2 KB 26, [1941] 1 All ER 480.

[18] *Union Rlys (North) Ltd v Kent County Council* [2008] 2 EGLR 183.

[19] [2009] EWCA Civ. 363, [2009] All ER (D) 56, [2009] 30 EGLR 68.

[20] The reliance on s 10 by the Lands Tribunal in the *Union Railways* case, as a provision conferring jurisdiction on the Lands Tribunal to determine compensation when land had been taken from the claimant, was because the Tribunal regarded itself as having no jurisdiction to determine compensation for land taken under s 6 of the Compulsory Purchase Act 1965 since that jurisdiction depended on an actual or deemed notice to treat having been served on the claimant, something which had not occurred in the case before the Tribunal. The Court of Appeal decided the case on a different basis. The question of whether a reference to the Tribunal can be made under s 10 claiming compensation for the land taken appears to be of more academic than practical significance. The answer to the question depends on whether the obiter dictum of Scott LJ in *Horn v Sunderland Corporation*, above n 17, is preferred to the recent decision of the Tribunal in the *Union Rlys* case.

head of compensation not provided for elsewhere in the legislation. It has been explained that injurious affection is a term which has been widely used in the law of compensation to mean damage to land.[21] This is its meaning in section 10(1) of the Compulsory Purchase Act 1965. It has been said that in this context the term 'injuriously affected' connotes '*injuria*', that is to say damage which would have been wrongful but for the protection afforded by statutory powers.[22] Given that section 10, as it has been interpreted, confers a separate head of compensation payable when a person's land has been damaged by the execution of works by an authority, but where no land or interest in land has been acquired from that person, the crucial question is that of knowing the exact circumstances in which a person in that situation is entitled to compensation for the injurious affection or damage to his land.

The underlying situation which must exist if section 10 of the Compulsory Purchase Act   10.14
1965 is to apply is less than clear. The nineteenth century decisions which followed the enactment of section 68 of the Lands Clauses Consolidation Act 1845 offer limited, and sometimes confusing, guidance on the question. Some degree of clarity has now been provided by the decision of the Court of Appeal in *Moto Hospitality Ltd v Secretary of State for Transport*.[23]

Section 10 itself simply states that compensation may be claimed in respect of land or an   10.15
interest in land which has been injuriously affected by the execution of the works for which the acquiring authority has not made satisfaction. From this it appears that there must be an acquiring authority and that there must have been works carried out by that authority. Section 1(1) of the Compulsory Purchase Act 1965 states that Part I of that Act, which includes section 10, applies in relation to a compulsory purchase to which Part II of the Acquisition of Land Act 1981 is applied, and in section 1(2) an acquiring authority is defined to mean a person authorised by a compulsory purchase order to purchase land. One would have supposed that for section 10 to become engaged at all there would have to be a compulsory purchase of some land and some works carried out by the acquiring authority. Section 1(4) states that the works mean the works of whatever nature authorised to be executed by the special Act. By virtue of section 1(2) the special Act means the enactment which authorises the compulsory purchase and the compulsory purchase order. An analysis of this thicket of definitions suggests that for a claim to be permissible under section 10: (a) there must be an enactment which confers a power of compulsory purchase, (b) there must have been a compulsory purchase of land under that enactment to which Part II of the Acquisition of Land Act 1981 is applied by the enactment, and (c) works must have been carried out by the acquiring authority under powers conferred by the empowering enactment. It is not stated that these works must have been carried out on land compulsorily acquired. As will become apparent recent authority states that the first and third of these conditions, but not necessarily the second, must be satisfied before a claim for compensation can be brought under section 10.

It must be remembered that by reason of section 10(2) section 10 is to be construed as giv-   10.16
ing the same right to compensation as section 68 of the 1845 Act has been construed as

---

[21] See ch 3, para 3.20.
[22] *Wildtree Hotels Ltd v Harrow LBC* [2001] 2 AC 1, [2000] 3 WLR 163, per Lord Hoffmann at p 7. See para 10.32 for the use of the latin expression '*damnum absque injuria*' meaning a loss suffered by a person without any actionable wrong having been committed against him.
[23] *Moto Hospitality Ltd v Secretary of State for Transport* [2007] EWCA Civ 764, [2008] 1 WLR 2822.

conferring. The link between a compulsory purchase of land and a right to compensation under section 68 appears from the authorities to have been looser than might be suggested by the above analysis of the current statutory language or of the equivalent language in the 1845 Act. The best example of this proposition is *Kirby v The School Board for Harrogate*,[24] in which an acquiring authority had purchased land by agreement for the building of school accommodation and in doing so had overridden a restrictive covenant applying to the land. The persons entitled to the benefit of the covenant were held to be entitled to compensation under section 68 even though no compulsory purchase was involved.[25]

10.17   In the *Moto* case[26] the Court of Appeal had to consider: (a) what was the necessary linkage between a compulsory purchase and the injury suffered by a claimant before a claim for compensation for the injury could be sustained under section 10, and (b) what were the works, and where did those works have to have been carried out, before such a claim could be sustained.[27] Moto Hospitality Ltd were tenants of a motorway service area at Ardley near an interchange on the M40 motorway and obtained much of their custom from traffic leaving or joining the motorway. The Secretary of State under powers in the Highways Act 1980 carried out a series of road improvements and alterations including the stopping up of certain roads in the vicinity of the service area the result of which was a reduction in traffic coming to the service area. A claim was made for temporary and permanent losses under section 10. The scheme was carried out under a package of powers and orders contained in or made under the Act including specific powers for the compulsory purchase of land and for the stopping up of public highways. The Acquisition of Land Act 1981 was applied to the compulsory purchase of land.

10.18   On the first question as stated in the last paragraph the Court of Appeal formulated the necessary link between compulsory purchase and the harm to the claimant's land. It was said that the inclusion of compulsory powers in the package of orders for the scheme being carried out, for at least a part of the land required, was enough to trigger the application of section 10 to the works as a whole.[28] At another point the principle was stated in much the same way when it was said that the inclusion of compulsory powers for part of the land is enough to apply section 10 to the effects of the whole of the scheme.[29] The essential criterion is therefore that there existed a power of compulsory purchase of land for the purposes of the scheme of the authority which carried out the works. It is not necessary that that power was exercised. On the other hand when examining the cases on section 68 of the 1845 Act the Court concluded that it was clear that 'A claim for compensation under section 68

---

[24] *Kirby v The School Board for Harrogate* [1896] 1 Ch 547.
[25] A further example of the proposition that no compulsory purchase of any land need exist is *Harpur v Swansea Corporation* [1913] AC 597, where compensation was held to be payable under s 68 even though no land had been acquired by the Corporation, either by agreement or by compulsion, for the scheme of laying pipes in a road which caused the damage to the land of the claimant. In *Horn v Sunderland Corporation* [1941] 2 KB 26, Scott LJ observed at p 42 that s 68 'has nothing to do with compulsory acquisition'. In *Westminster City Council v Ocean Leisure* [2004] EWCA Civ 970, [2004] RVR 219, it was conceded by the Council that works to a highway could trigger a claim under s 10 regardless of the link between those works and any acquisition of land whether by agreement or by compulsion.
[26] Above n 23.
[27] The law is illuminated by the careful decisions of the then President of the Lands Tribunal, George Bartlett QC, both in the *Moto* case and in the previous case of *Wagstaff v Department of the Environment* [1999] 2 EGLR 108.
[28] See the *Moto* decision, n 23, at para 53.
[29] Ibid, at para 57.

did not depend on the inclusion of compulsory purchase powers in the provisions authorising the works'.[30] Since section 10(2) of the Compulsory Purchase Act 1965 expressly requires
that section 10 is to be given the same interpretation as was previously accorded to section
68 of the 1845 Act it is difficult to see how the Court could reach this last conclusion, which
it did on the ambit of section 68, and then add an additional requirement for the operation
of section 10, namely that within the package of powers available to the authority carrying
out the works there must be a power of the compulsory acquisition of land. What is apparent as an answer to the second question before the court is that a claim under section 10 (as
under section 68) does not depend on the works which cause the injurious affection to the
land of the claimant being carried out on land which was compulsorily acquired.[31]

It was at one time thought that a claim under section 10 could not succeed when the injury   10.19
to the land of the claimant was caused by a stopping-up of a highway under statutory powers. The origin of this view was the decision of the Court of Appeal in *Jolliffe v Exeter
Corporation*.[32] Prior to the decision in *Jolliffe* in 1967 it does not seem to have been suggested that the stopping-up of a highway could not be something which in appropriate
circumstances might give rise to a claim under section 68 or section 10.[33] In *Jolliffe's* case a
stopping-up order was made under the Town and Country Planning Act 1947. The claimant's garage was left at the end of a cul-de-sac with reduced trade and a reduced value. The
Court of Appeal held that no compensation was payable to the claimant since the Act which
authorised the stopping-up contained no provision for compensation. In *Moto* the Court
of Appeal confined the absence of compensation for a stopping-up to cases where the stopping-up was carried out under a separate statute and did not apply to a situation where
there was a compendium of statutory powers, including a power of compulsory purchase
and a power of stopping-up, so that in the latter case compensation under section 10 could
in principle be available as a result of a stopping-up of a highway.[34] It is noticeable what
narrow and unsatisfactory distinctions have to be drawn in this area of the law.

It was suggested in argument in the *Moto* case that when there were some works such as the   10.20
obstruction to or stopping-up of a highway which affected the land of the claimant there
could not be a claim under section 10 unless the rights of the claimant were appurtenant to
his land and the works in question were sufficiently proximate to his land. Neither limitation found favour with the Court. The suggested limitations were bound up with the principle that the works of the authority had to be such as would have constituted an actionable
civil wrong against the claimant apart from the statutory authority to carry them out and
the rule that a public nuisance, such as the obstruction of a highway, can only be the subject
of a civil action if some particular harm has been suffered by the claimant over and above
that suffered by the generality of the public.

---

[30] Ibid, at para 40.
[31] The view that the works in question had to be on land compulsorily acquired was put forward by Lord
Denning in *Joliffe v Exeter Corporation* [1967] 1 WLR 993, [1967] 2 All ER 1099, but was not essential to the majority view of the Court of Appeal in that case. See the *Moto* decision at para 45.
[32] *Joliffe v Exeter Corporation* [1967] 1 WLR 993, [1967] 2 All ER 1099.
[33] See *Chamberlain v West End of London and Crystal Palace Rly Co* (1862) 2 BCS 605. Erle CJ at p 635 accepted
that the value of shop properties had been reduced and that a claim lay for compensation 'because the highway was
stopped up and the easy access which before existed to [the shop] was taken away'. The stopping up in this case was
for the purpose of railway works. See also *Wadham v North Eastern Rly Co* (1884) 14 QBD 747.
[34] See the *Moto* decision n 23, at paras 44–49.

10.21   Rights which are appurtenant to land are generally considered to comprise certain proprietary rights which burden one piece of land for the benefit of another, usually neighbouring, piece of land such as easements and restrictive covenants. The rights are appurtenant
in the sense that they have to benefit the land of the person entitled to exercise the rights
and that they normally pass to a new owner on a transfer of the ownership of the land benefited.[35] Certainly a claim for compensation can be made under section 10 when such rights
are overridden by statutory authority[36] but other rights such as the right to use a public
highway and the right not to suffer a nuisance to land are of a more general character and
there is no requirement that such rights are 'appurtenant' to the land adversely affected in
the sense in which that word is used in the law of real property before a claim can be
brought under section 10.[37]

10.22   If by proximity is meant that the roads obstructed or other works of the authority have to
be next to, or within a certain distance of, the land adversely affected by those works there
is no absolute requirement for such proximity before a claim can be made under section 10.
However, the damage to the land of the claimant cannot be too remote in the legal sense
of the concept of remoteness just as losses for which common law damages for a tort or for
a breach of contract are recoverable cannot be too remote. It is sometimes said, as in the
Moto decision, that the damage to the land of the claimant under a section 10 claim for
compensation must be 'direct', and the degree of physical proximity between the works of
the authority and the damage to the land of the claimant could have a bearing on this
question. The question of remoteness of damage in connection with claims under section
10 is discussed separately later in this chapter.[38] The claim for compensation in the *Moto*
case failed in the end because of the view of the Court of Appeal that the claim was too
remote.

10.23   In so far as it is possible to state clearly the linkage between a claim under section 10 and the
power of compulsory purchase of land, and the circumstances which must exist before a
claim can be made for compensation for injury to land caused by works carried out by a
public authority under section 10, the law following the *Moto* decision may be summarised
as follows.

(i)   There must be an enactment which confers some power of compulsory purchase
for the purposes of a scheme to be carried out by a body exercising powers under
that enactment.

(ii)   That enactment must be one which either directly, or through the application of
the Acquisition of Land Act 1981, applies the Compulsory Purchase Act 1965 to a
compulsory purchase under the enactment.

(iii)   The works in question must be works carried out under the compendium of
powers conferred by the enactment.

(iv)   The works may be, but need not be, on land acquired by compulsion.

(v)   It appears that while a power of compulsory purchase must exist within the package of statutory powers for the implementation of the scheme it is not necessary
that this power has actually been exercised as regards any land.

---

[35] See section (e) of this chapter.
[36] See the *Moto* decision n 23, at paras 61–63.
[37] Ibid, at paras 64–72.
[38] See section (e) of this chapter.

(vi) The works which cause harm to the land of the claimant can in principle be the stopping-up of a highway.

Having established that section 10 has little if any significance as regards compensation for   10.24
land acquired from a claimant, and having described the linkage which has to exist between a compulsory purchase and a claim under section 10 before such a claim can in principle be sustained, it is now possible to examine the conditions which have to be satisfied before a claimant can claim compensation under section 10 for injurious affection to his land caused by the works carried out by an authority with a power of compulsory purchase.

(D) THE RIGHT TO COMPENSATION

Section 10 offers little guidance on the exact circumstances in which a person can claim   10.25
compensation in reliance on it. As explained in the previous section of this chapter all that is stated as section 10 has been interpreted is that the land of the claimant must have been injuriously affected and that the injurious affection must have been caused by the execution of works which are authorised by an Act which authorises the compulsory acquisition of some land for those works. It was observed in the House of Lords in an early decision that section 68 of the Lands Clauses Consolidation Act 1845 did not define the conditions under which the person whose land has been in any way affected is to be entitled to compensation, but rather assumed that the right to compensation had been given in other enactments, and contented itself with pointing out the manner in which the compensation was to be obtained.[39]

Once it became established that section 68 did create a separate and substantive right to   10.26
compensation over and beyond that available under other enactments and that the entitlement arose when a person, none of whose land had been taken from him, suffered injurious affection to his land from works carried out by an acquiring authority it fell to the courts in the Victorian era to specify by a form of judicial legislation what exactly were the conditions which had to be satisfied before a claim for compensation could be made. It is possible today to state these judge-made conditions but it must be borne in mind that they were not laid down in a single and authoritative decision but instead emerged from a series of sometimes conflicting decisions on individual circumstances by which the law was gradually built up.[40]

It has been pointed out by Lord Hoffmann in the leading modern decision on the applica-   10.27
tion of section 10 of the 1965 Act that the decisions of the courts in the decades following the Lands Clauses Consolidation Act 1845 were motivated by different social and economic conceptions of what should be the rights of landowners and the rights of promoters of

---

[39] *Hammersmith and City Rly Co v Brand* (1869) LR 4 HL 171, per Lord Cairns at pp 217–18.
[40] The main decisions in chronological order are *Re Penny and South Eastern Rly Co* (1857) 7 E & B 660; *Ricket v Metropolitan Rly Co* (1865) 5 B & S 149, (1867) LR 2 HL 175; *Hammersmith and City Rly Co v Brand* (1867) LR 2 QB 223, (1869) LR 4 HL 171; *Metropolitan Board of Works v McCarthy* (1874) LR 7 HL 243; *Caledonian Rly Co v Walker's Trustees* (1882) 7 App Cas 259; and *Ford v Metropolitan and Metropolitan District Rly Co* (1886) 17 QBD 12. Certain of the principles laid down in *Ricket's* case did not survive subsequent judicial examination; see paras 10.38 and 10.39. This is a brief list of the main authorities and there were, of course, numerous other cases in which s 68 of the 1845 Act was considered some of which are referred to in this chapter.

undertakings such as railways.[41] On the one hand there was the view that losses to owners of property attributable to the new railway should be borne by the operators of the railway and reflected in the fares charged for the use of the facilities. On an extreme view this approach would have provided compensation for a wide variety of losses such as compensation for persons whose business, for instance that of running a coaching inn, was adversely affected by a railway built in its vicinity. On the other hand there was the view that new facilities such as railways served a public interest and that the operation of the facilities and the sums charged to users of them should not be unduly burdened by having to pay compensation to nearby property owners. [42] The result of the differing approaches was inevitably a compromise in the limitations on a claim for compensation, although it can be said as a generality that the second of the two approaches just described had the more powerful influence, something which is apparent from the various judicially created limitations on claims under section 10 which will be described in the remainder of this section of the chapter. A notable success of the advocates of the more restrictive approach to the entitlement to compensation was the limiting rule established by a decision of the House of Lords in 1869 that compensation was payable only for the effect of the execution of the works, for example the construction of a railway, and not for the effect of the operation of the facilities provided by the construction of the works, such as the actual operation of the trains.[43]

10.28   The conditions which have to be satisfied in order to found a claim for compensation for injurious affection are sometimes called the McCarthy rules after the decision of the House of Lords in *Metropolitan Board of Works v McCarthy*[44] although the derivation of the conditions is from a much wider span of decisions. There are five conditions which a claim for compensation must satisfy. The conditions will be explained in detail but may first be summarised as that: (a) the works must have been executed pursuant to statutory powers, (b) the execution of the works must have been lawful, (c) the injurious affection suffered by the claimant must have been that which would have given him an action in private law against the persons executing the works had it not been for the statutory authorisation of the works, (d) the injurious affection must have been damage to the land of the claimant, as opposed to a personal or purely financial loss, and (e) the injurious affection must have been caused by the execution of the works and not by their use.[45]

1. Condition 1: Use of Statutory Powers

10.29   The right to compensation under section 10 is confined to cases in which the works carried out and which caused the injurious affection to the land of a landowner are carried out pursuant to statutory powers. This is apparent from the definition of 'the works' in section 1(4) of the Compulsory Purchase Act 1965 where that expression is stated to mean the works authorised to be executed by the special Act. The special Act means the enactment

---

[41]   *Wildtree Hotels Ltd v Harrow LBC* [2001] 2 AC 1, [2000] 3 WLR 163.
[42]   In economic jargon burdens and costs borne involuntarily by persons not a part of the commercial enterprise, such as various forms of pollution caused by the enterprise, are called 'externalities'.
[43]   *Hammersmith and City Rly Co v Brand* (1869) LR 4 HL 171.
[44]   *Metropolitan Board of Works v McCarthy* (1874) LR 7 HL 243.
[45]   The conditions and the principles justifying them are summarised by Lord Hoffmann in *Wildtree Hotels Ltd v Harrow LBC*, above n 41, at p 7.

under which a compulsory purchase is authorised and the compulsory purchase order itself. Of course if it is the land or any part of the land of the claimant which has been acquired by the compulsory purchase then his claim will be under the general entitlement to compensation for the value of land acquired, or for injurious affection to any part of the land retained by him, and he will not need recourse to section 10. There could be many occasions on which a person is harmed in some way by works carried out by persons or bodies of persons other than under statutory powers and any remedy of a person whose land is so harmed will be under the private law of nuisance.[46] It will normally be public bodies such as highway authorities who will execute works under statutory powers which cause injurious affection to people in the vicinity whose land is not taken but what is critical is not the status of the body which carries out the works but the fact that the works are carried out under statutory powers. Today a wide variety of statutory powers to execute works are given to bodies which are profit making commercial entities, such as privatised utility companies, although generally the works are those considered necessary or desirable in the public interest. While the most usual cause for claims under section 68 of the Lands Clauses Consolidation Act 1845 may have been the construction of railways in the middle part of the nineteenth century (sometimes with consequential obstruction or alteration of highways needed to facilitate the works of constructing the railway) the most usual case in which a claim under section 10 may arise today is the obstruction, temporary or permanent, under statutory powers of a highway over which a landowner has a right of passage. The three leading modern cases on the meaning and operation of section 10 of the Compulsory Purchase Act 1965 fall into this category.[47]

2. Condition 2: Lawful Works

The second condition is that the execution of the works which have caused the injurious affection must have been lawful in the sense that they were within, and authorised by, the Act in question. If an authority acts outside the powers conferred on it by the Act then what it does is, or may be, unlawful and if there is any remedy for a person whose land is injuriously affected that remedy is under the ordinary law of tort. In *Imperial Gas Light and Coke Co v Broadbent*[48] an action was brought for an injunction and damages in connection with the construction of gas works. In the House of Lords reference was made to section 68 of the Lands Clauses Consolidation Act 1845 and in this connection Lord Campbell observed: 10.30

> [I]t has been determined over and over again, in every court in Westminster Hall, that under [section 68] there is no ground for seeking compensation except for that which is done under the powers conferred by the legislature. If there is wrong which is not authorised by those powers, the common law right of action exists for it.[49]

[46] It is said that the essence of nuisance is a condition or activity which unduly interferes with the use or enjoyment of land. See Buckley, *The Law of Nuisance*, 5th edn (LexisNexis, 2011). Effects on land such as noise, fumes or smell are typical nuisances. The obstruction of a highway is a public nuisance for which a person particularly affected may claim damages and today this is the type of action authorised by statute which is most likely to found a claim under s 10. See para 10.34 for this type of nuisance.

[47] *Argyle Motors (Birkenhead) Ltd v Birkenhead Corporation* [1975] AC 99, [1973] 2 WLR 487; *Wildtree Hotels Ltd v Harrow LBC* [2001] 2 AC 1, [2000] 3 WLR 163; *Moto Hospitality Ltd v Secretary of State for Transport* [2007] EWCA Civ 764, [2008] 1 WLR 2822.

[48] *Imperial Gas Light and Coke Co v Broadbent* (1859) 7 HL Cas 660.

[49] (1859) 7 HL Cas 666 at p 612.

The reason for this condition is apparent. If the actions of the public authority are not authorised by statute the authority has no immunity from an ordinary action at common law and a landowner should be left to his ordinary rights in private law. Although they are usually stated separately, the first and second conditions are in truth aspects of one principle which is that to found a claim under section 10 the works carried out must have been carried out under statutory authority and within the bounds of that authority.

3. Condition 3: Works Actionable in Absence of Statutory Authorisation

10.31   The third condition is that the execution of the works would have been an actionable injury in private law against the claimant if they had not been authorised by statute. The effect of a statutory power to execute works is that the works are lawful whether or not they would have been lawful apart from the statutory authorisation. Naturally some works authorised by statute would not have been an actionable injury to anyone even if there was no statutory authorisation. Works in this last category are not the subject of compensation under section 10 of the Compulsory Purchase Act 1965. If the works in question would not have constituted a wrong to the claimant, so giving rise to damages at common law, there is no reason why a landowner should be able to claim compensation for the works merely because they were carried out pursuant to a statutory power given to an authority or other persons or bodies who need statutory authorisation in order to be able to carry out certain actions or activities.

10.32   In *Metropolitan Board of Works v McCarthy*[50] the lessee of a property in close proximity to a dock which opened onto the Thames near Blackfriars in London had a right to the use of the dock as a member of the public. The dock was destroyed by works carried out under statutory authority by the Metropolitan Board of Works for the establishment of an embankment along the Thames. It was held that the claimant was entitled to compensation for the loss suffered to his land as a result of the removal of access to the dock. Lord Penzance explained the law in the following way:

> A rule has been established in these cases from which you would, I think, be disastrous to depart. It is this, that whether damage can be recovered under the words 'injuriously affected' depends upon whether it might have been the subject of an action if the works which caused it had been done without the authority of Parliament.
>
> There are many things which a man may do on his own land with impunity, though they seriously affect the comfort, convenience, and even pecuniary value which attached to the lands of his neighbour. In the language of the law these things are '*damna absque injuria*', and for them no action lies. Why then, it may surely be asked, should any of these things become the subject of legal claims and compensation, because instead of being done, as they lawfully might, by the original owner of the neighbouring land, they are done by third persons who for the public benefit, have been compulsorily substituted for the original owners?[51]

In *Re Penny and South Eastern Railway Co*[52] Lord Campbell said: 'Unless the particular injury would have been actionable before the company had acquired their statutory powers,

---

[50]   (1877) LR 7 HL 243.
[51]   *Metropolitan Board of Works v McCarthy* (1877) LR 7 HL 243 at p 261.
[52]   *Re Penny and South Eastern Rly Co* (1857) 7 E & B 660.

it is not an injury for which compensation can be claimed'. For example, in the absence of some contractual provision such as a restrictive covenant, a landowner does not have a right to privacy or a right to a view so that works by an authority which interfered with a person's privacy or outlook could not create a claim for compensation under section 10.

A good illustration of the operation of this condition is where the execution of the works   10.33
under statutory authority substantially reduces the access of natural light to premises in the proximity of the works. If the person whose lights are reduced has no easement of light, arising by an express or implied grant or by prescription, he has no right to compensation for any reduction in the light passing over other premises to his premises. The reason is that if the works had been carried out other than under a statutory power then in the absence of an easement he would have had no remedy against the person who reduced his light by carrying out those works. Conversely, if the person whose lights are reduced by the works carried out under statutory authority had an easement of light which would have been infringed by those works had they been carried out without statutory authority, then he may be entitled to compensation against the body which carries out the works.[53]

The works which give rise to a potential claim for compensation under section 10 may be,   10.34
and often are, an obstruction or interference with a public highway by an authority under statutory powers. The obstruction of a highway is a public nuisance for which the primary remedy is a criminal prosecution on indictment. A person who alleges that he is affected by the obstruction to the highway and has suffered loss, if he is to succeed in an action for damages in private law against the persons who have obstructed the highway and committed the public nuisance, must show a particular and greater loss than that suffered by the generality of the public who have been affected by the loss of use or the reduced use of the highways obstructed.[54] Such a particular loss can be shown if the property of the claimant is particularly affected by the obstruction to the highway; for example, in an extreme case a person's access to the public highway system may be cut off altogether by the obstruction to a particular part of a public highway adjacent to his property. In any event the important matter to note for present purposes is that if the works of the authority under statutory powers do amount to an obstruction of a highway a person will only be entitled to compensation under section 10 of the Compulsory Purchase Act 1965 if he can show that, apart from the statutory authorisation for them, the works of obstruction would have constituted not only a public nuisance but also a nuisance for which he could have obtained damages by reason of the fact that he had suffered a particular loss above and beyond that suffered by the public as a whole.[55]

---

[53] See *Wigram v Fryer* (1867) 36 Ch D 87.

[54] *Benjamin v Storr* (1874) LR 9 C & P 400; *Blundy Clark & Co v London and North Eastern Rly* (1931) 100 LJKB 401. See *Clerk and Lindsell on Torts*, 20th edn (London, Sweet and Maxwell, 2013) at paras 20-181 et seq.

[55] *Wildtree Hotels Ltd v Harrow LBC*, above n 41, per Lord Hoffmann at p 7. Despite the analysis of Lord Hoffmann and the well established law on this subject in *Moto Hospitality Ltd v Secretary of State for Transport* [2007] EWCA Civ 764, [2008] 1 WLR 2832, Carnwath LJ described the public nuisance analogy as 'almost meaningless' in the context of works to a major trunk road junction. What is difficult to understand is why the public nuisance criterion is of central importance when a highway is obstructed in connection with the construction of a railway but is almost meaningless when the same obstruction occurs in connection with improvements to a trunk road. One would have thought that legal principles operated in the same way irrespective of the exact purpose of particular works, and that public bodies providing a transport system today should be treated by the law in the same way as Victorian private railway developers.

10.35   If building or construction works carried out under statutory authority cause a nuisance by way of noise or dust or vibration, or similar effect to the land of the claimant, he may have difficulty in establishing a claim for compensation under section 10 because of the rule in the law of the tort of nuisance that building works which are reasonably carried out with all reasonable steps being taken to ensure that undue inconvenience is not caused to nearby landowners do not as a matter of private law constitute the commission of the tort of nuisance. This matter is considered below.[56]

4. Condition 4: Damage to Land

10.36   Injurious affection means damage to land. It does not encompass a purely personal loss or a monetary loss which is not reflected in the value of land. If a person suffers a bodily or personal injury from the execution of the statutorily authorised works he may have some remedy in private law against those who were executing the works, or their contractors, but he will not have a right to compensation for his loss under section 10 of the Compulsory Purchase Act 1965. The question is what is meant by damage to land. Land of course includes buildings.[57]

10.37   There are suggestions in some of the Victorian cases that the concept of damage to land is to be given a narrow and restricted meaning. One possible meaning is that land is only damaged by the execution of works if it is physically damaged such as by an effect on the foundations of buildings or by a reduction in the light which buildings receive. Even the last effect could be said not to be physical damage to the land in the sense of a physical alteration to it but only a reduction in the amount of light which it receives and so a reduction in its amenity.

10.38   An early instance of this restrictive approach was the majority decision of the House of Lords in 1867 in *Ricket v Metropolitan Railway Co*[58] in which it was held (applying a provision in the Railways Clauses Consolidation Act 1845 similar to section 68 of the Lands Clauses Consolidation Act 1845) that the owner of a public house called 'the Pickled Egg' in Clerkenwell in London could not recover compensation for the effect on the property and the business which resulted from the temporary closure of highways in the vicinity for the purposes of the construction of a railway. It may be that the limitation on compensation claims owed something to the distinction which was being made at about the same time in the law of nuisance between a nuisance which caused physical or material injury to property and a nuisance which caused personal disruption to the owners or occupiers of property without physical injury to the property being caused. The ingress of water to a property would be an example of the first category and noise would be in the second category. A purpose of the distinction was that as regards nuisances of the second category a degree of mutual tolerance was necessary between neighbours before there could be said to be an actionable nuisance; for example in residential areas it is necessary to put up with some noise from the ordinary activities of neighbours such as the noise of motor mowers or of works of repair to property.

---

[56] See paras 10.40 and 10.41.
[57] See s 1(2) of the Compulsory Purchase Act 1965 and see sch 1 to the Interpretation Act 1978.
[58] *Ricket v Metropolitan Rly Co* (1865) 5 B & S 149, (1867) LR 2 HL 175.

The very restrictive view of the requirement that the damage must be to land stated in 10.39
Ricket's case has been overtaken by more recent authority. Within the next two decades the
House of Lords held that compensation was payable where a property was adversely affected
because its access to a dock on the River Thames was cut off[59] and where a property was
affected by the closing of an access to a main street in Glasgow.[60] Any lingering effect of the
restrictive view of the concept of damage to land in this context has been removed by the
leading modern authority in the House of Lords, *Wildtree Hotels Ltd v Harrow LBC*,[61] in
which it was held that compensation could be claimed under section 10 of the Compulsory
Purchase Act 1965 in respect of a reduction in the rental value of land caused by the obstruction or closure of roads and pavements leading to premises used as a hotel. The loss was not
damage in a physical and material sense. Although the need for physical damage to the land
or buildings on it is not necessary in order to sustain a claim for compensation for damage
to land there are two areas of possible damage as to which problems may remain.

The first problem occurs where the damage to the land caused by the execution of works is 10.40
that caused by noise, vibration, smell, fumes or some similar effect. In such a case there are
three principles which have to be considered. The first is the principle, already explained,
that a claim under section 10 can only be made in respect of actions which, if they had not
been authorised by statute, would have constituted an actionable tort, usually the tort of
nuisance, against the claimant. The second principle is that when temporary works, such as
building works or construction works or civil engineering works, are being carried out the
law is that everybody has to put up with a certain amount of discomfort to his occupation
of neighbouring land because operations of that kind cannot be carried out without a certain amount of noise and dust and similar effects. The law, therefore, is that persons who
carry out such temporary works are not liable in private law under the tort of nuisance
providing the works have been reasonably carried on and that all proper and reasonable
steps have been taken to ensure that no undue inconvenience is caused to neighbours.[62] The
third principle is that when works are carried out under statutory authority the statutory
authority is subject to the implied condition that the works will be carried out and conducted with all reasonable regard and care for the interests of other persons.[63]

A person making a claim under section 10 for compensation in respect of noise, smell, 10.41
fumes, etc arising from temporary construction works is therefore in a dilemma. If it
appears that the works have been carried out in a reasonable fashion and with due regard
for his interests then, even apart from the statutory authorisation, he would have no claim
under the law of nuisance and consequently will have no claim under section 10. On the
other hand if the works have been carried out without proper care and regard for his interests then they will not have been authorised by the statute at all and he will have a remedy
in private law, something which again will prevent his claim under section 10. This was the
situation which arose in connection with noise, vibration, etc caused by road improvement
works near the hotel in the *Wildtree* case when it was held that for this reason no claim was
sustainable for compensation in respect of these effects. It is not impossible that a case
could arise in which a claimant could escape the dilemma just explained but it is not easy to

[59] *Metropolitan Board of Works v McCarthy* (1874) LR 7 HL 243: see para 10.32.
[60] *Caledonian Rly Co v Walker's Trustees* (1882) 7 App Cas 259.
[61] *Wildtree Hotels Ltd v Harrow LBC* [2001] 2 AC 1, [2000] 3 WLR 163.
[62] *Andreae v Selfridge & Co Ltd* [1938] Ch 1, [1937] 3 All ER 255.
[63] *Allen v Gulf Oil Refining Ltd* [1981] AC 1001, [1981] 2 WLR 188.

envisage such circumstances. Nor is this situation unjust. If the owners and occupiers of land are bound to put up with a degree of inconvenience from the effects here discussed, when building and construction work is being carried out by private persons or companies, there seems no reason why they should have a statutory right to compensation when such works are being carried out under statutory powers.

10.42   The second area of possible difficulty is where the damage is of a financial or economic character and creates a loss which affects a business carried on at the land of the claimant. The loss for which compensation can be claimed is a loss to the value of land and is not a loss to a business carried on at the land as such. However, a fallacy which sometimes emerges is to believe that an adverse effect on a business carried on at a piece of land cannot itself affect the value of that land. This subject has been explored in some detail in section (h) of chapter 4. The fact is that where land is suitable for the carrying on of a business something which adversely affects the continuation of that business, and so reduces its profits, can itself affect the value of the land. To take an extreme but obvious example, if a piece of land could only be used as a shop and there was some action which prevented it from being used as a shop then plainly that action would affect the value of the land. The principle and reasoning which has today found favour was put cogently by Lord Westbury in his dissenting opinion in *Ricket's* case:[64]

> The true principle and the only rule is, that, in the enquiry whether the interests of the occupier of a messuage or building is damaged, that is, injuriously affected, you should estimate the value of the messuage or building to the occupier with reference to the use that he makes of it, and the beneficial purpose for which he has hired it and fitted it up, and for which he has paid and pays to the landlord a larger annual sum than the building per se would command; and if you find this use and enjoyment impaired by the works of the railway, you are bound to decide that the interest of the occupier is pro tanto damaged, that is, injuriously affected.

In a decision only seven years after *Ricket's* case the House of Lords upheld an award of compensation in *Metropolitan Railway Board of Works v McCarthy*[65] where the injury in question was to the value of a building used by a contractor for supplying builders with lime, bricks, and other building materials and as a dealer in sand and ballast brought about when his access to a dock on the River Thames was cut off. More recently in the Court of Appeal in *Argyle Motors (Birkenhead) Ltd v Birkenhead Corporation*[66] Buckley LJ said that 'if [the appellants] can prove that the loss of profitability affects the value of their interests in the land they can recover compensation for this loss of value'. In the *Wildtree Hotels*[67] decision compensation was awarded under section 10 for a reduction in rental or annual value of the hotel which ensued while its means of access was affected by the obstruction or closing of nearby public highways such that the hotel business was adversely affected. In

---

[64] (1867) LR 2 HL 175, at p 204; see also at p 205. See also *Wadham v North Eastern Rly Co* (1884) 14 QBD 747, in which it was held that an arbitrator was correct to award compensation for the diminution of the value of an hotel and public house caused by the stopping up of roads. In this case the court was careful to point out that the sum assessed by the arbitrator was the diminution in the value of the property and was due to 'a depreciation in the trade': see per Mathew J at p 752.

[65] *Metropolitan Rly Board of Works v McCarthy* (1874) LR 7 HL 243. In *Chamberlain v West End of London and Crystal Palace Rly Co* (1862) 2 B&S 605, compensation under s 68 of the 1845 Act was awarded when the value of shops was reduced by the stopping up of a highway for the purposes of railway works.

[66] *Argyle Motors (Birkenhead) Ltd v Birkenhead Corporation* [1975] AC 99, [1973] 2 WLR 487, at p 114. See also per Lord Wilberforce at pp 130–31.

[67] [2001] 2 AC 1, [2000] 3 WLR 163.

Moto Hospitality Ltd v Secretary of State for Transport[68] a claim under section 10 for damage caused to a motorway service station, due to reduced custom as a result of road works in the vicinity, failed because the damage was held to be too remote but it appears that in principle the adverse effect on the business carried on could have constituted injurious affection for which compensation was recoverable. Thus today an effect on the business carried on at a property, or the profitability of that business, can be damage to land which ranks as injurious affection for the purposes of assessing compensation under section 10 of the Compulsory Purchase Act 1965 where the effect on the business or its profitability is reflected in a reduction in the capital or rental value of the land on which the business is carried out. It is still necessary to be cautious at this point. A reduction in the profitability of a business carried out on land does not necessarily mean that the value of the land is reduced by the same amount as the profits are reduced. The relationship between a reduction in the profits of a business and a reduction in the value of the land on which that business is conducted is a matter for expert evidence.

On a similar topic it was at one time argued that compensation was not recoverable under   10.43
section 10 where the damage was temporary, such as would normally be the case where the damage was a temporary closure of a road or the carrying out of works of construction. Again there are observations in the older authorities which supported this argument[69] but the *Wildtree* case shows that the argument was wrong and that where the value of land, if necessary in the sense of its rental value, is adversely affected for a temporary period while works are carried out or roads are obstructed that effect on value can be damage to land, and so can attract compensation, for present purposes.

5. Condition 5: Execution of the Works

A person may be entitled to compensation under section 10 of the Compulsory Purchase   10.44
Act 1965 for damage or injurious affection caused to his land by the execution of works under statutory authority but he is not entitled to compensation under that provision for loss caused by the use or operation of those works once constructed. This is a further limitation which became established in the Victorian cases and has remained as a restriction since. In *Hammersmith and City Railway Co v Brand*[70] in 1869 the House of Lords held, by a majority and having considered the opinion of the judges, that no compensation was recoverable under section 68 of the Lands Clauses Consolidation Act 1845 for damage or injurious affection caused to a house by vibration emanating from the operation of trains on a railway which had been constructed in the vicinity of the house. The claimant was entitled under a different item of claim to compensation for damage to the garden by lime, dust and smoke which occurred in the course of constructing the railway. The limitation on the ambit of compensation under section 68 was motivated by a number of considerations, one of which was the words 'injuriously affected by the execution of the works' in section 68 and another of which was that a less restricted operation of the statutory provision might open the floodgates to a large number of claims.

---

[68] [2007] EWCA Civ 764, [2008] 1 WLR 2822. See para 10.17 et seq.
[69] See, eg *Ricket v Metropolitan Rly Co* (1867) LR 2 HL 175, per Lord Chelmsford.
[70] *Hammersmith and City Rly Co v Brand* (1869) LR 4 HL 171.

10.45   The limitation on the operation of section 10 is a causative rather than a temporal limitation. If damage has been caused to a property by the execution of works, such as the permanent closure of a highway, the fact that the damage continues after the execution of the works for the closure of the highway has been completed does not prevent compensation being obtained for the permanent damage. What is not available is compensation for the operation and use of the works once constructed. Compensation is today available, under Part I of the Land Compensation Act 1973, for a depreciation in the value of certain interests in land caused by certain physical factors, such as noise or vibration or fumes, which result from the use of public works. This is an entirely different head of compensation and is the subject of chapter 13.[71]

(E) ASSESSMENT OF COMPENSATION

1. General Principles

10.46   The assessment of compensation due under section 10 of the Compulsory Purchase Act 1965 for injurious affection caused by the execution of works is said to proceed on the same principles as the assessment of damages in tort.[72] This is understandable since the compensation is given for losses caused by acts carried out under statutory authority which would be an actionable injury in the absence of the statutory authority. The difficulty is that the rules which apply to damages in tort are not capable of being stated in a single short proposition or even a series of such propositions. A distinction is sometimes usefully made in the law of damages between: (a) the determination of the kinds of loss for which damages are recoverable, and (b) the measure of damage in the sense of the method by which a kind of loss for which damages may be recoverable is translated into a monetary sum payable as damages. The first matter is sometimes described as a question of the remoteness of damage and the second question is sometimes described as a question of the measure of damages. When considering the assessment of damages for any particular loss it is logical to determine first whether the loss is too remote and then, if the loss is not too remote, to go on to determine the measure of damages for the loss. Even so it is convenient in this description of the law to examine first the second question of the measure of the compensation before coming to the matter of remoteness.

2. The Measure of the Compensation

10.47   The law on the second question is easy to state since the general principle is that the person who has suffered a loss which is not too remote must, as far as money can do so, be placed in the position he would have been if that particular loss had not occurred.[73] Obviously in cases of personal injury it is difficult to represent something, such as the loss of the use of a leg, as a monetary sum suitable as recompense. In the case of compensation under section

---

[71] See para 10.6(ii).
[72] *Clift v Welsh Office* [1999] 1 WLR 796, (1999) 78 P & CR 32, per Sir Christopher Slade at p 801.
[73] *Robinson v Harman* (1848) 1 Exch 850. The principle is sometimes described as one of *restitutio in integrum*.

10 the position is more tractable since, as explained, the compensation is for damage to land and that damage generally comprises a reduction in the value, whether capital value or rental value, of the land. The process of assessment is in principle not different from the assessment of compensation in other instances of loss of value to land which give rise to claims for compensation. Thus if the injurious affection or the damage is a reduction in the capital value of the land affected the capital value of that land, with and without the works of the acquiring authority, will normally be ascertained by envisaging hypothetical sales of the land in the open market in the two different circumstances.[74]

For example, if the claimant owns the freehold interest in a hotel and access to the hotel by customers and others is adversely affected by the closure of a nearby road then in principle the compensation is the reduction in the value of the hotel caused by that adverse effect on the business which can be carried on at it and expert valuers can calculate this reduction as they can any similar question. Where, as sometimes occurs with road works, the adverse effect is temporary while the works are being carried out it should in principle be equally practical to assess the reduction in rental value of the property while the works were being carried out and, perhaps, for a period afterwards until the previous level of business was restored.[75] Where the claim under section 10 is for compensation for the overriding of third party rights under statutory powers the assessment of damages may proceed on a some- what different basis as explained in section (f) of this chapter.   10.48

A question which is sometimes raised in this context is that of betterment. What is normally and properly meant by betterment in the context of compensation is that a person is deprived of his land by a compulsory acquisition, or a person's land is reduced in value in some way for which compensation is recoverable, but other land of the same person is increased in value by the same project of the public authority.[76] Betterment then means that the increase in value of the other property should be deducted from the compensation which is payable for the property which is acquired or for the property the value of which is reduced. There are general and specific provisions for the setting off of betterment in this sense against the compensation payable and this subject is considered separately else- where.[77] Unfortunately the word 'betterment' is sometimes used confusingly in respect to different effects from a single project of an authority on the same piece of land. Obviously the execution of works by an authority under statutory powers may contain components of the total works which reduce the value of the land, if looked at separately, and components which increase the value of the land, again if looked at separately. What is important in such a case is the overall effect of the execution of the works and compensation should only be recoverable if, and to the extent, that, that overall effect is a reduction in the value of the particular piece of property concerned.   10.49

Early decisions do not wholly follow this principle. For example, in one case the construc- tion of a railway reduced the light to commercial premises, which in itself would have given   10.50

---

[74] See ch 4 for the principles which govern the ascertainment of the open market value of land and see ch 14 for a more detailed explanation of valuation matters. An example of the assessment of compensation by this process is *Wadham v North Eastern Rly* (1884) 14 QBD 747, where an hotel and public house was adversely affected by the stopping up of a road in connection with the construction of a railway and it was held that an arbitrator was cor- rect in assessing that compensation as the diminution in the value of the property caused by the works.

[75] *Wildtree Hotels Ltd v Harrow LBC* [2001] 2 AC 1, [2000] 3 WLR 163.

[76] See ch 6, para 6.42.

[77] See ch 6, section (d).

a right to compensation for the reduction in value of the premises occasioned by the reduced light, but no offsetting effect was allowed for the increase in value of the same premises caused by the new railway.[78] A recent judgment of Lord Hoffmann in the Court of Final Appeal in Hong Kong may establish the position on a sounder footing. There compensation for injurious affection was due when commercial premises were deprived of their access to the sea when land reclamation of the adjoining sea-bed was to be carried on pursuant to statutory powers. It was held that in assessing the compensation regard must be had to the anticipation at the date of the removal of the access to the sea of the opportunity of future development of the land, which might be facilitated by the scheme of land reclamation pursuant to which the rights were removed, and to any increase in the value of the land which was attributable to that expectation.[79] Of course every case must depend upon the precise language of the statute which gives a right to compensation but there is nothing in section 10 of the Compulsory Purchase Act 1965 which requires that any ameliorating aspects of the project, for which the statutory powers are exercised on the land the subject of the claim, should be ignored when the compensation is assessed. For example, a road project carried out by a highway authority might block up a road which provided one means of access to commercial premises but replace that road with a new road which provided better access to the benefit of the premises. It would obviously be unsatisfactory that the owner of the premises should receive compensation for the effect of the road closure ignoring the effect of the new road when the overall effect of the road works was to increase the value of his property. Compensation is payable for a loss and not for a gain.

3. Remoteness

10.51   There remains the question of when a reduction in the value of land caused by the execution of works can be said to be too remote to be the subject of a claim for compensation under section 10.[80] It is here that the principles of remoteness of damage in the law of torts provide no single and comprehensive answer but may offer some guidance. The principles differ depending on the tort involved, a distinction sometimes being drawn between the tort of negligence and other torts, and a further distinction sometimes being drawn between physical damage and what is called pure economic loss. The tort which would normally be constituted by the execution of works if there was no statutory authority is the tort of nuisance. Nuisance is a tort of strict liability in that as regards the type of nuisance caused by the execution of works, such as the closing off of a public highway, the claimant has to show a special loss over and beyond that of the public as a whole but does not have to show negligence on the part of the defendant.[81] The principles of remoteness of damage may not be the same for torts of strict liability as for the tort of negligence. It was at one time said that a defendant should be liable for all the 'direct consequences' attributable to his tort.[82] This formulation states rather than answers the question of remoteness since it inevitably gives rise to the second question of when a loss or a consequence is direct. This approach has

---

[78] *Eagle v Charing Cross Rly* (1867) LR 2 CP 638: see also *Senior v Metropolitan Rly* (1863) 2 H & C 258.
[79] *Penny's Bay Investment Co Ltd v Director of Lands* (2010) 13 HKCFAR 287. The two decisions mentioned in n 76 had been cited in support of the opposite conclusion.
[80] See paras 10.22 and 10.46.
[81] See para 10.34.
[82] *Re Polemis* [1921] 3 KB 560.

been superseded to a large extent by the principle that, subject to other matters, a loss is not too remote if it is of a kind reasonably foreseeable by the person whose actions are alleged to create the liability.[83] A similar problem arises in cases of claims for compensation for disturbance or other loss under rule (6) of section 5 of the Land Compensation Act 1961 and in relation to claims of this character it has been suggested that the criterion of direct-ness may not be as unhelpful as some have thought.[84]

There seems no reason in principle why the general approach to remoteness of damage in tort should not be applied to the question of remoteness in claims for compensation under section 10 of the Compulsory Purchase Act 1965, particularly as the general principles of assessing damages in tort are said to apply to the assessment of section 10 compensation. It seems reasonable to consider the position of the authority carrying out the works in ques-tion and to ask whether loss of the kind suffered by a landowner as the claimant could have been reasonably foreseen by the authority as a consequence of its works at the time when it commenced to carry out those works. This at least would provide a coherent approach to the question of remoteness in this context. That, however, is not how the law has recently developed.   10.52

The decision of the Court of Appeal in *Moto Hospitality Ltd v Secretary of State for Transport*[85]   10.53
is mainly of significance for the clarity which is brought to the question of what link there has to be between the loss suffered by a landowner from the execution of works and the compulsory purchase of land if a claim under section 10 is to be available. This subject has been fully discussed.[86] A further question considered in that case was whether the loss was too remote.[87] Certain formulations of the test on the subject of remoteness in nineteenth-century cases were considered, two of them being that a loss, if it was to attract compensa-tion under section 68 of the Lands Clauses Consolidation Act 1845, had to be 'direct and proximate'[88] or 'particular, direct and substantial'.[89] At the date of those decisions there was of course no modern learning on the question of remoteness of damage in tort. It appears that the Court of Appeal alighted on the test that the damage had to be 'sufficiently particu-lar, direct and substantial' as that to be applied today certainly in the type of case before the court involving works to roads.[90] The decision of the Court of Appeal was that the loss caused to the motorway service area of the claimants by the new road system as a whole at the motorway interchange was too remote to found a claim under section 10. It was said that a claim might have succeeded in respect of a direct interference with the access to an individual site which went beyond what was ordinarily incidental to the traffic objectives of the scheme as a whole.[91] These perhaps general observations and phraseology must be seen in their factual context and are affected by two considerations. First, where the works of an authority are the stopping up or other interference with a road or some similar works, there is always the question of whether the works would have given a civil remedy to persons on

[83] *The Wagon Mound (No 1)* [1961] AC 388, [1961] 2 WLR 126.
[84] *Director of Buildings and Lands v Shun Fung Ironworks Ltd* [1995] 2 AC 111, [1995] 2 WLR 404, per Lord Nicholls at p 126.
[85] [2007] EWCA Civ 764, [2008] 1 WLR 2822.
[86] The facts of the case are summarised in para 10.17.
[87] See the *Moto* decision n 85, at paras 75 et seq.
[88] *Caledonian Rly Co v Walker's Trustees* (1882) 7 App Cas 259.
[89] *Metropolitan Board of Works v McCarthy* (1874) LR 7 HL 243.
[90] See the *Moto* decision n 85, at para 81.
[91] Ibid, at para 81.

the basis that those persons had suffered special damage above that caused to the public as a whole, a question which is in some ways similar to the question of remoteness.[92] Secondly, as the Court of Appeal stated, the nineteenth-century cases were concerned with the type of highway works carried out, not as a part of some road project as such, but with works having a different effect (eg *McCarthy's* case was concerned with the loss of access to a dock on the Thames) or with works to roads for a non-highway purpose such as the construction of a railway. In contrast the *Moto* case was a case concerned purely with highway works and this is something which appears to have affected the approach of the Court of Appeal.[93] The difficulty is of course to know when a loss is or is not sufficiently particular, direct and substantial. There is no criterion save the unexplained and unelaborated view of a particular judge who has to apply these adjectives to the facts of any specific case.[94]

10.54   It is difficult to provide any further concise and helpful guidance on the subject of remoteness. All that can be said is that a claimant for compensation under section 10 must show: (a) that works have been executed as part of a scheme with the power of compulsory purchase of land for that scheme available to the authority against whom the claim is made, (b) that the loss has been caused by the execution of the works at least in the sense that the loss would not have occurred if those works had not been executed, (c) that the case satisfies the other conditions explained in section (d) of this chapter, and, (d) that there has been or will be a reduction in the value of his land or interest in land, and (e) that the connection between the works and the reduction in value is not so indirect, thin or tenuous that it is to be concluded that the loss is too remote.

(F) THIRD PARTY RIGHTS

1. General Principles

10.55   The instances of and the authorities on the operation of section 10 of the Compulsory Purchase Act 1965, and of its predecessor, section 68 of the Lands Clauses Consolidation Act 1845, so far considered have concerned mainly the infringement of what might be termed rights of a public character, such as the use of a public highway or an access to a dock over which the public have a right. The statutory provisions have been held also to apply to instances where the infringement has been of a private right. A leading example and statement of the principle is a decision of the Court of Appeal in a case where land was acquired by a school board for the purpose of erecting a school on it under the Elementary Education Act 1870. The land was subject to a restrictive covenant that no building should be erected without the consent of an adjoining owner within a specified distance of the

---

[92] See para 10.34.

[93] See the *Moto* decision n 83, at para 80. When it comes to the damage to his land suffered by a particular landowner from the execution of works it is not apparent why any distinction should be drawn between the provision of transport facilities, such as roads by a public authority, or the provision of transport facilities such as railways by a private developer. See also n 55.

[94] This was the very difficulty explained by Viscount Simonds in *The Wagon Mound (No 1)* [1961] AC 388, [1961] 2 WLR 126, where he pointed out that the use of an adjective such as 'direct' to describe whether a loss was or was not too remote caused never-ending and insoluble problems of causation. The concatenation of adjectives – particular, direct and substantial – does not seem to add much to the single word 'direct'.

boundary of the land of that owner. It was held that the school board was entitled to erect the school pursuant to statutory authority and that no action in private law lay for damages but the board was required to make compensation to the person with the benefit of the restrictive covenant under section 68 of the Lands Clauses Consolidation Act 1845. The right to compensation arises whether the land burdened with the restrictive covenant has been acquired by agreement or acquired compulsorily.[95]

The same principle applies when there is an acquisition and use under statutory powers of land which is burdened by an easement such as a right of way. The right of a person to use the easement is removed insofar as it is inconsistent with the exercise of the statutory powers.[96] The breach of an easement is usually classified as the commission of the tort of nuisance. The land over which an easement is exercisable is called the servient land and the land which has the benefit of the easement is called the dominant land. It is of the nature of an easement that the rights over the servient land must in some way benefit the dominant land. The person entitled to compensation in the case of the overriding of an easement will therefore be a person with an interest in the dominant land who is entitled to exercise the easement. One particular easement which may be overridden as a result of the exercise of statutory powers is a right or easement of light. It should be remembered when compensation is sought for the infringement of an easement of light that what constitutes an infringement of the easement is not any reduction in the light which passes to an aperture in a structure on the dominant land, but only a reduction in the amount of light which leaves that land with light that is insufficient according to the ordinary notions of mankind for the comfortable use of the premises as a dwelling or, in the case of business premises, for the beneficial use of the premises for the business.[97] It must also be borne in mind that there is no natural right to light and that an easement must exist if the access of internal light is to be protected, that easement being created by an express or implied provision in a deed or by prescription (usually by 20 years or more of uninterrupted access of light over the servient land under section 3 of the Prescription Act 1832). The Law Commission published a consultation paper on 18 February 2013 proposing major changes to the law of rights to light. 10.56

Interferences with other rights pursuant to statutory powers may give a similar right to compensation, an example being an interference with the right of access to and use of a 10.57

---

[95] *Kirby v School Board for Harrogate* [1869] Ch 437; *Long Eaton Recreation Ground Co v Midland Rly Co* [1902] 2 KB 574. It was in part a consideration of this decision which led the Court of Appeal in *Moto Hospitality Ltd v Secretary of State for Transport* [2007] EWCA Civ 764, [2008] 1 WLR 2822, to hold as a matter of principle that a claim could be made under s 10 of the Compulsory Purchase Act 1965 for compensation caused by injurious affection due to the execution of works even though the works were not carried out on land which had been compulsorily acquired and even though no power of compulsory acquisition had been exercised over any land by the authority which carried out the works: see paras 10.14 et seq.

[96] *Clark v School Board for London* (1874) 9 LR Ch App 120. The principle was said by Lord Selborne LC to be that the legislation which gave a right to acquire land compulsorily gave the acquiring authority that land 'absolutely free from any *ius tertii* which would control their domination over it for the purpose of the duty which they have to discharge'. The removal or curtailment of the right to extract water from a stream by reason of the taking of water further up the stream under statutory powers may also create an entitlement to compensation under s 10: *Bush v Trowbridge Waterworks Co* (1875) LR 19 Eq 291. The removal of support to a house following the compulsory acquisition of an adjoining house may give rise to a claim under s 10: *Tile v Finchley Borough Council* (1953–54) 4 P & CR 362. In an appropriate case an interference with a right of access to a sewer to keep it in repair which was interfered with by works of an authority could found a claim under s 10: *Mayor of Birkenhead v London and North Western Rly* (1885) 15 QBD 572.

[97] *Colls v Home & Colonial Stores Ltd* [1904] AC 179.

river, a right which is called a riparian right.[98] In a recent case in the Court of Final Appeal in Hong Kong, to which reference has been made earlier, the interference was the removal of rights of access from land to the sea. [99] In that case a specific right to compensation for injurious affection was given by the statute which authorised the reclamation of the sea-bed but in England and Wales, and in the absence of a similar statutory provision, a right to compensation would be available under section 10 of the Compulsory Purchase Act 1965.

10.58   An option to acquire land, or the benefit of a specifically enforceable contractual right to purchase land, is in a sense a proprietary right over that land. These two rights are equitable interests in the land and can be classified as corporeal interests in that they do or may give to the owner of them a right to possession of the land. These rights confer an entitlement to compensation against the acquiring authority under section 7 of the Compulsory Purchase Act 1965, the compensation being the value of the interest, and the claimant is not dependent on section 10 for his compensation.[100]

10.59   Where development is carried out on land under statutory powers, in such a way as to infringe what would otherwise be enforceable third party rights, those rights are not necessarily permanently extinguished in the same way as, for example, a restrictive covenant would be extinguished by an agreement to discharge it or an order of the Lands Tribunal for its discharge under section 84 of the Law of Property Act 1925. In the type of case here under consideration the third party rights, such as under a restrictive covenant, remain in being but are merely unenforceable where the enforcement would prevent or hinder the exercise of the statutory powers. It follows that when the statutory powers have been fully executed the restrictive covenant which remains in being could be enforced in future circumstances. For example, an authority which acquires land for statutory purposes and carries out development in accordance with its statutory functions might in the future sell on the land for different and private development. In those circumstances the covenant would in principle remain enforceable against the successor in title of the public authority which was carrying out a purely private and non-statutory function on the land.[101] Where the exercise of the statutory powers involves the construction of some building which is likely to last for a substantial time, and perhaps to be replaced by a further building under statutory powers, although a third party right such as a restrictive covenant or an easement which would be infringed if the development had been for private purposes remains in theory exercisable in the future, the situation may in practical terms be akin to a permanent extinguishment of that third party right. When compensation is paid under section 10 to the owner of the benefit of a restrictive covenant it is sometimes agreed between the parties that the covenant will be wholly extinguished.

---

[98]   See n 94.

[99]   *Penny's Bay Investment Co Ltd v Director of Lands* (2010) HKCFAR 287.

[100]   See section (c) of ch 3.

[101]   *Hawley v Steele* (1877) 6 Ch D 521; *Ellis v Rogers* (1885) 29 Ch D 661; *Marten v Flight Refuelling Ltd* [1962] Ch 115, [1961] 2 WLR 1018. In *Marten's* case land subject to a restrictive covenant confining its use to agricultural purposes was compulsorily acquired by the Air Ministry for defence purposes. The Air Ministry permitted a commercial company to occupy the land. An injunction was issued to prevent use of the land by the company in breach of the restrictive covenant but the injunction was framed so as not to prevent use for the defence purposes for which the land had been acquired.

2. Basis of Assessing Compensation

The assessment of compensation under section 10, where a third party right is overridden   10.60
by the exercise of statutory powers, should follow the same lines as the assessment of damages for an infringement of that third party right. Of course where no statutory powers are
involved the owner of the third party right may be able to obtain an injunction to prevent
the infringement or the continued infringement of that right so that damages do not
become as important as a remedy. Where in the realm of private law damages are the only
appropriate remedy, or in a case where only damages are sought, the method of the assessment of damages has changed radically over the last few decades. It was at one time thought
that the usual method of assessing damages was to assess the diminution in the value of the
land with the benefit of the third party right caused by the infringement of that right.
Damages would then be equal to that reduction in value. Damages may still be assessed in
this way in certain cases but it has today become the general practice to assess damages on
what, for want of a better expression, might be described as the 'voluntary agreement'
basis.[102] The reasoning is that if the owner of the third party right had permitted actions
which would otherwise have infringed that right then he would have been able to negotiate
a sum to be paid to him under a voluntary agreement in return for his releasing or modify-
ing the right. If he is in fact deprived of his right by a wrongful act then his damages should
be equal to the amount which he would have been able to negotiate in a voluntary agreement for the release or modification of his right. The assessment of damages in this fashion
has received the imprimatur of the House of Lords and is routinely applied by the courts.[103]
This method of assessing damages may be used where the infringement is of a restrictive
covenant or an easement or of other incorporeal interests.

The logic of the situation suggests that compensation under section 10 for the overriding of   10.61
a third party right should be assessed on a similar basis. If a person is deprived of the right
to enforce a covenant or an easement in the public interest, by reason of the exercise of
statutory powers, then he should be entitled to compensation which is at least equal to the
sum which he would have received as damages if the actions of the authority exercising
statutory powers had been by a person who did not have those powers. There is no theoretical conflict between assessing compensation in that way and the principle that compensation is given under section 10 for damage to land which is normally measured by the
diminution in the value of the land. Where a person is entitled to enforce a right, such as the
benefit of a restrictive covenant, a part of the value of his land is that he is able to obtain, if
he so wishes, a sum of money from a person who intends to carry out development or other
actions which are an infringement of that right where the person with the benefit of the
right can release it in return for a sum of money. Unfortunately the Court of Appeal has
held that, whatever may be the position as to the assessment of damages, compensation
under section 10 is not to be assessed on the 'voluntary agreement' basis.[104] There was at the

---

[102] *Wrotham Park Estates Co v Parkside Homes* [1974] 1 WLR 798; *Jaggard v Sawyer* [1995] 1 WLR 269; *Amec Developments v Jury's Hotel Management* [2001] 1 EGLR 81. Of course unless it is agreed between the parties that the covenant will be permanently extinguished the assessment of compensation should take account of the fact that the covenant might become enforceable in the future: see para 10.59.
[103] *Attorney General v Blake* [2001] 1 AC 268, [2000] 3 WLR 625.
[104] *Wrotham Park Settled Estates v Hertsmere Borough Council* [1993] 2 EGLR 15. The claim for compensation in this case was under s 287 of the Town and Country Planning Act 1990 which applied s 10 of the Compulsory

time of this decision some doubt as to whether the assessment of damages on that basis was acceptable in law although that doubt has now been decisively resolved in favour of the assessment of damages on a 'voluntary agreement' basis in many cases. The only reason given for the decision was that the assessment of compensation on a 'voluntary agreement' basis was not in accordance with the intention of the statutory provisions, although it is not clear why this should be so. The present state of the law on this subject creates potential injustice and may be something which should be re-visited either by the Supreme Court or by statutory amendment.

(G) VALUATION DATE

10.62   It is sometimes asked what is the correct valuation date for the assessment of compensation under section 10 of the Compulsory Purchase Act 1965. It is true that where compensation is assessed by comparing the value of a piece of land in two circumstances, one without the exercise of the statutory powers and one with the exercise of those powers, the valuations have to be carried out as at a certain date since no valuation of land is a comprehensible exercise unless it is anchored to a valuation date.[105] Where the execution of works under statutory powers has an effect which is likely to be permanent, or at any rate to last for some considerable time into the future, it may be sensible to take a valuation date and to compare the value of the land injuriously affected at that date with and without the exercise of those statutory powers. In such a case the valuation date for the carrying out of the two valuations will normally be the date on which the value of the land injuriously affected was reduced by the commencement of the execution of the works. On the other hand not all claims under section 10 will fall into this category. There may be cases where the effect of the execution of the statutory works is temporary only such as the closure of highways for a limited period while works are carried out. It may occur that by the time the matter comes for the determination of compensation the works are well under way or may even have ended. Section 10 does not prescribe a valuation date nor does it state that the injurious affection has to be assessed in any particular fashion. Therefore, in a case of the nature just described, it would be correct to consider the actual loss which had occurred over the period of the works (and

Purchase Act 1965 to the assessment of the compensation. See para 10.9, n 12. See also *BP Petroleum Developments v Ryder* [1987] 2 EGLR 233. The same conclusion was reached by the Lands Tribunal in *Halliday v Breckland District Council* [2012] UKUT 193 (LC), [2012] 3 EGLR 95. The denial of 'voluntary agreement' compensation in that case, also an assessment of compensation under s 237 of the Town and Country Planning Act 1990 which applied s 10 of the Compulsory Purchase Act 1965, was founded on the reasoning that what was being given was compensation for injurious affection to land and not compensation for the value of land acquired. This is of course correct but the basis of compensation for injurious affection to land is the reduction of the value of that land caused by the loss of the rights in question and where the owner of a piece of land is able to obtain a substantial sum of money in return for giving up that right to someone who needs it the existence of the potential to obtain that sum of money is a part of the value of land and it seems in principle wrong, and unjust, that that element of the value of the land which the owner has and which is taken away from him against his will should not be reflected in the compensation due to him. A similar exclusion of the 'voluntary agreement' basis of compensation has been said to apply when compensation for the discharge or modification of a restrictive covenant is assessed under s 84 of the Law of Property Act 1925: see *Winter v Traditional and Contemporary Contracts Ltd* [2007] EWCA Civ 1088, [2008] 1 EGLR 80; *Re Stupinsky's Application* [2005] RVR 269. A complaint was made to the European Court of Human Rights that compensation assessed without regard to the voluntary agreement element was contrary to art 1 of the First Protocol to the Convention in *S v United Kingdom* [1984] 41 DR 226, but was rejected by the Commission under the procedural system then in force.

[105]   See section (e) of ch 4.

if necessary to assess any loss which will occur over any remaining period of the works) and to award that sum as the compensation. The compensation will still be for damage to land in the sense that the rental value of the land affected is reduced during the period of the temporary works and temporary closure of a highway.[106] The important point to bear in mind in the assessment of compensation under section 10 is that, unlike with other heads of compensation, there is no prescribed valuation date.[107] The most that can be said is that for the purposes of certain methods of assessing the compensation it may be useful to take a particular date as a valuation date as part of the process of quantifying the injurious affection.

If the compensation under section 10 is assessed by taking a valuation date and by compar-   10.63
ing the value of the land affected in two different situations on that date, one with and one without the overriding or removal of the third party rights, it would be appropriate in accordance with ordinary principles of valuation to value the land on both bases taking account only of what was known at the valuation date and that which was reasonably anticipated at that date.[108] On the other hand if the valuation in respect of a temporary effect is carried out by considering what has actually happened then there is no impediment to considering events which have occurred up to the date on which the Tribunal determines the amount of the compensation; indeed in such a case the assessment of the compensation could proceed in no other way.[109]

(H) SUMMARY

Section 10 of the Compulsory Purchase Act 1965 is the only provision in the compensation   10.64
code which provides for compensation to a landowner whose land is reduced in value by the execution of works under statutory powers but none of whose land has been acquired from him, whether compulsorily or by agreement.[110] The rules which govern the availability of this head of compensation have been largely worked out by the courts with scant regard to the sparse and unhelpful statutory provision. A person who claims compensation under this head has a number of hurdles to overcome. In the absence of precise statutory language and guidance it is helpful to summarise the nature of, and limitations on, claims for compensation under section 10.

(i)   A landowner can claim compensation only if his land has been injuriously affected or damaged, that is to say normally has been reduced in value, whether in capital or rental value.

(ii)   The compensation is available to a landowner none of whose land has been acquired, compulsorily or by agreement, by the authority which has executed the works.

---

[106] *Wildtree Hotels Ltd v Harrow LBC* [2001] 2 AC 1, [2000] 3 WLR 163.
[107] The valuation date for the primary head of compensation, the value of the land acquired, assessed under r (2) of s 5 of the Land Compensation Act 1961, is prescribed by s 5A of that Act: see section (e) of ch 4. The valuation date for claims under Pt I of the Land Compensation Act 1973 is 'the first claim day': see section (d) of ch 13.
[108] *Penny's Bay Investment Co Ltd v Director of Lands* (2010) 13 HKCFAR 287, per Lord Hoffmann.
[109] *Wildtree Hotels Ltd v Harrow LBC,* above n 104.
[110] Part I of the Land Compensation Act 1973 provides for compensation payable to a person whose land is reduced in value by public works where none of his land is acquired but the compensation is for the use, as opposed to the execution, of public works: see ch 13, para 13.5.

(iii)   Nonetheless there must be a linkage between the injurious affection and compulsory purchase. The necessary linkage is that a claim under section 10 is in principle only sustainable if the execution of the works by the authority has been carried out under a package or compendium of statutory powers which include a power of compulsory purchase. It is not necessary either that the works in question were carried out on land acquired by compulsion or even that any land for the implementation of the scheme was acquired by compulsion.

(iv)   The injurious affection must have been caused by the execution of works carried out on other land pursuant to statutory powers. Injurious affection caused by the use of works as opposed to their execution does not confer a claim for compensation.

(v)   A claimant, in order to succeed in his claim, must show: (a) that the works were lawfully carried out pursuant to statutory powers, and (b) that in the absence of the statutory authorisation the execution of the works would have been an actionable injury against him.

(vi)   The compensation is available for injurious affection to land in the sense of damage to land and is not available for a purely personal or economic loss not reflected in the value of land. However, the value of a piece of land may be affected by profits which are, or can be, earned from a business carried out on the land so that an interference with a business may result in a reduction in the value of the land on which the business is carried out.

(vii)   The compensation is generally assessed on the same principles as apply to the assessment of damages for a tort. The method of assessment is not prescribed and there is no prescribed or universally applicable valuation date for all claims. In many cases in which the execution of the works has caused a permanent reduction in the value of the land affected the claim will be assessed by the carrying out as at the date of the commencement of the works: (a) a valuation of the land ignoring the effect of the execution of the works, and (b) a valuation of the land taking account of the effect of the execution of the works, so that the compensation is the amount by which the first value exceeds the second value. However, where the works are of a temporary character the injurious affection or damage to land may be calculated in a different fashion.

(viii)   Compensation is also payable under section 10 to persons who hold incorporeal or third party rights over the land acquired compulsorily, or by agreement, by an authority, when those rights are overridden by the exercise of statutory powers on that land. In such a case the compensation will generally be the difference between the value of the land to which the rights are appurtenant before and after the rights are overridden. When a 'before and after' valuation is carried out for this purpose, in assessing the diminution in the value of the land which has the benefit of the rights account should not be taken of a loss which is assessable on the 'voluntary agreement' basis which is now regularly applied in many cases of the assessment of damages in tort when an action lies in private law for a wrong committed.

11

Additional Statutory Payments

(A) INTRODUCTION

The primary elements of compensation for the compulsory purchase of land are: (a) compensation equal to the open market value of the land acquired (under rule (2) of section 5 of the Land Compensation Act 1961), (b) compensation for disturbance or any other matter not directly based on the value of land (under rule (6) of section 5 of the 1961 Act), and (c) compensation for injurious affection to land retained when only a part of the land of an owner is acquired (under section 7 of the Compulsory Purchase Act 1965). Each of these elements was provided for in, or arose by judicial interpretation of, the Lands Clauses Consolidation Act 1845. It became usual under that Act to add an amount, usually 10 per cent, to the compensation which would otherwise be assessed to take account of the acquisition being compulsory and as some recompense to the owner for having his land removed against his will. There was no statutory authority for this addition. It was stated to be unnecessary in the report of the Scott Committee in 1919 (*Second Report of the Committee dealing with the Law and Practice Relating to the Acquisition and Valuation of Land for Public Purposes* (Cd 9229, 1918)) and was removed by rule (1) of section 2 of the Acquisition of Land (Assessment of Compensation) Act 1919, a rule now in effect as rule (1) in section 5 of the Land Compensation Act 1961.

More recent legislation has restored the rule that in addition to the primary elements of compensation certain additional payments are to be made to persons who lose their interest in land or are displaced from land by the compulsory acquisition of the land. One of these additional payments, the basic loss payment, is available in most cases when an interest in land is compulsorily acquired but the others are dependent on the claimant having been in occupation or possession of the land and having been physically displaced from it. The legislation to this effect is contained in the Land Compensation Act 1973 with substantial amendments and substitutions introduced by the Planning and Compensation Act 1991 and the Planning and Compulsory Purchase Act 2004. A major new entitlement, created by sections 37 and 38 of the Land Compensation Act 1973, was a right to a disturbance payment which arose when a person in lawful possession of land was displaced as a consequence of the compulsory acquisition of the land but had no interest in the land, such as that of a lessee, which entitled him to compensation under the primary elements of compensation just mentioned. Disturbance payments are separately considered in chapter 12. Disturbance payments are made to compensate persons for a definite and quantifiable loss for which they would not otherwise be compensated. They are therefore different in principle from the payments explained in this chapter which are not calculated, or wholly calculated, by reference to any

11.1

11.2

specific loss to the person displaced from land and are payments additional to any compensation payable under the three primary heads of compensation referred to in the last paragraph.

11.3   There are four types of additional payment which are considered in this chapter:

(i)   basic loss payments;
(ii)   occupier's loss payments;
(iii)   occupier's loss payments for agricultural land; and
(iv)   home loss payments.

Some of the additional payments are cumulative such as a basic loss payment and an occupier's loss payment. However a basic loss payment and an occupier's loss payment are not available in respect of a property or part of a property for which a home loss payment is payable.[1]

(B) BASIC LOSS PAYMENTS

11.4   A person whose interest in land is acquired compulsorily is entitled to a basic loss payment from the acquiring authority if his interest is a qualifying interest.[2] Acquisitions under blight notices and under purchase notices served pursuant to the Town and Country Planning Act 1990 are treated as compulsory acquisitions for this purpose.[3] An interest in land is a qualifying interest if it is a freehold or leasehold interest and it has subsisted for a period of a year or more at the earliest of: (a) the date on which possession of the land is taken by a notice of entry under section 11 of the Compulsory Purchase Act 1965,[4] (b) the date of entry under the procedure for obtaining entry in schedule 3 to that Act,[5] (c) the vesting date under a general vesting declaration,[6] (d) the date on which compensation is agreed, and (e) the date on which the amount of compensation is determined by the Lands Tribunal.[7] Of course more than one person may own a qualifying interest in the same land so that two or more persons may be entitled to a basic loss payment in respect of the same piece of land.

11.5   The amount of a basic loss payment is the lower of 7.5 per cent of the value of the qualifying interest and £75,000.[8] The value of an interest is its value for the purpose of determining the amount of compensation payable in respect of the acquisition. That value is its open market value at the valuation date determined in accordance with rule (2) of section 5 of the

---

[1] See paras 11.7 and 11.15.
[2] Land Compensation Act 1973, s 33A(1), (3). In the following notes to this chapter the Land Compensation Act 1973 is referred to as 'LCA 1973'.
[3] A blight notice is a notice which can be served under ss 149–71 of the Town and Country Planning Act 1990 by the owners of certain interests in land requiring the purchase of their interest by a public authority when the land falls within the location of certain types of proposed public project, such as a new road, the existence of which blights the land in the sense of making it more difficult to sell or making it saleable only at a reduced price. A purchase notice is a notice served under ss 137–48 of the same Act when planning permission has been refused and the land has become incapable of reasonably beneficial use in its existing state. It is also a notice which requires the local planning authority to purchase the land.
[4] See ch 2, para 2.96.
[5] See ch 2, para 2.97.
[6] See ch 2, para 2.133.
[7] LCA 1973, s 33A(4).
[8] Ibid, s 33A(2). Thus for interests worth £1 million or more the basic loss payment remains fixed at £75,000.

Land Compensation Act 1961.[9] It has been suggested that for this purpose the value of an interest includes any amount of compensation for disturbance or other matter not directly based on the value of land assessed under rule (6) of section 5 of the 1961 Act. The reason for this suggestion is that technically, and for historical reasons, compensation under rule (6) may be regarded for some purposes as a part of the value of the land.[10] The better view is that for present purposes the value of an interest in land means the open market value determined under rule (2) of section 5 of the 1961 Act and that value alone. In the first place the Land Compensation Act 1973 is to a significant extent founded on the fundamental rules for the assessment of compensation contained largely in the Land Compensation Act 1961. Since the 1961 Act contains a clear distinction between the value of the land acquired (rule (2) of section 5) and disturbance and other matters not directly based on the value of land (rule (6) of section 5) it is likely that the 1973 Act adopts the same distinction and meanings. Secondly, it makes good sense that the additional basic loss payment should be related to the inherent and basic value of the land acquired rather than be extended to other financial losses under rule (6) which by their definition have nothing to do with the value of land as that concept is normally understood. For example, one item of compensation which may be claimed under rule (6) is the reasonable expenses incurred in preparing a claim for compensation. It is difficult to see why the amount of the basic loss payment should have any relation to this sum.

In certain circumstances the compensation for the acquisition of an interest in land can be assessed on the basis of the reasonable cost of equivalent reinstatement of the land.[11] In such a case the value of the interest is taken to be nil for present purposes.[12] The effect is that basic loss payments do not apply to a case where the compensation is assessed on the equivalent reinstatement basis. 11.6

The basic loss provisions apply to a person with a qualifying interest only to the extent that he is not entitled to a home loss payment in respect of any part of the interest. If the interest giving an entitlement to a home loss payment consists partly of a dwelling and partly of other land a basic loss payment and a home loss payment may be payable but the value of the interest for the purposes of calculating the basic loss payment is the value of the whole interest less the value of that part of it constituted by the dwelling.[13] 11.7

There are a number of supplementary provisions relating to basic loss payments which also apply to other types of additional payments and these are considered together in section (e) of this chapter. 11.8

[9] Ibid, s 33A(6).
[10] The historical reason is that there was no separate provision for disturbance compensation under the Lands Clauses Consolidation Act 1845 so that when such compensation for disturbance came to be awarded the award was justified in legal terms on the basis that the disturbance compensation was a part of the value of the land acquired for which compensation was provided under s 63 of the 1845 Act. See ch 3, para 3.15, and see *Hughes v Doncaster Metropolitan Borough Council* [1991] 1 AC 382, [1991] 2 WLR 16.
[11] See r (5) of s 5 of the Land Compensation Act 1961, and see section (a) of ch 6.
[12] LCA 1973, s 33A(8).
[13] Ibid, ss 33A(1), (7). A dwelling means a building or part of a building occupied or, if not occupied, last occupied, as a private dwelling and includes a garden and other appurtenances: ibid, s 87(1). For home loss payments under ss 29–33 of the LCA 1973, see section (f) of this chapter.

(C) OCCUPIER'S LOSS PAYMENTS

11.9   This section covers occupier's loss payments other than for agricultural land. A person in occupation of land, not being agricultural land, whose interest is acquired compulsorily is entitled to an occupier's loss payment from the acquiring authority if he holds a freehold or a leasehold interest in the land and has occupied it for the same minimum period as is specified for the subsistence of an interest for the purposes of a basic loss payment.[14] An occupier's loss payment is payable in addition to a basic loss payment.

11.10   The amount of the occupier's loss payment is the highest of: (a) 2.5 per cent of the value of the claimant's interest, (b) the land amount, and (c) the buildings amount. The maximum payment in respect of an interest in land is £25,000.[15] Therefore the maximum amount which could become payable as a basic loss payment and an occupier's loss payment together in respect of an interest compulsorily acquired is £100,000.

11.11   The rules for determining the value of an interest are the same as those for the purposes of a basic loss payment.[16] The same apportionment of value as for the purposes of assessing a basic loss payment applies if the interest of the claimant consists partly of a dwelling in respect of which he is entitled to a home loss payment.[17] The claimant remains entitled to a home loss payment but the amount of the occupier's loss payment is reduced. As with basic loss payments if the compensation under rule (5) of section 5 of the Land Compensation Act 1961 is assessed as the reasonable cost of equivalent reinstatement the value of the interest acquired is taken as nil.[18] However, there could still be an occupier's loss payment founded on the land amount or the buildings amount.

11.12   The land amount is the higher of: (a) £2,500, and (b) £2.50 per square metre (or part of a square metre) of the area of the land acquired. If only a part of land in which a person has an interest is acquired the figure of £300 is substituted for the figure of £2,500. The substitution of a figure of £300 applies equally whether only a small part, say 5 per cent, of a person's land is acquired or nearly the whole of it, say 95 per cent, is acquired.[19] Where a large part of a person's land is acquired the amount of the land amount will be likely to be determined by the £2.50 per square metre calculation.

11.13   The buildings amount is £25 per square metre or part of a square metre of the gross floorspace of any buildings on the land acquired. The gross floorspace is measured externally.[20] The gross floorspace of a building measured externally means the aggregate of the floorspace at each level measured including the width of all external walls and ignoring any internal division of the floors into rooms or other areas.[21]

---

[14] Ibid, s 33C(1), (4). The period is the period of not less than a year ending with the expiration of the earliest of the five dates set out in para 11.4.

[15] Ibid, s 33C(2), (3).

[16] Ibid, s 33C(5). See para 11.5.

[17] Ibid, s 33C(6).

[18] Ibid, s 33C(7).

[19] Ibid, s 33C(8), (9).

[20] Ibid, s 33C(10), (11).

[21] See the *Code of Measuring Practice* published by the Royal Institution of Chartered Surveyors and the Incorporated Society of Valuers and Auctioneers. External measurement of floor areas is the method of measurement normally used for town planning purposes.

There are a number of supplementary provisions relating to occupier's loss payments which   11.14
also apply to other types of additional payments and these are considered together in section (e) of this chapter.

(D) OCCUPIER'S LOSS PAYMENTS FOR AGRICULTURAL LAND

Where a person is displaced from agricultural land by a compulsory acquisition of his free-   11.15
hold or leasehold interest in that land he is entitled to a payment from the acquiring authority on terms which are the same as those applicable to an occupier's loss payment for other
land save as to the land amount. The qualifying conditions including the minimum period
of occupation are the same as for other occupier's loss payments. The payment is again the
highest of 2.5 per cent of the value of the claimant's interest, the land amount, and the
buildings amount, with a maximum amount of £25,000. The ascertainment of the value of
the interest is subject to the same principles as apply to other occupier's loss payments
including a reduced value where there is an entitlement to a home loss payment and including a provision that the value of the interest is nil if the general compensation is assessed on
the equivalent reinstatement basis.[22]

The land amount is calculated differently. There is a minimum amount of £300. Subject to   11.16
the minimum the land amount is: (a) if the area does not exceed 100 hectares, £100 per
hectare or part of a hectare, and (b) if the area exceeds 100 hectares, £100 per hectare or part
of a hectare for the first 100 hectares and thereafter £50 per hectare or part of a hectare for
the next 300 hectares.[23]

The buildings amount is £25 per square metre or part of a square metre of the gross floor-   11.17
space of any buildings on the land measured externally.[24]

A person whose interest in agricultural land is compulsorily acquired may be entitled to an   11.18
occupier's loss payment under the above provisions in the Land Compensation Act 1973
and may be entitled to an additional payment in consequence of the compulsory acquisition of an agricultural holding under section 12(1) of the Agriculture (Miscellaneous
Provisions) Act 1968. A person in that position is entitled to a payment under only one of
his statutory entitlements. If a person makes a claim under both provisions he must be paid
in accordance with the entitlement which produces the greater amount.[25]

There are a number of supplementary provisions relating to occupier's loss payments for   11.19
agricultural land which also apply to other types of additional payments and these are considered together in section (e) of this chapter.

---

[22] LCA 1973, s 33B(1)–(7). See n 11. Agriculture has the same meaning as in s 109 of the Agriculture Act 1947:
see LCA 1973, s 87(1).
[23] Ibid, s 33B(8).
[24] Ibid, s 33B(9)–(10). See n 21.
[25] ibid, s 33H. Section 12(1) of the Agriculture (Miscellaneous Provisions) Act 1968 provides for an additional
payment to a tenant of an agricultural holding whose interest is compulsorily acquired by reference to the compensation for disturbance payable to such tenants by the landlord under s 60 of the Agricultural Holdings Act 1986
on the determination of the tenancy.

(E) OTHER PROVISIONS RELATING TO BASIC LOSS AND OCCUPIER'S LOSS PAYMENTS

11.20   There are a number of provisions of a substantive or procedural nature which apply generally to basic loss payments and to both types of occupier's loss payment. These are explained
together in this section of this chapter.

11.21   The right to a basic loss payment and to either type of occupier's loss payment is excluded
in two sets of circumstances. Both relate to a situation in which the land has been allowed
to fall into an unsatisfactory condition. The first set of circumstances is where certain types
of statutory notice have been served on the person who would otherwise be entitled to a
payment requiring him to take some action arising from the unsatisfactory state of his land
and where the notice has not been complied with. The notices are a notice served under
section 215 of the Town and Country Planning Act 1990, a provision which confers a power
to require proper maintenance of land, a notice served under section 11 or section 12 of the
Housing Act 2004, that is an improvement notice relating to certain types of hazard, and a
notice served under section 48 of the Planning (Listed Buildings and Conservation Areas)
Act 1990, that is a notice prior to the acquisition of a listed building where the building is in
an unsatisfactory state. The right to a payment is lost if the notice served has effect or is
operative on the date on which a compulsory purchase order made by an authority other
than a Minister is confirmed, or a compulsory purchase order prepared in draft by a
Minister is made by the Minister, and if the person concerned has failed to carry out any
requirement of the notice.[26]

11.22   The second set of circumstances in which a right to a payment is excluded is where an order
under certain statutory provisions has been served on the person who would otherwise be
entitled to the payment and the order has not been quashed on appeal. The orders are an
order made under section 20 or section 21 of the Housing Act 2004, that is prohibition
orders relating to certain types of hazards, an order served under section 43 of that Act, that
is an emergency prohibition order, and an order made under section 265 of the Housing
Act 1985, that is a demolition order relating to certain hazards.[27]

11.23   A person entitled to a basic loss payment or an occupier's loss payment may die before a
claim for the payment is made. In these circumstances a different person may make the
claim for a payment provided: (a) that person has occupied the land acquired for a period
of at least a year ending with the date on which the deceased person was displaced from the
land, and (b) he is entitled to benefit on the death of the deceased person under a will, or
under the law of intestate succession, or under the right of survivorship between joint tenants.[28] More than one person may fulfil these conditions and presumably more than one
person may become entitled to a payment.

---

[26] LCA 1973, s 33D(1), (3), (4), (6). See sections (e), (f) and (g) of ch 2 for the making and confirmation of
compulsory purchase orders by Ministers and other authorities. Where a compulsory purchase is directly authorised by an Act of Parliament without the need for a compulsory purchase order the Act often provides that for
certain purposes the Act itself has effect as a compulsory purchase order.

[27] Ibid, s 33D(2), (3), (5). See s 2 of the Housing Act 2004 for the hazards and the meaning of hazards and for
'category 1' and 'category 2' hazards.

[28] LCA 1973, s 33G. There is a similar provision relating to claims for home loss payments under LCA 1973, s
32(4) although in that case the successor must not be a minor: see para 11.41. There are two types of co-ownership
of land, a joint tenancy and a tenancy in common. The right of survivorship, sometimes called the *ius accrescendi*,

It may occur that a person entitled to a basic loss payment or an occupier's loss payment has   11.24
insolvency proceedings started against him before a claim for a payment is made. Insolvency
proceedings mean proceedings in bankruptcy or proceedings under the Insolvency Act
1986 for the winding up of a company or proceedings for the winding up of a partnership.
In the event of insolvency proceedings instead of a claim by the person against whom the
proceedings are started a claim may be made, in the case of an individual by a receiver,
trustee in bankruptcy or the official receiver, or, in the case of a company or a partnership,
by an administrator, administrative receiver, liquidator or provisional liquidator or the official receiver.[29]

A claim for a basic loss payment or an occupier's loss payment must be made in writing to   11.25
the acquiring authority. There is no prescribed form of claim but the claimant must give
such particulars as that authority may reasonably require for the purpose of deciding
whether a payment is to be made and the amount of any payment.[30] In practice many
acquiring authorities make their own investigations as to whether one or more of the additional payments is payable, and as to the amount of it, so that an estimate can be made by
that authority of its full liability to pay compensation. A person's right to recover a payment
is subject to the six year limitation period prescribed by section 9 of the Limitation Act 1980
for actions for sums recoverable by statute. Limitation periods run from the date on which
a right of action has accrued. A right of action to recover a basic loss payment is taken to
have accrued at the end of a year following whichever is the earliest of the date on which the
acquiring authority takes possession of the land under a notice of entry pursuant to section
11 of the Compulsory Purchase Act 1965, or enters the land under the procedure in schedule 3 to that Act, or the vesting date within the meaning of the Compulsory Purchase
(Vesting Declarations) Act 1981, or the date on which compensation is agreed between the
claimant and the acquiring authority, or the date on which the amount of compensation is
determined by the Lands Tribunal.[31] In the case of a claim for an occupier's loss payment of
either type the right of action to recover a payment is taken to have accrued on the date of
the displacement of the claimant from the land.[32] What these provisions amount to is that
the right of a person to recover a basic loss payment or an occupier's loss payment is lost
unless within six years of the accrual of his right of action as just stated that person: (a) has
made a claim in writing to the acquiring authority for the payment, and (b) if his claim has
not been met he has made a reference to the Lands Tribunal to determine his entitlement
to, or the amount of, the claim.

Any dispute as to the amount of a basic loss or occupier's loss payment is to be deter-   11.26
mined by the Lands Tribunal.[33] The jurisdiction of the Tribunal includes that of determining not only the amount of the payment but also whether a person is entitled to a

---

means that when one person has an interest in land as a joint tenant on his death his interest passes automatically,
and irrespective of the terms of any will, to the other joint tenant or tenants. As it is put in *Coke upon Littleton* 'ius
accrescendi praefurtur ultimate voluntati': Co Litt 185b. The right does not apply to persons holding land as tenants
in common.

[29] LCA 1973, s 33F.
[30] Ibid, s 33E(1)–(3).
[31] Ibid, s 33E(4)(a). The dates specified are by reference to LCA 1973, s 33A(4).
[32] Ibid, s 33E(4)(b).
[33] Ibid, s 33I(1). The procedure for bringing claims and the general procedure before the Tribunal are described
in ch 15.

payment.[34] Where a basic loss payment is due it must be paid by the acquiring authority by the latest of: (a) the last day of the period mentioned in section 33A(4) of the 1973 Act,[35] (b) the end of three months from the date on which the claim for the payment is made, and (c) the day on which the amount of the payment is determined.[36] Once the date for payment is reached the acquiring authority must pay the amount due even if other items of compensation remain unresolved or unpaid, although if a matter such as the value of the land is not agreed it may not be possible to determine the amount of the basic loss payment so as to render it payable. As regards either type of occupier's loss payment the payment must be made by the acquiring authority by the latest of: (a) the date the claimant is displaced from the land, (b) the end of three months from the date on which the claim is made, and (c) the day on which the amount of the payment is determined.[37] The determination of the amount of an occupier's loss payment may be dependent on the value of the interest of the claimant so that the amount of the payment may not be able to be determined until the value of the interest of the claimant is itself agreed or determined.

11.27   Where the only matter which prevents a payment being made is that the amount of the payment has not been determined the acquiring authority may, at its discretion, make an advance payment to the claimant. When the amount due is finally determined, and if it differs from the amount of the advance payment, the balance must be paid by or to the acquiring authority.[38]

11.28   Interest is payable on a basic loss or occupier's loss payment.[39] Interest accrues from the date specified in section 33A(4) of the 1973 Act in the case of a basic loss payment, and from the date the person is displaced from the land in the case of an occupier's loss payment, until the payment is made. If requested the acquiring authority may at their discretion make a payment on account of interest due.[40]

11.29   An interest in land may be acquired by agreement by an authority which has power to acquire the land compulsorily. If the interest is a qualifying interest for the purposes of a basic loss payment,[41] and if the interest is acquired from a person who would be entitled to a basic loss or occupier's loss payment if the interest was acquired compulsorily, the authority acquiring the interest by agreement may make a payment to that person equal to the basic loss or occupier's loss payment which would be due on a compulsory acquisition.[42] Where land is acquired by agreement the agreement will itself state the price to be paid or contain a provision on how the price is to be determined. A provision sometimes found is that the price shall be the compensation which would have been payable if the acquisition had been compulsory, with that amount to be determined by the Lands Tribunal or some

---

[34] The general jurisdiction of the Tribunal to determine compensation claims includes the power to determine whether a person is entitled to compensation at all: *Union Rlys (North) Ltd v Kent County Council* [2008] 2 EGLR 183, [2008] 2 P & CR 22.

[35] See para 11.4.

[36] LCA 1973, s 33I(2).

[37] Ibid, s 33I(3).

[38] Ibid, s 33I(4), (5). See section (c) of ch 15 for other advance payments.

[39] The rate is that prescribed under s 32 of the Land Compensation Act 1961. See section (d) of ch 15 for other provisions for the payment of interest on compensation.

[40] LCA 1973, s 33I(6)–(8). See ch 12, para 12.20, for a reference to the duty of an acquiring authority to exercise lawfully its discretion to make payments having regard to general principles of administrative law.

[41] See para 11.4.

[42] LCA 1973, s 33J.

other person acting as an arbitrator if the amount cannot be agreed. The effect of such a provision is that the purchaser under the agreement may have a contractual duty to pay the amount of a basic loss and occupier's loss payment as part of the price specified in the agreement if such an additional payment would have been due on a compulsory acquisition.

Basic loss and occupier's loss payments are calculated as specific amounts or as percentages   11.30
of other amounts. The Secretary of State has power to substitute by regulation a different amount or percentage in any case. If the change is to an amount, and is made because the Secretary of State thinks that the change should be made by reason of changes in the value of money, the power to make the change by regulation is not further constrained. However, if the change is to a percentage or is a change to an amount made for a different reason, the statutory instrument containing regulations making the change must be laid in draft before each House of Parliament and approved by resolution.[43] As at present no changes have been made to the amounts or percentages specified in the primary legislation.

(F) HOME LOSS PAYMENTS

1. Entitlement

A person who is displaced from a dwelling in consequence of the compulsory acquisition of   11.31
an interest in the dwelling is entitled to a home loss payment from the acquiring authority provided that he can satisfy two conditions.[44] The conditions are: (a) that throughout the period of a year ending with the date of displacement[45] he has been in occupation of the dwelling, or a substantial part of it, as his only or main residence, and (b) that he has been in such occupation by virtue of a specified interest or right.[46] It should be noted that the

---

[43] Ibid, s 33K.

[44] Ibid, s 29(1). For the meaning of a dwelling see n 12. There must be a displacement from the dwelling. This involves a degree of compulsion. A council tenant who applies to an authority to be moved to a new dwelling and then moves voluntarily may not be displaced and so may not be entitled to a home loss payment: *Ingle v Scarborough Borough Council* [2002] EWCA Civ 290, [2002] 2 EGLR 161. The question of whether a person has been displaced from a dwelling is one of fact. Displacement is said to be something to be decided by an objective test: see *Caplan v GLC* [1980] HLR 104, per Brandon LJ at p 109. In *Follows v Peabody Trust* [1983] 10 HLR 62, Cumming-Bruce LJ said at p 69 that the test of whether there is a displacement is an objective test and added that if an occupier went voluntarily from the premises he was not displaced. It seems curious that a person who co-operates with an authority and moves voluntarily to new premises may often not obtain a home loss payment whereas a person who moves only by compulsion will obtain such a payment. See also LCA 1973, s 29(3) which provides that a person may claim a home loss payment even though he has not been required by the acquiring authority to move from the premises acquired. See para 11.35.

[45] The date of displacement is of course the date on which a person is physically displaced from the property and is not necessarily the same as the valuation date or the vesting date: *Joyce v St Albans DC* [2007] EWCA Civ 179. Home loss payments are also payable to persons displaced from dwellings by certain other actions of public authorities such as demolition or closing orders under housing legislation. These entitlements are outside the subject matter of this book.

[46] LCA 1973, s 29(2). A requirement of occupation of a dwelling as a person's only or main residence was contained in the Leasehold Reform Act 1967 as enacted as a condition of the right to acquire the freehold or an extended lease. That requirement was removed by the Commonhold and Leasehold Reform Act 2002. There is no entitlement to a home loss payment for what are called second homes or holiday homes. For a decision in which the claimant was held not to have satisfied this requirement, see *Joyce v St Albans DC* [2006] RVR 106. See [2007] EWCA Civ 179, for the refusal by the Court of Appeal to give permission to appeal, and see n 45.

entitlement to a home loss payment depends on the claimant being displaced from a dwelling and on the interest or right in the dwelling held by the claimant and it is not necessary that that particular interest or right has been acquired. Indeed some of the rights which create the entitlement to the payment are unlikely themselves to be the subject of a compulsory acquisition. Consequently a tenant of a dwelling may be entitled to a home loss payment when he has to leave a dwelling as a result of his landlord's interest being acquired even though his tenancy is simply allowed to expire and is never acquired. The interests or rights necessary to satisfy the second condition are as follows:

(i)   An interest in the dwelling. This means a proprietary interest[47] and in practice is likely to be a freehold or leasehold interest.

(ii)   A statutory tenancy under the Rent Act 1977 or the Rent (Agriculture) Act 1976. Statutory tenancies under the Rent Acts are now infrequent.

(iii)   A restricted contract to which section 19 of the Rent Act 1977 applies. A restricted contract is a contract whereby one person grants to another a right to occupy a dwelling as a residence in consideration of a rent which includes payment in respect of furniture or services. Such contracts may amount to a licence.

(iv)   A right to occupy the dwelling under a contract of employment.

(v)   A right to occupy the dwelling under a licence to which certain statutory provisions apply.[48]

In general, and subject to the above categories of licence (including licences under subparagraphs (iii) and (iv) above), a right to occupy a dwelling under a licence is not enough to satisfy the second condition. Ordinary lodgers are generally licensees since they do not have exclusive possession of any part of the property and so are generally not entitled to home loss payments upon displacement. The rationale behind home loss payments is that a person who is required in the public interest to leave what has become his home should receive a reasonably modest additional payment (in many cases 10 per cent of the value of the interest of the occupier) for this disturbance in his life over and beyond the ordinary entitlement to compensation.

11.32   There are two circumstances in which the requirement to satisfy the conditions stated in the last paragraph are modified or relaxed:

(i)   A claimant may have satisfied the two conditions, occupation of the dwelling as his only or main residence and the holding of a specified interest or right, for the latter part of, but not the whole of, the year ending with the date of displacement. In that case the claimant can treat as a period during which he has satisfied the two conditions any immediately preceding period throughout which he resided in the dwelling as his only or main residence but without holding a specified interest and another person did satisfy those conditions. For example, a father who owns the freehold of a house may have occupied the house as his only or main residence with his son for the first three months of the year prior to the displacement but dies after three months of the year leaving the property to his son who then continues to occupy it as his only or main residence by virtue of his freehold for the remainder

[47] For the meaning of a proprietary interest in land, see ch 2, para 2.27.
[48] The statutory provisions are the Rent (Agriculture) Act 1976, Pt IV of the Housing Act 1985 (secure tenancies), Pt I of the Housing Act 1988 (assured tenancies), and ch 1 of Pt V of the Housing Act 1996.

of the year. The son can add together the three months and the nine months of the year as a period during which he has satisfied the two conditions and so may claim a home loss payment.[49]

(ii) A claimant may have satisfied the two conditions for only the latter part of the year ending with the date of displacement (the same situation as mentioned in sub-paragraph (i)). He is entitled to treat as a period during which he has fulfilled the conditions in relation to the dwelling any immediately preceding period or successive periods during which he satisfied the conditions in relation to another dwelling or dwellings.[50]

One spouse or civil partner (A) may have an entitlement to occupy a dwelling by reason of   11.33
an estate or interest or contract or statutory entitlement whereas the other spouse or civil partner (B) does not have that entitlement. In certain circumstances the spouse or civil partner without that entitlement may have a right to remain in the dwelling or to enter and occupy it under Part IV of the Family Law Act 1996. The rights of (B) are termed matrimonial home rights. For the purposes of a claim to a home loss payment (B) is treated as occupying the dwelling by virtue of an interest or right which is a specified interest or right (and so satisfies the second condition stated earlier) so long as the matrimonial home rights continue, and so long as (B) is in occupation of the dwelling and (B) is not otherwise treated as occupying the dwelling by virtue of a specified interest or right.[51]

A building may contain a number of single rooms or groups of rooms not constructed or   11.34
structurally adapted for use as a separate dwelling. This room or group of rooms may still constitute a dwelling and a person may have successively been in occupation of or resided in different dwellings in the same building. The conditions to be satisfied for the purposes of a claim for a home loss payment, as described above, then have effect as if those dwellings were the same dwelling.[52]

In certain cases a displacement from a dwelling does not give rise to a right to a home loss   11.35
payment. One case is where a person gives up his occupation of the dwelling before the acquiring authority was authorised to acquire an interest in the dwelling. The authority becomes authorised to acquire an interest upon the confirmation or making of the compulsory purchase order. Subject to this rule it is not necessary for the acquiring authority to have required the claimant to give up his occupation of the dwelling in order for him to be able to make a claim. In other words the claimant may still be taken to have been displaced from the dwelling despite not having been required by the acquiring authority to move from it.[53] A second case is that a person is not treated as displaced from a dwelling by reason of the compulsory acquisition of part only of a garden or yard or of an outhouse or appurtenance belonging to or usually enjoyed with the building which is occupied or intended to

---

[49] LCA 1973, s 32(3).
[50] Ibid, s 32(3A).
[51] Ibid, s 29A. The second condition is stated in para 11.31.
[52] Ibid, s 32(5).
[53] Ibid, s 29(3). See, however, n 44 for the need for an element of compulsion before there can be a displacement and a claim to a home loss payment. It is not clear what is the position if a person moves from a dwelling after the making of a compulsory purchase order but the acquiring authority does not proceed with the purchase, for example it never serves a notice to treat or withdraws a notice to treat so that possession of the dwelling is never taken. In such a case the displacement of the claimant may never be due to a compulsory acquisition of the dwelling. The making of the compulsory purchase order would probably be treated as a sufficient compulsory acquisition to create an entitlement to a home loss payment notwithstanding any subsequent events.

be occupied as the dwelling. A third case is that a person is not treated as displaced from a dwelling in consequence of the carrying out of any improvement to the dwelling unless he is permanently displaced from it in consequence of the carrying out of that improvement.[54] A person who himself requires the acquisition of his property by serving a blight notice under Part VI of the Town and Country Planning Act 1990 may be entitled to a home loss payment.[55]

11.36   An authority possessing compulsory purchase powers may acquire the interest of a person in a dwelling by agreement. If that occurs then any person who is displaced from the dwelling in consequence of the acquisition and who would be entitled to a home loss payment if the acquisition were compulsory becomes entitled to such a payment even though the acquisition was not compulsory.[56]

11.37   Where an interest in a dwelling is vested in trustees, other than a sole tenant for life within the meaning of the Settled Land Act 1925, and a person beneficially entitled, whether directly or derivatively, under the trusts is entitled or permitted by reason of his interest to occupy the dwelling, that person is treated for present purposes as occupying the dwelling by virtue of an interest in the dwelling. In other words a beneficiary under a trust in occupation of the dwelling is entitled to a home loss payment providing that he can satisfy the condition relating to occupation throughout the period of the year ending with the date of displacement.[57]

11.38   It may occur that at the date of displacement a person is in occupation of the dwelling, or a substantial part of it, as his only or main residence, and is in occupation by virtue of an interest or right which qualifies him for a home loss payment, but he cannot satisfy these conditions throughout the period of the year ending with the date of the displacement. In these circumstances he is not entitled as of right to a home loss payment but the acquiring authority is entitled at its discretion to make to him a payment of an amount not exceeding that to which he would have been entitled if he had satisfied the conditions throughout the requisite one year period.[58]

2. Amount and Payment

11.39   The amount of a home loss payment depends on the interest in the dwelling which is held by the person who is displaced from it. If the claimant has an interest other than an owner's interest the amount is £4,700. If the claimant has an owner's interest at the date of the displacement the amount is 10 per cent of the market value of the interest subject to a maximum of £47,000 and a minimum of £4,700.[59] An owner's interest means an interest held by a person, other than a mortgagee who is not in possession, who is for the time being entitled to dispose of the fee simple of the land whether in possession or in reversion or a tenant

[54] Ibid, s 29(3A), (3B).
[55] Ibid, s 29(5), which was to the opposite effect, was repealed by the Planning and Compensation Act 1991.
[56] LCA 1973, s 29(6).
[57] Ibid, s 29(8).
[58] Ibid, s 29(2). See ch 12, para 12.20, for a reference to the duty of an acquiring authority to exercise lawfully its discretion on whether to make a payment to a person displaced having regard to general principles of administrative law.
[59] Ibid, s 30(1), (2). Lower sums were specified for displacements which occurred prior to 1 September 2008.

under a lease or agreement for a lease the unexpired term of which exceeds three years.[60] The market value of an interest means the amount assessed for the purposes of the acquisition as the value of the interest. For these purposes the dwelling is taken to include any garden, yard, outhouses and appurtenances belonging to or usually enjoyed with the dwelling.[61]

A claim for a home loss payment must be made in writing to the acquiring authority. There 11.40 is no prescribed form of claim but the claimant must give such particulars as the authority may reasonably require to determine his entitlement to the payment and its amount.[62] In practice acquiring authorities often take steps to inform persons displaced from a dwelling of their entitlement to a home loss payment and make arrangements to pay it. For the purposes of the six year limitation period, prescribed by section 9 of the Limitation Act 1980 for actions for sums recoverable by statute, a right of action to recover a home loss payment accrues on the date of displacement.[63]

If a person entitled to a home loss payment dies without having claimed the payment a 11.41 claim may be made by any person who is not a minor who: (a) has resided in the dwelling or a substantial part of it as his main residence for a period of at least a year ending with the date on which the deceased person was displaced, and (b) is entitled to benefit under the will of the deceased person or under the law of intestate succession, or under the right of survivorship between joint tenants.[64]

The acquiring authority must make the home loss payment to a person entitled by the latest 11.42 of: (a) the date of displacement, (b) three months from the making of the claim, and (c) where the amount of the payment is to be determined as 10 per cent of the market value of the interest in the dwelling, the day on which that market value is agreed or finally determined.[65]

There is provision for a payment in advance of the whole or a part of a home loss payment. 11.43 Where the payment is the fixed sum of £4,700, in respect of an interest other than an owner's interest, there is no need for an advance payment since the fixed amount can be paid by the date on which payment is required. Provision for an advance payment is needed where the payment is in respect of an owner's interest and the amount of it depends upon the market value of that interest since it may take some time for that value to be determined. In such a case the acquiring authority may make a payment in advance at their discretion at any time. If the date of displacement and a period of three months from the making of the claim have passed, and the market value of the owner's interest has not been agreed or finally determined, the acquiring authority must make a payment in advance of a specified amount. They must pay this specified amount even if they have made a previous advance payment. The specified amount is the lesser of £47,000 or 10 per cent of the acquiring

---

[60] Ibid, s 30(7); Acquisition of Land Act 1981, s 7(1).
[61] Ibid, s 30(3)(a), (4). The value of an interest will not include any sum payable as compensation under r (6) of s 5 of the Land Compensation Act 1961: see para 11.5.
[62] LCA 1973, s 32(1).
[63] Ibid, s 32(7A). See para 11.25 for the effect of the limitation provision.
[64] Ibid, s 32(4). For the right of survivorship, see n 28.
[65] Ibid, s 32(2). See para 11.40 for the limitation period for references to the Lands Tribunal to determine disputes as to the entitlement to an amount of a home loss payment. An acquiring authority may be able to set off against a home loss payment due an amount owing to it by a claimant, such as arrears of rent, where the authority was the landlord of the claimant: *Khan v Islington LBC* [2001] RVR 62.

authority's estimate of the market value of the owner's interest. If it subsequently emerges that the amount due as a home loss payment is greater or less than the amount paid as an advance payment the balance must be paid by or to the acquiring authority.[66]

11.44   If two or more persons are entitled to make a claim for a home loss payment in respect of the same dwelling the amount of the payment is divided by the number of claimants and an equal part is payable to each claimant.[67] Such a situation may occur where persons are in joint occupation. For example, two persons may be in occupation of a house worth £300,000, being co-owners of the freehold under a tenancy in common. The home loss payment will then be 10 per cent of the market value of the house, that is £30,000, and each of the tenants in common will be entitled to £15,000 as a home loss payment. The same principle applies where a person displaced is entitled to a home loss payment but does not have an owner's interest so that the payment is £4,700. If two persons are in occupation without an owner's interest, for example two persons who share a dwelling under a contract of employment, the £4,700 will be shared equally between them. The two or more persons in occupation do not have to be in occupation in the same capacity for the present provision to apply. It is possible to envisage a situation in which one person is entitled to a home loss payment calculated on a value basis by virtue of an owner's interest and another person is entitled to a home loss payment of £4,700 in respect of the same dwelling by virtue of an interest which is not an owner's interest. An example would be the freehold owner of a dwelling and a live-in employed housekeeper. Such a situation is not likely to be a frequent occurrence and does not fit into the statutory provision on sharing the payment. The possible answer in such a situation is that both claimants are entitled to a full payment.

11.45   An interest in a dwelling may be acquired by agreement by an authority possessing compulsory purchase powers. In that case the authority may, at its discretion, make to the person holding the interest acquired a payment corresponding to the home loss payment which the authority would be required or authorised to make if the acquisition were compulsory and if the authority had been authorised to acquire the interest before the person in question gave up occupation.[68]

3. Caravan Dwellers

11.46   Home loss payments are available for certain caravan dwellers. In general the home loss payment provisions apply to persons residing in a caravan on a caravan site who are displaced from that site as they apply to persons displaced from a dwelling. A caravan site means land on which a caravan is stationed for the purpose of human habitation and land used in conjunction with that land. [69] However, a home loss payment is only payable to a caravan dweller where no suitable alternative site for stationing the caravan is available to him on reasonable terms.[70]

---

[66] LCA 1973, s 32(2A), (2B). See section (c) of ch 15 for a general consideration of advance payments.
[67] Ibid, s 32(6).
[68] Ibid, s 32(7). See para 11.29. See ch 12, para 12.20, for a reference to the duty of an acquiring authority to exercise lawfully its discretion on whether to make a payment to a person displaced having regard to general principles of administrative law.
[69] Ibid, s 33(1), (7).
[70] Ibid, s 33(2).

The provisions of sections 29–32 of the Land Compensation Act 1973 relating to home loss   11.47
payments have effect in general as though a reference to a caravan site was substituted
for any reference to a dwelling or land.[71] Subject to this general provision certain specific
modifications are made:

(i)   The basic requirement for an entitlement to a home loss payment, contained in sec-
      tion 29(1) of the Land Compensation Act 1973, namely that a person is displaced
      from a dwelling in consequence of the compulsory acquisition of an interest in the
      dwelling, is replaced by a reference to a person residing at a caravan site being
      displaced from the site.[72]

(ii) The conditions which the displaced person has to satisfy in order to entitle him to a
      home loss payment, (as contained in section 29(2) of the 1973 Act) are modified so
      that they become a condition that he has been in occupation of the caravan site by
      using a caravan stationed on it as his only or main residence and a condition that
      he has been in such occupation of the site by virtue of an interest or right to which
      section 29 applies.[73]

(iii) Section 30 of the 1973 Act provides for the amount of a home loss payment depend-
      ing on the nature of the interest which the claimant has in the dwelling from which
      he is displaced. For present purposes references in section 30 to a person occupying
      a dwelling and to his interest in the dwelling apply to a person occupying the cara-
      van site by virtue of an interest in it.[74]

(iv) In certain parts of section 32 of the 1973 Act references to a dwelling are replaced by
      references to a caravan or a caravan on a caravan site.[75]

(v)   There is a further provision applicable to caravans which applies to the requirement
      in section 29(2) of the 1973 Act that a person must have occupied a dwelling as his
      only or main residence for a minimum period of a year if he is to be entitled to a
      home loss payment.[76] Where any land comprises two or more caravan sites, and the
      claimant has successively been in occupation of or has resided in a caravan on dif-
      ferent caravan sites on that land, the above requirement has effect as if the sites were
      the same site. Amended provisions are also applied to certain other matters.[77]

---

[71] Ibid, s 33(6).
[72] Ibid, s 33(1).
[73] Ibid, s 33(3).
[74] Ibid, s 33(4).
[75] Ibid, s 33(5).
[76] See para 11.31.
[77] See s 33(5)(c) which substitutes a different s 32(5) for the purposes of caravan sites. The provisions affected
are ss 29(2), 33(3)–(5).

12

Disturbance Payments

(A) INTRODUCTION

12.1   Most persons who are in possession of land which is compulsorily acquired will hold a legal or equitable interest in the land entitling them to compensation which will include compensation for loss due to their physical disturbance in being dispossessed of the land. Freehold owners, lessees, sub-lessees, mortgagees in possession, and holders of equitable interests such as equitable leases, fall into this category. Such persons, as well as being compensated for the open market value of the land, will also be entitled to compensation for disturbance under rule (6) of section 5 of the Land Compensation Act 1961. Persons in possession of land generally fall into one of four categories. They may be: (a) freehold owners (legal or equitable), (b) lessees or sub-lessees (legal or equitable), (c) licensees, or (d) trespassers. A mortgagee of the interests of persons in the first two categories may be in possession of the land. Persons in the first two categories are entitled to compensation under the principles just mentioned. Trespassers, of course, are not entitled to any compensation (although it is possible that persons in adverse possession of land and building up a possessory title may be entitled to a notice to treat and to some compensation).[1] It is to losses caused by disturbance to persons in the third category, licensees, when they are required to remove themselves from land as a result of the compulsory acquisition of that land, that the remainder of this chapter is directed.

12.2   A licensee is someone who is permitted to enter the land of someone else with the permission or licence of that other person but without having a proprietary interest in the land. It is this permission which prevents the entry being a trespass.[2] Licences are traditionally divided into three categories. (a) A bare licence is a permission to enter land granted otherwise than for consideration and not as a contract or a part of a contract. A neighbourly act such as a person allowing his neighbour to park on his land for a short time while his neighbour's access is repaired would be the grant of a bare licence. A bare licence is revocable at any time. (b) It is the second class of licences, contractual licences, with which this chapter is mainly concerned. The essence of a contractual licence is that a person is allowed to enter and remain on the land of another person in return for some, usually monetary, consider-

---

[1] See ch 4 for the assessment of compensation for the value of the land acquired under r (2) of s 5 of the Land Compensation Act 1961 and ch 8 for compensation for disturbance under r (6) of s 5. Compensation under r (6) relates to other matters as well as losses caused by physical disturbance. Persons in occupation of land may be entitled to an occupier's loss payment, in addition to their general entitlement to compensation, under s 33C of the Land Compensation Act 1973 (see ch 11). See section (c) of ch 3 for a summary of the categories of persons entitled to claim the seven main heads of compensation. For the possibility that a person building up a possessory title by a period of adverse possession may have certain rights in relation to a compulsory purchase of the land see section (c) of ch 3, para 2.85 of ch 2, and see *Perry v Clissold* [1907] AC 73.

[2] *Thomas v Sorrell* (1693) Vaugh 330, 124 ER 1098.

ation. A person who pays to enter a car park or a cinema is a contractual licensee. Contractual licences are revocable in accordance with the terms of the contract. (c) The third class is what is called a licence coupled with an interest. Some interests in the land of other persons, for example a right of shooting game birds (a *profit á prendre*), include of their nature the right to enter the land of the other person for the exercise of the right. Such licences cannot be revoked while the interest to which they are coupled exists. Such a licence may best be regarded as an intrinsic aspect or component of the interest in land to which it is ancillary rather than a right of its own.

It is obvious from the above description of the nature of licences that a licence can cover a wide variety of situations. At one extreme a licence may be no more than a temporary permission to walk across land. At the other extreme it may include a right to be in possession of land for a substantial period. It is necessary here to explain the distinction between a lease and a licence.[3] If a person is granted exclusive possession of land for a fixed period or on a periodic basis he will usually become a lessee of the land under a lease. This will be so in law even though the arrangement is described as a licence and even though the parties may wish that their arrangement is only a licence. The law imposes upon the parties the legal classification of their relationship as one of landlord and tenant.[4] There may still be cases in which persons have lawful possession of land but are not lessees. For example, the possession may not be exclusive possession so that the arrangement cannot be a lease since exclusive possession is an essential attribute of a lease. Licences creating possession of land by the licensee may arise out of informal arrangements such as when one company in a group of companies allows another company in the same group to take possession of land without any formal documentation. The law sometimes requires that somewhat esoteric distinctions are drawn between occupation and possession and between physical possession and legal possession.[5] In the present explanation of an aspect of the law of compensation possession means ordinary physical possession of land the existence of which can generally be shown as a matter of fact and common sense. 12.3

In order to explain the law of disturbance payments it is necessary to draw attention to two aspects of the law of licences. One aspect is that a licence is not a proprietary interest in land. The nature of proprietary interests has been explained in chapter 2.[6] In summary a proprietary interest in land is an interest which is capable in principle of binding not only the owner of the land when the interest is created but all successors in title to the interest of that owner. A licence (other than a licence coupled with an interest) does not enjoy this status. Consequently if the owner of a piece of land grants a licence to enter it, or enjoy possession of it, and the owner subsequently sells his interest the licensee cannot enforce his licence against the successor in title of the interest of the owner.[7] The interest of a licensee is 12.4

---

[3] See ch 4, para 4.91 and n 123 for the nature and categories of leases.

[4] *Street v Mountford* [1985] AC 809, [1985] 2 WLR 877. A reason which at one time induced persons to describe their arrangement for the occupation of residential property as a licence, even though exclusive possession was given, was a desire to avoid the operation of the Rent Acts which applied to lessees but not to licensees. No new tenancies may now be created with the protection of the Rent Act 1977 and the number of subsisting tenancies with that protection is now small.

[5] See, eg *Heath v Drown* [1973] AC 498, [1972] 2 WLR 1306, for the distinction between physical and legal possession. The nature and quality of the possession of land may also be important for the gaining of title by a period of adverse possession as a trespasser.

[6] Chapter 2, para 2.27; *Ashburn Anstalt v Arnold* [1989] Ch 1, [1988] 2 WLR 706.

[7] *Ashburn Anstalt v Arnold*, ibid. If the licensee is a contractual licence the licensee may be entitled to damages against the licensor as the other party to the contract for the loss suffered by his inability to continue to enjoy the

therefore a fragile and usually a purely contractual interest. The result of this aspect of the law of licences is that when an acquiring authority acquires the interest of the owner of the land, that is the interest of the licensor, it takes that interest free of any rights of the licensee.

12.5   The second aspect of the law is that since a licensee does not hold a proprietary interest in land he is not entitled to claim compensation in the ordinary way for the loss of his rights or for loss caused to him by reason of his being disturbed from the land. A company which held a contractual right to supply refreshments at a theatre was held to possess only a licence, and not a lease, and not to be entitled to compensation when the property was acquired.[8] It is possible that a licence could ripen into a proprietary interest in land under the doctrine of proprietary estoppel, and so become an interest which gave an entitlement to compensation if the land was compulsorily acquired, but it would take exceptional circumstances for this to occur.[9]

12.6   It is these aspects of the law of licences which give rise to what was perceived as a possible injustice. A licensee in possession of land who is displaced from the land by the compulsory acquisition of the land might suffer a significant loss, for example the expenses of removal and an adverse effect on a business carried out on the land, yet that person could recover no compensation from the acquiring authority under the general provisions which gave an entitlement to compensation. Sections 37 and 38 of the Land Compensation Act 1973, which are explained in this chapter, were enacted to provide some measure of compensation for displaced licensees by way of disturbance payments. It is therefore necessary to describe the circumstances or conditions which give rise to an entitlement to a disturbance payment and then the assessment of the amount of that payment.

12.7   In order to avoid confusion it is necessary to distinguish clearly between: (a) a disturbance payment under section 37 of the Land Compensation Act 1973, which is the subject matter of this chapter, and (b) compensation for disturbance or other matters under rule (6) of section 5 of the Land Compensation Act 1961. Disturbance payments are available to licensees who are displaced from land by the compulsory acquisition of the land.

---

licence in accordance with the terms of the contract. It was at one time thought that a contractual licence must give rise to a constructive trust which bound a purchaser of the land subject to the licence who had notice of the existence of the licence when he purchased the land, but this understanding was also held to be incorrect in *Ashburn Anstalt v Arnold*, above.

   [8] *Warr (Frank) & Co Ltd v London County Council* [1904] 1 KB 713. This was one of the decisions relied upon by the Court of Appeal for its holding in *Ashburn Anstalt v Arnold*, above, that a licence did not create a proprietary interest in land. The course of reasoning appears to be that s 7 of the Compulsory Purchase Act 1965 creates a right to compensation equal to the value of the land purchased by the acquiring authority and a licence is not an interest in land and so cannot count as land. Nor is compensation payable to a licensee under s 20 of the Compulsory Purchase Act 1965 (see section (i) of ch 4 for compensation under s 20).

   [9] A classic definition of the doctrine of proprietary estoppel was given by Oliver J, on the basis of submissions by counsel, in *Taylors Fashions Ltd v Liverpool Trustees Co* [1982] QB 133n, at p 144 in the following terms: 'If A under an expectation created or encouraged by B that A shall have a certain interest in land, thereafter, on the faith of such expectation and with the knowledge of B and without objection by him, acts to his detriment in connection with such land, a Court of Equity will compel B to give effect to such expectation'. An early decision on the doctrine in the context of a claim for compensation for compulsory acquisition is *Plimmer v Mayor of Wellington* (1883–84) LR 9 App Cas 699. A person who held from the Crown a licence of a jetty in Wellington in New Zealand was allowed or encouraged to extend the jetty and build on it facilities needed for the reception of immigrants into the young colony which was establishing itself following the Treaty of Waitangi and the end of the Maori wars. When the jetty was compulsorily acquired it was held by the Privy Council that the person who had carried out the works was entitled to an interest in the land by virtue of an estoppel which was sufficient to confer on him a right to compensation.

Compensation for disturbance or other matters under rule (6) is available to a person who has a proprietary interest in the land acquired. The same person cannot claim both payments in respect of his rights over the land acquired. It is, of course, possible that different persons may have different rights over the same piece of land so entitling one person to a disturbance payment and the other person to compensation under rule (6).[10]

(B) THE CORPORATE VEIL

Before coming to the details of the entitlement to, and assessment of, disturbance payments mention needs to be made of one problem which has given rise to a previous possible harsh result and which can still arise today. It is a not uncommon practice for those who own and control a company through ownership of its shares to allow the company to occupy land owned by the controlling entity for the purposes of a business conducted at the land. The controlling entity may be a person, or may be a parent company in a group, which allows a subsidiary company to take possession of land owned by the parent company.[11] Such arrangements may be the subject of a formal and documented licence (or even a lease) but sometimes no formality is present and there is no documentation. The result is that the company in possession of the land is normally a licensee only.[12] If the land was compulsorily acquired there were, prior to the Land Compensation Act 1973, great difficulties in obtaining compensation for the disturbance of the business. The company which held the proprietary interest in the land was entitled to compensation for the value of that interest but not to any compensation for being disturbed from possession, or for the disturbance to the business, since that company was not in possession of the land and did not carry on the business. The company in possession of the land and carrying on the business was not entitled to compensation of any sort since its status was that of a licensee only and it held no proprietary interest in the land.

12.8

It was the *DHN* case in which circumstances of the above nature arose which may have provided the impetus for sections 37 and 38 of the Land Compensation Act 1973.[13] In that case the freehold interest in land was vested in a subsidiary company but the possession of the land and the business were enjoyed and carried on by the parent company, DHN Food Distributors Ltd. When the land was compulsorily acquired the Lands Tribunal held that, on the reasoning explained in the last paragraph, no compensation was recoverable for the disturbance to the business. The Court of Appeal reversed this decision, holding that it was possible in law to ignore the existence of the separate companies and that the claim for compensation for the value of the land, and for disruption to the business, could be made by and in the name of the parent company.[14] If this conclusion, founded on ignoring the

12.9

---

[10] An example is *Wrexham Maelor Borough Council v MacDougall* (1995) 69 P & CR 109, the facts of which are summarised in para 8.26 of ch 8.

[11] In some instances it is convenient for the land to be vested in the subsidiary company and for the parent company to be allowed into possession of the land to carry on the business. This was the situation in the *DHN* case which is discussed in para 12.9.

[12] The lease may be a bare licence if, as often happens, no monetary sums are payable or, if there is some payment or other consideration, it may be a contractual licence. See para 12.2.

[13] *DHN Food Distributors Ltd v London Borough of Tower Hamlets* [1976] 1 WLR 852, [1976] 3 All ER 462.

[14] The entitlement to compensation for disturbance was also explained by the Court on two further bases. (a) It was held that there was a resulting trust since the subsidiary company had acquired the land with money

distinction between separate companies, is correct the new provisions in the 1973 Act may not have been as necessary as was supposed.

12.10   The disregard of the distinction in law between separate but associated companies is usually called lifting or piercing the corporate veil. It might be thought that following the provisions in sections 37 and 38 of the Land Compensation Act 1973 this subject no longer had any significance as regards the law of compensation for disturbance. That is not so. As will be explained the entitlement to a disturbance payment under the provisions of the 1973 Act does not exist unless the claimant was in possession of the land at the date of the publication of the making of the compulsory purchase order, and a considerable time may elapse between that date and the valuation date, so that there is scope for a company to go into possession as a licensee only at a date before the valuation date in circumstances in which it has no claim to a disturbance payment under the 1973 Act.[15] The obtaining of compensation for disturbance may then depend on a claim being sustainable under the general provisions for compensation for disturbance under rule (6) of section 5 of the Land Compensation Act 1961 which in turn may depend on whether it is possible in law to lift the corporate veil as was done in the *DHN* case.

12.11   The Lands Tribunal has recently held that when it is necessary to do so in compensation cases it is permissible to lift the corporate veil in the sense just explained.[16] The reason was that the *DHN* decision of the Court of Appeal was said to remain good law in the area of compensation for compulsory purchase. There is strong reason to doubt whether this conclusion can be correct and whether it would survive a challenge in an appellate court. The reasons for this doubt are briefly explained here. An account has been given in chapter 4 of the nature of companies and other corporate bodies which are accorded legal personality as fictitious persons in English law.[17]

   (i)   The existence, status and powers attributable to companies as fictional legal persons depend on the rules of law in the statutory provisions which create or permit the creation of such persons, that is the rules of attribution.[18] The Companies Act 2006 which contains the rules of attribution for companies says nothing about merging the legal personality of different companies.

   (ii)   The fundamental rule in English law has long been established by the House of Lords as being that however closely a company may be controlled by a person or

ultimately provided by the parent company. On the long established principle in such cases as *Dyer v Dyer* (1782) 2 Cox Eq Cas 92, 30 ER 42, these facts were sufficient to create a resulting trust with the subsidiary company holding the land in trust for the parent company, thus giving the parent company an equitable proprietary interest in the freehold which entitled it to claim compensation in its own right. This reasoning can be justified on orthodox principles under the law of implied trusts but depended on the particular facts of the case. (b) It was held that the licence in favour of the parent company rendered that company a beneficiary under a constructive trust. This holding is unsustainable in the light of later developments in the law: see para 12.4, n 7.

[15] Where the acquisition takes place under the authority to acquire land granted directly by an Act of Parliament, rather than by a compulsory purchase order, the time during which a person has to be in possession may be even greater; see para 12.16.

[16] *Bishopsgate Parking (No 2) v Welsh Ministers* [2012] UKUT 22 (LC), [2012] RVR 237, in which the issue was examined by the Tribunal. See also *Roberts v Ashford Borough Council* (2004) (Lands Tribunal); *Million Add Development Ltd v Secretary for Transport* [1997] CPR 316 (Lands Tribunal, Hong Kong) in both of which cases the corporate veil was lifted although in neither case was there any examination of the principles of law involved.

[17] See ch 4, para 4.20.

[18] See per Lord Hoffmann in the appeal to the Privy Council from New Zealand in *Meridian Global Funds Management Asia Ltd v Securities Commission* [1995] 2 AC 500, [1995] 3 WLR 413, at pp 566–67.

persons or by another company that first company still retains its separate legal personality.[19]

(iii)   Following the *DHN* decision in the Court of Appeal the House of Lords in a Scottish case, concerning a claim for compensation and the question of the lifting of the corporate veil, has doubted whether the Court of Appeal applied the correct principle in the *DHN* case.[20]

(iv)   The question of lifting the corporate veil was considered comprehensively in 1990 by the Court of Appeal.[21] The conclusion reached, and the law stated, was that as a matter of general principle the only circumstances which permit the lifting of the corporate veil are: (a) where statute so states, (b) where a contract so states, and (c) where the corporate structure is a sham or façade which conceals the true situation. The circumstances which arose in the *DHN* case, and those considered recently by the Lands Tribunal, do not fall within any of these exceptions. This clear principle so established by the Court of Appeal has been applied in a series of subsequent authorities, spanning areas of commercial law and family law, in which the corporate veil was not lifted.[22]

(v)   The only way in which the *DHN* decision could be justified today would be on the footing that there was some special rule of law applicable to compensation claims which took those claims outside the normal thread of legal principle. Such an approach to the law of compensation has recently been deprecated by the House of Lords. The law of compensation is not an area of law in which general principles of the law can be ignored where it seems convenient to do so.[23]

Any residual doubt which may have existed as to the legal propriety of piercing the corporate veil in compensation cases has now been removed following the decision of the Supreme Court in *Prest v Petrodel Properties Ltd*.[24] The decision concerned the jurisdiction of a court to make an order for the transfer of property from one party to a marriage to the other following a divorce under section 24 of the Matrimonial Causes Act 1973 but the principles were explained as applicable generally and to all areas of the law in the judgment of Lord Sumption.[25] One of the cases considered by Lord Sumption was *Woolfson v Strathclyde Regional Council*.[26] It is not necessary for present purposes to consider the decision of the Supreme Court in detail. Two important principles were enunciated. One principle was that the corporate veil can only be pierced in very limited circumstances which were derived from the rule that there had to be some impropriety involved before there   12.12

---

[19]   *Salomon v Salomon & Co* [1897] AC 22.
[20]   *Woolfson v Strathclyde Regional Council* 1978 SLT 159. This was a Scottish appeal but the same legislative provisions and principles were applicable as in England. It is generally considered that English courts are bound by decisions of the House of Lords in Scottish appeals unless the House has itself said otherwise: *Re Tuck* [1978] Ch 49, [1978] 2 WLR 411, per Lord Denning MR at p 61. This principle of the law of procedure does not seem to have been considered by the Lands Tribunal in the *Bishopsgate Parking* decision.
[21]   *Adams v Cape Industries Plc* [1990] Ch 433, [1990] 2 WLR 657.
[22]   *Ord v Belhaven Pubs Ltd* [1998] BCCC 607, per Hobhouse LJ at p 615f; *Kensington Investments Ltd v Republic of the Congo* [2005] EWHC 2684 (Comm), per Cooke J at para 177; *Ben Hashem v Ali Shayif* [2009] 1 FLR 115.
[23]   *Commissioner of Taxation v Ryan* [2000] 201 CLR 109, per Kirby J at p 146 (High Court of Australia), cited by Lord Walker in *Transport for London v Spirerose Ltd* [2009] UKHL 41, [2009] 1 WLR 1797, at para 25. The relevant passage from the judgment of Kirby J is set out in para 5.79 of ch 5.
[24]   *Prest v Petrodel Properties Ltd* [2003] UKSC 34, [2013] 3 WLR 1.
[25]   Lord Sumption did not mention in his reasoning the *DHN* decision. Insofar as that decision relates to piercing the corporate veil it must be regarded as a decision which is wrong in law today.
[26]   *Prest v Petrodel Properties Ltd* [2003] UKSC 34, [2013] 3 WLR 1 at para 21.

could be such a piercing of the veil. The second principle, of importance to the present case, is that a general principle of law cannot be ignored, or described as something not applicable, where there is some particular specialist jurisdiction involved. Thus the general principle cannot be ignored in the area of compensation for compulsory purchase. The law as stated by Lord Sumption[27] is that there is a limited principle of English law which applies when a person is under an existing legal obligation, or liability, or subject to an existing legal restriction which he deliberately evades or whose enforcement he deliberately frustrates by interposing a company under his control. The court may then pierce the corporate veil for the purpose, and only for the purpose, of depriving the company, or its controller, of the advantage that they would otherwise have obtained by the company's separate legal personality. The principle is properly described as a limited one, because in almost every case where the test is satisfied, the facts will in practice disclose a legal relationship between the company and its controller which will make it unnecessary to pierce the corporate veil. It is therefore clear that in cases of assessing compensation for compulsory purchase there will be very limited circumstances in which the corporate veil can be pierced and certainly the suggestion which emerges from the *Welsh Minister's* case in the Lands Tribunal that there is some special rule applicable to the area of law constituted by the assessment of compensation appears to be radically misplaced.[28]

(C) THE ENTITLEMENT TO A DISTURBANCE PAYMENT

12.13   A person who is displaced from any land in consequence of the acquisition of the land by an authority possessing compulsory purchase powers is entitled to a disturbance payment from the acquiring authority providing that certain conditions are fulfilled.[29] A payment is due if the acquisition is by agreement as well as if it is compulsory (subject of course to the terms of the agreement). Disturbance payments are also due in other cases under housing legislation and where land previously acquired or appropriated by an authority is improved or redeveloped.[30] Payments in these circumstances which are not concerned with compulsory purchase are not further considered here. In order for a disturbance payment to become due following a compulsory acquisition of land four further conditions have to be satisfied.

12.14   The first condition is that the person displaced must be in lawful possession of the land from which he is displaced.[31] The entitlement to a payment is intended to apply to persons who are in possession of land as licensees and thus with the consent of the freeholder or tenant of the land and not to extend to trespassers who are, of course, not in lawful possession of the land. A person who has been in possession of the land for some substantial period of time, but without the consent of the owner, remains a trespasser unless and until he can show a sufficient period of adverse possession to establish himself as the owner by a

---

[27] [2003] UKSC 34, at para 35 per Lord Sumption. See also Lord Neuberger at para 60.
[28] *Bishopsgate Parking (No 2) v Welsh Ministers* [2012] UKUT 22 (LC), [2012] RVR 237.
[29] Land Compensation Act 1973, s 37(1)(a). An acquiring authority and an authority possessing compulsory purchaser powers have the same meaning as in s 39(1) of the Land Compensation Act 1961: Land Compensation Act 1973, s 87(1).
[30] Land Compensation Act 1973, s 37(1)(b)–(d).
[31] Ibid, s 37(2)(a).

possessory title.[32] Despite this principle there is some reason to believe that a person who is in possession of land without the consent of the owner and is building up a claim by adverse possession, but has not yet achieved the 12 years necessary to obtain a possessory title, may be entitled to compensation under the general rules relating to compensation and not by way of a disturbance payment.[33]

The second condition is that the person displaced from the land had no interest in the land for the acquisition of which he is entitled to compensation under any other enactment.[34] What this condition amounts to is that the displaced person must have no interest, such as a freehold or leasehold interest, legal or equitable, which entitles him to compensation for the acquisition of his interest under section 7 of the Compulsory Purchase Act 1965 or a short tenancy which entitles him to compensation under section 20 of that Act. In effect claims for a disturbance payment are confined to claims made by licensees in possession of the land. The condition prevents double claims for compensation.   12.15

The third condition relates to the date on which the claimant for the disturbance payment first went into lawful possession of the land from which he was displaced by the acquisition. It is considered that a person who went into possession when he knew, or should have known, of the compulsory acquisition ought not to be entitled to a payment for his disturbance from the land since he knew or should have known of the prospect of the disturbance when he took possession. The time limit is derived from this policy. The time limit depends on the procedure used for the acquisition. If the acquisition was under a compulsory purchase order a person displaced is not entitled to a disturbance payment unless he was in lawful possession of the land when notice was first published of the making of the order or of the preparation of the order in draft.[35] If the land was acquired under an Act which specified the land as subject to compulsory acquisition a person disturbed is not entitled to a payment unless he was in lawful possession of the land when the provisions of the Bill for the Act were first published.[36] If the land was acquired by agreement a person displaced is not entitled to a payment unless he was in lawful possession of the land when the agreement was made.[37] A considerable period may elapse between the first notice of the making or preparation in draft of a compulsory purchase order and the date when the acquiring   12.16

---

[32] There may be some doubt on the status of an unlawful sub-tenant, that is a person who has been granted a sub-tenancy in breach of the terms of the headlease. Such a person has an estate in land notwithstanding the unlawfulness of the grant of the estate by sub-letting: *Parker v Jones* [1910] 2 KB 32. The better view is that an unlawful sub-tenant may make an ordinary claim for compensation and so cannot be entitled to a disturbance payment by reason of the second condition mentioned next. Of course the value of his interest may be little since it may be liable to forfeiture by the head landlord. See also r (4) of s 5 of the Land Compensation Act 1961 which prevents compensation being claimed for any increase in the value of land by reason of a use of premises at the land which could be restrained by any court or is contrary to law. However, that provision is not applied to claims for disturbance payments. Furthermore what is unlawful in the case of an unlawful sub-tenancy is the grant of the sub-tenancy and not necessarily the use to which the unlawful sub-tenant puts the land.

[33] See ch 2, para 2.85; *Perry v Clissold* [1907] AC 73.

[34] Land Compensation Act 1973, s 37(2)(b).

[35] These two dates refer to the process for the making of an order by an authority other than a Minister and for the preparation of an order in draft by a Minister. In both cases notice of the making or preparation in draft of the order has to be published: see section (e) of ch 2 for a description of the procedure.

[36] See ch 2, para 2.5. In such cases the making of a compulsory purchase order is not necessary since the Act itself authorises the acquisition of any land within the area specified. Where the compulsory purchase is for the purposes of a specific project, such as the Crossrail scheme in London, the Act which authorises the construction project, in that case the Crossrail Act 2008, usually itself specifies the geographical limits within which land may be compulsorily acquired.

[37] Land Compensation Act 1973, s 37(3).

authority takes possession of the land, a time which may be taken up with dealing with objections to the order and other procedural matters. Equally there may be a considerable time between the first publication of a Bill authorising a public project and the acquisition of land for that project and the taking of possession of land by the acquiring authority. Persons who enter into possession of land as licensees during this period should therefore understand that they will not be entitled to a disturbance payment or any other form of compensation if they are displaced from the land by an acquiring authority.

12.17   The fourth condition is that there is no right to a disturbance payment when the land from which a person is disturbed is used for the purpose of agriculture.[38]

12.18   The person displaced may be a tenant of business premises from the acquiring authority as his landlord. In such a case the tenant may be entitled, by reason of his disturbance from the land let to him, to compensation from the acquiring authority as his landlord under section 37 of the Landlord and Tenant Act 1954. A right to compensation can arise under the 1954 Act when the tenancy of a tenant of premises occupied by him for the purposes of a business is determined under that Act and the court is precluded on certain grounds, such as that the landlord intends to redevelop the premises, from ordering the grant of a new tenancy to the tenant. The compensation is a multiple of the rateable value of the premises, the multiple depending on how long the business has been carried on at the premises.[39] If the tenant also qualifies for a disturbance payment under the Land Compensation Act 1973 he has an option on whether to receive compensation under the 1954 Act or the disturbance payment. He cannot receive both.[40] It is not clear in what circumstances an entitlement to both payments could arise. If the claimant in possession of the land is a tenant he may be entitled to compensation under the 1954 Act where the protection of the Act and the right to compensation are confined to persons who are tenants. In these circumstances he will not be entitled to claim a disturbance payment since he will have an interest in the land for the acquisition of which he is entitled to compensation under the general rules relating to compensation and so is prevented from claiming a disturbance payment.[41] On the other hand, if the claimant in possession of the land is a licensee, he may be entitled to claim a disturbance payment but he cannot have any rights under the 1954 Act since such rights are confined to tenants.

12.19   Where a person is disturbed from land in consequence of the acquisition of the land by an authority possessing compulsory purchase powers but is not entitled as against the acquiring authority to a disturbance payment, or to compensation for disturbance under any other statutory provision, the acquiring authority may still in its discretion make a disturbance payment to him.[42] The cases in which the practical prospect of such a discretionary payment being made are limited. The person displaced may not be entitled as of right to a disturbance payment for a number of reasons. (a) He may have a sufficient interest in the

---

[38]   Ibid, s 37(7). Agriculture has the meaning given in s 109 of the Agriculture Act 1947: ibid, s 87(1).

[39]   The grounds are stated in s 30(1) of the Landlord and Tenant Act 1954 and the provisions for compensation are in s 37 of that Act. The entitlement to a minimum payment of the compensation which would be payable under s 37 of the 1954 Act also applies to claims for compensation under s 20 of the Compulsory Purchase Act 1965 when possession is taken of land subject to a short tenancy: see s 39(2) of the Landlord and Tenant Act 1954 and see para 4.14 of ch 4.

[40]   Land Compensation Act 1973, s 37(4).

[41]   Ibid, s 37(2)(b)(i), and see para 12.15.

[42]   Ibid, s 37(5).

land, for example a tenancy, which entitles him to compensation for disturbance under rule (6) of section 5 of the Land Compensation Act 1961. In that event there is no possibility of a discretionary payment to him. (b) His possession of the land may be unlawful. It is difficult to think of circumstances in which an acquiring authority would wish to make a payment to someone whose possession is unlawful. A possibility might be someone who has been in adverse possession of the land as a trespasser for a substantial period of time, but not for the whole of the 12 years needed to entitle him to gain a possessory title.[43] (c) The land may be used for agriculture. It is difficult to think that an acquiring authority would wish to make a discretionary payment in respect of agricultural land when that land has been expressly taken out of the ambit of such payments. (d) The most likely possibility of a discretionary payment being made is where the claimant has been in lawful possession of the land for a significant period but first went into lawful possession after the date which constitutes the time limit for a claim for a disturbance payment.[44] Even so when Parliament has laid down a definite time limit of this nature it is not easy to envisage the circumstances in which public money should be expended in making a payment to someone whose claim is not within the time limit.

If the authority exercises its discretion to make a disturbance payment then the amount of   12.20
it has to be that which would be determined in accordance with section 38 as the amount of the disturbance payment to the claimant if he was entitled to that payment. It seems, therefore, that there is no power in the acquiring authority to make a disturbance payment of an amount which is less than that which would be the full entitlement. There may be circumstances in which the authority might feel that a payment less than the full entitle-ment was justified but it seems that they are precluded from making such a limited pay-ment. The decision of the acquiring authority on whether to make a statutory payment is entirely within its discretion. It cannot be reviewed as a matter of its ordinary merits by any court or by the Lands Tribunal. However, like all decisions of public bodies the decision of the acquiring authority is subject to the normal constraints of administrative law including the principle that in making its decision the authority must take into account all relevant considerations and must not act in a way which is so unreasonable that no reasonable authority could act in that way. A decision of an acquiring authority not to make a discre-tionary payment is therefore subject in principle to judicial review in the same way as other administrative actions. The Lands Tribunal, as the Lands Chamber of the Upper Tribunal, may obtain a statutory right itself to determine proceedings for judicial review in certain circumstances.[45]

(D) THE AMOUNT OF A DISTURBANCE PAYMENT

A disturbance payment may have two components. One is a sum equal to the reasonable   12.21
expenses of the person entitled to the payment in removing from the land from which he is displaced. The second component applies if the person displaced was carrying on a trade or business on the land and is a sum equal to the loss which that person will sustain by reason

[43] See para 12.14.
[44] See para 12.16.
[45] Tribunals, Courts and Enforcement Act 2007. See ch 15, para 15.90. No such power exists at present.

of disturbance of that trade or business consequent upon his having to quit the land.[46] Interest is payable from the date of displacement until the date of payment.[47] The first component creates no questions of principle in its assessment. The assessment of loss under the second component, disturbance to a trade or business, gives rise to three questions.

12.22　The first question is how the loss is to be assessed. The person displaced is under the same duty to mitigate his loss as any other claimant for compensation. If any loss to his business can be reduced by relocating the business to other premises he must do so.[48] If there is a relocation his removal expenses will be a part of the disturbance payment, as well as any loss to his business caused by the move, such as temporary disruption or a temporary loss of profits. If relocation of the business is not possible, or practical, the person dispossessed is entitled to payment for the loss of the profits which would have been made from the business. In these circumstances the business is said to be totally extinguished. It is likely that in such a case the loss will be calculated by reference to the loss of future anticipated net profits from the business. One way of calculating this loss would be to take the average net profits made from the business over the last few years and to apply an appropriate multiplier to that annual sum so as to produce a capital payment for the loss of those profits in future years. The difficulty is to know what is the appropriate multiplier. Obviously the greater the risk associated with earning profits in the future and the shorter the future period during which the profits would be likely to be earned had the acquiring authority not dispossessed the claimant the lower the multiplier is likely to be.[49] A more sophisticated method of assessing a sum to represent the loss of future profits is to carry out a discounted cash flow analysis so as to find the present day value as at the date of possession of the future stream of anticipated profits. This process is described in more detail elsewhere[50] but its essential elements are: (a) an estimate of future assumed net profits from year to year, (b) an estimate of the future period over which those profits would be likely to have been earned if the business had not been extinguished, and (c) the determination of the discount rate used to convert each annual sum of net profits (the profit stream) to a present day value.[51]

12.23　The second possible question is the likely duration of the licence. Obviously the amount of the loss of anticipated future profits consequent upon the extinguishment of a business

---

[46] Land Compensation Act 1973, s 38(1).

[47] Ibid, s 37(6). For the rate of interest prescribed, and the payment of interest generally on compensation, see section (c) of ch 15.

[48] There is a general duty on all claimants for any form of compensation to take reasonable steps to mitigate their loss: see *Director of Buildings and Land v Shun Fung Ironworks Ltd* [1995] 2 AC 111, [1995] 2 WLR 904, at p 126. The relevant passage from the opinion of Lord Nicholls is set out in ch 4, para 4.79, n 111. For the duty of a claimant for compensation under rr (2) or (6) of the Land Compensation Act 1961 to move his business elsewhere in order to mitigate his loss, see ch 4, para 4.79. The duty is emphasised as regards claims for disturbance payments by the provision in s 37(2) of the Land Compensation Act 1973 that in estimating the loss due to the disturbance of a business regard shall be had to the availability of other land suitable for the purposes of the business. This must mean that the claimant for compensation is bound to relocate his business in available alternative premises where doing so would reduce the loss to him caused by his displacement from the land acquired. If he does not relocate his business to other premises, where it would be reasonable to do so and where doing so would reduce his loss, the disturbance payment will be assessed as though the relocation had taken place.

[49] For the difficulty in selecting an appropriate multiplier when that method of assessment is used see *Clibbett v Avon County Council* (1975) 16 RVR 131.

[50] See section (d) of ch 14.

[51] See the description given by Lord Nicholls in *Director of Buildings and Lands v Shun Fung Investments* [1995] 2 AC 111, [1995] 2 WLR 904, at p 132. An example of a discounted cash flow analysis is given in section (e) of the Appendix.

depends in part on how long the business would have continued apart from the extinguishment and that in turn depends on how long the licence would have been likely to have
continued. In the case of a formal licence for a specific period there is no difficulty since the
end date of the licence is fixed. Many licences to take possession of land are informal in
nature with no specified duration. Such licences are normally determinable on the giving of
reasonable notice. Where the person dispossessed of the land held under a lease, determinable by a notice to quit in the case of a periodic tenancy or determinable under the terms of
a break clause in the lease, the law is clear. It has to be assumed in assessing compensation
that the lease would be determined at the earliest date on which it could be determined by
an appropriate notice served by the landlord at the valuation date.[52] The same rule should
apply to licenses. There is no reason why, as regards compensation for disturbance, a licensee
who claims a disturbance payment under the Land Compensation Act 1973 should be in a
better position than a lessee who is entitled to compensation under the general provisions
of the law of compensation.

The third question follows from the second. The anticipation of future profits from a busi-   12.24
ness carried on by a licensee on land may depend not only on how long his licence will
endure but also on whether the licence will be renewed on its termination. Licences are not
protected under Part II of the Landlord and Tenant Act 1954 so that a renewal of a licence
in the future must be a matter of probability only dependent on the future agreement of the
licensor and licensee. At this point there emerges a difference between the position of a
person who carries on business on the land as a lessee and a person who carries on business
as a licensee. It appears, although the law in England and Wales is not wholly certain, that
the expectation of an agreed and voluntary renewal of a lease is not to be taken into account
when compensation is assessed.[53] Whatever is the exact principle for leases the position is
made clear for licences and claims for disturbance payments by an express provision in the
1973 Act that in estimating the loss by reason of disturbance to a business reference shall be
made to the period for which the occupation by the claimant may reasonably have been
expected to be available for the purposes of the business of the claimant.[54] The result of this
provision seems to be that if there is good reason to believe that the licence current at the
date of dispossession will be renewed on its termination, for example because the licensor
and licensee are associated companies, the prospect of renewal is to be taken into account
in assessing the loss caused by the disturbance to the business. That prospect will be relevant to the estimate of the loss using one of the methods discussed earlier.[55] To this extent a
licensee who claims a disturbance payment may be in a better position than a lessee who
claims compensation for disturbance under rule (6) of section 5 of the Land Compensation
Act 1961. One possible view is that the provision here described not only allows the expectation of a renewal of a licence to be taken into account but also overrides for the purpose
of disturbance payments and licences the rule applicable to leases that subject to their

---

[52] *Bishopsgate Space Management Ltd v London Underground Ltd* [2004] 2 EGLR 175. See ch 4, paras 4.95–4.97.
There is a possible argument that for the purposes of claims for disturbance payments this rule is removed by
s 38(2) of the Land Compensation Act 1973. Section 38(2) is considered in the next paragraph.

[53] *Minister of Transport v Pettitt* (1968) LGR 449. This rule rests in part on a Scottish decision and observations
in a more recent case in the Court of Final Appeal in Hong Kong by Lord Millett: see ch 4, para 4.99. As there
explained the justification for the rule, if indeed it applies in England and Wales, is uncertain.

[54] Land Compensation Act 1973, s 38(2).

[55] See para 12.22. The strength of the expectation of the renewal of the licence may be relevant to the ascertainment of the multiplier or the discount rate.

nature or their contractual terms they are to be taken to be determined by a notice given at the valuation date.[56]

12.25   It should be understood that a disturbance payment is not a payment for the value of land or for the value of an interest in land. Indeed the claimant will not have an interest in land in the sense of a proprietary interest as that concept is normally understood in the law of real property. The payment is for two possible forms of monetary loss. The second form is not strictly the value of the business of the claimant since the claimant may be able to establish his business in alternative premises in which case he will not have lost the value of the business. If such a reinstatement is impossible and the business is totally extinguished the compensation may be equivalent to the value of the business.

12.26   A person may be displaced from a dwelling in which structural modifications have been made for meeting the special needs of a disabled person where assistance for the making of the modifications was provided (or where assistance would have been provided if an application had been made) under section 29 of the National Assistance Act 1948. If the displaced person moves to a different dwelling the disturbance payment is to include the amount of any reasonable expenses incurred by the person entitled to the displacement payment in making comparable modifications to the new dwelling. This provision applies whether or not the person entitled to the disturbance payment made the original modifications. It applies, therefore, where a previous owner or occupier of a dwelling acquired made the modifications.[57]

12.27   Any dispute as to the amount of a disturbance payment is to be determined by the Lands Tribunal.[58] It is likely that the jurisdiction of the Tribunal includes that of determining not only the amount of a disturbance payment but also whether a person is entitled to such a payment.[59] There is a limitation period of six years from the accrual of the cause of action under section 9 of the Limitation Act 1980. The cause of action accrues as the date on which the claimant is displaced from the land.[60]

---

[56]   See para 12.23 and see n 52.
[57]   Land Compensation Act 1973, s 38(3).
[58]   Ibid, s 38(4).
[59]   The general jurisdiction of the Lands Tribunal to determine compensation claims includes the power to determine whether a person is entitled to compensation at all: *Union Rlys Ltd v Kent County Council* [2008] 2 EGLR 183. For the procedure in references to the Lands Tribunal, see ch 15.
[60]   See *Hillingdon LBC v ARC Ltd (No 1)* [1999] Ch 139, [1998] 3 WLR 754, and see section (e) of ch 15.

13

Compensation for the Use of
Public Works

(A) INTRODUCTION

This book is primarily concerned with compensation due when a person's land is compul-   13.1
sorily acquired. This includes the case in which a part of a person's land is acquired and that
person is entitled to compensation for a reduction in the value of the land retained by him
due to its severance from the land acquired or due to the exercise by the acquiring authority
of its statutory powers on the land acquired or on other land. This last head of compensation has been a part of the main compensation provisions since the Lands Clauses
Consolidation Act 1845 and is considered in chapter 9. In addition there are two main
provisions in the general corpus of the compensation legislation which permit a landowner
to obtain compensation from an authority for the adverse effect on his land of public works
or other activities carried out by that authority even though none of his land has been
acquired. The first of these provisions, which relates to damage caused to a person's land
by the execution of works by an authority which has a power of compulsory purchase
of land in connection with its project, again goes back to the Lands Clauses Consolidation
Act 1845 and is now in section 10 of the Compulsory Purchase Act 1965. It has been
explained in chapter 10. The second set of provisions is that in Part I of the Land
Compensation Act 1973, and so is of comparatively recent origin, and it is considered in
this chapter.

Many people own land which is reduced in value by lawful acts carried out on nearby land.   13.2
A house with a view of the open countryside may have its view and its setting affected by
the construction of a new housing estate with a resultant loss in value. A new use of land in
the locality such as the opening of a new public car park on adjoining land may reduce the
amenities and the value of a property. In general persons are expected to put up with these
misfortunes where the change of use or development is by a private developer or landowner. The law of nuisance may afford a remedy in tort and in private law in the more
extreme cases of an adverse effect. Until 1973 much the same position applied where the
development which created the depreciation in the value of an interest in land was public
works carried out in the public interest. If a person's land was acquired for the public works
he would, of course, obtain compensation equal to the value of his land disregarding the
effect on that value of the public works. If a part of a person's land was acquired he would
obtain compensation for any reduction in the value of his retained land caused by the public works. However, the usual principle was that a person whose land was adversely affected
by a project such as a new road or a new railway, but none of whose land was acquired for
the project, had no entitlement to compensation for a reduction in the value of his land.

Even the possibility of an action in private law for damages for nuisance was often impossible since the statute which authorised the carrying out of the works might expressly or impliedly exclude any liability in nuisance on the part of the promoters of the project in respect of the carrying out or the use of the public works.

13.3   This situation was thought to be unsatisfactory when there was a project of works carried out by a public body for the benefit of the public. In an age when more and more people demand compensation for the vicissitudes of life it was thought hard that when the public in general benefited from the use of public works, such as a motorway, the small section of the public whose land in the locality of the works was reduced in value by the use of the works should obtain no recompense for that reduction in value. It was this general situation which was remedied by Part I of the Land Compensation Act 1973.[1] In a sense these new provisions constituted a new chapter in the ongoing debate, which originated in section 68 of the Land Clauses Consolidation Act 1845 and the series of subsequent decisions in Victorian times on the application of that provision, relating to the circumstances in which a private landowner should be compensated for the adverse effects on this property of schemes in the locality carried out for the public benefit.[2]

13.4   A general right to compensation for the depreciation in the value of a person's interest in land due to the use of public works was created by this legislation. The right to compensation is far from universal. The depreciation in value has to be caused by one or more of specified physical factors due to the use of the public works if compensation is to be recoverable. The loss of a view caused by public works may reduce the value of a nearby property but a loss of view is not a physical factor which creates a right to compensation. By no means all owners of interests in land can claim compensation. Nor can compensation be recovered where there is no statutory immunity from actions for nuisance in respect of the use of the works. In the case of no such immunity being conferred a landowner is left to any common law remedy for damages or other relief in respect of a nuisance which he can assert. There are two important dates to be borne in mind in the operation of the statutory provisions. The first is the relevant date which is the date on which the public works were first used after their completion.[3] The second date is the first claim day which is the day 12 months after the relevant date and is the first day on which a claim for compensation can be made.[4] The nature of the entitlement to compensation and the above and other important limitations on that entitlement will be explained in the remainder of this chapter.

---

[1] Other Parts of the Land Compensation Act 1973 introduced important reforms to the law of compensation which are covered elsewhere in this book. The main provisions in the Act were explained in the White Paper, *Description and Compensation – Putting People First* (Cmnd 5124, 1972).

[2] The historical and policy aspects of this subject were considered by Lord Hoffmann in the leading modern decision on s 10 of the Compulsory Purchase Act 1965, *Wildtree Hotels Ltd v Harrow LBC* [2001] 2 AC 1, [2009] 3 WLR 163.

[3] See para 13.15.

[4] See para 13.23.

(B) PUBLIC WORKS AND PHYSICAL FACTORS

1. The Works and the Physical Factors

The depreciation in the value of an interest in land must be caused by the use of public works if compensation is to be payable.[5] It is the use of the works and not the carrying out of the works which creates the entitlement to compensation. A property may be affected and reduced in value by the disruption and other matters caused by the carrying out of the public works but no compensation under the Land Compensation Act 1973 is recoverable for these matters. This rule is reinforced by the further rule that, as explained later, in assessing the depreciation of the value of an interest in land it is necessary to focus on the situation as it was after the public works had been in use for a year.[6]   13.5

Public works are defined as any highway, any aerodrome, and any works other than the two just mentioned, provided or used in the exercise of statutory powers. The word 'works' usually means the carrying out of works which result in development such as a highway or an aerodrome. In the present context the works mean the result of the construction works, namely the highway or aerodrome or other development which is then used. For present purposes a highway includes a part of a highway and means not every highway but only a highway maintainable at the public expense, as defined in section 329(1) of the Highways Act 1980. A claim cannot be made if at the relevant date the highway was not maintainable at the public expense and it does not become so maintainable within three years from that date.[7] It should be noted that for works in the third and general category to constitute public works they do not have to be carried out by a public body, in the sense of a body which is publicly owned, or which obtains its funds from the public purse. The relevant criterion in that the works are carried out in the exercise of statutory powers. The Land Compensation Act 1973 was enacted prior to the decades of privatisation in the 1980s and 1990s and today works carried out in privatised industries by ordinary commercial companies, such as in the water or electricity industries, are often carried out in the exercise of statutory powers so that in principle compensation can be claimed against the privatised utility companies. The word 'works' is not defined but it clearly connotes the result of physical operations and activities on land as opposed to a change in the use of land.   13.6

[5] Land Compensation Act 1973, s 1(1). In the remainder of the notes to this chapter the Land Compensation Act 1973 is usually referred to as 'LCA 1973'.
[6] See para 13.23. A landowner may in certain limited circumstances be entitled to compensation for the execution of public works under s 10 of the Compulsory Purchase Act 1965: see ch 10.
[7] LCA 1973, s 19(1), (3). Highways maintainable at the public expense are defined in s 329(1) of the Highways Act 1980. The great majority of highways are maintainable at the public expense. Some highways may not have this status, for example a highway created by an express or implied dedication of land as a public highway but which has not been adopted by the highway authority. A highway may be a highway not maintainable at the public expense because it was constructed by a highway authority on behalf of some person who is not a highway authority: Highways Act 1980, s 36(2)(a). A common practice is that roads are constructed by developers as part of an agreement with a highway authority and are opened for public use but are not adopted as a highway maintainable at the public expense until a date which is more than three years after it was opened for public use. Read literally s 19(3) would prevent a claim in these circumstances. In *Thomas v Bridgend CBC* [2011] EWCA Civ 862, [2012] QB 512, the Court of Appeal were able to interpret s 19(3) as not having this effect because the rule would, if so applied in the circumstances before the Court, have been inconsistent with art 1 of the First Protocol to the European Convention on Human Rights. The court did not state how exactly the statutory provision should be read so as to avoid the perceived inconsistency.

13.7   It is not enough that there have been public works which have been put into use. A claim for compensation for a depreciation in the value of an interest in land can be sustained only if the depreciation is due to physical factors caused by the use of the public works.[8] The physical factors in question are specified and are noise, vibration, smell, fumes, smoke and artificial lighting and the discharge on the land in question of any solid or liquid substance.[9] Smell usually means the operation of one of the senses rather than a physical factor but that sense is usually aroused by particles in the air which are a physical factor. Fumes probably mean gaseous emissions which include emissions of a harmful nature even though not perceivable by the sense of smell. It is difficult to think of any adverse effect which might be caused to land through the use of public works and by physical factors which are not one of the specified physical factors. Other matters do not give rise to a potential claim for compensation. The matters which do not create such a claim are non-physical effects such as the loss of a view or social effects such as the use of land for public housing which can decrease the value of nearby private housing (save perhaps where a claim for compensation may be sustainable as a result of certain physical factors such as noise or artificial lighting). For example, the use of a refuse tip on land near to the land affected may have caused a reduction in the value of that land but the reduction did not create a right to compensation since it was not shown to be due to one of the defined physical factors.[10]

13.8   The general rule is that a claim for compensation is only sustainable if the depreciation in value is due to physical factors the source of which is on or in the public works.[11] This may be an important limitation. For example, the use of an item of public works, such as the use of an electricity generating station, may affect the value of local properties by reason of increased heavy traffic on local roads delivering fuel and supplies to the station. There will not be a claim for compensation for any depreciation in the value of the properties caused by the traffic since the source of the physical factors of increased noise or vibration from the traffic will not be on the public works which are the generating station itself. There is one exception to this restriction. Physical factors caused by aircraft arriving at or departing from an aerodrome are treated as caused by the use of the aerodrome whether or not the aircraft is within the boundaries of the aerodrome.

2. Limitations on the Works and the Physical Factors

13.9   There are three limitations on the public works or physical factors which can give rise to a claim for compensation.

13.10   First, there is no claim for compensation in respect of physical factors caused by public works, other than a highway, unless an enactment relating to those works expressly or impliedly confers immunity from actions for nuisance.[12] A nuisance is one of the categories

---

[8]   LCA 1973, s 1(1).
[9]   Ibid, s 1(2). See *Blower v Suffolk County Council* (1994) 67 P & CR 228 as regards glare from street lights.
[10] *Shepherd v Lancashire County Council* (1977) 33 P & CR 296.
[11] LCA 1973, s 1(5).
[12] Ibid, s 1(6): see *Marsh v Powys County Council* (1998) 75 P & CR 538 (no claim because no immunity from liability for nuisance under the Education Act 1944 in the case of the use of a new school). In the case of an aerodrome and physical factors caused by aircraft a claim is excluded if the aerodrome is one to which s 72(2) of the Civil Aviation Act 1972 (which confers immunity from actions for nuisance) applies.

of torts the commission of which gives a right of action for damages (and at the discretion of the court an injunction to prevent the commission if it has not occurred or to prevent its continuation) on the part of a person harmed. A tort is in general terms a civil wrong independent of contract. A nuisance has been defined as a condition or activity which unduly interferes with the use or enjoyment of land.[13] All of the physical factors as described[14] are matters which could in principle constitute a nuisance in private law. A claimant is usually better off if there is a statutory immunity from nuisance in respect of the works so that a statutory claim for compensation is possible. In the case of an immunity all that the claimant has to show is that his property has been decreased in value by the physical factors. If there is no immunity the claimant, in order to recover monetary recompense by way of common law damages for nuisance, will have to show not only that there has been an adverse effect on his property but also that the use of the public works does constitute an actionable nuisance. He will also, of course, have to pursue his claims through the ordinary civil courts. However, if there is no statutory immunity from actions for nuisance the claimant might in principle be able to bring about the cessation of any nuisance caused by the public works by obtaining an injunction instead of, or in addition to, an award of damages. It seems probable that most landowners who suffer from the use of public works will find that a claim for statutory compensation for a reduction in the value of their property is a preferable remedy to have available.

A result of the above limitation is that the authority responsible for the public works may resist a claim for compensation under the Land Compensation Act 1973 by contending that no enactment confers immunity from nuisance in respect of the use of the public works which founds the claim. If such a contention is made, and as a result compensation is not payable, then the owner may subsequently bring an action in tort for damages for nuisance in respect of the use of the works. In that event the responsible authority is bound by its contention and no enactment relating to the works which was in force at the date of the contention can be used as a defence to the proceedings in nuisance.[15] This rule gives statutory effect to a result which might otherwise be reached by way of the common law doctrine of estoppel. · 13.11

The second limitation is that no compensation can be claimed in respect of physical factors caused by accidents involving vehicles on a highway or accidents involving aircraft.[16] · 13.12

The third limitation is now only of historical interest. No claim for compensation can be made where the public works were first used before 17 October 1969.[17] This date is three years before the publication of the White Paper (Cmnd 5124) in which the proposals which culminated in the Land Compensation Act 1973 were first published. [18] · 13.13

---

[13] See Buckley, *The Law of Nuisance*, 5th edn (LexisNexis, 2011). See also ch 10, para 10.31 et seq, where it is explained that the execution of works which would be a nuisance apart from statutory authorisation is relevant to claims for compensation under s 10 of the Compulsory Purchase Act 1965.

[14] See para 13.7.

[15] LCA 1973, s 17.

[16] Ibid, s 1(7).

[17] Ibid, s 1(8).

[18] *Development and Compensation – putting people first* White Paper (Cmnd 5124).

(C) QUALIFYING INTERESTS

13.14   As mentioned earlier only the owners of certain interests in land may claim compensation for the depreciation in the value of their interest by physical factors caused by the use of public works. There are a number of factors which determine whether an interest in land is an interest which qualifies for compensation, namely: (a) the date on which the interest was acquired, (b) the nature of the interest, (c) the use to which the land is put, (d) whether the claimant is in occupation of the land, and (e) the annual value of the land. Some of the criteria are drawn from the provisions relating to blight notices in the Town and Country Planning Act 1971, provisions which are now contained in Chapter II of Part VI of the Town and Country Planning Act 1990.[19] The existence or otherwise of a qualifying interest is determined by the application of four criteria.

13.15   The first criterion is that an interest only qualifies for compensation if it was acquired by the claimant before the date on which the public works were first used after their completion. If the works were highway works that date is the date on which the highway was first open for public traffic. The date is called the relevant date.[20] If an interest is acquired or a tenancy granted pursuant to a contract the interest or tenancy is treated as acquired at the date of the contract.[21] Accordingly a person may claim compensation if he has contracted to acquire the fee simple or take a tenancy of the land before the relevant date even though the actual transfer of the freehold or the grant of the tenancy to him occurs on a date after the relevant date. The effect of public works on the value of land may be felt from the date when those works were first proposed or even from when rumours of the works arose.[22] Suppose, to take an example, that a highway project is announced on 10 January 2012 and after the process of an inquiry and other procedural events work starts on 10 January 2014 and is completed so that the highway becomes open to public traffic on 10 January 2016. The diminution in the value of nearby land may start from the date of the announcement of the highway or from even earlier if there were rumours of it. If the land is sold in, say, July 2013 the purchaser will be a person who has acquired the land before the relevant date and so can make a claim for compensation. However, the value of the land will already have been depreciated at the date that he purchases the land. It could therefore be argued that he can claim compensation for a depreciation of the value of the land even though he has purchased the land at an already depreciated value. The answer to the seemingly unsatisfactory

---

[19]   The general nature of the blight provisions is that when the value of land is reduced by certain proposals for public works, such as highways, the owners of certain qualifying interests in the land may serve on the authority proposing to carry out the works a notice, called a blight notice, which compels the authority to acquire the land at the value it would have had if there had been no such proposals. The interests which permit the service of a blight notice requiring their acquisition are defined in a way which is similar to the definition of those interests which qualify for the making of a claim under Pt I of the Land Compensation Act 1973.

[20]   LCA 1973, s 2(1). If the highway has not always since 17 October 1969 been a highway maintainable at the public expense it is not necessary in order for a claim to be made that the highway was maintainable at the public expense when it was first open to public traffic but if the relevant date falls at a time when the highway was not so maintainable a claim for compensation may only be made if the highway becomes so maintainable within three years of the relevant date: see s 19(3). Where a developer constructs a road on behalf of a highway authority the road may become a highway maintainable at the public expense at its completion: *O'Connor v Wiltshire County Council* [2007] EWCA Civ 426, [2007] RVR 179.

[21]   LCA 1973, s 19(2).

[22]   A person whose land is reduced in value by proposals for public works may be able to serve a blight notice under Pt VI of the Town and Country Planning Act 1990: see n 13.

nature of this situation may be that since the purchaser knows that he will in due course obtain compensation he will pay for the land not just its depreciated value but also an additional element which includes the whole, or a part of, the compensation which he expects to obtain for the depreciation in value.

The reason for denying compensation to a person who has purchased the land affected by   13.16
the public works after the completion of these works is that such a person can be expected to have paid a price for the land which reflects the reduced value of the land caused by the use of the public works. The restriction does not apply to a person who has acquired his interest in the land by inheritance from a person who acquired the land before the completion of the works.[23] If it were otherwise there might be no person who could claim compensation for the reduced value of the land. A person acquires an interest by inheritance if the interest devolves to him under a will, or under the law of intestacy, or by way of the right of survivorship between joint tenants. The first two processes are apparent. In the case of joint tenancies of land the right of survivorship means that on the death of one joint tenant his interest in land passes as of right to the remaining joint tenant or tenants. Where a person acquires an interest in land by way of its appropriation in satisfaction of a share in the estate of a deceased person that process is treated as devolution of the interest by a direct bequest.[24] The general rule on the date of acquisition is also modified where a tenant for life under a settlement under the Settled Land Act 1925 dies and his interest passes to the claimant as the next tenant for life or where the claimant becomes entitled to an interest on the termination of the settlement.[25]

The second criterion is that the interest in land must be what is called 'an owner's interest'   13.17
which means either the legal fee simple or a tenancy granted or extended for a term of years of which at least three years remain unexpired at the date of the notice of the claim for compensation.[26] When freehold land is subject to a trust the claim must therefore be made by the trustees as the owners of the legal estate and not by a beneficiary with an equitable interest. Of course any compensation paid will be held by the trustees on the terms of the trust. It is provided that where an interest is subject to a trust of land the compensation is to be dealt with as if it were proceeds of sale arising under the trust.[27] It appears that a claim may be made by an equitable lessee, that is a person who has the benefit of an agreement for a lease which is specifically enforceable. There is nothing to prevent the owner of the landlord's interest under such a lease claiming compensation if he is the owner of the legal fee simple and satisfies any other qualifying conditions. For present purposes a tenancy includes a sub-tenancy or other derivative leasehold interest provided that at least three years of the term remain unexpired.[28]

The two criteria just mentioned, that is the date of the acquisition of the interest in the land   13.18
affected by the claimant and the nature of the interest, apply to all claims. In order to consider the remaining criteria it is necessary to distinguish between land which is or is not a dwelling since different criteria apply to the two categories of use. The third criterion applies

---

[23] LCA 1973, s 10.
[24] Ibid, s 10(3).
[25] Ibid, s 10(4), (5).
[26] Ibid, s 2(2)(a), (4).
[27] Ibid, s 10(2).
[28] Ibid, s 87(1), which states that a tenancy has the same meaning as in the Landlord and Tenant Act 1954.

to an interest in land which is a dwelling and the fourth criterion applies to land which is not a dwelling.

13.19   Land is a dwelling if it comprises only a building or part of a building occupied or, if not occupied, last occupied or intended to be occupied as a private dwelling. The dwelling includes any garden, yard, outhouses and appurtenances belonging to or usually enjoyed with the building or part of the building.[29] The third criterion is that insofar as the interest in land of the claimant is in land which is a dwelling: (a) the interest is an owner's interest, and (b) where the interest carries the right to occupy the land the land is occupied by the claimant in right of that interest as his residence.[30] An 'owner's interest' has just been described. The requirement of occupation of the land as a residence of the claimant needs no further explanation, although it should be noted that the occupation need not be as the only or main residence of the claimant. A person can claim compensation if he occupies the land as a second home. The requirement of occupation as a residence only applies where the interest of the claimant carries the right to occupy the land. In general, of course, a freehold or leasehold interest in land does carry the right to occupy that land. Therefore a freeholder who has not let the dwelling, but does not occupy it as his residence, will have no claim to compensation. It is possible that the freeholder has granted a lease so that both interests are an owner's interest. In that event the freehold interest will not carry the right to occupy the land since that right will have been divested to the tenant. Therefore the freeholder can maintain a claim for compensation for a depreciation in the value of his interest even though he does not occupy the dwelling since he has no right to occupy it. Turning to the position of the tenant, assuming that he has not sub-let the property, his leasehold interest will carry the right to occupy the dwelling and he will not be entitled to claim compensation unless he does occupy the dwelling pursuant to that right. Similar considerations apply where there is a sub-tenant of the land or any further derivative leasehold interest. Thus in the case of dwellings two or more persons may have a different interest in the same land which entitles each person to make a claim for compensation in respect of the depreciation in the value of his interest.

13.20   A fourth and different criterion operates if the interest in land is not in land which is a dwelling. The fourth criterion has two parts.[31] The first part is that the interest must be that of an owner-occupier. An owner-occupier means a person who occupies the whole or a substantial part of the land in right of his owner's interest, that is his freehold or leasehold interest.[32] When an interest in land is vested in trustees, and a beneficiary occupies the land, the requirement of occupation in right of the owner's interest operates as if the occupation was by the trustees in right of their legal estate.[33] For example, the owner of an office or a warehouse who has let the property is not entitled to compensation. The tenant may be entitled to compensation unless the property exceeds an annual value as specified in the second part of the fourth criterion.

13.21   The second part of the criterion depends on whether the land is in agricultural use. If the land is, or forms part of, an agricultural unit then if the interest in the land is that of an

---

[29] Ibid, s 87(1).
[30] Ibid, s 2(2).
[31] Ibid, s 2(3).
[32] Ibid, s 2(5).
[33] Ibid, s 10(4).

owner-occupier a claim for compensation may be made, that is only the first part of the criterion is relevant. In the case of land not in agricultural use the second part of the criterion requires not only that the occupation is that of an owner-occupier but that an additional requirement is satisfied which is that the land is, or forms part of, a hereditament of which the annual value does not exceed a prescribed limit.[34] The prescribed annual value is that which is prescribed for the purposes of the blight provisions in planning legislation. The definitions of 'annual value' and 'hereditament' are also taken from the planning legislation. The date for the ascertainment of the annual value is the date on which notice of the claim for compensation is made.[35] The current limit is £34,800.

It is apparent that there are substantial differences in the entitlement to compensation as between residential and non-residential land. As regards residential land the claimant need only be in occupation of the dwelling if his interest entitles him to occupy it. As regards other land it is only a claimant who occupies the land who can claim compensation. For example, the owner of a commercial property who has let it and so cannot and does not occupy it is not entitled to compensation. Furthermore, where the property is in non-residential use, other than agricultural use, there is no claim for compensation if the annual value of the property exceeds a prescribed limit. Thus owners and occupiers of higher value non-residential commercial property, other than agricultural units, are as a matter of policy denied compensation for a depreciation in the value of their interest caused by the use of public works. 13.22

(D) CLAIMS

1. The Time for the Claim

A claim for compensation is made by the claimant to the responsible authority whose duty it is to pay any compensation due. The responsible authority is the highway authority when the public works are a highway and, in relation to other public works, is the person managing the works.[36] The responsible authority is, of course, the body which promotes, designs, oversees, and pays for the works and then uses them not the contractors or other persons who physically carry out the works. The legislation does not define what is meant by managing the works. It is possible that when in use the works are managed, that is operated and controlled, by persons other than those who constructed the work and in that event it is the former persons who will be responsible for dealing with, and paying claims for, compensation. 13.23

A claim for compensation cannot be made earlier than the expiration of 12 months after the relevant date. As explained the relevant date is the date when the public works are first used or, if they are a highway, when that highway is first opened to public traffic. This first date for the making of a claim is called the first claim day.[37] The reason for the delay in 13.24

---

[34] Ibid, s 2(3)(b).
[35] Ibid, s 2(6). See s 149 of the Town and Country Planning Act 1990 for the prescription of the value limit.
[36] LCA 1973, s 1(2).
[37] Ibid, s 3(2). It will be a matter of fact in each case what exactly constitutes the public works particularly in respect of a large and ongoing scheme carried out in phases: see *Davies v Mid-Glamorgan County Council* [1979] 2 EGLR 158 (alterations to an airport); *Price v Caerphilly CBC* [2005] 1 EGLR 157 (road constructed and opened in stages).

permitting claims is that an assessment of the effect of physical factors caused by the use of the public works can then be made as a result of experience after a year of the use of the works and so is not simply a matter of prognostication.

13.25   In one exceptional case a claim can be made in the year between the relevant date and the first claim day. The exception arises when in that year a claimant has made a contract to dispose of his interest or, save where the interest is a dwelling, for the grant of a lease and when he makes a claim for compensation before the disposal of the interest or the grant of the lease. If in this exceptional case a claim is made before the first claim day the compensation is still not payable before that day.[38]

2. The Procedure for Making and Responding to a Claim

13.26   The claim is made by a notice served on the responsible authority containing certain specified particulars. The notice must be in writing since only a document can be served. There is no prescribed form of notice of claim. The following particulars must be contained in the notice. (a) Particulars of the land in respect of which the claim is made must be included. What is required is a general description. It is good practice to describe the land by reference to a plan such as the title plans issued by HM Land Registry. (b) Particulars of the claimant's interest and the date on which, and the manner in which, that interest was acquired must be given. It should be stated whether the interest is freehold or leasehold and, if the latter, the date of the grant and the term of the lease. The interest of the claimant will normally have been acquired by a transfer or the grant or assignment of a lease but may have been acquired by inheritance or the passing from one tenant for life to another of an interest under a settlement. (c) Particulars of the claimant's occupation of the land must be given except where his interest qualifies for compensation without occupation by him. The purpose for which the claimant occupies the land and any other relevant facts relating to occupation, for example that it is shared with others, should be stated. The only instance in which an interest can qualify for compensation without the claimant being in occupation of the land is the interest of a freeholder of a dwelling subject to a tenancy or the interest of a tenant subject to a sub-tenancy so that the claimant has no right to occupy the land. (d) Particulars of any other interests in the land so far as known to the claimant must be given. It is possible for there to be two interests in the same land which qualify for compensation, such as the freehold and a tenancy of a dwelling, but particulars should be given of all interests in the land. An interest in land means a proprietary interest in the sense of an interest which is in principle capable of binding successors in title of the land. Particulars must be given not only of other interests which give a right to occupation of the land, for example a particular tenancy, but also of third party or incorporeal interests such as easements or the benefit of restrictive covenants over the land.[39] The existence of interests of this latter type may be significant when it comes to assessing the amount of the depreciation of the value of the claimant's interest caused by the use of the public works. Particulars of any mortgage or contract of sale affecting the land should be given since these are likely to affect the assessment of compensation and the person to whom the compensation is to be paid as

---

[38]   LCA 1973, s 3(3).
[39]   See ch 2, para 2.20 for an explanation of proprietary, corporeal and incorporeal interests in land.

explained in section (f) of this chapter. (e) Particulars must be given of the public works to which the claim relates. (f) Particulars of any land contiguous or adjacent to the claimant's land to which the claimant is entitled in the same capacity on the relevant date must be given. This information is needed because, under a provision for betterment dealt with below, the compensation may be reduced if other land of the claimant is increased in value by reason of the use of the public works. (g) Particulars must be given of the amount of the compensation claimed. [40]

A notice which omits certain particulars, or contains errors as to certain particulars, is not 13.27 necessarily an invalid notice. The general principle is that a notice which fails strictly to comply with the statutorily required particulars may still operate as a valid notice if either: (a) the defect is immaterial, or (b) the defect has been waived by the recipient of the notice, or (c) the defect has not caused any significant prejudice or risk of significant prejudice to the recipient.[41] Nonetheless the omission of important matters in a notice of claim may mean that the Lands Tribunal does not have jurisdiction to adjudicate upon the claim.[42] If a notice is vitiated because of some omission or error which cannot be disregarded under this principle there is nothing to prevent the claimant serving a further and effective notice unless there is some impediment to his doing so such as that he has disposed of the land or six years have elapsed since the claim day so that he would have no means of enforcing his claim by proceedings in the Lands Tribunal.[43]

As will be explained under the next section of this chapter the compensation is the amount 13.28 of the depreciation in the value of the claimant's interest caused by the use of the public works assessed as at the first claim day. In most cases the claimant will need professional advice in estimating this amount and, as will also be explained, the reasonable expenses of obtaining that advice are payable in addition to the compensation. Valuation is not normally a precise process and, while clearly the amount of the claim should not be underestimated, it is not good practice to include an exaggerated claim since to do so may reduce the prospect of an early settlement of the claim and may lose the sympathy of the Lands Tribunal if the claim has to be litigated before that body. Although the only particulars required to be given are the amount of the claim, so that a single stated figure is all that is strictly needed, it may be good practice and something likely to lead to an early settlement if the basic calculation underlying the claim is given, for example the assessment of the value of the interest with and without the adverse physical factors caused by the use of the public works. It may assist the responsible authority and lead to an early settlement of the claim if other supporting information is given, for example details of comparable transactions from which the value of the land with and without the effect of the use of the public works is derived.[44]

When a responsible authority has received a claim any person authorised by the authority 13.29 may, on giving reasonable notice, enter the land to which the claim relates in order to survey

---

[40] LCA 1973, s 3(1). Certain additional particulars are required where a claimant for compensation is exercising his right to acquire the freehold or an extended lease under the Leasehold Reform Act 1967: see para 13.73.

[41] *R v Home Secretary, ex parte Jayeanthan* [2000] 1 WLR 354; *Newbold v Coal Authority* [2013] EWCA Civ 584.

[42] *Fennessy v London City Airport* [1995] 2 EGLR 167 (particulars of the amount of the claim held to be insufficient when stated as 'an amount in excess of £50 to be agreed'); *Donaldson v Hereford and Worcester County Council* [1997] RVR 242.

[43] See para 13.30.

[44] Valuation is described in more detail in ch 14.

it and estimate its value.[45] It is an offence to obstruct a person exercising this power. In practice unless the claim is immediately agreed there is likely to be a period of discussion between the representatives of the responsible authority and the claimant or his professional representative.

13.30   Any proceedings before the Lands Tribunal to establish a claim must be commenced within the period of six years generally prescribed for sums due under statute by section 9 of the Limitation Act 1980. The period runs from the first claim day.[46] It is therefore essential that a notice of claim and, if the claim or its amount is not agreed, a reference to the Lands Tribunal are made within six years from the first claim day. There is no minimum period following the service of a notice of claim for a reference to the Tribunal but good practice demands that a notice of claim is given in good time so as to permit assessment of it, and so as to permit the parties to make their position clear, and to conduct any negotiations prior to any reference to the Tribunal being necessary.

(E) THE ASSESSMENT OF THE COMPENSATION

1. The First Value and the Second Value

13.31   The compensation payable is for the depreciation of the value of the interest in land of the claimant due to physical factors caused by the use of public works.[47] The assessment of the compensation must plainly be carried out by comparing two values of the interest on the same date. The first value is the value of the interest with the existence of the physical factors and their expected continuation and the second value is the value of the interest on the assumption that the factors do not exist and will not exist. The compensation is the amount by which the first value is lower than the second value. Having stated the nature and purpose of the process it is necessary to explain more closely the details of the assessment of the compensation. In that explanation the two values as just described will be called the first value and the second value.

13.32   All valuations are dependent on a precisely defined valuation date.[48] For present purposes the valuation date is the first claim day and the claim for compensation has to be assessed by reference to prices current on the first claim day.[49] Furthermore in assessing compensation account is to be taken of the public works as they exist on the first claim day.[50] In addition account is to be taken of any intensification that may then be reasonably expected of the use of the works.[51] The nature of the interest of the claimant and the condition of the land are taken to be as they were at the date of the service of the notice of claim.[52] The date of the service of the notice cannot be earlier than the first claim day (save for the exceptional

---

[45] LCA 1973, s 3(4).
[46] Ibid, s 19(2A); *Bateman v Lancashire County Council* [1999] 2 EGLR 203.
[47] Ibid, s 1(1).
[48] See section (e) of ch 4.
[49] LCA 1973, s 4(1).
[50] Ibid, s 4(2).
[51] Ibid, s 4(2).
[52] Ibid, s 4(4)(a).

case of a contract to dispose of an interest or grant a lease in the year before that day) but may be later. In summary the rules as to the valuation date are: (a) land prices and values are to be taken to be as they were at the first claim day, (b) the use of the public works is to be taken to be as it was at the first claim day but including any intensification of the use reasonably expected at that date, and (c) the nature of the claimant's interest and the condition of the land are taken to be as they were at the date of service of the notice of claim. There are other facts and circumstances which can affect the value of a piece of land, for example other development being carried out in its vicinity. These factors and circumstances, other than the condition of the claimant's land, are presumably to be taken to be as they were at the first claim day.

Even if the notice of the claim is served after the first claim day it is only an anticipated   13.33 intensification of the use of the public works as that anticipation existed on the first claim day which should be taken into account in the valuation process. For example, it may have been anticipated on the first claim day that traffic on a new road would increase by 5 per cent over the next three years. If a notice of claim is served three years after the first claim day it may by then be known that traffic has increased by 15 per cent over the three years. Strictly speaking it is only the 5 per cent increase anticipated which should be taken into account in the valuation process. The same principle of course applies if the intensification of the use of the works proves less than was anticipated on the first claim day.[53] Alterations in the works themselves, as opposed to changes in the use of the works, are considered in section (h) of this chapter.

It needs to be emphasised that the difference between the two valuations is not that of the   13.34 existence and non-existence of the public works. The difference is between the existence and non-existence of the specified physical factors caused by the works which affect the value of land. That this is so is apparent not only from the language of the legislation but also from more general considerations. If the public works themselves were assumed not to exist for the purposes of the determination of the second value the compensation would take into account a reduction in the value of land brought about by matters such as the visual effect of the works, or physical factors caused by the works but with a source other than the site of the works, which are not intended to be the subject of compensation. A further consideration is that if the public works were assumed not to exist at the first claim day the need for those works would remain and the prospect of the same or similar works being carried out might have to be factored into the valuations. This difficulty is avoided if it is assumed for the purposes of both the valuations to be compared that the public works exist but that for the purposes of the first value the effect of the use of the works is as it actually is as regards the specified physical factors but for the purposes of the second value these physical factors are assumed neither to exist nor be likely to exist in the future in so far as they cause a reduction in the value of the claimant's interest. The assumed situation for the purposes of the second value is therefore artificial. On the one hand the valuer assumes for the purposes of the first value that the works exist and are in use and that the specified physical factors, such as noise, which have an adverse effect on value actually exist and may in future be intensified. On the other hand for the purposes of the second value the valuer

[53] This principle was applied by the Lands Tribunal in *Dhenim v Department of Transport* (1990) 60 P & CR 349. The so-called Bwllfa principle was not applicable since what was being determined under the legislation was land values on a specified date and not the assessment of damages: see section (f) of ch 4.

assumes that the public works exist and are in use but that there is no adverse effect on value attributable to the specified physical factors, such as noise, caused by the use of the works. It is these two valuations which are to be compared and which determine the amount of the compensation. For example, if a new highway is built and open to traffic near a residential property: (a) that property must be valued with the highway in use and producing noise, vibration and fumes from the traffic, and (b) the property must then be valued with the highway in use but notionally not producing noise, vibration or fumes or any other adverse physical factors. The second situation is obviously artificial.[54]

13.35   The relevant date, the date when the public works are first used, has a further part to play in the valuation process in that in valuing the claimant's interest no account is to be taken of: (a) any building, or improvement or extension of a building, on land if the building or the improved or extended building was first occupied after the relevant date, or (b) any change in the use of the land to which the claim relates made after the relevant date.[55]

13.36   The general nature and process of the valuation are to be those described in rules (2)–(4) of the Land Compensation Act 1961.[56] These rules have been considered in detail earlier.[57] In particular the value of the claimant's interest is to be assessed as the amount which that interest, if sold in the open market by a willing seller, might be expected to realise. The normal attributes and circumstances of a hypothetical sale in the open market are therefore envisaged. The special suitability or adaptability of the land for any purpose shall not be taken into account if the land could only be applied to that purpose in pursuance of statutory powers and there is no market apart from the requirements of any authority possessing compulsory purchase powers.[58] An increase in the value of land by reason of an unlawful use is not to be taken into account.[59] These are general rules applicable to assessing compensation for the compulsory acquisition of land and are applied to the valuations necessary in order to assess a claim under Part I of the Land Compensation Act 1973.

2. Development Value

13.37   The usual principle applied in valuing land is that the land is valued with all its potentialities including its potential for development which may greatly add to its value. It is for this reason that when land acquired compulsorily is valued there is in the legislation an elaborate scheme for determining what particular planning permissions are assumed to enure to the land.[60] For present purposes this principle is abandoned. It is to be assumed that planning permission will not be granted on the land affected for any development subject to a

---

[54] The two situations to be contrasted have been described as the 'switched-on' and the 'switched-off' value: *Nesbitt v National Assembly for Wales* [2003] RVR 302. As all valuations there is no prescribed method of valuing although knowledge of local conditions is likely to be significant: *Hallows v Welsh Office* (1995) 70 P & CR 117. It may not be an easy valuation exercise to distinguish the valuation effect of the existence of public works (for which compensation is not payable) and the effect of physical factors caused by the use of those works (for which compensation may be payable): *Toms v Secretary of State for Transport* [2011] UKUT 48 (LC), [2011] RVR 320.

[55] LCA 1973, s 4(5). See para 13.15 for the relevant date.

[56] Ibid, s 4(4), (5).

[57] See chs 4 and 6.

[58] See r (3) of s 5 of the Land Compensation Act 1961: see section (a) of ch 6.

[59] See r (4) of s 5 of the Land Compensation Act 1961: see section (c) of ch 6.

[60] See ch 7.

minor exception. It is also to be assumed that if a planning permission exists that permission has not been granted insofar as it relates to development which has not been carried out.[61] The development value of the land is therefore generally excluded from the valuations. The exception is that it is to be assumed that planning permission would be granted for any development of a class specified in paragraphs 1 and 2 of schedule 3 to the Town and Country Planning Act 1990. Paragraph 1 of that schedule refers to the rebuilding of buildings so long as the cubic content of the original building is not exceeded by a specified amount and paragraph 2 relates to the use as two or more separate dwellinghouses of any building which was used as a single dwellinghouse. The first of the assumed planning permissions is subject to the condition set out in schedule 10 to the Act which relates to the maximum gross floorspace which may exist in the rebuilt building.[62] The assumed permissions do not extend to the rebuilding of a building or the resumption of a use when an order has been made for the removal of the building or the discontinuance of the use under the Town and Country Planning Act 1990 and compensation has become payable by reason of that order. These provisions of the Land Compensation Act 1973 are heavily dependent on the provisions of the Town and Country Planning Act 1990 and expressions used in both Acts have the meaning given to them in the 1990 Act. The description of items of minor development in schedule 3 to the Town and Country Planning Act 1990, sometimes called 'third schedule development', is a remnant of the 'nationalisation' of the development value of land effected by the Town and Country Planning Act 1947. The forms of minor development in question were exempted from that legislation.[63]

In some cases the general exclusion of development value will be irrelevant since if a piece of land is vacant and ready for development it is not likely to be occupied so that no claim for compensation will arise in respect of an interest in the land. On the other hand in some cases the exclusion of development value will be important. An example would be a freehold house occupied by the owner with planning permission, or the expectation of planning permission, to erect a further house in its grounds or to extend the existing house. The value of the potential to carry out the development could be affected by noise from a new road as much as could the value of the existing house. In such cases the exclusion of compensation for the depreciation in the development value is a matter of policy rather than being based on any particular logic.[64] 13.38

3. Other Matters

Statutory provisions exist for the carrying out, or the payment of, grants towards the carrying out, of works on properties affected by public works which are designed to reduce the adverse effect of the public works. There are general provisions for such ameliorating works within Part II of the Land Compensation Act 1973 and, as regards noise from aircraft, 13.39

[61] LCA 1973, s 5(4). This is in effect the concept of existing use value. See ch 3, para 3.19(i).
[62] Ibid, s 5(2).
[63] Ibid, s 5(3). This historical remnant of the law lived on for other purposes in the law of compensation. There was an assumed planning permission for third schedule development under s 15 of the Land Compensation Act 1961 until this was removed by the Localism Act 2011.
[64] The decision not to provide compensation for the effect of the use of public works on the development value of land was stated in the White Paper (Cmnd 5124) which preceded the Act. See n 1.

under legislation dealing with aviation. Account is to be taken of the benefit of such ameliorating works in assessing compensation and, as regards such works or grants for such
works for which there is an entitlement, it is to be assumed that the works have been carried
out. If the relevant authority has a discretion whether to carry out works or pay a grant the
assumption that the works have been carried out is made only if the authority has undertaken to carry out the works or pay the grant.[65]

13.40   Where a person is entitled to compensation he is entitled to receive from the responsible
authority, in addition to the compensation, any reasonable valuation or legal expenses
incurred by him in preparing or prosecuting his claim. The expenses incurred will normally
be those of a solicitor in advising on whether there is a claim for compensation and those
of a valuer in assessing the depreciation in the value of the land. The additional sum is only
obtainable where compensation is payable. No expenses may be recovered if no compensation is payable whether because the claimant has no entitlement in law to compensation or
because he cannot show any depreciation in the value of his interest in land. The right to the
additional sum is without prejudice to the power of the Lands Tribunal to award costs in
the ordinary way if the claim cannot be agreed and there is a reference to the Tribunal.[66]
The powers of the Tribunal on costs are described in chapter 15.[67] The entitlement to the
additional sum is akin to the right of a person whose land has been compulsorily acquired
to obtain as additional compensation the reasonable costs of preparing his claim under rule
(6) of section 5 of the Land Compensation Act 1961, these costs being often called 'pre-
reference costs' in that they are incurred prior to a reference to the Lands Tribunal.[68]

13.41   There is an exclusion of very small claims. No compensation is payable where the depreciation in the value of the interest acquired is £50 or less. [69] In any event valuation of land is
not a precise process and it would be difficult to demonstrate a reduction in value of the
order of £50 or less.

13.42   Interest on the compensation is payable by the responsible authority to the claimant in
respect of the period between the first claim day and the date of payment of the compensation. The rate of interest is that prescribed from time to time for interest on compensation
for compulsory acquisition under section 32 of the Land Compensation Act 1961.[70]

(F) MORTGAGED LAND AND CONTRACTS FOR SALE

1. Mortgaged Land

13.43   When a piece of land is mortgaged, that is charged by way of security with the repayment
of a sum of money, both the mortgagor (the borrower) and the mortgagee (the lender) own
interests in the land. The mortgagor's interest is often called the equity of redemption and

---

[65] LCA 1973, s 4(3).
[66] Ibid, s 3(5).
[67] See section (m) of ch 15.
[68] See section (d) of ch 8.
[69] LCA 1973, s 7.
[70] Ibid, s 18. See also section (d) of ch 15.

the amount by which the value of the land exceeds the amount remaining to be repaid under the mortgage is sometimes called the mortgagor's equity or the equity of redemption. Mortgages may be legal or equitable although most mortgages of dwellinghouses are legal mortgages created by way of a charge by way of legal mortgage under section 85 of the Law of Property Act 1925. This form of mortgage is often called a legal charge.

Special rules apply when compensation is payable in respect of an interest subject to a   13.44
mortgage. Normally if land is subject to a mortgage and is sold without the prior discharge of the mortgage the sale price will be similar to the value of the seller's equity since the purchaser will remain with the burden of the security for the money due. In practice, when a property which is mortgaged is sold, the purchase price is used to discharge the mortgage and the property is sold free of the mortgage. The value of the mortgaged land is therefore the value of the equity of redemption. However, for the purposes of a valuation for assessing compensation under Part I of the Land Compensation Act 1973 the mortgaged interest is to be valued as if it were not subject to the mortgage.[71] No compensation is payable in respect of the interest of the mortgagee. Nonetheless either the mortgagor or the mortgagee may make the claim for compensation. Since no compensation is payable for the mortgagee's interest if it is the mortgagee who makes the claim he is taken to do so as if he were entitled to the mortgagor's interest. The vital question is what is to be done as to the payment of the compensation. It is payable by the responsible authority to the mortgagee (even if it is the mortgagor who has made the claim) or, if there is more than one mortgage, to the first mortgagee. The mortgagee must then deal with the compensation as if it were proceeds of sale of the mortgaged property.[72] Under statute, and under the terms of most mortgages, the mortgagee is entitled to sell the mortgaged property if the mortgagor defaults on his payments under the mortgage. [73] The mortgagee must apply the price obtainable on the sale first to the discharge of sums due to him, then to the discharge of sums due to subsequent mortgagees whose interests are postponed to that of the first mortgagee who effects the sale, with any balance being payable to the mortgagor. In most cases of ordinary mortgages of residential property there will be only one mortgagee and in any event the amount of the compensation is unlikely to be enough to do more than reduce the amount of the debt to the first mortgagee.

The process may be illustrated by an example. A house worth £1 million might be subject   13.45
to a mortgage with £600,000 outstanding and to be paid. The value of the mortgagor's equity of redemption is £400,000. The house might be reduced in value, ignoring the mortgage, by £100,000 as a result of the use of a new road near it. Either the mortgagor or the mortgagee may make the claim for the compensation of £100,000 but whoever makes the claim the responsible authority must pay the £100,000 to the mortgagee. The mortgagee must then use the £100,000 to reduce the mortgage debt to £500,000. The owner of the mortgaged house will therefore end up with a property worth £900,000 but subject to a mortgage of only £500,000, that is his equity of redemption in the property will remain at £400,000. In effect the owner of property subject to a mortgage who is entitled to compensation for the depreciatory effect on the value of the property due to the use of public works is not entitled to receive the compensation for his own immediate use but is obliged to treat

---

[71] Ibid, s 4(4)(c).
[72] Ibid, s 10(1).
[73] See s 101(1)(a) of the Law of Property Act 1925.

it as reducing the amount of his mortgage. The reason for the rules just described is that a mortgagee should not be required to see the value of his security reduced by reason of the use of public works. There is nothing to prevent a mortgagor and a mortgagee agreeing, if they wish, that the compensation shall be paid to the mortgagor and that the mortgage debt and the sum secured on the property shall remain as before, although if that does occur the value of the security will obviously be reduced.

2. Contracts for Sale

13.46   If land is sold subject to a contract to sell it or to grant a tenancy of it to someone else the right and the obligation to complete the contract will pass to any other purchaser of the property and he will pay a price which takes account of that burden. Again this rule is reversed for the purposes of valuations to determine the compensation payable. In valuing the land the contract of sale, and the contract to grant a tenancy if made after the relevant date, are ignored and the land is valued as if the contract did not exist. The compensation is payable to the seller or grantor of the lease. The person with the benefit of the contract of sale, the contractual purchaser, himself has an equitable interest in land called an estate contract but cannot make a claim for compensation since he does not own the legal fee simple of the land. Of course the compensation payable to the seller under the contract may be retained by him. To take an example, a person may own a house worth £800,000 and finds that it is reduced in value to £700,000 as a result of traffic noise from a new highway constructed near it. He contracts to sell the house for £700,000 which is its value having regard to the effect of the highway. Prior to the completion of the contract he may make a claim for compensation. The value of the land is to be assessed ignoring the contract so that the compensation is £100,000 and is payable to the seller, who is the person who has suffered the loss. An owner of land with a claim for compensation who intends to sell his land should make his claim before contracting to sell it or at any rate before completing the contract while he remains the owner of the legal interest in the land. Once the contract of sale has been completed no claim will be possible. The vendor will no longer have an interest in the land and the purchaser will have acquired his interest after the relevant date.[74]

(G) BETTERMENT

13.47   The term betterment is not a statutory term but is often used in describing the law of compensation to mean some increase in the value of land of an owner other than the land primarily affected and for which compensation is being assessed. The principle is that the compensation for the land primarily affected should be reduced by any increase in the value of other land of the same owner caused by the same project. This is generally seen as a just result. Where land is acquired compulsorily there is a general provision for taking account of betterment in this sense in section 7 of the Land Compensation Act 1961, and other more specific provisions exist such as in respect of compensation for land acquired for highway

[74] See para 13.15.

purposes. The same general principle applies to claims for compensation for the effect of public works.[75]

The betterment provisions have two aspects, an increase in the value of the interest in land 13.48 in respect of which the claim is made, and an increase in the value of other land in which the claimant has an interest.

The first aspect of the provisions might at first glance seem curious. Plainly the use of pub- 13.49 lic works could have an effect on a piece of land near to them which was in part adverse, for example increased noise, and in part beneficial, for example the provision of better access to the land. If compensation is to be payable for the effect of the use of the works then it might be thought that the rational process would be to consider both effects together, to set off one effect against the other, and if at the end the net effect on value was a reduction in value to provide compensation for that net reduction. Indeed when betterment is considered more generally as an aspect of the law of compensation this last observation holds good and to speak of a beneficial effect on the land primarily affected, and in respect of which compensation is claimed as betterment, leads to confusion.[76] The structure of the legislation here being explained precludes this simple approach. The compensation is confined to the effect on land of physical factors brought about by the use of the public works such as noise or vibration. If the legislation had stopped at this point no account could be taken of any increase in value to the land acquired brought about by matters such as improved accessibility since such matters are not physical factors. The nature of the valuation process required to assess compensation, the first value and the second value as described earlier, makes it necessary to include this first aspect of the betterment provisions since the valuation process is focussed purely on the valuation effect of the use of the public works leaving out of account factors such as improved access with the result that any beneficial effect of such a factor can be taken into account only by way of the specific betterment provisions.[77] It is for this reason that the compensation has to be reduced, or in an appropriate case eliminated, by an increase in the value of the interest in land of the claimant in respect of which compensation is claimed attributable generally to the existence or the use or prospective use of the public works to which the claim relates.[78]

The second aspect of the betterment process applies where there is an increase in value, 13.50 attributable to the existence or use or prospective use of the public works, in any interest of the claimant in land contiguous or adjacent to the land in respect of which compensation is claimed to which the claimant was entitled in the same capacity on the date on which the public works were first used or the highway first opened to public traffic. The increase in value of the interest of the claimant in the contiguous or adjacent land is to be deducted from the compensation payable in respect of the interest primarily affected and in respect of which the claim is made.[79] The betterment reduction only applies where the interest increased in value by the public works is in contiguous or adjacent land. One piece of land is contiguous to another in its strict sense if its boundary adjoins the other land, that is there is a common boundary. One piece of land is adjacent to another if the two pieces of land are

---

[75] See section (d) of ch 6 for a general consideration of betterment when land is compulsorily acquired. There is a specific betterment provision in s 261 of the Highways Act 1980.
[76] See ch 6, paras 6.41 and 6.42, for a further discussion of this point.
[77] See para 13.34.
[78] LCA 1973, s 6(1)(a).
[79] Ibid, s 6(1)(b).

situated reasonably close to each other but without necessarily having a common bound-ary.[80] There is therefore a limit to the ambit of the second aspect of the betterment provisions. Some public works, for example a highway or new drainage facilities, may benefit land within a wide area. If the benefited other land of a claimant is some distance away from the land the subject of the claim for depreciation in value the two areas of land may not be adjacent and there will be no offsetting of the benefit to the other land against the compensation for the land primarily affected and the subject of the claim. The result would have been otherwise if the betterment provisions had simply referred to 'other' land in which the claimant had an interest.[81]

13.51   If there is to be a reduction in compensation under the second aspect of the betterment provisions the claimant must hold his interest in the other land in the same capacity as he holds his interest in the land in respect of which he claims compensation. For these purposes a person holds an interest in two pieces of land in the same capacity if either he is entitled to both interests beneficially or he holds both interests as trustee of one particular trust or holds both interests as the personal representative of one particular person.[82]

13.52   Where land other than the land in respect of which the claim is made has to be valued in order to apply the second aspect of the betterment provisions the usual principles for the valuation of land as enshrined in rule (2) of section 5 of the Land Compensation Act 1961 apply so that the value of the land with and without the existence or use or proposed use of the public works has to be assessed as the amount which the land if sold on the open market by a willing seller might be expected to realise. The difference between the two values of the other land, assuming that the value taking account of the public works is greater, is the increase in value of that land which is then to be deducted from the compensation for the land in respect of which the claim for compensation is made. For these purposes it must be assumed that both areas of land would not obtain planning permission, and that any existing planning permission which has not been carried out had not been granted, save for the limited exception for 'third schedule' development referred to earlier, as in the case of the valuation of the land in respect of which compensation is being claimed.[83] Again, therefore, most development value is to be ignored in the valuation process.

13.53   A further rule is necessary if the second aspect of the betterment process is to apply fairly in all circumstances. It could occur that the interest in the other land or in a part of the other land, the increase in the value of which has been deducted from the compensation payable, is subsequently acquired compulsorily whether for the public works which give rise to the claim for compensation or for some other purpose. The general rule for the assessment of compensation for a compulsory acquisition is that any increase in value of the land acquired

---

[80]   For a fuller discussion of these expressions see section (d) of ch 6. The expression 'contiguous' can have a wider meaning which is little different from the expression 'adjacent'. The application of the concept of adjacency is necessarily an imprecise question: see *Wellington Corporation v Lower Hutt Corporation* [1904] AC 773.

[81]   The expression 'contiguous or adjoining' is probably derived from the same expression used in the general betterment provision for the purposes of compensation for compulsory acquisition contained in s 7 of the Land Compensation Act 1961. The expression is considered more fully in section (d) of ch 6. It may be noted that when compensation is claimable for injurious affection to land retained by a landowner when only a part of his land is acquired there is no rule that the land retained has to be contiguous or adjacent to the land acquired. See ch 9, para 9.4.

[82]   LCA 1973, s 6(1)(b), (4).

[83]   Ibid, s 6(2), (4) and (5). The limited exception is planning permission for development of a class specified in paras 1 and 2 of sch 3 to the Town and Country Planning Act 1990: see para 13.37.

due to the scheme underlying the acquisition is left out of account in accordance with the detailed provisions to this effect in section 6 of the Land Compensation Act 1961.[84] It would be unfair that this should happen when an increase in the value of the land in question had already been used to reduce the compensation payable under the provisions considered in this chapter. Accordingly in such a case the reduction in the compensation for compulsory acquisition which would otherwise be required under section 6 of the 1961 Act does not apply. The exclusion of the section 6 reduction applies whether at the time of the subsequent compulsory acquisition of the other land the claimant for compensation in respect of the use of the public works remains the owner of that interest or that interest has passed to a successor in title.[85]

The process involved can again be illustrated by an example. Suppose that a claimant owns   13.54
the freehold of a house and of adjoining commercial property and occupies both. The house is reduced in value from £600,000 to £500,000 by the effect of noise from a newly constructed highway but the commercial property is increased in value from £400,000 to £440,000 by the improved access to it created by the new highway. The compensation will therefore be £100,000 (the reduction in value of the house) less £40,000 (the increased value of the commercial property), so as to amount to £60,000. The landowner therefore starts with £1 million, the value of the two properties together ignoring any effect of the new road, and ends up with £1 million, being: (a) the house with its reduced value of £500,000, (b) the commercial premises with its increased value of £440,000, and (c) the £60,000 compensation in respect of the house. If the commercial premises are subsequently compulsorily acquired for the same highway scheme, or any other scheme, it may be that a part of the value of £440,000 would have had to be deducted because of section 6 of the 1961 Act. If, say, £40,000 of the value of those premises was so disregarded the owner would be left with a total value of less than £1 million, that is the house worth £500,000 and the reduced compensation of £400,000 for the commercial premises and the £60,000 compensation for the reduction in value of the house, that is £960,000 in all. This injustice is avoided by assessing the compensation for the commercial premises at £440,000 which is brought about by ignoring the effect of section 6 of the 1961 Act which would otherwise and generally apply.

It has been mentioned that when land is compulsorily acquired the compensation has to be   13.55
reduced by the amount of any increase in the value of contiguous or adjacent land of the claimant caused by the scheme underlying the acquisition. This reduction is required by section 7 of the Land Compensation Act 1961.[86] It would again be unfair if this was done when the land acquired had already had an increase in its value taken into account so as to reduce the compensation for the effect of the use of public works on other land under the provisions of Part I of the Land Compensation Act 1973 here being explained. Consequently in these circumstances there is no deduction of the increased value under section 7 of the 1961 Act when land is compulsorily acquired. The provisions as explained in this and the last paragraph are applied to what are called corresponding enactments, that is other enactments requiring the taking into account of betterment, which include in particular section 261(1) of the Highways Act 1980.[87]

---

[84] These provisions are examined in detail in ch 5.
[85] LCA 1973, s 6(3).
[86] These provisions are examined in section (d) of ch 6.
[87] LCA 1973, s 6(3).

(H) ALTERATIONS AND CHANGES OF USE IN THE PUBLIC WORKS

13.56   Public works may be altered in some way after they have come into use and the alteration may cause depreciation or further depreciation to nearby land. A claim for compensation may be made in respect of the depreciation caused by such alterations.[88] A new notice of claim is needed. Such a claim may be brought whether or not a previous claim has been made in respect of a depreciation in value caused by the original or unaltered works. If a previous claim has been brought a new claim is still necessary. It seems that if at the time of the alterations no claim has been made in respect of the original or unaltered works a sepa-rate claim must be made for those works (provided the six year limitation period has not expired) and that a new claim must be made in respect of the altered works.

13.57   There are three types of alterations or changes which may give rise to a claim. (a) The car-riageway of a highway may be altered after the highway has been opened to public traffic. For present purposes there is only an alteration if an additional carriageway is provided, which may be beside an existing carriageway or over or above it (eg a flyover or underpass), or if the location, width or level of the carriageway is altered. Re-surfacing does not consti-tute an alteration. (b) Any other public works may be reconstructed, extended, or otherwise altered after they have been first used. (c) The third change is a change of use in respect of any public works other than a highway or an aerodrome.[89] An intensification of an existing use is not a change of use for present purposes.[90] This last limitation is to be a degree miti-gated by the rule, stated earlier, that when the depreciation of the value of a piece of land is assessed as at the first claim day, that is the day when the works have been in use for a year, account is to be taken of any intensification of the use of the works which might have been reasonably expected at that date.[91] In practice, of course, there may be a subsequent inten-sification of use beyond that reasonably expected in the early days of the use of the works and no further compensation is recoverable in such a case.[92] It seems that in order for there to be a claim for further compensation based on a change of the use of the works the change of use must be from one use which constitutes public works to another use which also con-stitutes public works but of a different sort. Public works are works provided or used in the exercise of public powers. Thus if the land or the works are sold so that they come into use for a purpose which is not public works this will not be sufficient to found a further claim for compensation.

13.58   Where there is an alteration or change of use of the public works there is a new relevant date for the purposes of a new claim for compensation. The new relevant date is the date on which the highway or part of the highway was first opened to public traffic after the com-pletion of the alterations to the carriageway, or the date on which the other public works were first used after the completion of the alterations, or the date of the change of use. The first claim day will be one year from the new relevant date. The claim for further compensa-tion is for the amount of the depreciation of the value of the claimant's interest in land

---

[88] Obviously the works must be changed in some way to justify a new claim by a new owner of the land: *Bannocks v Secretary of State for Transport* [1995] 2 EGLR 157.

[89] LCA 1973, s 9(1), (5).

[90] Ibid, s 9(7).

[91] See para 13.32.

[92] See para 13.33.

which would not have been caused but for the alterations or change of use.[93] Thus if the original works did not create any depreciation in value to the claimant's interest the claim will be for the whole of the depreciation caused by the alterations or change of use whereas if the original works did cause some depreciation there may be a claim for compensation for any additional depreciation in value caused by the alterations or change in use. The same principles apply as to the assessment of the depreciation and compensation as apply to a claim founded on the effect of the original works.[94] The depreciation in value must be due to one or more of the specified factors caused by the altered public works. The amount of the depreciation in value must be assessed by references to prices current on the first claim day for the altered works or change of use.

The additional depreciation in value caused by the alteration of the location, width or level   13.59
of the carriageway of a highway must be caused by one or more of the specified physical factors the source of which is the use of the altered length of carriageway. If the alteration consists of an additional carriageway on a highway the additional depreciation must be caused by physical factors the source of which is the use of the additional carriageway together with the corresponding length of the existing highway.[95]

In order that a claim can be founded on alterations to an aerodrome, and on physical fac-   13.60
tors caused by aircraft, the alterations must be runway or apron alterations. Runway altera-
tions mean the construction of a new runway, the major re-alignment of an existing runway, or the extension or strengthening of an existing runway. Apron alterations mean a substantial addition to, or alteration of, a taxiway or apron whose purpose or main purpose is to provide facilities for a greater number of aircraft.[96]

A claim notice in respect of depreciation caused by alterations or a change of use must   13.61
specify, as well as the other matters required to be stated, the alterations or change of use alleged to give rise to the depreciation. The same provision as to a reduction from the com-
pensation on account of betterment to other land of the claimant applies as with a claim in respect of the original works but of course the increase in value of contiguous or adjacent premises will only be taken into account if it is due to the alterations or change of use.[97]

(I) SUCCESSIVE CLAIMS

The general, and unsurprising, policy of Part I of the Land Compensation Act 1973 is that   13.62
there shall be one claim and one claim only under the Act for compensation for the depre-
ciation of the value of an interest in land caused by the use of public works. The Act has the equally important purpose that compensation for the same depreciation shall not be recoverable under Part I and under any other enactment.

As mentioned when an interest in land is depreciated in value by physical factors caused by   13.63
the use of public works there is a six year period running from the first claim day during

---

[93] LCA 1973, s 9(2).
[94] See paras 13.31–13.34.
[95] LCA 1973, s 9(5).
[96] Ibid, s 9(3), (6). See *Brunt v Southampton International Airport Ltd* [2005] EWCA Civ 93, [2005] 2 EGLR 105.
[97] Ibid, s 9(4).

which a reference to the Lands Tribunal may be made following a claim for compensation for depreciation made by a claim notice served by a person who holds that interest.[98] If the interest is in land other than a dwelling there is only one person who can bring the claim, namely the owner of an interest which is that of an owner-occupier. In that case only one claim can be made relating to the works on the land. Once a claim has been made in respect of an interest no subsequent claim can be made in relation to the same works and the same land or even by someone who holds a different interest in that land. However the making of a claim only prevents a subsequent claim if compensation has been paid or is payable on the claim.[99]

13.64   For example, if A is the freehold owner and in occupation of a commercial building he has six years from the first claim day to refer his claim to the Lands Tribunal. If he has served a notice of claim and compensation is paid or payable he cannot make a subsequent claim in relation to the same public works and the interest in land which he owns. If A sells his freehold the purchaser cannot make a claim in relation to the same public works whether or not A has made a claim. The reason is that the purchaser acquired the freehold after the relevant date. Nor can A make a claim after he has sold the freehold since at the time of the making of such a claim he will not be an owner-occupier. If a claim is made by A, and it is rejected after disputed proceedings in the Lands Tribunal, there can be no other claim by A by reason of the ordinary principles of *res judicata* or issue estoppel. On the other hand if a claim is made and is rejected by the acquiring authority, perhaps on the basis that there is no depreciation in the value of the interest of the claimant, while the claimant cannot make a fresh claim he has until the end of the six year limitation period to refer his claim to the Tribunal. If a claim is made by the person who has served a notice of claim near to the end of the six year period the claimant should be aware that he will have only a limited time up to the end of that period to refer his claim to the Tribunal and that a failure to do so within the period will render his claim unenforceable.

13.65   The above rules relate to land not in residential use. Where the land is a dwelling the owner of the freehold and the owner of a tenancy in the dwelling may have separate claims for the depreciation of the value of their respective interests.[100] Each such person may make a claim within the six year limitation period.[101] In this case also a claim cannot be made in respect of an interest when a person has sold the interest since after the sale the seller will not hold an owner's interest and the purchaser will not have acquired the interest before the relevant date. As a generality the rule can be stated as being that as regards the freehold interest or a tenancy in a dwelling only one claim for a depreciation in the value of each interest can be made and this claim must be made by a person who acquired his interest before the bringing into use of the public works (the relevant date) and who continues to own that interest when the claim is made.

---

[98]   See para 13.30.
[99]   LCA 1973, s 8(1).
[100] See para 13.19.
[101] LCA 1973, s 8(1).

(J) AVOIDANCE OF DOUBLE COMPENSATION

The legislation contains a general provision that compensation shall not be payable in   13.66
respect of the same depreciation under both Part I of the Land Compensation Act 1973 and
under any other enactment.[102] The general rule is that a claimant has a choice as to whether
to claim the compensation under one provision or the other. A possible instance of the
operation of this principle is that circumstances could create an entitlement to compensation under Part I of the 1973 Act and under section 10 of the Compulsory Purchase Act
1965 and the same depreciation in value might figure in both claims.[103] In this context the
same depreciation means depreciation in the value of the same interest caused by the same
factor or factors. If a claim could be made for the depreciation in the rental value for a
period of an interest in land under section 10 of the Compulsory Purchase Act 1965 due to
the temporary closure of a road for the purposes of highway improvements the making of
that change and the receipt of compensation for that damage to land would not prevent a
claim under Part I of the 1973 Act in respect of a fresh depreciation in the value of the land
caused by noise from the same improved highway.

The most likely potential overlap of claims is under section 7 of the Compulsory Purchase   13.67
Act 1965 and Part I of the Land Compensation Act 1973. The 1973 Act contains a specific
provision for this type of overlap the effect of which is that a claimant must make his claim
under the 1965 Act and cannot sustain a claim under Part I of the 1973 Act.[104] In this case
the specific provision overrides the general provision that there is a choice of claims as
stated in the last paragraph. Claims for compensation for injurious affection to land under
section 7 of the 1965 Act are an important element of the compensation payable for the
compulsory acquisition of land and are dealt with elsewhere.[105] In summary where a part of
an owner's land is compulsorily acquired he is entitled to compensation under section 7 of
the 1965 Act not only for the value of the land acquired but also for any injurious affection
to the part of his land which is retained by him. In such a case where the land acquired is
acquired for the purposes of any public works no claim for compensation may be made
under Part I of the 1973 Act for compensation for depreciation of the value of the retained
land after the date of the service of notice to treat on the claimant. The exclusion applies
whether or not any sum is paid or payable under section 7 of the 1965 Act in respect of
injurious affection to the retained land. A claim under section 7 is not necessarily assessed
in the same way as a claim under Part I of the 1973 Act. For instance, claims under section
7 do not have the first claim day as the valuation date and the valuation date for the assessment of compensation for injurious affection to the retained land is usually the date on
which the acquiring authority takes possession of the land acquired. In any event, where the
acquisition is for the purposes of public works, the landowner must bring any claim for loss
to the retained land under section 7 of the 1965 Act.

---

[102] Ibid, s 8(7).
[103] See ch 10 for claims to compensation for injurious affection to land under s 10 of the Compulsory Purchase
Act 1965. It is unlikely that claims under s 10 of the 1965 Act and Pt I of the Land Compensation Act 1973 could
much overlap since claims under s 10 must relate to injurious affection caused by the execution as opposed to the
use of works (see ch 10, paras 10.44 and 10.45) whereas claims under Pt I of the 1973 Act must relate to the use
rather than the execution of works.
[104] LCA 1973, s 8(2). See *Lall v Transport for London* [2008] RVR 183.
[105] See ch 9.

13.68   On an acquisition of land for the purposes of public works, where the owner retains land in respect of which there is or may be a claim for compensation under section 7 of the Compulsory Purchase Act 1965, the acquiring authority is required to deposit particulars of the retained land and of the nature and existence of the public works with the local authority in which the retained land is situated. In England this is the District Council or London Borough Council. In Wales it is the Welsh Borough or County Borough. The deposited particulars are a local land charge under the Local Land Charges Act 1975. Thereafter for the purposes of any claim under Part I of the Land Compensation Act 1973 the public works are to be taken to be those in the deposited particulars.[106] The purpose of these provisions is that a purchaser of the retained land prior to the date of the completion of the public works can search the register of local land charges and so ascertain that he will not have a claim under the 1973 Act in respect of the use of the public works.

13.69   There is one exceptional case in which a claim for compensation may be made under Part I of the Land Compensation Act 1973 even though it relates to retained land following a compulsory acquisition of a part of the land of a landowner. The exceptional case occurs when following the acquisition the compensation for injurious affection falls, or will fall, to be assessed otherwise than in accordance with section 44 of the 1973 Act and is in respect of public works situated elsewhere than on the land acquired. In order to explain this exception it is necessary to summarise again the nature of claims for compensation for injurious affection to retained land, a subject which has been explained more fully in chapter 9.[107] When land is compulsorily acquired from an owner, and he retains a part of his land, compensation is payable under section 7 of the Compulsory Purchase Act 1965 for injurious affection to the retained land caused by the exercise of the powers of the acquiring authority. The exercise of the powers which creates the entitlement to compensation is not confined to the carrying out of works but in the great majority of cases it will be the works carried out by the acquiring authority which cause injurious affection to the retained land. The provisions of section 7 of the Compulsory Purchase Act 1965 are a repetition of provisions in section 63 of the Lands Clauses Consolidation Act 1845 and in a series of decisions, culminating in the decision of the Court of Appeal in *Edwards v Minister of Transport*,[108] it was held that the compensation for injurious affection to the retained land of the owner was confined to compensation for the effect on the retained land of works by the acquiring authority on the part of the owner's land which had been acquired from him and did not extend to compensation for injurious affection to his retained land caused by works on other land. In the case of a project of public works, such as a road scheme, this limitation could greatly reduce the compensation payable for the retained land since the greater part of the injurious affection was likely to come from the use of the length of road built on other land. This situation was thought to be unsatisfactory and section 44 of the Land Compensation Act 1973 provided that where works were carried out on the land acquired from the owner and on other land the compensation to the owner for injurious affection to his retained land should be assessed by reference to the whole of the works of the acquiring authority. The exception to the provision which is considered under this paragraph applies only to a case where section 44 does not apply. Since section 44 applies to circumstances where public works are carried out by the acquiring authority on the land acquired from

---

[106] LCA 1973, s 8(3), (4), (4A).
[107] See in particular section (e) of ch 9.
[108] *Edwards v Minister of Transport* [1964] 2 QB 134, [1984] 2 WLR 515.

the claimant and on other land the exception must apply when the public works which cause injurious affection to the retained land are carried out wholly on land other than the land acquired from the landowner. It has been suggested that in such a case, as compensation is payable by virtue of the exception under Part I of the Land Compensation Act 1973, it cannot also be claimable under section 7 of the Compulsory Purchase Act 1965 since, if compensation were so claimable, there would be a possibility of double compensation. This question is considered more fully in chapter 9.[109]

(K) OTHER MATTERS

All questions of disputed compensation are to be decided by the Lands Tribunal.[110] In an exceptional case where a claim can be made before the first claim day there cannot be a reference to the Tribunal before that day but normally a reference will follow the making of a claim for compensation after the first claim day where that claim is rejected by the responsible authority or the amount of the claim cannot be agreed. The general procedure before the Tribunal in compensation claims is considered in chapter 15.   13.70

Given the importance to the operation of the legislation of the relevant date the responsible authority is required to keep a record of the date on which a highway was first opened to public traffic, of the date on which other public works were first used after completion, and, in the case of public works other than a highway or aerodrome, the date on which there was a change of use in respect of the public works. A certificate given by the Secretary of State under these provisions stating that runway or apron alterations have or have not been carried out at an aerodrome and the date on which an aerodrome was first used after the completion of the alterations is conclusive evidence of the facts stated.[111]A record must also be kept of when a public highway was first opened to traffic after completion of alterations to a carriageway or on which other public works were first used after the completion of alterations to those works.   13.71

Any compensation payable under Part I of the Land Compensation Act 1963 in respect of land which is ecclesiastical property is to be paid to the diocesan board of finance for the diocese in which the land is situated. Ecclesiastical property means land belonging to an ecclesiastical benefice of the Church of England or which is, or forms part of, a church subject to the jurisdiction of a bishop of any diocese, or the site of such a church, or is or forms part of a burial ground subject to the jurisdiction of the bishop of a diocese. The compensation paid to the diocesan board of finance is to be applied for the purposes of which the proceeds of a sale by agreement of the land would be applicable under any enactment or measure authorising, or disposing of the proceeds of, such a sale.[112]   13.72

Special rules apply where a person is entitled to acquire the freehold or an extended lease under Part I of the Leasehold Reform Act 1967. The conditions for the exercise of the entitlement have been relaxed and the properties to which the entitlement applies have been   13.73

---

[109] See section (e) of ch 9.
[110] Ie the Lands Chamber of the Upper Tribunal.
[111] LCA 1973, s 15. See *R v Secretary of State, ex parte Plymouth City Airport Ltd* (2001) 82 P & CR 20.
[112] Ibid, s 13.

extended since the 1967 Act was passed. The rules apply where at the relevant date, that is the date on which the public works were first used after their completion,[113] a tenant has given notice of his claim to have the freehold or an extended lease but has not acquired that interest. The special rules which apply in this situation are as follows:[114]

(a) The tenancy is treated as an owner's interest even if there are less than three years of it unexpired when a notice of claim for compensation is served.[115]

(b) If the claimant has acquired the freehold, or an extended lease, he may still make a claim for compensation by virtue of his previous tenancy and as if he were still entitled to it. For the purposes of such a claim the rule that in assessing the compensation the nature of the interest of the claimant and the condition of the land must be taken to be as they subsisted on the date of service of the notice of the claim[116] is replaced by a rule that these matters must be taken to be as they subsisted at the relevant date. However, no claim may be made after the former tenant has ceased to be entitled to the freehold or extended lease which he has acquired, for instance after he has disposed of it. A tenant who acquires the freehold or an extended lease therefore loses his right to make a claim for compensation when he disposes of his new interest, but there is an exception to this exclusion if the claim is made by him between the making of a contract to dispose of the new interest and before the actual disposal of that interest and the claim is made before the first claim day, that is the day one year after the relevant date. Where this exceptional case applies compensation is still not payable until the first claim day.

(c) A notice of claim made under these special rules must contain, in addition to other matters required to be included in the claim notice, a statement that the claim is made in respect of a tenancy to which these special provisions apply and must contain sufficient particulars to show that it falls within the relevant provisions which have just been set out.

13.74 The Leasehold Reform, Housing and Urban Development Act 1993 created new rights for leaseholders of flats who became entitled to collective enfranchisement of the building containing the flats or to a new long lease of any individual flats. Provisions were added to Part I of the Land Compensation Act 1973 similar to those described as applying when a tenant of a house has given notice of a claim under the Leasehold Reform Act 1967.[117]

---

[113] See para 13.15.
[114] LCA 1973, s 12.
[115] See para 13.26 for a notice of claim.
[116] See LCA 1973, s 4(4)(c) and see para 13.32.
[117] Ibid, s 12A.

14

Valuation

(A) BASIC CONCEPTS

1. Introduction

Valuation may be regarded as the putting into practical effect of the rules of law which govern the assessment of statutory compensation. It is by the process of valuation of land that the actual amount of compensation payable is determined. In nearly all cases this process requires the assistance of a qualified surveyor or valuer. In more complicated cases the input of other experts such as accountants or planners may be needed. The ultimate rule in the assessment of compensation for land acquired is that contained in section 7 of the Compulsory Purchase Act 1965 which simply states that in assessing compensation regard shall be had to the value of the land acquired and to any damage caused by severance or other injurious affection to land which is retained. The first part of this rule is now supplemented by rule (2) of section 5 of the Land Compensation Act 1961 which states that the value of land shall be taken to be the amount which the land if sold in the open market by a willing seller might be expected to realise. Most of the valuation process used to assess the amount of the compensation flows from these two basic rules.

14.1

In most cases compensation is assessed by way of a valuation of interests in land. The primary element of compensation for the land acquired is the open market value of that land on the valuation date assessed in accordance with rule (2) of section 5 of the 1961 Act as just stated. Compensation in respect of land retained by the landowner generally requires two valuations of the land, one before its severance from the land acquired and the other after that severance, with the compensation being the amount by which the first value exceeds the second value.[1] Other areas of compensation, such as compensation for injurious affection to land under section 10 of the Compulsory Purchase Act 1965, or compensation for the depreciation in the value of land caused by the use of public works under Part I of the Land Compensation Act 1973, also demand land valuations. In one area of compensation, that for disturbance under rule (6) of section 5 of the 1961 Act, the assessment may not involve a valuation of land, for instance compensation for removal expenses or for a temporary loss of profits while a business is relocated to new premises which requires a purely monetary calculation.

14.2

This book is not a textbook on the law of valuation of land, and valuations of land are required for many purposes besides the assessment of compensation, from rent reviews under leases to the assessment of inheritance tax. The aim of this chapter is to provide at

14.3

[1] See ch 9.

least an outline of the valuation process, and its methods, principles and techniques, particularly for the assistance of those who are involved in compensation claims but are not themselves expert qualified valuers. The same processes and methods are, of course, widely used in land valuations carried out for other purposes. It is intended to start by summarising certain basic concepts which are not always kept fully in mind. After that a description will be given of the main methods of valuing land and this will be supplemented by worked examples and explanations of them which are in the Appendix. A fuller explanation of some basic concepts and legal principles relevant to the meaning and determination of the open market value of the land acquired and of land retained is given in chapter 4. The important matter of disregarding the effect on value of the scheme of the acquiring authority, something which is an integral aspect of most compensation valuations, is explained in chapter 5. The more detailed and practical aspects of valuation procedures and techniques cannot be fully understood or carried out without some grasp of the legal principles explained in chapter 4.

14.4   The most basic concept is that of value itself. In every day terms the value of a piece of land is what that land would sell for. In essence this is what rule (2) of section 5 of the 1961 Act states. What is involved is the sale of the land in the open market and the further expressions 'market value' and 'open market value' are often used. There is no difference in the meaning of these last two expressions.² A less crude and more authoritative definition of value (that is of the value of assets generally and not just of the value of land) can be found in the publications of two bodies.

14.5   The first body is the International Valuation Standards Council which is an independent organisation and which seeks to build confidence and public trust in the valuation process by creating a framework for the delivery of credible valuation opinions. Accordingly it creates and maintains international valuation standards. The Council publishes the *International Valuation Standards Framework* which contains generally accepted valuation concepts and principles on which international valuation standards are based. The current *International Valuation Standards Framework* has as its effective date 1 January 2012.³ The definition of value contained in the framework is:

> The estimated amount for which an asset or liability should exchange on the date of valuation between a willing buyer and a willing seller in an arm's length transaction after proper marketing wherein the parties had each acted knowledgeably, prudently and without compulsion.⁴

14.6   The Royal Institution of Chartered Surveyors publishes *RICS Valuation – Professional Standards Effective from 30th March 2012.*⁵ This publication is commonly called the 'Red Book'. The *Red Book* states that its standards are fully compliant with the *International Valuation Standards* and that the *International Standards* are, in some instances, supplemented by the *RICS Standards*. The *Red Book* defines market value in the same way as does the *International Valuation Standards Framework.*⁶

14.7   The essence of the application of rule (2) of section 5 of the 1961 Act, and of the two authoritative definitions of market value just mentioned, is that there has to be imagined a

---

² See section (b) of ch 4.
³ *International Valuation Standards Framework*, (International Valuation Standards Council, 2012).
⁴ Para 30 of the *Framework*.
⁵ *RICS Valuation Professional Standards*, (Royal Institution of Chartered Surveyors, 2014).
⁶ See ch 4, para 4.19 where the *Red Book* definition is set out.

hypothetical sale of the land being valued at the valuation date. That hypothetical sale takes place between a hypothetical willing seller and a hypothetical willing buyer. The meaning of these hypothetical entities has been fully explained in chapter 4.[7]

The concept of value is to be distinguished from the concept of worth. These concepts have   14.8
been explained in chapter 4 but it is worth setting out again the essence of the distinction since it is crucial to an understanding of value and to the valuation process. Expressions such as 'value', 'worth', 'price' and 'cost' are often used in a loose fashion in valuing land and it is helpful to define what exactly is meant by these words and how they relate to each other before coming to details of the valuation process. In every day parlance the two concepts of value and worth may not be distinguished and it may seem natural to say that the value of an asset is simply what it is worth. However, for the purposes of land valuation generally, including the process of assessing compensation for compulsory purchase, a distinction must be drawn between the two concepts. Value is an objective concept in the sense that it can be ascertained as the amount which would be paid for the land being valued if that land was exposed to the market. Worth is a subjective concept and is the worth of the land in question to the person who owns it. Obviously that worth may not be the same when expressed as a numerical amount (where indeed it can be so expressed) as the amount which would be paid for the land if it was put on the market and sold. A prime reason for the difference is that the owner of the land may have his own personal and subjective reasons for attributing a worth to that land which neither a particular purchaser nor the market as a whole would share. Worth is sometimes called subjective value. It can also be referred to as investment value. Worth is defined in the *Red Book* as 'the value of an asset to the owner for individual investment or operational objectives'.[8] The *International Valuation Standards Framework*, while not referring to worth as such, applies exactly the same definition to the expression 'investment value'. The *Framework* goes on to refer to investment value as:

> [A]n entity-specific basis of value. Although the worth of an asset to the owner may be the same as the amount that could be realised from its sale to another party, this basis of value reflects the benefits received by an entity from holding the asset and, therefore, does not necessarily involve a hypothetical exchange. Investment value reflects the circumstances and financial objectives of the entity for which the valuation is being produced.[9]

Since the assessment of compensation for compulsory purchase is based on value there may   14.9
be circumstances, as explained earlier, in which a dispossessed landowner does not receive as compensation what he can reasonably regard as the true worth of the property to him. An example might be where an owner had expended money on improvements to a property which were of particular worth to him but where the cost of those improvements was not reflected, or fully reflected, in the amount which purchasers in the market would pay for the property The reason is that purchasers generally may not have the same aspirations or concerns or pleasures as did the owner of the property when expending his money on works to that property. Indeed sometimes the works which create worth in the eyes of the owner can reduce, rather than merely add nothing to, the value of the land in the market. A further important instance of where worth is not the same as value in the context of

---

[7] Section (c) of ch 4.
[8] Ch 4, para 4.3.
[9] Para 38 of the *Framework*.

compensation for compulsory purchase would be where a person carried on a profit making business on land and the expectation of future profits was of obvious worth to that
owner as a businessman. Purchasers in the market would no doubt pay a sum for the land
which included the expectation of themselves continuing to make a profit from a business
but the amount which such purchasers would pay, the value of the land, would not necessarily be equivalent to the worth which the owner attributed to his own expectation of
himself making future profits.[10]

14.10   A further expression often used is 'price'. This simply means the amount which a purchaser
would pay for the land if it was put on the market. Another word used is the 'cost' of land.
The cost of the land to a purchaser is the amount which he has to expend in order to obtain
that land. In this context the cost to the purchaser is therefore equivalent to the value of the
land together with the other expenses of acquiring it, such as legal and agents' fees and
stamp duty land tax. The value of the land is the price which the purchaser would pay to
acquire it less these other expenses.

14.11   Other important concepts, including the concept of a special purchaser and the concept of
marriage value, have been explained earlier.[11] It should be noted that the existence of a special purchaser, and the additional amount which he would pay to acquire land, are relevant
to assessing the value of the land for the purposes of compensation for compulsory purchase whereas the *International Valuation Standards Framework* and the *Red Book* exclude
the existence of a special purchaser and of any additional amount which he would pay to
obtain the land from the definition of market value. To this extent the general published
definitions of value differ from the concept of value as understood for the purposes of
assessing compensation for compulsory purchase.

2. The *Stokes v Cambridge* Principle

14.12   It is appropriate at this point to mention separately a subject which engenders some general
interest in valuations, the so-called *Stokes v Cambridge* principle. This is no more than a
common sense valuation technique. In *Stokes v Cambridge Corporation*[12] land was acquired
with the potential for industrial development on it. The implementation of that development depended upon access being obtained over other land. It was considered, obviously
reasonably, that the owner of the other land would wish to share in the development value
which would be released if he gave his consent to the access. The reasoning of the Tribunal
was that the owner of the access land would only agree to provide access over his land if he
was paid a proportion of the development value of the land being valued attributable to his
doing so. Therefore, at least prima facie, the value of the land being valued should be
reduced by the amount which the owner of that land would have to pay in order to obtain
that access. In the absence of any reason to the contrary it could be reasonably supposed
that the owner of the land which was to be developed, and the owner of the land who was
to provide the access to permit that development, would divide between themselves on an
equal basis, a 50/50 basis, the development value which would be released by their agree-

[10]   See in particular section (h) of ch 4.
[11]   Section (e) of ch 4.
[12]   *Stokes v Cambridge Corporation* (1961) 13 P & CR 77.

ment. Therefore on the face of it the value of the land to be developed and which was being valued should be reduced by 50 per cent of the development value which it would otherwise have borne.

Of course circumstances are not always as simple as that. On the facts under consideration 14.13
in the *Stokes* case the owner of the land over which the access would take place would himself benefit from the development of the land being valued in that it might bring forward the date on which his land could be developed. This was a special consideration which, in the view of the Tribunal, meant that the amount which the owner of the land to be developed would have to pay for his access would not be 50 per cent of the development value but only one-third of it. Plainly there could be many other circumstances which would result in a different split between the two owners of the development value released. One important point, however, to be grasped at the outset is that what was to be split was not the whole of the value of the land which was to be developed but only that part of that value which represented the additional value brought about by the development. The land being valued might have had an existing use value and that value could have been realised and continued without any co-operation from the person who was to provide the access.

Thus, to take a numerical example, if a piece of land had an existing use value of £250,000 14.14
and a total value of £750,000 if it could be developed using an access over other land, the additional value, or development value, released by the obtaining of that access would be £500,000. Thus it would be reasonable to suppose that, in the absence of any other circumstances, the person whose land was to be developed and the person who was to provide the access which would permit that development would divide between themselves not the total value of the land being valued, that is £750,000, but the additional or development value of that land, that is £500,000, so resulting in a division of that development value of £250,000 to each of them. On this simple hypothesis, the value of the land to be developed would be £250,000 plus its share of the development value which was also £250,000, namely £500,000 in all.

The above explanation assumes that the land which provides an access, and so unlocks the 14.15
development value of other land, has itself no significant value save for its potential to provide the access. Of course this may not be so and it could be that the land providing the access had a value for a use which would be lost if it came to be used as an access to other land, and in that case the value of that use would have to be brought into the bargaining and the analysis. Again what is meant may be illustrated by a simple example. Suppose that plot A contains a house with a road frontage. It has adjoining it a strip of land within its curtilage used as an off-road parking space and a garden shed. Plot B is open land behind plot A and could be developed by building a house on it save that it has no access to the road. The land adjoining plot A could be used to provide that access if the garage and shed were removed. Plot B has a value of £30,000 as grazing and amenity land and £150,000 for development by a house. The strip adjoining plot A has a value of £10,000. Logic suggests that before he would sell his strip to the owner of plot B to be used as an access the owner of plot A would seek a half of the development value of plot B plus a recompense for the loss to him of the strip. The bargaining might then be that the owner of plot A sold the strip for a half of the development value of plot B (50 per cent of (£150,000 − £30,000)), that is £60,000, plus the value to him lost on the strip of £10,000, a total sale price of £70,000.

14.16   The division of the development value on an equal basis between seller and buyer is only a starting point. It may be the most likely result of a negotiation where the parties have equal bargaining power and an equal interest in securing the development value. There may be other factors which lead to the conclusion that the percentage of the development value which would be paid by a developer to obtain an access or other benefit is less than 50 per cent. An obvious reason would be where there were two pieces of land which could provide an access for the developer. The developer would then be likely to be able to bargain down the person whose land he actually bought for an access by threatening that if a deal was not done with that person the developer would make an arrangement with the person who could provide the alternative access even if that alternative access might be less convenient. The result would be likely to be that the person able to provide the access would agree to do so for a sum which was less than 50 per cent of the development value released.[13] A further possibility is that the development of the land for which an access was being provided might itself produce some benefit to the person who was providing the access, for example it might make it more likely that the person providing the access could himself obtain planning permission for a valuable development of his land. It has been explained that these were the circumstances in the decision in *Stokes v Cambridge Corporation* and resulted in the payment being not 50 per cent but only a third of the development value.

3. Methods of Valuation

14.17   There is no legally prescribed method of arriving at the value of a property, that is at arriving at the sum which a hypothetical willing buyer would agree to pay and which a hypothetical willing seller would be willing to receive. In practice there are four principal valuation methods:

   (a) a valuation using comparable transactions;
   (b) a residual valuation;
   (c) a profits valuation; and
   (d) a depreciated replacement cost valuation.

14.18   It is for the valuer to choose which method or methods to use in any particular case. It is generally considered that a valuation carried out by comparing similar transactions, agreements and settlements, often referred to as the comparables method, is the most satisfactory and reliable method when it is possible. To some extent the other valuation methods themselves rely on comparables, but within the framework of their own methodologies. Clearly effective use of this first method depends on the availability of good comparables and their proper analysis and weighting; generally comparison of market transactions such as lettings carry rather more weight than comparison of non-market transactions such as rent reviews and lease renewals under statutory compulsion. It is sometimes useful to use more than one valuation method. If they are used accurately and correctly the different methods should provide the same, or much the same, result and if they do so that fact

---

[13] See, eg *Persimmon Homes (Wales) Ltd v Rhondda Cynon Taff CBC* [2005] RVR 59 (45% held to be the correct proportion of the development value); *Crown House Developments Ltd v Chester City Council* [1997] 1 EGLR 169, [1997] RVR 33 (30% of the development value); *Kaufman v Gateshead Borough Council* [2012] RVR 128 (15% of the profit having regard to the factors which would have affected the hypothetical negotiation).

increases confidence in the accuracy of the result. On occasions a primary method of valuation may be used and a secondary method used as a check on the primary method.

It is sometimes said that valuation is an art and not a science. What is meant is that the 14.19 valuation of land does not purport to arrive at a result which is accurate in the same way as scientific or mathematical measurements. If a vehicle travels at an average speed of 30 mph for 2 hours it will travel 60 miles. If the initial data is accurate it would be inaccurate and incorrect to say that the vehicle travels 59 or 61 miles in the 2 hours. By contrast if a piece of land is being valued a valuer may conclude with some confidence that its value is of the order of £650,000. However, he could not say with any confidence that the value was exactly that sum and not £649,000 or £651,000. In other words there is an inevitable range or spectrum of correct values when virtually any valuation of land is produced. This principle is reflected when proceedings are brought against a valuer for alleged negligence in producing his valuation. It will be rare that a breach of his duty of care by a valuer can be established where his valuation has been within a range, which may be a span of 5 per cent or 10 per cent or more, depending on the nature of the property and the circumstances, from what others believe is the 'true' value.[14] The reason for this inevitable degree of imprecision in any valuation is that valuations depend to a significant degree on subjective rather than objective judgements. Even when good comparables are available the valuer may have to exercise a degree of judgement, or weighing of the exact differences, between the circumstances of the comparable transaction and those of the hypothetical sale of the property which he is valuing and of the effect on value of these differences and he may wish to attach different comparative weights to different comparables. Most valuations contain a series of points at which the judgement and experience of the valuer have to be exercised. Different valuers may therefore reach different conclusions on precisely the same data by reason of differences of subjective judgement. In principle, of course, the more a valuation judgement can be backed by hard evidence, that is usually evidence of what others have done in similar circumstances in the past in the market, the more reliable it is likely to be. It is for this reason that the comparables method of valuation is regarded as the most reliable method. It is a method founded on the hard evidence of the undisputed facts of transactions which have actually happened.

There is a further process which is sometimes referred to as a 'spot' valuation. What this 14.20 means is that the valuer, instead of employing some particular process such as considering a series of comparables and adjustments to the comparables, simply uses his experience and judgement and states that a property has a certain value. Evidence of this nature is acceptable in principle and the weight to be given to it may depend on the experience and judgement of the valuer. However, the function of the Lands Tribunal in disputed cases (as of any expert tribunal) is not itself to value a property but to use the skill and experience of the member to evaluate the opinions and evidence of valuers as to the value of that property.[15] As a result the Tribunal is normally bound to examine the reasoning behind competing valuations and it is rare for a witness to rely only on a spot valuation.[16]

---

[14] See, eg *Singer & Friedlander Ltd v John D Wood* [1977] 2 EGLR 84; *Merivale Moore Plc v Strutt & Parker* [2000] PNLR 498, per Buxton LJ at p 515.

[15] See the explanation given by the member, Mr Walmsley, in *Marson v Hasley* [1975] 1 EGLR 157. The process can be described as 'valuing the valuers'. See also para 14.38.

[16] A spot valuation was upheld in the Privy Council on an appeal from Mauritius: *Mon Tresor v Ministry of Housing and Lands* [2008] 3 EGLR 13.

(B) VALUATIONS BY COMPARABLES

1. The Nature of the Process

14.21   The word 'comparables' means transactions which have occurred, usually and preferably in the market, which are similar in their circumstances to those of the hypothetical sale of the property being valued (the subject property) such that the amounts agreed as a part of the comparable transactions provide a guide to the amount which would be agreed between the hypothetical parties in the hypothetical transaction in the subject property. Comparables may also include evidence which is itself a hypothetical reflection of what the market may have done. A common example is a rent review settlement.[17] If a valuer is asked to value a particular property his first task will generally be to do his best to find out what comparable transactions exist so as to give him the guidance just mentioned. If a valuer is asked to value one house in a row of 10 almost identical houses and six of them have been sold in the previous six months at prices between £400,000 and £420,000 in a steady market this is a good initial indication that the value of the house being valued is in this range. Of course the valuer's task does not end there and he must consider among other matters whether there are some unusual circumstances relating to the subject property, for instance extensive improvements carried out to it, or a planning permission restricting its use, which takes its value out of the range. The first valuation example in section (b) of the Appendix is a valuation of a suburban house which has been acquired for the purposes of a road improvement. It is a valuation based on an analysis of the prices obtained on sales of similar residential properties in the locality.

14.22   Cases as obvious as that just described may be unusual. Nevertheless it is because of the logic and obvious utility of the process described that the comparables method of valuation is normally preferred as a valuation method when it is possible to use it. It reduces the number of uncertainties and subjective judgements which often exist more abundantly when other methods of valuation are applied. The uncertainty and scope for doubt which does exist, even in a valuation by comparables, is frequently that of adjustments which have to be made to the results of the comparable transactions. There are nearly always differences between the circumstances of the comparable transaction and the circumstances of the hypothetical transaction on the subject property so that adjustments have to be made for these differences in order to use the comparables as an indicator of the value of the subject property. Even in the plain and obvious case of the valuation of a house in a row of identical or almost identical houses, such as mentioned in the last paragraph, there may need to be an adjustment for the time of the comparable transactions. If the housing market is rising steeply the price agreed for a house six months before the valuation date for the subject property may need to be adjusted upwards if it is to provide an accurate guide to the value of the subject property. A good deal of time may be spent by valuers in disputed cases in discussing whether such adjustments are necessary and, if they are, the amount of each of the adjustments.

---

[17] In this latter type of case the comparable is not what parties have directly committed themselves to in the market but only of what parties have agreed that which they think other parties would have committed themselves to in the market in hypothetical circumstances. Comparables in this latter category are sometimes thought to be of less weight than actual transactions because they are one step further from the actual market. See also para 14.37.

2. The Six Stages

When carrying out a valuation using comparables, once the valuer has inspected the prop-   14.23
erty to be valued and has established its factual characteristics, including the nature of the
legal interest to be valued and planning constraints and opportunities, there are six stages
in the valuation process which can be considered in a logical and sequential fashion,
although they may inter-relate with each other as matters unfold.

(i)   The valuer must identify those transactions and agreements[18] which appear, given
        information initially available, to merit use as comparables.
(ii)   He must then obtain all possible relevant information on the comparable transac-
        tions to confirm the decision that the evidence may be relevant and to make the
        best possible use of it.
(iii)   He must consider the differences between the circumstances of the comparable
        transaction and those of the hypothetical sale of the subject property which may
        require adjustments to the amount agreed in the comparable transactions. Even at
        this stage he may discard some evidence, for example on the basis that analysis and
        adjustments would become too extensive or unwieldy.
(iv)   He must determine the amount of any adjustment required for any relevant dif-
        ference.
(v)   He must weigh the results of the various comparables when adjusted since not all
        comparables are likely to be of equal weight or merit.
(vi)   Finally he must arrive at his valuation of the subject property in the light of the
        whole of the process.

Each of these stages is now considered in more detail. The six stages are considered and
explained in the first valuation example in section (b) of the Appendix.

The first stage is a search for comparables. It is useful first to define a geographical area of   14.24
search and a time over which the search should take place. The area within which comparables can usefully be found depends on the type of property being valued and the availability of comparables. The valuation of an ordinary suburban house is likely to be assisted
by a number of readily available comparables and a search beyond the general locality of the
subject property may be unnecessary and unproductive. A valuation of an asset, such as a
large quarry or parts of an airport, may require a much wider search for comparables perhaps extending throughout the United Kingdom. It is impossible to prescribe a cut-off date
for comparables. If only a small number of recent comparables is available it may be necessary to search further. Also much may depend on how well general price trends for the type
of property in question between the date of the comparable and the valuation date (whether
earlier or later) are recorded and how volatile prices have been. If prices for the type of
property being valued have fluctuated rapidly it may be difficult to gauge the reliability of
a sale which is some time before or after the valuation date as a guide to values on the

---

[18] By agreements is meant lease renewal agreements, rent review settlements, independent expert determina-
tions and arbitration awards. Not all may be admissible evidence, but that might not necessarily restrain the valuer
who will use his own judgement. Previous decisions of the Lands Tribunal could be of assistance although they
may be more useful for matters of valuation technique, methodologies and principle rather than for the exact
numerical result of the decision.

valuation date. It must be remembered that in principle comparable transactions after the valuation date are admissible as evidence so that a search each side of that date is necessary.[19]

14.25   Having made at any rate a provisional determination of an area and time for his search for comparables the valuer will use all available means actually to find the comparables. A number of sources of information will be available including the personal knowledge of the valuer, the records of his firm, information from other firms, information from the property press, information obtainable from HM Land Registry, rating lists, property websites, and simple verbal enquiries and word of mouth conversations. It is difficult to carry out a perfect and comprehensive search and in disputed cases a useful and frequent practice is that at an early stage the valuers advising each party exchange information, often in the form of lists of comparables, so that when analysing the comparables each valuer can be confident that he is analysing many, if not all, transactions which are or may be relevant.[20]

14.26   The second stage is that the valuer collects and records all relevant information on the property transactions which he has ascertained as those which are, or may be, useful comparables. It is impossible to provide a comprehensive list of the information which needs to be gathered and in principle anything which is relevant to the value of the property should be ascertained. The main items of data to be ascertained in most cases are: (a) the location of the property, (b) the use and size of the property, (c) the date of the transaction, (d) other terms of the transaction which may have a bearing on value, (e) the price or rent agreed in the transaction, (f) the parties to the transaction (and/or their agents), (g) other relevant physical characteristics of the property such as the standard of its mechanical and electrical services if it is a commercial property, (h) the terms on which the property is held, for example if it is held on a lease its rent and other terms and if a reversion on a lease the rent and terms of the lease to which it is subject, (i) the planning status of the property, (j) the rateable value of the property, (k) the state of repair of the property, (l) whether the property has any potential for development, (m) whether there are any particular burdens affecting the property such as difficulties of access or the existence of a restrictive covenant or easement over the property, (n) any proposals for development or public works in the locality which may have an effect on the value of the property, (o) whether the transaction was a true arm's length transaction, (p) whether the property was properly marketed, and (q) whether the contractual terms of the transaction are unusual in any way such as the payment of the sale price in instalments or some collateral benefit allowed to one or other party. The valuer may need to look carefully at a transaction if it is a sale by a mortgagee following default by the mortgagor under the mortgage. A mortgagee is obliged to obtain the best price reasonably obtainable if he exercises his power of sale but suspicions remain that in such a sale there may not have been the same assiduity in getting the best price as would have been applied by an ordinary seller. A list of this nature cannot be comprehensive and other characteristics and factors may be important in a particular case. A purpose in collating this information is to see whether there are particular features of the property the subject of the transaction which distinguish it from the circumstances of the hypothetical sale of the property being valued. What are not important are the particular

[19] *Melwood Units Pty Ltd v Commissioner of Main Roads* [1979] AC 426, [1978] 3 WLR 520; *Segama NV v Penny Le Roy Ltd* [1984] 1 EGLR 109.
[20] For the procedure in references to the Lands Tribunal, see ch 15, paras 15.84–15.86. An exchange of comparables with full details of them will certainly be required as part of the preparation for any hearing.

circumstances and position of the dispossessed landowner of the property to be valued since the hypothetical sale which determines the value of the property is made by a hypothetical willing seller and not by the claimant for compensation.

It is possible that the gathering of information at this second stage may result in a decision   14.27
that the transaction in question is not comparable and therefore merits no further consideration. For example, information obtained may reveal that the sale of a property was between connected persons and was not an arm's length transaction so that no reliance can be placed on it as an indicator of what might happen in a true open market situation. The gathering of information will reveal the nature and scale of the differences between the circumstances of the comparable transaction and the circumstances of the hypothetical transaction on the subject property. The valuer may decide at this stage that the differences are so many and so great that cumulatively they mean that the transaction in question should not be relied upon as a useful comparable. It is possible that so many potential comparables are ruled out at this stage because of some particular deficiency, or the cumulative effect of differences in circumstances, that the valuer decides to go back and extend either or both the geographical area of his search and the time period for his search for comparables. It is possible that important aspects of the comparable transaction cannot be ascertained because, for instance, they are regarded as commercially sensitive by the parties and this situation may lead the valuer to decide that the comparable is too unreliable to be used in his valuation or that only reduced weight should be placed on it.

If the valuation is in dispute it is good practice that the valuers should exchange all relevant   14.28
data on any comparable transaction on which either or both of them wishes to rely. Such data should then generally be capable of agreement or may merit further investigation. If the claim is referred to the Lands Tribunal it is likely that the Tribunal will require the parties to carry out this process.[21]

Coming to the third stage of the process, by this point the valuer should have a list of com-   14.29
parable transactions together with the relevant information which can be ascertained for each of those comparables. The third stage involves ascertaining how each comparable is to be used as an indicator of the value of the subject property. This is the stage which involves adjustments. Each piece of relevant information relating to each comparable should be considered. If there is no, or no significant, difference between this particular item of information on the comparable and the equivalent circumstances of the hypothetical transaction on the subject property then no adjustment is necessary. For example, if the subject matter of the comparable transaction is next to or close to the subject property it may not be necessary to make any adjustment for locational differences. On the other hand if the comparable property is some distance away from the subject property the difference in location may make the subject property more or less valuable, everything else being equal, than the comparable property. In that event an adjustment must be made to the price or rent of the comparable property to take account of this difference. If the comparable property is in a less favourable or attractive location than the subject property the price paid on a sale of the comparable property should be adjusted upwards so as to bring it into line with the price which would be paid for it if it was in the same location as the subject property. In other words the valuer attributes the relevant characteristic, such as location, of the subject

---

[21] See n 18, and see ch 15, paras 15.84–15.86.

property to the comparable property and adjusts the price or rent agreed on the comparable property upwards or downwards to that which in his judgement it would have been if the comparable property had shared that particular attribute of the subject property. The third stage of the process is, therefore, one of considering all relevant characteristics or attributes or circumstances of the subject property and of a particular comparable and deciding for that comparable what are the differences for which an adjustment, upwards or downwards, needs to be made to the price or rent agreed for the comparable. Obviously this process needs to be carried out for each of the comparables.

14.30   The fourth stage follows closely from the third stage and is that of deciding the amount of the adjustment required for each characteristic of each comparable where an adjustment has been determined to be necessary. This can be a difficult and sometimes disputed exercise and it is a central part of the valuer's art. In some cases the adjustment can be found by applying known facts. A good example of this type of adjustment is an adjustment needed for the date of the comparable transaction. Records of sales in the market may show how prices of properties of the type in question have moved generally over past months and years. Details of movements in property prices are provided by way of property value indices published by various organisations such as firms of surveyors and building societies. Some such indices are divided or sub-divided into particular localities or different types of property. In London values of residential sales prices are divided into locations such as Kensington or Mayfair and divided into houses and flats. Prices and rents for offices are also published with similar divisions and sub-divisions such as Central London generally, the City, the West End, and Docklands. Geographical definitions of these areas are given by those who produce the indices of price movements but there is no overall agreement on exact boundaries and obviously one area merges into another. In the absence of such detailed records and indices recourse may be had to the retail prices index published monthly by the Government through the Office for National Statistics, although it is everyone's experience that property prices do not necessarily move in tandem with general inflation but are much more volatile in an upwards or downwards direction. It should be borne in mind that when considering the date of the transaction on a comparable property which is important is not the date of the completion of that transaction but its 'effective date' which is the date on which the parties to the transaction enter into a legal binding commitment to carry out the transaction on certain terms. This may be a significant point when property values were moving rapidly at the date of the transaction.[22] A similar instance of where an adjustment may be made by reference to hard evidence is an adjustment for the location of the property. Records of past transactions may show that properties, otherwise broadly similar, may sell or let at a particular difference in prices or rentals of, say, 10 per cent if located in one particular area as opposed to another. Statistics on property values in general locations, especially areas of large cities, can only give a general indication of an adjustment needed for a particular comparable. The exact location of the comparable within an area, such as its proximity to public transport facilities, may be important.

14.31   One adjustment which may in principle be susceptible of fairly precise analysis is an adjustment for the state of repair of a property. If the property the subject of the comparable transaction is in a very poor state of repair it may be possible to calculate the amount of money needed to put it into proper repair so that that amount represents the correct adjust-

---

[22]   See ch 4, para 14.16.

ment. In the same way if the subject property has been improved in some particular respect as compared with the comparable the cost of carrying out the improvement to the comparable may be an appropriate adjustment. However, this reasoning rests on the proposition that the amount spent on a property in repairing it, or improving it, results in an equal increase in the value of the property, and this proposition may itself be queried when considering actual properties. As a general rule cost does not amount to value.

An adjustment which often figures in valuations is an adjustment for size. It is obvious that a larger property will normally command a higher price or rent in overall terms than a smaller property. For this reason rents are often analysed in terms of a rent per square foot of the property (for offices of the net internal area or net lettable area) or prices analysed in terms of a price per square foot for the purposes of a capital value as is often done for houses or flats. An adjustment for size which is made is based on the proposition that, everything else being equal, the price or rent per square foot of a larger property may be less or more than that of a smaller property. The concept is similar to that of a discount for bulk in the sale of goods. Care needs to be taken that such an adjustment is justified by the evidence and is not simply an assumption. Evidence should be available that larger properties and of a particular type, and in a particular locality, do in general command a greater or lesser value per unit of their area if the adjustment is to be justified. Whether this is so may depend heavily on the balance of supply and demand for larger or smaller properties. A substantial demand for larger properties, not balanced by a level of availability of such properties, may result in a higher price per unit of area being obtainable for larger as compared to smaller properties. Even when some adjustment for size can be justified as a matter of principle it is often very difficult to quantify that precise adjustment. Again the amount of any adjustment should be backed by hard evidence from actual transactions if that is possible. 14.32

Other necessary adjustments may be much more subjective and not capable of being supported by concrete evidence. For example, the planning status of a property may raise some doubts. The exact meaning of a planning permission or its conditions may be in doubt or it may be uncertain whether certain use rights have been established by long user which has created an immunity from planning enforcement action.[23] The particular planning difficulties and doubts which attach to a particular property are unlikely to have been reproduced in other properties which are subject to transactions so that there may be no evidence from which the scale of any necessary deduction for the existence of planning difficulties can be ascertained. The matter is then left to the judgement of the valuer, a judgement which maybe sometimes informed or fortified by expert planning advice. A similar situation could arise where a property was subject to a restrictive covenant which prohibited alterations save with the consent of an adjoining owner with that consent not to be unreasonably withheld. It would be difficult to prognosticate in what circumstances an adjoining owner might reasonably refuse his consent to alterations and even more difficult to calculate what effect the existence of such a restriction would have on the value of the property burdened by it. 14.33

The traditional method of making adjustments to a comparable transaction so as to bring it into line with the circumstances of the hypothetical transaction on the subject property is by way of a percentage addition or deduction. If this is done the various upwards or 14.34

---

[23] Rule (4) of s 5 of the Land Compensation Act 1961 provides that no account is to be taken of an increase in the value of the land acquired due to an unlawful use. See section (c) of ch 6.

downwards percentage adjustments can be cumulated at the end so as to provide one figure for the necessary net adjustment to that comparable. When the valuer has carried out this process for each of the comparables he is able to arrive at an adjusted figure for each comparable. At the end of this stage of the valuation process the valuer will therefore be left with a list of comparables each of which provides a capital or rental value which can be applied to the subject property. The overall process can then be taken to the next stage. Where the valuer has made adjustments to a number of comparables he should take care that he does so consistently. To take a simple and obvious example, if the property being valued has a single garage and certain of the comparables have double garages the valuer might decide to make a downwards adjustment to the comparables of, say, 3 per cent to take account of this difference, a judgement which rests on his general experience of properties in the area and the importance which purchasers attach to a double garage. The valuer could be criticised if he had, without good supporting reason, made a different percentage adjustment for different comparables.

14.35   Care should be taken in the way in which adjustments to the price for a comparable are cumulated so as to arrive at an adjusted price to be applied to the subject property. Suppose that the price paid on the sale of the comparable property was £100 per square foot (psf). Two downwards adjustments may be necessary, one of 20 per cent because of the poorer location of the subject property and one of 10 per cent because of the poorer access arrangements to the subject property. The adjusted price for the comparable may be reached by an additive or a multiplicative process. The additive process would be to add up the two adjustments to reach a 30 per cent downwards adjustment and so an adjusted price of £70 psf. A multiplicative process would be to apply one adjustment, say 20 per cent, so as to reduce the adjusted price to £80 psf, and then to apply the second adjustment to the price reached by the application of the first adjustment, that is 10 per cent of £80 psf in the example, so giving an adjusted price of £72 psf. The difference to the end result reached by using the two arithmetical processes of course becomes greater the larger the number of adjustments that are required to be made. The multiplicative process is generally considered to be preferable and more accurate. For one thing if there was a sufficient number of downwards adjustments, and all of them were simply added up as percentages, the end result could be a negative value for the subject property. It should also be noted that if the multiplicative process is used the order in which the adjustments are made makes no difference to the end result. In the above example the end result would be £72 psf whether the 20 per cent or the 10 per cent adjustment was applied first.

14.36   At the fifth stage it is possible that the valuer has available only one comparable which he is satisfied is so good that with any appropriate adjustments applied to it that comparable proves the value of the subject property. A more likely situation is that the valuer has a series of transactions which he has used as comparables. He may have adjusted each one as described earlier and each one as so adjusted may have produced a price, say a capital value per square foot or a rental value per square foot, which he can then apply to the subject property. His problem at this stage is that the comparables will not all show the same value per unit area to be applied to the subject property. There are various techniques for dealing with this situation. The first technique is that one of a list of comparables may show a result which is at substantial variance with all of the others. Four of the comparables may have results which cluster fairly closely together and the fifth may be entirely out of line. In such a case the valuer, exercising his judgement, may simply decide that the fifth comparable has some oddity about it, for instance an absence of information on some point or some special characteristic or circumstance which is not known, or is simply out of line with the general market, so that it should be rejected from the list of comparables to be used in the final valuation. Where none of the comparables can be rejected in this way, and there is no particular reason for attaching more weight to one than another, a second technique sometimes used is that of simply averaging the results of the comparables and applying that average to the subject property. A third more sophisticated, and possibly more accurate, technique is to attempt to attribute different weights to different comparables. The obvious criterion for attaching greater weight to one comparable than another is that in the case of the first comparable there are less differences between it and the subject property so that less adjustments have to be made. The more adjustments there are the greater the scope for doubt and the less reliable the comparable. Using this criterion if there are, say, four comparables the valuer might decide to attribute a 40 per cent weight to one of them and only a 20 per cent weight to the other three. In this way he becomes able to take forward a final figure to be applied to the subject property which he is satisfied is the more reliable because he has taken into consideration all the comparables but has attributed the greatest weight to the most reliable comparable or comparables and a lesser weight to the other comparables. The end result at this stage of the analysis of the comparables is that the valuer has a rate, say a rate in pounds per square foot or per square metre, as a capital or a rental value which he can apply to the property being valued. There is unfortunately still no overall uniform practice on whether metric or imperial units are used in valuations and analyses. All that can safely be said is that no valuer should mix his use of the two forms of spatial measurement.

It is possible to consider comparable transactions in accordance with a general hierarchy of   14.37 their weight. The best comparables are likely to be actual open market sales and lettings at arm's length with both parties competently advised. A past transaction involving the property being valued may be of particular weight.[24] The next tier down may be agreements or settlements of some sort such as rent review settlements under a lease or an agreement on the price under an option to acquire an interest in land. Here the parties are agreeing what hypothetical parties would do in the market. The lowest tier is likely to be decisions by courts or tribunals or arbitrators. In this last type of case the decision is even more removed from the market since it is a judgement on value by one person, say an arbitrator, based on what experts have told him (usually with disagreements between the experts) that they believe hypothetical parties would have done in certain circumstances.

The final stage is to apply the result of the comparables, determined by the various pro-   14.38 cesses as just indicated, to the subject property. In principle this should be a simple arithmetical exercise. The comparables provide a final indicator of £x per square foot and the subject property has y square feet. A multiplication of x by y gives the value of the subject property at the valuation date. Even so the careful valuer will still at this stage stand back. He will weigh up all the information which he has; he will consider each stage in the process and the reliability of it; and he will apply his own general experience and knowledge of property transactions of the type and in the area in question. This may lead him to make some end adjustment so that the final valuation is not in precise accord with the arithmetical process just described. It is impossible to describe this last element of the process by

[24] *Windward Properties Ltd v Government of St Vincent and the Grenadines* [1996] 1 WLR 279.

ratiocinative means but the carrying out of this final or stand back overview is a legitimate part of the overall exercise carried out by a valuer. The valuer may often conclude from his overview that no end adjustment of this nature is justified. The valuer must arrive at a final figure and the arithmetical exercise just described, even if tempered by the final or 'stand back' step, will produce an exact numerical figure. Property transactions in the real world are normally concluded at fairly rounded figures. Thus at the final juncture before arriving at his valuation the valuer may round up or round down the figure arrived at by the arithmetic to a rounded sum such as would actually be agreed between the hypothetical willing parties. For example, a value of £584,651 would be likely to be rounded up to £585,000.

14.39   A valuer who has carried out a valuation by comparables, utilising all or most of the stages which have been described, should be prepared to justify his conclusion by explaining each stage and by explaining the whole of his detailed reasoning and calculations at each stage. If the matter comes to proceedings before the Lands Tribunal the valuer who can explain his valuation approach clearly and logically and by way of a series of sequential stages or steps will assist the Tribunal and may gain a substantial advantage for the party who instructs him.

14.40   The explanation of a comparables valuation which has been given has concentrated on the use of comparables to provide a capital value or a rental value for the property being valued. If it is necessary to arrive at a capital value for a property, say an office property which is let, the valuer will need to capitalise the annual rents by determining the appropriate yield and then applying a years' purchase multiplier to the rents. The ascertainment of the correct yield can also be carried out by the use of comparables and in this instance the comparables will be the yields which have been used in the capitalisation process in transactions on other property when these are known. Of course other data may be used as an aid to determining the correct yield, such as the general level of interest rates at the valuation date or the financial standing of tenants or likely tenants. An example of the valuation of interests in a property which is compulsorily acquired at a time when it is let in part to office tenants and in part to shop tenants is contained in section (c) of the Appendix as the second valuation there explained.

(C) RESIDUAL VALUATIONS

1. The Nature of the Process

14.41   A residual valuation is a method of valuing land which is ready or may become ready for development. In principle such land can be and should be valued by the use of comparable transactions when that can be done. It is often less easy to find comparable transactions which can be analysed reliably involving land which is a development site than it is to find comparables of developed land, so that resort is necessary to other means of valuing development land and the residual method is that normally selected. A residual valuation may be used when the land being valued is a site cleared, or to be cleared, for new development or when it contains a building which is to be substantially altered and refurbished such as the conversion of an office building into flats.

The nature of a residual valuation is that the valuer estimates the value of the land assuming   14.42
it has already been developed and deducts from that value the estimated costs of the development and the profit which the developer would require for carrying out the project. The
residue after the deductions is the amount which the prospective developer would pay to
acquire the land for the development. It is for this reason that the process is termed a residual valuation. A difficulty with this method is that it involves so many judgements on
inputs, such as the value of the completed development (itself dependent on matters such
as use, rent, yield and so on) and the amount of the cost of construction and the time the
development would take, and that small changes in some of the inputs can make a large
difference to the residual value at the end. For this reason it has often been said in the Lands
Tribunal that residual valuations are a method of valuation which should only be used
when no satisfactory comparables are available. Nonetheless as valuation models have
become more sophisticated, aided by computer technology, such valuations have become
more commonplace and perhaps more reliable.[25]

Despite these strictures the residual method is not infrequently used both in actual transac-   14.43
tions and in evidence before the Lands Tribunal in valuing land with a potential for
development.[26] Indeed there is a case for saying that if this is the way in which actual parties
in real market transactions value land then despite the theoretical imperfections of the
method it is a methodology which a valuer should use when trying to replicate for the
hypothetical parties envisaged in a valuation that which would happen between actual persons in the actual market. In practice a residual valuation is likely itself to involve the use of
comparables in determining some of the components or inputs of the valuation. For
instance, the value of the completed development may only be ascertainable by way of
lettings or sales of comparable properties which have been developed. When undertaking
residual valuations the valuer usually assumes rents and yields and other inputs, including
costs, as at the valuation date rather than attempting to forecast such inputs at a future date.
It is sometimes the drift from this important aspect of the methodology which leads to differences between valuers in the results of their appraisals. Because of the difficulties in accurately assessing the values of the inputs, and because of disagreement on the level of
the developer's profit which would be required, the use of residual valuations in disputed
cases tends to result in opposing valuations which are a long way apart. This is less likely to
occur when there are good comparables and it is another reason why the comparables
method of valuation is preferred by the Lands Tribunal. Of course, when it is practical to
do so, a comparables valuation and a residual valuation can be used as a check on each
other.

Residual valuations have a traditional format. The task of the valuer is today lightened but   14.44
also extended by the availability of computer programmes which can be purchased. The

---

[25] An analysis of the difficulties inherent in residual valuations was provided by the Lands Tribunal in *Clinker
and Ash Ltd v Southern Gas Board* (1967) 18 P & CR 372, and the reluctance of the Tribunal to rely on this type of
valuation when comparables are available has been repeated in a number of later decisions: see, eg *Snook v Somerset
County Council* [2005] 1 EGLR 147; *Essex Incorporated Congregational Union v Colchester Borough Council* [1982]
2 EGLR 178; *Mon Tresor v Ministry of Housing and Lands* [2008] 3 EGLR 13 (Privy Council on appeal from
Mauritius). In *Cripps on the Compulsory Acquisition of Land*, 11th edn (Sweet and Maxwell, 1962) it was stated at
para 4-200 that the residual method of valuation would not be applied where the open market value of the land
was otherwise ascertainable.
[26] An example is *Blakes Estates Ltd v Government of Montserrat* [2006] 1 WLR 297, where the use of this method
of valuation by the Board of Assessment in Montserrat was not challenged in the Privy Council.

valuer enters into the programme his opinion of the various inputs and a residual value is produced (often somewhere in the course of the workings rather than as an express end result). As well as convenience and speed of use a programme has the advantage that different valuations of the land using the same programme can be easily compared and that the sensitivity of the residual land value to changes or combinations of changes in the inputs can be quickly seen. Opposing valuers should be prepared to make their programmes available to each other on proper terms.

14.45   There are nine major inputs to most residual valuations and these will now be briefly considered. They can be considered within three main categories which are: (a) the value and other attributes of the completed development, (b) the cost of achieving that completed development, and (c) the level of the developer's profit. Of course not all inputs necessarily apply to all residual valuations. As will be explained planning matters, for example, may justify an additional input of costs in some valuations but not in others. Any particular valuation may require some particular additional input within the categories. For example, there may be a remaining sitting tenant in a part of a development site and the cost of persuading the tenant to leave would then be an additional factor in the cost of the development. A development of land for office, retail and residential purposes is mainly used in this explanation although in principle the residual method of valuation can be used to value land for any form of development.

2. The First Category of Inputs

14.46   The aim of this initial part of the valuation is to find the capital value of the completed development. It is obvious that a residual valuation can only be carried out if the precise form and content of the development are known. In some cases there may be a dispute over not only whether a purchaser of the land would assume that he could develop it but also the form or scale of the likely development. Such disputes must be determined by the valuer as a preliminary matter before decisions relating to the residual valuation can take place. It is possible to proceed directly to the value of the completed development although in practice it is usual with office developments to assess the rental value before finding the capital value by capitalising those rents since the usual assumption is that such developments are let and then sold to an investor once the income is known (even though it may not necessarily be received by the date of the assumed sale since, for instance, a lease may be subject to a rent free initial period). Therefore, the first input is usually the rental value of the completed office building or buildings, and this necessarily entails judging the length and other characteristics of the lease or leases which the development would attract and which an investor buying the completed development would expect. If the building is residential, or is a mixed use building with in part a residential content, it is more usual to go directly to the capital value of the residential component as that is often how completed residential development is sold (normally by way of the grant of long leases at a nominal rent and subject to a service charge in the case of flats). If the assumed development is a major office development different rental values may be applied to different areas, such as different floors and reception areas, and ancillary areas for storage or other purposes. Should it be envisaged that the building is likely to be let in parts for shared occupation a decision will have to be taken on how a common area such as a reception area is to be valued.

It is usual with office buildings to find a rental value attributable to each unit of net internal   14.47
area (sometimes called net lettable area). This is the first major input. The net internal area
of an office building is the internal area available for office use after excluding areas such as
corridors, stairs, lifts, toilets and washrooms, kitchens, and areas used for plant such as heat-
ing and air conditioning. This is to be compared to the gross internal area which is the
whole of the internal area of the building including the above areas and excluding only the
thickness of internal walls. The gross internal area is the area to which construction costs
are often applied. In the case of residential buildings it is more usual to assess the capital
value of the building by reference to the gross internal area including such areas as entrance
halls and bathrooms and toilets, as well as using that area when estimating construction
costs.[27]

When leases are granted of commercial properties it is often agreed that there will be a rent   14.48
free initial period, say the first six months of the term of the lease. The justification may be
that the incoming tenant is to have a period free of rent while he fits out the premises and
so is unable to put them to the use of his business, but rent free periods often exceed the
time estimated as that necessary for fitting out particularly in a tenants' market when supply exceeds demand. The existence and length of rent free periods are important for: (a)
determining the rent payable after the rent free period has expired (obviously the longer the
rent free period the higher the rent which becomes payable at the end of that period is likely
to be), and (b) the capitalisation of the right to receive rent under the lease (as explained
below). It is usual to describe the rent which becomes payable at the end of a rent free
period as the 'headline' rent.

It is at this rental value stage that the use of comparables comes most forcefully into the   14.49
process. The rental value of a completed office building can usually only be ascertained by
way of the rent payable for existing buildings with the need for adjustments in the usual way
as has been described when examining the method of valuation by comparables. The valuer
will need at this stage to have at least a general idea of the physical standard of a building,
for instance the existence of air conditioning and a good lift service and an adequate storage
area in an office building, since these items will be important to a valuation based on comparables. The same is true in principle as regards the capital value per unit area of residential buildings. The same general observations as apply to the use of comparables when a
valuation is by the comparables method apply also to the use of comparables in this part of
a residual valuation. Indeed, it can be said that a residual valuation is an amalgam of comparable evidence, relevant to all three parts or categories of a residual valuation. The more
reliable the comparables, the more reliable the residual valuation assuming the inputs have
been properly applied.

Where the completed value of the developed building is estimated by way of rental values,   14.50
and the rent free periods which may apply, the second major input is the capitalisation of

---

[27] See the *Code of Measuring Practice* published by the Royal Institution of Chartered Surveyors and the
Incorporated Society of Valuers and Auctioneers. This document provides precise definitions and illustrations of
the various bases of measurement. A further basis of measurement is gross external area which includes all internal
areas and the thickness of external walls. This is used for planning purposes and for the calculation of parts of
occupier's loss payments due under the Land Compensation Act 1973 (see section (c) of ch 11). The volume of
buildings, as opposed to their floor area, is not normally used for valuation purposes although some unusual feature, such as an unusually small dimension between the top of a raised floor and the bottom of a suspended ceiling
in an office building, could mean that the anticipated level of rent was reduced.

those rental values. A capitalisation multiplier has to be applied to the rents in order to convert them into a capital value (this multiplier often being called a years' purchase (or YP) multiplier). The ascertainment of the multiplier depends upon the yield or return for his investment which a purchaser of the completed development, subject to leases of the nature envisaged at the estimated rents, would require having made allowance for any rent free periods which are assumed. Assuming that the purchaser is buying a freehold and so will be entitled to the value in perpetuity the YP multiplier is found by dividing the required yield into 100, deferred only for any rent free period. For example, if the purchaser would require a 5 per cent yield on the investment of his money by the purchase of the reversion to the lease or leases then the YP multiplier will be 20, that is 100 divided by 5, assuming no rent free periods are involved. The estimated total annual rents for the building will then be multiplied by 20 so as to find its capital value. The same process is in principle applied in finding the value of a reversion which is itself a leasehold when the YP multiplier will take account of the length of the unexpired residue of the lease. Valuation tables are published to assist in this and other calculations, each of which has a formula. In determining the yield required, and thus the YP multiplier, the valuer will take into account, inter alia, general prevailing rates of interest at the time, the nature and standard of the property, the covenant strength of the expected lessees, the type and certainty of length of lease which can be expected to be entered into, and yields disclosed by actual sales of reversions of other properties (ie comparables) where they are known. The underlying principle is that the greater the risk associated with the investment the higher the yield which a purchaser of it will require. Obviously the higher is the yield required the lower will be the capital value of the completed development derived from the years' purchase multiplier produced by that yield.

14.51   It is important to note that the rental and capital values which are used in the process are values as at the valuation date. In reality the developer will not realise the value of the completed development until it has been completed sometime in the future and can be sold on, but for this first category of inputs the time difference between the valuation date, at which point the development has yet to start, and the anticipated date of its completion and sale is ignored. Clearly values may increase or decrease over the period of the development although the usual expectation is that of an increase. The general practice is to disregard the possibility of an increase or decrease in property values (and changes to the cost components mentioned later). The hope of an increase in value and the risk of a decrease in value are something which may be taken into account at a later stage when considering the level of developer's profit, which itself may be affected by the optimistic or cautious nature of the inputs used.

14.52   By this stage the valuer should have available a figure which represents his view of the value as at the valuation date of the completed development as if it had then been completed and this comprises the first category in the total residual valuation process.

3. The Second Category of Inputs

14.53   Moving to the second main category of inputs, the cost of achieving the completed development and the resultant investment to be sold, the principle is that every component of cost which the developer who is purchasing the land would expect to incur from the moment of his purchase to the moment of the receipt by him of the capital value of the completed development when it is sold on by him should be included.

The main item of cost, and the third major input into the valuation process, is the building   14.54
costs. Building costs can often be estimated from published documents which give a range of costs per unit area of the development, the range depending on the type of development, its location and its standard. The advice of a quantity surveyor, or sometimes of a building surveyor, will usually be needed at this stage. Obviously the detailed estimate of cost will be affected by such factors as the standard of facilities which are to be provided, for example air conditioning, and matters such as difficulties of access for carrying out the works where the development is in a dense urban area. Sometimes, and in order to achieve a cautious result, an inflation element is built into costs even though there is no inflation in rental or capital values. This is a matter of judgement for the valuer, having had comments from those advising on such costs, although his decision should be made explicit in his workings and can be expected to influence the extent of the developer's profit used. Such an inflation adjustment may be relevant when the period between the valuation date and the start of the principal works is lengthy. Adjusting the costs but not the income for inflation creates a tension in the methodology which is usually best avoided. The risk of unanticipated problems in the construction process which could cause additional cost and delay can be reflected in the rates adopted for building costs, including the extent of contingencies, and is one of the factors which can be taken into account in deciding the level of the developer's profit. As well as building costs, in the sense of a sum payable to building contractors, sums must be included for professional fees as a part of the total costs. Such fees may include those of architects, quantity surveyors and mechanical and electrical engineers.

As a fourth major input, planning costs are sometimes included. If there exists at the valu-   14.55
ation date a full planning permission for the development then there should be no further planning costs in the sense of the costs of planning consultants and planning fees. It will be otherwise if there is no permission in place or if approval of reserved matters under an outline planning permission has to be obtained. An important component of this general item is the sums which may have to be paid to the planning authority or others by virtue of planning obligations such as matters relating to archaeology, or a contribution towards the costs of highway works, or towards the costs of public amenities in the area. In major cases the advice of a planning expert and a highways engineer may be necessary on this input.[28]

The fifth major input relates to the holding costs prior to and during the development, such   14.56
as business rates, security and insurance.

---

[28] Planning obligations are entered into under s 106 of the Town and Country Planning Act 1990. Some planning authorities publish indications of the type and scale of contributions which will be required when planning permission is granted for different forms of development. The scale of contributions required for actual grants of permission in the past may offer guidance. A further item of planning costs may be the fees payable on making planning applications. See also ch 7, para 7.4. The whole of the system of planning obligations under ss 106–106B of the Town and Country Planning Act 1990 is being gradually replaced by a system of community infrastructure levy under the Planning Act 2008 (and see the Community Infrastructure Levy Regulations 2010 (SI 2010/948)). A system of levies produced by local planning authorities and approved by the Secretary of State will provide formulae and standards by reference to which developers may be required to make a contribution to infrastructure costs. There will remain other matters to be the subject of s 106 obligations which may have a bearing on the costs, or anticipated costs, of a development.

14.57   A sixth possible major input is that sometimes it is anticipated that expenditure to satisfy rights held by owners of nearby property will be required, so that this may form a sixth input covering matters such as rights to light. If the rights to light appurtenant to a neighbouring property would be infringed by the development it is likely that a sum will have to be negotiated and paid to those with interests in the neighbouring property to secure the release of their rights. Obviously account must be taken of this in a residual valuation.

14.58   The seventh major input is the costs of lawyers, agents and others in effecting the various land transactions which are involved in the overall development project. These costs are: (a) the costs involved in acquiring the land being valued, (b) the costs of lawyers and agents of marketing and letting any of the developed property envisaged as let and the same costs of disposing of parts of it such as flats sold on long leases, and (c) the costs of the ultimate disposal by the developer of the completed and let development to a purchaser such as a financial institution or fund. Such ultimate purchasers as investors usually require that their own costs of solicitors and others are paid by the developer to them or borne by the developer and this is a further part of the last head of costs. Where stamp duty land tax will be payable by the developer that should also be included. Consideration should be given to whether value added tax will be payable on any costs and not recoverable.

14.59   The eighth major input, and last item of costs within the second main category of inputs, is the cost of finance. A developer will expect to borrow money to carry out the development (or, what amounts to the same thing, to lose the return otherwise obtainable on his own funds if they are used) and the cost of finance should therefore be added to the total costs of the project within the appraisal. An appropriate cost of obtaining finance should be assessed as should the period over which the finance will be required. For example, the construction costs of a substantial development are likely to be incurred by way of stage payments over a period of time while the construction is carried out and the cost to the developer of raising finance to meet these payments might be adjusted accordingly. One method of doing this is to take for this purpose a half of what would be the cost of financing the construction works over the whole of their period. One cost is the cost of acquiring, at the outset, the land which is being valued and the cost of finance should include the cost of financing this purchase.

14.60   As with other inputs relating to the overall costs of the development the date on which the expenditure is expected to be incurred by the developer is important. The cost should be deferred until the date on which it is likely to be incurred. Where costs are likely to be payable in stages over a period, such as under interim certificates issued by an architect in most standard forms of building contracts, a practice sometimes adopted is to defer the costs to a date half way through the assumed period of the construction. Computer programmes allow a choice of payment regimes, one commonly adopted being known as an 'S' curve.

4. The Third Category of Inputs

14.61   The third category of inputs, and a critical factor in the whole exercise, is the percentage required as a developer's profit. This can be regarded as the ninth major input. Obviously the purpose of a developer in acquiring the land being valued and carrying out the development is to make a profit at the end of it, that is to end up with a sum which exceeds the whole of his costs including the initial cost of acquiring the land to be developed. This component of the valuation is put into effect by adding a percentage to the whole of the costs of the developer. Those costs will include the cost of acquiring the land being valued in the first place and the various items of costs which have just been outlined. The percentage profit which a developer would require in order to acquire the land and carry out the project of development is a matter for the judgement of a valuer. The amount of profit which a developer would require would in part depend on the degree of risk which he was taking in carrying out the project. A development project has within it certain inherent risks. One is obviously the risk that the rents obtained on the letting of the developed property and the price on its ultimate sale are less than estimated. Market conditions can change in unpredictable ways over the period of a development and before the time comes for the letting or disposal of the developed property. Time itself is a risk affecting many of the inputs. There can be overruns in time and a resultant increase in costs for which the developer may have to bear the burden, matters which again cannot be predicted or estimated at the stage at which the residual valuation is carried out. Residual valuations are carried out by developers and others and the valuer may find assistance in fixing the level of the required developer's profit by considering what level has been used in other valuations which have been a part of sales of land for development or of other arrangements. This is another point at which the use of comparables can play a part in a residual valuation.

While certain elements of risk, such as those just mentioned, are common to some degree   14.62
with most developments there may be other elements of risk which are particular to the development which is envisaged on the land being valued. If there exists a full planning permission, or an outline permission with approval of all reserved matters, and any planning agreements and other similar arrangements are in place, then risks attendant on those matters will not be present. On the other hand if there is still a need to obtain permission or other planning uncertainties exist then this may be something which substantially increases the risk and so the level of developer's profit. If the risks attendant on a particular project are very large or unusual in character and can be quantified, at least in general terms, it may be considered preferable to include in the valuation a more normal level of developer's profit such as would be attributable to a more normal project but then to make a further and specific deduction for uncertainty at the end of the process when deciding how much the land being valued would obtain if sold on the market for development. The valuer should always guard against double counting; he should not use some component of risk or uncertainty as a reason for increasing the level of developer's profit and then use that same matter as a reason for a final deduction for uncertainty or for some other adjustment to the inputs. For instance, if an unusually large allowance for contingencies is made in estimating the building costs because of some special uncertainty or risk perceived in the construction process the valuer should think carefully before using this same risk as something which justifies a higher rate of developer's profit than would normally apply to a project of the nature being evaluated.

There is often merit in undertaking a sensitivity analysis. A characteristic of development   14.63
appraisals is that they are sensitive to the inputs used. Testing the sensitivity of the appraisal by inputting changes to some key figures, such as rent, yield and construction costs, will sometimes help the valuer to arrive at an answer with which he will be more confident. The software programmes habitually used today include the capacity to adjust inputs or combinations of inputs in this way so that the task of sensitivity checks and weighing is relatively

straightforward. The checking of the residual valuation and the results it produces at various stages can also usefully be undertaken by referring back to comparable evidence. For example, the value per square foot of the completed development could be compared with actual sales per square foot of other investments.

14.64   It is plain from the account which has just been given that a residual valuation can be a complex exercise. It may be carried out with various degrees of detail. Thus a general estimate can be made of building costs derived from published figures for the cost of projects of the nature under consideration. On the other hand all projects are different and if the project was ever actually carried out it would be likely to be necessary to prepare some more detailed schedule of the works or fully itemised bills of quantities. One task of the valuer is to decide the level of detail into which he goes (perhaps assisted by others) on matters such as estimated costs when carrying out his valuation. The Lands Tribunal has protested against an unreasonable level of detail which adds greatly to the time and costs of a hearing, and this can be a further ground of complaint as to the use of residual valuations as a valuation technique. The principle which should guide the valuer in deciding on the level of detail in the valuation he prepares should be what he believes would be done by a purchaser of the property in the market. The underlying task of the valuer is to replicate as best he can what a hypothetical willing purchaser would do in the market. If a hypothetical willing purchaser would carry out a residual valuation, either because there are no comparables or as an adjunct to a valuation based on comparables, then the valuer may feel justified in himself carrying out a residual valuation in the same way. The level of detail which he employs should depend on his judgement of the level of detail which would be used in a residual valuation carried out by, or on behalf of, the hypothetical willing purchaser.

14.65   At the end of this process the calculation, or the computer programme used to effect the calculation, will provide a value which is the residual value of the land being valued. It is this value which is the estimated open market value of the land and which provides its value for the purposes of assessing compensation under rule (2) of section 5 of the 1961 Act.

14.66   An example of a residual valuation with a further explanation of the various steps within it is included as the third example in section (d) of the Appendix.

(D) PROFITS VALUATIONS

1. The Nature of the Process

14.67   The essence of a profits valuation is that the value of land is found with the assistance of an estimate of the profits that can be expected to be made from activities, usually of course business or commercial activities, to be carried out on the land. It is important to be clear at the outset that the purpose is not to value the business but to gain an indication from the profits anticipated to be made from the business of what a willing buyer would pay to acquire the land in order to be able to use it to make those profits. This method of valuation is most frequently used when there is an existing business on the land acquired and being valued since the future net profits can be estimated from records of past profits. In principle the method can also be used when, apart from the compulsory acquisition, it is anticipated that a new business could be commenced on the land. The value of a business and the value of the land on which the business can be carried out are by no means necessarily the same.[29]

Profits valuations are sometimes carried out when ascertaining the rental value of property.   14.68 The process then used is to estimate the annual net profits of a business, in substance the excess of annual gross receipts over costs taking account of such matters as the depreciation of assets, and then to reason that the landlord and tenant would agree to divide the annual net profit between them with the landlord's share being the rent payable to him in return for the grant of the lease. Calculations of this nature can be used in determining the rent to be paid under leases particularly of premises in the leisure and entertainment fields such as restaurants, pubs, hotels and cinemas. The same technique can be used to determine rents on rent reviews. A similar technique is also sometimes used in valuations for rating purposes in the absence of comparable transactions. The Lands Tribunal has indicated that valuations based on comparables are to be preferred to profits valuations where satisfactory comparables are available.[30] The reason, as with residual valuations, is that profits valuations are dependent on a number of factors which may be in dispute and which are difficult to assess accurately such as the expected level of future profits, or the correct multiplier to apply to the estimated profits, or the discount rate to be used in a discounted cash flow analysis.[31]

2. The Profits Multiplier

Where it comes to an assessment of the capital value of a property which has been acquired,   14.69 when using the profits method of valuation the simplest method of proceeding is to make a reasonable estimate of the anticipated future annual profits and to apply to that estimate a multiplier so as to arrive at a capital sum for the value of the loss of those profits. Where there is an existing business at the property, which will usually be the case, the amount of the anticipated future profits can be ascertained by looking at records of past profits and by taking an average of those profits over a reasonable period in the past, say three years. It is necessary to be careful that there are no special circumstances which apply to one or more of these years which would not operate in the future since otherwise the record of historical profits might give a distorted view of what could be expected in the future. Once the average annual net profits have been so ascertained a multiplier is applied to the average so as to find the capital value of those profits as anticipated to be earned in the future, and thus to assist in finding the value of the land acquired having regard to the extinguishment of the business and the availability of the profits. The difficulty, of course, is to find the appropriate multiplier. This topic has been considered in relation to disturbance payments under section 37 of the Land Compensation Act 1973[32] but the process is one which can be applied generally to a profits valuation used in an assessment of the value of the land acquired. The important factors are the period of years in the future over which the profits are anticipated to be earned and the strength or likelihood of the anticipation of those profits being earned over that period. The longer the period and the stronger the anticipation of the profits

---

[29] See section (h) of ch 4.
[30] *Snook v Somerset County Council* [2005] 1 EGLR 147.
[31] See paras 14.71 et seq for discounted cash flow analyses.
[32] See ch 12, para 12.22.

being earned the higher will be the multiplier. Conversely the shorter the period and the greater the risk as to whether or not the profits will be earned the lower will be the multiplier. This is a crude and imprecise process but is one often used and in smaller cases can give a speedy and acceptable result. As always it must be understood that the result achieved by the ascertainment of the rate of likely profits and the application of a multiplier to that rate is something which provides a value for the loss of the profits in question caused by the compulsory acquisition. It does not necessarily provide the value of the land on which those profits will be earned by way of a business carried out on that land. Little further guidance can be given as to the multiplier and this is a matter for the judgement of an individual valuer or accountant informed, where that is possible, by the rate of multiplier which has been used in other cases.[33]

14.70 An approach similar in concept where a property is being valued by, or by reference to, its capacity to earn profits from a business carried on at the property is the use of a prices/earnings (a P/E) ratio. The P/E ratio is the numerical relationship of the total value of the shares of a company (the capitalisation value of the company or the price per share multiplied by the number of shares) and the annual earnings or profits of the company. If the company carried on its business solely on a particular piece of land the application of the P/E ratio might give an indication of the value of that land. It is necessary to be careful about what exactly is meant by earnings. One basis of assessment of earnings is the EBITDA basis (earnings before interest, tax, depreciation and amortisation).[34]

3. Discounted Cash Flow Analyses

14.71 A discounted cash flow (DCF) analysis proceeds by an estimate of the net profits likely to be made over a series of future years. In order to carry out the process it is necessary to estimate revenues and costs for each year. When land is compulsorily acquired the business which generates the net profits is often an existing business so that future revenues and costs can be estimated from past records. When an amount of net profit has been attributed to each future year that amount for each year is discounted back to a base year, usually the valuation date. The discounted sums are then aggregated to produce a present value (or PV) at the base year of an anticipated stream of future profits. It is possible that in some future years a loss rather than a profit will be anticipated, perhaps because of a particular item of expenditure which will inevitably fall in some years, in which case the amount of the discounted loss for that year will be included in the estimate of the present value. That value may then be described as the net present value (or NPV). An example and an explanation of a DCF analysis and valuation are provided as the fourth example in section (e) of the Appendix.

14.72 It is apparent that there are three components in the carrying out of a DCF analysis. First, the number of years over which the profits (or exceptionally losses) are expected to be made must be determined. Secondly, the amount of the anticipated profit or loss for each future year during this period must be estimated. Thirdly, an appropriate discount rate must be

---

[33] See the observations of the then President of the Lands Tribunal, Sir Douglas Frank QC, in *Clibbett Ltd v Avon County Council* (1975) 16 RVR 131.

[34] This matter is discussed in *Optical Express (Southern) Ltd v Birmingham City Council* [2005] 2 EGLR 141.

applied to the profit or loss in each future year so as to bring it back to a value at the base year.[35]

The period over which the analysis takes place is a consequence of the nature of the interest   14.73
in land being valued and of the nature of the business to be carried out on that land. If a leasehold interest is being valued then the analysis will be carried out over the unexpired residue of the lease. In the case of leases which are protected by Part II of the Landlord and Tenant Act 1954 statute provides that the expectation of a new lease being granted under the provisions of the Act is to be taken into account.[36] The business which generates the profits may be such that it has a finite life, for example a right to extract sand and gravel clearly has a life determined by the amount of sand and gravel available for extraction and the annual rate of extraction anticipated. There may be some other factor which limits the anticipated period over which profits can be expected to be earned, for example the expiration of a planning permission if there is no prospect of its renewal. It should be noted that the expectation of the renewal of a lease by agreement and other than under a statutory provision giving a right to renewal probably cannot be taken into account in assessing compensation and so must be ignored in a DCF analysis.[37] Of course, the longer the period of the discounted cash flow, the more discounted are the future profits or losses in the later years of the period and so, when discounted back to the base date, the lesser the impact of the flows in those years. In general terms the first 10 years are the years which have the greatest impact on the present day capital value of anticipated future profits as described later.

The second component, the amount of future annual profits (or losses), is of course a mat-   14.74
ter for a valuer or an accountant to estimate. All elements of future cost should be included, examples being the burden of replacing physical assets, or a duty which may arise under planning conditions or from some other source to carry out restoration or remediation work to land. Obviously an estimate must be made of the year in which such future burdens will come into effect since when a discount rate is used the year in which a particular burden falls will be an important factor in leading to the end result. The burden of having to replace physical assets such as plant and machinery in future years may be reflected in the costs by including an annual sum for the depreciation of the asset. A process often used is 'straight line' depreciation. For instance, if a piece of machinery costing £150,000 is estimated to have a life of 15 years with no residual value at the end, the annual sum for depreciation will be £10,000. In reality, of course, depreciation may not occur by equal annual sums and the machinery may need replacement at an earlier date.

The third component, the discount rate, is often the most contentious. A discount rate   14.75
determines the value today of receiving a specified sum of money at some specified future date. A person may be willing to pay £100 today for the certainty of receiving £100 today.

[35] *Director of Buildings and Lands v Shun Fung Ironworks Ltd* [1995] 2 AC 111, [1995] 2 WLR 904, per Lord Nicholls at p 132.
[36] Ch 4, paras 4.100 et seq. It may therefore be correct in such a case to assess the profits as likely to be earned even after the contractual expiry date of the current lease but account should be taken: (a) of the possibility that no new lease will be granted because the landlord may be able to resist the grant of a new lease by showing that he intends to redevelop the property or on some other ground available to him under s 30 of the Landlord and Tenant Act 1954, and (b) of the fact that on the grant of a new lease the rent will be adjusted to the open market rental value at the time.
[37] See ch 4, para 4.99.

He will certainly not pay £100 today for the right or expectation of receiving £100 in three years time (at least in the absence of anticipated currency deflation). The reasons are obvious, namely: (a) that the person receiving the £100 will not have the use of it, and the ability to invest it, during the three years, (b) that there must be some degree of doubt as to whether the sum, or the whole of it, will actually be received at the end of the three years, and (c) that the sum paid as a nominal sum of £100 at the end of the three years will have a reduced real value because of the impact of inflation and a drop in the value of money over the three years. The discount rate is therefore set by taking into account these three factors and so translates the amount that is to be received in a future year into an amount which represents the value at the base year of the right to receive that amount in the specified future year. The higher the discount rate the lower will be the value at the base year of the right to receive the specified amount at the specified future year. For example, a right to receive £100 in seven years time at a discount rate of 5 per cent is worth £71.06 today. The right to receive the same sum at the same time at a 15 per cent discount rate is worth £37.59 today. Because of the reduction in the present value of a right to receive a sum of money in future years the amount anticipated to be received in the early years of the analysis is much more important to the amount of the present value than the amount anticipated to be received in later years when the effect of the discounting, particularly if a high discount rate is used, will mean that the present value of sums receivable at later years substantially into the future becomes less significant.[38]

14.76   Because of the reducing effect on the present value of sums anticipated to be received in later future years the carrying out of the analysis may sometimes be truncated at a particular year. To take an extreme example, the value today of the right to receive £100 after 99 years at a discount rate of 10 per cent is the very small sum of £0.007. If the analysis is truncated at a particular future year for this reason it is sometimes possible to estimate a specific amount which represents at that future year the right to receive the income over future years from that year and then to discount that specific amount back to the base year.

14.77   As just mentioned there are three reasons why the right to receive a sum of money at a future time is of less value than the right to receive that same sum of money immediately. It is these same three factors which determine the level of the discount rate. The process of determining a discount rate by reference to these factors is the same as that of determining the interest which a lender of money or an investor would require for lending or investing money repayable at a fixed future time, for instance a purchaser of corporate bonds.

   (i)   The first of the three determinants is the risk free rate. If a sum of money is to be received as a matter of right at a future year and there is a total certainty that it will be so received then (ignoring inflation) the only reason for reducing the present value of that right to a level below the value of the sum of money itself is that it will not be received until that future year so that the person entitled to receive it loses the use of it over that period. The person entitled to receive the money could have invested it in a risk free investment if it had been receivable today and not at a future date. The return available for risk free investments can be derived from published financial data at the time when the valuation is being made or from past records of such data. In strict theory no investment is wholly risk free. The nearest approxima-

---

[38] See the example given in the next paragraph.

tion to a risk free investment is said to be an investment in government bonds issued by stable governments, for example US treasury bonds or British 'gilts' or bonds issued by the German or Swiss Government. The return on such risk free or nearly risk free investments can be found from data published daily. This element of the discount rate can be called the usury rate since it represents no more than a return for money lent ignoring any compensation to the lender for risk or inflation. It is possible for the usury rate to be nil, or even negative, in volatile circumstances, such as those which existed during the worst of the economic crisis following the collapse of Lehman Brothers on 15 September 2008. At times of economic uncertainty the risk free rate is likely to be low since investors may seek bonds issued by stable governments as a safe haven for their investments so that such governments can borrow money by issuing bonds at low rates of interest.

(ii) The second factor is the additional rate of return, or the additional rate of discount, required for the risk that the sum in question will not be paid, or paid in full, at the stipulated future year. Plainly the critical matter in determining the level of this risk and this component of the discount rate is the riskiness of the business enterprise in question. Sophisticated techniques have been developed for making the whole or a part of this estimate. The extra risk which is involved, and so the extra return required, for investing in equities, that is predominantly ordinary shares, can be found from records of past returns that have been obtained from investments in equities. This additional factor may be called the equity risk premium. Another concept employed is the beta coefficient which is a measure of the volatility in the value of the shares in a particular company compared with the average volatility of shares quoted on a particular stock exchange or market such as the London Stock Exchange or the alternative investment market (AIM). The average volatility is taken as 1 so that a beta of 1.3 for a company would mean that its shares were more volatile than the average. The greater volatility is considered to represent a greater risk and so to justify an increased discount rate. It is beyond the scope of this book to comment on these techniques in any detail. They involve the use of such processes as the weighted average cost of capital and capital asset pricing models. In most cases it is this second factor in the determination of the discount rate which brings about the largest component of the total rate. It is also a factor which is most likely to be a major cause of dispute in DCF valuations.

(iii) The third factor is the risk of inflation. Here an estimate has to be made of the likely future rate of inflation over the period of the DCF analysis. Discount rates are calculated as real or monetary discount rates depending on whether the anticipated annual stream of future profits is itself adjusted for the impact of an anticipated rate of future inflation.

Discounted cash flow analyses have other uses besides that of an adjunct to the valuation of   14.78
land. They can be used to compare the comparative economic viability or attractions of different projects. For example, in a decision whether to construct further gas fired power stations as opposed to nuclear installations a DCF analysis may be useful in comparing the low initial construction costs but high fuel and running costs of a gas fired station as against the high initial costs but low fuel and running costs of a nuclear power station.

The remaining question to consider is the role which a DCF analysis can properly play in   14.79
the valuation of land. The use of such an analysis was considered and explained in *Director*

of Lands v Shun Fung Ironworks Ltd,[39] an appeal to the Privy Council from Hong Kong, where the purpose of the agreed use of the DCF process was to assess business loss under a specific Hong Kong Ordinance which provided compensation for such a loss. There was in that decision no issue, and thus no consideration, of the use of a DCF analysis as a means of valuing land.

14.80   Plainly the value of a piece of land may be strongly influenced by a commercial use which can be carried out, or continued to be carried out, on the land and by the expected level of profit from that use. Nonetheless when good evidence of comparable transactions is available it will be infrequent that a DCF analysis will provide a good indicator of the value of land. Two identical shops might be being sold and their value might be capable of being assessed on the basis of good comparables. It is unlikely that the value of one shop will be significantly increased above that of the other because the purchaser of the first shop intends to carry out a form of retail trade which will bring in more profits than the retail trade to which the other shop is to be put. On the other hand where comparables are scarce, or in an extreme case where there are no comparables, a DCF analysis may provide a much stronger indication of the value of land. What is wrong in principle for present purposes is to suppose that the land has one value and that there is some additional value of a business which may be carried out on the land. The truth is that the main function of a valuation for compensation for compulsory purchase is to find the value of the land acquired under rule (2) of section 5 of the Land Compensation Act 1961 and not to find the value of a business or to find the worth of the land to its owner as opposed to the value of the land in the market. These matters, which are more matters of legal principle and valuation concept, are examined in greater detail in chapter 4 where the concept of the value of land as the primary component of compensation is considered.[40]

(E) DEPRECIATED REPLACEMENT COST VALUATIONS

14.81   A valuation by way of depreciated replacement cost (DRC) is something of a last resort and is unlikely to find favour where a valuation by using comparable transactions is possible. The nature of a DRC valuation is that: (a) the present day cost of constructing structures on the land is estimated, and (b) a deduction is applied to that cost to take account of the fact that usually the actual structures on the land are not new, may be in need of repair or maintenance or improvement, and may for various reasons be to a degree obsolete for present purposes. The first part of the process may be carried out with reasonable precision on the basis of publications which indicate the cost of construction. The second part of the process is more debatable. In addition the methodology omits a number of factors which are important to value, such as the location and convenience of the land and its means of access, unless further specific adjustments are made to take account of these matters.

---

[39] *Director of Lands v Shun Fung Ironworks Ltd* [1995] 2 AC 111, [1995] 2 WLR 904.
[40] See section (h) of ch 4.

(F) OTHER VALUATION METHODS

As mentioned earlier no rational method of valuation can be excluded as a matter of law. It   14.82
is a matter for the judgement of valuers in any individual case whether to use any particular
method or series of methods. On occasions entries in the rating valuation list may be of use.
The rateable value of properties (now only commercial properties since residential properties are subject to the payment of the council tax) is intended to be the rental value of the
property on the assumption of an annual tenancy as at the rating valuation date. In England
and Wales rateable values have in the recent past been revised at five yearly intervals. The
entry into the valuation list prepared at the beginning of the five year period is assessed by
reference to values at a date two years earlier, called the antecedent valuation date. The law
and practice of rating has produced its own techniques of valuation engendered in part by
the fact that for certain types of property there is no evidence, or virtually no evidence, of
any actual lettings of the type of property being valued let alone lettings on the basis of an
annual periodic tenancy. One such approach to rating valuations, the contractor's test, is
much the same as the depreciated replacement cost type of valuation described under the
immediately preceding section of this chapter. The profits method is also sometimes used.
Valuations for the purposes of assessing compensation may be assisted by entries in the
valuation list although it must be remembered that those entries are rental values, that they
are rental values on the basis of an assumed annual tenancy which is something not
frequently found in commercial properties, and that the valuation is by reference to a particular date, the antecedent valuation date as just mentioned. The purpose of a hypothetical
valuation is to replicate, so far as possible, that which would have occurred in a real sale of
the property being valued at the valuation date. Since petrol filling stations are often sold by
reference to a price per unit of petrol sold that method of valuation was used in valuing
such a property when it was compulsorily acquired,[41] and this illustrates that in principle
the varieties of valuation techniques which may be used are not closed. A further example
is that property used as a casino might be valued by reference to 'the drop', that is the
amount of money wagered by customers over a given period of time.

Where a substantial amount of property in an area is being acquired for the purposes of a   14.83
major scheme, settlements of the amount of compensation payable for properties acquired
may form a valuable guide to the correct amount of compensation in other and later cases.
A difficulty is that although the amount of a settlement may be known the way in which the
parties arrived at that settlement may be less easy to ascertain. It is always open to a party in
a later valuation and claim to contend that the settlement of an earlier claim for compensation proceeded on some wrong method of law or principle, or in ignorance of certain
relevant facts, and so is for that reason of little utility as a guide to the value of land in a later
case. Of course a determination of the Lands Tribunal in an earlier decided case can be
included in the overall body of relevant evidence but such a decision may not rank high in
the hierarchy of useful evidence since it is not evidence derived from the result of an actual
transaction in the market, and is not even evidence of what valuers have agreed would have
been done in the market. A decision is at best a conclusion reached on the basis of what
different valuers have stated in evidence they think would have happened in the market.

---

[41] *Telegraph Service Stations Ltd v Trafford BC* [2000] EGLR 145.

There is an inevitable cost and delay and risk to a claimant in referring his claim to the Lands Tribunal and claimants, especially those with small claims, may prefer to take the compensation offered to them rather than incur the risks and burdens of litigation. The result may be a number of settlements of compensation affected by these factors and it may be contended before the Tribunal that the evidential value of such settlements is thereby reduced.[42]

---

[42] This effect is called the 'Delaforce' effect after the decision of the Tribunal regarding references under the Leasehold Reform Act 1967 in *Delaforce v Evans* (1970) 22 P & CR 770, in which it was discussed. Cf *Lewicki v Noneaton & Bedworth BC* [2013] UKUT (LC) 0120, [2013] RVR 196.

15

Procedure

(A) INTRODUCTION

A pivotal position in the procedure for claiming and assessing compensation is occupied by   15.1
the Lands Chamber of the Upper Tribunal. This court was first established by the Lands
Tribunal Act 1949 as the Lands Tribunal and replaced the former official arbitrators, and
before that juries, magistrates and arbitrators, who determined claims for compensation
and similar matters. The Lands Tribunal has extensive other jurisdiction relating to land
including the hearing of rating appeals, the hearing of applications for the discharge or
modification of restrictive covenants under section 84 of the Law of Property Act 1925, the
determination of issues under the Leasehold Reform Act 1967 and later legislation on
the same subject, the determination of claims for compensation for mining subsidence and
the determination of some procedural matters relating to rights to light. The Tribunals,
Courts and Enforcement Act 2007 brought about a reorganisation of tribunals in England
and Wales. Most tribunals are today organised into two tiers called the Upper Tribunal and
the Lower Tribunal and each tier is divided into a number of chambers. The Lands Tribunal
became the Lands Chamber of the Upper Tribunal and that remains its official and proper
designation today. The transfer of jurisdiction to the Lands Chamber was in June 2009. A
frequent practice among practitioners remains to call the Lands Chamber by its former
name of the Lands Tribunal and that practice is generally adopted in this book.

The jurisdiction, powers and procedure of the Lands Tribunal are derived from six main   15.2
sources. (a) The Lands Tribunal Act 1949 established the Tribunal and conferred on it jurisdiction to determine disputed claims for compensation for compulsory purchase. (b) A
number of provisions within the legislation on compensation confer a specific jurisdiction
on the Tribunal to determine particular components of compensation. All main heads of
compensation are covered by these provisions.[1] (c) A series of other statutory provisions

---

[1] (a) Section 1 of the Land Compensation Act 1961 states that where under any statute land is authorised to be
acquired compulsorily any question of disputed compensation shall be referred to the Lands Tribunal.
(b) Section 6 of the Compulsory Purchase Act 1965 states that where a person has been served with a notice
to treat and the compensation is not agreed the question of the disputed compensation shall be referred
to the Lands Tribunal. A notice to treat includes the deemed notice to treat which arises from the making
of a general vesting declaration.
(c) Section 10 of the Compulsory Purchase Act 1965 states that any dispute relating to claims for compensation
for injurious affection under that section shall be referred to the Lands Tribunal.
(d) Section 16(1) of the Land Compensation Act 1973 states that any question of disputed compensation
under Pt I of that Act (compensation for depreciation in the value of land due to the use of public works)
shall be referred to the Lands Tribunal.
(e) Section 38(4) of the Land Compensation Act 1973 states that any dispute as to the amount of a disturbance
payment shall be referred to the Lands Tribunal.

confer other land related areas of jurisdiction on the Tribunal, for example claims for compensation for mining subsidence. This jurisdiction is outside the scope of this book. (d) The powers and procedure of the Tribunal, as a part of the Upper Tribunal, were extended or altered by the Tribunals, Courts and Enforcement Act 2007. In particular the categories of persons who could sit as members of the Tribunal were extended and subject to the making of a Ministerial order the Tribunal was given a power of judicial review. (e) The Tribunal has its own procedural rules, the Tribunal Procedure (Upper Tribunal) (Lands Chamber) Rules 2010.[2] These Rules govern the general procedure in the Tribunal and some are of particular application to claims for compensation. (f) There are Practice Directions of the Tribunal, issued on 29 November 2010, which amplify and explain the practice and procedure adopted by the Tribunal in exercising its various areas of jurisdiction.[3] Some of the directions are general and others are more specifically directed to the determination of compensation claims.

15.3   The Tribunal consists of a President, who has always been a lawyer, and a number of other members. The President for some years was Mr George Bartlett QC who on his retirement in 2012 was replaced by Lindblom J. It was announced in May 2013 that a Deputy President had been appointed and he is currently Mr Martin Rodger QC. There are currently three other members who are qualified surveyors. Since the reconstitution of the Tribunal as the Lands Chamber of the Upper Tribunal by the Tribunals, Courts and Enforcement Act 2007 all Judges of the High Court and Lords Justices of Appeal have been entitled to sit as members of the Tribunal although this appears rarely to have happened. Those who sit in the Tribunal are generally described as the President, the Deputy President, judge or member. The general administration of the Tribunal is conducted under the supervision of the President by a Registrar who also deals with certain decisions on procedural matters subject to a right of appeal to the President. A practice statement issued on 29 November 2010 under rule 4 of the Tribunal Procedure (Upper Tribunal) (Lands Chamber) Rules 2010[4] provides that many functions of the Tribunal may be carried out by the Registrar subject to the right of a party within 14 days of receiving notice of the decision to apply for the decision of the Registrar to be considered afresh by a judge. Under this procedure the Registrar may exercise the general case management powers of the Tribunal under rule 5 of the Rules. Other persons may be appointed to hear particular proceedings before the Tribunal and currently certain circuit court judges exercise that function. The Tribunal sits in London at

(f) Section 30(3) of the Land Compensation Act 1973 states that any dispute as to certain valuation matters needed to assess a home loss payment is to be determined by the Lands Tribunal.

(g) Section 33I(1) of the Land Compensation Act 1973 states that any dispute as to the amount of a basic loss or occupier's loss payment is to be determined by the Lands Tribunal.

The seven main heads of compensation are summarised in section (b) of ch 3. In addition the legislation provides that certain specific matters which may arise in the course of a compulsory purchase are to be determined by the Lands Tribunal in default of agreement. These additional areas of jurisdiction are noted when the relevant topics are described. Examples are the assessment of the compensation which may be due to a landowner when a notice to treat served on him is withdrawn (see section (j) of ch 2), the question of whether an acquiring authority which proposes to acquire a part of a person's land can be compelled to acquire the whole of his land (see section (b) of ch 9), arrangements between a mortgagor, a mortgagee and the acquiring authority (see section (m) of ch 2), and, as a recent addition under the Localism Act 2011 to the jurisdiction of the Tribunal, the hearing of appeals against decisions of local planning authorities on applications for certificates of appropriate alternative development (see section (d) of ch 7).

[2] Tribunal Procedure (Upper Tribunal) (Lands Chamber) Rules 2010 (SI 2010/2600).

[3] 'Tribunals Judiciary. Practice Directions. Lands Chamber of the Upper Tribunal', 29 November 2010.

[4] Tribunal Procedure (Upper Tribunal) (Lands Chamber) Rules 2010 (SI 2010/2600).

premises in Bedford Square and hearings are conducted there and at other locations throughout the country. Many cases not involving complex issues of law are decided by a single surveyor member. Cases involving legal issues are more likely to be allocated to the President, who may sit alone or with one or more surveyor members, or to the Deputy President or one of the circuit court judges who sit as members from time to time. More detailed aspects of the procedure before the Tribunal in compensation claims are explained later in this chapter. There are equivalent Lands Tribunals who decide disputed questions of compensation for compulsory purchase in other jurisdictions, for example the Scottish Lands Tribunal, the Northern Ireland Lands Tribunal, and the Hong Kong Lands Tribunal, and important decisions on the law of compensation in England and Wales originated or were concluded in these Tribunals.[5]

The Lands Tribunal has power to determine the amount of compensation payable for the compulsory acquisition of land and compensation in other cases of a similar nature where no land is acquired. It also has power to decide on whether a claimant is entitled to compensation at all.[6] This power may lead to the Tribunal having to decide questions such as the title to, or interest in, the land acquired held by a claimant for compensation. It has no general powers in connection with the operation of a compulsory purchase. If a landowner is unwilling to comply with his statutory obligations under the legislation, such as by refusing to allow an authority entry to survey the land or to provide information, the remedy of the authority is to seek an injunction in the High Court or the County Court. Should an acquiring authority refuse to comply with its obligations, for instance by refusing to make an assessment of the compensation and to make an advance payment on the basis of that assessment or by refusing to pay interest on compensation as prescribed by statute, the remedy of a landowner would also be through the ordinary courts, possibly in the first case by seeking an order for judicial review. In the unlikely event of the compensation having been settled by a decision of the Tribunal and the acquiring authority not paying it the means of enforcing payment would be by recovery of the sum determined as payable as though it was a sum payable under an order of the High Court or of the County Court.[7]   15.4

There is a right of appeal from the Lands Tribunal to the Court of Appeal with permission of one or other court, and ultimately the possibility of an appeal to the Supreme Court. The appellate procedure is explained later.[8]   15.5

The Lands Tribunal is also entitled, though not bound, to act as an arbitrator to settle disputes. The general practice of the Tribunal is to accept an appointment as an arbitrator when the subject matter of the arbitration is that which, had there not been an agreement to arbitrate, would have been within the ordinary jurisdiction of the Tribunal. It not infrequently occurs that instead of an acquiring authority acquiring land compulsorily the land is acquired by agreement, but with a provision that the price is to be equal to the amount of the compensation which would have been payable if the acquisition had been compulsory. Such agreements often provide that in the absence of agreement on the price it shall be   15.6

---

[5] Eg a leading case on the assessment of compensation for disturbance loss is *Director of Lands v Shun Fung Ironworks Ltd* [1995] 2 AC 111, [1995] 1 All ER 846, a decision of the Privy Council which started in the Lands Tribunal in Hong Kong. The current law on compensation for losses incurred by a landowner prior to the acquisition of the land results from the adoption by English courts of decisions of the Scottish Lands Tribunal. See ch 8.

[6] *Union Rlys Ltd v Kent County Council* [2008] 2 EGLR 183.

[7] Tribunals, Courts and Enforcement Act 2007, s 27(1).

[8] See section (n) of this chapter.

determined by the Lands Tribunal acting as an arbitrator, and in cases of this nature the general practice of the Tribunal is to accept the position of an arbitrator. Where there are proceedings by consent of this type many of the general rules governing the procedure in the Tribunal and the Practice Directions of the Tribunal as well as certain of the provisions in the Arbitration Act 1996 apply to the reference by consent.[9]

15.7   This chapter explains the procedure to be used in making and pursuing a claim for compensation. It also explains two matters which are partly substantive and partly procedural, namely the making of an advance payment of compensation, including advance payments to mortgagees, before the final determination of the compensation and the payment of interest on compensation.

(B) EVENTS PRIOR TO A REFERENCE

15.8   Proceedings before the Lands Tribunal to determine the amount of compensation are called a reference to the Tribunal. In many cases the process of the acquisition of land for public purposes, including agreement on and payment of the price, is completed by agreement and without the need for a reference. The normal course is that an authority which wishes to acquire land seeks to do so by agreement and the Secretary of State has indicated that he expects a full attempt to be made to acquire land by agreement before he is willing to confirm a compulsory purchase order.[10] If there is a single piece of land to be acquired the whole process may be concluded by agreement so that there is no need to initiate any compulsory purchase procedure. In larger cases where there is a diversity of areas of land and of ownership the acquiring authority may think it expedient to make a compulsory purchase order at an early stage over the whole of the land but that does not of course prevent subsequent negotiations for a sale by agreement. One reason for the making of a compulsory purchase order is that there may be land with uncertain title or persons with interests unknown to the acquiring authority and this situation can be dealt with more easily within the compulsory purchase procedure.[11] A general vesting declaration can be made which has the automatic effect of vesting interests in land within the area covered by the declaration in the acquiring authority.[12]

15.9   If compulsory purchase is necessary the acquiring authority must either serve a notice to treat or operate the general vesting declaration procedure which operates as a constructive notice to treat. A notice to treat is a document which has to state that the acquiring authority is willing to treat for the purchase of the land and as to the compensation to be made for the damage which may be sustained by reason of the execution of the works. The service or constructive service of a notice to treat has certain procedural consequences which are dealt with elsewhere but the obvious purpose of the notice is to initiate discussions as to the

---

[9] References by consent are discussed in section (o) of this chapter.

[10] Circular 06/2004, para 24.

[11] Another reason for the making of a comprehensive compulsory purchase order covering all land where there is not a binding agreement for its acquisition is that when it comes to determining the compensation the provisions in s 6 and Case 1 in sch 1 in the Land Compensation Act 1961 for disregarding the effect on value of certain development apply only to development of land within the area of the compulsory purchase order: see ch 5, sections (d) and (e), and see *Wilson v Liverpool City Council* [1971] 1 WLR 302, [1971] 1 All ER 628.

[12] See section (p) of ch 2.

compensation payable for the acquisition of the land if these have not already occurred.[13] Most acquiring authorities are willing to give informal advice to landowners and to meet them for informal discussions. Often the advice which is given is that the landowner should himself take professional valuation advice and, certainly in more complicated cases, legal advice as to his claim. It is usually explained to landowners that the reasonable costs of obtaining such advice are themselves claimable as an item of compensation. Often this process results in fruitful discussions and on an agreement being reached as to the price or compensation.

If and when there are disputed proceedings by way of a reference to the Lands Tribunal a   15.10 landowner may find himself penalised in costs if he has not presented a proper claim to the acquiring authority. The action required of a landowner is that he delivers to the acquiring authority, in time to enable it to make a proper offer, a notice in writing of the amount claimed by him containing certain particulars. The particulars are the exact nature of the interest in respect of which compensation is claimed and details of the compensation claimed distinguishing the amounts of compensation under separate heads and showing how the amount claimed under each head is calculated. Different heads of compensation include the value of the land acquired, any injurious affection to other land retained by the owner, and any claim for disturbance or other compensation under rule (6) of section 5 of the Land Compensation Act 1961. Owners of land should remember that the costs of presenting such a claim, providing they are reasonable in nature and amount, are normally claimable as a part of the compensation under rule (6) of section 5 of the Land Compensation Act 1961.[14] A failure to give proper notice in good time of a claim can result in adverse consequences in costs for a landowner if his claim cannot be agreed and is referred to the Lands Tribunal. This matter is explained later in this chapter.[15] The service of a notice to treat is important to the initiation of a reference to the Tribunal since no reference may be made earlier than one month after the date of service or constructive service of a notice to treat or, if no such notice is served or deemed to be served, earlier than one month of the notice of claim made by the claimant.[16]

It may occur that an acquiring authority makes a payment of compensation to a claimant   15.11 beyond that properly due as a result of an error by the authority. For example, the authority may believe that the claimant had an interest in the land which he did not have or may not have been aware of some encumbrance on the land, such as a restrictive covenant, which reduced its value. Where a general vesting declaration has been made under the Compulsory Purchase (Vesting Declarations) Act 1981 there is a statutory express provision which permits recovery of the compensation or the excess compensation in the circumstances just mentioned.[17] In other cases the authority may be able to recover the compensation agreed and paid by mistake under the general doctrine of the law of restitution that money paid under a mistake of fact or of law may be recovered.[18] It is, however, most unlikely that an acquiring authority would be able to recover money paid simply because it has made an error of judgement in its valuation, for example a misjudgement as to the significance of a comparable.

[13] See section (j) of ch 2.
[14] See section (d) of ch 8.
[15] See paras 15.128 and 15.129.
[16] Para 15.32.
[17] Compulsory Purchase (Vesting Declarations) Act 1981, s 11. See section (q) of ch 2.
[18] See Burrows, *The Law of Restitution*, 3rd edn (Oxford, Oxford University Press, 2010), ch 9.

(C) ADVANCE PAYMENTS

1. General Rules

15.12   A considerable time can pass between the date on which an acquiring authority takes possession of land and the date on which the compensation for the acquisition is agreed or
determined and then paid. Negotiations on the amount of the compensation, or even on
the question of an entitlement to an item of compensation, can take some time and the
conclusion of a reference to the Lands Tribunal, particularly in a complex case, is not likely
to be speedy. There is also the possibility of an appeal on law from the Tribunal. Interest is
payable on the amount of the compensation from the date of possession to the date of payment[19] but there could obviously be hardship if a dispossessed landowner did not receive
the capital sum due to him or any part of it for a period of years. In order to meet this
problem the Land Compensation Act 1973 introduced a scheme for the making of compulsory advance payments by the acquiring authority in certain circumstances.

15.13   A person entitled to compensation may make a request in writing for an advance payment.
The request must give particulars of the claimant's interest in the land acquired (so far as
not already given pursuant to a notice to treat) and has to be accompanied or supplemented
by such other particulars as the acquiring authority may reasonably require to enable it to
estimate the amount of the compensation.[20] Although an advance payment does not have
to be paid until the acquiring authority has taken possession of the land it seems that a valid
request for such a payment can be made in advance of possession being taken.[21]

15.14   When an acquiring authority has taken possession, and has received a request for an advance
payment, it is the duty of the authority to make that advance payment on account of the
compensation payable. If an authority has taken possession of a part of land in respect of
which a notice of entry has been given, or a payment into court has been made, the advance
payment is to be calculated by reference to the compensation payable for the acquisition of
the interest in the whole of the land.[22] There is no specific procedure for challenging the
estimate of the compensation made by an acquiring authority. If an authority refuses to
make a genuine estimate of the compensation, or refuses to make a payment, the performance of the duty could be enforced by an application for the general remedy of judicial
review as available in administrative law to control the actions of public bodies. A difficulty
in such a course might be that the obtaining of permission to apply for judicial review and,
in a contested case, the hearing of the application itself are not usually quick processes and
may not achieve the desired result of an early receipt of an advance payment or of a properly assessed advance payment. In practice if the decision of the acquiring authority not to
make an advance payment is because of an issue of legal or valuation principle between the

---

[19] See section (d) of this chapter.
[20] Land Compensation Act 1973, s 52(2). In the remainder of the notes to this section of this chapter the Land
Compensation Act 1973 is described as LCA 1973.
[21] This is inherent in s 52(4) of the LCA 1973 dealing with the date of payment, which contemplates that a request
may be made before possession is taken by the acquiring authority. The date for payment is stated in para 5.16.
[22] LCA 1973, s 52(1), (1A), (1B). The giving of notice of entry and the payment into court of the estimated
compensation are methods available to the acquiring authority for obtaining possession of the land before the
compensation is paid: see section (k) of ch 2.

parties there is little that a claimant can do except to pursue his claim for the full amount before the Lands Tribunal.

The amount of an advance payment is 90 per cent of the amount of the compensation if the   15.15 claimant and the acquiring authority have agreed the amount. In any other case it is 90 per cent of the amount estimated as the compensation by the acquiring authority.[23] An acquiring authority is, of course, required to make a genuine estimate of the compensation on the basis of proper consideration and advice. To do so the authority may be dependent on information supplied by the landowner. Claimants are therefore well advised to provide full particulars of their claim as soon as possible and are well advised to answer as fully as possible queries put to them by the acquiring authority.

The acquiring authority is required to make the advance payment by the later of three   15.16 months from the making of the request for the payment and the date when possession is taken.[24] This can cause difficulty for an acquiring authority which has received a request for an advance payment but, despite seeking it, has inadequate information to make a realistic estimate of the compensation or of components of the compensation due. For instance, a claim may be made for compensation under rule (6) of section 5 of the Land Compensation Act 1961, that is for compensation for disturbance, but the acquiring authority may have no means of establishing the amount of the claim without information which may be available only to the claimant. Where the component of the compensation involved is the value of an interest in land acquired an estimate may be easier but even so an acquiring authority may be dependent on information provided by a claimant such as the rents receivable for a property. An acquiring authority can scarcely make a reasonable estimate of the likely compensation, and can scarcely be required to make an advance payment, unless it has a reasonable amount of information when it has sought it. On the other hand if an estimate can be made of components of the compensation, or an estimate can be made of the minimum amount of compensation likely to be payable, an acquiring authority which receives a request for an advance payment should make a payment on the basis of the best estimate it can make with the possibility of a later and further payment as further information becomes available. The compensation for which an advance payment is to be made under these provisions is the compensation payable under section 7 of the Compulsory Purchase Act 1965, namely the value of the land acquired, compensation for disturbance, and compensation for injurious affection to land retained by the claimant, and does not extend to additional statutory payments such as a basic loss payment under Part III of the Land Compensation Act 1973 as to which special provisions for the making of advance payments apply.[25] When land is settled land under the Settled Land Act 1925 the advance payment should be made to the person entitled to give a discharge for capital money under the terms of the settlement and the legislation.[26] The advance payment provisions apply to the acquisition of rights over land as they apply to the acquisition of corporeal interests in land with any necessary modifications and as if references to taking possession of land were references to entering the land to exercise the rights acquired.[27]

[23] LCA 1973, s 52(3).
[24] Ibid, s 52(4).
[25] For these additional payments see ch 11. The special provisions for advance payments on these sums are described in para 15.20 and in ch 11.
[26] LCA 1973, s 52(7).
[27] Ibid, s 52(12). The provisions for making advance payments to mortgagees do not apply where rights over land are acquired: see para 15.24(i).

15.17   An advance payment of compensation is only on account of the compensation which will become payable when that compensation has been finally agreed or determined. Consequently if the compensation as finally agreed or determined is less than the advance payment made the excess must be repaid by the recipient of the advance payment to the acquiring authority. Equally if an advance payment is made to a person and it is later discovered that he was not entitled to it the amount of the payment is recoverable by the acquiring authority from that person.[28]

15.18   It may occur that a person to whom an advance payment has been made subsequently disposes of his interest in the land or creates a new interest in the land in favour of someone other than the acquiring authority. A purchaser of land in such circumstances needs to be aware that an advance payment has been made. Consequently an acquiring authority, before it makes an advance payment in respect of an interest in land, must deposit with the council of the district or London borough in which the land is situated particulars of the payment to be made and the compensation and the interest in land to which it relates. The particulars deposited are a local land charge for the purposes of the Local Land Charges Act 1975. A prospective purchaser of the land can find out that the advance payment has been made and can find out particulars of it by searching the local land charges register. The amount of the advance payment can then be set off by the local authority against any compensation payable by that authority to a person to whom the disposal of the interest in land has been made or in favour of whom the new interest has been created.[29] A person who has received a notice to treat is still entitled to dispose of his land. However the rule explained in this paragraph may be of limited practical effect since normally an advance payment will not be made until possession of the land has been taken by the acquiring authority and it is unlikely that a landowner will dispose of his title to the land being acquired after possession has been taken from him.

15.19   One of the procedures by which an acquiring authority can gain title to the land acquired is by tendering or paying into court the amount of the compensation agreed or awarded and then executing a deed poll which vests the land absolutely in the authority.[30] Where an advance payment has been made, and the compensation is subsequently agreed or determined, a deed poll may be executed under this procedure upon tender or payment into court of the balance remaining unpaid of the total compensation.[31]

15.20   The acquiring authority may, at its discretion, make an advance payment on account of a basic loss payment or an occupier's loss payment (including an amount on account of interest due on such payments) under the Land Compensation Act 1973.[32] An acquiring authority has a power to make, and in certain circumstances has a duty to make, an advance payment on account of a home loss payment under the same Act.[33]

---

[28] Ibid, s 52(5).
[29] Ibid, s 52(8), (8A), (9).
[30] See s 9 of the Compulsory Purchase Act 1965 and see ch 2, para 2.121.
[31] LCA 1973, s 52(10).
[32] See ch 11, paras 11.27, 11.28.
[33] See ch 11, para 11.43.

2. Mortgaged Land

Special provisions as to the making of advance payments apply where the land acquired is   15.21
subject to a mortgage.[34] The provisions differ depending on whether the principal debt
outstanding and secured by the mortgage (or mortgages) is 90 per cent or less than 90 per
cent of the amount of the compensation as agreed or estimated by the acquiring authority.
If the sum outstanding is 90 per cent or less the acquiring authority must reduce the advance
payment to the owner by the amount which it thinks will be required to secure the release
of the mortgage (or all of the mortgages if there is more than one). If the claimant for compensation so requires in writing, and his request is accompanied by the written consent of
the mortgagee, the acquiring authority must then pay to the mortgagee the amount it
thinks will be required to discharge the mortgage and so secure the release of the mortgagee's interest. Any balance is then available for an advance payment to the claimant. The
amount of the advance payment to the claimant and the amount paid to a mortgagee or
mortgagees must not exceed 90 per cent of the agreed or estimated compensation. The
claimant must provide to the acquiring authority the information required for it to give
effect to these provisions. If there is more than one mortgage affecting the land acquired the
provisions are applied to each mortgagee individually but one mortgagee cannot be paid
until the interest of any mortgagee with priority to him is released.[35] If the acquiring authority makes an increased estimate of the compensation then on a request from the claimant
the above provisions must be reapplied on the basis of the revised estimate.

To take an example of the operation of these provisions, suppose that land estimated to be   15.22
worth £200,000 is burdened by a mortgage debt of which £160,000 remains payable. Apart
from the mortgage the acquiring authority would be required to make an advance payment
to the claimant of £180,000, 90 per cent of the estimated compensation. As it is the acquiring authority must reduce the advance payment by the amount due under the mortgage so
that the amount of the advance payment will be reduced to £20,000. The balance of
£160,000 will be available for the authority to use to secure the release of the interest of the
mortgagee. If it receives a request to do so, the authority will pay the £160,000 due to the
mortgagee and deduct that from the £180,000 which would otherwise be payable as an
advance payment to the owner of the land, so again making the advance payment to the
claimant a sum of £20,000. The aggregate sum paid will be £180,000 which does not exceed
90 per cent of the estimated compensation. If no request is received the acquiring authority
can wait until the amount of the compensation is agreed or determined and can then proceed to secure the discharge of the mortgage by a payment to the mortgagee under section
14 of the Compulsory Purchase Act 1965.[36]

A different set of provisions applies if the land acquired is subject to a mortgage (or mort-   15.23
gages) and the principal debt outstanding and secured by the mortgage exceeds 90 per cent
of the amount of the compensation as agreed or estimated by the acquiring authority.[37] In
such a case no advance payment is to be made to the dispossessed claimant. However, if the

---

[34] LCA 1973, ss 52ZA, 52ZB, 52ZC.
[35] Mortgages are generally ranked in priority according to the date of their creation. See *Megarry and Wade on the Law of Real Property*, 8th edn (London, Sweet and Maxwell, 2012), ch 26.
[36] See section (m) of ch 2.
[37] LCA 1973, s 52ZB.

claimant so requests in writing and his request is accompanied by the written consent of the mortgagee the acquiring authority is required to pay to the mortgagee the lesser of the value of the land acquired and the principal debt outstanding under the mortgage. The value of the land is to be calculated in accordance with rule (2) of section 5 of the Land Compensation Act 1961, that is it is the amount which the land if sold in the open market by a willing seller might be expected to realise.[38] If the value of the land for this purpose is not agreed between the claimant and the acquiring authority it is to be estimated by that authority. Again the amount paid to a mortgagee or mortgagees must not exceed 90 per cent of the value of the land. If there is more than one mortgagee payment must not be made to a mortgagee until the interest of any other mortgagee with priority is released. If the acquiring authority considers that the estimate of the value of the land which it has made is too low it may revise its estimate and, on receipt of a written request, it must pay to a mortgagee the balance due on the basis of the revised estimate.

15.24 A mortgagee who receives a payment under either of the above sets of provisions must apply the sum received towards the discharge of capital, interest and costs due under the mortgage. The acquiring authority will therefore obtain title to the land acquired discharged from the mortgage or discharged to the extent that the sum it has paid to the mortgagee reduces the amount charged on the land. A sum so paid to a mortgagee is taken into account as a reduction in the compensation due to the owner of the land. For example, if land estimated to be worth £200,000 is encumbered by a mortgage debt of £120,000 and the acquiring authority pays £120,000 to the mortgagee under the first of the sets of provisions just described the land is discharged from the mortgage and the acquiring authority is entitled to treat the payment of £120,000 as a part payment of the compensation, so leaving £80,000 payable to the owner as the compensation due to him. In addition the sum paid to a mortgagee reduces the amount of unpaid compensation on which interest is payable.[39] It also reduces the sum for which a bond would have to be given by the acquiring authority if the authority has used the procedure in schedule 3 to the Compulsory Purchase Act 1965 to obtain possession of the land.[40] There is a further procedure in sections 14–16 of the Compulsory Purchase Act 1965 under which an acquiring authority can pay a sum to a mortgagee and obtain title to the land acquired free of the mortgage. If that procedure is used, and after payment or tender of the required sum to him the mortgagee refuses to convey or release his interest to the acquiring authority, that authority can pay a sum into court and execute a deed poll vesting in it the interest of the mortgagee.[41] A sum paid to a mortgagee under the provisions described above reduces the amount which is required to be paid into court.[42]

15.25 There are four circumstances in which no payment can be made to a mortgagee under the provisions just described:

(i) No such payment can be made where the compulsory acquisition is of a right over land as opposed to a corporeal interest in land.[43]

---

[38] Other provisions applicable to the r (2) calculation, such as the disregard of the effect on value of certain development required under s 6 of the Land Compensation Act 1961, will also have effect.

[39] For the payment of interest on compensation see section (d) of this chapter.

[40] See ch 2, para 2.97. This provision is little used today.

[41] See section (m) of ch 2.

[42] LCA 1973, s 52ZC(7).

[43] Ibid, s 52ZC(9)(b).

(ii)   No such payment can be made where the acquiring authority has exercised its power under section 14(2) of the Compulsory Purchase Act 1965 to pay to the mortgagee the amount due under the mortgage and so secure the release of the land acquired from the mortgage.[44]

(iii) No such payment can be made where the acquiring authority has exercised its power under section 14(3) of the Compulsory Purchase Act 1965 to make payments to the mortgagee and so secure the release of the land acquired from the mortgage.[45]

(iv)   Where the mortgage debt exceeds the value of the land acquired, or where the acquisition is of a part of the land subject to the mortgage, it may be necessary that the parties agree the value of the land or a part of it and the amount of the compensation or that these amounts are settled in default of agreement by the Lands Tribunal under the procedures in sections 15 and 16 of the Compulsory Purchase Act 1965. No sum can be paid to a mortgagee under the present provisions where such an agreement has been made or the matter has been referred to the Lands Tribunal.[46]

The general effect of the last three of the four excluded cases is that when the acquiring authority has adopted the procedure for the discharge of mortgages under the provisions of sections 14–16 of the Compulsory Purchase Act 1965 the present provisions for discharge of mortgages in whole or in part by the making of a payment to a mortgagee do not apply. The two procedures for dealing with mortgaged land are therefore to this extent alternatives. An acquiring authority can use the procedure in sections 14–16 of the Compulsory Purchase Act as of right in which case the procedure here described for advance payments to mortgagees is not available. The procedure here described relating to payments to mortgagees is only available if the claimant for compensation and the mortgagee agree to it.

(D) INTEREST ON COMPENSATION

A person whose land is compulsorily acquired is likely to suffer a loss which should be the   15.26
subject of compensation at least from the date when he is dispossessed of the land. Some time may pass following that date before the compensation is agreed or determined by the Lands Tribunal and is paid. The delay is mitigated by the provision for an advance payment of compensation explained in section (c) of this chapter. It is just that a landowner in these circumstances should obtain interest on the compensation over the period during which it remains unpaid. Interest on compensation is payable by the acquiring authority in respect of the period from the date of entry onto the land acquired until the date of payment of the compensation. Under the Lands Clauses Consolidation Act 1845 an acquiring authority which had not paid compensation because it had not been agreed or determined was entitled to take possession of the land in advance of the payment if it paid into court the sum claimed as compensation (or the sum as settled by a surveyor) and gave a bond to secure payment of the compensation. Interest at 5 per cent per year was payable from the date of

[44] Ibid, s 52ZC(10)(a).
[45] Ibid, s 52ZC(10)(b).
[46] Ibid, s 522C(10)(c).

entry until the date of receipt by the claimant of the compensation.[47] A similar procedure for obtaining entry in advance of the payment of compensation is available today but is rarely used.[48] Instead entry in advance of the payment of compensation is normally secured either by service of a notice to treat and notice of entry or by virtue of the right of entry which arises following the making of a general vesting declaration. Section 11(1) of the Compulsory Purchase Act 1965 provides for notice of entry and for the payment of interest from the time of entry once the compensation is paid. Under section 10 of the Compulsory Purchase (Vesting Declarations) Act 1981 interest is payable from the vesting date as if entry had been taken on that date under section 11(1) of the Compulsory Purchase Act 1965.[49] The rate of compensation today, payable from the date of entry until the date of payment when compensation has not been paid prior to the date of entry, is that rate which is prescribed from time to time by regulations made by the Treasury. This rate replaces the 5 per cent which was specified under the Lands Clauses Consolidation Act 1845.[50] Following the enactment of this provision in the Land Compensation Act 1961 successive regulations frequently changed the rate of interest with the rate at one time rising to 17 per cent per annum. A more sensible system was introduced by Regulations in 1995 and since that date the rate of interest has been 0.5 per cent below bank base rate.[51] For some time the rate of interest has been 0 per cent in the light of the very low bank base rates that have prevailed in recent years as a matter of monetary policy. As and when general interest rates rise and bank base rate rises interest rates payable on unpaid compensation will also rise again. Interest on unpaid compensation is simple interest and there is no jurisdiction to award compound interest or to increase the compensation because simple interest or the statutory rate may not be an adequate recompense for a claimant who is kept out of his money.[52]

15.27   Interest as just stated will be payable in respect of the three main heads of compensation when a person is compulsorily deprived of an interest in land, namely: (a) compensation for the value of the land acquired (under rule (2) of section 5 of the Land Compensation Act 1961), (b) compensation for disturbance or other matters (under rule (6) of section 5 of the 1961 Act), and (c) compensation for damage by severance or injurious affection to the retained land when a part of a person's land is compulsorily acquired (under section 7 of the Compulsory Purchase Act 1965).[53] Interest is also payable on compensation assessed on an equivalent reinstatement basis under rule (5) of section 5 of the Land Compensation Act 1961 from the date of possession until the cost of the reinstatement (or the last instal-

[47] Lands Clauses Consolidation Act 1845, s 85.
[48] See ch 2, para 2.97 for this process.
[49] For notices of entry see section (k) of ch 2 and for general vesting declarations see section (p) of ch 2.
[50] Land Compensation Act 1961, s 32.
[51] Acquisition of Land (Rate of Interest after Entry) Regulations 1995 (SI 1995/2262). The Regulations specify the exact method of ascertaining bank base rate at any time.
[52] *Meghnagi v Hackney LBC* [2008] RVR 122. The provisions as to interest are wholly statutory and do not involve the Tribunal in any decisions. It was held in the Court of Appeal in *Knibb v National Coal Board* (1984) 49 P & CR 426, that a similar power must have been intended to be available to the Tribunal under the Coal Mining (Subsidence) Act 1957 when deciding claims for compensation for mining subsidence, but no such question arises as regards claims for compensation for compulsory purchase where there is express statutory provision for compensation under the provisions described in this paragraph. It was long considered to be the general law that interest could not be awarded to a claimant as part of his loss when he obtained an order for the payment of a debt or for damages for a breach of contract or a tort. That rule was reversed by the House of Lords in *Sempra Metals Ltd v IRC* [2008] 1 AC 561, [2007] 3 WLR 354, so that such orders can now include sums for simple or compound interest. This alteration in the law does not affect the terms of a statutory power to award interest as explained in this section of the chapter.
[53] For the heads of compensation, see section (b) of ch 3.

ment if the cost is paid by instalments) is paid.[54] Claims for compensation under rule (6) can in principle relate to loss or expenditure incurred prior to the date of possession so that as regards such items a person may be kept out of his interest on compensation relating to such losses in respect of a period which occurs prior to the date of possession since interest runs only from the date of possession.

Other provisions state that interest is payable on other items of compensation which may   15.28
become due. In all cases the rate of interest is that prescribed by the 1995 Regulations.

(i)   Interest is payable on compensation under section 10 of the Compulsory Purchase Act 1965 (compensation for injurious affection caused by the execution of works when no land of the claimant is acquired) from the date of the claim for compensation until payment.[55]

(ii)   Interest is payable on compensation due under Part I of the Land Compensation Act 1973 (compensation for the depreciation of the value of land caused by the use of public works) from the date of the service of a notice of claim until payment.[56]

(iii)   Interest is payable on disturbance payments due under section 37 of the Land Compensation Act 1973 (compensation due when a person is disturbed in his possession of land by a compulsory acquisition but has no entitlement to compensation by reason of a proprietary interest in that land) from the date of displacement from the land until payment.[57]

(iv)   Interest is payable on basic loss and on occupier's loss payments under sections 33A–33C of the Land Compensation Act 1973 from the date specified for payment until payment.[58]

(v)   Interest is payable on the additional compensation which may become payable where there is a planning decision to grant planning permission for additional development within 10 years of the acquisition under section 29 of the Land Compensation Act 1961 from the date of the planning decision until payment.[59]

(vi)   Where a notice to treat ceases to have effect three years after its service because action has not been taken under it notice must be given to those affected that the notice to treat has ceased to have effect and compensation may become payable to those persons. Interest is payable on that compensation from the date on which notice should have been given of the lapsing of the notice to treat until payment.[60]

Since 1 July 2013 the Tribunal is given a general power to order the payment of interest   15.29
where a decision provides for a sum to be payable. Certain statutory provisions, such as section 35A of the Senior Courts Act 1981 and section 17 of the Judgments Act 1838, are applied as if the proceedings in the Tribunal were proceedings in a court to which these statutory provisions apply.[61] The specific powers to award interest in compensation cases

---

[54]   *Halstead v Manchester City Council* (1998) 76 P & CR 8. See section (a) of ch 6 for the equivalent reinstatement basis of compensation.
[55]   Land Compensation Act 1973, s 63.
[56]   Ibid, s 18.
[57]   Ibid, s 37(6).
[58]   Ibid, s 33I(6). See ch 11.
[59]   Land Compensation Act 1961, s 23(5). See section (e) of ch 6.
[60]   Compulsory Purchase Act 1965, s 5(2E). See section (j) of ch 2.
[61]   Rule 51A of the Tribunal Practice (Upper Tribunal) (Lands Chamber) Rules 2010 (SI 2010/2600), added by the Tribunal Procedure (Amendment No 3) Rules 2013 (SI 2013/1188). See r 10 of the Amendment Rules for traditional provisions.

stated in the previous paragraphs continue to apply to amounts payable covered by those specific provisions. As far as compensation references are concerned the main impact of the new powers may be that it permits the award of interest on costs and this subject is explained later in this chapter.[62]

15.30 An advance payment of a part of the compensation due is often made and in such a case interest is only due on the unpaid balance. When making an advance payment the acquiring authority should also make a payment of interest to the claimant in respect of the period from the date of entry to the date of the payment. The interest should be on the total of the agreed or estimated amount of the compensation even though the advance payment is to be only 90 per cent of the total amount.[63]

15.31 If the acquiring authority refuses to pay interest due, or the entitlement to interest, or the amount cannot be agreed the remedy of a landowner is to issue proceedings in the courts to recover what he contends is due to him.[64]

(E) STARTING PROCEEDINGS IN THE LANDS TRIBUNAL

1. Notice of Reference

15.32 Most courts and tribunals have a prescribed process for the initiation of proceedings. The usual method of initiating proceedings before the Lands Tribunal is by sending to the Tribunal a notice of reference. It is this procedure which has to be used to initiate a claim for compensation following the compulsory acquisition of land.[65] In the great majority of cases a notice of reference is issued by the claimant for compensation but there is no reason why the acquiring authority should not issue a notice and this is sometimes done. It may be done, for example, where a claimant is unreasonably delaying the progress of his claim or because the acquiring authority wishes to know its financial liability at an early stage following a compulsory acquisition of land. As mentioned earlier a notice of reference cannot be issued earlier than one month after the service of a notice to treat on the claimant or, if there is no such notice, within one month from the notice of claim.[66] If the acquiring authority has used the general vesting declaration procedure to acquire the land a constructive service of a notice to treat occurs at the date of the execution of the vesting declaration and the one month time period which must elapse before a notice of reference may be issued then runs from that date.

15.33 There is no prescribed form of a notice of reference but the Rules require that the notice is signed and dated and that it states certain matters.[67] The main matters which must be specified in a notice of reference are: (a) the name and address of the person making the refer-

---

[62] See para 15.136.
[63] Land Compensation Act 1973, s 52A(2), (6). For advance payments see section (c) of this chapter.
[64] *Halstead v Manchester City Council* [1998] 1 All ER 33, (1998) 76 P & CR 8.
[65] The Tribunal Procedure (Upper Tribunal) (Lands Chamber) Rules 2010 (SI 2010/2600), r 28. In the ensuing text and notes in this chapter these Rules are referred to as the Rules and any reference to a rule is to one of these Rules.
[66] Rule 28(6). See para 15.10.
[67] The Tribunal Procedure (Upper Tribunal) (Lands Chamber) Rules 2010, rule 28(3) (SI 2010/2600).

ence and of his representative if he has one, (b) the address or description of the land to which the reference relates, (c) the name and address of every other person with an interest in that land, (d) the statutory provision under which the reference is made (this will usually be section 1 of the Land Compensation Act 1961 or section 6 of the Compulsory Purchase Act 1965), (e) the amount claimed as compensation and an explanation of how that amount is calculated and a summary of the reasons for making the claim (it is usual at this stage to state these matters in the notice of reference with some generality; for example a stated sum may be said to be claimed as the open market value of the interest in land acquired at the valuation date and that the reason for the making of the claim is that no agreement has been reached with the acquiring authority on that amount), and (f) whether it is desired that the reference should be determined without a hearing (this matter is considered later). The person making the reference must send with it a copy of any notice to treat or notice of entry that has been served and any notice of claim made by the claimant in pursuance of section 4 of the Land Compensation Act 1961.[68] A fee of £250 is payable on the lodging of a notice of reference. References relating to compensation are given a reference number such as ACQ/10/2013, the last figure denoting the year in which the reference was made. Although any notice of reference which complies with the requirements of the Rules will be valid a form to be used as a notice of reference is available and the completion of this form will ensure that all relevant matters are stated. The form is accompanied by useful notes as to its completion. While the notice of reference is an essential part of all compensation proceedings, in more complicated cases most significant material in the notice soon becomes elaborated in further pleadings or documents passing between the parties and the Tribunal.

The parties to the proceedings before the Tribunal are the person who makes the notice of reference and any person named as a party in the notice of reference.[69] Normally, of course, a notice of reference made by a landowner will name the acquiring authority as the other party to it. The Rules define a party for purposes of the present type of reference as the claimant and the acquiring authority or compensating authority.[70] It is these terms which should be used in any title of the reference as the parties to it. The acquiring authority or compensating authority is in practice sometimes called the respondent.   15.34

When the Tribunal has received a notice of reference it sends copies of the notice and accompanying documents to the persons who are named in it other than the person making the reference.[71]   15.35

A person who receives a copy of the notice of reference from the Tribunal is required, within one month of receiving the notice, to send a response to the Tribunal and to the party who made the reference. That response must be signed and dated and must state whether the person making the response intends to take part in the proceedings. The main other matters which must be stated in a response are: (a) the name and address of the person making the response and of his representative if he has one, (b) a summary of the contentions of the person making the response (as with the notice of reference the material which is provided under this requirement is often very short in form, for example that the acquiring authority   15.36

---

[68] Rule 28(3), (4). See para 15.12 for particulars of claims to be provided under s 4 of the 1961 Act.
[69] Rule 28(2).
[70] Rule 1(3). There may be references where no land of the claimant is acquired such as where the claim is under s 10 of the Compulsory Purchase Act 1965 (see ch 10) or under Pt I of the Land Compensation Act 1973 (see ch 13). In the remainder of this chapter references to the acquiring authority include a compensating authority.
[71] Rule 28(8).

disputes the amount claimed as compensation), and (c) whether the person making the response wishes the reference to be determined without a hearing. Where the person making the response is a claimant, that is where the notice of reference has been given by the acquiring authority, the person making the response must state the amount of compensation claimed and an explanation of how that amount is calculated and a summary of the reasons for making that claim, that is the material which would have had to be included in a notice of reference if that notice had been issued by the person seeking compensation.[72]

15.37   On receiving a response to a notice of reference the Tribunal must direct either that the notice of reference and any response to it shall stand as the statement of case of the party in question or that the party making the reference and the person making a response must deliver to the Tribunal and to each other a statement of case within a specified period. [73] Except in the simplest cases the notice of reference and the response are unlikely to provide an adequate statement of a party's case so that further documents are needed. The matter of statements of case and pleadings is dealt with below.

2. Limitation Periods

15.38   Limitation of actions means that a person may only bring an action in order to enforce a right when he does so before the expiry of a certain period from the date on which his cause of action to enforce that right accrued. All limitation periods are statutory and today under the Limitation Act 1980 the general limitation period for actions based on contract or tort in the courts is six years.[74] There are a number of limitation periods which bear on references to the Lands Tribunal to determine compensation.

15.39   When the acquiring authority has used the general vesting declaration procedure, so that a notice to treat is deemed to have been served, a reference must be made within six years from when the claimant, or a person under whom he derives title, first knew, or could reasonably be expected to have known, of the vesting of his interest in the acquiring authority by virtue of the Compulsory Purchase (Vesting Declarations) Act 1981.[75]

15.40   Where the acquiring authority has used the notice to treat procedure no specific limitation period is prescribed in the compensation legislation. However the Limitation Act 1990 provides in section 9(1) that an action to recover any sum recoverable by virtue of any enactment shall not be brought after the expiration of six years from the date on which the cause of action accrued. A reference to the Lands Tribunal is considered for these purposes to be an action to recover a sum of money recoverable by virtue of an enactment. The cause of action is taken to have accrued at the date of entry onto the land by the acquiring authority. Consequently when the notice to treat procedure is used there is a limitation period for the making of references to the Lands Tribunal of six years running from the date of entry by the acquiring authority.[76]

---

[72] Rules 29(1), (2).

[73] Rule 29(3).

[74] Limitation first arose under the Limitation Act 1623. The general limitation period for claims in contract and tort is prescribed by ss 2 and 5 of the Limitation Act 1980.

[75] Compulsory Purchase (Vesting Declarations) Act 1981, s 10(3). See section (p) of ch 2, for general vesting declarations.

[76] *Hillingdon LBC v ARC Ltd (No 1)* [1999] Ch 139, [1998] 3 WLR 754.

The result of a failure to make a reference within the six year limitation period is that the   15.41
right to claim compensation is wholly lost. Nonetheless it appears that there may be a
waiver or estoppel arising out of the actions of the parties the operation of which means
that the right of the acquiring authority to rely on the limitation period as defeating a reference is itself lost.[77] There may also arise a separate agreement between the acquiring authority and the claimant for the transfer of the land or the payment of compensation which will
be enforceable in the ordinary way as a separate agreement and will be subject to its own
limitation period.[78]

The six year limitation period just mentioned applies to claims for the three main heads of   15.42
compensation, compensation for the value of the land acquired, disturbance and other
compensation under rule (6) of section 5 of the Land Compensation Act 1961, and compensation for injurious affection to land retained. There are other specific limitation
periods for other heads of compensation which have been stated when those heads of compensation have been explained. In summary the other limitation periods are as follows:

(i)   A reference to the Lands Tribunal to assess compensation under Part I of the Land
      Compensation Act 1973 (compensation for the effect of the use of public works)
      must be made within six years from the first claim date.[79]
(ii) A reference to the Lands Tribunal to determine the amount of a basic loss payment,
      or an occupier's loss payment, or a home loss payment under the Land Compensation
      Act 1973, or a claim for payment of the amount due must be made within the six
      year period prescribed by section 9 of the Limitation Act 1980.[80]
(iii) Section 9 of the Limitation Act 1980 applies to claims for disturbance payments
      under sections 37 and 38 of the Land Compensation Act 1973.[81]
(iv) The cause of action for the recovery of interest due on compensation under section
      11(1) of the Compulsory Purchase Act 1965 accrues (and thus the limitation period
      under section 9 of the Limitation Act 1990 starts to run) when the amount of com-
      pensation on which interest is payable is agreed or determined.[82]

---

[77] *Hillingdon LBC v ARC Ltd (No 2)* [2004] EGLR 97, (2000) 80 P & CR D29 (no estoppel on the facts);
Co-operative Wholesale Society v Chester-le-Street District Council [1993] 3 EGLR 11; *Bridgestart Properties Ltd v
London Underground Ltd* [2004] EWCA Civ 793 (no estoppel on the facts). The type of estoppel which would
normally be relied on would be either a promissory estoppel, that is some promise by the acquiring authority that
it would not insist on the observance of the limitation period, or an estoppel by convention, that is an assumption
shared between the parties and known to each of them that the limitation period would not be insisted on so that
it was inequitable to allow the acquiring authority to insist on the observance of that period. The elements of an
estoppel by convention were described by Lord Steyn in *Republic of India v India Steamship Company (No 2)*
[1998] AC 878, [1997] 3 WLR 818, at p 913 as being: 'It is settled that an estoppel by convention may arise where
parties to a transaction act on an assumed state of facts or law, the assumption being either shared by both of them
or made by one and acquiesced in by the other. The effect of an estoppel by convention is to preclude a party from
denying the assumed fact or law if it would be unjust to allow him to go back on the assumption'.
[78] The service of a notice to treat followed by an agreement on the amount of the compensation creates an
enforceable contract of sale in its own right which may be enforced by ordinary proceedings: see ch 2, para 2.91,
and see *BP Oil UK Ltd v Kent County Council* [2003] 3 EGLR 1; *Bhattacharjee v Blackburn and Darwen Borough
Council* [2002] RVR 55.
[79] See ch 13, para 13.30 and see *Bateman v Lancashire County Council* [1999] 2 EGLR 203.
[80] See ch 11, paras 11.28, 11.40.
[81] See ch 12, para 12.27. There are other time limits for making claims for certain types of compensation, for
example a six month period for making claims for additional compensation when additional development is carried out on the land acquired in the 10 years following the completion of the acquisition: see section (e) of ch 6. In
such cases the six year period for making a reference to the Lands Tribunal if the compensation is not agreed under
s 9 of the Limitation Act 1980 may also apply.
[82] *Halstead v Manchester City Council* (1998) 76 P & CR 8.

(F) THE FOUR PROCEDURES

15.43   The Practice Directions of the Tribunal of 29 November 2010 state that the Tribunal will follow one of four procedures in dealing with notices of reference.[83] They are the simplified procedure, the written representations procedure, the special procedure and the standard procedure. It is for the Tribunal to decide which of those procedures will be followed in dealing with any particular reference. The Tribunal will assign a reference to one of the procedures when it has sufficient information to enable it to do so. This power may be exercised by the Registrar or a member of the Tribunal at any stage although it is usual that the procedure is decided at an early stage so that directions for pleadings and for a hearing in accordance with the selected procedure can be made. The Practice Directions require that a party should state which procedure it considers should be followed when issuing a notice of reference or a response to a notice of reference.[84] As indicated above the Rules[85] require that the notice of reference and the response shall state whether the person issuing that document wishes the reference to be determined without a hearing and the written representations procedure is such a determination. The Tribunal will take account of the expressed wishes of the parties when allocating the reference to one of the four procedures.[86] If it is operated sensibly by the parties the procedure before the Tribunal is helpful and simple. It may be compared with the detail and complexity of the Civil Procedure Rules which regulate proceedings in the High Court and the County Court.

1. The Simplified Procedure

15.44   The simplified procedure is suitable for a case in which no substantial issue of law or of valuation practice or substantial conflict of fact is likely to arise and is often suitable where the amount at stake is small. It is not normally appropriate for cases where there will be more than one expert witness. The usual course is that a date for the hearing, almost always not to exceed a single day, is fixed when the reference is allocated to the simplified procedure and that date is normally about three months ahead. The hearing will be informal and strict rules of evidence will not apply although statements of case will be required. It is not entirely clear what is meant by strict rules of evidence but what is envisaged is that the parties can present what they have to say without formality or observing the usual procedures which are observed in courts. In practice in modern civil proceedings there are few technical rules of evidence which create difficulty. The parties will still be required to observe fundamental principles which span the law of evidence and the law of procedure such as that statements made without prejudice are not disclosed to the Tribunal and that an expert witness brings all relevant facts known to him to the attention of the Tribunal.

15.45   Under the simplified procedure as well as statements of case the parties must exchange copies of all documents on which they intend to rely not later than a month before the hearing

---

[83] Practice Directions, paras 3.1–3.5. In the remainder of this chapter the Directions are referred to as 'Practice Directions'.

[84] Practice Directions, para 3.1(2).

[85] Rule 29(2)(e).

[86] Practice Directions, para 3.1(2).

date and not later than 14 days before that date they must file and exchange an expert's report if they intend to rely on expert evidence and a list of the witnesses they intend to call at the hearing.

Apart from the principles as to costs set out in section 4 of the Land Compensation Act   15.46
1961, and save in exceptional cases such as where an offer of settlement has been made and refused when it should have been accepted, no order for costs will be made under the simplified procedure. The simplified procedure is in some ways akin to the small claims procedure operated in the County Court under Part 26 of the Civil Procedure Rules.[87]

2. The Written Representations Procedure

Rule 46 of the Rules provides that the Tribunal may make any decision without a hearing.   15.47
If there is no hearing then the case for the parties must be presented by way of written representations and it is to this process that the next procedure, the written representations procedure, is directed.[88] In deciding whether to make a decision on the basis of only written representations the Tribunal is required to have regard to the views of the parties. The Practice Directions state that the consent of the parties will usually be required if the written representations procedure is to be adopted but there is no statutory requirement for their consent.[89] The decision of the Tribunal on whether to adopt the written representations procedure will depend on the issues in the case and the desirability of minimising costs. The written representations procedure will generally be quicker and involve less costs than a hearing. That procedure may be most appropriate where there is no disputed expert evidence and no, or no significant, disputed questions of fact. If there is disputed expert evidence or disputed questions of fact then the ordinary process of oral evidence and cross-examination will generally be more appropriate. A case in which the written representation procedure could be followed would be where there was a clearly defined preliminary point of law. In larger cases the Tribunal often follows the practice of completing the oral evidence and then inviting the parties to make their final submissions in writing on the basis of the evidence and the pleadings. In this way a combination of an oral hearing and written representations is obtained. The benefit of such a process, as last described, is that the parties and the Tribunal can be sure that every substantial contention is set out and taken fully into account in the final decision. Also the representations of the parties on costs, usually given after a draft of the decision has been distributed, are normally made by way of written representations.

There is no set form of procedure for a decision made wholly on the basis of written repre-   15.48
sentations. The Tribunal will give its directions for the filing of representations and documents. The essential point is that each party should have a full opportunity both of putting its own case in writing and of commenting on the case for the opposing party or parties. The fairest, and probably most convenient, procedure is that both parties are required to submit and exchange their initial written representations within a specified period and then each party is given an opportunity within a further specified period to respond to and

---

[87] Ibid, para 3.3.
[88] Ibid, para 3.5.
[89] Ibid, para 3.5(1).

comment on the representations of the other party. This procedure only works well if both parties do put forward their full case in their initial submissions and the opportunity to respond to the submissions of the opposing party is confined to just that and does not involve introducing wholly new facts or arguments. In order for the procedure just mentioned to work well it is best that the issue or issues between the parties are defined with reasonable precision before the exchange of written submissions starts so that each party can know from the outset the matters to which his written submissions can be directed. An alternative process, which could be used within the written representations procedure, would be for the claimant to provide the initial representations with a response by the acquiring authority and a final reply by the claimant confined to any new matters raised by the acquiring authority in its response. Such a process would follow generally the process of pleadings in the courts where there is a particulars of claim, a defence and a reply.

15.49   Under the written representations procedure costs are not generally awarded and will only be awarded if there has been an unreasonable failure to accept an offer to settle, or unreasonable conduct by one party, or some other exceptional circumstances.[90] The direction seems to suggest that, like the simplified procedure where a similar principle regarding costs applies, the written representations procedure is expected to apply mainly in smaller and simpler references. If the claim is larger or more complex there seems no reason why the general principles on costs should not apply even though the written representations procedure is applied.

3. The Special Procedure

15.50   The special procedure is appropriate where the complexity or the amount in issue, or the wide importance of the case, renders it necessary that its case management should be by a member. A main feature of the special procedure is that there should be a case management hearing before the member at an early stage. In cases of particular complexity, or where substantial issues of law are involved, it is likely that the President or Deputy President of the Tribunal will conduct the case management hearing and in due course the hearing of the reference itself. At the hearing if there are complex valuation issues the President or Deputy President may sit with a surveyor member. The parties should consider and seek to agree the terms of any order or directions which will be made as a result of the case management hearing. They should seek to agree a position statement summarising the subject matter of the case and the issues at least seven days before the date fixed for the case management hearing. The parties should also state the areas of expertise and general scope of the evidence of any expert witness on whom they propose to rely. The question of a preliminary issue or issues should be considered in the position statement and this question can be resolved at the case management hearing.[91] Experience shows that in some cases where large sums of money and complex issues are involved the parties sometimes cannot agree the appropriate procedural directions and the areas of dispute have to be resolved at a case management hearing, perhaps with legal representatives present. In such a case it is preferable that rather than engaging in a forlorn attempt to provide an agreed position

[90]   Ibid, para 3.5(3).
[91]   Ibid, para 3.4.

paper the parties should assist the Tribunal to resolve the procedural issues by each producing their own position paper explaining what is or is not agreed and why they ask for certain directions.

4. The Standard Procedure

The last procedure is the standard procedure which is that which will apply if the reference 15.51
has not been allocated to one of the other procedures. Where the standard procedure applies
the Registrar will hold a case management hearing in an appropriate case. Procedural directions will be given as a result of that hearing, or without it if it is not necessary, by the
Registrar for the further progress of the reference.[92] The standard procedure can be used
across a wide span of cases and in some instances it will be appropriate that directions are
given which are similar to those which would be given if the special procedure applied.

It is apparent that the four procedures do not involve standard or detailed programmes for 15.52
directions and the procedural conduct of the case and that there is a great deal of flexibility
as to the details of the procedure which is appropriate for each particular case. It has been
the practice of the Tribunal to convene a case management hearing where neither party has
taken any step in the reference for a considerable period so that the parties can be required
to obtain directions on how the reference is to proceed. The Rules of course apply to all
procedures. It is possible that a case will be transferred from one procedure to another if it
becomes apparent that that is necessary. The Rules state that the overriding objective is to
enable the Tribunal to deal with cases fairly and justly. The Tribunal must seek to give effect
to this overriding objective when it exercises any power under the Rules or interprets its
Practice Directions and the parties are required to help the Tribunal to further the overriding objective as well as to co-operate with the Tribunal generally.[93]

(G) PLEADINGS

The expression 'pleadings' is one taken from the long established practice of the ordinary 15.53
courts where the parties are required to set out the essence of their case by way of, on the
part of a claimant, particulars of claim and, on the part of a defendant, a defence. At one
time such pleadings were complex documents which dealt in formal terms with each allegation and might contain such technicalities as a general traverse (a formalised statement that
all contentions in the opposite side's pleading which were not specifically admitted or otherwise dealt with were denied or not admitted). Following the introduction in 1998 of the
Civil Procedure Rules, which now govern most proceedings in the High Court and the
County Court, this antiquated system has been replaced in those courts by a requirement
that a party gives a more general and more intelligible account of his case by way of his
pleadings. In former times the Lands Tribunal had no such system of pleadings and parties
were sometimes required to find out what precisely was being alleged by the other party

---

[92] Ibid, para 3.2.
[93] Rule 2. In the event of an extreme case of non co-operation a party may find that his case, or a part of it, is struck out: see para 15.67 et seq.

only when the hearing started. Fortunately a more rational system has now emerged in that the Practice Directions require what are called statements of case by both parties. It is required that each party to a reference shall provide a statement of its case. It is said that each statement of case must set out the basis of fact and law on which the party relies. The statement should be in summary form but must contain particulars sufficient to tell the other party the case that is being advanced and to enable the Tribunal to identify the issues.[94] The Practice Directions state that a statement of case must be contained in, or be provided with, the notice of reference or the response to the notice of reference.[95] The matters which in accordance with the Rules a notice of reference and a response must contain have been explained. If a notice of reference or response does not contain or provide a statement of case application should be made at the time of the notice or response for an extension of time for providing it.[96] In practice, and except in the simplest cases, the material normally provided in a notice of reference and a response does not come anywhere near meeting the requirements of a proper statement of case by either party. The Practice Directions state that if a statement of case has not been provided with the notice of reference or response the Tribunal will order that a statement of case be provided.[97] A party who considers that another party has failed to provide a statement of case can apply to the Tribunal for an order that a statement of case should be provided.[98]

15.54   In practice in nearly all cases, save the simplest, a statement of case from both parties will be required following the initial notice of reference and response. The parties may provide these voluntarily or the Tribunal will order them of its own volition, perhaps as a result of a case management hearing. The best procedure is that the claimant for compensation first produces his statement of case and the acquiring authority then produces its statement of case replying to the claim. The idea of pleadings setting out separate and sometimes unhelpful allegations which have to be dealt with by formal denials or non-admissions or admissions and sentence by sentence should be consigned to history. The statement of case of the claimant should make clear what he is claiming and why he is claiming it and the heads under which he claims it and the legal justification for his claim and the calculations which underlie his claim. The statement of case of the acquiring authority should contain an equivalent format and content. Although a statement of case is intended to be a summary of the case for a party in more difficult and complex cases it is good practice that at least a reasonable summary of the reasoning and justification for the way a case is framed should be set out. This saves time and costs since the same will have to be done in any event at a later stage (for example in expert reports or in a skeleton argument) and assists the Tribunal in an appropriate case in deciding how to deal with the matter by further directions and, of some importance, whether there should be preliminary issues and, if so, what those preliminary issues should be. The philosophy which underlies modern legal proceedings is that they are, to use a jargon phrase, front loaded. For example, a party who seeks permission to appeal to the Court of Appeal must produce his skeleton argument with a sound indication of his case at the time when he seeks that permission and not wait until a later date.[99] A statement of case may properly include with it supporting documents where they elucidate

[94] Practice Directions, para 6.1(2).
[95] Ibid, para 6.3(1).
[96] Ibid, para 6.3(3).
[97] Ibid, para 6.3(4).
[98] Ibid, para 6.3(5).
[99] Civil Procedure Rules (CPR), Pt 52 Practice Direction (PD), para 5.9.

the case and its justification. It is to be hoped that in future in larger and more complicated cases the Tribunal will insist on a full and proper statement of case at an early stage, something which will save time later, will assist the parties, and will generally much assist the Tribunal.

A party can apply for a clarification of a pleading which has been served on him, a process   15.55 which in the courts used to be called a request for further and better particulars. Such an application should first be made by letter. In accordance with the practice in the ordinary courts it is good practice to state in such an application a reasonable period during which the clarification sought should be given.[100] Of course if a request for clarification is not answered, or adequately answered, the party making the request may make a formal application to the Tribunal for an order that the information requested should be given.[101] Although the statements produced by both parties are called a statement of case in the Practice Directions it assists clarity if the expression 'statement of case', is applied to the statement on behalf of a claimant and an expression such as 'statement of case in reply' is reserved for the statement of case of the acquiring authority.

(H) HEARING OF PRELIMINARY ISSUES

A particular feature of references allocated to the special procedure is that a determination   15.56 of a preliminary issue or issues may be appropriate. Such a process is less likely under other procedures though it is still possible.[102] There is a specific power in the Rules for the hearing of preliminary or separate issues.[103] The parties should consider the question of a preliminary issue or issues for the purposes of a case management hearing. Preliminary issues are often issues of law and can be determined without the calling of evidence. However, preliminary issues which are in whole or in part questions of fact can also be determined if it is appropriate and in such cases evidence of fact or expert evidence may be needed for the purposes of the preliminary issue. The current general practice of the Tribunal is to encourage the hearing of preliminary issues where that can reasonably be done. The purpose of a preliminary issue is that it may cut down the time and expense of the proceedings as a whole if that issue is determined separately and at an early stage. For example, a claimant may put his case forward on one basis of law and the acquiring authority may put its case forward on a different basis of law. If there is no preliminary issue both parties would probably need to adduce expert evidence on two alternative bases since they cannot know which party will be held to be correct on the issue of law. If the issue of law is determined as a preliminary issue the parties will then know which basis of law is correct so that the whole of their evidence and subsequent argument will need to be addressed to that basis only. Another possible occasion on which a preliminary issue is useful is if the determination of that issue one way would dispose of the proceedings or a part of the proceedings altogether. For example, it may be contended that the Tribunal has no power to determine a particular issue because of past events or some defect in past proceedings. In that case if the Tribunal

---

[100] See CPR Pt 18 PD, para 1.1.
[101] See paras 15.65 and 15.66 for the procedure for the making of applications.
[102] Practice Directions, para 7.
[103] Rule 5(3)(e).

decides as a preliminary issue that it has no jurisdiction that is obviously the end of the reference whereas if there had been no preliminary issue the parties might have had to call extensive evidence on the subject matter of the claim only to find at the end of the day that the whole of what was done was purposeless since the Tribunal held that it had no power to deal with that claim.

15.57 While the principle of determining preliminary issues is clear, and the instances just mentioned as well as others will sometimes justify it, the superior courts have often been critical of a process of trying elaborate preliminary issues without a full hearing of the evidence and determination of the facts since to do so may in the end cause the parties more delay and expense than if the whole of the facts had first been elucidated. It is inappropriate to try to determine a question as a preliminary issue when that issue may depend in part on evidence which may have to be called at a later stage.[104] A process which the parties may sometimes agree to follow, with the approval of the Tribunal, is that certain claims or facts may be assumed to be correct but only for the purposes of the preliminary issue. The decision one way on the preliminary issue may then mean that a dispute on the facts need never be resolved. On the other hand if the preliminary issue is decided in a way which makes it necessary to do so the Tribunal can then proceed to determine the facts. On many occasions the parties may agree that there should be a determination of a preliminary issue and its terms but it is open to the Tribunal to direct that there should be an issue even if one or both of the parties does not agree to that course. The formulation of the preliminary issues is important so that the parties can know exactly what is to be determined at that stage. Even so the general approach adopted by the Tribunal is that it is not bound by the exact wording of preliminary issues provided that the general ambit of that which is to be decided is clear. The parties must always understand the proposition that they can agree anything they wish as a matter of fact. In contradistinction to this the parties cannot agree the law. The law must always be stated and applied by a court or tribunal as that which is determined to be correct by the court or tribunal. Thus one party may assert that proposition A is the law and the other party may assert that proposition B is the law. It is open to a court or tribunal to decide that proposition C is the law. Indeed it must do so if it concludes that that is correct. In the same way although the parties may agree between themselves what is the law on a certain subject a court may refuse to accept the agreement and may determine that some other view of the law is correct.

(I) PROCEDURE PRIOR TO THE HEARING

1. General Procedure

15.58 The Tribunal has wide powers to regulate and control references before they come to a hearing which are contained in the Rules.[105] Subject to anything contained in the Tribunals,

---

[104] *Harrison & Hetherington Ltd v Cumbria County Council* [1985] 2 EGLR 37, (1985) 50 P & CR 396; *GPE (Hanover Square) Ltd v Transport for London* [2012] UKUT 417 (LC), at para 2. See the observations of Litton NPJ in *Penny's Bay Investment Co Ltd v Director of Lands* (2010) 13 HKCFAR 287, and in *Commissioner of Rating & Valuation v Agrila Ltd* (2001) 4 HKCFAR 83.

[105] See in particular Pt 2 of the Rules.

Courts and Enforcement Act 2007 and subject to any specific provision in the Rules, the Tribunal may regulate its own procedure.[106] There are many detailed aspects of legal proceedings, such as the times of sitting and interposing witnesses to suit their reasonable convenience or hearing issues in a particular order, which cannot be covered by procedural rules and, providing it observes the basic principles of justice, the Tribunal can give directions on such matters. For example, the Tribunal could limit the length of cross-examination if it appeared that the questioning was inordinately long or was serving little purpose, but could probably not prevent cross-examination at all, or prevent cross-examination of a particular witness at a hearing.[107] Where there is no specific provision in the Rules the Tribunal may find it convenient to follow the practice which is adopted in the courts under the Civil Procedure Rules and has indicated that in certain areas, such as in awarding costs, it will normally do so.[108]

Except where the Rules make express provision as to what is to be done the procedure prior to a hearing is controlled by directions issued by the Tribunal, either by a member or by the Registrar. [109] A direction may be given at any time including a direction which amends an earlier direction. The most important procedural powers available to the Tribunal are now summarised.   15.59

The Tribunal may permit or require a party or another person to provide documents, information, evidence or submissions to the Tribunal or to another party.[110] This is an important power which is similar in part to the procedure for disclosure of documents which exists in the civil courts under the Civil Procedure Rules. Disclosure, formerly called discovery, means that a party has to produce a list of documents which are, or have been, in his control relevant to the issues in dispute.[111] A party can also be ordered to allow another party to inspect the documents and to take copies of them. Disclosure may be ordered in relation to all issues in the case or only in relation to a particular issue or issues. Disclosure can be a costly and time consuming process and in deciding whether to order it the Tribunal will balance the gain likely to ensue from the process against the time and cost involved. A party directed to disclose documents may indicate that certain documents are privileged from disclosure; for instance documents may be communications between a solicitor and his client and so be covered by legal professional privilege. Disclosure may be ordered against a person who is not a party to the proceedings, called third party disclosure, but this is a power which is sparingly exercised. Disclosure is not normally needed in disputes involving only valuation issues and expert evidence but may be more necessary where there are disputed issues of fact. It may also be helpful in claims which involve disturbance compensation where the actions of a claimant in incurring expenses for which he claims compensation   15.60

---

[106] Rule 5(1).

[107] Like any other court the Tribunal must observe the basic rules of natural justice such as the *audi alteram partem* rule, that is the right of a party to put forward his own case and deal with any allegations made against him.

[108] See Practice Directions, paras 12.2 and 12.3, and see paras 15.119 and 15.121 of this chapter. Proceedings in the Court of Appeal and in the High Court and the County Courts are governed by rules called the Civil Procedure Rules (SI 1998/3132) first promulgated in 1998 which are supplemented by a series of Practice Directions. The Civil Procedure Rules replaced the former Rules of the Supreme Court (which provided for the procedure in the Court of Appeal and the High Court) and the County Court Rules (which provided for the procedure in the County Courts). The new Rules were intended to unify and simplify the procedure in general civil litigation. The House of Lords, and now the Supreme Court, had or have their own separate rules of procedure.

[109] Rule 5(2).

[110] Rule 5(3)(d).

[111] See CPR, r 31.8.

may be important. The Tribunal can prohibit the disclosure or publication of specified documents or information relating to the proceedings.[112] Such an order might be made where a party has revealed in disclosure, or has put in evidence, commercially sensitive documents.

15.61   The power to order the provision of information by a party can also be very useful. Parties sometimes fail to reveal in their pleadings, or in reports exchanged, what is the reasoning or information which leads to a certain conclusion, sometimes because they cannot readily do so or because they think that doing so may weaken their case or because they wish to cause difficulties to another party by keeping back matters until the last moment. The Tribunal can prevent such a process and achieve better justice by ordering the disclosure of information at an early stage. For example, a party might be ordered to provide a full list and details of the comparable transactions on which it relies in support of a valuation, or a party may be ordered to provide information on the carrying on of its business where a loss of profits is relevant to the claim, or a party may be ordered to disclose the results of tests which it has carried out.

15.62   The Tribunal can order the consolidation or hearing together of two or more sets of proceedings or parts of proceedings raising common issues and can order that a case be treated as a lead case.[113] This power may be exercised where a series of claims raise similar issues of principle or similar questions of valuation. There is little practical difference between the consolidation and the hearing together of proceedings. Where proceedings are consolidated the parties may still instruct separate experts or separate advocates if they wish but if one witness or one advocate can deal with a matter on behalf of all claimants then obviously time and costs may be saved. Where proceedings are consolidated or heard together then the decision in the proceedings binds all parties to the various sets of proceedings. Where a case is treated as a lead case the decision in that lead case does not formally bind parties to other sets of actual or potential proceedings but is likely to give general guidance which is useful in the sense that that general guidance given in the lead case may lead to the settlement of other cases and is unlikely to be departed from if those other cases still come to a hearing. Sometimes in a particular case the Tribunal takes the opportunity to explain its general approach or thinking on procedural or evidential matters. An instance is the preference which the Tribunal feels for valuations based on evidence of comparables, as opposed to residual valuations or other methods of valuation, where adequate comparables are available. This matter is explained in chapter 14.

15.63   The Tribunal may stay proceedings.[114] A stay means that no other steps are to be taken in the proceedings or in a part of the proceedings while the stay is in force. There are many reasons why a stay may be ordered but one is that a claimant has failed to comply with a direction made so that it is just that nothing further is done to further the claim until he does comply. A further possible reason for a stay might be that some event or decision was awaited, for instance a decision on an application for planning permission or the result of an appeal in another case, which is of central importance to the proceedings and it would be unreasonable for further procedural steps to be taken until that decision is known. Another possibility is that the Tribunal stays one part of the proceedings until another part is decided on the

[112] Rule 15.
[113] Rule 5(3)(b).
[114] Rule 5(3)(j).

reasoning that the decision on the second part is likely itself to provide an answer to, or at any rate valuable guidance on, the first part.

The Tribunal may require a party to produce a bundle for a hearing.[115] It is vital for the   15.64
proper conduct of a hearing that agreed bundles of documents are produced in advance. The agreement of documents does not mean that either party accepts the truth of the content of the documents but merely that the parties are willing that the documents should be before the Tribunal. It is rare that documents are not agreed, at any rate in this limited sense, but if there are any documents which cannot be agreed in this way, for instance because one party claims privilege in respect of them, then that issue will have to be decided before the hearing or at the hearing before the documents are tendered in evidence. It is important that bundles of documents are properly page numbered, divided into appropriate files with dividers in large cases where there are many documents, and contain an index of the documents. The burden of producing an agreed bundle or bundles of documents is usually initially that of the claimant. In cases which involve disputed legal issues and decided authorities a bundle of authorities (decided cases and statutory materials) will also need to be produced.

2. Applications

The Tribunal may give a procedural direction on its own initiative. As mentioned one occa-   15.65
sion on which it may exercise this power is if neither party has taken any steps in proceedings for some substantial time and the Tribunal wishes to know whether the proceedings are to be continued. The Tribunal may at any time direct that there shall be a case management hearing to decide the procedure to be adopted and the directions which should be made. Apart from these cases a particular direction is normally made as a result of an application by one or more of the parties.[116] An application may always be made orally during the course of a hearing but a party who wishes to obtain a direction in advance of the hearing must send or deliver a written application for the direction to the Tribunal and the application must include the reason for making it. Often directions are made by the consent of each party and in such a case the application must be accompanied by consents signed by or on behalf of each party. If an application is made, but without the consent of every other party, the applicant must provide a copy of the proposed application to every other party before it is made and must notify every other party of the right of that party to make any objection when he receives the application. The party who receives an application then has 10 days from the date on which he is sent a copy of the application to send written notice of his objection to the Tribunal and the applicant. The Rules therefore contemplate that a party making an application which is not made by consent first sends a copy of the proposed application to every other party and then makes the application itself and sends to every other party a notice of that application. In practice what often occurs is that an application is made and a copy of the application is at the same time sent to the other party. Applications to the Tribunal are rarely made out of the blue and are often preceded by a request that the opposite party acts in some way such as by producing certain documents.

---

[115] Rule 5(3)(i).
[116] Rule 6.

15.66   When the Tribunal has received the application and any objection to it, it makes its decision on the application and notifies the parties. In most cases the decision of the Tribunal can be made on the basis of the written application and written objection but in matters of importance or complication the Tribunal may convene a hearing to consider and decide on the application. In a case where the application is of substantial importance and is likely to be contested it is good practice to accompany, or follow up, the application with a witness statement which establishes the relevant facts, exhibits any relevant documents, and explains or amplifies the reasons for the application. If the application depends on legal or procedural arguments to be considered at an oral hearing the parties will often assist the Tribunal if they produce a position paper or skeleton argument in advance of the hearing, a procedure which is insisted on in procedural applications in the courts. The party who has received notice of the direction from the Tribunal may challenge it by applying for another direction which alters the first direction. If the direction has been made by consent a ground for alteration may be that circumstances have significantly changed. If a direction has been made without an objection to the application a party may put forward the view that he has now realised that an objection should have been made and its grounds. If a direction has been made having considered objections, whether in written form or orally, it will obviously be more difficult for a party to persuade the Tribunal to amend its previous direction. However, the procedure is flexible and even in such a case a change of circumstances or further information may justify an amended direction.

3. Striking Out

15.67   The Tribunal has power to strike out the whole or a part of the proceedings.[117] Thus a particular claim may be struck out leaving the remainder of the proceedings to continue. A particular ground of objection or resistance to a claim by an acquiring authority could be struck out in an appropriate case. Striking out is a draconian procedure and will be used only if there is good reason for it. There are two broad sets of circumstances in which striking out is appropriate, namely: (a) where a claim is wholly and clearly without merit, and (b) where there is a default by a party in complying with the Rules and directions made. These are considered in turn.

15.68   The whole or a part of the proceedings may be struck out if the Tribunal considers there is no reasonable prospect of the case of the claimant, or part of it, succeeding. Since an acquir-

---

[117] Rule 8. Every court and tribunal has an inherent power to control its own procedure and this involves a power to strike out proceedings or a part of proceedings. The former Lands Tribunal had such a power: *Mean Fiddler Holdings Ltd v London Borough of Islington* (2003) 44 *Estates Gazette* 170. However, now that there are elaborate rules which provide for striking out, it seems likely that the Tribunal in its present form of the Lands Chamber of the Upper Tribunal will proceed mainly in accordance with its statutory powers under the Rules. It is possible that a claim is made which cannot be struck out under one of the specific Rules but is what is called an abuse of the process. An instance would be when a party brought a claim which was in substance the same as a previous claim which had been decided and when there was no later change of circumstances. Sometimes, but not always, such a claim could be prevented by invoking the principles of estoppel *per rem judicatam* or issue estoppel. If those principles do not provide a solution and in an extreme case of an abuse of the process the Tribunal may still have an inherent jurisdiction to strike out a claim. The circumstances which could give rise to such abuses of the process are probably less likely in compensation claims than in other areas of jurisdiction exercised by the Tribunal. See also para 15.77, and see *Johnson v Gore Wood* [2002] 2 AC 1, [2001] 2 WLR 72, for the principles which apply to an abuse of the process of the nature here being discussed.

ing authority is not a claimant, as defined in rule 1(3), it appears that no part of the case for an acquiring authority can be struck out under this provision. A claimant who wishes that a part of the case for the acquiring authority is disposed of at an early stage could apply for a decision on the validity of that part of the case by way of the determination of a preliminary issue. A reason for a party having no reasonable prospect of success on its case, or a part of its case, may be that the factual allegations supporting the case are wholly implausible or that there is some legal impediment to the case succeeding. If the question is one of law or principle it may be more appropriate that the matter is decided as a preliminary issue rather than as one of striking out although the end result for a claimant who fails is the same, being that he cannot proceed with his claim or with the aspect of his claim which is in question. A further reason for a striking out direction, akin to that last considered, is that the Tribunal concludes that it does not have jurisdiction in relation to the proceedings or any part of them and is not exercising its power to transfer the proceedings to another court or tribunal.[118]

There are five powers which can be used by the Tribunal if a party fails to comply with the Rules or with directions. The provisions on this matter seem inordinately complex. All that is needed is a simple provision that the Tribunal may strike out the whole or a part of a case of a party if satisfied: (a) that the case or a part of it has no reasonable prospect of success, or (b) that the party has failed to comply with the Rules or a direction of the Tribunal and that the latter power may be exercised to have effect at once or on the failure of the party in default to comply with a further direction. 15.69

First, the Tribunal has a general power to strike out the whole or a part of the proceedings if the claimant has failed to co-operate with the Tribunal to such an extent that the Tribunal cannot deal with the proceedings fairly and justly.[119] It should be noted that this power is not confined to a case of a failure to comply with specific rules or directions. It could be used, for example, if a party refused to co-operate by answering questions or failed to attend at the date fixed for proceedings to be heard. It should also be noted that this particular power to strike out applies only to a failure of co-operation by a claimant and not by an acquiring authority. It is presumably thought that acquiring authorities can be relied upon not to act in a wholly unco-operative fashion. It may be that striking out proceedings is thought to be equivalent to striking out the claim. 15.70

Secondly, where a party has failed to comply with the Rules or a practice direction or a direction of the Tribunal, then the Tribunal, either on its own initiative or as a result of an application made to it, may take various courses of action including waiving the requirement or simply issuing a direction or further direction requiring the failure to be remedied. However in an appropriate case the Tribunal is permitted to exercise its power under rule 8 to strike out a party's case.[120] The power to strike out under rule 8 is presumably the power to strike out for a failure of co-operation, that is the first power (although, as mentioned, this particular power to strike out applies only to the case for claimants). It will be an unusual case in which the party's case is struck out simply for an initial failure to comply with some requirement or direction. Normally the party will be given a second opportunity. 15.71

---

[118] Rule 8(3)(c).
[119] Rule 8(3)(b).
[120] Rule 7(2).

15.72   This leads to the third power of the Tribunal. When issuing a direction the Tribunal may
state that failure by a party to comply with the direction will lead to that party being automatically barred from taking further part in the proceedings or part of the proceedings.[121]
Such a direction is sometimes called an 'unless order', since it takes the form that a party will
be barred from taking part in the proceedings unless he performs certain actions within a
certain time. An instance of the use of such a power could be where a party is ordered to
produce a statement of case dealing with certain matters and fails to do so. A further order
could then be made by the Tribunal that he will be barred from taking further part in the
proceedings unless he complies with the initial order within a specified time. A party who
is barred may apply to the Tribunal for a lifting of the bar by an application made in writing
and received within 14 days of his having received from the Tribunal notification of the
bar.[122] If a bar has come into effect and has not been lifted the Tribunal need not consider
any response or other submissions made by the party who is barred and may summarily
determine all and any issues against that party.[123] To revert to the example just mentioned,
if a claimant fails to deliver a statement of case, and a bar has taken effect, the Tribunal may
then summarily determine the issues raised by the claim against the claimant and in effect
dismiss the claim.

15.73   The fourth power is that a direction issued by the Tribunal may state that failure by a party
to comply with the direction could lead to the striking out of the proceedings or part of
them. If the party then fails to comply with the direction the whole or a part of the proceedings may be struck out.[124] This power is similar to the power mentioned in the last paragraph. The difference is that if a direction is made, as described in that paragraph, referring
to an automatic bar the bar comes into effect automatically whereas if a direction is made
stating that there could be a striking out the Tribunal must then make a further decision as
to whether there will in fact be a striking out as a result of a failure to comply with the direction.

15.74   The fifth power is akin to the third power but is automatic in its effect. When it makes a
direction the Tribunal may state that failure by a party to comply with a direction will lead
to a striking out of the proceedings or a part of them. If the party in question then does fail
to comply with a direction the proceedings or a part of them will automatically be struck
out.[125] The only difference between this power and the fourth power, explained in the last
paragraph, is that in the present case the strike out is automatic. The present power is therefore more severe in its effect than the fourth power and the Tribunal will consider which of
the powers to put into effect when it makes the initial direction in accordance with such
considerations as the importance of the direction and the previous conduct of the party
against whom the direction is made.

15.75   If the Tribunal is giving consideration to making a striking out order on the ground of lack
of jurisdiction, or a failure by a party to co-operate, or there being no reasonable prospect
of a case or a part of it succeeding, the party against whom the order may be made must be
given an opportunity to make representations in relation to the proposed striking out.[126] If

[121] Rule 7(3).
[122] Rule 7(4), (5).
[123] Rule 7(6).
[124] Rule 8(3)(a).
[125] Rule 8(1).
[126] Rule 8(4).

the proceedings have been struck out under the fourth or fifth of the powers just described the party against whom the order has been made may apply for the proceedings, or a part of them, to be reinstated. That application must be made in writing and must be received by the Tribunal within 14 days after the Tribunal has sent notification of the striking out to the party in question.[127]

4. Withdrawal and Substitution of Parties

A party may withdraw the whole or any part of its case either before a hearing by sending   15.76
to the Tribunal and all other parties a written notice of withdrawal or orally at a hearing. The withdrawal will only have effect if all other parties consent or the Tribunal consents. However an application for permission to appeal may be withdrawn by the applicant even without the consent of the Tribunal or of all other parties. A party which has withdrawn its case, or a part of it, may apply to the Tribunal for the case to be reinstated. The application for reinstatement must be made in writing and received by the Tribunal within one month after the receipt of the notice of withdrawal, or the date of the oral withdrawal, at a hearing.[128] If a party withdraws its case or a part of its case the Tribunal will usually only consent to the withdrawal if that party pays to the other party the costs thrown away by the previous promotion of the case or part of it which is withdrawn. The consent to a withdrawal will therefore usually be on such terms as to costs. It is not clear what happens if a party wishes to withdraw its case but the Tribunal does not consent. Presumably the case is not then withdrawn but it may subsequently be struck out for lack of co-operation. It is difficult to envisage circumstances in which a party is not permitted to withdraw the whole or a part of its case if it wishes to do so and pays the costs thrown away by the previous promotion of its case.

There is no express provision which prevents a party who has withdrawn its case from start-   15.77
ing new proceedings of the same or a similar nature.[129] It is possible that in some circumstances a party who acts in this way could find its new proceedings struck out as an abuse of the process either under rule 8 or under the inherent jurisdiction of the Tribunal to control its own procedure. [130]

Where proceedings have been commenced a person who is not a party may apply to the   15.78
Tribunal to be added or substituted as a party.[131] The Tribunal may give a direction adding, substituting or removing a party in any proceedings and may give consequential directions. It is unusual in claims for compensation for parties to be added or substituted. On occasions acquiring authorities make arrangements with other parties, such as developers, to

---

[127] Rule 8(5), (6).
[128] Rule 20.
[129] It may be that the limited opportunity to apply for the reinstatement of a case which has been withdrawn under r 20, as mentioned in the last paragraph, is inconsistent with the commencement of new proceedings which are substantially the same as proceedings which have been withdrawn and not reinstated. Under the CPR applicable in the High Court and the County Court a party who has discontinued his proceedings needs the permission of the court to make another claim against the same defendant where the discontinuance is after the defendant has filed a defence and the other claim arises out of facts which are the same or substantially the same as those relating to the discontinued claim: CPR, r 38.7.
[130] *Johnson v Gore Wood* [2002] 2 AC 1, [2001] 2 WLR 72. See n 11.
[131] Rule 9.

fund the payment of compensation. In such a case it would be normal for the acquiring authority alone to contest the proceedings and any arrangements for assistance to the authority would be informal arrangements with the party providing the funds not entitling that party to be a participant in the proceedings.

5. Witness Statements and Reports of Experts

15.79   It is a feature common to all modern civil litigation that parties are required to produce their evidence in written form prior to the commencement of an oral hearing. Evidence is either evidence of factual matters or expert evidence, that is opinion evidence on an expert subject by someone qualified in the field. Where factual evidence is necessary the Tribunal will normally direct that all witnesses giving that evidence shall prepare and serve a witness statement in advance of the hearing. That statement should set out the factual evidence of the witness and should have exhibited to it, or be accompanied by, any documents to be produced or relied on in support of that evidence. A witness statement must contain the words 'I believe that the facts stated in this witness statement are true' and must be signed by the person who makes it.[132] It should be understood that the function of a witness statement of fact is to state relevant facts and not to contain expressions of opinion or to try to argue the case for or against a party. This principle may be somewhat relaxed in witness statements which accompany a procedural application since an explanation and sometimes submissions made in the witness statement may be the most practical way of bringing the detailed grounds of the application to the attention of the Tribunal and the other party.

15.80   An expert witness of course owes a contractual duty of care to his client, and he is not immune from civil proceedings which seek damages for a breach of that duty.[133] However, it is stated in the Rules that it is the duty of an expert to help the Tribunal on matters within the expert's expertise and that this duty overrides any obligation to the person who instructs or pays the expert.[134] Indeed this is the principle which governs the participation of expert witnesses in all civil proceedings. Expert evidence has to be given in a written report unless the Tribunal directs otherwise.[135] In nearly all cases there will be a direction that an expert's report is provided well in advance of the hearing. That report must contain a statement that the expert understands the duty just stated, must be signed by the expert, must contain the words 'I believe that the facts stated in this report are true and that the opinions expressed are correct', and must comply with any practice direction as regards its form and content.[136] The Practice Directions of the Tribunal require that an expert's report is addressed to the Tribunal and not to the party who instructs the expert and must give details of the expert's qualifications, give details of any literature or other material on which he has relied, state who carried out any inspection or investigations which the expert has used for the report and whether or not the investigations have been carried out under the expert's supervision,

---

[132] Rule 16(4).
[133] *Jones v Kaney* [2011] UKSC 13, [2011] 2 AC 398. Prior to this decision of the Supreme Court it had been supposed that no proceedings for breach of a duty of care could be brought against an expert witness either as regards the giving of evidence or as regards the preparation of evidence for proceedings by way of an expert's report or similar material.
[134] Rule 17(1).
[135] Rule 17(4).
[136] Rule 17(5).

and give the qualifications of the person who carried out any such inspection or investigations. Where there is a range of opinion on the matters dealt with in the report it must summarise the range of opinion and give reasons for the expert's own opinion. The report must contain a summary of the conclusions reached and must contain a statement setting out the substance of all material instructions received by the expert, whether written or oral. This statement should summarise the facts and instructions given to the expert.[137] Although such instructions are not privileged against disclosure the Tribunal will not permit any questioning on the instructions, other than by the party who instructed the expert, unless there are reasonable grounds to believe that the statement made by the expert of his instructions is inaccurate or incomplete.[138]

In simpler cases an exchange of experts' reports should be sufficient. In longer and more complicated cases it is usually of value that following the initial exchange of experts' reports there are rebuttal reports in the sense that each expert provides a further report which explains where and why he disagrees with the report of an expert on the same subject who has produced a report for the other party. The value of such rebuttal reports is that it prevents anyone being taken by surprise and cuts down the time taken in oral evidence at a hearing. The time taken up in preparing useful rebuttal reports is often better spent than is time taken up in negotiating bland and unhelpful statements of agreed facts between experts who fundamentally disagree.[139]   15.81

An expert witness should be wholly independent and impartial and should not have any connection, direct or indirect, with the outcome of the proceedings. As an extreme example it would be most undesirable for a valuer to give expert evidence where his fee depended on the result of the proceedings.[140] It is not possible to state a precise rule which establishes what precise connection with one of the parties or with the issues prevents a person giving evidence for a party as an expert witness. It is frequent practice that employees or officers of public bodies give expert evidence on valuation and other matters on behalf of their employer.[141] If there is an unacceptably close connection between the expert and the party who wishes to call him to give evidence the court may refuse to admit the evidence.[142] Even if the evidence of an expert is admitted, despite his connection with the party who calls him to give evidence, that connection may reduce the weight which the Tribunal accords to his evidence. Where a party has any doubt on the independence of an expert to be called by him or by another party he should raise this matter at the earliest possible time. If there is a dispute on the question the matter should, wherever possible, be decided at a preliminary stage rather than waiting for trial.[143]   15.82

---

[137] Practice Directions, para 8.2(1).

[138] Practice Directions, para 8.2(2).

[139] See paras 15.84 et seq.

[140] *R (Factortame) Ltd v Transport Secretary (No 2)* [2003] QB 381, [2003] 3 WLR 1104. An undertaking by an expert witness to bear the costs of his client if a claim is unsuccessful is plainly objectionable: *Hallows v Welsh Office* (1995) 70 P & CR 117.

[141] *Field v Leeds City Council* [2001] 2 CPLR 129. An expert has been permitted to give evidence for a party even though he was an employee of a related company: *Gallagher Industries Ltd v Tiais Enterprises Ltd* [2007] EWHC 464. A general summary of the principles on this subject is found in *The Ikarian Reefer* [1993] 2 Lloyd's Rep 68, at pp 81–82.

[142] *Liverpool Roman Catholic Archdiocesan Trust v Goldberg (No 3)* [2001] 1 WLR 2337; *Toth v Jarman* [2006] 4 All ER 1276.

[143] *R (on the application of Factortame) Ltd v Transport Secretary (No 2)* [2003] QB 381, [2003] 3 WLR 1104.

6. Case Management Hearings

15.83   It is the practice of the Tribunal to convene, either at its own initiative or at the request of the parties, a case management hearing (sometimes called a case management conference) in more complicated proceedings. This is the usual course where a case is allocated to the special procedure.[144] There may need to be more than one case management hearing. Matters which can usefully be dealt with at a case management hearing include the following. (a) The need for and terms of preliminary issues can be determined. (b) Directions can be given as to the number of expert witnesses on each side. (c) Directions can be given for exchange of witness statements of fact. (d) A timetable can be laid down for the exchange of experts' reports. (e) An order for disclosure of documents can be made, together with an order for parties to provide information or answer questions raised by the other party. (f) Directions can be given for meetings between experts to agree material. (g) Directions can be given about the preparation of bundles of documents and bundles of authorities. (h) An estimate can be made of the expected length of the hearing. (i) Further pleadings or clarification of pleadings can be ordered. (j) Directions can be given for steps leading to the hearing including the exchange of skeleton arguments. It is sometimes directed that a date be fixed for the hearing which is to be not before some specified date which allows time for preliminary procedural matters and steps to be completed. The Tribunal generally has a full list of cases awaiting trial and if a hearing is likely to take more than a short time there is likely to be a considerable delay before a hearing date is available.

7. Agreements in Advance of the Hearing

15.84   The Practice Directions require that where more than one party intends to call expert evidence in the same field the experts should take steps to agree all matters of fact relevant to their reports before preparing or exchanging the reports. The facts include those relating to comparable transactions on which the experts rely. Steps should also be taken to agree plans, documents or photographs intended to be relied on in the reports.[145] While this is obviously a useful practice there is far from universal compliance with this requirement of the Practice Directions. What is often more useful is that, as explained below, the experts meet to try to see what can be agreed after reports have been exchanged when the parties and their experts will have a better idea of what are the expert contentions of the opposing party.

15.85   A party may put written questions about the report of an expert instructed by another party. This should be done within a month of service of the report and should be only for the purposes of clarification. An answer should be given within three weeks. The Tribunal may order that the question must be answered. If the question is not answered pursuant to a direction an order may be made that the party calling the expert may not rely on the evidence of that expert.[146]

---

[144]   Practice Directions, para 3.4(1).
[145]   Practice Directions, para 8.1.
[146]   Practice Directions, para 8.3.

The Practice Directions also require that when the reports of experts have been exchanged   15.86
the experts should usually meet, and where the Tribunal directs must meet, in order to
reach agreement as to facts and to agree plans, photographs, etc, so as to identify the issues
in the proceedings and where possible to reach agreement on an issue. The Tribunal may
also direct that following such a discussion the parties prepare a statement showing those
facts and issues on which the experts agree, and on which they disagree, and a summary of
their reasons for disagreeing.[147] Experts tend to be cautious in that which they will and
will not agree. Often agreement is reached only on basic facts such as the description of
the property being valued, the facts of comparable transactions, and matters such as the
valuation date. As a result statements of agreement and disagreement tend to be more bland
than helpful. The contents of the discussions between the experts cannot be referred to at
the hearing unless the parties agree. They are in effect without prejudice discussions.
Furthermore the content of an agreement does not bind the parties unless they expressly
agree to be bound by the agreement. One supposes that, even if the agreement is not formally binding, propositions which opposing experts have agreed will be strong evidence of
the truth of those propositions. Parties who instruct experts to attend discussions of the
present nature sometimes also take a cautious approach and tell the expert that he is not to
reach any formal agreement until it has been approved by the lawyers representing the parties.

An attempt is sometimes made between the parties to produce a statement of agreed facts   15.87
in advance of the hearing. General experience is that such statements tend to refer only to
obvious matters such as the date of entry into the property, the service of notice to treat and
similar matters not susceptible of dispute. Much effort is sometimes put into negotiating
these agreed statements with little useful result. A difficulty is that even when the facts are
largely and basically agreed parties tend to believe that the way in which the opposing party
wishes to state the facts contains nuances which favour that party. The background to the
proceedings can often be usefully stated at the beginning of experts' reports or witness
statements.

A party may apply for an order that expert evidence in the proceedings should be given by   15.88
a single joint expert jointly instructed by the parties. A single joint expert may give evidence
relating to one issue among others before the Tribunal. Before giving a direction for a single
joint expert the Tribunal will take into account a number of circumstances including
whether it is proportionate to have separate experts for each party on a particular issue and
whether the instruction of a single joint expert is likely to assist the parties and the Tribunal
to resolve the issue more speedily and in a more cost-effective way.[148] The use of a single
joint expert is not often popular with the parties and in valuation disputes it is not a procedure which is frequently adopted before the Tribunal. The Tribunal can itself impose the
giving of evidence by a single joint expert even though it has not received an application
from one party that that should be done.[149]

---

[147] Practice Directions, para 8.4.
[148] Practice Directions, para 8.6(2).
[149] Rule 16(1)(c) permits the Tribunal to give a direction that the parties must appoint a single expert to give
expert evidence. The Practice Directions in para 8.6(1) refer to a party applying for an order that evidence should
be given by a single joint expert. Under r 6(1) the Tribunal may give a direction on its own initiative and this could
include a direction for a single joint expert.

15.89   Where parties propose to rely upon computer-based valuations they should agree to employ a common model which can be made available for use by the Tribunal in the preparation of its decision. Directions should be sought on this matter if there is likely to be difficulty in reaching agreement.[150] In valuation disputes the preparation of residual valuations and of discounted cash flow analyses as valuation techniques is often aided by computer models. These and other valuation methods are explained in chapter 14. What is often done is that the parties agree, subject to conditions as to confidentiality, that the details of their computer-based valuations shall be made available to the opposite party. Arrangements can then be made for supplying the model for the use of the Tribunal in its decision. The point, of course, is that the operation of the model depends on the inputs into it which will be a matter of valuation judgement. When the Tribunal reaches its decision on the appropriate inputs it may need the model in order to enable it to produce a final result.

8. Judicial Review

15.90   Judicial review is a process under which since medieval times the superior courts have controlled the proceedings of lower courts and of administrative bodies. It is a process which is today carried out by the Administrative Court of the Queen's Bench Division under Part 54 of the Civil Procedure Rules. The Lands Tribunal as part of the Upper Tribunal is itself in principle controllable by process of judicial review.[151] The Upper Tribunal, including the Lands Chamber, has been given a limited power to grant certain types of relief by way of judicial review under the Tribunals, Courts and Enforcement Act 2007. The powers available include relief by way of an injunction or a declaration or a quashing order. A quashing order means that the decision of some other person or body is quashed on the basis that it is unlawful. The occasions and circumstances in which the jurisdiction of the Tribunal can be exercised are limited both as to when an order may be made and as to the persons sitting in the Tribunal who may make the order.[152] As yet no steps have been taken under the Tribunals, Courts and Enforcement Act 2007 needed before the Lands Chamber of the Upper Tribunal becomes entitled to exercise a power of judicial review. In any event it appears unlikely that there will be many circumstances in references to determine compensation in which the power of judicial review will become relevant.

9. Security for Costs

15.91   There is a power in the High Court and the County Court under the Civil Procedure Rules whereby the court can in certain defined circumstances order a claimant to give security for costs.[153] The purpose is to guard against a situation in which a claimant is ordered to pay the costs of the proceedings but is then found to have insufficient funds to do so. There is no separate power in the Rules or in the Tribunals, Courts and Enforcement Act 2007 which allows the Tribunal to order security for costs. There was formerly a statutory power to

---

[150] Practice Directions, para 8.5.
[151] *R (on the application of Cart) v Upper Tribunal* [2011] UKSC 28, [2012] 1 AC 663.
[152] See ss 15–18 of the Tribunals, Courts and Enforcement Act 2007.
[153] CPR, rr 25.12 and 25.13.

order a company which was a claimant to give security for costs under section 726(1) of the Companies Act 1985. This was repealed as from 1 October 2009 by the Companies Act 2006 and was not replaced since the statutory provision duplicated one of the circumstances in which a court could order security for costs against a company. The Lands Tribunal could formerly have ordered security for costs under this provision against a company which made a claim for compensation. Today, following the repeal of the statutory provision, there is no power for the Tribunal to order security for costs. In some ways this seems an unfortunate situation, although an order for security for costs is always discretionary and would sparingly be ordered against any genuine claimant for compensation particularly if the result of the order might be to prevent that claimant from pressing his claim.[154]

(J) PROCEDURE AT THE HEARING

1. General Procedure

The procedure at a hearing before the Tribunal is, subject to the Rules, at the discretion of   15.92 the Tribunal.[155] All courts and tribunals have an inherent power to conduct and control proceedings before them. The Tribunal is given an express power under the Rules to decide the form of any hearing and to adjourn or postpone a hearing.[156] The procedure adopted in any particular case will vary according to which of the four procedures a reference has been allocated. If the reference is allocated to the simplified procedure the hearing will be informal and strict rules of evidence will not apply.[157] At such a hearing in some cases the parties may be represented by valuers rather than lawyers or a claimant may not be represented at all but may conduct his own case. In such cases legal formalities which are otherwise important, such as the strict separation of evidence and representations based on evidence, may have little impact. In references under the other procedures where there is an oral hearing, the special procedure and the standard procedure, the procedure at a hearing will generally accord with that usual in the High Court and the County Courts and the rules of evidence will apply.[158] The hearing must be held in public.[159] If a party fails to attend a hearing the Tribunal may proceed with the hearing if it is satisfied that the party has been notified of the hearing, or that reasonable steps have been taken to notify him of the hearing, and it is in the interests of justice to proceed with the hearing.[160] Therefore if a claimant fails to attend a hearing the Tribunal may in an appropriate case proceed to determine the compensation with only the acquiring authority present and calling evidence. One of the circumstances which permit the Tribunal in its discretion to set aside a decision is that a party or his representative was not present at a hearing.[161]

---

[154] In *Transport for London v Spirerose Ltd* [2009] UKHL 44, [2009] 1 WLR 1797, the Lands Tribunal at an interlocutory stage held that it had power to order security for costs under s 726(1) of the Companies Act 1985 but declined to make an order since the effect of doing so was likely to be to prevent the claimant from pressing on with its claim.

[155] Practice Directions, para 9.1.

[156] Rule 5(3)(g).

[157] Practice Directions, para 3.3(2).

[158] Ibid, para 9.1.

[159] Rule 48(1), (3).

[160] Rule 49.

[161] See para 15.111.

15.93   The general procedure adopted in the courts is well known. The parties usually instruct legal representatives, either a solicitor or a barrister. The claimant may make an opening statement. It has become a useful practice adopted in some courts that at this stage, and before any evidence is given, the defendant or respondent is invited also to make an opening statement. In this way the court is enabled to know at an early stage what is the substance of the case for both parties insofar as that is not already apparent from statements of case.[162] It is also the general practice that each party is required in advance of the hearing to provide a skeleton argument which summarises the main components of his case. Although described as skeleton arguments these documents often amount to a fairly full exposition of the case for a party and take the form of what is in effect a written opening statement.[163] If the statements of case on behalf of both parties and the skeleton arguments are full documents there should not normally be any reason for long opening statements at the oral hearing. The Tribunal may itself during any opening statements choose to put questions to the representatives of the parties so as to understand what are the true issues in the case and what is the contention of a party on those issues.

15.94   The next stage is that evidence is called by the claimant. Where a witness has made a witness statement that witness statement stands as the evidence in chief of the witness save that with the permission of the Tribunal the witness may amplify the statement and may deal with new matters which have arisen since the witness statement was provided.[164] The report provided by an expert will normally stand as the evidence in chief of that expert but some amplification may be necessary. The purpose of expert reports and reports in rebuttal is that a good deal of time should not be taken up at the hearing with giving oral expert evidence in chief. It is the usual practice in criminal trials that a witness stays outside the courtroom until he comes to give his evidence, the reason being that he should not be influenced by what earlier witnesses have said. The Tribunal has power to direct that a witness in the proceedings before it shall be excluded until he gives evidence.[165] This power is rarely exercised in compensation hearings. Each witness is subject to cross-examination by the representative of the other party and to re-examination by his own representative. When the evidence for the claimant has been completed a similar process is followed with the evidence for the acquiring authority. Where there are a number of issues, and these can be clearly separated, a procedure which is sometimes adopted is that the evidence of the claimant is given on one issue followed by the evidence of the acquiring authority on that issue and then the same process is followed for other issues. The benefit of this course is that the Tribunal then hears the evidence of opposing experts on a particular issue one after the other rather than there being a time separation between them. Whether such a procedure is adopted is a matter for the discretion of the Tribunal. If the parties wish such a procedure the Tribunal will normally permit it.

15.95   The final stage in the proceedings is closing submissions. In smaller cases these can be made orally when the evidence has been completed. The acquiring authority makes its submissions before those of the claimant. In larger cases the practice has increasingly become that the Tribunal requests written submissions by the parties with a period allowed for this and

---

[162] In the Lands Tribunal in Hong Kong this useful procedure is standard practice in complex cases.

[163] It would be a useful practice if in complex cases the pretence of 'skeleton' arguments was abandoned and a full written opening statement from each party was required at least a week before the beginning of the hearing.

[164] Rule 16(5).

[165] Rule 48(7).

with the acquiring authority making its submissions first followed by those of the claimant. If this written submissions procedure is adopted then there may be a final oral hearing, at the request of the Tribunal or at the request of one of the parties, at which final submissions can be made and any outstanding queries from the Tribunal answered.

2. Representation

A party is entitled to represent himself at a hearing. He may appoint a representative, whether a legal representative or not, to represent him.[166] If he does he should send written notice to the Tribunal and to each other party of the name and address of his representative.[167] In larger cases parties are normally represented by a barrister or a solicitor. In smaller cases a valuer who advises a party may also represent him at a hearing, and under the simplified procedure this is a course frequently adopted. When it comes to the hearing the Tribunal may give permission for any person to act as a representative of a party or to assist in some other way in presenting a case for that party at the hearing.[168]   15.96

3. Number of Witnesses and the Giving of Evidence

The Tribunal has a substantial degree of control over the number of witnesses who may be called. It may give directions as to whether the parties are permitted to provide expert evidence.[169] It will be an unusual case in which a party is refused permission to call expert evidence of any sort. Obviously if one party is permitted to call expert evidence the other party must also be permitted to do so. The Tribunal may limit the number of witnesses whose evidence a party may put forward whether in relation to a particular issue or generally.[170] This limitation applies to expert witnesses or witnesses of fact. There are then specific limitations on the number of expert witnesses. The general rule is that no party may call more than one expert witness without the permission of the Tribunal. This is qualified in proceedings relating to mineral valuations or business disturbance where the rule is that a party may call not more than two expert witnesses without the permission of the Tribunal.[171] In compensation claims it is often necessary to call more than one expert witness, for example a witness on valuation and a witness on planning matters. The Tribunal will generally give permission to do this. If a party genuinely cannot advance some aspect of his case without the support of expert evidence it will be rare for the Tribunal to refuse permission for that evidence (and of course evidence in reply from the other party if requested) to be given.   15.97

---

[166] Rule 11(1).
[167] Rule 11(2). The operation of this rule is often ignored or overlooked.
[168] Rule 11(5).
[169] Rule 16(1)(c).
[170] Rule 16(1)(d).
[171] Rule 17(2), (3). The reference to two expert witnesses in those two cases seems to hearken back to previous rules which governed proceedings in the Lands Tribunal. It is obvious that different cases call for different numbers of expert witnesses and a modern and sensible rule would simply enable the Tribunal to limit the expert witnesses in each case according to what is in issue and what is reasonable.

15.98   The Rules state that the Tribunal may admit evidence whether or not the evidence would be admissible in a civil trial in England or Wales.[172] This suggests that the rules of evidence may not be applied but the Practice Directions of the Tribunal state that save where the simplified procedure is applicable the rules of evidence will be applied.[173] In addition the Rules allow the Tribunal to exclude evidence which would otherwise be admissible where the evidence was not provided within the time allowed by a direction or was not provided in a manner which complied with a direction or it would otherwise be unfair to admit the evidence.[174] The primary principle of evidence in civil courts is that evidence is only admissible if it is relevant to some fact in issue in the proceedings. If evidence is tendered which has been provided in accordance with the directions of the Tribunal and is relevant it is not easy to see when it would be unfair to admit that evidence. A possible occasion for refusing to admit evidence might be where the evidence, although not strictly irrelevant, was of only tangential significance and a consideration of it and of any evidence in rebuttal would add substantially to the time and costs of the proceedings. The wide powers given to the Tribunal to limit the giving of evidence is a part of the modern tendency of courts to play a more active role in controlling procedure than was formerly the case. That having been said, the exercise by the Tribunal of its wide powers and discretions is subject to the overriding principle that a party is entitled to a fair opportunity to present its case and to meet the case of the opposing party, that is the *audi asteram partem* rule as a component of the rules of natural justice.

15.99   The Tribunal may consent to a witness giving, or may require a witness to give, evidence on oath.[175] In practice evidence is not often given on oath. If there is a suggestion that evidence is or may be dishonestly given then the taking of it on oath might be appropriate. An effect of evidence being given on oath is that the deliberate giving of untrue evidence constitutes the crime of perjury.

15.100 The Tribunal has power to compel the attendance of persons to give evidence. This may be done by the Tribunal issuing a summons, on the application of a party or on its own initiative, requiring any person to attend as a witness at a hearing. The summons must give 14 days notice of the hearing or such shorter period as the Tribunal may direct and, if the person served with a summons is not a party, the summons must make provision for that person's necessary expenses of attendance to be paid. In addition the Tribunal may order any person to answer any question or produce any documents in his possession or control which relate to any issue in the proceedings. The person who receives a summons or has an order made against him may apply to the Tribunal for it to be varied or set aside. No person may be compelled to give evidence or produce any document unless he could be compelled to give that evidence or produce the document at a trial of an action in a court of law. In other words in this instance the ordinary principles as to the compellability of witnesses and the admission of documentary evidence apply.[176]

15.101 It is not always apparent what is meant today by the rules of evidence, or the strict rules of evidence, in civil proceedings. It is said that the strict rules of evidence do not apply to references allocated to the simplified procedure and in any event the Tribunal has a wide discre-

---

[172] Rule 16(2)(a)(i).
[173] Practice Directions, para 9(1).
[174] Rule 16(2)(b).
[175] Rule 16(3).
[176] Rule 18.

tion under the Rules to admit, or not admit, evidence in proceedings before it.[177] Evidence is an oral or written statement which is relevant to one or more of the issues in the reference. Subject to the exclusion of irrelevant material there are few rules left today which can be called technical rules of evidence. The old 'best evidence' rule, that is the rule that only the best evidence of a matter could be introduced so that, as an example of its operation, generally the originals and not copies of documents had to be produced, has gone. There was at one time some difficulty with the exclusion of hearsay evidence. Hearsay evidence is evidence in a statement, written or oral, made by someone other than the giver of the evidence in order to prove the truth of the statement. It is generally someone who comes forward to say in evidence what someone else has told him. A result of the hearsay rule was that in valuation cases the valuers could not give evidence of what they had ascertained about the facts of a comparable transaction because that would be to give evidence of what people had told them with the result that the person who was himself involved in the transaction, either as a principal or agent, had to be called to prove these facts.[178] The hearsay rule was abolished in civil proceedings by the Civil Procedure Act 1995.

Apart from the technical rules of evidence (some of which still apply in criminal proceedings) there are other rules which are sometimes called rules of evidence but are perhaps better categorised as rules of procedure or fairness. For example, the content of without prejudice discussions cannot be disclosed without the consent of all involved in the discussions. A person cannot be required to disclose advice given to him by his legal representatives, a principle called legal professional privilege. Although this may not often arise in a compensation case the rule against self-incrimination should not be forgotten, that is the general immunity of a witness from being competent to answer questions the answers to which may indicate his guilt of a criminal offence.[179] When a witness is being cross-examined he should not speak to anyone about the case until his cross-examination has finished. The observance of rules of this nature is essential to a fair hearing and it is to be expected that these rules will be enforced by the Tribunal. 15.102

It is also necessary to be clear about the distinction drawn between the admissibility of evidence and the weight of evidence. The question of admissibility is a question of whether as a matter of principle and in law the evidence may be tendered to the Tribunal at all. Thus evidence of without prejudice discussions is inadmissible as stated in the last paragraph. Once evidence has been admitted it is then a matter for the Tribunal to decide what weight it accords to the evidence. Obviously the weight accorded to any particular item of evidence may vary from that item being compelling evidence of some matter to it being very slight evidence of the matter. Indeed it is possible that evidence is admitted and when the Tribunal has considered and evaluated the evidence it is decided that it can be accorded no weight. The admissibility of evidence is as matter of law subject to the general and wide discretion given to the Tribunal by the Rules to admit or not admit evidence. Obviously the weight which the Tribunal accords to a particular piece of evidence is a matter for the decision of the Tribunal having heard that evidence in the context of the reference as a whole and generally having heard the giver of the evidence cross-examined. 15.103

---

[177] See para 15.98.
[178] *English Exporters (London) Ltd v Eldonwall Ltd* [1973] Ch 415, [1973] 2 WLR 435.
[179] See *R v Director of the Serious Fraud Office, ex parte Smith* [1993] AC 1, [1992] 3 WLR 66, per Lord Mustill. There is at least one recent instance in which a person has been prosecuted in the Crown Court for making a fraudulent claim for disturbance compensation.

4. Site Inspections

15.104   The Tribunal may enter and inspect the land the subject of the proceedings and any other land relevant to the proceedings. The consent of the occupier is necessary and the Tribunal must give reasonable notice of its intended entry to the occupier and the parties to the proceedings. Unless otherwise agreed the Tribunal at its inspection will be accompanied by one representative from each party. The purpose of an inspection is to assist the Tribunal in its decision by viewing the premises and no further evidence, written or oral, may be given during the inspection. The result of an inspection is sometimes described as real evidence. The Tribunal may make an unaccompanied inspection if it can do so without entering private land.[180] A visual inspection is often an important part of the valuation process. The usual practice is that at the close of the proceedings the Tribunal considers with the assistance of the parties whether it needs to make a site inspection and, if it does, makes arrangements for it including arrangements for the member to be accompanied by a representative of each of the parties. When the valuations are based on comparable transactions it may be useful for the Tribunal to view the sites of the comparables. The party relying on a comparable transaction is expected to make arrangements with the owners and occupiers of the property in question if an internal inspection is necessary.

(K)   THE DECISION

15.105   While a decision of the Tribunal may be given orally at the conclusion of the hearing the normal practice is for the Tribunal to reserve its decision and to provide it later in writing. When it has made its decision, either a decision disposing of all issues or a decision on a preliminary issue or issues, the Tribunal must provide to each party a decision notice. The decision notice must provide or be accompanied by written reasons for the decision unless the decision was made by consent or the parties have consented to no reasons being given. Notice must be given of rights of review or appeal against the decision. There are two types of decision to which the requirement of a decision notice and written reasons do not apply, these being: (a) decisions correcting, setting aside or reviewing decisions of the Tribunal, and (b) decisions on interlocutory matters.[181] The Tribunal may provide written reasons for these decisions if it wishes.[182]

15.106   The Tribunal may make a consent order at the request of the parties and where it considers it appropriate it may do so without holding a hearing.[183] Parties sometimes settle their proceedings and wish for this to be recorded in formal terms by a consent order. Doing so may assist in the enforcement of the order or may provide a useful record for future cases. If exceptionally a decision is given orally notice of the decision with reasons in writing must still be given later if the decision is one which finally disposes of all issues or disposes of a

---

[180] Rule 19.
[181] Rule 51. For these purposes a decision on a matter ordered to be tried as a preliminary issue is regarded as a final and not an interlocutory decision.
[182] Rule 51(4). Reasons for decisions on important procedural issues are often sent.
[183] Rule 50.

preliminary issue or issues unless the order is by consent or the parties have consented to no reasons being given.

The usual practice of the Tribunal is that when it makes a decision on substantive issues, 15.107 including preliminary issues, it sends out a notice of decision with full reasons. It then invites written submissions on costs and finally sends out the decision with an addendum on costs.[184] Procedural and interlocutory applications are dealt with by a decision in writing if the application has been made and opposed by written representations or if there is a hearing the decision may be given orally at the hearing or, in more complex cases, by a separate written decision.[185]

Most cases on the law of compensation start in the Lands Tribunal and most end in that 15.108 court without any appeal. It follows that the decisions of the Tribunal form valuable guidance for practitioners. It is clearly important that where possible that guidance is consistent in the decisions of the Tribunal. The quality of, and the care taken in, decisions of the Tribunal on points of law over recent years is certainly equal to that of decisions of the High Court and the Court of Appeal, a sentiment which would be shared by most practitioners before the Tribunal. The Tribunal, however, is not bound by its own decisions in the way it is bound by decisions of the Court of Appeal and the House of Lords and the Supreme Court. It is free to depart from its previous decisions if it thinks it right to do so. It has been said in the Court of Appeal that decisions of the Tribunal on points of law should be treated with great respect even when given by a surveyor member but should not be regarded as binding and that it is important that such decisions should be carefully scrutinised and, if necessary, rejected particularly in cases which raise points of law of substantial importance.[186] Decisions on valuation, including a consideration of valuation techniques, do not form any sort of precedent in the same way as decisions on points of law but can sometimes provide useful guidance for future cases. For example, the reluctance of the Tribunal to place weight on residual valuations or profits based valuations where good comparables are available as an aid to valuation is well established in decisions of the Tribunal.[187] Decisions on procedural and interlocutory matters may also constitute useful guidance for the conduct of future cases.

(L) AMENDING DECISIONS

An appeal may be made against a decision of the Tribunal with permission and appeals are 15.109 described in section (n) of this chapter. The Tribunal itself has four limited opportunities to amend its decision in some way without an appeal from the decision.

---

[184] See section (m) for costs.

[185] Decisions of the Tribunal which contain points of general importance are reported with headnotes in specialist law reports such as the *Estates Gazette Law Reports* (EGLR) and the *Property and Compensation Reports* (P & CR). A full record of decisions of the Tribunal is published in the *Rating and Valuation Reporter* (RVR). The Tribunal also publishes its decisions on its website with an indication of any cases that are subject to appeal.

[186] *West Midland Baptist (Trust) Association Inc v Birmingham Corporation* [1968] 2 QB 188, [1988] 2 WLR 535, per Salmon LJ at p 210.

[187] See section (c) of ch 14. The Tribunal has on occasions set out to give general guidance on important matters of valuation such as in the valuations which have to be conducted under the legislation dealing with leasehold reform and enfranchisement: see *Earl Cadogan v Sportelli* [2007] 1 EGLR 153. See, however, the observations of the then President of the Tribunal, Douglas Frank, in *W Clibbett Ltd v Avon County* Council [1976] 1 EGLR 171. See also *Arbib v Earl Cadogan* [2005] 3 EGLR 139.

1. Clerical Mistakes

15.110 There has long existed in the courts what is known as 'the slip rule' whereby a decision of the court can be amended so as to rid it of any clerical and other similar errors. The Tribunal has a similar power under the Rules to correct any clerical mistake or other accidental slip or omission in a decision or record of a decision. The correction may be made at any time. The Tribunal must send to all parties notification of the amended decision or a copy of the amended record and must make any necessary amendment to any information published in relation to the decision or record.[188]

2. Setting Aside a Decision

15.111 Where it considers that it is in the interests of justice to do so the Tribunal may set aside a decision, or part of a decision, which disposes of proceedings and may re-make the decision or the relevant part of it. The Tribunal can only exercise this ostensibly drastic power if one or more of four conditions are satisfied. The conditions are: (a) a document relating to the proceedings was not sent to, or was not received at an appropriate time by, a party, (b) a document relating to the proceedings was not sent to the Tribunal at an appropriate time, (c) a party or its representative was not present at a hearing related to the proceedings, and (d) there has been some other procedural irregularity in the proceedings. The power to set aside a decision is therefore confined to cases of procedural errors or irregularities.

15.112 A decision may be set aside pursuant to this power on the application of a party which must be made by a written application to the Tribunal and all other parties and received no later than one month after the sending of notice of the decision to the party.[189] The exercise of the power to re-make a decision may involve the consideration of further evidence or a further hearing. An example of when this power may be exercised would be if written closing submissions were sent to the Tribunal but not received by it. The Tribunal, if it were to exercise its power, would then need to consider the further submissions and the result might be an alteration of its decision.

3. Review of a Decision

15.113 The Tribunal may review and amend a decision but only if it has received an application for permission to appeal and then only in limited circumstances. The circumstances are: (a) that when making the decision the Tribunal overlooked a legislative provision or binding authority which could have had a material effect on the decision, or (b) since the decision a court has made a decision which is binding on the Tribunal and which, had it been made before the decision of the Tribunal, could have had a material effect on that decision.[190] The

---

[188] Rule 53.

[189] Rule 54.

[190] Rule 56(1). It should be noted that the omission of the Tribunal to take account of one of its own previous decisions is not a ground for review since the Tribunal is not bound by its own previous decisions. Decisions of the High Court, although of strong persuasive force, are not formally binding on the Tribunal.

Tribunal is of course bound by legislative provisions and is bound by decisions of the Court of Appeal and the House of Lords and the Supreme Court. If it emerges following a decision that there was such a provision or binding decision, or a further binding decision has been given, apart from the power of review the only recourse of a party would be to appeal. The necessity for an appeal in such circumstances can be avoided by the Tribunal itself reviewing its decision and, in effect, and where necessary, amending its decision to that which it would have made had it been aware of and applied the legislative provision or binding authority in question. The Tribunal must notify the parties in writing of the outcome of the review and any rights of review or appeal in relation to that outcome. The Tribunal will normally not make a decision following a review without giving every party an opportunity to make representations but if every party has not been given that opportunity the notification to the parties must state that any party did not have that opportunity and that such a party may apply for the decision of the Tribunal on the review to be set aside and for the decision to be reviewed again. If the Tribunal decides not to review its decision, or reviews its decision but decides to take no action in relation to its decision, it must then go on to consider whether to give permission to appeal.[191] There is no time limit on the power of review but the exercise of the power is discretionary and if a considerable time has passed since the decision, or if a party has acted on the decision, the Tribunal may decline to carry out a review.

4. Amendment before Formal Order

When the High Court makes a decision it retains a power to correct its decision at any time 15.114 until a formal order is drawn up. The Tribunal, as mentioned, normally sends out notice of its decision, then invites submissions on costs, and then sends out the decision again with an addendum dealing with costs. It appears that pursuant to this general principle which applies in the courts the Tribunal retains a power to reconsider and amend what it has done at any time until the formal notification of the decision with the addendum as to costs is sent out.[192] There is no formal recognition of this process in the Rules or in the Practice Directions of the Tribunal.

The applications which may be made to the Tribunal after notification of its decision are 15.115 therefore an application for a decision to be corrected, for it to be set aside, for it to be reviewed, or an application for permission to appeal against the decision. There may be some understandable confusion on the part of parties as to which application it is most appropriate to make and provision is made to meet this difficulty. The Rules provide that the Tribunal may treat any of the applications just referred to as an application for any other

---

[191] Rule 56(2).

[192] *Charlesworth v Relay Roads Ltd* [2000] 1 WLR 230, [1999] 4 All ER 397; *Stewart v Engell* [2000] 1 WLR 2268, [2000] 3 All ER 518. For the power of the Tribunal to reconsider its decision at any time until it has issued its final decision including any determination on costs, see *Shraff Tip Ltd v Higgins Agency (No 2)* [1999] RVR 322, a decision of the Lands Tribunal approved by the Court of Appeal in *Railtrack Plc v Guinness Ltd* [2003] 1 EGLR 125. In principle new evidence can be received at this stage. However, in *Ridgeland Properties v Bristol City Council* [2011] RVR 232, the Tribunal refused to allow new evidence to be adduced in support of a different method of valuation after it had issued its decision in draft, but before it had issued its decision on costs, and the Court of Appeal refused to interfere with this exercise of its discretion by the Tribunal.

one of those matters.[193] It needs to be emphasised that the general principle is that once any court has delivered its judgment it has completed its function and, in the latin expression sometimes used, the court is *functus officio*. This principle applies to the Lands Tribunal so that the Tribunal has no general power to reconsider its decision once made. The power to reconsider and alter a decision is restricted to cases of clerical errors, procedural irregularities and the overlooking of binding authority. In brief terms a party cannot ask the Tribunal to alter or amend its decision simply because he believes that the decision was wrong. His only recourse in such a case is to seek permission to appeal, and then on a point of law only.

(M) COSTS

15.116 The Tribunal has power to make an award of costs on an application or on its own initiative.[194] The power to award costs covers proceedings for compensation for compulsory purchase and proceedings for injurious affection to land.[195] It seems that these words can cover references to the Tribunal in relation to the seven main heads of compensation and other questions relating to compulsory purchase where the Tribunal has jurisdiction.[196] The discretion to award costs is exercisable on certain principles some of which are of general application and some of which are of particular application to claims for compensation. The Rules state that in making an order for costs in proceedings for compensation for compulsory purchase, or for injurious affection of land, the Tribunal must have regard to the size and nature of the matters in dispute.[197]

1. Procedure and Powers

15.117 As mentioned earlier the usual procedure adopted by the Tribunal is to issue a decision dealing with the substantive issues and then to invite the parties to make any application for costs by way of written submissions.[198] The best course is that if one or other or both parties

---

[193] Rule 58.

[194] Section 29 of the Tribunals, Courts and Enforcement Act 2007; r 10. (1) A new form of r 10 came into effect on 1 July 2013 pursuant to the Tribunal Procedure (Amendment No 3) Rules 2013 (SI 2013/1188). Certain other amendments were made to the Rules at the same time which are referred to as necessary in this chapter. The new r 10 and other amendments to the Rules apply to references made before 1 July 2013 as well as on and after that date. In respect of references made before 1 July 2013 there is a transitional provision in para 10 of the Amendment Rules which gives the Tribunal the power to apply any provision of the Rules which applied before 1 July 2013 and to disapply any amendment made by the Amendment Rules. In exercising its power the Tribunal must ensure that the proceedings are dealt with fairly. In addition the Tribunal in exercising its discretion must have regard to all relevant considerations: *Wootton v Central Land Board* [1957] 1 WLR 424, (1957) 8 P & CR 121.

[195] Rule 10(2)(a), (6).

[196] See section (b) of ch 3 for the seven main heads.

[197] Rule 10(8).

[198] See para 15.107. Under r 10(10) of the Rules the application must be made within 14 days of the sending of the notice of the decision which finally disposed of all issues in the proceedings. The practice of the Tribunal is to state this time limit when notice of the decision is sent. If a notice of withdrawal of proceedings is sent to the Tribunal with the consent of all parties, or the Tribunal sends notice to the parties that a withdrawal which ends the proceedings has taken effect, the 14 days for making the application for costs runs from the date of the sending of the notice: r 10(10)(b), (c). The Tribunal may extend time for making an application for costs under r 5(3)(a).

wishes to make an application for costs that application is made in writing with the other party then given an opportunity to respond with written submissions. If the response raises new matters or new arguments fairness requires that the applicant should be given a final opportunity to reply to this material. It may of course occur that both parties apply for an order for costs. A timetable may be imposed for this process of the exchange of submissions. The Tribunal then re-issues its decision with an addendum dealing with costs. The period prescribed for an application for permission to appeal does not start to run until the costs decision has been issued.[199]

Orders may be made as to the costs of interlocutory procedural applications such as an application for disclosure of documents or for directions for pleadings and for the hearing. The Tribunal will sometimes make a separate order for the costs of such applications, certainly if they involve an oral hearing. Where the interlocutory or procedural application is necessary for the disposal of the reference an order often made is 'costs in the reference'. This means that when a final order is made for costs at the end of the proceedings the costs of the application become a part of those general costs. For example, if a claimant is in the end awarded his costs of the reference against the acquiring authority the costs will include the costs of the application in respect of which such an order was made. As mentioned earlier a case management hearing is often held, especially in more complex cases, to determine aspects of the future conduct of the proceedings and it is a frequent practice to order the costs of such a hearing to be costs in the reference. On the other hand if a party has behaved unreasonably in making or resisting an interlocutory application, or sometimes even if he has just been unsuccessful in making or resisting the application, so that costs have been incurred unnecessarily that party may be ordered to pay the costs of that application in any event. Thus a party who fails in a particular interlocutory application, such as by seeking an order for disclosure of documents which is refused by the Tribunal, may have to pay the costs of the unsuccessful application. The approach to costs stated in this paragraph accords with the general practice in civil courts.[200] The Tribunal may make an order ordering a party to pay costs if it considers that the party has acted unreasonably in bringing, defending or conducting the proceedings (a wasted costs order).[201]   15.118

The Tribunal may direct that no order for costs may be made against one or more specified parties in respect of costs subsequently incurred.[202] This power, introduced by amendment in 2013, reflects the practice of the courts in certain circumstances. For example, if one   15.119

An application for costs must be made in writing and sent to the Tribunal and to the person against whom it is proposed the order be made: r 10(9)(a). In practice applications for the costs of interlocutory matters are often made orally during the course of proceedings and an order is made there and then. The Tribunal must give a person against whom an order for costs is made an opportunity to make representations: r 10(11).

[199] See para 15.141 .

[200] Various other forms of costs order are sometimes made. One is that the costs of interlocutory proceedings shall be 'costs reserved'. What this means is that the decision about costs is deferred to a later occasion but if no later order is made the costs will be the costs in the reference. Another variation is that an order is made for the claimant's or the acquiring authority's 'costs in the reference'. This means that if the party in whose favour the costs order is made is awarded costs at the end of the proceedings that party is entitled to his costs of the part of the proceedings to which the order relates. If any other party is awarded costs at the end of the proceedings the party in whose favour this form of costs order is made is not liable to pay the costs of any other party of the part of the proceedings to which the order relates.

[201] Section 29(4) of the Tribunals, Courts and Enforcement Act 2007; r 10(3).

[202] Rule 10(7). A written application for such a direction should be made to the Tribunal and the application must include the reasons of the person making it as to why the conditions or circumstances relevant to making a direction apply.

person brings proceedings which are in effect a test case with many other persons having a similar interest in the result (or if proceedings are brought against such a person) it may be appropriate to make a direction of the present sort to ensure that the person who has taken the burden of the proceedings (or who has had the proceedings brought against him) does not run the personal risk of a heavy order for costs being made against him.

2. The General Principle

15.120   Where the reference is determined under the simplified or the written representations procedure costs will only be awarded in exceptional circumstances such as if there has been an unreasonable failure on the part of a claimant to accept an offer or if either party has behaved in some unreasonable fashion.[203] If the reference is allocated to the standard or special procedure more general considerations govern an award of costs.

15.121   The general rule adopted by the courts is that costs follow the event and this is now enshrined in the Civil Procedure Rules.[204] What this means is that a successful party is generally entitled to have his costs paid by the unsuccessful party. However, this is only a starting point and in general litigation some different order for costs may often be justified. A party may be deprived of the whole or a part of his costs even though he has been successful overall if there are particular issues which have been considered separately and he has failed on those. For example, a defendant may resist proceedings against him on two alternative grounds. He may succeed on the first ground so that he obtains judgment but fail on the second ground. If the second ground was considered separately, with separate evidence and separate arguments, it is possible that the defendant will be awarded some but not the whole of his costs. Another situation is that a party may be awarded his costs even though he is not successful or wholly successful where he has made an offer to settle and then has done better at the end of the proceedings than his offer. Irrespective of the result of the remainder of the proceedings the person who made the offer may then be awarded his costs from the date of the offer or from a reasonable date following the offer and needed to consider the offer at the end of which it should have been accepted. Of course a party, although successful, may be deprived of the whole or a part of his costs if he has behaved in some unreasonable fashion in relation to the litigation, for example by not co-operating with the court or by inordinately dragging out the proceedings. The Tribunal follows these general principles in exercising its discretion on costs.[205]

15.122   The general rule that costs follow the event is not easy to apply where the dispute is one of the valuation of land. In many civil proceedings a party either succeeds or fails; for instance he either succeeds in showing that there has been a breach of contract or a tort committed against him or he does not. It is much less usual for a party to a valuation dispute wholly to succeed in this way. It is more likely that the decision of the body which decides the dispute will be that the value falls somewhere between that contended for by each of the parties. It is not always easy in such circumstances to say that one party has wholly or mainly succeeded in the litigation. In arbitration, and other forms of determination of valuation,

---

[203]   Practice Directions, paras 3.3(4), 3.5(3).
[204]   CPR, r 44.3(2)(a).
[205]   Practice Directions, paras 12.2, 12.3.

disputes where the result is somewhere between the two extremes contended for by the parties the result is often that no order for costs is made. However, when the claim is a claim for compensation for land compulsorily acquired a different and important principle comes into play. It is considered that the costs and expenses of establishing the amount of the compensation due to him are a part of the loss imposed on a landowner by the compulsory purchase. Consequently, unless there are special circumstances, the general principle is that the claimant for compensation in a reference to the Tribunal is entitled to his costs.[206] This principle is similar in its rationale to the rule that a claimant is normally entitled to the reasonable costs incurred by him in preparing his claim for compensation prior to a reference to the Tribunal under rule (6) of section 5 of the Land Compensation Act 1961.[207] In short the general rule in civil litigation that costs follow the event is superseded in compensation references before the Lands Tribunal by the general principle just mentioned which is of course more favourable to claimants than the general rule that costs follow the event. There are three main exceptions to this general principle.

3. The Three Exceptions

The first exception mirrors the practice in the courts. A claimant may still be deprived of the 15.123 whole or a part of his costs if he has acted in some way which is unreasonable. A claimant may have unnecessarily delayed the proceedings in some procedural fashion or called unnecessary evidence. He may have exaggerated his claim in some way. He may have included in his claim items which are dealt with separately and which prove unsustainable. On the other hand a claimant who has conducted his case sensibly and without exaggeration and waste of time is likely to be awarded the whole of his costs of the reference even though the amount of compensation which he is awarded falls substantially below that which he has claimed. The leading case in the Court of Appeal on this subject is an example of where a claimant who obtained before the Lands Tribunal a higher sum of compensation than had ever been offered to him was awarded only 75 per cent of his costs on the ground that he had introduced certain comparables which the Tribunal found unhelpful.[208] Despite this decision it has now been established on high authority that a claimant, otherwise entitled to his costs, should only fail to obtain an order for the whole of his costs on the ground that his claim was excessive where the exaggeration has given rise to an obvious and substantial escalation in the costs over and above those which it was reasonable for the claimant to incur. If a reduction is justified the amount should have regard to the amount of waste of time and costs properly attributable to the claimant's acts and omissions.[209]

---

[206] *Purfleet Farms Ltd v Secretary of State* [2002] EWCA Civ 1430, [2003] 1 EGLR 9; *Emslie P Simpson Ltd v Aberdeen District Council* [1995] RVR 159; *Blakes Estates Ltd v Government of Montserrat* [2006] 1 WLR 297. The same principle was applied under the Lands Clause Consolidation Act 1845 to arbitrations which were one of the methods of determining compensation prescribed by that Act: *Fisher v Great Western Rly* [1911] 1 KB 551.

[207] See ch 8, paras 8.23–8.25.

[208] *Purfleet Farms Ltd v Secretary of State*, above n 200. The Court of Appeal in this case, having explained the general principle, declined to interfere with the decision of the Tribunal to award the claimant only 75% of his costs. In *English Property Corporation v Royal Borough of Kingston on Thames* (1999) 77 P & CR 1, the Court of Appeal held that a decision of the Lands Tribunal ordering the claimants to pay to the acquiring authority the costs of a part of the total claim on which the claimants had failed was correct in principle.

[209] *Blakes Estates Ltd v Government of Montserrat* [2006] 1 WLR 297, at p 307. It is questionable whether the decision in the *Purfleet Farms* case to reduce the costs by 25% is justifiable in the light of this later guidance.

15.124 The second exception arises out of the making of an offer to settle the claim. An acquiring authority may make such an offer at any time, before or after the reference to the Tribunal. If the offer is made before the reference it is usually made in the form of a 'Calderbank' offer which means that the offer cannot be referred to in any proceedings relating to the claim except in relation to costs. It is usual to mark the letter clearly at the top with some expression such as 'without prejudice save as to costs'.[210] If the offer is made after the reference to the Tribunal has been issued the Practice Directions of the Tribunal state that the offer must be made by sending a copy of it to the Tribunal within a sealed envelope enclosed with a covering letter. The member hearing the case will not see the offer or be informed of its existence until after the proceedings, save as to the question of costs, have been determined.[211] Such offers are often called 'sealed offers'. Despite this advice in the Practice Directions there is no reason why a party, even after the issuing of the reference to the Tribunal, should not make an offer in any form that it wishes.[212] The sealed offer may be made in any form but the Practice Directions suggest that it must clearly identify which part of the proceedings or the issue it relates to and that it should also state whether or not it is open for acceptance indefinitely or for a specified period of time, whether or not it includes interest, and whether or not it includes an agreement to pay the other party's costs.[213] A typical and properly framed offer by an acquiring authority will state that the authority is willing to pay a specified sum in full and final settlement of the compensation (or some specified sum in settlement of certain stated items of the compensation) and that the authority is also willing to pay interest at the statutory rate from the date specified by statute until the date of payment and that the authority is willing to pay the costs of the claimant up to a reasonable date following the receipt of the offer during which the offer can be considered. What is a reasonable date will depend upon the complexity of the case but normally a few weeks should be sufficient.

15.125 Obviously a sealed offer by an acquiring authority will be pitched at a level somewhere in excess of the compensation figure which it contends is correct through its evidence. This is partly because of the imprecise nature of the valuation process and partly because an authority may be willing to pay a sum somewhat in excess of its estimate of the correct compensation in order to avoid the costs and delay and uncertainty attendant on legal proceedings. That having been said an authority could be criticised if it made a sealed offer grossly in excess of the figure put forward in its evidence. It is the duty of an authority to pay the correct compensation, not the lowest compensation, and a very high sealed offer could be criticised as showing either: (a) that the authority had no faith in the valuation of its own expert, or (b) that it was willing to pay out of the public purse a sum much greater than its estimate of the total value of the property acquired.

---

[210] The practice derives from *Calderbank v Calderbank* [1976] Fam 93, [1975] 3 WLR 586, a decision of the Court of Appeal in a matrimonial matter in which the practice was first approved. It is now a procedure used widely in litigation and arbitration.

[211] Practice Directions, para 12.7(3).

[212] Tribunals, Courts and Enforcement Act 2007, s 29. See *Director of Buildings and Lands v Shun Fung Ironworks Ltd* [1995] 2 AC 111, [1995] 2 WLR 904, for observations on the desirability of giving weight to every attempt to settle proceedings in whatever form made.

[213] Practice Directions, para 12.7(2). If a sealed offer does not expressly refer to interest it would probably be considered as an offer to pay compensation in the sum stated together with interest on that sum as provided by statute: *Tollgate Hotels Ltd v Secretary of State for Transport* [2006] RVR 315.

The normal consequence which flows from the making of an offer by the acquiring authority   15.126
is that if the offer is not accepted, and the claimant in the end is awarded compensation
which is no higher than the amount of the offer, the acquiring authority is likely to be ordered
to pay the costs of the claimant up until the date on which the offer should have been accepted
and the claimant is likely to be ordered to pay the costs of the acquiring authority from that
date onwards. This approach to costs has statutory recognition in that it is provided in section 4(1)(a) of the Land Compensation Act 1961 that where an acquiring authority has
made an unconditional offer in writing of any sum as compensation to any claimants and
the sum awarded by the Tribunal to those claimants does not exceed the sum offered the
Tribunal shall, unless for special reasons it thinks proper not to do so, order the claimants to
bear their own costs and to pay the costs of the acquiring authority insofar as they were
incurred after the offer was made.[214] The statutory rule does not refer to the acquiring authority paying the costs of the claimants up to the date when the offer should have been accepted
but that it should do so follows from the general principle explained above. Acquiring
authorities are in a potentially difficult position in compensation references since even if
they successfully resist the greater part of the claim and the award is much closer to their
assessment of the compensation rather than that of the claimants an authority may still have
to pay the whole or a part of the costs of the claimants by reason of the general principle
explained. An acquiring authority can guard itself against this risk by making a Calderbank
offer or a sealed offer on the basis explained. The making of such an offer puts pressure on
claimants to settle their claim because of the risk that they may not achieve an award greater
than the offer with the resultant likely penalty in costs against them.

It is open to an acquiring authority to make an open offer. An open offer means an offer   15.127
which can be referred to at any time by either party. It is unusual for open offers to be made
but such offers may sometimes be useful from the point of view of a confident authority. An
open offer can also indicate to the Tribunal the reasonableness of the position being taken
by an acquiring authority. A claimant can also, of course, make an offer to settle which may
be on a Calderbank basis or an open offer. There is less inducement for a claimant to make
an offer to settle because of the privileged position as to costs which he occupies by reason
of the principle explained above. If one offer has been made by a party a further and later
offer may be made on more favourable terms to the other party. There is nothing to prevent
an offer being withdrawn after it has been made unless the offer itself states that it will be
kept open for a particular time. One method of bringing pressure on an opposing party is
to state that an offer is open only for a particular time since the pressure on the other party
to settle quickly is then the greater. The risk in taking this course is that a party making a
time limited offer of this nature may not put himself in such an advantageous position as
to costs as he would be if his offer had been open for acceptance up until the determination
of the proceedings. In any event an offer should never contain a term that it is to lapse
before the recipient has had a reasonable time to consider whether it should be accepted.[215]
An acquiring authority which has made a sealed offer may decide to make a later and higher
offer because it has come to understand the strength of a claimant's case.[216]

---

[214] Rule 10(2)(b) provides that where s 4 of the 1961 Act applies an order for costs must be in accordance with
the provisions of that section.
[215] One possible difficulty about a time limited offer is that the claimant may say that at the time of the offer he
had not received all the information necessary for his decision on whether to accept the offer and that by the time
full information had become available to him the offer had lapsed.
[216] *Azzorpardi v London Development Agency* [2010] RVR 112.

15.128 The third exception also derives from section 4(1) of the Land Compensation Act 1961. It arises where the Tribunal is satisfied that a claimant has failed to deliver to the acquiring authority, in time to enable the authority to make a proper offer, written notice of the amount claimed. An acquiring authority may need full information and particulars of such matters as the terms of a lease or the amount of a claim for removal expenses in order for it to be able to estimate accurately the total compensation. The notice must state the exact nature of the interest for which compensation is claimed and must give details of the compensation claimed distinguishing the amount claimed under separate heads and show how the amount claimed under each head is calculated.[217] If the Tribunal is satisfied that a notice has not been delivered in good time by a claimant it must, in the absence of special reasons, order the claimant to bear his own costs of the reference and pay the costs of the acquiring authority after the time when in the opinion of the Tribunal the notice should have been delivered. The period during which this exception operates presumably ends if a notice, or an adequate notice, is belatedly delivered. A claimant is therefore well advised to give full particulars of his claim before or at the time of a reference to the Tribunal. It is not enough just to state a sum as the total claim without including the specified particulars and details. In many cases a reference to the Tribunal is thought of as a last resort and is not made until there has been some discussion on the claim so that the amount and the nature of the claim will often have been made known to the acquiring authority when the reference is made. In such cases there will be no scope for the present exception. One recourse open to the acquiring authority where a claimant will not provide full information on his claim is itself to make a reference to the Tribunal and so put the claimant at risk as to the costs of the reference under the present rule. Once proper notice of the claim has been delivered the general principle regarding costs in compensation references will apply, namely that generally the acquiring authority will be required to pay the costs of a claimant unless the claimant has behaved unreasonably or obtains no more compensation than he has already been offered.

15.129 There is a further provision in section 4 of the Land Compensation Act 1961 which reinforces, rather than constitutes, an exception to the general principle. When a claimant has delivered proper particulars of his claim and has himself made an unconditional offer to accept a sum as compensation then if the amount of compensation awarded by the Tribunal is equal to or exceeds that sum the Tribunal must, unless there are special reasons, order the acquiring authority to bear its own costs and to pay the costs of the claimant from the time when the offer was made.[218] Such an order for costs would in those circumstances be in accordance with the general principle. Indeed the general principle suggests that provided a claimant has given proper particulars of his claim he should also be awarded his costs before he has made the offer unless he has behaved in some way unreasonably.

4. Assessment and Payment of Costs

15.130 The procedure for the making of, and resisting an, application for costs has already been described.[219] The application must be made in writing and within 14 days of the date on

---

[217] Land Compensation Act 1961, s 4(1)(b), (2).
[218] Ibid, s 4(3).
[219] See para 15.117.

which the Tribunal sends a decision notice which finally disposes of all issues in the proceedings except costs and other ancillary matters such as an application for permission to
appeal.[220]

There are three methods for the determination of the amount of costs to be paid under an   15.131
order:

(i)   The costs may be summarily assessed by the Tribunal. What is involved is that a
      person seeking a summary assessment of the costs must prepare a schedule of his
      costs and send it with, or in advance of, his application for costs to the Tribunal and
      to the other party.[221] The Tribunal then makes an immediate assessment of the total
      sum payable as costs. Sometimes both parties prepare costs schedules and when this
      is done the Tribunal is assisted in considering the reasonableness of particular items
      of costs by comparing what the two parties have estimated. This procedure is appro-
      priate in a simple case or where the Tribunal is dealing with the costs of an inter-
      locutory matter. An application for costs may be made at any time during the
      proceedings and applications for the costs of interlocutory proceedings will often
      be made orally at the end of those proceedings even though the Rules require that a
      person making an application for an order for costs must deliver a written applica-
      tion to the Tribunal.[222]

(ii) The parties may agree a specified sum as to the amount of the costs.[223]

(iii) There may be a detailed assessment of the whole, or a specified part of, the costs. As
      in the ordinary courts costs may be awarded on a standard basis or an indemnity
      basis. The detailed assessment may be carried out by the Tribunal itself or, if the
      Tribunal directs, by way of an application to the Senior Courts Cost Office or to a
      County Court.[224] The practice is that the Registrar of the Tribunal carries out the
      assessment. A party dissatisfied with that assessment may apply to the Registrar for
      a review and, if still dissatisfied, may apply to the President for a further review.[225]

In civil litigation as a whole the general rule is that costs are awarded on the standard basis   15.132
and indemnity costs are only awarded against a party where such an order for costs is justified by the fact that the conduct of the party has been outside that which is expected and
acceptable in the normal run of litigation. An example of the award of costs on an indemnity basis in the courts is where serious allegations of dishonesty have been made in support
of a hopeless case and have then been withdrawn.[226] The practice of the Lands Tribunal has
been to follow this general rule in compensation cases so that, although a claimant is in a
favoured position in obtaining an order for costs by reason of what has been described as
the general principle,[227] any award of costs in his favour would still be on the standard basis
as just explained.[228] There appears to be no decision of the Tribunal in which it has awarded

[220] Rule 10(3).
[221] Rule 10(9)(c), (12)(a).
[222] See r 10(9)(a).
[223] Rule 10(12)(b)
[224] Rule 10(12)(c).
[225] Practice Directions, para 12.10.
[226] *Three Rivers District Council v Bank of England* [2006] EWHC 816 (Comm), [2006] All ER D 175.
[227] See para 15.122.
[228] The underlying rule for the assessment of both standard and indemnity costs is that an item of costs incurred
is recoverable unless it is unreasonable. The essential difference between the two bases is one of the burden of
proof. Where costs are assessed on the standard basis the person assessing the costs shall resolve any question of

general costs against an acquiring authority on an indemnity basis. The result is that a claimant who has been awarded his costs will not generally obtain all of his expenditure on the litigation from the party who has to pay his costs. The whole of the expenditure is likely to be recovered where costs are awarded on an indemnity basis but where costs are awarded on a standard basis parties are sometimes advised by their legal advisers that they could expect to recover something in the order of 70 per cent of the amount actually expended by them on the proceedings.[229] The justification for the general principle that a claimant is normally awarded his costs in compensation claims, unless he has behaved unreasonably, is that a person who has been dispossessed of his land against his will and in the public interest should obtain all sums expended by him in asserting his claim for compensation unless it is shown that he has acted unreasonably in some way. An award of what may prove to be only 70 per cent of his costs is scarcely consistent with the underlying reasoning for an award of costs in favour of a claimant. Nor would it be in accord with the principle of equivalence which is said to underlie the whole of the law of compensation. A general principle that costs are to be awarded to a claimant on an indemnity basis would be more in accord with the general principle adopted by the courts. This reasoning has been held to be correct in a powerful decision of the Court of Appeal of the Cayman Islands in reliance on general principle and what was said in the Court of Appeal in England in the *Purfleet Farms* decision.[230] It remains to be seen whether the clear logic of this approach will find favour with the Lands Tribunal in England. The question of the general applicability of indemnity costs in compensation cases where costs are awarded to a claimant has never been argued before the Lands Tribunal or the superior courts in England and Wales so that the matter remains an open question.[231] The basis of costs was not in issue in the *Purfleet Farms* decision before the Court of Appeal.

15.133   As explained in chapter 8 one of the items of compensation which may be recoverable under rule (6) of section 5 of the Land Compensation Act 1961 is 'pre-reference costs', that is the costs of a claimant in preparing his claim and presenting it to the acquiring authority prior to a reference to the Tribunal. If such an item of compensation is allowed and the amount is not agreed the member of the Tribunal hearing the case will have to determine the amount payable in a similar way to that in which ordinary costs are determined.[232]

15.134   The provisions of the Civil Procedure Rules apply, with necessary modifications, to the process of assessment as if proceedings in the Tribunal had been proceedings before a court to which those Rules apply.[233] Fees paid by a party to the Tribunal will normally be taken into account in an award of costs but if that has not been done, including in a case where no

---

reasonableness in favour of the party who has to pay the costs. In addition, on this basis, for costs to be recoverable they must not only be reasonable but must also be proportionate having regard to the amount of money involved, the importance of the case, and the complexity of the issues. When costs are assessed on the indemnity basis all costs are to be allowed unless they are of an inordinate amount or unreasonably incurred and any doubts on these matters are to be resolved in favour of the party who is to receive the costs. See CPR, 44.4.

[229]   This practice is by no means confined to England and Wales. In the United States there is no general rule that a successful party is awarded his costs as in England and Wales. In New Zealand a successful party is less likely in the end to obtain even 70% of his costs than he is in England.

[230]   *The National Roads Authority v Bodden* (2013) (CICA 10 of 2012).

[231]   Despite the importance of the question the first occasion on which it appears to have been raised as a legal principle was by Ms McClymont before the Chief Justice in the Grand Court of the Cayman Island in the *Bodden* litigation, ibid.

[232]   See section (d) of ch 8.

[233]   Rule 10(12).

award of costs has been made against a party, the Tribunal may make a specific order that one party pays to another an amount equal to the whole of any fees paid.[234] The Tribunal may in any case disallow the cost of counsel.[235] This last power will presumably be exercised if counsel has been instructed in a case which is so short and simple as not to justify that course.

There are two methods by which the acquiring authority may recover the amount of any 15.135 costs awarded to it. It may deduct the amount of the costs from the amount of compensation payable. Alternatively it may recover the amount of the costs summarily as a civil debt.[236]

Where an order for costs is made in the courts it has become frequent practice, where the 15.136 amount of the costs is not summarily assessed but is left to a subsequent assessment, to order a party to make a payment on account to the party who has gained the benefit of the order for costs. The usual practice is to ask for an estimate of the costs of the party who is entitled to the order and then to order a payment on account at an early date of a proportion of the costs as so estimated. It is also a common practice to order the payment of interest on costs from the date on which the costs were incurred until they are paid. There is specific provision in Part 44 of the Civil Procedure Rules for this to be done in the Court of Appeal, the High Court and the County Court. A welcome amendment to the Rules has conferred on the Tribunal the power to order that an amount be paid on account of costs.[237]

The Civil Procedure Rules applicable in the High Court and the County Court contain 15.137 specific provisions in CPR 44 for the payment of interest on costs. With effect from 1 July 2013 a new rule 51A has been inserted into the Rules which provides that where the decision of the Tribunal provides for a sum to be payable, including a sum awarded in respect of the costs of the proceedings before the Tribunal, certain statutory provisions apply with necessary modifications as if the proceedings in the Tribunal were proceedings in a court to which those provisions apply.

One of the provisions so applied is section 35A of the Senior Courts Act 1981. Section 35A 15.138 states that simple interest can be ordered to be paid from the date when the cause of action accrued to the date of the decision at such rate as the court thinks fit. The necessary modification as regards an order for costs in the Tribunal is that the words 'accrual of the cause of action' in section 35A should be replaced by the words 'the date on which an item of costs was incurred'. It seems just that a party who has incurred costs and then obtains an order in his favour for the payment of the costs by another party should in general be awarded interest on each item of his costs from the date on which that item was incurred until the date of the order made by the Tribunal. The Tribunal must fix a rate of interest which should be a reasonable commercial rate. In the circumstances of mid-2013 with very low general levels of interest rates a rate of 4 per cent has sometimes been ordered in the courts. Of course this can be expected to change if and when general interest rates rise to levels which have in the past been more typical.

---

[234] Ibid.
[235] Land Compensation Act 1961, s 4(4).
[236] Land Compensation Act 1961, s 4(5), (6). A sum recoverable as a civil debt is recoverable under the Magistrates Courts Act 1980.
[237] Rule 10(13) which came into effect on 1 July 2013.

15.139 The above provision deals with interest on costs from the date on which an item of costs was incurred until the order of the court. In practice costs may not be paid until some significant time after an order of the Tribunal, even taking into account the current power of the Tribunal to make an order for a payment on account of costs. Rule 51A also applies section 17 of the Judgments Act 1838. This provision in 1838 states that every judgment debt (which includes costs) shall carry interest at 8 per cent from the date of the judgment until the date of payment. No modification of this provision is necessary for present purposes. The provision simply operates and should be reflected in the order of the Tribunal. The statutory rate of 8 per cent cannot be altered by the Tribunal and is, of course, a high rate in circumstances which have recently existed.

(N) APPEALS

15.140 A party to a decision of the Tribunal may appeal to the Court of Appeal. The right of appeal is limited in two ways. First, it is an appeal on a point of law only. Secondly, permission to appeal must be obtained from the Tribunal or from the Court of Appeal. The application for permission to appeal must be made to the Tribunal in the first instance. It is only if permission to appeal is refused by the Tribunal that an application for permission may be made to the Court of Appeal.[238]

1. Permission to Appeal

15.141 The application to the Tribunal for permission to appeal must be made in writing and must be made within one month after the latest of the dates on which the Tribunal sent to the applicant: (a) the relevant decision notice, (b) written reasons for the decision if the decision disposes of all issues in the proceedings or disposes of a separate or preliminary issue, (c) notification of a decision on costs, (d) notification of amended reasons for a decision or the correction of a decision following a review, and (e) notification that an application for a decision to be set aside has been unsuccessful. The general rule is, therefore, that when the Tribunal has issued a decision on a preliminary issue an application for an appeal can be made within the stipulated one month in respect of that decision without waiting for the determination of the remainder of the reference. However, the Tribunal may direct that the period for delivering an application for permission to appeal against a decision on a separate or preliminary issue shall run from the date of the decision that disposes of all issues in the proceedings. In that case a person wishing to appeal will have to wait until the full and final determination of the Tribunal on the reference before it.[239] The normal practice is that the Tribunal sends to the parties its written decision with reasons and then, after further written submissions if necessary, sends an addendum dealing with costs.[240] The one month limited for an application for permission to appeal therefore runs in most cases from the

---

[238] Tribunals, Courts and Enforcement Act 2007, s 13(1)–(5).
[239] Rule 55(1), (2), (2A). For amending decisions of the Tribunal by process of review and for setting aside decisions see section (l) of this chapter.
[240] See para 15.107.

receipt of the addendum on costs. The Tribunal may extend the time for an application for permission to appeal provided it receives an application for an extension with reasons given as to why the application for permission to appeal was not made in time.[241]

The application for permission to appeal must be made in writing and must identify the deci- 15.142 sion of the Tribunal to which it relates and the alleged error or errors of law in the decision. It must also state the result which the applicant seeks from an appeal.[242] The result may be that a different decision should be made on a preliminary issue, or that a different sum should be awarded as compensation, or that the matter should be referred back to the Tribunal for further hearing or consideration. Where there is a question of law before the Tribunal, and when it is practical and convenient to do so, the Tribunal sometimes follows the procedure of deciding the question of law and stating the amount of the compensation on that basis and then stating what would have been the amount of the compensation awarded if the question of law had been decided differently. The advantage of this course is that, if an appeal on the question of law is allowed, the Court of Appeal can substitute the second amount (sometimes called the alternative award) for the sum actually awarded as compensation and so avoid the need to refer the matter to the Tribunal for further hearing.[243] One course which the Tribunal may take on receiving an application for permission to appeal is to review its decision in accordance with the limited power available for that purpose.[244] If the decision is amended as a result of a review a party has the opportunity again to seek permission to appeal to the Court of Appeal within one month of the decision on the review.[245]

When it receives an application for permission to appeal the Tribunal will generally notify 15.143 the other party to the decision, if he has not already been notified by the proposed appel-lant, and then consider written representations from both parties before making its decision on whether to give permission to appeal. A permission to appeal may be limited in certain ways. The most frequent form of limitation is that the permission is on one par-ticular issue or issues only. If permission is given in general terms without any limitation it appears that the appellant may argue any question of law that he wishes before the Court of Appeal. If permission to appeal is given, but limited to a particular issue, a proposed appellant may ask the Court of Appeal for permission to appeal on a further issue or issues.

2. Appellate Proceedings

If the Tribunal gives permission to appeal the procedure on the appeal to the Court of 15.144 Appeal is governed by Part 52 of the Civil Procedure Rules and by the Practice Directions

---

[241] Rules 5(3)(a) and 55(5).

[242] Rule 55(6).

[243] Eg in the decision in *Transport for London Ltd v Spirerose Ltd* [2009] UKHL 44, [2009] 1 WLR 1797, the Tribunal stated the compensation as one figure on the basis that there was in law a certainty that a particular plan-ning permission would be granted on the land acquired in the absence of the scheme of the acquiring authority and awarded that sum as compensation but went on to state that the award would have been a specified lesser sum if as a matter of law there was not a certainty but only a hope of obtaining that planning permission. The House of Lords held that the correct conclusion was that only a hope of obtaining a planning permission should be taken into account and so was able to substitute the second figure arrived at by the Tribunal as the compensation without the necessity of the matter being reconsidered by the Tribunal.

[244] See para 15.113.

[245] Ibid.

given under Part 52. Details of the procedure can be found in 'the *White Book*' or 'the *Green Book*' which contains the Rules and the Practice Directions and a detailed commentary.[246] The general procedure is that the appellant must file an appellant's notice setting out the grounds of the appeal and a skeleton argument explaining his case in summary form. A respondent to the appeal must serve a respondent's notice if he intends to support the decision of the Tribunal on a ground other than those stated in the decision. What this means is that a party, say an acquiring authority, may resist the claim for compensation under grounds (a), (b) and (c). The Tribunal may uphold ground (a) and either decide that grounds (b) and (c) are not good grounds of resistance or not reach a decision on those grounds. If a respondent in these circumstances wishes to support the decision of the Tribunal on grounds (b) or (c) he must serve a respondent's notice indicating that he wishes to do so. The Court of Appeal has wide powers in dealing with an appeal including any powers which the Lands Tribunal itself had and a power to affirm, set aside or vary any order made by the Tribunal and to make an order for a new hearing. The Court of Appeal will also deal with the costs of the appeal and, so far as necessary, with the costs of the previous proceedings before the Tribunal.[247] The general rule as to costs in the Court of Appeal is that costs follow the event.[248]

15.145   If the Lands Tribunal refuses permission to appeal a proposed appellant may seek the permission of the Court of Appeal. He must do so within 28 days of the decision of the Tribunal refusing him permission to appeal.[249] In recent years the Tribunal has been sparing in itself giving permission to appeal and a party with a substantial point of law need not be deterred from asking the Court of Appeal for permission. In one of the leading cases on the general principles of the law of compensation over the last decade permission to appeal to the Court of Appeal was refused by the Tribunal although in the end the House of Lords unanimously overruled the decision of the Tribunal and of the Court of Appeal.[250] The method of applying to the Court of Appeal for permission to appeal is by way of an appellant's notice. A skeleton argument summarising the case for the proposed appellant has to be served with the appellant's notice or shortly after it.[251] The decision of the Court of Appeal on whether to grant permission to appeal will be given initially by a single Lord Justice and by way of a brief written decision. If the proposed appellant is dissatisfied with a written refusal of permission to appeal from the Court of Appeal he is entitled to an oral hearing of his application.[252] If the application is refused after an oral hearing then that is the end of any possibility of an appeal as far as a proposed appellant is concerned. The Court of Appeal will only give permission to appeal where it considers that the appeal would have a real prospect of success or there is some other compelling reason why the appeal should be heard.[253] A compelling reason might be that some point of law or principle of general importance was involved or that there was some risk of real injustice occurring if the matter was not considered by the Court of Appeal.

---

[246] The *White Book* (Sweet & Maxwell) and *Civil Court Practice (Green Book)* (LexisNexis Butterworths). The appellant's notice must be filed within 28 days of the date of the decision of the Tribunal: CPR, Pt 52 PD, para 21.9.

[247] CPR, r 52.10.

[248] See para 15.121.

[249] CPR 52DPD4, para 3.3(2).

[250] *Transport for London Ltd v Spirerose Ltd* [2009] UKHL 44, [2009] 1 WLR 1797.

[251] CPR, r 52.4; Pt 52C PD, paras 3(1)(g), 31.

[252] CPR, r 52.3(4).

[253] CPR, r 52.3(6).

There is a possibility of a further and final appeal from the Court of Appeal to the Supreme 15.146 Court. The Supreme Court now exercises powers which until a few years ago had been exercised for centuries by the House of Lords. The permission of the Court of Appeal or of the Supreme Court is needed for an appeal to the Supreme Court. Permission is sparingly given particularly by the Court of Appeal. It is unlikely that permission will be given by either Court unless either there is some point of law of major importance involved or there has been disagreement between the three Lords Justices who normally constitute the Court of Appeal in deciding an appeal. If the Court of Appeal refuses permission to appeal to the Supreme Court an application to the Supreme Court for permission may be made under the Supreme Court Rules 2009.[254] If the Supreme Court refuses permission there is no further appeal. It has been explained elsewhere that in this country a hierarchical system of jurisprudence operates, the meaning being that a decision of the Court of Appeal thereafter binds both that Court and, of course, any other lower court such as the Lands Tribunal. A decision of the Supreme Court binds every lower court and, although it technically does not bind the Supreme Court in that it may reconsider its previous decisions, it will be rare that the Supreme Court exercises that power and generally a decision of the Supreme Court on the law establishes the law on that subject unless and until there is some statutory amendment.

3. Point of Law

It has been explained that an appeal from a decision of the Lands Tribunal is an appeal on 15.147 a point of law only. There is no appeal on matters of fact or on the exercise of discretions. The boundary between what are matters of law and what are other matters is an imprecise one. It is very unlikely that a decision of the Tribunal on detailed valuation matters would be considered to be a point of law. It is unlikely that an attempt by an appellant to change the method of, or essential elements in, his valuation would meet with success in an appellate court.[255] On the other hand the construction of statutes is a matter of law and matters of general principle, such as the operation of the principle of equivalence or the presumption of reality, are likely to be considered to be points of law. There is an overriding principle that although the decision of the Tribunal may be one which on the face of it is one of fact if there is no evidence on which the Tribunal properly directing itself could reach that conclusion of fact then that decision may itself for that reason be erroneous in point of law and susceptible to an appeal.[256] An appeal against a decision which involves the Lands Tribunal

---

[254] Supreme Court Rules 2009, r 10–17 (SI 2009/1603).

[255] In *Director of Buildings and Lands v Shun Fung Ironworks Ltd* [1995] 2 AC 211, [1995] 2 WLR 904, the Privy Council disapproved the decision of the Court of Appeal in Hong Kong in allowing the claimants to alter certain aspects of their valuation in an appeal to that Court. The Privy Council also restored the decision of the Lands Tribunal on the question of whether the commencement in China of a new business was the relocation of a business carried on at the land acquired, observing that this was a question of fact for the Tribunal and it was not correct for an appellate court to reverse conclusions reached on the basis of primary findings of fact as the Court of Appeal in Hong Kong had purported to do. The Lands Tribunal is a specialist tribunal and will sometimes need to form its own judgments which may not necessarily be founded on some specific item of evidence: see *Abbey Homesteads v Northamptonshire County Council* (1992) 64 P & CR 372, per Glidewell LJ at p 390.

[256] *Edwards v Bairstow* [1956] AC 14, [1955] 3 WLR 410; *Ashbridge Investments Ltd v MHLG* [1965] 1 WLR 1320, [1965] 3 All ER 371, per Lord Denning; *Mahon v Air New Zeeland Ltd* [1984] AC 808, [1984] 3 WLR 884; *Coleen Properties Ltd v MHLG* [1971] 1 WLR 433, [1971] 1 All ER 1049.

exercising a discretion may involve a point of law if the Tribunal has misdirected itself in some way in exercising its discretion or has exercised it in a way which goes outside the boundaries of what can be regarded as reasonable. It appears that an error by the Tribunal on some matter, such as double counting, in reaching its award may constitute an error of law which can be corrected by the Court of Appeal.[257] A material breach of the rules of natural justice, or other procedural irregularity, will be an error of law. For example, if a party is not given an opportunity to deal with some point which is decided against him or which adversely affects his case an appeal is likely to succeed on that ground.[258] In judicial review proceedings although such proceedings do not involve an appeal on the facts when a decision is reached upon an incorrect basis of fact due to misunderstanding or ignorance a remedy may lie.[259] In English law the correct interpretation of a document such as a notice is always a matter of law and so may be the subject matter of an appeal to the Court of Appeal.[260]

15.148   The Lands Tribunal, as the Lands Chamber of the Upper Tribunal, is in principle susceptible to control by proceedings for judicial review. However, it is most unlikely that judicial review would in practice be obtainable against a decision of the Tribunal both because there is a limited right of appeal and because it will only be in extreme circumstances that the High Court, exercising its power of judicial review, would think it proper to consider judicial review against any part of the Upper Tribunal.[261]

(O)   REFERENCES BY CONSENT

15.149   It has been explained that the Tribunal will generally accept a reference to determine matters as an arbitrator where the subject matter is that which would come within the statutory jurisdiction of the Tribunal and the reference is then known as a reference by consent.[262] The rules as to procedure described in this chapter apply generally to references by consent as they apply to other references to determine compensation. The procedural powers of arbitrators are those conferred by the parties in the arbitration agreement or conferred by the Arbitration Act 1996. The Rules provide that, unless the parties have agreed otherwise, certain specified provisions in the Arbitration Act 1996 apply to a reference by consent.[263] The specified provisions in the Act are: (a) section 8 (whether agreement discharged by death of a party), (b) section 9 (stay of legal proceedings), (c) section 10 (reference of interpleader issue to arbitration), (d) section 12 (power of the court to extend time for begin-

---

[257]   *Railtrack Plc v Guinness Ltd* [2003] 1 EGLR 124; *English Property Co v Kingston upon Thames London Borough Council* (1998) 77 P & CR 1.

[258]   *Faraday v Carmarthenshire County Council* [2004] EWCA Civ 649, [2009] 2 EGLR 5, where an appeal was allowed when the Tribunal made a deduction from compensation for loss of profits for time which it thought that the claimant could have spent on other business without giving him an opportunity to deal with the deduction. In *Ridgeland Properties v Bristol City Council* [2011] RVR 232, the Court of Appeal declined to interfere with a decision of the Tribunal to refuse a party permission to adduce further evidence supporting a different method of valuation when the tribunal had issued its decision in draft form and all that was awaited was a decision on costs.

[259]   *R (on the application of Alconbury Development Ltd) v Secretary of State* [2001] UKHL 23, [2001] 2 WLR 1389, per Lord Slynn at para 53.

[260]   *Newbold v Coal Authority* [2013] EWCA Civ 584.

[261]   *R (on the application of Cart) v Upper Tribunal* [2011] UKSC 28, [2012] 1 AC 663.

[262]   See para 15.6.

[263]   Rule 20.

ning arbitral proceedings, etc), (e) section 23 (revocation of arbitrator's authority), (f) section 57 (correction of award or additional award) insofar as it relates to costs, and (g) section 60 (agreement to pay costs in any event). There are other procedural provisions in the Arbitration Act 1996, such as the wide powers given by section 34 of that Act to an arbitrator to order pleadings and disclosure of documents, which are not applied to a reference by consent since the Rules provide ample procedural powers for the Tribunal in most cases.

The principle therefore is that the Rules and other provisions relevant to the Lands Chamber 15.150 of the Upper Tribunal apply generally to references by consent and are supplemented by certain additional provisions found in the Arbitration Act 1996. For example, an appeal on a point of law against a decision of the Tribunal acting as an arbitrator and on a reference by consent lies to the Court of Appeal as for any other decision of the Tribunal so that it is not appropriate or necessary to operate the particular provisions for appeals in the Arbitration Act 1996 which are not applied to references by consent.[264]

One feature of arbitrations, and one of their attractions to parties, is that arbitration pro- 15.151 ceedings are confidential and hearings are held in private. The general rule that all compulsory purchase compensation references must be held in public is altered when the Tribunal sits as an arbitrator on a reference by consent which must be held in private unless the parties agree otherwise.[265]

---

[264] See ss 67–71 of the Arbitration Act 1996 for provisions for an appeal or other challenge to decisions of arbitrators.

[265] Rule 48(4). Where the hearing is to be held in private the Tribunal can determine who is entitled to attend the hearing or a part of it.

16

Reform

(A) INTRODUCTION

16.1   One conclusion which is reached by everyone concerned with the operation of the law of compulsory purchase and compensation is that it is in need of comprehensive reform. The underlying provisions of the current law go back to the Lands Clauses Consolidation Act 1845 but since then there has been over the years a plethora of interpretations, additions and alterations, the latest being in the Localism Act 2011. A significant part of the processes is antiquated and of little use today. There are still important areas of uncertainty. For example, the principle that a dispossessed owner is entitled to compensation for his disturbance in addition to the ordinary value of the land acquired was established even before the 1845 Act was passed,[1] and was given statutory form in 1919 and again in 1961, but even today there is fundamental uncertainty over the extent to which events prior to the date of dispossession can give rise to claims under this principle.[2] The legislation is contained in what sometimes appears to be a haphazard fashion in a series of Acts. Clearly new legislation is needed which sets out the procedure for compulsory purchase and the law on the assessment of compensation in a comprehensive modern code. A way forward was proposed by the Law Commission in two reports in 2003 and 2004[3] but the Government has been unwilling to take these proposals forward into legislation.[4] This is a textbook on the law of compulsory purchase and compensation and it seeks to state the law as it is with all its doubts and imperfections. Nonetheless it may be helpful to practitioners and others to suggest in outline some of the main areas in which reform should take place.

16.2   The main suggestions relate to the law of compensation which is where the greatest changes are needed. This is not to say that the procedure for effecting a compulsory purchase is not itself in need of very substantial overhaul and amendment. It certainly does have that need but the reforms in this area are likely to be less controversial than those needed in the law of the assessment of compensation. A few examples may be given of areas of compulsory purchase procedure which need substantial reform:

    (i)   The alternative procedures of notices to treat and general vesting declarations as means of putting into effect a power of compulsory purchase of land are unneces-

---

[1] *Jubb v Humber Dock Co* (1846) 9 QB 443.
[2] See section (e) of ch 8.
[3] Law Com No 286, 2003 'Towards a Compulsory Purchase Code (Compensation)' and Law Com No 281, 2004 'Towards a Compulsory Purchase Code (Procedure)'. These reports are now a decade old but they contain considerations of principle and recommendations for comprehensive reform which will be invaluable if and when such a reform is introduced.
[4] Certain of the recommendations of the Law Commission relating to planning assumptions were put into effect by the Localism Act 2011 by way of substituting new ss 14–18 of the Land Compensation Act 1961.

sary and unacceptable. They need to be replaced by a single procedure which should be a simplified form of the general vesting declaration procedure. All that in essence a vesting declaration need do is state that interests in land in an area specified are vested in the acquiring authority on a date which is stated. The only other procedural requirement needed is that of full publication and notification of the making of the vesting declaration. A vesting declaration should not be capable of being withdrawn except by consent.

(ii)   It needs to be made clear that any power of compulsory purchase can be used, subject to any constraints in the empowering Act and subject to it being for the purpose stated in that Act, to acquire any interest in the land authorised to be acquired, to acquire any existing rights over land, to acquire any newly created rights over land, and to acquire any strata within a particular piece of land.

(iii)   The separate procedures for making compulsory purchase orders by Ministers and by other authorities should be simplified into a single method of the making of a compulsory purchase order, a consideration of objections, and then the confirmation or non-confirmation of the order.

(iv)   The process for confirming compulsory purchase orders is unnecessarily complex as is clear from the explanation of it in section (f) of chapter 2. All that is required is that anyone should in principle be entitled to object to the order, that the confirming Minister should be entitled to reject an objection which is plainly irrelevant when he has seen its terms, and that remaining objections are considered at a public local inquiry or by written representations. The Minister should be entitled to impose the written representations procedure where he considers that procedure to be appropriate having regard to the nature and extent of objections.

(v)   The special parliamentary procedure is an unnecessary complication. When particular types of land, such as commons, or particular landowners, such as statutory undertakers, have a special need of protection that can be taken into account by the confirming Minister as part of the normal process of considering objections.

(vi)   A reasonably short time limit for challenging compulsory purchase orders in the court is required so that finality can be achieved. However the rigidity of the present statutory limits is unfortunate and the court should have a power in exceptional circumstances to extend the time for making an application to challenge the validity of an order such as in cases where an objector through no fault of his own has been unable to obtain information which would be important to a challenge.

(vii)   The gaining of possession by use of a notice of entry under section 11 of the Compulsory Purchase Act 1965 works well and should be the sole method of obtaining entry applicable to all land.

(viii)   The present distinction between short tenancies and other interests is unnecessary, both in terms of procedure and in terms of the provisions for the assessment of compensation.

(ix)   The provisions relating to untraced or absent owners (which in any event does not apply when a general vesting declaration is made) are unnecessary. The interests of all persons in the land the subject of a vesting declaration should automatically vest in the acquiring authority at the vesting date. The provisions relating to acquiring authorities entering land and finding that they have mistakenly not acquired all interests is also unnecessary. A single procedure, modelled on a simplified form of the present general vesting declaration procedure, should bring about the automatic vesting in the acquiring authority of all legal and equitable interests in the land the subject of the declaration save for: (a) the interests of mortgagees and rentchargees (such of the latter as may remain today), and (b) the interests of third parties over the land acquired such as easements. Separate provisions for compensating persons with these interests can be readily provided (and the latter type of interest is separately considered later).[5]

16.3   One approach is that new legislation should provide that compensation should in all cases be assessed in accordance with some widely expressed principle, for example the principle of equivalence. By this means the linguistic complexities of putting detailed rules into appropriate language and providing for exceptions could be avoided. This is a counsel of despair and is inconsistent with the nature of legislation in highly developed legal systems. It would create unacceptable uncertainty and would result in a body of case law being built up over the next century which would become a substitute for the necessary statutory rules.

16.4   A further initial point to be made is that, while the legislation as a whole is certainly in need of overhaul and amendment, certain of the fundamental principles which guide the assessment of compensation are well founded and have been shown to work well over the years. It is perhaps obvious that the basic principle of compensation should be that the owner who is dispossessed of his land should be paid the open market value of his land at the date of the dispossession. Another principle is that when the owner is left with remaining land he should obtain compensation for damage to that remaining land caused by the removal of the land which has been acquired from him. In addition it has been established for well over a century that the compensation due to someone who is dispossessed of his land against his will should not be confined to the amount which he would have obtained if he had voluntarily sold the land but should include other elements of loss which are borne by him as a consequence of the compulsory dispossession. An important recurring problem is to place some realistic limits on the extent of compensation which is to be provided for this last area of loss.

16.5   It does therefore seem reasonably apparent that the three main heads of compensation available to a person whose land has been acquired as described in this book, the value of the land acquired, compensation for damage to other land of the owner, and certain consequential losses, should be retained as the primary components of compensation. A century and a half of experience has shown that overall compensation founded on these three primary heads is fair and reasonable and deals comprehensively with the losses suffered by landowners. One head of compensation, the additional basic loss, occupier's loss and home loss payments, are not further mentioned in this chapter. Such payments are not compensation for any specific loss and whether they should be paid, and if so how they should be computed, is more of a social and practical question than a legal question.

(B) ENTITLEMENT TO COMPENSATION

16.6   That having been said, what is plainly required is a simple and comprehensive statement of the persons entitled to compensation under each of these heads. This should be fairly simple to attain. As regards the first head, the value of the land acquired (assuming that the

---

[5] See para 16.9.

acquiring authority acquires all interests in the land), the persons entitled to compensation should be all those persons with a legal or equitable proprietary interest in the land.[6] The same persons should be entitled to compensation for consequential losses under the third head. As regards the second head, damage to retained land, any person entitled to compensation for the land acquired should in principle be entitled to compensation for any reduction in the value of any proprietary interest owned by him in his retained land caused by the acquisition of the land acquired. There are four exceptions to, or comments on, this general principle.

First, as stated earlier, the special rules currently applied to short tenancies are unnecessary. They go back to conditions in the first half of the nineteenth century and are untenable today. A person with a periodic tenancy or with a tenancy with a short unexpired residue of the lease should in principle be compensated in the same way as anyone else with a proprietary interest.   16.7

Secondly, mortgagees are treated separately under current legislation. The essence of the rules is that the acquiring authority pays sufficient of the compensation to a mortgagee to secure the discharge of the mortgage. In exceptional cases of 'negative equity' the payment of the whole of the compensation is made to the mortgagee whose mortgage is then still discharged. This is a sensible and practical system so that the proprietary rights of mortgagees are not acquired upon a compulsory purchase of the land but are dealt with in this way.   16.8

Thirdly, there is the position of persons with third party interests annexed to other land but exercisable over the land acquired such as easements or the benefit of restrictive covenants. In practice it is normally only these two types of interest which need separate treatment. Persons with equitable interests such as rights under a specifically enforceable contract to purchase land or an option to acquire land should be entitled to compensation for the value of those interests under the first three heads when the land in respect of which the interest subsists is compulsorily acquired. At present the owners of these third party rights annexed to other land are treated in a special way. (a) Their rights or interests are 'overridden' in the sense that they remain in being but cannot be enforced so as to affect the implementation of the purposes of the acquiring authority. (b) They receive compensation under section 10 of the Compulsory Purchase Act 1965 for injurious affection to the land to which the benefit of these interests is annexed. Simplification is here needed. Two new rules are required: 16.9

(i)   An acquiring authority should be required to state at the time of the vesting declaration whether or not it elects that all or any of such third party interests are extinguished. There may be cases where the purposes of the acquiring authority can be carried out without affecting such third party interests in which case nothing more need be done.

(ii)   If the acquiring authority elects to extinguish a third party interest, as will usually be the case, the owner of that right should be entitled to compensation for any loss caused to him by the extinguishment of that right. The basis of this compensation is at present unsatisfactory and is mentioned again below.[7]

---

[6] A proprietary interest is defined in para 2.27 of ch 2. The law of real property over its centuries of development has defined what are these interests.

[7] The basis of this compensation is mentioned later in paras 16.30 and 16.31. It would, of course, be open to the parties to agree some modification of the covenant or easement such as would permit the project of the acquiring authority to be carried out subject to agreed compensation if they wish.

16.10   Fourthly, persons may be displaced from land by a compulsory acquisition when they have no proprietary interest which entitles them to compensation under the above principles. In practice it is licensees who fall into this category. At present such persons have a right to a disturbance payment in certain circumstances. This seems fair and reasonable and its essential elements should be retained. The calculation of such a disturbance payment should in principle be the same as the calculation of compensation for consequential losses to persons who have a proprietary interest in land, that is the third of the main heads of compensation. This subject is also mentioned again later in this chapter.[8]

(C) VALUE OF THE LAND ACQUIRED

1. The Basic Rule

16.11   The basic rule is that the first and primary head of compensation is the amount which the land acquired would realise if sold in the open market at the valuation date. A hypothetical sale of this nature is fundamental to all valuations of land and to the valuation of most other assets. It serves this purpose well in the area of compensation law and no alteration is needed. The concept is well understood by valuers and others.

16.12   Nor is there any need for a change in the concepts of a hypothetical willing seller and a hypothetical willing purchaser as parties to the hypothetical sale which are also well understood by practitioners and applied in many areas of land valuation.

16.13   The status of a special purchaser has had a fluctuating history in the assessment of compensation. The existence of a special purchaser was upheld as a legitimate factor in valuing land by the Court of Appeal in 1914. In 1919 the Scott Committee wished to eliminate the role of a special purchaser in compensation valuations and an attempt to do so was made in the Acquisition of Land (Assessment of Compensation) Act 1919 and repeated in the Land Compensation Act 1961, only for that attempt to be removed by the Planning and Compensation Act 1991.[9] Valuation standards published by the Royal Institution of Chartered Surveyors exclude the effect of a special purchaser in the general valuation of land. The thesis which underlies the first head of compensation for compulsory purchase is that the dispossessed owner shall receive as compensation what he would have obtained if he had sold the land in the market at the valuation date. If at the valuation date a special purchaser had existed, and the amount received for the land would have been enhanced by the existence and bid of such a special purchaser, there is no reason for excluding that element of the value from the compensation for compulsory acquisition. The existence of the special purchaser as a possible relevant factor in valuations should therefore be retained.

[8] See para 16.64.
[9] See section (d) of ch 4.

2. The Valuation Date

A further area of the law in which a generally satisfactory situation has been reached after   16.14
earlier fluctuations is the determination of the valuation date. It was at one time considered
that the date of the notice to treat was the valuation date but as a result of decisions of the
courts and subsequent statutory intervention the valuation date is now fixed as the vesting
date when the general vesting declaration procedure is used or the date of entry onto the
land by the acquiring authority when the notice to treat procedure is used. If, as suggested
above, the vesting declaration procedure supersedes the use of notices to treat in all cases
then the vesting date would become the valuation date generally applicable. The only exception would be the unusual circumstances in which the tribunal assessing the compensation
carried out its assessment before the valuation date. Even this complication could be
avoided by providing that there could be no reference to the tribunal to decide compensation until a general vesting declaration had been made. Indeed this is the effect of the present law since a reference to the Tribunal cannot be made until a notice to treat has been
served and a general vesting declaration operates as a constructive notice to treat. There is
an exception to the principle of the valuation date in that where equivalent reinstatement is
the basis of compensation the cost of the equivalent reinstatement is to be that at the date
on which it was first reasonable to put the reinstatement into effect. Obviously this exception should be retained.

One of the consequences of a valuation date is that no regard can be had in the valuation   16.15
process to facts or events which took place after the valuation date although of course the
anticipation at the valuation date of future events can be taken into account where relevant
to the value of the land. This straightforward and logical rule is so often forgotten in practice despite its reiteration by courts of the highest authority that it deserves a prominent
place in any future compensation code.[10]

The valuation date determines the levels of values and prices pertaining at a particular   16.16
moment as that applicable to the valuation of the land acquired. There is unfortunately
some doubt as to the extent to which the valuation date fixes other circumstances relevant
to the valuation of the land. There is a remnant of the supposed old rule, that the date of the
notice to treat was the valuation date, in the notion that the nature of interests in land is to
be fixed at the date of the notice to treat even though the valuation of those interests may
have to be carried out as at a later valuation date. A simple way of dealing with this notion
would be, as suggested, that the service of notice to treat as a method of implementing a
compulsory acquisition is abolished and replaced with the more modern and satisfactory
system of a general vesting declaration. If that were done and the vesting date, as stated in
the declaration, was in all instances the valuation date then the fundamental rule could
become that all facts and matters, including the nature of the interests in land to be valued,
should be determined as at the valuation date. For example, the physical state of the land,
the physical state of all surrounding land, Government policies and other similar matters
relevant to value, and the unexpired residue of a lease where a leasehold interest was being
valued, should all be determined and applied as at the valuation date. Only two exceptions
are required to this simple and universal principle.

[10] See also n 29 to para 16.52.

16.17   The first exception is a rule, equivalent to the rule at present in force, that any increase in the value of the land should be left out of account if it is attributable to any actions carried out at any time prior to the valuation date, for example the creation or alteration of an interest in land, the carrying out of development or other works to land, or a change in the use of land, with a view to the obtaining of compensation or increased compensation.

16.18   The second exception is that in certain circumstances the nature or qualities of an interest in land may have been affected by the scheme of the acquiring authority. The best example of this today is that the expectation of a tenant of premises within the protection of Part II of the Landlord and Tenant Act 1954 of obtaining the grant of a new tenancy may be reduced by the scheme of the acquiring authority which would entitle that authority successfully to resist an application for a new tenancy against it when it had become the landlord by reason of its intention to carry out a redevelopment of the land. Such alterations in the nature or quality or attributes of an interest may have to be left out of account in the valuation process. This is a subject which is bound up with the important topic of the disregard of the scheme. The principle should be that if the effect of the scheme of the acquiring authority is to reduce the statutory protection available to a tenant of the land acquired that effect should be left out of account. Since it is reasonable that the landlord's interest and the tenant's interest in the land acquired should be valued on the same basis the same principle should apply to the valuation of both interests.[11]

3. Leasehold Interests

16.19   It is generally recognised that the valuation of a leasehold interest acquired should proceed on the same basis and in accordance with the same rules as the valuation of any other interest in land. It has already been pointed out that there is no justification for continuing the special treatment currently accorded to short tenancies. There are, however, certain principles relating to the valuation of leasehold interests which have been introduced by decisions of the courts and which need radical reconsideration.

16.20   The current rule is that where an interest in land is a periodic tenancy it has to be assumed that that tenancy would be brought to an end at the earliest date at which it could be brought to an end by a notice to quit served at the valuation date. It is unclear why this artificial rule was introduced. A person who acquires a periodic tenancy by way of an open market transaction will take his own view of how long the tenancy will be likely to last. It may have already lasted for a considerable time and the purchaser may feel that there is every expectation that it would continue to last for some substantial future period, possibly with agreed adjustments to the rent from time to time. It can scarcely be repeated too often that the underlying rationale of the assessment of compensation for an interest in land is the determination of the sum which would be obtained for that interest if it was exposed to the market at the valuation date. If a purchaser would pay a sum of money for a periodic tenancy in the reasonable expectation that it would be continued for some substantial period there is no reason of justice or logic why the tenant under that tenancy should be deprived of any value attributable to that thinking of a hypothetical purchaser by some artificial rule that the tenancy has to be taken to be determined at some early future date.

[11]   See para 16.38.

Very much the same considerations apply to cases where a tenancy is subject to determina- 16.21
tion by a break clause which can be operated by a landlord. The present rule is that it has to
be assumed that that tenancy would be determined by the operation of the break clause at
the earliest date on which it could be so determined by a notice given by the landlord at the
valuation date. There is, again, and for the same reasons, no justification for the making of
such an artificial assumption.

The next matter is the principle, perhaps allied to the principles presently operating and 16.22
discussed in the last two paragraphs, that any hope or expectation that a tenancy would be
renewed upon its determination is to be left out of account in assessing compensation.
Once again if a purchaser of the tenancy would pay a sum which took into account such a
reasonable hope and expectation there is no reason of principle or justice why that element
of the value of the tenancy should be left out of account in assessing compensation. The
thesis which underlies what has been written in this, and the last two paragraphs, is the
simple one that the prospect of the tenancy being ended by a notice to quit or by a break
clause or the prospect of it being renewed should be a factor, perhaps a cardinal factor,
which would be taken into account by a hypothetical willing purchaser and the function of
a tribunal in valuing the leasehold interest in question should be to attempt to reproduce
that thinking, and the result of that thinking, in a sum of money which would be offered
by a hypothetical willing purchaser. This can be done without recourse to rigid and artificial
assumptions introduced by the courts. The Law Commission in its report, Law Com
No 286, [12] in 2003 drew attention to the fact that under the Australian Commonwealth
Code there was a provision that if the interest being valued was terminable by some person
or was limited in time there was to be taken into account 'the likelihood of the continuation
or renewal of the interest and the likely terms and conditions on which any continuation or
renewal would be granted'.[13] This appears to be a fair and succinct statement of the correct
principle which we should borrow from Australia.

4. Unlawful Uses

A further candidate for reform is the present rule that no account shall be taken in valuing 16.23
the land acquired of any uses which are unlawful. The fundamental theory underlying the
assessment of compensation again comes into play, namely that the dispossessed landowner
should receive that which he would have obtained if he had put his land on the market at
the valuation date. If a use is being carried on which is unlawful in any sense of that word it
is likely to reduce, or even eliminate, the value which the property has and this will be
reflected in the valuation in the ordinary way. On the other hand there are instances in
which the unlawfulness of a use will have little, if any, effect on the amount which a purchaser would pay. An instance would be where a purchaser believed that there would be
little likelihood of any effective steps being taken by anyone to prevent the unlawful use.
There is no reason why the compensation rules should do anything other than assess
and reflect that which the market would itself have done. The compensation rules are concerned not with some abstract morality or with becoming a secondary means of enforcing

---

[12] 'Towards a Compulsory Purchase Code (Compensation)' (n 3).
[13] Law Com No 286, 'Towards a Compulsory Purchase Code (Compensation)' at para 5.5.

restrictions but are concerned with the ordinary concept of value in the sense of what the market would pay for a piece of land.

16.24   The present rule, rule (4) in section 5 of the Land Compensation Act 1961, does not state what exactly is meant by an unlawful use and in particular does not state whether the unlawful uses which have to be left out of account are those which are unlawful by reason of some public law provision (for example planning controls) or are unlawful because of some restriction which exists in the private law field such as a restrictive covenant or a covenant in a lease. An uneasy compromise has been suggested to the effect that it is only breaches of aspects of the public law which should be left out of account in valuing the land or even that, because of the uncertainty of the subject, the tribunal assessing compensation should have a discretion either to leave out of account or take into account the effect of an unlawful use. Such complex distinctions and uncertain discretions appear to be the very matters which should be eliminated from an up to date and simplified compensation code.

5. Equivalent Reinstatement

16.25   It seems just that where land is devoted to a purpose for which there is no general market or demand, so that the compensation assessed on the normal basis would be small and insufficient to allow the landowner to reinstate the purposes for which the land is used, compensation should exceptionally be assessed on an equivalent reinstatement basis. It appears that the present power of the Lands Tribunal to award compensation on this basis has been exercised in a successful and satisfactory way. It seems just that the power to award compensation on this basis should remain to be exercised in limited and controlled cases.

16.26   The Law Commission in its report, Law Com No 286,[14] in 2003 suggested certain amendments to the present law on equivalent reinstatement as contained in rule (5) of section 5 of the Land Compensation Act 1961, for example that the award of compensation should be made conditional upon the payment being used for the purpose of reinstatement and certain other clarifications of the law. Some modernisation of the wording and the inclusion of such a condition are necessary but the fundamental rule should clearly remain. In particular, where other conditions are satisfied, the tribunal assessing compensation should have a discretion as to whether to award compensation on the equivalent reinstatement basis and a comparison between the cost of equivalent reinstatement and the amount of compensation which would be awarded on the ordinary open market basis will be an important consideration in the exercise of this discretion although it should not necessarily be the only factor to be taken into account.

6. Betterment

16.27   The statutory provisions at present contain a general provision for a deduction from the compensation for betterment, that is an increase in the value of land held by the dispossessed owner other than the land acquired where that other land is increased in value by the

---

[14] 'Towards a Compulsory Purchase Code (Compensation)' (n 3).

scheme of the acquiring authority. In addition other statutory provisions contain specific requirements for a deduction for betterment, notably section 261 of the Highways Act 1980. The principle of whether there should be a deduction for betterment can be the subject of conflicting arguments. On the one hand it may seem to many to be fair that when a land-owner is compensated for the full market value of the land acquired from him, including any increase in value of that land attributable to the planning permission for the proposals of the acquiring authority which has to be assumed to be in force, and the same scheme of the authority increases the value of other land which he retains he should have that increase in value deducted from his compensation. He will on this reasoning receive at the end of the day a sum equivalent to that which in overall terms he has lost. On the other hand there may be other landowners in the area none of whose land is acquired but whose land is also increased in value by the scheme of the acquiring authority. They obtain the benefit of this increase in value without being required to give up any of that increase. It might be asked why a person whose land is acquired from him should be treated in a different way as regards his other or retained land.

There is no wholly fair or wholly logical answer to this question. The Law Commission in its report in 2003 recommended, after substantial consultation on the subject, that there should be a form of compromise solution in that in general there should be no deduction from the compensation payable for the land acquired by reason of betterment but that where an owner owned other land and claimed compensation for a reduction in the value of that other land due to its severance from the land acquired, or due to injurious affection caused to it by the scheme of the acquiring authority, he should be required to deduct from that claim for a reduction in value any increase in value to further land which he owned which was also brought about by the scheme.[15] This appears to be a reasonable and defensible approach which could well find its way into a new compensation code. It would have the merit of somewhat simplifying the legislation. Similar alterations would be needed to other legislation which deals with betterment.   16.28

7. Planning Permissions after the Valuation Date

Section 23 of the Land Compensation Act 1961 provides for additional compensation to be paid in certain circumstances where a planning permission for further development of the land acquired is granted in the 10 years following the acquisition. It appears that this provision is little implemented particularly since a new permission for development for the functions or project of the acquiring authority does not count for the purposes of this additional compensation. In addition the open market value of the land acquired at the valuation date will take account of its potential for future development and the expectation of that development taking place. In these circumstances the Law Commission in its report in 2003, and again as a result of consultations as well as its own reasoning, recommended that this provision for additional compensation should not form part of any new code.[16] This appears to be eminently reasonable and represents a further welcome simplification of the system.   16.29

---

[15] See para 3.31 of the report.
[16] See paras 8.35 et seq of the report.

8. Valuation of Third Party Interests

16.30   Under the present law when a third party interest in the land acquired, such as an easement or the benefit of restrictive covenant, is overridden by the need to implement the project of the acquiring authority compensation to the owner of that interest is payable under section 10 of the Compulsory Purchase Act 1965. The result of overriding the interest is considered to be injurious affection to the land to which it is annexed. It has been suggested earlier that where such third party interests are to be overridden they should be extinguished and compensation payable for the extinguishment.[17] The basis of that compensation can be considered as a part of the valuation of land. It was at one time thought that the method of assessing damages for the infringement of an interest, such as the benefit of a restrictive covenant, was to assess the diminution in the value of the land to which the interest was annexed caused by the infringement. It has been established over recent decades that in many cases a fairer way of assessing damages is to award as damages the sum which would be agreed for a voluntary release of the interest such as to permit what would otherwise be an infringement, and this process has been commended by the House of Lords.[18]

16.31   The 'voluntary agreement' method of assessing damages is fairer and also often leads to a substantially higher award of damages than would otherwise be the case. Unfortunately the Court of Appeal has held that when it comes to assessing compensation for the overriding or extinguishment of a covenant or easement this more modern and fairer method of assessment cannot be applied.[19] It is patently unjust that a person whose rights are infringed or removed by a private developer can obtain damages on one basis but that a person whose rights are overridden or extinguished by a public authority obtains compensation only on a different and often reduced basis. This is an area of the law which is ripe for reform. The compensation for the extinguishment of third party interests should plainly be assessed on the same basis as would damages for the infringement of those interests, that is on what has been called the 'voluntary agreement' basis.

(D) THE SCHEME

1. Introduction

16.32   The most difficult subject on which to investigate a comprehensive reform is that of the effect of the scheme on valuation. The history of this subject has been stated in detail in chapter 5. The matter of the disregard of the scheme has had two phases in its development. Following the passing of the Lands Clauses Consolidation Act 1845 and up until 1959 the courts developed and applied a principle which in brief terms can be stated as that in valuing the land acquired there was to be left out of account any increase or decrease in the value

---

[17] See para 16.9.

[18] *Attorney General v Blake* [2001] 1 AC 268, [2000] 3 WLR 625. See ch 10, paras 10.60 et seq.

[19] *Wrotham Park Estates Co v Parkside Homes* [1974] 1 WLR 798. See n 100 to ch 10, para 10.60. This decision was at a time when the 'voluntary agreement' basis of assessing damages was in the infancy and was regarded by some as a doubtful innovation. As mentioned that basis of assessment has now won general approval.

of that land due to the scheme of the acquiring authority which underlay the acquisition. The second phase was the enactment in the Town and Country Planning Act 1959, and then its consolidation in the Land Compensation Act 1961, of a system of statutory rules designed to achieve the same object. For a long time it was assumed that the statutory rules did not wholly replace the 'common law' rule but that the common law rule remained available so as to fill any obvious gap in the statutory provisions. This view of the law was shown to be wrong by the decision of the House of Lords in *Transport for London Ltd v Spirerose Ltd*[20] where it was held that the statutory rules constituted a complete code on the subject in question.

The principle that it is necessary 'to disregard the scheme' has engraved itself in the thinking 16.33 of those who practice in the area of the law of compulsory purchase and compensation. There is general agreement that the present statutory rules are not satisfactory and that a radical rethinking on the subject is necessary. Views that have been expressed on the nature of any reform have differed widely. The reason for this is not so much one of technical law but rather one of the fundamental approach to what is, or is not, just in relation to the disregard of the scheme. Accordingly this section of the present chapter attempts to consider four questions:

(i) the extent to which a principle requiring the disregard of the scheme of the acquiring authority for valuation purposes is needed;
(ii) the ascertainment and content of the scheme;
(iii) the cancellation assumption; and
(iv) the scheme and planning permissions.

2. The First Question: The Need for the Principle

An initial consideration is that the scheme of the acquiring authority may either decrease or 16.34 increase the value of land that is acquired pursuant to it. The justification for an owner being compelled by law to sell his land is the public interest that a particular scheme shall be implemented, say a major new road or railway built. It would be patently unfair that when the owner of land was required to give up his land the value which he received in return should be depressed by the existence of the public scheme and the need which justified the dispossession. No one would voluntarily sell his land at such a reduced price and it is clearly unfair that an owner should be compelled to do that. A good starting point is therefore to say that the effect of the scheme must be left out of account in valuing the land acquired when the scheme reduces the value of that land.

The situation when the scheme increases the value of the land acquired is different. Victorian 16.35 judges, in their development of the value to the owner principle and the disregard of the scheme, would have stated that such an increase in value had to be left out of account. However, that is clearly not the current law as can be seen from section 15(1) of the Land Compensation Act 1961, retained by the Localism Act 2011, which provides that planning permission for development of the land acquired in accordance with the proposals of the acquiring authority is to be assumed to be in force at the valuation date. If the implementation

---

[20] *Transport for London Ltd v Spirerose Ltd* [2009] UKHL 240, [2009] 1 WLR 1797.

of that planning permission would add value to the land acquired then that development, which is of course a part of the scheme, is to be taken into account in valuing the land acquired. Under the present law development, or the prospect of development, on land other than the land acquired sometimes has to be left out of account on the basis that it is a part of the scheme.[21] This is an uneasy and unsatisfactory compromise. It is considered just that an acquiring authority should compensate a landowner for the value given to his land by development on the land under the scheme of the authority, a value which of course accrues to the authority following the purchase, but that any effect on value of his land of the rest of the scheme should, at any rate in some cases, be disregarded.

16.36   There is a strong case for saying that where an acquiring authority carries out a scheme, with the result that all increases in the value of land attributable to the scheme within the area of the scheme accrue to the authority, it should pay to persons who are dispossessed by compulsion of their land the full value of that land attributable to the whole of the scheme. This is what would happen if a private developer acquired land to carry out a development project. If a developer wishes to build houses on plots A to D, each plot being owned by a separate owner, he will have to pay that which would be agreed in a market negotiation to each owner taking account of the prospect of development on the land of that owner and the prospect of development on the land of the three other owners. It is difficult to see why an acquiring authority should be in a different position. Under the present law when plot A is acquired the owner of it will be paid the value of that land for the development proposed on it but, at any rate sometimes, ignoring the prospect of the proposed development of plots B to D. If the owner happens to own the whole of plots A to D then he will obtain the whole value of the development over all the plots. All of this seems arbitrary.

16.37   The unsatisfactory nature of the above situation is compounded when one considers forms of major development. Suppose that there is a project to build or substantially extend a regional airport. There may be two properties in the vicinity both ran as guest houses, properties A and B. Both will be increased in value by the airport scheme since it will bring increased custom both during its construction and during its use. Property A lies just outside the confines of the new or expanded airport so that its owner benefits from the increased trade. Property B lies just inside the confines of the new or expanded airport and is acquired in order to build a new access road for the purposes of the scheme. The owner of property B will not receive the increased value of his property attributable to the airport project. Thus the owner of property A, who is undisturbed, obtains the benefit of the increase in value due to the scheme whereas the owner of property B, whose land is compulsorily taken from him in the public interest, obtains no such benefit. It is hard to justify an overall situation such as this.

16.38   There are contrary arguments. Some would say that a landowner should never benefit from the increase in the value of his land brought about by public investment, although of course as explained in the last example many do so benefit. There is probably no perfect solution and the state of the law may in the end be determined by the different social and economic perspectives of those concerned rather than by logic or any purely legal considerations. Nonetheless, for reasons just mentioned in outline, the present law on the effect of an increase in the value of land compulsorily acquired brought about by the scheme of the

---

[21] Land Compensation Act 1961, s 6 and sch 1.

acquiring authority appears lacking in both logic and justice. The clear solution would be to value land acquired with the effect and benefit of the scheme of the acquiring authority where that scheme increases the value of the land.[22] Whether legislators, concerned at the level of public expenditure, or others involved in giving advice on this subject would be willing to embrace what appears a fair and simple solution to an old problem is another matter.

3. The Second Question: The Ascertainment and the Content of the Scheme

The delineation of the scheme is thus a necessary part of the valuation process. It would   16.39
certainly be so if increases in the value of the land acquired as well as decreases in the value of that land had to be left out of account. It would still be so even if, as just suggested, only decreases in the value of the land acquired due to the scheme had to be left out of account. In the latter case the disregard of the scheme so far as it brought about a decrease in the value of the land acquired would have two aspects, the general aspect of the scheme as a factor reducing the value of the land acquired (for example, the effect of a new road because of its noise and disruption) and the more specific effect of the scheme in reducing or eliminating the prospect of obtaining a planning permission for development of the land acquired.

Three systems have been devised to ascertain the extent and content of the scheme: 16.40

(i)   When the value of the owner principle was being developed as a judge-made doctrine it was said that the ascertainment of what was the scheme, and thus of what was to be left out of account in the valuation process, was a matter of fact to be decided by the court or tribunal which assessed the compensation. It was at this time not entirely clear whether it was only the scheme of the acquiring authority as proposed to be carried out on the land acquired which had to be disregarded as opposed also to the scheme as proposed to be carried out on other land. It has today become clear that it is the effect of the scheme on both areas of land which has to be disregarded when it comes to a reduction in the value of the land acquired brought about by the scheme.[23]

(ii) The statutory provisions at present in section 6 and schedule 1 in the Land Compensation Act 1961 are an attempt to bring precision to that which had previously been taken to be simply a matter of fact. It is widely recognised that this attempt has to a considerable extent failed in its purpose. Leaving aside the extreme linguistic complexity of the provisions there are plain instances where that which ought to be a part of the scheme is outside the statutory provisions. It is this difficulty which led to the 'lacuna theory' which is explained in detail in chapter 5, that is the theory that the previous rules remained so as to plug gaps in the legislation.

---

[22] There is a possible exception where an increase in the value of a person's interest in the land acquired due to the scheme should be left out of account. That is where the landlord's interest and the tenant's interest in the land are affected by the removal of a statutory protection by the scheme and the removal of that protection should be disregarded in the valuation of both interests. See para 16.18.

[23] This is the combined effect of ss 6 and 9 of the Land Compensation Act 1961: see ch 5.

(iii) The last attempt at defining the scheme is that recommended by the Law Commission in Law Com No 286 in 2003.[24] What this amounts to is that the old description of a scheme is replaced by the new description of a 'statutory project' and that the statutory project is taken to be the implementation of the project of the acquiring authority within the area of the compulsory purchase order save that it can be shown to be part of a wider project although the Lands Tribunal is precluded from hearing evidence of such a wider project except in special circumstances. There is much to be commended in the carefully phrased provisions of these recommendations, in particular: (a) the assumption that the statutory project has been cancelled at the valuation date, (b) the principle that actions taken prior to the valuation date in pursuance of the project by a public authority are to be left out of account, and (c) the rule that no other project to meet the same or substantially the same need will be carried out with the exercise of compulsory purchase powers. The change of linguistic description from scheme to project is trivial but the fundamental difficulty in the recommendations is the close linkage of the scheme to the area of a compulsory purchase order. One obvious difficulty is that in the case of schemes carried out under an Act of Parliament, which authorises a specific scheme, such as the Crossrail Act 2008, there is no compulsory purchase order as such. Secondly, aspects of what is in substance the same scheme may be implemented by more than one compulsory purchase order (as in the *Waters* decision).[25] Thirdly, acquiring authorities may either own, or have acquired by agreement, much of the land needed for the purposes of their scheme so that no compulsory purchase order need be made in relation to that land. Fourthly, it is unclear what are the special circumstances in which evidence can be given of a wider scheme or why there have to be special circumstances for such evidence to be admitted.

16.41 The fact is that attempts to define or constrain the scheme by statutory provisions and descriptions run into difficulties. A reason is the wide variety of circumstances of public schemes or projects and the different process of authorising a compulsory acquisition. Even the latest attempt by the Law Commission leaves it open to the parties to argue in exceptional circumstances that the scheme (or statutory project) is wider than that which is primarily said to be its ambit. The original approach of the courts is the best solution. Since there is such a wide variety of circumstances which may constitute a single scheme it is best to leave it to the parties to agree what that scheme is with the Lands Tribunal with its wide experience of these matters being able to make a factual determination in the absence of agreement. That which will have to be determined involves the nature of the scheme, its geographical extent, and the time when it started.

16.42 One important advance, already mentioned, does emerge from the considerations and recommendation of the Law Commission. The attempt to define the scheme in the Land Compensation Act 1961 confined the scheme to development or the prospect of development. Certainly this will be a major aspect of any scheme. Nonetheless other aspects of the scheme are important to land valuation. For example, if land has been assembled in the past by a public authority or by a developer for the purposes of a scheme that in itself may have an effect on the valuation of a particular piece of land acquired. The sensible approach is

---

[24] See Pt VII of the report 'Towards a Compulsory Purchase Code (Compensation)' (n 3).
[25] *Waters v Welsh Development Agency* [2004] UKHL 19, [2009] 1 WLR 1304.

that, once the geographical ambit and general nature of the scheme have been established, all actions in the past prior to the valuation date pursuant to that scheme and for its purposes should be left out of account. These actions will be actions by a public authority implementing the scheme but may also be actions of other bodies, such as a developer who has assembled land for the purposes of the scheme in co-operation with the acquiring authority. These actions should all be left out of account. In other words both the geographical ambit of the scheme and the actions taken for the purposes of the scheme are matters of fact which in the event of dispute should be determined by the Tribunal as matters of fact and, if held to be part of the scheme, should be left out of account.

For example, to look at the circumstances in *Waters v Welsh Development Agency*[26] it would   16.43
have been for the Tribunal assessing compensation to decide whether the acquisition and use of land for a nature reserve, needed as a replacement when an area of land 10 miles away had been acquired for major development, was a part of one scheme including the major development so that the impact of the whole scheme on the value of agricultural land acquired for the nature reserve had to be left out of account. The question in such a case only arises if, contrary to that suggested earlier, the effect of an increase in value has to be left out of account in the valuation process.

4. The Third Question: The Cancellation Assumption

It has been explained in chapter 5 that one of the routes taken by the courts, now seen to be   16.44
plainly wrong, is the building up of an adjusted world, that is a notional or hypothetical world which would or might have existed over a substantial period prior to the valuation date if there had been no scheme. The creation of an adjusted world depended on the assumption of there never having been in existence the scheme of the acquiring authority. As explained in chapter 5 this has now been shown to be an unacceptable approach. The Law Commission recommended that the proper assumption was that the scheme should be taken to have been cancelled as at the valuation date. The previous approach sometimes taken of assuming that the scheme had never existed would be stated to be incorrect. This is plainly sensible. It means that there is no need or justification for an investigation of what might have happened in the past had there never been a scheme at any time. It is of course a corollary of this approach that it must be assumed, as the Law Commission recommended, that there should be disregarded the prospect of the same or any other project intended to meet the same or substantially the same need. It would be ridiculous to ignore the effect on valuation of one scheme only to have it replaced by the impact on valuation of the same or a similar scheme. Therefore when the disregard of the scheme rule applies there would be disregarded the effect on the value of the land acquired of actions taken prior to the valuation date as part of the scheme but there would be no investigation of what else might have happened in that period in the absence of the scheme. This can be achieved by the cancellation assumption.

---

[26] Above n 25. See ch 5, para 5.57 for the facts of the *Waters* case.

5. The Fourth Question: The Scheme and Planning Permissions

16.45   A landowner may wish to establish that in the absence of the scheme he would have obtained a particular planning permission. The existence of the scheme in the past may have prevented his obtaining planning permission but this is nothing to the point and the matter must be looked at as at the valuation date. If the existence of the scheme at the valuation date would prevent the landowner obtaining what would otherwise be a valuable planning permission then plainly the scheme should be disregarded for this purpose as for other purposes connected with valuation. This matter is dealt with more fully under section (g) of this chapter which covers the important and separate topic of planning permissions. However, the answer to the problem which is raised is apparent. It should be assumed that the scheme has been cancelled at the valuation date so that the landowner is able to establish whatever prospect there would have been of obtaining a particular planning permission at that date in the absence of the scheme and he should have the benefit of that expectation in so far as it affects the value of his land. As will be explained more fully in section (g) dealing with planning that expectation should be what it is stated to be, namely an expectation of obtaining a planning permission which like all expectations may be high or low, and not a certainty that the planning permission would be granted or that it is in force.

(E) RETAINED LAND

16.46   It has always been recognised that when a part of an owner's land is acquired he is entitled to compensation for any damage to his remaining or retained land. As explained in chapter 9 that compensation is available under section 7 of the Compulsory Purchase Act 1965 and takes the form of compensation for severance or for other forms of injurious affection. It is plainly correct that this head of compensation should remain and remain broadly in the form which it now takes. As well as the provision for compensation there are certain further, and in part antiquated, provisions of some complexity which entitle a landowner a part of whose land is sought to be acquired to require the acquiring authority to take the whole of his land. This last aspect of the law may have more to do with the procedure for compulsory purchase than the assessment of compensation but it is convenient to mention it here. It is an area of the law ripe for rationalisation and reform.

1. The Land Retained

16.47   The present legislation does not limit the location of the land retained by an owner in respect of which he may claim compensation. The expression 'contiguous or adjacent land', with its inherent imprecision, which is found in other parts of the legislation is not applied to this head of compensation.[27] In principle no geographic limitation is necessary. If a landowner whose land is acquired is the owner of other land adversely affected by the

---

[27] Eg s 7(1) of the Land Compensation Act 1961.

acquisition, and the proposed works of the acquiring authority, he should be entitled to compensation whatever the geographical location of his other land. Some schemes of public authorities, such as a motorway or a new railway, can affect land within a wide area and a limitation on the right to compensation, such as that the retained land of an owner must be 'adjacent' to the land acquired would be imprecise in its application and in some cases unfair. Equally compensation should be available for an adverse effect on other land whatever proprietary interest the landowner has in that other land.

2. Adverse Effects

At present under section 7 of the Compulsory Purchase Act 1965 compensation is payable   16.48
for an adverse effect on retained land caused by the severance of that land from the land acquired or by the exercise of its powers by the acquiring authority, the latter effect being usually the result of works carried out by the authority. The language of this dual entitlement goes back to the Lands Clauses Consolidation Act 1845. No radical change is needed to the principle involved but the rule would benefit from a modernisation of the phraseology so that it becomes one of compensation being available for damage to the land retained by the owner caused by the acquisition of the land acquired or by the exercise of the powers of the acquiring authority under the Act which conferred the power of compulsory purchase.

A more controversial question is that of knowing exactly what adverse effects on the land   16.49
retained can be the subject of the compensation. As explained in chapter 9 the general, although not the invariable, view taken has been that the adverse effect which founds a claim for compensation must be a diminution in the value of the owner's interest in the retained land caused by the factors just mentioned. This view flows from the reference to injurious affection in section 7 of the Compulsory Purchase Act 1965 and the nature of injurious affection to land which is normally a diminution in the value of that land. Certainly it is this adverse effect which must form the primary component of the compensation.

It is arguable that in addition to a diminution in the value of his land the claimant may suf-   16.50
fer forms of financial loss not directly based on the value of the retained land and that if he can show that the loss is a result of the acquisition of a part of his land, or the result of the exercise of the powers by the acquiring authority under the empowering Act, he should be entitled to compensation for that loss in addition to any diminution in the value of his land. An instance of such a monetary loss might be that the owner feels that he is in practice compelled to sell the retained land because it is of no further use to him and he incurs the costs of the sale or the costs of moving or that he suffers a temporary loss of profit in a business carried out on the retained land which is not reflected in any reduction in the capital value of that land. Claims for losses of this nature would be similar to claims under rule (6) of section 5 of the Land Compensation Act 1961 in respect of the land acquired. It does seem fair and reasonable that the owner of retained land should be compensated for additional and limited losses of this nature. Such an entitlement to compensation is best considered under the general subject of further losses not based on the value of land which is the third main head of compensation. It should, however, be made clear that any claims for

such further or additional monetary losses are likely to be of a limited nature and that there is no question of substituting some general claim for purely business or monetary loss for the primary claim which must be based on a diminution in the value of the land retained caused by the acquisition of the land acquired and the exercise by the acquiring authority of its powers under the empowering Act. Of course an adverse effect on a business carried on at retained land may reduce the value of that land.

16.51 There is one matter which has engendered some speculation amongst lawyers and which can be swiftly resolved. It is clear that when retained land is adversely affected by the scheme of the acquiring authority that adverse effect can be taken into account in assessing compensation when the works of the acquiring authority are on the land acquired from the claimant or on that land and other land. This position has come about as the result of an amendment of the previous law by the Land Compensation Act 1973 and which was intended to reverse the effect of the decision of the Court of Appeal in *Edwards v Minister of Transport*.[28] The doubt is as to whether a claim for an adverse effect on land retained can be made where the works of the acquiring authority are wholly on land other than the land acquired from the claimant. This can be swiftly resolved by providing that the right to compensation for an adverse effect to retained land operates taking into account the works, and any other actions under its statutory powers, of the acquiring authority whether on the land acquired or on any other land or on both areas of land.

3. The Valuation Date

16.52 The present legislation prescribes a valuation date for assessing compensation for the value of the land acquired. No valuation date is prescribed for the purposes of a claim for compensation in relation to retained land. Nonetheless if compensation in respect of retained land is to be based primarily on a diminution in the value of that land then a valuation date is as much needed for this purpose as it is needed for the valuation of the land acquired. There is no reason to take a valuation date in respect of the retained land which is any different from that in respect of the land acquired. Accordingly the valuation date for determining the diminution in the value of the land retained by the claimant as the primary component of any claim for compensation under that head should be the date of the vesting declaration on the assumption that the general vesting declaration procedure will have to be used in every case. This will mean that in accordance with general and basic valuation principles the only matters which may be taken into account in assessing the diminution in the value of the land retained are those facts and events which are known at the valuation date or those matters which are anticipated at that date so far as relevant to the value of the retained land. There is no reason for varying or making exceptions to this fundamental valuation principle in this instance than there is in any other case relating to the valuation of land, whether for the purposes of compensation or anything else.[29]

---

[28] *Edwards v Minister of Transport* [1964] 2 QB 134, [1964] 2 WLR 515; Land Compensation Act 1973, s 44. See ch 6, paras 9.63 et seq.

[29] The general principle in valuing land is that all matters known to the hypothetical parties at the valuation date can be taken into account, as can their anticipation of matters which they reasonably believe would occur at that date, but that future events which do not fall within these categories must be left out of account: see, eg *Lynall v Inland Revenue Commissioners* [1972] AC 680, [1971] 3 WLR 759. The principle is explained by Lord Hoffmann

The observation in the last paragraph applies to the assessment of compensation based on   16.53
the diminution in the value of the land retained. If a secondary item of compensation can
be claimed for further or additional monetary losses then that item of claim will be akin to
a claim for damages. Where such a claim is available under rule (6) of section 5 of the Land
Compensation Act 1961 it is permissible under the present law to consider events after the
valuation date in order to know what is the true extent of the loss under such a claim.
Obviously this same principle would apply if further and additional claims of a secondary
nature are permissible in respect of the retained land.[30]

4. Valuation Methodology

The remaining matter to consider in relation to this head of compensation is the method of   16.54
assessing the compensation for a reduction in the value of the retained land. As explained
in chapter 9 both the language of the current legislation and decided authority show that
the correct way of assessing the compensation is by: (a) carrying out a valuation of the
retained land as it was and by itself ignoring the scheme of the acquiring authority, and (b)
carrying out a valuation of the retained land as it became following, and taking into account,
the acquisition of the land acquired and the scheme of the acquiring authority. The compensation in respect of the retained land is then the amount, if any, by which the first value
exceeds the second value. Of course the compensation for the land acquired (and the compensation due under any other head) is added to the compensation in respect of the retained
land, assessed as just mentioned, so as to constitute the total compensation payable. It has
also been explained that valuations have in practice often been carried out using a different
methodology, namely that the value of the whole of the land of the claimant, the land
acquired and the retained land, is assessed prior to the acquisition of the land acquired and
ignoring the scheme of the acquiring authority and then the value of the retained land
alone is assessed following the acquisition of the land acquired and taking into account the
scheme of the acquiring authority. The difference between the two sums is then said to be
the total compensation for both the land acquired and for a reduction in the value of the
land retained. The second method is said to be simpler and, possibly, fairer than the first
method. In practice the two methods may lead to the same result although this is not necessarily so.[31]

There is room here for a simplification of the process. The second methodology described   16.55
in the last paragraph, although not strictly in accordance with the present statutory provisions, is certainly in most cases simpler to apply than the correct methodology and is something which will generally lead to a fair result. On the other hand it is possible that the
application of the more correct, but more complex, methodology will lead to a higher

---

in *Penny's Bay Investment Co v Director of Lands* (2010) 13 HKCFAR 287, at para 43. There seems to be a powerful
tendency among those who adjudicate on, and suggest reform of, the law of compensation to forget or to water
down or to provide exceptions to this principle on the reasoning that it is or can be unfair in its operation. The rule
is not unfair. It would add to certainty, clarity and fairness in the valuation of land for compensation purposes
generally, as well as in the area here under consideration, if the simple and fair rule as stated by Lord Hoffmann
and others was observed.

[30]   See ch 8, para 8.32.
[31]   See the discussion in sections (c) and (d) of ch 9.

award of total compensation and for that reason can be said to be fairer and a truer representation of the loss suffered by a landowner in some circumstances. The way forward may be to allow a claimant for compensation, when a part of his land has been acquired, to assess his total compensation by whichever of the two methodologies he considers more appropriate in his case.

5. Purchase of the Whole

16.56   There are provisions at present in force under which a landowner, a part of whose land is acquired, can require the acquiring authority to purchase the remainder of his land. These provisions are outmoded and thoroughly unsatisfactory. They are spread among three separate sets of provisions, one applying when a notice to treat is served, the other applying when a general vesting declaration has been made, and the third applying only to agricultural land. It is obvious that these provisions need to be combined into a single composite provision. The existence of the separate provisions is unfortunately typical of the way in which the law of compulsory purchase and compensation has grown up. The first two of the three sets of provisions mentioned are also unsatisfactory in that, instead of applying to all types of land, they apply only to land which has the somewhat antiquated descriptions of 'house, building or manufactory' or land which forms part of a garden or park attached to a house.

16.57   Two extreme views can be taken of whether a landowner should be entitled to require the purchase of the whole of his land when the acquiring authority wishes to acquire only a part of it. One view is that a landowner should always be able to require the acquisition of the whole of his land. This is an untenable view since in some cases the retained land of the landowner may not be affected in any significant way by the acquisition or the proposed scheme of the acquiring authority or only a small sliver of his land may be taken and it would be unrealistic to require that the acquiring authority should purchase the whole of it. The other extreme view is that there should be no entitlement on the part of an owner to require the acquisition of the whole of his land, the reasoning being that the owner is in any event compensated for the value of the land which is acquired from him and for any reduction in value to his retained land and that this should amount to a satisfactory recompense for his loss. On the other hand it seems more consonant with justice and a fair system that a landowner who retains an amount of land which is significantly affected by the scheme should be able to require in appropriate circumstances that the whole of his land is taken.

16.58   The reform which is needed is that of producing an uncomplicated system which has the following characteristics. A landowner a part of whose land is acquired should be entitled to request the acquiring authority to acquire also the whole or any part of land which is retained by him. If the authority is willing to do so then no further difficulty arises. If the authority is not willing to do so then the owner should be entitled to refer the matter to the Lands Tribunal for decision. The Lands Tribunal would then have the following powers. If the Tribunal is satisfied that the retained land of the owner is not significantly adversely affected by the acquisition of the land proposed to be taken from him by the acquiring authority and by the scheme of the authority then the landowner should have no further entitlement to require that his retained land is purchased. On the other hand if the Tribunal

determines that the retained land, or any part of the retained land, of the owner is significantly adversely affected as just stated then the Tribunal should be entitled to determine
that the whole, or any part, of the land of the landowner which he requires to be purchased
should be purchased by the acquiring authority if it is reasonable to do so. Upon such a
determination by the Tribunal the landowner should then have an option, to be exercised
within a short time, of whether or not he requires the whole or that part of his retained land
as determined by the Tribunal as that which should be acquired to be purchased from him.
Such a system should of course apply uniformly to all types of land. It will enable substantial justice to be done as between the public authority and the landowner when land is
retained by him without placing an undue and unreasonable burden on the public authority in any particular case.

(F) CONSEQUENTIAL LOSSES

There is an explanation in chapter 8 of the way in which it became established by the courts   16.59
that a person dispossessed of his land was entitled to compensation not only for the open
market value of that land but also for any losses which he would not have suffered apart
from the compulsory acquisition. An example of the type of consequential loss covered is
the expense of moving to other premises. This entitlement was given statutory form in 1919
and it is today in rule (6) of section 5 of the Land Compensation Act 1961. The claimant is
entitled to compensation for disturbance and any other matter not directly based on the
value of the land taken from him. The entitlement to compensation under this head has
been given a wide interpretation by the courts and today an issue of some importance is
that of establishing reasonable limits to the ambit of this head of compensation.

Few would dispute that a right to such additional compensation should in principle remain.   16.60
Unfortunately the scope of the right has of recent years become uncertain and in some ways
unacceptably wide. A reason for this situation is that in *Director of Buildings and Lands v
Shun Fung Ironworks Ltd*[32] Lord Nicholls in the Privy Council laid down three general rules
for the assessment of all types of compensation and these have been applied by the Lands
Tribunal in a literal fashion and as if they were themselves legislation to provisions in force
in England and Wales which were not before the Privy Council and which are materially
different from the Hong Kong Ordinance which was before the Privy Council. The most
recent example of this process is *Pattle v Secretary of State for Transport*[33] in which it was
held that a landowner was entitled under rule (6) to compensation for his inability to
develop his land years before it was acquired when that inability was brought about by the
prospect of the works of the acquiring authority, there the Channel Tunnel rail project.

The present situation, apart from its uncertainty, is unacceptable for a number of reasons.   16.61
The application of the present approach to rule (6) compensation can involve a notional
reorganisation of that which has actually happened for a substantial period into the past,
the very process which has been repeatedly condemned by the House of Lords. It appears to
provide an unlimited right to compensation for any opportunities to use or deal with land

---

[32] *Director of Buildings and Lands v Shun Fung Ironworks Ltd* [1995] 2 AC 111, [1995] 2 WLR 904.
[33] *Pattle v Secretary of State for Transport* [2010] 1 P & CR DG 1.

lost by an owner of land for an indefinite period into the past where he can show that that loss of opportunity was the prospect of the scheme of the acquiring authority being carried out. What appears to be arising as a sidewind of the application of rule (6) is a general and unconstrained right to compensation for past blight to land when: (a) Parliament has enacted in the Town and Country Planning Act 1990 specific and limited provisions which give relief against blight, and (b) it is only persons fortunate enough to have their land acquired who obtain this wide 'blight' compensation created by the Lands Tribunal. When rule (6) was first enacted it was said that it did not introduce any new head of compensation but merely put into statutory form the existing law. Those who were prepared to allow a degree of additional compensation for consequential losses when that doctrine developed would have been surprised at the lengths to which that principle has at present been taken.

16.62   There are other uncertainties in the present application of rule (6):

(i)   Compensation may be recovered for losses which occurred before the date of dis-possession of the claimant, and it is right that in certain instances compensation for such losses should be recovered. However, there seems to be no limit on how far back one can go. In the *Shun Fung* case compensation was awarded for a loss of profits for four years before the date of the acquisition caused by the prospect of the acquisition.

(ii)   It is sometimes suggested that under this head of compensation there can be recovery for losses to land other than the land acquired.[34] This is clearly unsatisfac-tory since there is a separate provision and head of compensation for losses caused to land retained by the landowner.

(iii)   It is generally agreed that claims for compensation should be confined to losses which are not too remote but no clear principle has been established for distin-guishing when a loss is or is not too remote.

(iv)   It is uncertain whether, and to what extent, business losses, that is usually loss of anticipated future profits, can be recovered as a consequential loss.

16.63   Most of these matters need to be clarified in a restatement of the rule which allows compen-sation to be recovered for consequential losses. It is not difficult to formulate at any rate the outline of such a rule. Compensation should be recoverable, in addition to the value of the land acquired, for any loss suffered by the person whose land is acquired subject to the fol-lowing five conditions:

(i)   The loss must have been caused by the compulsory acquisition or the prospect of the compulsory acquisition of the land of the claimant.

(ii)   The loss must have been due to an event or events which occurred: (a) if there is a compulsory purchase order, not before the date of the notification of confirma-tion of the order, or (b) if the land acquired has been specified in a statute dealing with a specific project, the date on which that statute received the Royal Assent.

(iii)   The loss must relate to the land claimed from the claimant.

(iv)   The loss must not be directly based on the open market value of the land acquired. This condition (which repeats the current law) is necessary to prevent any overlap between compensation for the value of the land acquired and compensation for consequential loss. For example, where the expectation of making profits from a

---

[34] See the *Pattle* decision, ibid.

business conducted on the land acquired is reflected in the value of that land, as will normally be the case, there would be no question of recovering a further sum for the loss of those profits as a consequential loss.

(v)   The loss must have been reasonably incurred and must not be too remote. A loss will be too remote if it is of a kind which could not have been reasonably anticipated by the acquiring authority at the date stated in sub-paragraph (ii). This condition reflects the general principle relating to remoteness of damage in tort.

Disturbance payments under sections 37 and 38 of the Land Compensation Act 1973 are at present a separate head of compensation and are available to persons who are displaced from land by a compulsory acquisition but do not have an interest in land, such as a free-hold or leasehold interest, which would entitle them to general compensation including compensation under rule (6) of section 5 of the Land Compensation Act 1961. There is everything to be said for bringing the entitlement to this further head of compensation into the general provisions for compensation for consequential losses. The rules just suggested could, with some adaptation, be applied to losses to persons required to give up possession of land but who do not have an interest in the land. Obviously the compensation would not be in addition to the value of an interest in land since there is no interest in land for which compensation would be paid. As under the present legislation a time would need to be specified as that after which a person who first goes into possession of land does not have an entitlement to compensation.   16.64

(G) PLANNING

1. Introduction

The existence or the expectation of a planning permission often determines, or largely determines, the value of a piece of land. It is a subject which is therefore central to the assessment of compensation for land compulsorily acquired. Many valuation disputes come down to disputes about planning permission and the planning status of land. The rule that the value of land includes any potential for development which the land has (its development value), and the principle in general force since 1948 that it is unlawful to carry out development without planning permission, place town and country planning at the core of many valuations of land.   16.65

It was not until 1959 that statutory rules were introduced into the law of compensation relating to planning permissions, first in the Town and Country Planning Act 1959 and then by way of consolidation in sections 14–17 of the Land Compensation Act 1961. New provisions in sections 14–17 of the 1961 Act were introduced by the Localism Act 2011. For reasons which will be explained it is questionable whether landowners or acquiring author-ities have been well served by these statutory rules including in some ways the most recent alterations to the rules.

2. The Defects of the Present System

16.67   The essence of the present system is that the land acquired is to be valued at the valuation date with the benefit of any actual planning permission then in force and with the benefit of certain other planning permissions assumed to be in force. One of the methods of obtaining an assumed planning permission is to obtain from the local planning authority a certificate of appropriate alternative development, that is a certificate that, ignoring the scheme of the acquiring authority, planning permission for a particular form of development would be granted at the valuation date. There are three substantial defects in the system as it stands.

16.68   First, the statutory provisions are complex. A planning permission may be assumed to be in force at the valuation date if it would reasonably have been expected to be granted at that date but the assessment of whether a permission would reasonably have been expected to be granted depends on matters such as finding the 'launch date' for the scheme of the acquiring authority and on rules for defining what exactly was the scheme and what it comprises and for the admissibility of evidence as to the ambit of the scheme. Simplification is needed.

16.69   Secondly, there is the system of obtaining certificates of appropriate alternative development as just mentioned. This requires the involvement of the local planning authority in deciding whether it would have granted a particular planning permission in hypothetical circumstances, followed by a right of appeal to the Lands Tribunal at which the whole question can be re-litigated *de novo* with new oral evidence. Obviously the system can operate so as to benefit the parties in some cases but it would be difficult to devise a more cumbersome and complex method for deciding what was the expectation of a planning permission being granted in the absence of the scheme of the acquiring authority. There is much to be said for getting rid of this system and replacing it with something much simpler (particularly since local planning authorities may feel little appetite for having to spend their time and resources in dealing with hypothetical planning questions, and sometimes find it difficult to understand just what it is they are supposed to be doing). The unsatisfactory nature of the process is compounded by the fact that the acquiring authority and the local planning authority may be the same body which then has to make planning judgments which affect its own liability to pay compensation.

16.70   Thirdly, and perhaps most importantly, there is one extraordinary aspect of the present system. When land is sold in the market and a planning permission for a particular development does not exist the valuer makes a judgement on the expectation of obtaining the necessary permission and values the land accordingly. This is something which is at the heart of valuation practice. No credible valuer would say that because the prospect of obtaining a particular planning permission was greater than even (greater than 50/50 as it is sometimes put) the land should then be valued as if that planning permission actually existed or was certain to be granted. Yet that is what two of the three present assumptions of planning permission require should happen. If it is concluded that in the absence of the scheme of the acquiring authority there would be a 45 per cent prospect of obtaining a particular planning permission the land is valued in the light of that prospect. If it is concluded that there is a 55 per cent prospect of obtaining that permission it has to be assumed that the planning permission is actually in force at the valuation date and the land has to be valued on the artificial basis of the existence of that permission on that date. Such a system, which defies reality and the ordinary practice of valuers, cannot be justified on any rational basis and has recently been described by the House of Lords as unsatisfactory and as logically incoherent.[35] The 50/50 system also rests on an apparent belief that the operation of the inherently flexible and uncertain system of planning control can be predicted with a degree of precision which is more appropriate to quantum physics than the realities of the planning world. This type of assumption derives originally from the system of certificates of appropriate alternative development as enacted in the Town and Country Planning Act 1959. This system is something which should be reconsidered and revised in any new compensation code.

3. The Way Forward

The alterations effected by the Localism Act 2011 appear to be based largely on recommen- 16.71 dations made by the Law Commission in 2003.[36] The alterations contain a number of features which should be welcomed and which should at any rate in substance certainly be taken forward into any new code. (a) The former assumptions in section 16 of the Land Compensation Act 1961 relating to provisions in development plans became outmoded as a result of changes in the nature and content of those plans and have been justifiably repealed. (b) The same can be said of the former assumption that planning permission would be granted for development as described in the third schedule to the Town and Country Planning Act 1990. (c) The altered provisions make it clear that, although the scheme of the acquiring authority must be disregarded in assessing the expectation of a planning permission being granted, there is no justification for going back years or decades into the past and asking what planning permissions might have been granted over those years in hypothetical circumstances. (d) A specific date is stated, called the launch date, which is the date on which the scheme of the acquiring authority is taken to be cancelled for the purposes of assessing the expectation of a planning permission being granted. (f) It is made clear that, subject to disregarding the scheme of the acquiring authority and past actions taken under that scheme, the expectation of a planning permission being granted is to be assessed in the light of all facts and circumstances relevant to that matter as at the valuation date and as they actually were at that date. (g) The imprecision of the old assumption that planning permission 'would be granted' is replaced by the more precise assumption that a planning permission is in force at the valuation date. All of these valuable advances should in principle be reflected in any new code.

---

[35] See *Transport for London Ltd v Spirerose Ltd* [2009] UKHL 44, [2009] 1 WLR 1797, per Lord Neuberger at para 62. Lord Walker, with whom all other members of the Appellate Committee agreed, described the system as not satisfactory: see para 38 of his opinion. None of this reasoning in the House of Lords prevented the draftsman from re-introducing this logically incoherent system a few years later in the Localism Act 2011. No attention seems to have been paid to the views of eminent judges in the United Kingdom's highest court, views which were almost self-evidently correct. It is unsatisfactory and piecemeal legislation of this sort which has done much over the years to bring the law of compensation into its unsatisfactory, and in this instance incoherent, state.

[36] Law Com No 286, 2003 'Towards a Compulsory Purchase Code (Compensation)'.

16.72   Any satisfactory modernised system should rest on three simple propositions:

   (i)   Account should be taken in valuing the land acquired at the valuation date of any planning permission which is actually in force at the valuation date for any development on the land acquired or on any land which includes the land acquired or on any other land.

   (ii) Planning permission should be assumed to be in force at the valuation date for development in accordance with the proposals of the acquiring authority.

   (iii) An assessment should be made of the expectation as at the valuation date of planning permission being granted for any other development in the absence of the scheme of the acquiring authority, and the land acquired should be valued in the light of that expectation and of the strength of that expectation. For these purposes the scheme should be taken to be cancelled at the valuation date.

16.73   The first proposition is obvious, and indeed, has formed a part of the legislation since it was first introduced in 1959.

16.74   The second proposition has also formed a part of the legislation on this subject since 1959. It rests on the reasoning that where an acquiring authority acquires land which has an enhanced value due to its scheme it should pay to the landlord that enhanced value. The whole subject of the disregard of the scheme has been explained in section (d) of this chapter.

16.75   The reasons for the third proposition have been explained, in particular its consonance with justice and the realities of valuation practice and the planning world. The application of the proposition is an aspect of the wider question of the scheme and the disregard of the scheme of the acquiring authority for certain purposes. The proposition is in general accord with the suggestions as to the way the scheme should be dealt with within the law of compensation as made in section (d) of this chapter.

(H) PUBLIC WORKS

1. The Principle of Reform

16.76   A landowner whose land is affected by works carried out by a public body, but none of whose land is acquired, may be entitled under the current law to compensation under two wholly different statutory provisions. (a) He may be entitled to compensation for a depreciation in the value of his land caused by the execution of the works under section 10 of the Compulsory Purchase Act 1965. This entitlement is constrained by a series of conditions developed by the courts which are explained in detail in chapter 10. The essence of the matter is that the landowner will be entitled to compensation if the loss is due to the execution of works (as opposed to their use) authorised by statute but which would be a private nuisance committed against him without that authorisation. The main area of such claims under section 10, certainly today, is that arising from the stopping up, permanently or temporarily, of highways. (b) The landowner may be entitled to compensation for a depreciation in the value of his land caused by the use of public works under Part I of the Land

Compensation Act 1973. This entitlement is also constrained by statutory limitations such as a value limit on non-residential properties in respect of which a claim may be made. The details of this system are explained in chapter 13.

It seems indefensible that two statutory provisions which deal with very much the same 16.77
subject matter should be spread amongst two statutes with different rules and conditions, one dating back to 1845 (section 68 of the Lands Clauses consolidation Act 1845 was the origin of section 10 of the Compulsory Purchase Act 1965) and one enacted in 1973. The Land Compensation Act 1973 provides in many ways a sensible system for dealing with claims for compensation of the present nature and the way forward is surely to bolt onto those provisions, with suitable amendments, an entitlement to compensation for loss caused to land by the execution of works by a public authority. Section 10 would then become unnecessary. While this appears sensible and logical the ultimate decision on it is as much political and economic as legal. It may be that some analysis ought to be obtained of the additional burden which will be placed on public authorities by an amalgamation of the two entitlements to compensation before a new compensation code proceeds as just suggested.

2. The Details of Reform

Any reform along the lines just indicated will need to address a number of matters of detail, 16.78
although again any amendments may have an economic impact on public authorities which will need to be considered. All that can be usefully done at present is to suggest possible alterations which may both simplify and improve the overall system.

(i)   If compensation for the execution of public works is brought within the system then a claim for that compensation should not normally be required to be assessed until the works have been completed or substantially completed. It is only then that the effect on the land of the claimant, whether a temporary effect or a permanent effect, can be known.

(ii) The rule worked out in relation to claims under section 10 of the Compulsory Purchase Act 1965 is that a claim may only be made in relation to the execution of works which would be, apart from their statutory authorisation, a private wrong, usually a nuisance. Indeed, as mentioned, this is the essence of claims under section 10. This principle as regards the execution of works should be retained. There seems no reason why a landowner should recover compensation from a public authority for the execution of works when, if those works had been carried out by a private individual or body, there would be no claim in private law for any damage or loss. This rule, if retained, would itself do much to reduce any additional burden on public authorities.

(iii) It has been suggested that the ambit of claims for compensation arising from the execution of works should be extended from its current limit under section 10 of the Compulsory Purchase Act 1965 of a reduction in the value of the land affected to other losses such as personal losses, monetary losses and losses to a business. The Law Commission in its report No 286 in 2003 drew attention to the Ontario Expropriations Act RSO 1900 which provided that as well as reductions in the value of the land of the owner 'personal and business damages, resulting from the construction of the works by the statutory authority, are recoverable if that authority would be liable were the construction not under the authority of statute'.[37] It is a provision of this nature which would be likely to extend substantially the burden on public authorities. The arguments in favour of such an extension are that an owner would be compensated for his whole loss and that, if he had a claim in private law for damages for nuisance, it may be that losses of this character could be included within the damages awarded. On the other hand the current provisions in Part I of the Land Compensation Act 1973 refer only to compensation for a depreciation in the value of land. Furthermore where the loss is caused by the execution of works and the result is a loss of anticipated profits from a business that loss of anticipated profits may readily be translated in many cases into a reduction, whether a reduction in rental value or a reduction in capital value, of the land affected. It is, therefore, not at all clear that the extension as suggested has everything to commend it.

(iv) At present section 10 of the Compulsory Purchase Act 1965 has been interpreted to provide compensation for two disparate elements of loss, the first being where the execution of works by an acquiring authority damages the land of a nearby landowner and the second being where the acquiring authority needs to override third party rights such as the benefit of restrictive covenants and easements which exist over the land acquired and the overriding of which is necessary for the implementation of the scheme of the acquiring authority when those rights are appurtenant to other land. The second element of section 10 can be replaced with a simple provision, such as mentioned earlier, whereby the acquiring authority may elect that third party rights over the land acquired shall, or shall not be, extinguished and if they are extinguished the authority shall pay compensation for that extinguishment equal to the damages which would be paid if there had been an infringement of the rights by a private developer.[38] Section 10 would not then be needed for these purposes.

16.79   There are certain aspects of the entitlement to compensation under Part I of the Land Compensation Act 1973 which merit substantial reconsideration.

(i)   The limitation on the annual value of non-residential properties (apart from agricultural properties) in respect of which a claim may be made seems arbitrary and scarcely just.

(ii)   A claim may generally be made in respect of residential property whether the person making the claim occupies the property or does not occupy it. Yet in respect of other properties it is only an owner-occupier who can make a claim. Again the limitation is one which needs to be reconsidered. If a person buys a block of flats as an investment he is able to make a claim even though he has let each of the flats to tenants whereas if he buys an office as an investment to let he has no claim under the present provisions.

(iii) At present, claims are confined to a reduction in the existing use value of land caused by the use of public works and cannot extend to loss of the potential value

---

[37]   Ontario Expropriation Act RSO 1990, s 1(1)(b).
[38]   See paras 16.9, 16.30 and 16.31.

for the development of land. The exclusion of losses to development value seems to be based on no particular logic and should be removed.

(iv) The present rule is that a depreciation in the value of land due to physical factors caused by the use of public works is only the subject of compensation if the source of the relevant physical factor is situated on or in the public works. This rule means that a person with land close to a public project can obtain compensation for the effect of noise or fumes emanating from the project but a person with land a little distance away cannot obtain compensation for a reduction in the value of his land caused by heavy vehicles passing to or from the project. This limiting rule also merits reconsideration.

Appendix

(A) VALUATION METHODOLOGIES

1. Chapter 4 highlighted the differences between 'value' and 'worth' and at paragraph 4.11 onwards explained the nature of the open market and the context within which value is to be assessed. The concept of value, and how it is to be distinguished from worth, is also dealt with in chapter 14 at paragraph 14.8, and what is meant by 'price' is explained in paragraph 14.10.

2. Having obtained a firm grasp of what is meant by value it is necessary to consider the methods of arriving at any particular value, and the relevance and applicability of those methods. As has been explained in chapter 14, and in particular in paragraph 14.17, there are various methods of valuation one or more of which a valuer may adopt to identify what he considers an appropriate value. Set out in this Appendix are examples of the principal methodologies (comparison; residual; discounted cash flow) used, and also an example of a claim for disturbance compensation. The method employed is the same in each case. Each example proceeds by, first, identifying the facts relating to the particular property being valued; secondly, each example summarises the valuation approach and the reasons for it; thirdly, there is the valuation itself; and finally the main examples conclude with an explanation of the steps and components which comprise the valuation.

3. The method of valuing property by comparison is that most commonly used and is often the most reliable, although it is not in every case a methodology which is available. As valuation by comparison is the most common form of valuation, two examples of comparison valuations are set out, the first relating to a residential property and the second relating to an office and retail commercial investment property. The discounted cash flow example which is later set out and explained utilises the same principal facts as the commercial comparison valuation example so that the characteristics and impacts of the different approaches may be more readily compared. The residual valuation example is less detailed, and involves a similar but smaller commercial development.

(B) A RESIDENTIAL PROPERTY COMPARISON VALUATION

4. Valuation by comparison is described generally in paragraph 14.21 et seq of chapter 14. The first of the two comparison valuation examples detailed below is of a residential property.

1. The Facts

5. The following facts are assumed:

    (i)   The property, 1 Vincent Crescent, is a suburban detached house built 10 years ago. The house is owner-occupied and is used as a single dwelling. There is no prospect of any other use for the property in the no-scheme world, and the interest being acquired is the unencumbered freehold interest.

    (ii)   The house comprises 2,000 sq ft gross internal floorspace on ground and first floors, with three reception rooms and a kitchen on the ground floor, and three bedrooms, one with an en suite bathroom, and one other bathroom. Externally there is a single garage and small front and rear gardens with external access along each side of the house.

    (iii) The aspect or siting of the house is poor, being adjacent to a commercial use and at the corner of a busy road junction, although the site itself is reasonably proportioned. The location of the property is good in terms of access to local amenities including schools and transport connections.

    (iv)   The house and garage are in good repair and the house has all modern amenities expected for the type and age of property.

    (v)   The road junction on the corner of which the property is sited is one which the acquiring authority intends to improve and extend, necessitating the compulsory purchase of the house. No other property is required to carry out the scheme and no other property nearby is adversely affected.

    (vi)   There are a number of similar properties in the area, a reasonably active sales market in the area, and during the last 12 months the economic outlook has remained stable with no discernible movement in residential values in the locality in either direction, and this situation is expected to remain stable for the foreseeable future. There are several comparable sales known in the market place, summarised in the table below, each of which enjoys a similar location. The details of the property acquired and being valued are on the second line of the table on the next page in bold.

2. The Approach to the Valuation

6. The assessment of the capital value of this property should be relatively straightforward. In this example the valuer has at the outset obtained confirmation of the legal interest to be valued and established the nature of any encumbrances. The valuer will also need to gather such facts as are relevant and available such as planning information, plans, floor areas, council tax banding, and energy performance information.

7. The valuer should also first, before undertaking the valuation itself, inspect the property and identify its characteristics, and note its condition. The valuer may not be expected to carry out a survey, but if there are aspects which trigger the need for a survey, or some investigation to be made on a matter which may actually or potentially affect the value of the property, the valuer should make this known to those instructing

Table 1

Address	Sq ft	Reception Rooms	Bedrooms	Bathrooms	Age (Years)	Garage	Aspect	Sale Date	Sale Price
1 Vincent Crescent	2,000	3	3	2	10	1	Poor	The valuation date	To be assessed
12 Vincent Crescent	2,200	3	3	3	9	1	Good	9 months ago	£350,000
3 Stanley Street	1,750	3	2	2	20	–	Poor	12 months ago	£225,000
40 Arthur Road	2,000	3	3	2	15	1	Fair	6 months ago	£300,000
5 Pinfold Lane	1,500	2	2	2	New	1	Good	The valuation date	£275,000
66 Broad Walk	2,400	3	3	2	5	1	Good	3 months ago	£375,000
17 Forge Avenue	2,100	3	3	2	10	1	Good	Available	£400,000 (asking)

him with a view to gaining the necessary information or advice.[1] Unfortunately it is sometimes the case that a valuer is only instructed after a property acquired has been demolished and in that case its physical state will obviously have to be ascertained from records and from looking at similar properties in the locality.

8. Thereafter the first valuation step involves deciding on the scope of a search for comparable evidence. The valuer will decide key criteria to search for, such as the range of time and the geographic extent of the search area. He or she may also decide to look only at three bedroom houses or be influenced by the age of the property and discard much older properties.

9. The second step is to obtain all possible information on the comparable properties to confirm the accuracy of the evidence which is at this stage considered to be relevant.[2] This will include matters such as those established for the subject property itself, although usually not to the same level of detail.

10. The third step is to take into account any significant differences between the evidence relating to the comparable properties and the property being valued. This may involve discarding some comparables or focusing on other comparables. For example, it may be that, although nearby, a particular property is in a different school catchment area or a different council tax area and the valuer considers that these matters are of such importance that transactions which would constitute good comparables but for these characteristics are unreliable.[3]

11. The fourth step is to determine the amount of the adjustment for each difference. This, for instance, might be undertaken by making a monetary adjustment where the subject property has smaller garden areas at the front and rear than other properties or where it only has a single garage whereas the other properties have double garages. The adjustments which the valuer may make for these characteristics are likely in turn to be the product of comparable evidence of which he may be aware as well as the application of his own general knowledge and experience.[4]

12. The fifth step is to weigh the different comparables. For example, the valuer may have identified that a sale of one of the comparables was an off market transaction, which might cast doubt as to whether the price obtained fully reflected the open market value. An off market transaction may be described as one where the property has not been freely and openly marketed and made available to all. Instead the property may not have been marketed at all, the seller having been approached direct by the buyer. Some agents and valuers refer to an off market transaction additionally as one which has only been offered to a handful of potential purchasers, usually on a confidential basis, whom it may be thought would show the highest interest for the property. Reasons for not openly marketing the property are varied; the seller may be reluctant and not wish to expose the property openly in the market place for fear of tainting it if a sale does not materialise; a purchaser may have special reasons for bidding more than others and in any event may be attracted to the prospect of buying something which no one else

---

[1] See ch 14, para 14.21.
[2] See ch 14, para 14.26.
[3] See ch 14, para 14.27.
[4] See ch 14, para 14.30

knows could be purchased in a market where there is strong demand – time and costs may not be wasted in entering into direct competition with others. The valuer might decide to attach less weight, or even in some cases no weight, to such off market evidence. Another scenario is that more weight may be attached to a property sold at auction a week before the valuation date than a property sold three months earlier having previously been on the market for a year because the vendor originally asked too much money.[5]

13. The final and sixth step is to arrive at a valuation in the light of the whole process. Having studied the property being valued, looked at the evidence, made adjustments and weighed the evidence, it is necessary for the valuer to stand back and consider whether the result remains representative of the sort of figure expected. An experienced valuer, whilst not prejudging the result, is likely to have a reasonable idea as to where the value lies in general terms or within a range either at the outset or as the valuation evolves. If the result of the exercise referred to above falls outside that expectation then a competent valuer will go back through the process, or at least some elements of it, to check whether the judgements and analysis undertaken along the way are correct. It may be found that an adjustment should be altered so that the final valuation figure in the light of the whole process becomes consistent with general expectations within the context of the evidence and the valuer's knowledge and experience. Mr JD Trustam Eve, a past President of the Royal Institution of Chartered Surveyors, in an article entitled 'Valuation and the Courts' in 1962 wrote that

> valuation is the art of comparison and depends ultimately on the sense of value possessed by the valuer. In rating it is customary to talk about basing valuation on rental evidence. In a long experience of rating valuations, I have yet to find that evidence of rents is ever sufficient of itself and, therefore, in every case the ultimate decision as to the value rests with the valuer and not with the rental evidence. In my view the primary duty of a valuer is to make a valuation and, only secondly, to borrow ideas from rental evidence. Indeed, rental evidence should be tested against valuation and not valuation against rental evidence.[6]

Valuers today are likely to hold similar views.

3. The Valuation

14. The valuer in this example is undertaking a valuation by comparison, and in so doing is likely to use a number of comparator yardsticks.

   (i)   No adjustment for time is necessary as over the 12 month period covered by the comparables there is no time impact on values in this particular case.
   (ii) Comparison on a per bedroom approach: three bedrooms at £110,000 per bedroom amounts to £330,000, again derived from an analysis of the comparables.
   (iii) Comparison on a per square foot approach: 2,000 sq ft for the subject property at £155 per sq ft, again derived from an analysis of the comparables. The result is £310,000.

---

[5] See ch 14, para 14.36.
[6] [1962] 2 *Rating and Valuation Reporter* 665.

(iv) Comparison with 12 Vincent Crescent which was sold nine months earlier at £350,000 in a static market. The subject property is one year older and has a poor aspect, whereas no 12 has a good aspect. Adjust say, by comparison with number 12, by £30,000 for the aspect, but assume no impact for the difference between a 10 year old property and a nine year old property. The result is £320,000.

(v) Comparison to check the aspect adjustment: consider the difference between: (i) 3 Stanley Street, which has a poor aspect very similar to that of the subject property, but which is 10 years older, and (ii) 5 Pinfold Lane, which has a good aspect but is new, both those properties having only two bedrooms and otherwise being very similar. The difference between the two is £50,000, 20 per cent of which is accounted for by the garage at 5 Pinfold Lane, absent at 3 Stanley Street, and 20 per cent of which is accounted for by the impact on value of the age of those two properties, a conclusion the valuer arrives at by considering the effect of the age factor on other properties and by applying his general knowledge and skill. The remaining element of the £50,000 difference, namely £30,000, can be attributed to the difference between good and poor aspects. As 12 Vincent Crescent is otherwise similar to the subject property (save as to having an extra bathroom), and the former sold for £350,000, a value of £320,000 can be supported for the subject property prior to making the bathroom adjustment. In this case the valuer knows from the market that an extra bathroom generally has a £10,000 impact on the price which can otherwise be achieved and so it is concluded that the value which appears to be indicated is in the order of £310,000. In this example the valuer has decided not to apply the percentage discounts, although such an approach could be justified; it is a matter for the valuer to judge.

(vi) The valuer then stands back and attributes a value to the subject property and considers whether the result is consistent with the checks and balances described above and his own instinctive view of value. His conclusion is that the value is £315,000, looking at all factors 'in the round'.

4. An Explanation of the Valuation Steps and Components

15. There has been no need to make any adjustments for time as the valuer has already concluded that the 12 month period over which the comparables are spread has seen no changes in capital values. Obviously, the valuer will need to be satisfied that this is a properly held view, which will be derived from his knowledge and experience as well as from the evidence. The valuer in this case has placed little or no weight on 17 Forge Avenue as it is an available property and therefore not evidence of any sale. The price asked may never be achieved. The greatest weight is placed on the sale of 12 Vincent Crescent because it is very similar in terms of age and accommodation and is close by in the same street. The only difference is the aspect or siting of the property and the lack of an extra bathroom. The valuer has therefore considered what impact these factors may have. The assessment of such an impact is often subjective, but the valuer has made an effort to establish whether an adjustment of £30,000 for aspect, which is the

valuer's instinct having regard to his knowledge and experience, is of the right magnitude. The check carried out, although by no means foolproof in this example, leads the valuer to the view that an adjustment of that amount is not unrealistic. The difference between 3 Stanley Street and 5 Pinfold Lane is a total of £50,000. Some of that difference is attributed to the age difference between those two properties (a new property versus one 20 years old), and some to the impact on value of a garage, leaving about £30,000 for the difference between the property with a poor aspect and a good aspect. All these matters are weighed up and lead to and support the ultimate estimate of the value of the subject property at £315,000.

(C) A COMMERCIAL PROPERTY COMPARISON VALUATION

16. The second of the two comparison valuation examples is of an office property, the principal facts relating to which are as follows.

1. The Facts

17. The appraisal shown as an example comprises the valuation of a well located commercial (office and retail) investment property in a major city let on three leases. One lease comprises about 30,000 sq ft of offices on ground to sixth floors inclusive let for 10 years from December 2009. Another comprises a ground floor retail unit with some lower ground floor storage totalling just under 8,000 sq ft let for 15 years from June 2010. The third lease comprises office accommodation let on a lease with some retail space totalling about 31,500 sq ft held on a lease for 10 years from December 2009.

18. In the case of the office and retail rents the passing rents payable under the leases are at or above the current estimated rental value, something which the valuer has established having regard to evidence of lettings in the area. As a result, a schedule of evidence setting out the office and retail rents is not here tabulated. The valuer has concentrated on the yield to be applied and the table below sets out evidence on which the yield was based and the adjustments which have been made to the transactions which are considered relevant in the area.

2. The Approach to the Valuation

19. The valuation approach principally comprises identifying existing and future streams of income for their actual or anticipated duration at a yield or rate which reflects the risks and opportunities involved. It is therefore necessary in this case to identify from comparable evidence rental values and to compare the estimated rental value with the rent actually paid or to be paid. The difference, positive or negative, is then capitalised applying one or more yield rates for the relevant periods. The appropriate yield or yields are in turn derived from comparable evidence.

20. The yield approach adopted, which utilises yields derived by comparison from the investment transactions, can be described as the 'All Risks Yield' or ARY approach. In other words it multiplies streams of income at a rate or 'years' purchase' which lumps risks together. Risks are implied in the sense that they are reflected implicitly within the yield, including re-letting risks, voids, fees and so on. This approach contrasts with the discounted cash flow approach referred to in the fourth example which explicitly identifies and quantifies various risks.

Table 2

11 Hough Street

ERV Headline rent: 3.49% £42.00 | Rent free net fit out months: 12 | Amortisation period months: 120 | Net effective rent: £37.80 | Sale date: Sold Jan-10

	19 Hough Square			18 Hough Square		
Equivalent Yield	Adjustment	Reason	Notes	Adjustment	Reason	Notes
	0.00%	Tenure	FH (same)	0.00%	Tenure	FH (same)
	0.00%	Age / Specification		0.15%	Age / Specification	
	-0.10%	Location		-0.10%	Location	
	0.50%	Length of Income	v. 2016	0.00%	Length of Income	v. 2016
	0.25%	Lot size	v. £13.7m	0.25%	Lot size	v. £13.7m
	0.00%	Covenant strength		0.50%	Covenant strength	
	0.15%	Time		0.15%	Time	
	0.80%			**0.95%**		

Implied EY for 19 HS: 4.29% | Implied EY for 18 HS: 4.44%

4 Tenpin Street

ERV Headline rent: 4.42% £35.00 | Rent free: 12 | Amortisation: 120 | Net effective rent: £31.50 | Sale date: U/o Dec-09

	19 Hough Square			18 Hough Square		
Equivalent Yield	Adjustment	Reason	Notes	Adjustment	Reason	Notes
	0.00%	Tenure	FH (same)	0.00%	Tenure	FH (same)
	0.25%	Age / Specification		0.40%	Age / Specification	
	-0.10%	Location		-0.10%	Location	
	0.75%	Length of Income	v.2023	0.25%	Length of Income	v.2023
	0.00%	Lot size	v. £27m	0.00%	Lot size	v. £27m
	0.00%	Covenant strength		0.50%	Covenant strength	
	0.00%	Time		0.00%	Time	
	0.90%			**1.05%**		

Implied EY for 19 HS: 5.32% | Implied EY for 18 HS: 5.47%

25 Hough Square

ERV Headline rent: 3.49% £40.00 | Rent free: 12 | Amortisation: 120 | Net effective rent: £36.00 | Sale date: Sold Dec-09

	19 Hough Square			18 Hough Square		
Equivalent Yield	Adjustment	Reason	Notes	Adjustment	Reason	Notes
	0.00%	Tenure	FH (same)	0.00%	Tenure	FH (same)
	0.30%	Age / Specification		0.45%	Age / Specification	
	0.00%	Location		0.00%	Location	
	0.50%	Length of Income	v. 2016	0.00%	Length of Income	v. 2016
	0.00%	Lot size	v. £25m	0.00%	Lot size	v. £25m
	0.00%	Covenant strength		0.50%	Covenant strength	
	0.00%	Time		0.00%	Time	
	0.80%			**0.95%**		

Implied EY for 19 HS: 4.29% | Implied EY for 18 HS: 4.44%

10 Beech Street

ERV Headline rent: 3.76% £37.00 | Rent free: 12 | Amortisation: 120 | Net effective rent: £33.30 | Sale date: Sold Mar-10

	19 Hough Square			18 Hough Square		
Equivalent Yield	Adjustment	Reason	Notes	Adjustment	Reason	Notes
	0.00%	Tenure	FH (same)	0.00%	Tenure	FH (same)
	0.25%	Age / Specification		0.35%	Age / Specification	
	-0.10%	Location		-0.10%	Location	
	0.15%	Length of Income	v. 2017 (3@2012)	0.00%	Length of Income	v. 2017 (3@2012)
	0.00%	Lot size	v. £30.25m	0.00%	Lot size	v. £30.25m
	0.00%	Covenant strength		0.50%	Covenant strength	
	0.30%	Time		0.30%	Time	
	0.60%			**1.05%**		

Implied EY for 19 HS: 4.36% | Implied EY for 18 HS: 4.81%

77 Gate Street

ERV Headline rent: 3.95% £38.75 | Rent free: 12 | Amortisation: 120 | Net effective rent: £34.88 | Sale date: Sold Dec-09

	19 Hough Square			18 Hough Square		
Equivalent Yield	Adjustment	Reason	Notes	Adjustment	Reason	Notes
	-0.35%	Tenure	FH v. LLH	-0.35%	Tenure	FH v. LLH
	0.35%	Age / Specification		0.50%	Age / Specification	
	0.00%	Location		0.00%	Location	
	0.75%	Length of Income	v. 2021 (av)	0.25%	Length of Income	v. 2021 (av)
	-0.15%	Lot size	v. £89.4m	-0.15%	Lot size	v. £89.4m
	0.00%	Covenant strength		0.50%	Covenant strength	
	0.00%	Time		0.00%	Time	
	0.60%			**0.75%**		

Implied EY for 19 HS: 4.55% | Implied EY for 18 HS: 4.70%

65 Gate Street

ERV Headline rent: 4.47% £41.00 | Rent free: 12 | Amortisation: 120 | Net effective rent: £36.90 | Sale date: Sold Jan-10

	19 Hough Square			18 Hough Square		
Equivalent Yield	Adjustment	Reason	Notes	Adjustment	Reason	Notes
	-0.35%	Tenure	FH v. LLH	-0.35%	Tenure	FH v. LLH
	0.35%	Age / Specification		0.50%	Age / Specification	
	0.00%	Location		0.00%	Location	
	0.50%	Length of Income	v. 2017 (av)	0.00%	Length of Income	v. 2017 (av)
	0.00%	Lot size	v. £35.5m	0.00%	Lot size	v. £35.5m
	0.00%	Covenant strength		0.50%	Covenant strength	
	0.15%	Time		0.15%	Time	
	0.65%			**0.80%**		

Implied EY for 19 HS: 5.12% | Implied EY for 18 HS: 5.27%

EQUIVALENT YIELD SELECTED AFTER WEIGHTING THE EVIDENCE USING VALUER'S JUDGEMENT: 5.12% | 4.68%

3. The Valuation

Table 3

REPORT	Property Valuation Example

Assumptions

Tenure	Freehold
Valuation Date	2nd December 2013
Software	Argus Valuation - Capitalisation
Valuation Tables	Annually in Arrear

Valuation Summary

Gross Valuation				£59,555,062
Capital Costs				£0
Net Value Before Fees				£59,555,062
Less	Stamp Duty	@ 4.00% of Net Value		- £2,251,609
	Agents Fee	@ 1.00% of Net Value		- £675,483
	Legal Fee	@ 0.50% of Net Value		- £337,741
	Fees include non recoverable VAT @ 20%			
Net Valuation				£56,290,229
			Say	**£56,290,000**

Equivalent Yield	4.5858%	True Equivalent Yield	4.7238%
Initial Yield (Deemed)	5.2370%	Initial Yield (Contracted)	5.2370%
Reversion Yield	4.4581%		

Total Contracted Rent	£3,118,882	Total Current Rent	£3,118,882
Total Rental Value	£2,655,037	Number of Tenants	3
Capital Value per ft^2	£807		

Running Yields

Date	Gross Rent	Net Rent	Annual	*Quarterly*
20/12/2013	£3,118,882	£3,118,882	5.2370%	*5.4130%*
21/12/2014	£2,944,822	£2,944,822	4.9447%	*5.1014%*
21/12/2016	£2,942,621	£2,942,621	4.9410%	*5.0974%*
02/06/2019	£2,655,037	£2,655,037	4.4581%	*4.5852%*

Yields based on £59,555,062

Table 3a

REPORT	Property Valuation Example

<u>Tenant:</u>	Office Occupier
Description	Offices
Use	Office suite
Status	Occupied and let
Lease	10 years from 21 Dec 2009
	Expiring 20 Dec 2019
	Rent reviews every 5 years upwards only
Parent Tenure	Freehold
Current Rent	£1,493,882
Rental Value	£1,206,298
Valuation Method	Hardcore (4.680%)

Areas

Areas	per ft^2	ft^2	% of ERV	+/-% adjust	Rent pa
Car Spaces	£3,500 each	22 (no)	100.00%	0.00	£77,000
6th Floor	£38.25	1,939	90.00%	0.00	£66,750
6th Floor Storage	£12.75	214	100.00%	0.00	£2,729
5th Floor	£38.25	5,529	100.00%	0.00	£211,484
4th Floor	£38.25	5,522	100.00%	0.00	£211,217
3rd Floor	£38.25	5,487	100.00%	0.00	£209,878
2nd Floor	£38.25	5,438	100.00%	0.00	£208,004
1st Floor	£38.25	5,439	100.00%	0.00	£208,042
Ground Reception	£38.25	522	50.00%	0.00	£9,983
Ground Storage	£12.75	95	100.00%	0.00	£1,211
		30,185			£1,206,298
					£1,206,298

Lease History

Date	Years	Months	Days	Event	Rent Paid
02/12/2009	5	0	0	Review	£1,493,882
21/12/2014	5	0	0	Fixed	£1,493,882
21/12/2019	0	0	0	Reversion	£1,206,298

Component Valuation

02/12/2013

Gross rent (current over-rented)	£1,493,882		
Rental Value	£1,206,298		
Net rent	£1,493,882		
Less Froth Deduction	- £287,584		
Valuation rent		£1,206,298	
Years' Purchase (YP) in perpetuity (perp)	@4.68%	21.3675	
			£25,775,599

<u>02/12/2013</u>

Gross rent	(Froth)	£287,584	
Valuation rent		£287,584	
YP for 5 years 11 months	@4.68%	5.1252	
21/12/2014			£1,473,916

Gross Value	**£27,249,516**

Table 3b

REPORT	Property Valuation Example

Tenant: Retail Occupier

Description   Retail Unit
Status   Occupied and let
Lease   15 years from 3/6/10
                      Expiring 2/6/25
                      Rent reviews every 5 years upwards only
Parent Tenure   Freehold
Current Rent   £225,000
Rental Value   £222,799
Valuation Method   Hardcore (4.680%)

Breaks

Act Date	By	Penalty
02/06/2016	Tenant	£0

Areas	per ft^2	ft^2	% of ERV	+/-% adjust	Rent pa
Zone A	£109.50	587	100.00%	5.00	£67,490
Zone B	£109.50	644	50.00%	5.00	£37,022
Zone C	£109.50	666	25.00%	5.00	£19,143
Zone D	£109.50	663	12.50%	5.00	£9,529
Remainder	£109.50	1,919	10.00%	0.00	£21,013
Remainder B1 space	£22.50	2,819	100.00%	0.00	£63,427
Lower Ground Storage	£7.50	690	100.00%	0.00	£5,175
		7,988			£222,799
					£222,799

Lease History

Date	Years	Months	Days	Event	Rent Paid
01/06/2010	4	11	29	Review	£225,000
01/06/2015	1	0	1	Review	£225,000
02/06/2016	0	0	0	Reversion	£222,799

Component Valuation

02/12/2013			
Gross rent (current over rented)	£225,000		
Rental value	£222,799		
Net rent	£225,000		
Less Froth Deduction	- £2,201		
Valuation Rent		£222,799	
YP perp	@4.68%	21.3675	
			£4,760,663
02/12/2013			
Gross rent	(Froth)	£2,201	
Valuation rent		£2,201	
YP 2 years 6 months	@ 4.68%	2.3088	
			£5,082
Gross Value			**£4,765,744**

Table 3c

REPORT	Property Valuation Example

Tenant: Office and Retail Occupier

Description	Offices and Retail
Status	Occupied and let
Lease	10 years from 21-12-2009
	Expiring 20-12-2019
	Rent reviews every 5 years upwards only
Parent Tenure	Freehold
Current Rent	£1,400,000
Rental Value	£1,225,940
Valuation Method	Hardcore (4.480%)

Breaks

Act Date	By	Penalty
21/12/2014	Tenant	£0

Areas	per ft^2	ft^2	% of ERV	+/-% adjust	Rent pa
Car Spaces	£3,500 each	15 (no)	100.00%	0.00	£52,500
5th Floor	£42.50	1,767	100.00%	0.00	£75,098
4th Floor	£42.50	1,747	100.00%	0.00	£74,248
3rd Floor	£42.50	5,734	100.00%	0.00	£243,695
2nd Floor	£42.50	6,451	100.00%	0.00	£274,168
1st Floor	£42.50	6,037	100.00%	0.00	£256,572
Ground Reception	£42.50	285	50.00%	0.00	£6,056
Ground Storage	£12.75	651	100.00%	0.00	£8,300
LG Storage (Retail)	£12.50	2,494	100.00%	0.00	£31,175
Ground Retail	£42.50	6,404	75.00%	0.00	£204,128
		31,570			£1,225,940
					£1,225,940

Lease History

Date	Years	Months	Days	Event	Rent Paid
21/12/2009	5	0	0	Review	£1,400,000
02/12/2014	5	0	19	Review	£1,400,000
21/12/2014	0	0	0	Reversion	£1,225,940

Component Valuation

02/12/2013			
Gross rent (current over rented)	£1,400,000		
Rental value	£1,225,940		
Net rent	£1,400,000		
Less Froth Deduction	-£174,060		
Valuation rent		£1,225,940	
YP perp	@ 4.48%	22.3214	
			£27,364,732
02/12/2013			
Gross rent	(Froth)	£174,060	
Valuation rent	@4.68	£174,060	
YP 1 year 0 months	@ 4.48%	1.0058	
			£175,070
Gross Value			**£27,539,802**

4. An Explanation of the Valuation Steps and Components

Table 3

21. The first page of the valuation is a summary of the valuation assumptions, including the valuation date, and also provides a summary of the results.

22. The appraisals assume that rent under the leases is payable annually in arrear notwithstanding the fact that the leases are held on the basis that rent is paid quarterly in advance as is normal in the market. The reason for applying the less advantageous annually in arrear approach is because this has been the normal approach taken historically in the market and it continues to be taken on the basis that by consciously understating the result of the valuation a small margin is inbuilt which acts as a contingency.

23. The valuation proceeds by identifying the gross valuation (in this case £59,555,062) which is the result of taking the gross values derived from the three leases.

24. There are no capital costs, but these would have included expenditure such as refurbishment or other one off costs had they arisen.

25. In this case the net value before accounting for fees is the same as the gross value as there are no capital costs to deduct.

26. Next it is necessary to deduct stamp duty, agents' fees and legal fees. The stamp duty rate is that relevant at the date of valuation and the agents' fees and legal fees are those which a property of this type and size would command. VAT is added to the fees at the relevant rate at the sale date on the assumption that VAT is not recoverable by the purchaser. Although some purchasers may be able to recover VAT it is usually the case, at least when valuing properties which may appeal to institutional investors such as pension funds, that VAT is included on the basis that it is non-recoverable, the assumption being that a pension fund or some similar purchaser may not be able to recover VAT. In other cases the inclusion of VAT on fees is something that could be argued to act as a margin or contingency.

27. The total figure is rounded down as is normally done, and in the example amounts to £56,290,000.

28. The remainder of table 3 shows the results of other analyses by indicating yields and other returns. The equivalent yield, which is one such analysis, may be described as the constant capitalisation rate or internal rate of return applied to all cash flows, including reversions to market rent, but disregarding changes that might occur in the market itself. Conventionally it assumes that rents are payable annually in arrear even though in reality they are usually payable quarterly in advance. The programme used allows the payment basis to be selected, but the default setting is annually in arrear. Such an assumption, when contrary to reality, in effect builds in a risk margin. If rents are receivable quarterly in advance then the equivalent yield may be described as the true equivalent yield. The initial yield, which is another analysis referred to, is the initial net income expressed as a percentage of the gross purchase price including the cost of

purchase. The initial yield (contracted) is calculated on the current rent that the tenant is still paying prior to conclusion of an outstanding rent review. The initial yield (deemed) is calculated on the valuer's assumption of the rent that will be achieved on settlement of any outstanding rent review. In the example there are no outstanding rent reviews so that the deemed and contracted initial yields are the same. The reversion yield referred to at the end of page 1 is the discount rate applied to the income on reversion. In this example the reversion yield is lower than the initial yield as the reversionary rent is lower. It would normally be the other way round. The total contracted rent to which reference is also made at the bottom of page 1 is the addition of the three rents payable at the valuation date. In the example it is the same as the total current rent. The total rental value is the addition of the three rental values in the example. The capital value per square foot is derived by dividing the net valuation by the number of square feet (irrespective of what are the characteristics of each square foot). It is therefore a relatively crude but nevertheless often useful analysis. Running yields are calculated by expressing the income as a percentage of the market value at a chosen date. In this example the running yields are expressed both annually and quarterly at the four chosen dates and are based on the total purchase price including the costs of acquisition.

Table 3a

29. This table deals with the first of the three leases which is the lease of a little over 30,000 sq ft granted to an office occupier. The initial information is largely self-explanatory and identifies that the offices are let by a freeholder to an occupier. The valuation method used is described as 'hardcore'. It is also sometimes known as the 'layer' method. A hardcore rent is a rent or part of a rent which is receivable from a property and which is sufficiently secure in relation to rental value to be judged as assured. This rent can be capitalised in perpetuity at a lower rate than any 'marginal' rent, which is a rent that is anticipated or estimated as an increase in rent which will become payable on a rent review or when a lease ends so that the property can be re-let.

30. Next, the floor areas are set out as well as the rent per square foot per annum for each part and its relation to 'ERV' (estimated rental value). The following part of the table entitled 'Lease History' records that this particular lease had a rent review in 2009 to a rent of £1,493,882 per annum, which is also stated as the rent likely to become payable at the next review in 2014. However, the rental value is only £1,206,298 so that on the termination of the lease (ie when the lease term ends in 2019, or rather in this case June 2016 at which time there is a break option in favour of the tenant) it is the lower rental value and not the passing rent which is capitalised from that date onwards.

31. The remainder of table 3a sets out the component parts of the valuation. First, the rental value is capitalised in perpetuity as it is less than the passing rent. In this case the valuer has chosen a yield of 4.68 per cent which is based on comparable evidence.

32. Secondly, the difference between the passing rent and the lower rental value is capitalised. The period of capitalisation is from the valuation date to the expiry of the tenant's break option in 2016, as the break may be operated and it would be unwise to assume that the higher rent would continue after that date. The rent review is irrelevant as the

amount is already fixed. This difference, the excess of the passing contractual rent over the rental value, is termed the 'froth' income. Froth income is a colloquial term for that part of an income which is greater than the open market rental value of a property at a particular time. What is being capitalised in this example is the difference between the present passing rent and the present rental value, in this case £287,584 per annum, for five years 11 months and here it is capitalised on the basis that the income is as certain as the passing rent. This is not strictly true since if the tenant defaulted the excess of rent over the market rent could not be recovered on a re-letting. However the valuer has made the judgement that the amount is relatively small and the period (two and a half years) is short so that in such a large overall valuation an adjustment is not necessary; it would be lost in the rounding.

Table 3b

33. This follows a similar process to table 3a, but relates to a retail unit. In this case the current rent is also above the rental value, but in this case by only £2,201 per annum for a period of two years and six months. The component valuation reflects that scenario.

Table 3c

34. This lease comprises both office and retail accommodation. It too has a passing rent which is higher than the rental value, which is therefore reflected in the component valuation.

35. In this particular case the yield is very slightly lower. Again, the yield is derived following analysis of comparable evidence, and in this case is influenced by the covenant strength of the tenant, which is seen as slightly better than that of the other two tenants. Covenant strength or weakness refers to the ability of the tenant to perform its covenants and obligations under the lease the most significant item usually being the payment of rent. A tenant who is less able to pay rent than another because, for example, its balance sheet is not as strong for one or more reasons may be regarded as a weaker covenant than a more financially sound tenant. Obviously, the greater the covenant strength the lower the actual or apparent risk of covenants being breached and therefore the lower the risk for the investor all others factors being equal.

(D) A RESIDUAL VALUATION

36. The next valuation methodology of which an example is given adopts the residual approach, often referred to as a development appraisal approach. The nature of the valuation process and the three categories of inputs are mentioned at paragraph 14.41 et seq of chapter 14. The methodology is used when site value needs to be identified ahead of an intended purchase of the land for development.

1. The Facts

37. The facts are broadly similar to those assumed in respect of the commercial property comparison example, although of course in this residual appraisal example the property has not yet been built. In this example the property which it is envisaged will be put on the site comprises 59,750 sq ft of predominantly office space and 9,350 sq ft of retail space. It is a well located site in a major city. The gross floor area is assessed as 85,550 sq ft.

2. The Approach to the Valuation

38. The purpose of the residual appraisal exercise is not to ascertain the value of the office investment asset once built and let (although the valuer will need to assess this as part of the residual appraisal). The purpose is to ascertain the value of the site on which the property would be built and then let. The value of the site is ascertained so that it can be acquired for the purpose of undertaking such a project. Each proposed development, by virtue of its size, shape, location, planning limitations and so on, will vary and even if comparables of sites sold for development can be found it is often the case that a comparison valuation will not be sufficiently detailed or accurate for the valuer to place any or enough reliance on a comparison with other sales of sites available for development and nothing else. Therefore residual appraisals are commonly adopted, the valuer often testing the site value outcome by undertaking detailed sensitivity analyses on key inputs before ultimately standing back and reaching an informed view of value utilising his own skill and knowledge.

3. The Valuation

39. Any residual appraisal is a complex exercise which realistically can only be undertaken using a dedicated computer software programme. The software programme most commonly used is available by licence from ARGUS known as 'Developer'. There is a sister programme known as ARGUS 'Valuation Capitalisation' which has as its focus streams of income of importance for investment purposes and which is not concerned with development inputs.

40. Set out immediately below in table 4 is the valuation (residual appraisal) using the 'Developer' software. There are many tabs and sheets and variations which can be used, and the appraisal below shows only the summary information and results.

4. An Explanation of the Valuation Steps and Components

41. As identified in paragraph 14.45 et seq of chapter 14, three categories of inputs can be identified, namely, first, those which identify the capital value of the completed and let development, secondly, the associated costs of completing letting and selling that

Table 4

Development Appraisal Summary (referred to in Chapter 14 at paragraph 14.50)

CATEGORY 1: REVENUE

Sales Valuation (Part of 1st input)

Residential   8 flats   8,000/ft² in total   at £1,250/ ft² = £1,250,000/flat   so Gross Sales = £10,000,000
(i) The £/ft² and £/flat total is derived from comparable sales transactions

Rental Summary (Part of 1st input)

Offices 5th	5,000 ft²	at a rent of £55.00/ft²	= £275,000 pa	
Offices 4th	8,000 ft²	at a rent of £50.00/ft²	= £400,000 pa	
Offices 3rd	10,000 ft²	at a rent of £50.00/ft²	= £500,000 pa	
Offices 2nd	10,000 ft²	at a rent of £50.00/ft²	= £500,000 pa	
Offices 1st	10,000 ft²	at a rent of £50.00/ft²	= £500,000 pa	
Offices Ground Reception	1,275 ft²	at a rent of £25.00/ft²	= £31,875 pa	
Retail Ground	9,350 ft²	at a rent of £75.00/ft²	= £701,250 pa	
Storage/Parking Basement	6,125 ft²	at a rent of £15.00/ft²	= £91,875 pa	
Totals	59,750 ft²		£3,000,000	

(ii) The rent/ft² is derived from comparable lettings

Investment Valuation (Yield or capitalisation, the 2nd input)

Offices 5th floor Market Rent	275000	YP @	5.00%	20	
(1yr Rent Free)		PV 1yr @	5.00%	0.9524	£5,238,095
Offices 4th floor Market Rent	400000	YP @	5.00%	20	
(1yr Rent Free)		PV 1yr @	5.00%	0.9524	£7,619,048
Offices 3rd floor Market Rent	500000	YP @	5.00%	20	
(1yr Rent Free)		PV 1yr @	5.00%	0.9524	£9,523,810
Offices 2nd floor Market Rent	500000	YP @	5.00%	20	
(1yr Rent Free)		PV 1yr @	5.00%	0.9524	£9,523,810
Offices 1st floor Market Rent	500000	YP @	5.00%	20	
(1yr Rent Free)		PV 1yr @	5.00%	0.9524	£9,523,810
Offices Ground Reception Market Rent	31875	YP @	5.00%	20	
(1yr Rent Free)		PV 1yr @	5.00%	0.9524	£607,143
Retail Ground Market Rent	701250	YP @	5.00%	20	
(0yrs 6mths Rent Free)		PV 0yrs 6mths @	5.00%	0.9759	£13,686,999
Storage/Parking Basement Market Rent	91875	YP @	5.00%	20	
(1yr Rent Free)		PV 1yr @	5.00%	0.9524	£1,750,000
					£57,472,713

(iii) The yield of 5% is derived from comparables investment sales
(iv) The deferment (PV) of 1 year or 6 months is derived from comparable lettings

GROSS DEVELOPMENT VALUE   £67,472,713

Purchaser's Costs   **(Part of 7th input)**   *(v) Costs comprise Stamp Duty, legal and agents fees*   5.41%   -£3,112,147

NET DEVELOPMENT VALUE (the capital value of the completed development)   **£64,360,565**

CATEGORY 2: OUTLAY

ACQUISITION COSTS

Residualised Price (i.e. the value of the land at the valuation date)		£20,000,000	*(vi) This is the value of the land prior to the appraised development*	
Stamp Duty	**(Part of 7th input)**	4.00%	£800,000	
Agent Fee	**(Part of 7th input)**	1.00%	£200,000	
Legal Fees	**(Part of 7th input)**	0.50%	£100,000	
Town Planning Consultancy	**(As part of 7th input)**		£10,000	
Survey	**(Part of 7th input)**		£20,000	
				£21,130,000

CONSTRUCTION COSTS (3rd input)

Offices (5th flor)	6,250 ft²	at £235 pf² =	£1,468,750	
Offices (4th floor)	10,000 ft²	at £235 pf² =	£2,350,000	
Offices (3rd floor)	12,500 ft²	at £235 pf² =	£2,937,500	
Offices (2nd flor)	12,500 ft²	at £235 pf² =	£2,937,500	
Offices (1st floor)	12,500 ft²	at £235 pf² =	£2,937,500	
Offices Reception (Ground floor)	1,500 ft²	at £235 pf² =	£352,500	
Retail (Ground floor)	11,000 ft²	at £175 pf² =	£1,925,000	
Storage/Parking (Basement floor)	7,200 ft²	at £175 pf² =	£1,260,000	
Plant (Roof)	2,500 ft²	at £235 pf² =	£587,500	
Residential flats	9,600 ft²	at £335 pf² =	£3,216,000	
Totals	85,550 ft²		£19,972,250	£19,972,250

(vii) The construction costs will be derived from comparable schemes, usually by quantity surveyors

Contingency		5.00%	£998,613
			£998,613

PROFESSIONAL FEES

Architect	**(Part of 3rd input)**	4.50%	£898,751	
Quantity Surveyor	**(Part of 3rd input)**	2.50%	£499,306	
Structural Engineer	**(Part of 3rd input)**	2.00%	£399,445	
Mechanical & Electrical Engineer	**(Part of 3rd input)**	1.50%	£299,584	
Project Manager	**(Part of 3rd input)**	1.00%	£199,723	
Construction and Design Manager	**(Part of 3rd input)**	1.00%	£199,723	
Other Professionals	**(Part of 3rd input)**	2.50%	£499,306	
				£2,995,838

MARKETING & LETTING

Marketing	**(Part of 7th input)**		£200,000	
Letting Agent Fee	**(Part of 7th input)**	1.50%	£450,000	
Letting Legal Fee	**(Part of 7th input)**	0.50%	£150,000	
				£800,000

DISPOSAL FEES

Sales Agent Fee	**(Part of 7th input)**	1.00%	£537,534	
Sales Legal Fee	**(Part of 7th input)**	0.50%	£321,803	
Residential flats	**(Part of 7th input)**		£250,000	
				£1,109,337

Additional Costs

Arrangement Fee	**(Part of 8th input)**	£50,000	
Empty rates liability/service charge voids	**(5th input)**	£140,000	
Planning Consultancy	**(Part of 4th input)**	£400,000	
Planning Application Fee	**(Part of 4th input)**	£35,000	
Planning Legal Fees	**(Part of 4th input)**	£75,000	
Public Realm incl highway	**(Part of 4th input)**	£250,000	
Other s106 costs (Art/CCTV etc)	**(Part of 4th input)**	£200,000	
Rights to Light	**(6th input)**	£50,000	
			£1,200,000

FINANCE

Debit Rate 7.0% Credit Rate 0.0%

Total Finance Cost	**(Part of 8th input)**	£7,759,672

TOTAL COSTS   **£55,965,708**

CATEGORY 3: PROFIT

Developer's Profit (calculated as a percentage of all costs)   at **15%** of Total Costs =   **£8,394,858**

development, and, thirdly, the profit which a developer requires to make for the trouble
and risk to which he will be put.

Category 1

Input 1

42. As identified in the example, the first input in a residual valuation focuses on annual
revenues and capital sums, that is to say the rents that can be expected on the letting of
the completed development and the way in which the right to receive the rents would
be capitalised by a purchaser wanting to purchase the property subject to and with the
benefit of the identified annual revenue. This first category of input therefore comprises two principal ingredients, the first being the rent and the second being the yield
(ie the rate of capitalisation), although obviously a capital receipt for, say, residential
flats which are to be sold on long leases will show the capital input directly.

43. It must be kept in mind that the valuer in undertaking the development appraisal
should input rents, yields and capital values which are current at the valuation date, as
if the development was already completed at that date and as if it had just been let at
that date. The rents, yields and capital values should not be those which it is hoped or
anticipated may be obtained or applied at some future time when the development is
completed. This is a key characteristic of development appraisals.

44. In the example used in this Appendix, the development has some residential flats. These
have been valued at a capital rate per square foot, although the valuer will also have
considered separately the capital figure obtained on a sale of each flat since it is possible
that the value of a flat of, say, only 600 sq ft may differ when expressed in per square
foot terms when compared with a flat of, say, 1,800 sq ft. In this development appraisal
example the flats are sold on a virtual freehold basis and therefore there are no rental
inputs required – the gross sales figure of £10 million forms part of the gross development value of the whole development. Obviously, to achieve those sales not only would
the purchaser of the proposed development have to incur building costs, but also the
costs of disposal of those flats. These costs are included in the second category of inputs
as part of the outlay referred to later.

45. Within the first category of inputs are office, retail and ancillary rents, since the remainder of the development involves those uses. The market expectation is that the space
built for those uses will be let and that the investment will then be sold. The various
rents per sq ft are derived from comparable lettings. It should be emphasised again that
they are not forecasted values at the likely future date of the letting or sale, but are figures assuming values at the date of the valuation. The top floor office rent is higher
simply because in this case it is thought that it would attract an enhanced rent due to
its good views, excellent natural light and the attractive addition of a terrace. The example indicates that the ground floor reception area has been rentalised. This is because it
is considered by the valuer in this case that the upper floor offices would be let as a
single letting with the result that a tenant would have control over the ground floor
office reception. Based on evidence of comparable transactions, the valuer has concluded that half the upper floor office rate is attributable to the ground floor reception
area. Had the valuer considered that the office element of the development would be let

on a floor by floor basis it would be unlikely that he would attribute any rental to the ground floor reception as no single tenant would have control of it. The ground floor retail element is at a higher rate per sq ft than the office element, and it is derived from current market letting evidence. It is possible that the valuer would zone the retail area so that the Zone A rate (usually the first 20 feet of depth and halving for each 20 feet of depth thereafter) would be higher than that stated as the overall rate. Finally, the storage and parking rentals will also be derived from market evidence. The parking rental could instead be expressed as an amount per car space. The square footage used for the flats and for the rented areas are lower than the areas used to calculate the construction costs since the construction costs are calculated on a gross internal floor area basis whereas the revenues are calculated on a net internal area basis (offices) or a gross internal area less some common circulation areas (flats).

46. The zoning method of valuation is commonly adopted for retail premises and is generally considered to assist comparison of one retail unit with another. The approach involves analysing or valuing retail premises in terms of a rental amount per unit of area in the most valuable part of the unit, generally taken to be the area of the first 20 feet of depth. In some locations which are particularly popular and valuable the depth adopted may be greater. Whatever depth is taken the area of each subsequent unit of depth is halved one after the other. This process does not go on indefinitely. Deep units may be divided into three or four depths and thereafter a 'Remainder' will unusually be applied. For example, if a zone A rate is £100 per sq ft, and the unit is of equal width throughout, having a total area of 1,000 sq ft, the rents per square foot using 20 feet zones would be: A £100; B £50; C £25; D £12.50; and the 'Remainder' would be £6.25 per sq ft. The total rent would be £38,750 per annum. In area terms the ITZA would be: A 200; B 100; C 50; D 25 and Remainder 12.50 so that the total would be 387.5 ITZA, which multiplied by the zone A rate of £100 produces £38,750 per annum. Basement and first floor retail areas may also be expressed as a proportion of the zone A rate. Specific differences as between comparables relating to matters such as return frontages, colonading or an internal area which is shielded may be specifically adjusted. A property such as a department store or other large retail unit may be assessed by looking at comparables on a non-zoning basis.

Input 2

47. The income is capitalised, in this case at a uniform yield of 5 per cent derived from investment sales evidence. The office elements are deferred for one year on the basis that a rent free period of one year would be granted to the lessee (although a shorter period of six months has been attributed to the retail space). These periods are derived from market evidence. The income duly capitalised, together with the residential gross sales figure, produces a gross development value of just under £67.5 million. From this is then deducted the purchaser's costs, assumed to be 5.41 per cent in this example, comprising stamp duty, legal and agents' fees. However, the percentage is not applied to the £10 million gross sales figure attributable to the residential space since it is assumed that those flats would be sold by the developer to occupiers and not to an investor.

48. It is assumed in the example, as is commonly the case, that the whole of the development is sold as soon as the lettings are in place (but not yet income generating) and it

is further assumed, for convenience, that all of the lettings take place at the same date. The reality may be different and the valuer may alter his appraisal accordingly.

Category 2

49. The next category is category 2, which relates to the outlay or costs of undertaking the development.

50. These costs, once deducted from revenues, culminate in the residualised price, that is the value of the land at the valuation date, which is £20 million in the example. This is what is judged to be the amount someone would pay for the property on the basis that they intended to carry out the scheme of development which has been appraised based on the inputs as to revenue and cost set out in the example. The purpose of the residual valuation is, of course, to arrive at the value of the undeveloped land which will be the compensation payable under rule (2) of section 5 of the Land Compensation Act 1961. It should be noted that the structure of the computer programme used is such that the sum which is critical for the purposes of valuing the undeveloped land, and thus for assessing the compensation, the £20 million, appears in the middle of the printout of the analysis.

Input 3

51. The third set of inputs is the construction costs themselves. These are likely to have been provided by quantity surveyors (or possibly building surveyors where the scheme is a less extensive refurbishment scheme). Often a contingency is added, the amount dependent on the complexity of the scheme and the confidence the cost adviser has in the figures provided which will be influenced by, inter alia, the detail available at the time the appraisal is undertaken. Often, at this stage, the scheme detail is not refined, something which emphasises the need for a contingency allowance. Sometimes in addition a developer's contingency is included where it is considered that there is further uncertainty from the developer's point of view, although this may instead be generally reflected in the level of the developer's profit referred to later.

52. Professional fees, usually calculated as a percentage of the construction costs prior to the application of any contingency, are then included. The percentages may be provided by the quantity surveyor or building surveyor, possibly with some input from a valuer. The professional fees are part of the third input.

Input 4

53. The fourth set of inputs relate to planning matters and will include an estimate of the consultancy fees needed to gain planning permission for the scheme envisaged and will include the planning application fee and the associated legal fees. It will also include costs that may be required, or anticipated to be required, relating to a planning obligation under section 106 of the Town and Country Planning Act 1990 such as public art and public realm work. These inputs in a scheme such as that described in the example may be derived from a planning expert instructed, but if not are a matter for the valuer to judge.

Input 5

54. The fifth input relates to holding costs such as empty rates which may be incurred whilst a scheme is finalised and once development has been completed but prior to any letting taking place. It will also include the cost of service charge items which cannot be recovered whilst the building, or parts of it, are unoccupied, usually after the development has been completed. These inputs will be for the valuer to assess and this will require a decision as to their duration and extent.

Input 6

55. The sixth input relates to possible payments to third parties such as payments to a person with rights to light over the land being developed and payments for crane oversailing. Advice on the former item may be provided by a rights to light expert in a complicated case but otherwise the sum is likely to be estimated by the valuer. Payments for matters such as crane oversailing rights may be estimated by the valuer although a quantity surveyor may have some experience of the likely amount of such payments.

Input 7

56. The seventh input relates to the cost of marketing and letting the commercial space and the disposal fees associated with selling the residential flats. Arguably the residential disposal fees could instead be included towards the end of the first category as a deduction from the gross development value to provide the net development value. That will be a matter for the valuer to decide.

Input 8

57. The eighth and final input within Category 2 is the important matter of finance. It will be noted from the example that the finance costs are over £7.75 million, that is approaching 40 per cent of the value of the land identified as £20 million. The finance cost is calculated using industry standard software by utilising a cash flow. In this appraisal the valuer has been informed by the planning expert how long it would take to get planning permission, and has been informed by the quantity surveyor how long it would take to draw up a specification, undertake a tender, mobilise labour and complete the construction phase of the scheme. The valuer, using today's expectations, then judges how long it would be before the development is let (or in the case of the residential units, sold). He then judges at what point the whole development would be sold. From the date of the initial purchase of the land by a developer until the sale date the expenditure identified in the appraisal has to be funded. The cash flow identifies the amounts and the timing and applies the finance cost, the valuer having chosen the debit rate. In cases where the valuer chooses to sell the development after some income has been generated, he may chose a credit rate, but that has not been applied in this example. Whereas the debit rate is the interest rate payable for borrowing money the credit rate is the percentage interest receivable for money lent.

Category 3

58. The third and final category of inputs relates to the profit that the developer requires in order to carry out the scheme envisaged. Normally this is calculated by taking a percentage of the total costs, the bracket being usually 15–20 per cent.

59. It is necessary for the valuer to exercise his judgement as to the level of developer's profit using his own knowledge, skill and experience. In the example the developer's profit is 15 per cent, reflecting the view that this is a relatively straightforward development in a market which is sound. In a very volatile market it is likely that the development would not proceed at all. The percentages for developer's profit may not often exceed 20 per cent as beyond that level the risk may be too great to persuade any developer to buy the land. In deciding what level of developer's profit to adopt the valuer will be conscious of how bullish or bearish various inputs elsewhere in the appraisal have been. Inevitably, rents, yields, flat sales, construction costs and the timing of the various stages of the development are a result of judgements made by the valuer or by others upon whom he is depending. There will be margins associated with these figures. The treatment of those inputs will help to influence the valuer as to whether he applies one level of percentage profit or another.

60. It is commonplace that the level of profit is a percentage of the costs incurred including the cost of buying the property at the outset. In this example the total profit is almost £8.4 million and is therefore a very significant figure. The way development appraisals work is that if the developer allowed for no profit the residualised price would increase by a corresponding amount. Therefore the level of profit directly dictates the price.

61. The developer's profit is, as the description implies, the profit which the developer may require as a return for undertaking the development venture. The profit will include a return for the risks involved, not merely a return for time and effort. It is possible to reflect some risks, to an extent at any rate, in the development appraisal. For example, the development appraisal is likely to capitalise rents annually in arrear whereas rents will be payable quarterly in advance. Another example of the reflection of risk outside the developer's profit allowance may be thought to be the adoption of current market values and current market yields even though lettings and the subsequent sale of the development may be two or three years distant. Development appraisals should however not use forecasted figures, whether rental or capital. Taking values current at the time of the appraisal may be considered to be equivalent to inflating rental and capital values and then deferring the results by the appropriate period. Development appraisals, using current values, do not defer the results. If the valuer considers that rents may increase that view may properly be reflected in the yield rate chosen current at the time the appraisal is undertaken.

62. The specific factors that affect the developer's profit and which will contribute to the return the developer will require may include for example matters relating to the risk of not obtaining a satisfactory planning permission or risks relating to a rights of light injunction. The valuer needs to take great care that there is no double counting or omissions. An appraisal might, by way of illustration, be criticised for reflecting the risk of not obtaining a satisfactory planning permission by being unduly conservative as to the amount of space that may be gained and attributing pessimistically large planning

fees. A development appraisal, rather than reflect some uncertainties within the developer's profit such as potential increases of build costs, may instead reflect risks in the appraisal elsewhere, such as in this example, a contingency for build costs, or by applying higher build costs. Developer's profit is normally a percentage of the costs of development; by increasing the build costs (or other costs) the developer's profit does not increase. This is because development appraisals are in this sense circular; the higher the build costs (or other costs) the lower the land value. As land value is one of the costs the total developer's profit will remain unchanged even though the make up of the costs themselves alters.

(E) A DISCOUNTED CASH FLOW (DCF) VALUATION

63. DCF methodology is commonly adopted when a series of inflows and outflows are expected over a number of years which by being stated explicitly can provide a more reliable valuation result than the traditional comparison or All Risks Yield valuation methodology mentioned earlier under the heading 'The approach to the commercial property valuation'.

1. The Facts

64. The facts are the same as those on which the commercial comparison valuation is based.

2. The Approach to the Valuation

65. As the name of the methodology suggests the approach involves identifying flows of income and expenditure over a period of time generated by the asset being appraised or valued, and then discounting the net flow of cash (whether positive or negative) as the period evolves to reflect the passage of time and the risks and opportunities involved.

66. The net flow of cash over the period selected, in this case 20 years, represents or is equal to the value of the asset. Selection of a longer period generally serves little purpose because of the discounting effect. A typical cash flow period is 10 years or so.

67. DCF appraisals often involve many inputs and therefore require computer programmes to record and process the data. In this example the DCF adopts 'ARGUS Valuation Capitalisation' software; only the summary sheet is presented below. In other cases bespoke spreadsheets may be created, perhaps using Excel software. It is for the valuer to judge what programme should be adopted or created and for him to select the period over which the DCF should run, and how frequently the inflows and outflows should be recorded (eg monthly, quarterly or yearly). These inflows (such as rent) and outflows (such as fees), as well as the discount rate itself, will also be matters for the valuer to judge based on evidence, knowledge and experience.

3. The Valuation

Table 5

Discounted Cash Flow Example	Start Date	Years 1-5	Years 6-10	Years 11-15	Years 16-20
Headings	Dec-13	Months 1 - 60 Dec '13-Nov '18	Months 61 - 120 Dec '18-Nov '23	Months 121 - 180 Dec '23-Nov '28	Month 181 Dec '28
Office Tenant	0	7,568,144	6,300,067	6,031,490	-79,727
Retail Tenant	0	1,134,235	1,113,995	1,113,995	-14,725
Office/Retail Tenant	0	6,394,288	6,129,700	6,129,700	-81,025
ACQUISITION					
Residual Value (Net Value)	-56,290,229	0	0	0	0
Acquisition Fee @5.80%	-3,264,833	0	0	0	0
Total Rental Income	0	15,096,667	13,543,762	13,275,185	-175,477
Total LH Ground Rent Payments	0	0	0	0	0
Total Operating Revenues	0	0	0	0	0
Total Capital Receipts	0	0	0	0	0
Total Operating Costs	0	0	0	0	0
Total Capital Expenditure (Gross Value)	-59,555,062	0	0	0	0
SUMMARY					
Interest/Service	0	0	0	0	0
Total Debt/Equity	0	0	0	0	0
Net Cash Flow	-59,555,062	15,096,667	13,543,762	13,275,185	-175,477
Net Cash Balance	-59,555,062	-44,458,396	-30,914,634	-17,639,449	-17,814,925

Cashflow Results

Gross Value (Total Capital Expenditure)	£59,555,062	
Acquisition Costs at 5.80%	-£3,264,833	
Net Value	**£56,290,229**	
Cash Flow Discount Rate for Office Tenant		4.68%
Cash Flow Discount Rate for Retail Tenant		4.68%
Cash Flow Discount Rate for Office/Retail Tenant		4.48%

Comments

This example is directly derived from the rule (2) 'Argus Valuation Capitalisation' appraisal described elsewhere here.

The overall discount rate used in the above cash flow is identical to the equivalent yield in the 'Argus Valuation Capitalisation' appraisal from which this cashflow is directly derived.

The equivalent yield is the description given to the yield applied to the income flow expected during the life of the investment, so that the total income discounted at this rate equals or is equivalent to the initial capital expenditure, i.e. the gross capital value.

An assessment of the equivalent yield is applicable to the valuation when using what is often described as the straight-line approach. The straight-line approach involves spreading the income and costs associated with the investment uniformly over the life of the investment.

The equivalent yield of 4.59% represents the difference between the discount rates of 4.48% and 4.68% shown above.

4. An Explanation of the Valuation Steps and Components

68. The first step is to input the income and expenditure data into the cash flow and spread it according to the valuer's estimate of when money will be spent and received. In the example above the income and expenditure have been bundled into five year tranches and spread evenly for brevity; in reality monthly, quarterly or yearly tranches are more likely to be adopted. The valuer may choose to reflect rent free periods or void periods explicitly, simply reflected by leaving the relevant time period in the cash flow blank.

69. Having selected an appropriate discount rate as the second step (in this particular case 4.59 per cent being a composite discount rate of the three rates referred to in the valuation), the third step is to multiply the income and expenditure by the discount rate for each time period using a Present Value formula.

$$PV = (S) \times ((1+i)^{-n})$$

Where:

$S =$ sum of income and expenditure
$i =$ discount rate adopted
$n =$ years (ie 5 for years 1–5; 10 for years 1–10)

In this example the calculations have been undertaken by software. Although they are not shown, the discounting calculations can be seen from the decrease in the figures as time advances.

70. The fourth step is to aggregate the total income and expenditure relating to each time period. In the case of the example above this is the net total of the office rental income and expenditure, the retail income and expenditure and office/retail rental income and expenditure, prior to discounting. The resultant figure is 'S' in the formula above. 'S' is then discounted, that is it is multiplied by the discount rate ('i') to the power of the time period ('n'). The result is 'PV' in the formula, as represented by the Net Cash Flow figure shown in the cash flow above. It is necessary for the valuer to undertake these steps in order to arrive at a figure which is relevant in terms of the value of money at the valuation date, that is the present value or PV.

71. The fifth step is to aggregate the PV amount for each time period. The example shows the result of this, namely the Gross Value figure of £59,555,062. The valuer must then deduct acquisition or purchaser's costs of 5.80 per cent to reflect the cost of Stamp Duty Land Tax at 4 per cent on sales of commercial property over £500,000, agents' fees at 1 per cent, legal fees at 0.5 per cent and VAT of 20 per cent on agents' fees and legal fees in order to arrive at the residual value or 'net present value' of the property or project that is the subject of the cash flow.

72. The discount rate adopted in the example of 4.59 per cent is the same as the equivalent yield, which is the net weighted average income return the property will produce based on the timing of the income received. A discount rate differs from an equivalent yield as the discount rate will have been selected by the valuer; it is not a product of the valuation, whereas an equivalent yield is. It is difficult for the valuer to select and rely upon an accurate equivalent yield as the equivalent yield by its nature requires assumptions

about the movement upwards or downwards of future rental payments and expenditure which are unlikely to be known by the valuer at the valuation date.

(F) A DISTURBANCE CLAIM

1. The Facts

73. The acquiring authority compulsorily acquired and took possession of the property, which operated as a hotel, exactly a year ago and that date is the valuation date in this example. The tenant, a company, held a leasehold interest in the property, which at the valuation date had an unexpired term of 10 years; the property was rented at full market value. The hotel comprised a modern property in a fashionable area of a large city. The tenant was able to acquire a new lease of another hotel property nearby, three months after the acquisition date, but in so doing incurred some temporary loss of profits, the losses ending a year after the valuation date. Although the relocation was to a property of similar size, but older and in the same general area, the compulsory acquisition meant that the tenant could not start operating its new hotel for six months following the valuation date, that is three months after the acquisition of the lease of the replacement hotel. It took a further six months for the profits of the business to be re-established to their prior level, the annual net profit being reduced pro rata by half during that six month period.

74. The tenant is entitled to compensation for loss of profits to its business during the temporary period while the hotel business was being relocated, as well as being entitled to reimbursement of removal expenses and the reasonable fees incurred prior to reference to the Lands Tribunal (the 'pre-reference' costs). The annual net profits would, but for the compulsory acquisition, have been £200,000. £34,000 was incurred as removal expenses, miscellaneous items totalled £1,000, and £5,000 is attributable to the pre-reference costs, that is the fees reasonably incurred by the tenant in obtaining advice on and assessment of the claim.

2. The Valuation

75. The claim for temporary loss of profits of the hotel business during relocation is assessed as follows, such loss being over and above the value of the land, the latter comprising a separate claim under rule (2).

Disturbance

1. Temporary loss of profits during the relevant relocation period not relating to rule (2).

2. Other disturbance costs and expenses.

Table 6: Temporary Loss of Profits

(i)	Loss of annual net profits before tax for six months:	£100,000	
(ii)	Loss of half of annual net profits for six months:	£50,000	
(iii)	Directors' time reasonably incurred dealing with the acquisition and claim:	£15,000	
(iv)	Forced sale of stock during non-trading period, and depreciation in value of stock (eg branded linen) not otherwise reflected in the net profits:	£10,000	
(v)	Notification of new address, stationery and promotion:	£25,000	
(vi)	Adaptation of new premises not representing an improvement on the previous facilities:	£ 50,000	**£250,000**

Table 7: Other Disturbance Costs and Expenses

Removal expenses:	£34,000	
Miscellaneous, including interest charges not otherwise reflected in the net profits:	£1,000	
Professional fees (pre-reference costs):	£5,000	
Total:		**£40,000**
TOTAL:		**£290,000**

76. The tenant in this example can recover the VAT charged on professional fees.

77. In summary the disturbance amounts comprise:

Loss profits of hotel business due to relocation:	£250,000
Removal expenses and pre-reference costs:	£40,000

DEDUCT:

Advance payments received (if any).

Glossary

The purpose of this glossary is to provide a brief explanation of words or expressions of a legal and technical nature used in this book. A full explanation of the words or expressions will usually be found in the various chapters and in the Appendix of the book.

Acquiring authority · The body which acquires land compulsorily and is required to pay compensation for that land. If an authority is required to pay compensation for damage (injurious affection) to land which it has not acquired it is more appropriately called the compensating authority.

Adjusted world · A notional situation or world in a locality which was sometimes built up by valuers as that which would be likely to exist at any given time if the scheme of the acquiring authority had never existed and some alternative developments or other events had occurred in the past in place of that scheme. This approach to valuation which at one time found favour has now been largely discredited.

Advance payment · A sum of 90 per cent of the compensation as agreed or as assessed by the acquiring authority paid at the request of a claimant under the Land Compensation Act 1973 in advance of the final determination and payment of the compensation.

All risks yield (ARY) · A yield which takes account of all risks associated with the receipt of a particular income in the future. For example, an ARY applied to rent payable under leases of a property let would take into account risks such as that a tenant would default in paying the rent or that there may be a period when no tenant can be found to take a lease.

Appropriate alternative development · Development for which it might reasonably be expected that planning permission would be granted if the scheme of the acquiring authority had been cancelled.

Assumptions · The assumed existence of a state of affairs contrary to the reality which under compensation provisions sometimes has to be made for the purposes of valuing land. The primary assumption is that at the valuation date the land is sold by a hypothetical willing seller to a hypothetical willing buyer whereas in reality the land is being acquired by the acquiring authority.

Basic loss payment · A sum based on the value of the interest acquired or the area of the land acquired (currently a maximum of £75,000) payable under

	the Land Compensation Act 1973 to persons whose interest in land has been compulsorily acquired.
Before and after valuation	The valuation of the same piece of land at the same date, one taking account of some action by a public authority and the other leaving out of account that action. The difference between the two valuations may in some cases be the basis of compensation, or a component of compensation, payable.
Betterment	An increase in the value of land other than the land acquired or the land in respect of which compensation is payable. In certain circumstances this value must be set off against the compensation due.
Break clause	A provision in a lease for a term certain under which either the landlord or the tenant or both can terminate the tenancy at a specified date by a notice given at a specified time before that date.
Bwllfa principle	The principle of law that when compensation is recoverable for loss or damage, as opposed to compensation recoverable for the value of land, it is generally appropriate to take into account all facts and matters known at the date of the assessment of the loss so as to calculate the loss or damage and the compensation. The name of the principle derives from the decision of the House of Lords in *Bwllfa & Merthyr Dare Steam Coal Co v Pontypridd Waterworks Co* [1903] AC 426.
Calderbank offer	An offer to settle a claim for compensation or other proceedings marked 'without prejudice save as to costs'. The existence and amount of the offer may not be referred to in any proceedings until all substantive matters have been determined and only the matter of costs remains to be determined. The name derives from the matrimonial case of *Calderbank v Calderbank* [1976] Fam 93, in which the process was first approved by the Court of Appeal.
Cancellation assumption	An assumption that the scheme of the acquiring authority has been cancelled at a specified date such as the date on which notice of the confirmation of a compulsory purchase order is first published.
Case management hearing	A hearing before the Lands Tribunal at which procedural matters are discussed and decided.
Certificate of appropriate alternative development	A certificate issued under section 17 of the Land Compensation Act 1961 (as substituted by the Localism Act 2011), sometimes called a 'section 17 certificate'. It is a certificate issued by the local planning authority, or by the Lands Tribunal on appeal, which states the development for which planning permission would be granted for the land being acquired in the absence of the scheme of the acquiring authority. Planning permission for the development certified is assumed to be in force at the valuation date.

Civil Procedure Rules   The rules of procedure which govern proceedings in the Court of Appeal, the High Court and the County Court.

Claimant's costs in the   An order for the costs of an interlocutory matter which means that:
reference (or cause)   (a) if the claimant obtains a final order for costs in his favour that final order will include the costs of the interlocutory matter, and (b) if the claimant does not obtain a final order for costs in his favour, or even if a final order for costs is made against him, he will not be required to pay the costs of the interlocutory matter. An order for 'respondent's costs in the reference' has a corresponding effect for a respondent.

Comparables valuation   A valuation of land based on transactions in properties similar to the hypothetical transaction in the land being valued with the application of appropriate adjustments. The comparable transaction may have taken place before or after the valuation date.

Compensation code   An expression which generally means the whole of the statutory provisions which govern the assessment and payment of compensation. These provisions are spread amongst a number of Acts of Parliament and are not a code in the true sense of that term.

Confirmation of   The decision by a Minister either to confirm a compulsory pur-
compulsory purchase   chase order made by some other body or to make a compulsory
order   purchase order prepared in draft by him.

Confirming authority   The Minister with power to confirm a compulsory purchase order with or without modifications.

Corporate veil   An expression which reflects the principle of law that save in very exceptional circumstances the separate identity of separate legal corporate bodies, mainly companies, is preserved and applied.

Corporeal and   A corporeal interest (or hereditament) is an interest in land which
incorporeal interests   confers on the owner of it a present or future right to possession of the land (eg freeholds and leaseholds). An incorporeal interest (or hereditament) is an interest in land which confers on the owner of the right certain rights over land of someone else but not the right of possession (eg easements and the right to enforce a restrictive covenant).

Costs in the reference   An order for the costs of an interlocutory matter which means that
(or cause)   the payment of the costs of that matter will follow the final order for costs in the reference whatever that final order is.

Costs reserved   An order for the costs of an interlocutory matter which means that the decision on the costs of that matter is left over to be determined at a later stage usually when a final order for the costs of the reference is made.

DCF analysis   Discounted cash flow analysis. A process by which a sum expected to be received at a future date is adjusted (or discounted) so as to become equal to an amount which would be paid at the base date, usually the valuation date, for the right at that date to receive that sum at that future date. The rate at which the sum is discounted is called the discount rate. The carrying out of this process for a series of sums to be received in the future is a DCF analysis. A similar exercise may be carried out as regards sums to be expended at a future date.

Deed poll	A deed executed by a single party. Provisions entitle an acquiring authority to execute a deed poll in certain circumstances the effect of which may be to vest land in itself when it cannot obtain title in a different way, for example when the owner of the land cannot be traced.
Deferment	An adjustment to a sum of money payable or to be received at a future date to reflect the fact that the payment will be at that future date. The percentage used to effect the adjustment is the deferment rate.
Developer's profit	A component of a residual valuation. It is the percentage of the anticipated total costs of a development of land which a developer would require to be deducted from the price which he was paying to acquire the land for that development as a profit to him for carrying out that development and in return for the risks which he would bear in carrying out that development.
Development value	(a) The value of land in excess of its existing use value which is attributable to the prospect of the development of the land (the stricter and more correct meaning). (b) The whole of the value of land which is available for development.
Disturbance compensation	(a) The compensation payable under rule (6) of section 5 of the Land Compensation Act 1961 to a person who is disturbed in his occupation of land by a compulsory purchase (the stricter and more correct meaning). (b) Any compensation payable under rule (6) whether for disturbance of occupation or not.
Disturbance payment	A payment due under sections 37 and 38 of the Land Compensation Act 1973 to a person who is displaced from land by a compulsory acquisition of the land but who does not have an interest in the land which would otherwise entitle him to compensation (eg a licensee in occupation of the land). A disturbance payment must be distinguished from disturbance compensation.
Doctrine of precedent	The doctrine of law which in general terms requires that a lower court or tribunal must follow and apply a principle of law established by a decision of a higher court. Sometimes called the doctrine of stare decisis.

Easement	A right over the land owned by some other person not normally entitling the owner of the right to possession of any part of the land of the other person, such as a right of way or of support or of the access of natural light across the land of the other person. Such rights are sometimes called incorporeal interests or third party rights or *iura in re aliena* or servitudes (the last description being taken from Roman Law and in use in Scotland).
Effective date	The date on which the parties to a transaction enter into a legally binding agreement to complete that transaction. When the transaction is used as a comparable the effective date is taken as the date of the transaction.
Empowering Act	An Act of Parliament which confers a right to acquire land compulsorily. The Act may confer that right either for the purposes of a particular project such as the Crossrail scheme or for some general purpose such as housing or the provision or improvement of highways. The empowering Act and a compulsory purchase made pursuant to it are 'the special Act'.
Equitable mortgage	A mortgage which is either: (a) a mortgage of an equitable interest, or (b) an agreement to execute a legal mortgage.
Equity of redemption	The interest and rights held by a mortgagor of land. The general right is that of redeeming the mortgage, that is securing title to the land free of the mortgage on payment of all sums due under the mortgage. The expression 'negative equity' means that the value of the property free of the mortgage is less than the amount remaining due to the mortgagee under the mortgage.
Equivalent reinstatement	A method of assessing compensation under rule (5) of section 5 of the Land Compensation Act 1961 which is an alternative to the open market value of the land acquired. In certain circumstances compensation can be assessed as the reasonable costs of reinstating in other premises the purpose for which the land acquired was used.
Estoppel	A general principle of law under which in certain circumstances a person is prevented from denying the truth or effect of: (a) a representation he has made (common law estoppel), or (b) a promise he has made (promissory estoppel), or (c) an assumption under which he has acted (estoppel by convention). Proprietary estoppel is also a variety of estoppel which is separately defined.
Existing use value	The value of land in its existing use and on the assumption that no development of the land can be carried out.
Fictional person (*persona ficta*)	Personality in law is attributable to: (a) real persons, and (b) corporate bodies. Corporate bodies are sometimes called fictional persons or *personae fictae*. The main example of corporate bodies is companies incorporated under the companies legislation, now the Companies Act 2006.

First claim date	The first date to which a claim can be made under Part I of the Land Compensation Act 1973 for compensation for the depreciation of the value of an interest in land caused by the use of public works. The first claim date is normally one year after the date on which works first come into use (known as the relevant date).
Froth	That part of a rent contractually payable at any time which exceeds the rental value of the property at that time. It is the converse of a profit rent.
General vesting declaration	A declaration made by an acquiring authority under the Compulsory Purchase (Vesting Declarations) Act 1981 which has the effect: (a) of vesting interests in the land the subject of the declaration in the acquiring authority, and (b) giving to the acquiring authority power to enter the land. It is an alternative to the notice to treat procedure as the means of putting a power of compulsory purchase into effect.
Goodwill	The expectation that customers of a business will return to the business, that expectation being created by reason of the carrying on of the business in the past. In property terms it is based on the expectation that customers will continue to return to the same premises notwithstanding that the same business (as opposed to the same use) is no longer there.
Headline rent	The rent which becomes payable under a lease following the end of a rent free period.
Home loss payment	A sum payable under Part III of the Land Compensation Act 1973 to persons displaced from a dwelling and payable in addition to general compensation.
Hope value	(a) That part of the value of land in excess of its existing use value which is attributable to the hope, although not the certainty, of being able to carry out a development on the land. The uncertainty may be created by any factor although it is often the uncertainty in being unable to obtain a planning permission which is most relevant (the stricter and more correct meaning). (b) The whole of the value of land in the above circumstances.
Hypothetical willing buyer (or purchaser)	A hypothetical or notional person who is taken to acquire the land being valued at the valuation date after it has been put on the market. The hypothetical willing buyer may be assumed to be an ordinary person or a corporate body but is not any actual person or actual company or other corporation.
Hypothetical willing seller (or vendor)	A hypothetical or notional person who is taken to sell the land which is being valued on the valuation date. The hypothetical willing seller is not the owner of the land acquired and is not any actual person or actual company or other corporation.

Indemnity costs — Costs ordered to be paid on an indemnity basis. The result of the order is that the person to be paid his costs is likely to recover either the whole of his costs incurred in the proceedings or at any rate a higher proportion of those costs than if the costs had been ordered to be paid on the standard basis.

Injurious affection — An expression used in the compensation legislation going back to the Lands Clauses Consolidation Act 1845. It means damage to land not acquired (usually a diminution in the value of that land) for which an acquiring authority is required to pay compensation. The two most frequent instances of the use of the expression are: (a) compensation due for injurious affection to land of an owner retained by him when a part of that owner's land is acquired, and (b) injurious affection to land caused by the execution of works by an acquiring authority when, apart from statutory authorisation, those works would constitute a civil wrong against the owner.

Judicial review — A legal remedy available since medieval times, now provided for in Part 54 of the Civil Procedure Rules, by which the High Court controls and supervises the legality of actions of administrative bodies and lower courts and tribunals.

Lands Tribunal — The Lands Tribunal was established in 1949 by the Lands Tribunal Act 1949 and replaced the official arbitrators (and before them arbitrators, magistrates and juries) who had assessed compensation under the Lands Clauses Consolidation Act 1845 and the Acquisition of Land (Assessment of Compensation) Act 1919. In 2009 the functions of the Lands Tribunal in determining compensation were transferred to the Lands Chamber of the Upper Tribunal pursuant to the Tribunals, Courts and Enforcement Act 2007. The Lands Chamber is still commonly called the Lands Tribunal despite its official designation. For purposes of convenience the Lands Chamber continues to be described as the Lands Tribunal in this book.

Legal mortgage or charge — A statutory form of mortgage provided for by section 87(1) of the Law of Property Act 1925. It is the only form of legal mortgage available today of freehold or leasehold land and is to be distinguished from an equitable mortgage.

Licence — A contractual right to enter or to take possession of land which is not a proprietary interest in the land such as a lease. Licensees who are displaced from land by a compulsory purchase of the land are not entitled to compensation under the general compensation provisions but may be entitled to a disturbance payment under sections 37 and 38 of the Land Compensation Act 1973.

Limitation — A statutory rule under which persons who have some enforceable right are bound to bring proceedings before an appropriate court or tribunal to enforce that right within a specified period from the date on which the right first arose. If they do not bring proceedings to enforce the right within that period then their right becomes unenforceable and worthless. There are a number of provisions within the law of compensation by which a limitation period of this nature is prescribed.

Locus standi	The right of a person to apply for a remedy or to commence or participate in proceedings before a court or tribunal because he has a sufficient interest in the subject matter of those proceedings.
Marriage value	When two pieces of land in separate ownership are combined in one ownership, or two interests in the same land in separate ownership are combined in one ownership, the value of the combined pieces of land or combined interests may exceed the aggregate of the value of the separate pieces of land or separate interests. The excess is called the marriage value. For example, if a freehold subject to a lease is worth £500,000 and the lease is worth £200,000 it may be that if the two interests are combined in one ownership the value of that combined interest, the freehold with vacant possession, is £800,000. The marriage value will then be £100,000. The parties to a transaction which produces a marriage value may divide that marriage value between them in some appropriate proportion.
McCarthy rules	A series of criteria which have to be satisfied before a person is entitled to compensation under section 10 of the Compulsory Purchase Act 1965 for injurious affection to his land caused by the execution of works carried out by a public authority. The name derives from the decision of the House of Lords in *Metropolitan Board of Works v McCarthy* (1874) LR 7 HL 243, although the criteria in question were worked out in this and a series of other cases in the mid and late nineteenth century.
Mitigation	Actions which a claimant for compensation is required to take in order to reduce the amount of his loss. Generally a claimant will not be entitled to compensation for any loss which he could have avoided by taking reasonable steps to mitigate his loss.
Net Present Value (NPV)	The sum of money representing the difference between the present value of all income and the present value of all expenditure discounted to their present value at a rate equal to a target rate of return or target cost of capital.
Nil certificate	A certificate issued by a local planning authority under section 17 of the Land Compensation Act 1961 that in the opinion of the authority there is no form of appropriate alternative development.
No-scheme world	The facts and circumstances which exist at any given time disregarding the scheme of the acquiring authority which underlies the acquisition of the land.

Notice of entry	A notice given under section 11 of the Compulsory Purchase Act 1965 following the giving of notice to treat which entitles an acquiring authority to enter land which is being compulsorily acquired.
Notice to treat	A notice given under section 5 of the Compulsory Purchase Act 1965 which requires the recipient to give particulars of his interest in the land the subject of the notice and states that the acquiring authority is willing to treat for the purchase of that land. A notice to treat is one of the two methods of proceeding to the acquisition of land which an acquiring authority is authorised to acquire. The other method is by the general vesting declaration procedure under the Compulsory Purchase (Vesting Declarations) Act 1981.
Occupier's loss payment	A sum payable to an occupier of land who is displaced from the land by its compulsory purchase. The sum is payable under Part III of the Land Compensation Act 1973 and is payable in addition to general compensation.
Open market value	The amount which land if sold in the open market by a willing seller might be expected to realise. This is the primary basis of compensation for the acquisition of land and is prescribed by rule (2) of section 5 of the Land Compensation Act 1961.
Periodic tenancy	A tenancy granted to run for a series of periods such as a year or a month and to continue until determined by a notice to quit given by one of the parties. It is to be contrasted with a tenancy for a fixed term or term certain where the commencement date and the term date of the tenancy are fixed.
Piercing the veil	Disregarding the separate existence in law of associated corporate bodies, something which is only very exceptionally permissible. Sometimes called lifting the veil.
Pointe Gourde principle	Another name for the main aspect of the value to the owner principle, that aspect being in general terms the rule developed by the courts following the Lands Clauses Consolidation Act 1845 that in valuing land for the purposes of assessing compensation the effect on the value of that land of the scheme of the acquiring authority is to be left out of account. The Pointe Gourde principle derives its name from the terse opinion of Lord MacDermott in *Pointe Gourde Quarrying and Transport Co Ltd v Sub-Intendent of Crown Lands* [1947] AC 565, a decision of the Privy Council on appeal from Trinidad and Tobago.
Preliminary issue	A separate and specific issue within legal proceedings which is ordered to be tried in advance of the determination of future issues. The preliminary issue may be one of law or of fact or of law and fact.
Premium	A capital sum payable by a tenant to a landlord in consideration of the grant of a lease or a capital sum paid by an assignee of a lease to an assignor in consideration of the assignment of a lease.

Pre-reference costs	Costs incurred by a claimant for compensation prior to a reference being made to the Lands Tribunal such as the costs of obtaining valuation and legal advice. Such costs, providing they are reasonable, are recoverable as an item of compensation under rule (6) of section 5 of the Land Compensation Act 1961.
Present value (PV)	The capital sum attributable at a given time to the expectation of receiving a stream of income over one or more future periods. The present value is determined by the discount rate applied to each of the items of future income. If a net expenditure or loss is expected in a future period that may also be discounted back to the present time and the total of the discounted items of income less the discounted items of expenditure is then the net present value or NPV.
Presumption of reality	The presumption that in valuing land all facts and circumstances relating to the land being valued and to other land are as they actually are at the valuation date unless there is some statutory provision which expressly or by necessary implication requires otherwise. Where some facts or circumstances are required to be taken into account contrary to the reality there is usually said to be an assumption of those facts or circumstances, for example an assumption that planning permission existed at the valuation date when it did not in fact exist.
Price	The amount which a vendor of a property receives, or which a purchaser of a property pays to acquire that property, not including incidental expenses of the disposal or purchase such as lawyer's fees or stamp duty land tax. The price may or may not be equal to the value of the property.
Principle of equivalence	The principle that the compensation shall be equal to the actual loss suffered by a claimant whose land has been compulsorily acquired or injuriously affected. The principle is applied in interpreting statutory provisions on compensation and in assessing compensation in individual cases in accordance with those statutory provisions.
Profit rent	The difference between the rent actually payable under a lease at any given time and the open market rental value of the property let at that time, assuming that the latter is higher.
Profits valuation	A valuation of land which proceeds with the assistance of the determination of a sum which at the valuation date is attributable to the expectation of earning profits in the future from a business carried on or to be carried on at the land. The two most frequent methods of carrying out such a valuation are: (a) by a discounted cash flow analysis, and (b) by applying a multiplier to the amount of the expected annual profits.

Proprietary estoppel	This is a form of estoppel but is defined separately because of its importance to the law of compensation. Unlike other forms of estoppel it is capable of resulting in the creation of an interest in land. If a person carries out work or carries out improvements on the land of a different person, encouraged by that second person to do so and in the expectation that he will obtain an interest in the land of that second person, then where it is just and equitable to do so the court may order that an interest in land of the second person is transferred to or created in favour of the first person. Interests which arise in this way by virtue of the doctrine of proprietary estoppel may in principle be capable of supporting a claim for compensation.
Proprietary interest	An interest in land which is in principle capable of being exercised in respect of the land whoever becomes the owner of the land, for example leases and easements and options to acquire the land. Other rights may have land as their subject matter but do not have the same characteristic. The best example of such non-proprietary interest is a licence. Thus if A, the freehold owner of a piece of land, grants a lease of a part of the land to X, grants an easement over the land to Y, and grants a licence to occupy a part of the land to Z, and then sells his freehold interest to B, B will be bound by the interests of X and Y but not by the rights of Z under his licence.
Rack rent	A rent equal to the full open market rental value of a property.
Ransom strip	A small piece of land which provides the only access to a public highway for a larger piece of land and so is essential to the development of that larger piece of land. The value of a ransom strip is usually only that of providing the access.
Ratio decidendi	The principle of law stated as the foundation of a decision of a court and by reference to which the decision before the court is made. The ratio or principle of law may then become a precedent in the sense that it is a rule of law binding on courts who make later decisions.
Rebus sic stantibus	A latin expression which may be literally translated as 'matters so standing'. It was at one time considered that valuations of land for compensation had to be carried out '*rebus sic stantibus*' as at the date of the notice to treat but this principle has now been shown by decisions of the courts and statutory intervention to be largely incorrect.
Reference	Proceedings before the Lands Tribunal which must be initiated by a notice of reference.
Rent free period	The initial period under a lease during which no rent is payable.
Rentcharge	A charge on land securing the payment of periodic sums of money which are not rent under a lease. No new rentcharge can have been

created after 1977.

Residual valuation	A method of valuing land, usually land which is to be developed or to be the subject of substantial refurbishment. The valuation proceeds: (a) by establishing the value of the completed development, (b) by estimating the total cost of carrying out the development, (c) by taking a percentage of those costs including the purchase price to be paid, as the developer's profit, and (d) taking away the costs and the developer's profit from the value of the completed development. The result is a residual value and this is the value which would be paid for the land which is being valued in order to carry out the development or refurbishment on it.
Restrictive covenant	A right over the land of some person which prevents or restricts that person from using or developing his land in certain ways. A restrictive covenant may in principle be enforced against successors in title to the person who entered into the covenant (the covenantor) and is in this in contrast to a positive covenant which may not be so enforced.
Retained land	The land retained by an owner when a part of his land is compulsorily acquired. The retained land may or may not adjoin the land acquired. An owner is generally entitled to compensation for the diminution in value of his retained land caused by the acquisition of the land taken from him.
Rule (2) compensation	The primary element of the total compensation for the acquisition of land which is determined under rule (2) of section 5 of the Land Compensation Act 1961. It is the amount which the land if sold in the open market by a willing seller might be expected to realise.
Rule (6) compensation	An element of the total compensation determined under rule (6) of section 5 of the Land Compensation Act 1961. This item is often, although inaccurately, called disturbance compensation.
Scheme world	The facts and circumstances as they exist at any given time in the light of the scheme of the acquiring authority which underlies the acquisition of land.
Sealed offer	An offer which a party to a reference to the Lands Tribunal makes to pay or to accept a specified sum as compensation. Such offers are usually offers to pay made by an acquiring authority. The making and the terms of the offer cannot be disclosed to the Tribunal until all substantive issues including the amount of the compensation have been determined. The making of a sealed offer may put the maker in an advantageous position as to costs.
Severance	A process whereby a part of the land of an owner is acquired leaving him as the owner of the remaining land which is then said to be severed from the land acquired.
Slip rule	A rule which entitles a court or tribunal to correct typographical or

other obvious errors in its judgment or order.

Special Act

In relation to a compulsory acquisition of land the special Act means the Act which confers the power of compulsory purchase together, when there is one, with the compulsory purchase order.

Standard basis costs

The normal basis for the assessment of costs in general civil litigation, to be compared with the indemnity basis of assessment. A party awarded costs on the standard basis rarely recovers the whole of the costs incurred by him in the litigation and as a rule of thumb it is said that he is likely to receive only about two-thirds of his costs.

Stokes v Cambridge principle

The principle that where the owner of property A requires the con sent of the owner of property B to enable him to develop property A, for example because of a restrictive covenant or because an access across property B to a highway is required, the owner of property A will pay a proportion of the development value of property A in order to obtain that consent. There is no fixed proportion but in the absence of special circumstances 50 per cent of the development value of property A may be a starting point. The result is that in these circumstances the value of property A is reduced by the amount which its owner would need to pay to the owner of property B and the value of property B is increased accordingly. The name of the principle derives from the decision of the Lands Tribunal in *Stokes v Cambridge Corporation* (1961) 13 P & CR 77.

Straight line depreciation

The depreciation of the value of an asset by an equal amount during each year of the anticipated life or use of the asset.

Striking out

A legal process whereby the whole or a part of the case of a party before a court or tribunal is summarily dismissed so that that party may no longer rely on it.

Tenancy at will

A tenancy under which either party may determine the tenancy at any time and immediately by notice.

Third party interests or rights

Interests in or rights over land which are held by someone other than the owner of the land. Good examples are easements or the benefit of restrictive covenants. A right of this nature is sometimes described as a *ius quaesitum tertio.*

Valuation date

The date by reference to which a piece of land is valued. The hypothetical sale which establishes the value of the land is assumed to take place on the valuation date. In general land values and other facts and events relevant to value are taken to be as they were on the valuation date. The valuation date is now prescribed for many purposes by section 5A of the Land Compensation Act 1961 and is normally either the date of entry onto the land by the acquiring authority or the vesting date if a general vesting declaration has been made.

Value
: The value of an asset is the amount which could be obtained on a sale of that asset in the open market by a hypothetical willing seller to a hypothetical willing buyer.

Value to the owner principle
: A principle developed by the courts following the Lands Clauses Consolidation Act 1845 as a gloss on the word 'value' as used in section 63 of that Act and subsequently in section 7 of the Compulsory Purchase Act 1965. The principle has two aspects. (a) The value of land is the value which it would have leaving out of account the effect on value of the scheme of the acquiring authority and its proposals for compulsory acquisition. (b) Certain costs incurred by the owner resulting from the compulsory acquisition of his land, such as removal costs, may be recovered as part of the value of the land and this is a part of the compensation even though such sums would not normally be regarded as a part of the value of land. These two aspects of the principle are today wholly or largely stated in legislation such as sections 6 and 9 and rule (6) of section 5 of the Land Compensation Act 1961. The principle is sometimes called the value to the seller principle.

Vesting date
: The date specified in a general vesting declaration on which interests in the land the subject of the declaration vest in the acquiring authority. The vesting date is also the valuation date.

Years' purchase (YP)
: See yield.

Yield
: In general terms the percentage annual return which a purchaser or investor would require on his investment. If the investment is the purchase of a freehold property subject to a lease at a rent the investor will pay that price to acquire the property which will mean that the annual rent provides the required yield. For example, if the required yield is 5 per cent and the rent is £100,000 per year the purchaser will pay £2 million for the freehold. A valuer can therefore determine a required yield and use it to translate a rent for a property into a capital value for that property. The percentage yield is divided into 100 and the result is the years' purchase (YP) multiplier to be applied to the rent to find the capital value of the property. In the above example $100 \div 5 = 20$ YP x £100,000 = £2 million. Yield may be expressed as net (of costs) or gross, and may only have regard to the initial rent receivable (initial yield) or be expressed as an equivalent yield (being the internal rate of return) or as an equated yield (being the discount rate applied in a cash flow so that the net income so discounted equals the capital outlay).

Worth
: The amount which an owner of an asset subjectively believes is its value to him. The worth of the asset may be greater than its value.

For example, the owner of the asset may have some sentimental attachment to it which means that it is worth more to him than would be realised if the asset was exposed to the open market.

Zoning

A method of valuation often applied to the valuation of retail premises. The premises are divided into a series of zones of a given depth, traditionally 20 feet, running back from the front of the shop. A rate per square foot is applied to the area which falls within the first 20 feet, the zone A rate, and a half of that rate per square foot is applied to the area within the next 20 feet back from the front. The process is repeated for successive depths of 20 feet with the rate per square foot halved again for each successive zone, zone B, zone C, etc. The rationale of the method is that for a shop the area which has a street or public frontage is usually the most valuable area.

Index